Louis Ritman. *Sunlight*. Oil on canvas, 39 x 39 inches. Courtesy R. H. Love Galleries, Chicago.

LOUIS RITMAN

From Chicago to Giverny

LOUIS RITMAN

FROM CHICAGO TO GIVERNY:

How Louis Ritman Was Influenced by Lawton Parker
and Other Midwestern Impressionists

By Richard H. Love

Haase-Mumm Publishing Company, Inc.
Chicago

Published by the Haase-Mumm Publishing Co., Inc., Chicago

Distributed by the Amart Book and Catalog Distributing Co., Inc.
100 East Ohio Street, Room B-20, Chicago, IL 60611

Printed in the United States of America

First Edition

Library of Congress Cataloging-in-Publication Data

Love, Richard H.
    Louis Ritman from Chicago to Giverny.

    Bibliography p.
    Includes index.
    1. Ritman, Louis, 1889-1963.   2. Painting, American.
3. Painting, Modern—20th century—United States.
4. Painters—United States—Biography.   5. Ritman, Louis,
1889-1963—Homes and haunts—France—Giverny.   6. Artist
colonies—France—Giverny—Influence.   I. R.H. Love
Galleries.   II. Title.
ND237.R565L68   1989   759.13   87-26091
ISBN 0-940114-28-3

Editor: Vytautas Babusis
Assistant Editor: Julie Love Hosier
Editorial Assistants: Susan Jensen
                      Kristina Vagenius
Photography and illustrations: Bruce C. Bachman

Typesetting and production: Northwestern Printing House

Jacket illustration: Louis Ritman. *Woman Gardening*. 1916. Detail. Private Collection.

Dedicated to
Maurice Ritman,
the artist's brother

Contents

FOREWORD

Every few years, the work of an artist of the past, previously unknown or little known, appears in museum exhibitions or on the market place, and suddenly commands attention and admiration, attracting the interest of scholars and collectors. Louis Ritman is one such painter, actually among the latest to be elevated in public attention. The awareness of Ritman's art is a phenomenon of only the last several years; previously, he was known only to the specialist in American impressionist painting and thought of as a figure involved in the circle around Frederick Frieseke, one of a group of American expatriates from the Midwest, working in Monet's home village of Giverny.

Frieseke himself, though he had never been forgotten, was subject to the same reevaluation of his career and the merits of his painting only a few years earlier. Yet, this sorting out and seizing upon one specific individual among the hundreds of candidates for artistic stardom is hardly confined to the practitioners of impressionism. Many of us can recall when *Ironworkers—Noontime*, (Fine Arts Museum of San Francisco), by Thomas Anshutz, an artist only dimly recognized previously, came to auction and suddenly elevated that late nineteenth-century painter to a hallowed rank in the American artistic pantheon.

Prior to the last few years, Ritman's work was, in fact,

viewed as similar to that of Frieseke. This was especially true of his subject matter, devoted as most of it was to rather monumental images of the female at leisure, often out-of-doors and in garden settings, and sometimes in the nude. The methodology also was comparable, in so far as both artists shared in the exploitation of impressionist strategies of broken brushwork, high coloration, and an interest in light. Yet, some differences were acknowledged, as they had been by contemporary writers who located a more highly structured aesthetic at work in Ritman's art, one as much related to Cézanne as to Frieseke's revered Renoir.

That distinction is valid, but as those of us know who have admired the paintings by Ritman that have recently surfaced in gallery and auction exhibitions, there is much more to Ritman's art, and a great deal that is very lovely. He is a painter ripe for exploration and analysis, and Richard Love, who may be credited with the initial resurrection of the artist back in 1975, here explores in depth Ritman's relationship with his native Chicago as well as his expatriate life in France, and reveals the individuality and distinction of a first-rate American painter.

William H. Gerdts
Graduate School of the City University of New York

INTRODUCTION

It is an irony of American history that major wars have often unleashed unusual economic and cultural prosperity. The Civil War especially was followed by the longest period of peace and prosperity in our history. The war spurred the country into industrialization, creating a much enlarged class of wealthy families eager to demonstrate their achievement in splendid homes furnished with the best art. The underlying premise was that culture at home was the product of a cultured mind, not just of the new money that paid for it. Real culture, if it has any validity, is a learned, not acquired, quality. Thus the post-Civil War era ushered in the European Grand Tour. American families sailed to the sources of civilization. Like pilgrims at Lourdes, they knelt at the monuments of Antiquity and its Renaissance, seeking to heal their provincial inadequacies. Having filled their eyes, and sometimes their minds, a few sought to insure a permanent cure by repatriating portable icons of their new cultural faith — bringing home crates of paintings by or after (in many cases only the artists knew which) the great masters.

This flood of European art and artifacts into the homes and museums of the new tastemakers put America's own art, no matter how highly accomplished, on the defensive. The landscapes of the Hudson River School, America's first and finest indigenous art movement, ebbed away under the wave. In retrospect, however, the seed of its demise could be seen in its own premise — the wonder of a growing country's wilderness would surely abate as the frontier came to a close. This cultural divide was marked by the celebration of the country's first hundred years, the 1876 Philadelphia Centennial Exposition, which also happened to coincide with the maturing of America. Coming of age engenders comparison with one's peers and begs for assurance about future success. Naturally Americans looked to Europe. They measured themselves for equality and found it ample in all but culture. The great acquisition was on. Scholars went to acquire new knowledge, students to acquire old knowledge, the rich to acquire the symbol, if not substance, of knowledge, and the rest to acquire a little of everything by osmosis.

For the art-going public in America, the Philadelphia Exposition became an eye opener to European art and convinced many artists that if they were to compete, they had to go to Europe to learn, or to learn to make a living, or both. European art, both old and new, dominated the American market as artists signed up at the academies, especially in Paris and Munich, to learn subjects and techniques that would bring them recognition. The irony of their arrival at the end of the 1870s was that just as they entered the state-supported art schools, seeking acceptance within the traditional salons, they found themselves surrounded by an artistic revolt.

Progressive artists in several centers in Europe had broken out in open revolt against the hidebound academic traditions of the schools and salons. The seminal event took place in Paris at the 1874 exhibition of paintings produced in a radical style by a group which centered around Edouard Manet. Instead of following accepted salon conventions, these artists used unmixed pure colors applied directly to canvas without neutral tones, blacks or greys. Intense prismatic effects were achieved by close placement of contrasting hues, which at a distance appeared to fuse. Combined with the application of thick impasto and diffused object outlining, the method created the illusion of flickering light and vibrating atmosphere. It was the artist Claude Monet's painting *Impression — Sunrise* that in time gave rise to the term by which this new style was to become known — impressionism.

While the new-found mode quickly caught the attention of American artists and critics, its broad acceptance in France and elsewhere was slow, meeting harsh criticism for being garish, unfinished, and worse. Just a few expatriate American artists experimented with it at first. By 1886 the original French impressionist group, the *Société anonyme*, held its final exhibition together as a last gasp. Their nearly bankrupt dealer, Paul Durand-Ruel, however, was invited to stage an exhibition in New York City that year. The show turned out to be a surprising financial success. In one stride America revived — and saved — French impressionism and gave birth to its own version.

Claude Monet had inherited the leadership of the impressionist movement on Manet's death in 1883, but characteristically he lived in semi-seclusion in the village of Giverny, an hour by train from Paris. As exile has enhanced the appeal of revolutionaries, so Monet's calculated isolation in time brought him acclaim as the greatest living artist, prices for his paintings to match, and an entourage of foreign artists who settled nearby in unrequited symbiosis.

The first American artists to descend on this quiet river village and its famous first citizen (who kept nearly all of them beyond his garden wall) were Theodore Robinson and Willard Metcalf in 1886, followed by other New England artists. Then seasonally or permanently still others followed during the 1880s and 1890s until Giverny became an art colony, displacing Barbizon as the place for American painters to find inspiration. Midwestern artists began to arrive in 1887, first Louis Ritter, then the next year Theodore Butler, both from Ohio. It was a decade later, however, before a second generation of American artists, mostly from the Midwest, began to invest their residence and talents in Giverny.

Prominent Midwesterners became involved in the American impressionist movement at this time. The catalyst was certainly the World's Columbian Exposition of 1893, which had a profound effect on Chicago and its art community. For the duration of the event, Chicago replaced Paris or New York as the art capital of the world. From then on, Chicago turned art-conscious on a new level.

While the art portion of the Columbian Exposition represented diverse international art styles, it is remembered for opening the floodgates to impressionism. America embraced the new mode before, or since, and its most articulate proponent, the Chicagoan Hamlin Garland, in a now famous defense, published in 1894, extolled its qualities, emphasizing that impressionism was equally applicable to American as well as to European subjects. He was admonishing American artists to make impressionism American. Garland's words were heard by eager young artists yearning for a fresh approach. The earliest school of American impressionist art, not surprisingly, came from this region, the Hoosier School of Indiana artists.

Later in New York a group of ten leading American masters — the Ten — officially organized themselves as self-styled impressionists, thus helping to propel the movement to wide acceptance by the establishment. In Chicago, on the other hand, the School of the Art Institute emphasized a thorough learning of academic skills and a preference for the human figure. Many eager students, however, soon began to combine this learning with the new impressionist manner. The attractive imagery and optimistic mood of their chosen new style must have closely paralleled their own feelings about the artistic future. They planned to extend their studies in Europe, as some of their mentors had already done.

One of those students was Frederick Frieseke from Michigan who had enrolled in the Art Institute classes during the Columbian Exposition, then transferred to New York's Art Students League, before arriving in Paris in 1898. Frieseke quickly assimilated the impressionist influences in Paris, specializing in figure paintings, specifically, comely females in gardens or interiors, which neatly preserved the years he had invested in figural draftsmanship in Chicago, while incorporating the new broken-color technique. He brought his intimist subject with him to Giverny, where he settled for a long period, becoming the de facto leader of the second generation of American artists there, almost all originating in the Midwest. Frieseke was to become one of the most internationally renowned American artists.

Another prominent Midwesterner who drew aesthetic sustenance from Giverny was Lawton Parker, a native of Nebraska, first a student and then instructor at the Art Institute of Chicago. He was a remarkable artist whose reputation among the Midwest artists was second to none, and his own visits to Giverny, beginning around 1900, had a cumulative effect on others who followed him. Richard Miller, for example, had been a student of his at the Saint Louis School of Fine Arts, and one of the first to find his way to Giverny. Like Frieseke and Parker, Miller shared a common style and subject matter. Within the next few years before World War I, several other artists from the fertile plains of the Midwest came through or stayed in Giverny to paint — Carl Anderson, Henry Hubbel, Karl Buehr, Alson Skinner Clark, and the gifted young Louis Ritman.

One of the most remarkable facts about American impressionism is that so many artists came from the Midwest. They showed attributes of diligent work, high standards, and a propensity to share ideas and subjects. The fact that so many of them congregated at Giverny and vicariously absorbed Monet's ideas reflected a communion of spirits intensified by the shared influence of place (Giverny) and art (Monet).

Ritman had come a long way when he reached Giverny. His father, Solomon Ritman, descended from an Austrian family of Jewish designers and weavers of clothing textiles. Later Solomon and his family moved to Kamenets-Podolsky in southwestern Russia to further his career. Louis was born there in 1889 and in youth showed a strong inclination to draw. A greater promise of life led the Ritman family to sail for America, where they settled in Chicago. Like so many immigrant families in that period, the Ritman's discovered that the Promised Land was not milk and honey, but ghetto housing, low-paid employment, and language barriers.

Solomon Ritman's job in textiles did not provide enough to support a family of six children, so Louis, only thirteen, worked full time at the Thomas Cusack Company, makers of signs. At night he eagerly took drawing lessons at Hull House. His preference ran to figure painting unlike the predilections of most students who concentrated on landscapes, following the lingering tradition of American landscape in Chicago. Since Louis drew in charcoal uncommonly well, his instructor, Enella Benedict, urged him to enroll in the life class at the School of the Art Institute. He began instruction in 1905 under the institute master John H. Vanderpoel. Louis's family-bred propensity for disciplined hard work suited Vanderpoel's rigorous instruction in draftsmanship of the human figure. Yet at the same time Louis admired the striking portraits and genre paintings of Lawton Parker, Chicago's

most renowned artist, depicting women engaged in pleasant activities. Induced by a scholarship, Ritman transferred to the Chicago Academy of Fine Arts, where Parker was the dominant personality. Studying under the respected instructor Wellington J. Reynolds, Louis soon became his favorite student at the academy, absorbing Reynolds's fine draftsmanship and skilled application of fat pigment, and finishing with a lively appearance of spontaneity.

Ritman mastered so well what Reynolds taught him that it affected his art for decades to come. Reynolds, for example, insisted that figures be painted in their proper environment, with appropriate background and suitable objects. Although Ritman's work reflected these features, given his determination to continually seek greater excellence, he chafed under these obvious limitations. While Chicago was one of the best and most innovative centers for American arts — theater, literature, and architecture — its contributors in the fine arts were surprisingly inadequate.

Within a year Louis's desire for wider experience was answered in the award of a scholarship to the Pennsylvania Academy of Fine Arts. Just to study there under William Merritt Chase, acknowledged as the greatest art instructor of his time in America, was a great achievement. Within months, however, Ritman returned to Chicago, apparently short of funds. He took a studio, as so many did, in the Tree Studio building and earned his way with portraits, determined to raise enough funds for a long-sought trip to France. Lawton Parker was no doubt the greater influence on his plans now. Parker had achieved an international reputation and was virtually commuting back and forth between Chicago, New York, Paris, and Giverny, all the while shipping paintings back for exhibitions. By 1909 Louis was just twenty years old, having spent half his life in America. Now he was returning to Europe, a very different Europe from what he may have remembered.

In Paris, Ritman was the archtype of a poor struggling artist. He enrolled in the famous Julian Academy to study under Jean-Paul Laurens and Tony Robert-Fleury, where his old teachers had at one time studied. Always ambitious, however, to learn more, Ritman then entered the grueling competition for admission to the Ecole des Beaux-Arts, the official school for more tradition-bound studies. Undoubtedly to his surprise, he was accepted to study under the master Adolphe Déchenaud, a two-time winner of the Prix de Rome, the most important award any academic painter could aspire to in France. At this time Ritman's work was traditional and quite acceptable under the academic standards of the Ecole. His move into impressionism was yet to come. Although Ritman was a newcomer to Paris, his first work submitted to the Paris Salon exhibition, a portrait of his roommate, was accepted — a truly extraordinary accomplishment. Exhibiting in subsequent salons, he began to receive the coveted approbation of the critics, a rare attitude among the xenophobic French. It was a result of his prodigious talent, boned by a disciplined, mature mind.

Outside of school work, activities among Ritman's fellow artists centered around café life in Paris. At the Café du Dôme, through Parker, Ritman finally met Frieseke and Miller and learned first-hand of their life in Giverny. Other expatriates joined them, forming a tight group of Midwesterners. At Giverny the influence of Monet, as always, remained inspirational and indirect. In subject matter, if not style, the Giverny group owed more to Renoir. Ritman showed this when he began to paint nudes, although unlike the same subject in French works, they were always discreetly posed. His characteristic rhythm of vertically patterned strokes created a tapestry-like background to the skillful manipulation of high-key pigment of the body, subtly rendered in pinks and lavenders. He excelled at expressing the variegated patterns of broken light, but the impressionistic juxtaposition of contrasted color strokes, however, was held back.

The Giverny expatriates showed mixed reactions both to the Armory Show of radical modernist art in 1913 and to the outbreak of World War I in 1914. Some accepted and became involved, others fled in horror, and still others remained unchanged and relatively unperturbed. Ritman belonged to the latter group. He continued to work at his usual diligent pace in Paris and Giverny as if unconcerned, motivated by a promised debut exhibition in Chicago and a desire to enter in the forthcoming Panama-Pacific Exposition in San Francisco. By the fall of 1914 he had completed his paintings and decided to return to America for the duration of the war. Having left Chicago as a very young, humble, poor, but promising artist, he returned in triumph. His exhibition was such a success that the Art Institute invited him to hold a solo show there, an honor some of his teachers had not yet attained. For the son of an emigrant family it was the fulfillment of the American dream.

Ritman's exhibiting activities culminated in a silver medal he won at the Panama-Pacific Exposition in 1915, especially prized as it was the most prestigious and competitive international exhibition of its time. It was also an impressive showing of the whole breadth and history of American impressionist painting, still the dominant aesthetic in America.

Ritman's stay in France and his triumphant exhibitions in Chicago only made him realize how much still had to be accomplished in his artistic life. He returned to war-

torn France in the spring of 1915 and volunteered, as had Frieseke, to serve in the French military hospitals. When the German invasion was halted, they both returned to Giverny to paint. In spite of a traumatic existence on account of the carnage of trench warfare continuing northeast of Giverny, Frieseke and Ritman were back at their easels. So was Monet, who overcame his initial inactivity with Premier Clemenceau's help and produced his great cycle of water lilies, including mural-sized works, which Clemenceau hoped would become a public monument to his art. By 1916 few expatriates remained in France.

Ritman settled down to his former routine of composing his model in domestic grace, but soon his paintings began to show a change. All over his canvas broadly brushed single strokes created a quiltlike pattern, forming a multicolored composition. It was his own working out of the impressionistic formula, distinct and personal. Now taking a cue from his neighbor Frieseke, he became fascinated with surface color per se, relegating his model to middle ground and making it almost disappear canvas-wide profusion of brilliant, high-key broken colored flowers. Around 1916 Ritman had reached an artistic divide in his life as much as the Great War would be for those around him. He purged his work of all traces of the years of academic training he had so consciously pursued and became a complete convert to high impressionism.

During 1917 and 1918 Ritman continued to paint in Paris and Giverny. Few of his known paintings can be dated to these hectic years, but some give a clue to his progress. His brushstrokes, still a juxtaposition of broken color, grow larger and bolder, becoming quite different from his earlier manipulation of pigment. Sometimes deeper pigments predominate, applied in flat, patchlike patterns. The palette knife came into play, giving the feeling of a Cézannesque manner. Indeed, Ritman moved away from impressionism, exploring Cézanne's aesthetic resolutions.

With the end of World War I in 1918, artists returned in droves to Paris. Yet Ritman decided to depart for New York. He wanted to capitalize on the reputation his exhibitions had brought him by seeking out a dealer. This resulted in an agreement for a solo show at the prestigious Macbeth Gallery in New York. At the same time he was elected a member of the *Société Nationale des Beaux-Arts* in Paris. On both sides of the Atlantic he now had the kind of recognition he had struggled to achieve for so many years. Reviews of his exhibitions were highly complimentary, suggesting that he was becoming the "Vermeer of the impressionist school". Returning to Giverny, he could feel the security of income as his paintings sold in Chicago, New York, and Paris. Giverny itself was an idyllic place to stay, comfortable, attractive, and by its very nature conducive to working out the possibilities of impressionism long after that movement had faded from the forefront of art elsewhere. Ritman remained basically a conservative artist, although modesty, even humbleness, made it possible for him to incorporate the suggestions of others. His innate skill at rendering beautiful imagery, not innovation, was the basis for his reputation. He continued as a productive artist in Giverny and Paris, regularly sending paintings to his dealers, patrons, and exhibitions in America while winning prizes and awards.

The art world in the 1920s, however, was moving at a rapid pace, and change has a disparaging way of casting shadows on its past champions. Many of those who had been so successful with impressionism, like Ritman, sought to prolong it by altering its aesthetic along the lines of Cézanne's style. This began to be perceived as formula painting which had nowhere to go. It was the end of American impressionism. Ritman continued as always with his favorite theme—intimism, but its highest and best expression was seen more and more to have been a product of its fortuitous convergence with brilliant high-key broken color. This event happened to coincide when a very talented young Ritman appeared in the right place and time for a fresh discovery of how perfectly that subject and style worked together.

The year 1929 was another watershed year for Ritman. He was offered a job as instructor of portrait and figure painting at the Art Institute of Chicago for a year. He remained there for thirty years. Throughout that time he produced many fine genre paintings of women and even some landscapes. He was considered an American master of a broadly executed realist style, changing as he did with the times. Many of his later paintings were powerful, even outstanding, but from the perspective of our era, it is his impressionist paintings, especially those executed during the years of World War I, that were to become his most brilliant legacy.

Roderic H. Blackburn

LOUIS RITMAN

FROM CHICAGO TO GIVERNY:

How Louis Ritman Was Influenced by Lawton Parker
and Other Midwestern Impressionists

CHAPTER ONE:
A LAND OF NEW VISION

A study of the early background of Louis Ritman encompasses two continents and a convergence of people and events from the four corners of the world. It was the appearance of the triumvirate of Lawton Parker, Frederick Frieseke, and Richard Miller from the Midwest, coupled with the later arrival of Louis Ritman from Russia, that resulted in an expatriate school of Midwestern impressionism, centering in Giverny, France. Indelibly affected by the Chicago art world, this Midwestern group exerted a great deal of influence on the younger immigrant, Louis Ritman. Parker, the most influential, came from Kearney, Nebraska; Frieseke, from Owosso, Michigan; and Miller from Saint Louis, Missouri. Inspired by their common experiences in Chicago and France, the three Midwesterners—Parker, Frieseke, and Miller—drew Louis Ritman into their midst to assist in maintaining their potent second-generation, expatriate American impressionism in Giverny, France. Although this group received a great deal of their inspiration from differing milieus in Paris and Giverny, where Monet, the father of French impressionism still worked, the mature results of their artistic endeavor revealed an inherently obvious American character, the basic fabric of which undoubtedly came from the Midwest, and more specifically, Chicago.

Our story begins in 1863 with the birth of Solomon Ritman, the father of Louis, in Austria, the core of the Hapsburg Empire. Solomon's father was a weaver of clothing textiles with which he designed men's wear. A time-honored profession in Eastern Europe, especially in Poland, Austria, and the western Ukraine, weaving-designing had been pursued by several generations of the Ritman family. The adult Solomon, of medium height and slender, maintained a certain aristocratic demeanor in spite of his family's lower-middle-class standing.[1]

Solomon's future wife, Rebecca Saltzman, was also born within the domain of the Hapsburg Empire in Austria or Poland. One of five daughters, young Rebecca was short, of slight build, and serious-minded. Exactly how or when Rebecca and Solomon met is unknown, but in accordance with Hebrew tradition, their marriage was arranged. Pursuing the family career, Solomon moved his family to Kamenets-Podolsky, a small city in southwestern Russia.[2]

In 1868, five years after Solomon Ritman's birth in Austria, an American farmer, J. S. Parker, and his wife celebrated the birth of their son Lawton in Fairfield, Michigan. In 1873, the Parker family moved to Kearney, Nebraska, where young Lawton soon proved to be the leading spirit among his schoolmates and even gained admirers among the adult residents of the town. Interestingly, it was in the same year that seven-year-old Robert Henry Cozad (the future Robert Henri) moved with his family from Cincinnati to a place on the Platte River about fifty miles north of Kearney. Robert's father, John Cozad had purchased 50,000 acres, which he named Cozad and began developing as a western community.[3] Although young Robert Henri and Lawton Parker did not know each other, they spent several years in the 1870s only fifty miles apart in Nebraska. In future years, the two would become well acquainted and their careers would mingle as they orbited around the greater master from Indianapolis, William Merritt Chase, who was just beginning his career in Germany with friends from Cincinnati, Frank Duveneck and John H. Twachtman. In Kearney, Lawton Parker's youthful efforts and occasional pranks met with the approbation—and even some cooperation—of those who knew him. A lively and enterprising farm boy, Lawton worked and played hard as he absorbed the fascinating Western life around him. Indeed, this life was very similar to that which Robert Henri observed on the Platte River farther west: "We see a great many herders and hunters here. They are fine riders and have beautiful ponies. Some of the hunters wear pretty suits of buckskin with fringe all around. I saw one who had rows of gold dollars on his suit for buttons. They wear their hair very long and a belt around the waist filled with pistols and great spurs on their boots."[4] As Lawton Parker grew up in Kearney, he, like Robert Henri, became a keen observer of his own environment, but in his youth, Lawton was more accomplished at recording his observations by drawing than by writing. Three decades later, Lawton Parker's magnetic and talented personality became a force in the art worlds of Chicago and Giverny. His artistic career would also serve as an inspiration in the artistic development of Louis Ritman, one of Solomon Ritman's sons born in Russia.

In 1874, only a year after the Parkers left Michigan, Herman C. Frieseke and his wife Eva Graham had a new addition to their family in Owosso, Michigan. Their son Frederick Carl was born on April 7. Shortly afterwards, the official birth of impressionism occurred in Paris, France, on 15 April 1874, when the original impressionists opened their first group exhibition at the studios of the photographer Nadar. Frederick's father was engaged in a different kind of enterprise. A son of German immigrants, he had a half-brother, also named Herman, and a sister, Edith. Raised in Owosso, the brothers operated a brick factory in partnership. Eva, Frederick's mother, was a descendant of the founders of Owosso, where he first attended grade school. Frieseke found beauty even in his father's brickyard, with its black wor-

kers singing improvised tunes.[5]

A sudden change in Frederick's environment brought about an early consciousness of his artistic inclinations. In 1881, when Frederick was only seven years old, his father took the children to Jacksonville, Florida, where he had landed a project of manufacturing bricks.[6] Frederick's mother had died, and the children were going to stay with "Uncle Albert's" family across the Saint John's River from Jacksonville. The family was to stay in Florida for several years, and the early impressions of its natural beauty remained with Frederick throughout his life.

Frederick remembers picking yellow jasmine flowers in Georgia woods when the train stopped on the way to Florida. Later, when he watched one of his relatives, a taxidermist, stuff alligators for tourists or Ransom paint Florida sunsets on rosy conch shells, he dreamed of becoming an artist. An ardent observer of the raw and pristine nature around Jacksonville, young Frederick Frieseke was captivated by the color and beauty of Florida and vividly reminisced about it fifty years later. Also, Frederick's protective elder sister, Edith, attempted to keep ugly sights away from her little brother, a circumstance Frieseke found to be of recurrent significance in his life.[7] Frederick had continued to attend grade school in Jacksonville and was ready for high school when the family returned to Owosso, Michigan.[8]

In evaluating Frieseke's early Florida experience with regard to his future relationship with Monet, it is interesting to note that the older French master also had perceived the color effects of brilliant southern light. At a different time and in a different place, Monet's experience had come about during his years of service with the French forces in North Africa. Unlike Monet, who was an adult when he discovered color through light, Frieseke had perhaps already become aware of a similar phenomenon when he was a child exploring and admiring the sunny glades and country roads around Jacksonville, Florida. That Frieseke's years in Florida made a profound impression on his aesthetic sensibilities may be gauged from the fact that, beginning in 1921, he painted a number of landscapes of Florida from memory—forty years after his observations of the scenery. All in all, however, Frieseke's consciousness of color through light lay dormant until it manifested itself through the influence of Monet.

Like Lawton Parker, Frederick was a talented youngster: he took singing lessons, but his baritone voice made him decide against a vocalist's career.[9] Like Parker and Miller, from his childhood Frederick showed a predilection for drawing, which soon turned him to cartooning. A visit to the Art Institute of Chicago provided the necessary inspiration that set Frieseke in pursuit of an artistic career.[10] After the initial period of training, he gravitated toward the progressive style of impressionism. His talents in that direction matured in Giverny over three decades later. Accordingly, Frieseke came to provide a powerful stimulant in the impressionist years of Louis Ritman.

One year after Frieseke's birth, the third member of the triumvirate, Richard Edward Miller, was born to Esmeralda and Richard L. Miller in the booming Midwestern city of Saint Louis, Missouri on March 22, 1875. A dreamer of dreams since adolescence, Miller early set his sights on the art world. By 1893 he was attending night classes at the Saint Louis School of Fine Arts, where he received excellent instruction in the academic tradition, especially the techniques of figure drawing. Among Miller's more outstanding teachers we find Edmund H. Wuerpel, Charles Percy Davis, and Charles A. Winter. Well prepared for illustration work by his studies, Miller became artist-reporter for the *St. Louis Post Dispatch* in 1897. In time he, too, would become one of the second-generation Giverny group, and in this role he would influence Ritman's art.

Back in Europe at this time, the Hapsburg regime was enjoying its most colorful period. Strong ties bound the Hapsburgs and France, and at times America was affected by certain shifts in the balance of power among European countries. For example, in the year of Solomon Ritman's birth, Napoleon III of France proposed to mediate peace in the American Civil War, an offer that was strongly rejected by a Congressional resolution as a subtle scheme for foreign intervention. In a last-ditch effort to maintain influence on the North American continent, Napoleon installed Archduke Maximilian of Austria as the Emperor of Mexico.

On a different sociopolitical level, many Europeans such as the Ritmans perceived America as the land of great opportunity; in their view, it was still the new land that had been prepared by great thinkers for those who wanted to escape European tyranny. However, during the American Civil War, when Solomon Ritman was born, few Europeans crossed the Atlantic in hopes of starting a new life. Actually, many Americans returned to Europe, some to escape the war, others simply to travel leisurely where high culture could be found at every turn.[11] The Conscription Act of 1863 provided that a man's military service might be compensated by the hiring of a substitute or by the remittance of a $300 commutation fee. The act angered many unskilled laborers, whose draft protests resulted in riots, but it provided safety for many wealthier Americans. There were those who seized the opportunity to make fortunes, some legally, some otherwise.

On the stock markets and gold exchanges, hordes of speculators thrived on the good and bad news of the war. The crafty railroad capitalist and speculator Daniel Drew recalled that he and his friends on "Wall Street had the fortunes of war to speculate about . . . . It's good fishing in troubled waters."[12] Andrew Carnegie, Jay Gould, J. P. Morgan, John D. Rockefeller, John Wanamaker, Philip Armour, and many others hired substitute soldiers, an exploit that allowed them to join the ranks of American entrepreneurs who virtually dominated the nation's economy between the Civil War and World War I. Once wealthy, the same financial moguls came to desire culture, some obsessively so; and eventually their art dilettantism resulted in stronger art communities, especially in New York and Chicago, where there was great economic expansion. Eventually, at the turn of the century, Solomon Ritman would leave Kamenets-Podolsky for Chicago, but in the meantime the American art community, which would subsequently incubate his son's talent, was undergoing an amazing transformation. Thus, an overview of this period will help the reader to properly understand the factors that came to contribute to the development of Louis Ritman's art.

Even prior to the Civil War, as Americans joined in the Grand Tour of Europe, their ideas about what culture should consist of changed drastically. The newly enlightened travelers wanted better art and architecture, the kind they saw in Europe. To bring it back to home soil or to send American artists to learn how to make it became acceptable: they rationalized that nearly everything American had its origins in Europe anyway. Therefore, pressure came to be exerted by America's affluent, dilettantes, and intellectuals alike to reestablish the goals of American culture via European criteria. High art became a priority for this select group, which began seeing itself as an elitist society, properly trained to establish and maintain high plateaus of culture in America. At the forefront of this cultural expansion was the acquisition of fine art, especially paintings. For example, in 1863, the year that Solomon Ritman was born, the *New York Times* reported that a "picture mania" had gripped society.[13]

Even earlier, American writers at *The Crayon* subtly suggested European standards in the series "Art Conversazione," while the *Cosmopolitan Art Journal* expressed warm appreciation for a show of European art at the National Academy of Design in New York.[14] Typical of the times was the response of someone like Henry Tappan, university president and educational philosopher, who, having seen his first Rubens, warned that learning art from books was not sufficient, and that "until we see with our own eyes what art has done by the hand of the great masters," we cannot discern the qualities of art.[15] This attitude, however, was not exclusive to the novice;

indeed, the influential American writer James Jackson Jarves found greatness in European paintings but little to praise even in the work of America's great landscape painters of the Hudson River School. In his disdain for the grandiose images of nature, which other cognoscenti found specifically *American* , Jarves incurred the wrath of many constituents. He had spent a good deal of time in Florence and was vehemently opposed by the Society for the Advancement of Truth in Art, an elitist clan whose Ruskinian ideas about America's vast nature were published in the magazine *New Path,* its official journal.[16]

Until the post–Civil War years, the American imagery presented to the public by the Hudson River School was not only highly regarded but also reflected all that was sacred. These paintings were considered to be grandiose images of God's majestic wilderness, artistic mirrors reflecting unique and hitherto secret places in America. In these works the artists had conveyed the sense of a special kind of sublimity which inspired the spirit of patriotism.[17] Writers for the *New Path* and other publications put forth many words of praise for luminist artists such as John F. Kensett, whose 1869 scene **Lake George** (Metropolitan Museum of Art, New York) has since been described as "exactly the point [James Fenimore] Cooper takes us to in the *Deerslayer,* when, as so many critics of American literature. . . have insisted, the new American is symbolically born."[18] In spite of cynics like Jarves, most of the American cultural community was inspired by this kind of imagery, for even Alexis de Tocqueville, the usually caustic French traveler and writer on America, reported that he found the "stillness so complete that the soul is invaded by a kind of religious terror." So compelling was this strange, non-European ambience that he thought the "forces of nature are paralyzed."[19] Huge canvases by "nature's brothers," Frederick Church, Albert Bierstadt, and Thomas Moran, depicting the Grand Canyon, the Yosemite, and other awe-inspiring places, were the manifestation of a new vision in American art; like Whitman, who saw his mission decreed by God, these artists made images of "Creation. . . all creation."[20] Alas, in these great works also, the indelible image of Europe crept through, since even to Washington Irving, the "lofty trees," sunshine, and mood in general were reminiscent of a Gothic cathedral and "the deep breathings of the organ."[21] Staunchly American painters like Eastman Johnson, who went to Europe to learn his craft, and Winslow Homer (ill. 1-1), who went to France in 1867, produced specifically American genre (ill. 1-2), but even their work was often considered second rate compared with that of European masters. Actually, it became difficult for American artists to create American art, and it was equally difficult for Americans

Ill. 1-1. Winslow Homer. Photograph. R.H. Love Galleries Archives, Chicago.

to support it in the face of growing pressure to replace it with European works.

Before the end of the nineteenth century, the historian Henry Adams declared that more changes had taken place since 1854 than during all the ages known in the history of mankind. It was a period of amazing industrial growth, which had contributed equally well to America's Civil War and to its peacetime expansion. In art, the Civil War served as a kind of watershed. Having witnessed an obvious change, the art critic S. G. W. Benjamin saw this great conflict not only as one which settled ideological and political accounts but one from which a new "era of mental development" came forth.[22] To bystanders there was no doubt that those who were seriously interested in America's cultural advancement "would have to establish models of national culture while celebrating material power."[23]

The astute art writer Henry T. Tuckerman was saddened by the fact that American artists still had "no appropriate medium whereby their labors [could] be known to the public," but he also recognized that "within the last few [post–Civil War] years the advance of public taste and the increased recognition of art in this country have been among the most interesting phenomena of the times."[24] To most, it seemed apparent that America had been expanding in every way but culturally, and that it was time to create a solid foundation for the establishment of a national art community. As one post–Civil War art writer put it, "what we need is art-culture, not that which produces the artist (who produces American scenes), but that which educates the connoisseur."[25]

As America grew and prospered in the post–Civil War years, businessmen and manufacturers accumulated unprecedented wealth with which they were anxious to obtain objets d'art from overseas. Encouraged by others in high places, they thought that by bringing European art home, they were contributing to the growth of American culture as well as to industry and business. If their ofttimes crude enthusiasm resulted in some tasteless acquisitions, that was to be excused for the cause of cultural expansion; yet even the discriminating Tuckerman observed that some "American travelers in Europe have secured admirable copies of the most renowned works of the old masters."[26] Ostensibly, of course, wealthy collectors contributed a great deal to America's new cultural foundation, but underlying each collection were secret motivations, not the least of which included the acquisition of art as a symbol of personal taste and social stewardship.[27] Even at this early date, the mystique of art as investment fascinated collectors, but an impressive collection of European art also demonstrated a special combination of intellectual and moralistic motivation on the part of the owner. Furthermore, it proved that Americans could be just as culturally minded as the Europeans who saw them as culturally deprived colonists. Some Americans were openly defensive about their roles as connoisseurs, while others openly admitted their ignorance; but in either instance, they sought European art.[28]

Thus, as the demand for European art reached new heights, Americans left for Europe in a near exodus to eagerly examine every nook and cranny of the Continent's cultural centers. This was a special segment of American society that struggled desperately to find or establish cultural opportunities equivalent to the rich prospects beckoning in agriculture, industry, and business. The American tourist looking for art became a familiar sight in Düsseldorf, London, Madrid, Paris, and Rome. Confident of his ability to pay the highest prices, he sought entry into the most sacred places and the most aristocratic homes, frequently with success. "With traditional American brashness, he often thought nothing of calling on

famous artists."[29] One observer pointed out that "the liberality of American travellers is well-known to European artists whose studios they frequent for purchase."[30] Realizing that American civilization was in its infancy, progressive urban leaders looked with renewed vigor to Europe for cultural inspiration, while prominent and wealthy figures of business and industry looked to Europe for art, especially paintings.

Ill. 1-2. Eastman Johnson. *The Card Players.* 1853. Oil on canvas, 21¾ x 28½ inches. Private Collection. Courtesy R.H. Love Galleries, Inc., Chicago.

Surely nowhere was this trend more evident than in New York in 1871, when William Tilden Blodgett brought back 174 important European paintings that he had purchased in London with the Metropolitan Museum "in mind."[31] Blodgett was praised by his curator-partner, Metropolitan Museum President John Taylor Johnston, who wrote that he had been "very magnanimous" in not keeping "some of those fine things when he had it in his power." Johnston, who owned a private gallery, admitted that he "would have had at least to have taken out that Van Dyck or perished."[32] The irony of the Blodgett-Johnston purchase was that it was acquired for a museum that did not yet exist. In fact, the museum had only recently acquired its name; and yet, in the honorable endeavor of providing "custody and protection of the highest of all works in the world," Blodgett and Johnston spent an amount equivalent to nearly one-half of the budget needed to implement the creation of the future Metropolitan Museum of Art.[33] If the acquisition seemed inappropriate or extravagant to some, it signaled to Europe's art community that a great revival of interest in their art was taking place among wealthy Americans, who were anxious to share the works with their fellow citizens.

In 1856, an art writer had described a painting by Asher B. Durand as a "purely American" image that "tells an American story out of American facts, portrayed with true American feeling, by a devoted and earnest student of Nature."[34] The post–Civil War era, however, fostered a society that was no longer so interested in what was "purely American." What had been considered traditionally American now seemed to have serious flaws. America became as painfully aware of its own cultural shortcomings as it was of its sociopolitical ones; in spite of the military victory for freedom, all things "purely American" became suspect. Many people reasoned that it was time to get back to basics, and the enlightened minds thought these basics were to be found in Europe. As a result, the post–Civil War era also fostered a new generation of art writers and critics who were just as anxious as collector-philanthropists to improve the status of American art. One of these writers was Clarence Cook of the *New York Tribune* and *New Path*, who had frequently challenged the conservative opinions of William Curtis, editor of *Harper's Weekly*. In effect, Cook blazed the trail for the acquisition of European art when he publicly criticized American artists for attempting to persuade Congress to impose a tariff to control the importation of foreign art. He stated flatly that regardless of how "pure" it was, American art was inferior to European art, and that American painters feared competition.[35] Writers and other cognoscenti were influenced by critics like Cook who made it plain that Americans were "indebted to foreign art." Cook told his readers that it was "in the improvement of public taste, that the difficulty lies." He continued: "The majority of our artists have been left behind by it [public taste], and are indisposed or unable to make the necessary exertions to catch up with it, and regain the public favor." Historian H. Wayne Morgan points out that "the new critics were determined to encourage the best painters, enlarge their audience, and develop canons of taste to sustain art into the future." Morgan underscores the fact that these art critics, "like the painters whose works they criticized . . . had multiple ambitions." He goes on to explain: "They [the critics] wished to equal the prestige and influence of counterparts in literary criticism, a better-established discipline. They realized that American art in the 1860's was old-fashioned, bound to change on the rising wave of new styles and intentions which they meant to ride to authority. They were also defensive, as educated people, about the Old World's cultural superiority. And they were eager to make art an important aspect of the national power they saw coming to the new industrial America."[36]

As the decade of the 1870s progressed, a large part of the established American art community finally abandoned its pursuit of American imagery for something still undefined but decidedly European. With the trend gaining momentum, it became increasingly difficult to find dealers, collectors, or even artists who wanted to be involved in traditional American art. The changes occurring during this period were summarized succinctly by the art historian Samuel Isham: "With the seventies [art] became an important business exploited with all the energy of the other newly found methods of gaining wealth." He continued:

As a rule the dealers were men of commercial integrity, making large profits, but making them by perfectly honorable dealing; one or two of them, however, were much more than that — connoisseurs in the best sense of the word, understanding and loving good painting, recognizing the great merits of some men still unappreciated in France, counselling and educating their patrons — men like Cottier and Samuel P. Avery, to whom the culture of the country owes much. They forced upon the hesitating purchasers the works of Corot and Millet and Daubigny, and with others brought over also the more readily comprehensible Meissoniers and Gérômes and Bouguereaus. These were for the wealthier and more enlightened patrons; for the others there was the whole school of Parisian *genre* painters with their brilliancy, their manifest skill, their deceptive imitation of textures, their amusing modern anecdotes or reconstruction of old fashions and costumes; and to them was added the new German school of Munich with its shiny bitumen and bold brush work beside which the old Düsseldorfian favorites seemed faded and prosaic. . . .The invasion was inevitable and on the whole beneficial. The growing prosperity forced a departure from the older, simpler mode of life. Men of ability and character found their wealth increasing far beyond their expectation. . . .taste had to be formed which could only be done by trying all things and cleaving to that which was good. The dealers' galleries were an education in painting. . . . Against this rising tide of foreign work the native painters struggled manfully, but for a while it was a losing battle."[37]

Therefore, by the late 1870s the American art community no longer prided itself on seeking and promoting something specifically "American"; instead, its leading members sought only that which was strictly European, hoping to transplant or at least reflect some "Old World" classicist superiority across the Atlantic. There were a few "unenlightened" Americans who still clung to pre–Civil War dreams of an autonomous American art and demanded only native imagery. Similarly, there were a few artists who made such images and a fewer number of art dealers who cared to promote them. Old established dealers, such as the Voses in Boston, sold both European and American art. Painters like Winslow Homer, Thomas Eakins, Thomas Hovenden, and others remained attached to the American vision (ill. 1-3). These art

Ill. 1-3. Thomas Hovenden. *Bringing Home the Bride.* Oil on canvas, 56 x 78 inches. Private Collection. Courtesy R.H. Love Galleries, Inc., Chicago.

makers, however, were motivated by a different set of principles from those of expatriate painters like Frank Duveneck, Mary Cassatt, Mark Fisher, or T. Addison Richards, whose illustrated handbook on travel helped many an American artist get around in Europe. Nor did the American idealists think like Albert Pinkham Ryder, whose trips to Europe and interest in Wagnerian opera resulted in a kind of universal imagery that fascinated the sophisticated collectors. To many American artists, the obvious obsession with European art on the part of their constituents was frustrating if not downright un-American. Interviewed in the 1870s, the master genre painter John George Brown stated: "Half of the foreign stuff that is sold here I feel is a swindle on the public." He explained: "I can show you in [Worthington] Whittredge's studio some of the most beautiful studies ever

made. . . . studies of American scenery seen with his own eyes. Why don't we worship Whittredge instead of worshipping foreigners. . . . the picture-dealers are the ones that do it. They have made it fashionable to buy European works."[38]

Eventually, American canvases began to look European. For example, the exhibition of Frank Duveneck's avant-garde paintings in Boston in 1875 ushered in the Munich School style to America. Duveneck's was a strikingly brushy bravura, promoted by liberal teachers at the Munich Royal Art Academy. His dark painting mode was modern, but it only remotely resembled French impressionism, the radical style that only a year earlier had been presented to the Parisian public by Edouard Manet and his so-called Batignolles group at Nadar's former photography studio in Paris. Actually, all of Europe's art communities were in flux, and a few progressive painters like Duveneck in Munich and John Singer Sargent in Paris and London reflected new trends in their art. This situation was perplexing to many young American expatriate art students, who stood by innocently as European progressives demolished their own academic traditions. Most American hopefuls now longed for acceptance in the great state-supported European art schools, openly seeking recognition within the official procedures of the salons. Many members of the art world were horrified by these seemingly anarchistic art movements, and American expatriates who absorbed the influences were considered radical if not quite un-American.

Certain liberal-minded American artists brought back from Europe innovative stylistic ideas, which they implemented locally in hopes of reforming their own art communities. As Marchal Landgren explains, these artists "had fresh ideas relating to all art matters, for many had been in contact with the rebellious movements abroad." He points out that "they created a new and vigorous interest in art that well complemented the vast sums that the rich had begun to lavish on art and art objects."[39] These artists, motivated by examples set by their counterparts in Europe, wanted reform, a liberalization of worn-out tradition. It was not just the artists themselves, however, who pushed for reform, but any liberal who had a cultural ax to grind. Among these personalities was the new generation of enlightened critics, who "understood and sought the role of cultural arbiter. Their opinions became part of the art process for both painter and patron."[40]

To most constituents of the art community it seemed that the greatest need for reform existed at the nucleus of the American art community, the National Academy of Design in New York. As a result, the Art Students

Ill. 1-4. Panorama of the 1876 Centennial Exposition in Philadelphia. Photograph. R.H. Love Galleries Archives, Chicago.

League was organized in 1875, when the young Wisconsin artist Theodore Robinson and other National Academy students banded together with their chief instructor, Lemuel Wilmarth, to found their own academy.[41] Soon this group controlled the league and broke relations with the National Academy. Most critics and the press in general supported their efforts. As the league was being formed, the liberal supporters of art, Richard Watson Gilder (assistant editor of *Scribner's*) and his painter wife Helena de Kay, made their home a unique meeting ground for artists who had recently returned from Europe.[42] The expatriate Will H. Low described the Gilder home as "an oasis in the first few years of our return to our desert home, as it appeared to us in comparison to the flowery regions of art whence we came."[43] At the same time, the Cottier and Company Gallery in New York City mounted an exhibition featuring the work of progressives like Albert Pinkham Ryder, William Morris Hunt, John La Farge, and others—the show served as an alternative to the one at the National Academy of Design and prompted some interesting discussion in New York newspapers.[44] In his position at *Scribner's*, Gilder supported the idea of holding exhibitions as alternatives to those presented by the National

Academy.[45] To make matters worse, in 1876 a controversy began at the academy which centered around a hanging-committee decision to put works by Frank Duveneck, Walter Shirlaw, William Merritt Chase, and other progressives "on the line."[46] These painters were all leading members of the American expatriate group who had recently returned from Munich, Paris, and elsewhere in Europe. The controversy that arose over the hanging of their radical work not only resulted in certain reforms at the academy but also opened the door for the establishment of the American Art Association, soon to be known as the Society of American Artists .[47] The premier exhibition of this very forward-thinking society, although billed ironically as "thoroughly American," was justifiably criticized for its European-trained membership and their "foreign-looking" art. Anxious to repel the potential for such criticism, the society reported that its members had "an unbounded appreciation of the future in store for art in this country." The group pointed out that its members intended to avail themselves of the freshest and most approved means of art culture, and that to this end, most if not all of them had studied in the leading schools of France and Germany.[48]

The American Centennial in 1876 was the result of the

Ill. 1-5. Main Building. Centennial Exposition of 1876, Philadelphia. R.H. Love Galleries Archives, Chicago.

efforts made by many cultural leaders to inspire a new spirit of nationalism, albeit one based on re-established European traditions.[49] Accordingly, the event culminated in the great Centennial Exposition (ill. 1-4; 1-5), which was held in Fairmount Park in Philadelphia and which served as an unprecedented forum for foreign, especially European, art. The park grounds provided an impressive view of the city proper and of the Schuylkill River. The Centennial Exposition section consisted of 450 acres; a board fence nine feet high and nearly three miles long enclosed the actual exhibition grounds.[50] Completely transformed, the area included many impressive spots of interest, not the least of which was the zoological gardens and the East Park, the site of the home of Benedict Arnold, and the great Lincoln Monument, a bronze by Randolph Rogers. The most impressive structure, known as Memorial Hall, was a huge art exhibition building, replete with an heroic figure of Columbus (see ill. 1-6).[51] For the occasion, the European and American cultural committees cooperated as never before: John Greenleaf Whittier wrote a special hymn for the event, and Richard Wagner composed a new march. Writers everywhere waxed eloquent about the exposition, and having viewed the huge art exhibition, most painters resolved either to go to Europe for the first time or to renew their expatriate status. Young artists like J. Alden Weir who were fortunate enough to already study there were advised to take advantage of every foreign opportunity, since there seemed to be little reward for one's efforts at home. In 1877, while he was studying at the Ecole des Beaux-Arts in Paris, young Weir received a letter from his brother John F. Weir, then director of the Yale School of Art, saying that it seemed a "great mistake" to return to America. The letter continued: "There is no

interest in Art here now—the outlook was never so discouraging. Stay over there as long as you can."[52]

By the late 1880s, there was little momentum left in the "pure" American art dream, even in the once very American Hudson River School. Appreciation for the meticulous realism of artists such as Frederick E. Church, J. F. Cropsey (ill. 1-7), and Albert Bierstadt was seriously waning among the enlightened cognoscenti. Indeed, according to J. K. Howat, "the bottom went out of Bierstadt's market, just as it did for Church and Cropsey."[53] Howat points out that Bierstadt must have been devastated when he read the *Official Report of the American Centennial Exhibition of 1876*, prepared by Professor John F. Weir of Yale University: "The earlier works of this artist [Bierstadt] showed a vigorous, manly style of art, that had its undeniable attractions. His pictures exhibited at Philadelphia indicate a lapse into sensational and meretricious effects, and a loss of true artistic aim." The huge majestic compositions, depicting scenes that conjured up ideas of primeval beauty even in the New York countryside or in the recently discovered panoramic vastness of the Yose-

Ill. 1-6. Memorial Hall with the Statue of Columbus. Centennial Exposition of 1876, Philadelphia. R.H. Love Galleries Archives, Chicago.

mite area in the distant West, were increasingly ignored for smaller easel paintings by French artists like Narcisse Virgile Diaz, Theodore Rousseau, and other Barbizon painters.[54] Lewis Mumford believed that this kind of art was the product of what he called the "Brown Decades."[55] When the Barbizon style was imitated by a slightly later group of Americans and carried on into the waning years of the century, it was called tonalism or the color of mood , as Wanda Corn so aptly described it.[56] The somber palettes and dramatic skies of those who worked in the Forest of Fontainebleau were fashionable, but even this approach did not appeal to those who loved academicism, the continuing heritage of the great neoclassicist Jacques Louis David, through Jean Auguste Ingres, to the great Salon masters like Ernest Meissonier, William Adolphe Bouguereau (ill. 1-8), and others. In the case of these government-supported masters, high art was nothing less than the so-called Salon style, consisting for the most part of the careful draftsmanship, formally designed compositions, and slick, meticulous realism of the age-old academic masters. The skillfully painted canvases of the Salon masters were highly regarded by American collectors, art dealers, and museum curators. As a result, genre works by Europeans came to be much more in demand than native productions. To stouthearted American artists like John George Brown (ill. 1-9) and others, it seemed that both they and their work had been abolished by their own countrymen.

Eventually, however, American painters saw the light—they learned that they could not row against the mainstream of the American art industry. To exist professionally, they were obliged to sacrifice not only native subjects and scenery but native styles as well for anything European, but especially French. Also, American painters found tempting rewards in becoming expatriates, if not permanently, at least for a couple of years until they had learned how to make their images look European—better yet, French. In this practical, yet fashionable endeavor to Europeanize their art consciousness and skills, several alternative routes were open to artists, each as complicated as the next. Of course, the Salon experience was paramount; and for landscapists, a painting sojourn in the Barbizon area was quite helpful. However, if American painters were either incapable or unwilling to continue the traditional Beaux-Arts Salon routine, there was motivation aplenty to make an alliance (officially or otherwise) with the avant-garde independent movements in Paris, Munich, or London. These three art capitals already boasted a few independent American stars, progressives like the controversial bohemian James A. M. Whistler and the cosmopolitan darling of international society, John Singer Sargent, both of whom figured prominently in the inner art circles of London and Paris.

Ill. 1-7. Jasper F. Cropsey. *Couple on a Bridge*. Oil on canvas, 9 x 14 inches. R.H. Love Galleries, Inc., Chicago.

Teachers recounted their own experiences in learning the expatriate routine, and that was usually enough to inspire most students to make their own pilgrimage to Europe. Other teachers actually arranged guided tours: for example, for many years, after the close of the National Academy of Design show in New York in March, William Merritt Chase took an entourage across the Atlantic to see the London Royal Academy show in April and the Paris Salon in May. In this way, he and his students experienced mainstream European art and reflected on it when they returned to New York, Chicago, and elsewhere.

The Munich School style was, in essence, the first foreign progressive art trend to be assimilated by the post-Centennial American expatriates. Actually voted into the curriculum by the student body, the Munich School style exerted a tenacious hold at the Art Students League; but

Ill. 1-8. William Adolphe Bouguereau. R.H. Love Galleries Archives, Chicago.

There were also Mary Cassatt in Paris, Frank Duveneck and J. Frank Currier in Munich, John La Farge in France and the Far East, and a host of other lesser-known expatriates who were not afraid to expand their imagery to plateaus beyond the limits of the Salon system.

Some of the Americans who embraced the new French and German styles returned to America to teach. Most of them stayed in New York or elsewhere on the East Coast; but a few came to Chicago, Saint Louis, and Cincinnati, and some went as far west as California.[57] At first, it was difficult for the hierarchy at the National Academy of Design in New York to accept the radical concepts of the European avant-garde; in time, however, most teachers came to advocate the international style, as it came to be known.[58] Vastly more liberal, the recently organized Art Students League of New York first promoted the Munich School style, then the international style, and finally impressionism through the enthusiastic guidance of teachers like William Merritt Chase.[59] In Boston, there were Joseph DeCamp, Edmund Tarbell, and Frank Benson; in Cincinnati, Twachtman, Louis Meakin, and Duveneck; and in Chicago, Lawton Parker, William Merritt Chase, Wellington J. Reynolds, and John H. Vanderpoel. Philadelphia had Thomas Eakins, Robert Vonnoh, William Merritt Chase, and Thomas Anshutz.

Ill. 1-9. John George Brown. R.H. Love Galleries Archives, Chicago.

during the early 1880s, it was replaced by the French international style.[60] Paris-trained artists such as Thomas Wilmer Dewing and William Sartain promoted the procedures of the French academicians, famous Beaux-Arts Salon masters like Benjamin Constant, Jules Lefebvre, Gustave Boulanger, and Léon Bonnat (ill. 1-10).

As a result of these many influences, scores of American art students sailed from New York to Europe to learn how to deal with the Salon routine. Some went to Lon-

Ill. 1-10 Leon Bonnat. R.H. Love Galleries Archives, Chicago.

don, others to Munich, a few to Holland and even to Florence and Rome, but most of them settled in Paris. Here, the vast majority began by attending either the Ecole des Beaux-Arts, the Julian Academy, or one of various private ateliers like that of the American favorite Tony Robert-Fleury or Emile Auguste Carolus-Duran, who had instructed John Singer Sargent, J. Carroll Beckwith, Theodore Butler, Theodore Robinson, and others.

In the 1880s, most American painters knew little about the controversial impressionists. For the most part, the movement was considered an underground activity resulting in a shallow product of a few French radicals, whose anti-Salon tendencies were dismissed as something bizarre and at best inconsequentially unique. The canvases that were seen by American expatriates had usually been characterized by their constituents as crude compositions, garish in color, and little more than sketches in oil, rather poor *esquisses*, as the French frequently called them. Even a decade after its genesis, impressionism was kept at arm's length by all but the most liberal Americans. If the words of Louis Leroy, *Le Charivari* critic whose caustic narrative resulted in the ironic sobriquet *impressionism*, did not stick in their minds, his response no doubt reflected the thoughts of many cynical Americans. After viewing the first impressionist show, Leroy wrote a description of the reactions of an imaginary conservative artist and himself: "'Ah! This is it, this is it!' he cried in front of n. 98. . . . 'What is this a painting of? Look in the catalogue.' *Impression, Sunrise.* 'Impression — I knew it. I was just saying to myself, if I'm impressed, there must be an impression in there. . . . And what freedom, what ease in the brushwork! Wallpaper in its embryonic state is more labored than this seascape!'"[61] From that point in 1874 on, impressionism became a movement that was visible to the public. Also, it was in Paris that the rest of the Western world looked for new ideas in art. Many American artists went there to search as well, but it took most of them quite some time to develop a serious interest to the point where they tried the aesthetic for themselves. One of the most observant and negatively straightforward analysts of impressionism was the New England painter Henry Bacon. In a report published in 1882, Bacon wrote:

> There are a number of painters in Paris whose works always figured in these [Independent] exhibitions, and they have at last formed themselves into a society under the title of 'Impressionistes,' which, as well as we can learn, intends to explain that they wish to present to the public their impression of nature. We have no reason to consider them dishonest, so we must conclude that they are afflicted with some hitherto unknown disease of the eye; for they neither see form nor color as other painters have given them to us, or as nature appears to all who do not belong to this association. Their models must be a regiment of monstrosities with green or violet flesh, the skies of their land-

scapes green, the trees purple and the ground blue.[62]

Ill. 1-11. Frédéric Bartholdi's Statue of Liberty with pedestal against a background view of New Jersey, Brooklyn and New York. R.H. Love Galleries Archives, Chicago.

About a year after Bacon's report, an event took place that was to serve as a positive influence on the impressionist movement in America: the Bartholdi Pedestal Fund Exhibition was mounted in New York (ill. 1-11). Organized by William Merritt Chase and J. Carroll Beckwith, teachers at the Art Students League, the exhibition contained a number of works by Edouard Manet and Edgar Degas. With the exception of a smaller and little-noticed show that was entitled the Foreign Exhibition and presented a few months earlier at the Mechanics' Building in Boston, the 1883 Bartholdi Exhibition was actually the first major showing of impressionism in America. Some harsh criticism surrounded the show; in fact, an anonymous *New York Times* critic viewed the exhibition and proclaimed: "Here, too, are 'impressionists' of the most pronounced kind — Manet. . . Degas (repulsively real ballet girls magnificently brushed in) and Whistler."[63] Still, the Bartholdi Pedestal Fund show actually fostered a modicum of public appreciation for the new French style.

As time went on, the American public demonstrated a good deal more receptivity to impressionism than did the French. Part of this irony resulted from the fact that Americans had been experiencing a gradual transition in culture — the replacement, as it were, of "pure" American art with European art, something they had become accustomed to in the course of the preceding two decades. It is also possible that a percentage of the American public "demonstrated its inferiority complex by suppressing pejorative criticism out of cultural intimidation."[64] One example of this attitude, which lingered long after the introduction of impressionism to America, is the response of an unidentified viewer to Monet's work. He recounted that "Tom Appleton said when the first Corots were brought to Boston they were the worst pictures and the worst painted by the worst artist that ever lived. . . and though that's about what I think of these Monets, I am not going to let anybody know it."[65]

Yet, if certain liberal segments of the American public were relatively receptive to impressionism, individual artists seemed somewhat less anxious to embrace the style because it meant self-imposed alienation from mainstream art. These artists hoped, instead, to gain recognition via the official and traditional channels, namely, the Paris Salon, the National Academy of Design, and the Royal Academy shows in London and Munich. Because of their proximity to the impressionists, a greater number of the growing expatriate group in Paris might have been expected to embrace the new French style, but art history records a different story. Prior to 1886 only a few expatriates had demonstrated any significant interest in impressionism: James A. M. Whistler (actually one of the first unofficial impressionist innovators), Mark Fisher (who studied with Monet, Alfred Sisley, and Auguste Renoir at Charles Gleyre's atelier), and Mary Cassatt (the only official American impressionist).[66] In fact, certain artists who later became impressionists bitterly condemned the early French innovators. One of these was J. Alden Weir, who, while a student at the Ecole des Beaux-Arts in Paris, was shocked at his first encounter with impressionism and sent home these disparaging words: "I went across the river the other day to see an exhibition of the work of a new school which call themselves 'Impressionalists' [sic] I never in my life saw more horrible things." He went on to say: "I understand they are mostly all rich, which accounts for so much talk. They do not observe drawing nor form but give you an impression of what they call nature."[67]

Regardless of anyone's view of impressionism during its evolution, the year 1886 was to effect a decisive change in the future of the movement. That spring, a few members of the *Société anonyme* (the original impressionist association) organized their last group show in Paris.[68] Unable to mount an exhibition for the previous three years because of disagreements on terms and logistics — especially as a result of Manet's death about that time — several charter members went their own ways.[69] Even Camille Pissarro, the ever-reliable member of the vanguard of impressionism, had become fascinated with new direction — pointillism, or scientific impressionism, a method in which small dots of high-key pigment were juxtaposed(neo-impressionism).[70] This new style had been demonstrated and explained to Pissarro by the much younger artist Georges Seurat, who centered his artistic experiments on the scientific theories of the American physicist Ogden N. Rood and the French chemist Eugène Chevreul. One formula set by Chevreul states that "under simultaneous contrast of colors are included all the modifications which differently colored objects appear to undergo in their physical composition, and in the height of tone of their respective colors, when seen simultaneously."[71] Since that time, studies have adequately

Ill. 1-13. The Paris Bourse (Stock Exchange) mirrored the French financial life of the nineteenth century. However, it was the more daring American business that saved the sagging fortunes of French impressionism. R.H. Love Galleries Archives, Chicago.

Ill. 1-12. Theodore Earl Butler. *Portrait of Paul Durand-Ruel.* 1911. Oil on canvas, 28¼ x 23½ inches. Mr. and Mrs. L. J. Berger Collection. Courtesy R. H. Love Galleries, Inc., Chicago.

proved that juxtaposed strokes of color do not mix in the retina.[72] Nonetheless, Pissarro was so taken by Seurat's scientific impressionism that he insisted that pointillist paintings be included in the last group show — a further indication that impressionism was splintering.[73]

"But just as impressionism was about to gasp its last breath, the movement was reborn into a more spiritual life through the merit of its champion, the French art dealer Paul Durand-Ruel." (ill. 1-12)[74] It was largely through the efforts of James F. Sutton, an enthusiastic member of the American Art Association of New York, that the nearly bankrupt Durand-Ruel was invited to show the work of his impressionists in New York.[75] The astounding show opened in April 1886 and evoked both harsh criticism and a surprising number of favorable comments by critics and some of the public. One reviewer for the *New York Daily Tribune* reported that the public found "the paintings of this school. . . utterly and absolutely worthless," while he believed that "these versatile and technically clever painters have done some work of fine quality."[76] To an anonymous critic writing for the *New York Tribune*, it was the "presence of vivacity and vitality which induces us to think less of faulty drawing and discordant colors." He reported that "these men paint as if they liked it, with an abandon in which there is a certain sensuous charm."[77] Even the ever-conservative, albeit pro-French, critic Clarence Cook suggested that visitors "allow for all exaggerations, deduct for all crudeness, and vain shooting at the sun, what every one must feel here is the work of men delighting in the excerise of their art, not working at a task for the sake of boiling the pot, not weaving rhymes. . . but singing as they paint, and facing the new world with the leaping wine of discovery in their veins."[78] Few observers in France had expected such a response from Americans , but the success inspired a new ideological momentum and brought economic salvation for both Durand-Ruel and his French impressionists, whose efforts had been consistently rejected by the Parisian art world for a dozen years. Thrilled with his success, Durand-Ruel wrote to Henri Fantin-Latour: "Don't think that Americans are savages. On the contrary, they are less ignorant, less bound by routine than our French collectors."[79]

So it was that 1886 marked the end of impressionism as a singular movement in France and signaled its beginning as a new movement in the United States. As a style that was replacing the French international style, impressionism was no longer the exclusive property of the original French few and their elitist circle of cultural isolationists (ill. 1-13). The actions of farsighted culture makers like Sutton implied that "if you don't like it, we do, and once adopted, we'll make it our own." In this regard, French impressionism, an art movement that symbolized revolution, freedom, and independence, became

available to anyone who wished to interpret or reinterpret its quality. Thus, impressionism became equally representative of American ideology in art and of French aesthetic thought. Of course, the American acceptance of impressionism did not come as a surprise because there existed a strong tradition of French support for the American revolution. Now America could return the favor on a cultural level. Accordingly, impressionism assumed new dimensions and headed in other directions through the retrospective and analytical inquiries of both its established and its younger practitioners. The distinctive contributions of the two age groups have been best delineated by John Rewald: "The history of the years after 1886 is thus the parallel history of two generations: the older one, still in the prime of its vigor and confident in its strength, and the younger, which first had to acquire the independence necessary to unfold its own potentialities. While audacity and initiative often remained with the newcomers, knowledge and experience were the prerogative of the old-timers."[80]

Notes

1. For the most part, the biographical data regarding the Ritman family is derived from various interviews with Maurice Ritman, the youngest son of Solomon and brother of Louis Ritman. Various family documents were also consulted in gathering biographical information. The original biographical chronology on Louis Ritman was compiled in 1976 for an exhibition catalog published by the Louis Ritman estate.

2. A city with a distinguished historical background going back to the twelfth century, when it became part of the Duchy of Galicia-Volhynia, Kamenets-Podolsky fell under Polish control during the fourteenth century and boasted a fortress. It was briefly held by the Turks at the end of the seventeenth century. In 1793, when Poland was divided, the city became part of Russia.

3. William Innes Homer, *Robert Henri and His Circle* (Ithaca, NY: Cornell University Press, 1969), pp. 11-13.

4. Robert Henri (Robert H. Cozad), "A Letter from Young America," *Hundredth Meridian,* 28 November 1876, quoted from Homer, p. 12.

5. Frederick C. Frieseke, "Uneventful Reminiscences," Reminiscences, Writings, Price Lists, Microfilm Roll no. N737, frames 0001-0005, Archives of American Art, Smithsonian Institution, Washington, DC.

6. Ibid., frames 0001-0002.

7. Ibid., frame 0004.

8. Nicholas Kilmer, Frederick Frieseke Questionnaire, R. H. Love Galleries Archives, Chicago.

9. Nicholas Kilmer to Moussa M. Domit, 26 August 1974, Raleigh, NC, photocopy, Frieseke File, R. H. Love Galleries Archives, Chicago.

10. Ben L. Summerford, *A Retrospective Exhibition of the Works of F. C. Frieseke*, exhibition catalog (San Francisco, CA: Maxwell Galleries, Ltd, 1982), p. 10.

11. Edgar P. Richardson and Otto Wittmann, Jr.,*Travelers in Arcadia, American Artists in Italy, 1830-1865* (Detroit, MI: The Detroit Institute of Arts and The Toledo Museum of Art, 1951). See also Thomas W. Leavitt, "Let the Dogs Bark: George Loring Brown and the Critics," *American Art Review,* I, no. 2 (January-February 1974).

12. Maury Klein, "The North At War," *Shadows of the Storm* (Garden City, NY: Doubleday & Co., Inc., 1981), vol. 1, p. 370. See also Bouch White, *The Book of Daniel Drew*, 1910.

13. *New York Tribune*, 4 April 1863. For a somewhat later historical review of the trend in the 1860s, see M. G. Van Rensselaer, "The New York Art Season," *Atlantic Monthly*, 48 (August 1881), pp. 193-202.

14. *The Crayon,* V (February 1958), p. 59; *Cosmopolitan Art Journal,* III (December 1959), p.236.

15. Henry P. Tappan, *A Step from the New World to the Old, and Back Again. . .* (New York, 1852), vol. I, p. 229.

16. The first issue of *New Path* appeared in May of 1863. Clarence Cook was one of its contributors while the society was guided by Charles Farrer, an English expatriate living in New York City.

17. For a complete overview of these topics, see Barbara Novak, *Nature and Culture: American Landscape and Painting, 1825-1875* (New York: Oxford University Press, 1980).

18. Vincent Scully, *New World Visions of Household Gods & Sacred Places* (Boston: Little, Brown and Company, 1988), p. 115.

19. Alexis de Tocqueville, *Journey to America*, trans. George Lawrence, ed. J. P. Mayer (Garden City, NY: Doubleday, 1971), p. 383.

20. James Fenimore Cooper, "The Pioneers," in *The Leatherstocking Saga*, p. 688.

21. Washington Irving, *A Tour on the Prairies* (1835; reprint ed., New York: Pantheon , 1967), p. 36.

22. S. G. W. Benjamin, *Contemporary Art in Europe* (New York: Harper, 1877), p. 7.

23. H. Wayne Morgan, *New Muses: Art in American Culture, 1865-1920* (Norman, OK: University of Oklahoma Press, 1978), p. 4.

24. Henry T. Tuckerman, *Book of the Artists* (1867; reprint ed., New York: James F. Carr, 1966), p. 11.

25. "Table Talk," *Appleton's Journal*, no. 6 (December 16, 1871), p. 695.

26. Tuckerman, p. 11.

27. Corinna Lindon Smith, *Interesting People* (Norman, OK: University of Oklahoma Press, 1962), pp. 141-44.

28. Sadakichi Hartmann, *A History of American Art* (Boston, MA: L. C. Page & Co., 1902), vol. II, p. 284.

29. Morgan, p. 11.

30. Philip Quilibit, "Art at the World's Fair," *Galaxy*, no. 21 (February 1876), p. 272.

31. Described as a "perspicacious" executive committeeman, Blodgett, with president of the Metropolitan Musem, John Taylor Johnston, borrowed the $116,180.27 for the purchase of the pictures, spoils from the war between France and Germany. See Leo Lerman, *The Museum* (New York: The Viking Press, 1969), p. 17.

32. Johnston, quoted in Lerman, p. 18.

33. Reverend Dr. Bellows, quoted in Lerman, p. 17.

34. *The Crayon*, III (May 1856), p. 150.

35. Clarence Cook, "The Cry from the Studios," *Galaxy*, 3 (15 February 1867), p. 439-440. Concerning the artist Peletin to Congress, see *New York Tribune*, 16 January 1867, p. 4, and 23 January 1867, p. 4.

36. Morgan, p. 40. See also "Another Look at Foreign Pictures in New York," *Nation*, 2 (11 January 1866), pp, 55-56. Regarding the motivational aspects of contemporaneous art critics, see Russell Sturgis, "What Is Art Criticism," *Art Journal*, no. 5, (January 1879), p. 29.

37. Samuel Isham, *The History of American Painting*, new edition with supplemental chapters by Royal Cortissoz (New York: The Macmillan Co., 1936), pp. 360-61.

38. G. W. Sheldon, *American Painters* (New York: D. Appleton and Co., 1879), pp. 141-42.

39. Marchal Landgren, *Years of Art: The Story of the Art Students League of New York* (New York: Robert M. McBride and Company, 1940), pp. 22-23.

40. Morgan, p. 42.

41. For more discussion about the Art Students League, see Frank Waller, *First Report of the Art Students League of New York* (New York, 1886).

42. Richard Watson Gilder was born in Bordertown, New Jersey, on 8 February 1844, and died in New York on 18 November 1909. The brother of Jeanette Leonard Gilder, the journalist-critic, and William Henry Gilder, also a journalist, Richard became involved with *Scribner's Monthly* in 1870 and later became the editor in chief of *The Century* magazine. As a prolific poet, he produced works including *The New Day*, written in 1875, and *The Celestial Passion*, published in 1887. Gilder and his wife were very important liberals in the New York art community, and Gilder's position at *The Century* provided impetus for the movement of impressionism in America.

43. Rosamond Gilder, ed., *The Letters of Richard Watson Gilder* (Boston, 1916), p. 89.

44. *New York Times*, 29 April 1875, pp. 2-4.

45. Richard Watson Gilder, "Some Other Pictures," *Scribner's Monthly*, no. 10 (May-October 1875), p. 253.

46. Lois Marie Fink, "American Renaissance: 1870-1917," in *Academy: The Academic Tradition in American Art*, exhibition catalog (Washington, DC: Smithsonian Institution Press, 1975), p. 77.

47. For a detailed accounting of the controversy, see Eliot Clark, *History of the National Academy of Design, 1825-1953* (New York: Columbia University Press, 1954), chapter VII.

48. *New York Times*, 30 October 1877, p. 4.

49. Philadephia Museum of Art, *Philadelphia: Three Centuries of American Art,* exhibition catalog (Philadelphia, PA: Philadelphia Museum of Art, 1976).

50. The actual exhibition grounds were formally transferred by the Commissioners of the International Exhibition on 4 July 1873, and Proclamation of the Exhibition was made by order of the President of the United States.

51. J. S. Ingram, *The Centennial Exposition* (Springfield, MA: Hubbard Bros., 1876).

52. John F. Weir to J. Alden Weir, New Haven, CT, 3 February 1877. Quoted in Dorothy Weir Young, *The Life and Letters of J. Alden Weir* (New Haven, CT: Yale University Press, 1960), p. 118.

53. John K. Howat, *The Hudson River and Its Painters* (New York: Penguin Books, 1978).

54. For an interesting study of this subject, see Fink.

55. Lewis Mumford, *The Brown Decades: A Study of the Arts in America, 1865-1895* (New York: Dover Publishers, 1931).

56. Wanda M. Corn, *The Color of Mood: American Tonalism, 1880-1910*, exhibition catalog (Washington, DC: Smithsonian Institution Press, 1975).

57. For research on this topic, see *Impressionism: The California View* (Oakland, CA: The Oakland Museum Art Department, 1981). See also Nancy Dustin Wall Moure, *Publications in Southern California Art*, no. 3, *Dictionary of Art and Artists in Southern California before 1930* (Los Angeles, CA: Dustin Publications, 1984).

58. Michael Quick, *American Expatriate Painters of the Late 19th Century* (Dayton, OH: The Dayton Art Institute, 1976), pp. 16-19.

59. When Walter Shirlaw and William Merritt Chase first taught at the Art Students League, students were offered the choice of voting for one of two European styles in which to work, either the Munich School or the French. See Ella Condie Lamb, "1881 to 1884," in *Fiftieth Anniversary of the Art Students League of New York* (New York, 1925), p. 37.

60. Landgren, pp. 33, 41.

61. Louis Leroy, "The Impressionist Exhibition," *Le Charivari*, 25 April 1874; English translation quoted from Charles F. Stuckey, *Monet: A Retrospective* (New York: Hugh Levin Associates, Inc., 1985), p. 57.

62. Henry Bacon, *A Parisian Year* (Boston, MA: Roberts Bros., 1882).

63. *New York Times,* 2 and 4 December 1883. The pedestal fund consisted of money raised for the construction of the base for the new French statue *Liberty Enlightening the World* by Frederic Auguste Bartholdi (1834-1904). The exhibition was organized to help raise funds for the sculpture pedestal in 1883.

64. Richard H. Love, *Theodore Earl Butler: Emergence from Monet's Shadow* (Chicago: Haase-Mumm Publishing Co., Inc., 1985), p. 26.

65. Unidentified newspaper clipping, 7 May 1892. Quoted in John I. H. Baur, *Theodore Robinson 1852-1896*, exhibition catalog (Brooklyn, NY: The Brooklyn Museum, 1946), p. 30, fn. 29.

66. Richard H. Love, *Cassatt: The Independent* (Chicago: R. H. Love Galleries, 1980).

67. J. Alden Weir to his parents, Paris, 15 April 1877. Quoted in Young, p. 123.

68. For an excellent discussion of the society and its exhibitions, see John Rewald, *The History of Impressionism* (New York: The Museum of Modern Art, 1961), pp. 313-38.

69. See Anne Coffin Hanson, *Manet and the Modern Tradition* (New Haven, CT: Yale University Press, 1977).

70. Robert L. Herbert, *Neo-Impressionism* (New York: The Solomon R. Guggenheim Museum, 1968).

71. Quoted in John Rewald, *Post-Impressionism: From Van Gogh to Gauguin* (New York: The Museum of Modern Art, 1956), p. 79, fn. 2.

72. J. Carson Webster, "The Technique of Impressionism — a Reappraisal," *College Art Journal*, November 1944.

73. John Rewald, ed., *Camille Pissarro: Letters to His Son Lucien,*" trans. Lionel Abel (New York: Pantheon Books, Inc., 1943).

74. Love, *Theodore Earl Butler*, p. 24.

75. Sutton was one of the first Americans to bring art objects to the United States from China. In 1880, he founded the Kurtz Gallery which became known later as the American Art Association, the auction house Sutton promoted.

76. "The French Impressionists," *New York Daily Tribune*, 10 April 1886.

77. Ibid.

78. Clarence Cook, "The Impressionist Pictures," *Studio*, 21 (17 April 1886).

79. Durand-Ruel to Fantin-Latour, New York, 1886. Quoted in F. Daulte, "Le marchand des impressionnistes," *L'Oeil*, June 1960.

80. Rewald, *The History of Impressionism*, p. 547.

CHAPTER TWO:
THE LINK BETWEEN PARIS AND GIVERNY

After Manet's death in 1883, Claude Monet remained the undisputed leader of the older generation of impressionists (ill. 2-1). Monet exploited *broken color*, the quintessential feature of impressionism, better than any of his constituents did, so his work seemed to typify the whole aesthetic. Degas, the only other leader type in the charter group, never really desired official membership; moreover, his work was mostly figurative, far too individualistic to typify impressionism as it was conceived of by most artists. Maintaining this dubious place of honor, Monet had been carrying his banner of leadership in self-imposed exile in Giverny, a small village located on the Seine and Epte rivers in Normandy northwest of Paris (map, ill. 2-2).

For quite some time prior to his arrival in Giverny, Monet had been living out of wedlock with Alice Hoschedé, the estranged wife of Ernest Hoschedé, one of the painter's early patrons.[1] The addition of Mrs. Hoschedé and her children made the Monet household quite large. The master and his children came to Giverny on 29 April 1883. Waiting for Alice Hoschedé to arrive, they first stayed at La Grenouillère, a small inn in the eastern part of Giverny.[2] Apparently, "Monet had not even finished uncrating his boxes on May 1, when the news reached him of Edouard Manet's death which occurred on the night before."[3] After a few days, the Monet-Hoschedé clan moved "into a house rented from Louis Joseph Singeot, a major landowner from the village, who had retired to Vernon."[4] Only a two-acre parcel of land, Monet's place had been traditionally known as Le Pressoir [The (Cider) Press]. The property was located between the high road (now rue Claude Monet) and Chemin du Roy, the main road connecting nearby Vernon and Gasny. The western projection from the central house was then a barn, which was later converted to a combination living room and studio. Almost immediately, Monet began cultivating the orchard and garden, situated between the front of the house and Chemin du Roy. Soon this special botanical environment became one of his chief interests, but he also acquired a great familiarity with the Seine, whether upstream near Port-Villez or farther down at Vernon. Often Monet painted as if viewing these subjects from the river bank, although he reached the locations in his "floating studio," one of the four boats that he had originally acquired in Poissy. There was also the fascinating little strip of land called the Ile aux Orties, located at the mouth of the Epte, a much smaller stream that emptied into the west bank of the Seine. Two other small picturesque islands in the Seine were Ile de la Merveille and Ile de la Flotte, farther downstream.

Monet's financial situation was so uncertain in the early 1880s that he wondered if he had made the right

Ill. 2-1. Claude Monet. *A Path on the Ile Saint-Martin, Vétheuil.*
1880. Oil on canvas, 31½ x 23¾ inches. The Metropolitan
Museum of Art. Bequest of Julia W. Emmons, 1956.

decision in moving to Giverny, but Durand-Ruel reassured him: "I hear Giverny is lovely, and I don't doubt for a moment that you will return with a mass of paintings, all of them masterpieces. . . . Don't forget that you are walking in Manet's footsteps and that in the eyes of the public you are at the head of that remarkable artistic movement in which France has set the example. Manet is dead! Long live Monet!"[5] Fully aware of his inherited position as the leader of impressionism, Monet worked for several years in Giverny in quiet seclusion, developing colorful gardens on his estate and painting in the surrounding countryside (ill. 2-3). He lived in this bucolic Norman village with his children and Alice Hoschedé and her children, one of whom, Suzanne, served as a replacement model for Monet's deceased wife, Camille.[6]

The master sought privacy, but his presence in Giverny was no secret to the Paris art community. Certain of Monet's friends visited him there, but it is not known exactly when the first Americans came to Giverny in hopes of meeting him. There is a remote chance that The-

odore Robinson, the American expatriate from Wisconsin, visited Monet with the French artist Deconchy as early as 1885, but it is more probable that he first went there in the spring of 1886.[7] Another of Robinson's artist friends, Willard Metcalf, was also there that spring of 1886, although Elizabeth de Veer has recently pointed out that Metcalf may have been there in 1885 during a trip to Fourges to visit Paul Coquand.[8] In any instance, tradition has it that some time in April or May of 1886, Willard Metcalf and a friend (probably Theodore Wendel and perhaps also Frederick Louis Ritter) were hiking in the area and by chance came upon Giverny. Anxious to spend time there, Metcalf set out to find lodging. He inquired at several local establishments and then at the general store-café managed by Angelina Ledoyen Baudy.[9] It seems that the bearded Metcalf looked so much like an American mountain man that Angelina feared to lodge him and slammed the door in his face. Exactly how Metcalf and Wendel discovered the path to Monet's door is unclear (perhaps via their mutual friend Robinson, who was already visiting there), but their reception at the master's place was cordial. In fact, it seems that they were invited to have lunch with Monet and his family. Moreover, it is reported that later that day the small group spent some time painting in the company of Blanche Hoschedé, one of Monet's stepdaughters. For the balance of the summer of 1886, the activities of these American artists are somewhat sketchy. Wendel's picture *Girl with Turkeys* attests to his having worked at Giverny; Metcalf's bird's egg records confirm his presence; and from various documents, it seems that Robinson spent a good deal of the summer there. By September 1886, Metcalf's relationship with the Baudys had so improved that they put him up at Ferme de la Côte, the family farm. It was also at this time that Metcalf became close to the Monet group. He even took Jean-Pierre Hoschedé and Monet's son Michel on nature hikes in the surrounding countryside, telling them about the habits of birds and other wild creatures. Indeed, by the end of 1886, a warm and cordial rapport existed among Monet, the Givernyites, and the young American visitors. How other friends happened to join Metcalf later in Giverny is unclear, but the story most frequently recounted is that after his return to Paris he came back to Giverny the following spring of 1887 with William Blair Bruce, Henry Fitch Taylor, Louis Ritter, John Leslie Breck, and Theodore Wendel. This time the proprietors took the Americans in as boarders. In fact, the Baudys were especially accommodating, giving up their own room and finding additional places in Giverny for the other artists. Once again Metcalf stayed at Mrs. Baudy's family farm.

Thus the excellent relationship that had begun a year

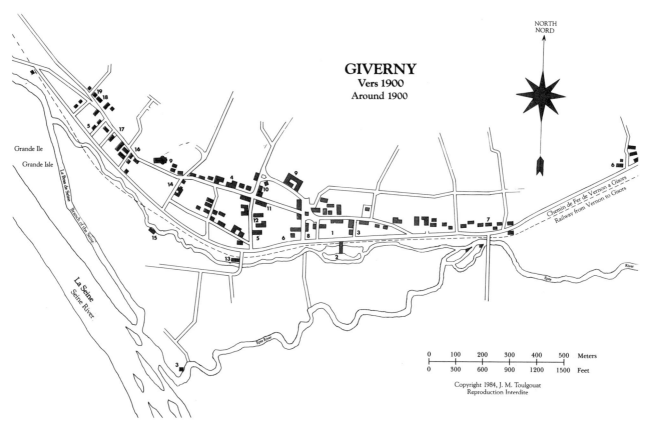

Ill. 2-2. Map of Giverny around 1900. Copyright Jean-Marie Toulgouat, reproduction interdite.

earlier between the Baudys and their foreign visitors continued in Giverny—and, it was to continue for at least another two generations; furthermore, the small store-café would soon expand to become the Hotel Baudy, hosting mostly English-speaking visitors, especially Americans.

Several canvases by Bruce, Wendel (ill. 2-4), Ritter, Metcalf, Robinson (and probably others yet to be discovered) confirm their presence in Giverny at this time. Intensely devoted to his art, each member of the group was determined to learn and to produce significant modern images. One of them, William Blair Bruce, a Canadian, left not only his art but a written record of his experiences of that spring and summer.[10] A fascinating letter from Bruce to his mother as early as 24 June 1887 is excerpted here in part: "I have unconsciously let the time slip by without giving you a word of the new settlement which we have formed here in this most beautiful part of France, the river Seine running by almost at our door. The village is far far ahead of Barbizon in every respect. We have rented a large and well furnished house

Ill. 2-3. Claude Monet. *Vétheuil in Summer.* 1880. Oil on canvas, 23⅜ x 39¼ inches. The Metropolitan Museum of Art. Bequest of William Church Osborn, 1951.

[Baudy residence] for a year, and find it much more comfortable than any hotel could be, there are six of us in the arrangement so it comes not too expensively upon us individually.''[11] As he continued his letter, Bruce made no mention of his proximity to Monet but wrote of various American friends: "Mr. Robinson's father is dead, he will not go to America. . . . Mr. [Henry Fitch] Taylor is here, one of the party, and with Mr. Wendel and Mr. Metcalf form our household." Bruce also discussed the promotion of art, mentioning the Cincinnati artist Louis Ritter, whom he described as "the noted painter and violinist of Boston." If Bruce's routine was typical of artists in the American pioneer group at Giverny, so was his dis-

Ill. 2-4. Theodore Wendel. *Flowering Fields, Giverny.* 1889. Oil on canvas, 12½ x 21½ inches. Private Collection. Courtesy Jeffrey R. Brown.

cipline. Their work habits were admirable and their seriousness obvious: "I get up at four or five these summer mornings," Bruce reported, "and take a good bath and proceed to paint in the open air — nothing could be more invigorating than this method of proceeding in such a salubrious climate."[12]

Bruce's serious ambition and his extraordinary talent were manifested at this time in an outstanding canvas known as ***The Bridge at Limetz*** (ill. 2-5). Signed and dated "87," the scene depicted is a multiarched stone bridge spanning a branch of the Epte River at the outskirts of Limetz, a village only a couple of miles from Giverny.[13] The lower third of the composition is devoted to a simplistically rendered open road that recedes from the picture plane at an oblique angle. Bright sunlight tends to segregate the cooler-toned lower half of the picture from the middleground, where the human activity is concentrated. Bruce has not yet incorporated a great deal of broken color into this work, but he proves his concern with the effects of light; his brushwork is spontaneous, as one might expect from a disciple of Eugène Boudin rather than of Monet. All in all, however, Bruce's picture indicates a definite transition on his part from the Barbizon style to that of impressionism.

Another artist of the young American group who worked in Giverny that summer of 1887 was John Leslie Breck. A report written years later for the *Boston Evening Transcript* by Edward Breck, John's brother, confirms the story of Giverny's discovery by Metcalf in 1886, but it also dates the arrival of the expanded group there in the summer of 1886 instead of a year later:

Leaving Fourge, Ritter and Metcalf strolled through the valley that grew more and more beautiful as it neared the Seine. At the little village of Giverny on the Ept [sic]. . . they wrote to their friends in Paris that Paradise was found. . . The invitation was answered by Theodore Robinson, Theodore Wendell [sic], Blair Bruce, and John Leslie Breck, who, with the present writer and his mother, formed the American colony that year and are the 'simon pure' original 'Givernyites.' Hardly had the little company begun eagerly to transfer the lovely motifs of the neighborhood to their canvases when they discovered that they were not the only painters in Giverny, that none other than Monet himself had already been living there for several years past. During that season, however, none of the Americans made the master's acquaintance.[14]

Ill. 2-5. William Blair Bruce. *The Bridge at Limetz.* 1887. Oil on canvas, 29 x 35½ inches. Private Collection. Courtesy R.H. Love Galleries.

Ill. 2-6. Facing pages of the Hotel Baudy guest register, Giverny. Philadelphia Museum of Art.

Whether it was Robinson or Metcalf who made the first contact with Monet is unclear, but it is certain that as time went on, the American group was gratified with Monet's response to them, since he usually ignored visitors. At first, the master visited them at Baudy's and even invited them to his home, where they discussed art and had a photograph taken with Bruce, Taylor, Breck, and the Hoschedé girls.[15] It is reported that he showed them some of his recent Giverny work. At that time Monet kept his canvases in his barn-studio, with its large door and dirt floor. One imagines that as he showed them his work, he smoked his cigarette as usual and pointed out certain favorite images. Perhaps he also told them that he worked on several canvases at a time, drawing in a few basics of

his scene with charcoal and then "attacking" them with fully loaded brushes; but, of course, such information would have been the only kind of instruction he provided, since he refused all students.

A remote possibility exists that in the summer of 1887, the American group also met John Singer Sargent when he visited Monet in Giverny. In fact, it has been suggested that Sargent's enthusiasm for Monet's Giverny was partly responsible for some of the American invasion that summer. In any instance, the Baudys were so pleased with their new guests and the business they generated that they officially renamed their establishment the *Hotel* Baudy. Furthermore, as of June 1887, they provided a guest register, in which the birthplaces, ages, and professions of

their visitors were recorded (ill. 2-6). The first few names
to appear in the register make up a significant portion of
the pioneer group: although an extant picture proves that
he was there earlier (ill. 2-7), Robinson first signed the
register in September of 1887 and checked out in January of the following year. Other names include John Leslie Breck, Theodore Wendel, and Theodore Earl Butler,
who came in the spring of 1888 (ill. 2-8). These young
painters were excited about their new place to paint.
Monet's presence there underscored their own assess-
ments of its quaint beauty. Before the summer was over,
the Baudys built a studio addition to the structure, apparently at Robinson's suggestion. At this time, Robinson
was the most vocal of the group — he prophesied that in
time, year-round guests would stay at the Hotel Baudy.
As the members of this group looked around, it became
quite apparent that the village was looking at them, "siz-
ing them up," as it were. It seemed obvious to nearly
everyone that an art colony was in the making. Another

Ill. 2-8. Area view of Butler's residence in Giverny around 1900.
Photograph. Collection of Jean-Marie Toulgouat, reproduction
interdite.

Ill. 2-7. Theodore Robinson. *Valley of the Seine, Giverny.* Oil on
canvas, 16¼ x 13 inches. Private Collection. Courtesy R. H. Love
Galleries, Inc., Chicago.

letter from Blair Bruce to his mother in October 1887
reported the enthusiasm and progress of the group: "You
are right that we have a fine lot of fellows in our house
and the house in a fine country. The natives are already
beginning to build studios and we presume that the
colony will soon be quite the thing to talk about just at
present however we are very exclusive and daily letters
arrive from fellows asking leave to visit us which we are
obliged to refuse — on account of the lack of accommo-
dation for them."[16]

It took only a short time for news of the Americans'
presence in Giverny to reach across the Atlantic. Even
before Bruce's letter to his mother, someone sent a report
early enough to be published in the October 1887 issue
of *The Art Amateur.* The short but accurate bit of hear-
say dealt with Monet's influence on the group: "Quite an
American colony has gathered, I am told, at Givernay

[sic], seventy miles from Paris, on the Seine, the home of Claude Monet, including our Louis Ritter, W. L. Metcalf, Theodore Wendell [sic], John Breck, and Theodore Robinson of New York. A few pictures just received from these young men show that they have got the blue-green color of Monet's impressionism and 'got it bad.' "[17] This report is surprising since art historians have traditionally held that for quite some time to come, the influence of Monet's high-key "blue-green" palette did not manifest itself in the work of even the pioneer group. Today, however, extant pictures by Bruce, Wendel, and Robinson prove the early influence of Monet on these young painters. Their assimilation of his style was exceedingly limited, but telltale signs of his influence are evident in a few Giverny canvases from this time. Typical is the conclusion reached by John I. H. Baur in his 1946 catalog on Theodore Robinson. Baur believed that Robinson "discovered Giverny in 1887, and his friendship with Claude Monet had probably begun then, but it was not until the following year that his Impressionist pictures were painted."[18]

By the spring of 1888, several other interested painters had abandoned Paris to work in Giverny. Not all the visitors stayed at the Hotel Baudy, but of those who signed the register, the most important was Theodore Butler, who had probably been urged to paint in Giverny by his Midwestern friends Robinson and Wendel. Like Wendel and Ritter, Butler was from Ohio; however, while Butler studied in New York, Wendel and Ritter were with Frank Duveneck in Munich where they learned to paint rapidly, seeking the raw essentials of the subject or scene. Soon, all of the pioneer group experimented with Monet's palette; and now that they were in Giverny, they could even analyze his manner of execution on their own. Each artist pursued the general features of Monet's style to a greater or lesser extent, but most of them (with the exception of Butler) refrained from fully adopting his high-keyed palette and broken-color technique. Furthermore, although all the artists trekked in and around the Giverny countryside, setting up their easels to work en plein air, Robinson also used photographs as visual aids. Ironically, Metcalf, the discoverer of Giverny, moved at a snail's pace in his response to impressionism. Apparently, Monet's presence there had little effect on him for many years.

Not every visitor to Giverny in the summer of 1888 was an artist or an American, but in his later years one who was, Dawson Dawson-Watson, revealed yet another story that is worthy of note here about the American discovery of Giverny. As reported by the painter Eliot Clark, Dawson-Watson had been told by John Leslie Breck that Giverny was discovered by chance in 1887, a year earlier than Dawson-Watson's own arrival there.[19] The story is

plausible, since it is in relative accord with other factual data, but the last part of the report is problematic: "The point made very dominant in that story [Breck to Dawson-Watson] was that the drawing card of Giverny was the fact that it was the home of Claude Monet." Dawson-Watson explained further that in the master's later years Giverny was well known as Monet's home, but insisted that "when the first group went it was not so." He said, "[W]hen I went it was not so for the simple reason, and the very simple reason that he was an unknown quantity and it was six months before I learned that he lived there."[20] Dawson-Watson's contention that Monet was "an unknown quantity" to either the French or the Americans is unconvincing. Even in his early years, and in these years especially, Monet was a controversial figure whose whereabouts were well known to the chauvinistic Paris art community and even to the local peasants, who found his behavior rather strange. Furthermore, Monet frequented the Baudy store-café, which was only a couple of blocks away from his home (map, ill. 2-2). It is quite possible that the first group of artists were drawn to Giverny by the same evanescent beauty that had attracted Monet; but if by the summer of 1888, Dawson-Watson or any other member of the pioneer group was ignorant of the French master's presence there, he would have had to live in abject isolation—which was not the case, since most of the expatriates came en masse and socialized extensively in Paris and then at the Hotel Baudy. By the fall of that year, Monet and impressionism was the talk of the American expatriate community in France.

Overnight, Giverny had become an art colony, and it would soon replace Barbizon as the place for American painters to find inspiration, to live inexpensively but comfortably, and to share the camaraderie of the new impressionists who had gathered in the shadow of Claude Monet. For the American painter in Giverny, however, life was dichotomous: both slow and fast, rural and cosmopolitan (in terms of art matters), immediate and futuristic, retarded and dynamic. It contained all these enigmatic qualities because of the special position of the village as an art colony. Beautifully situated in rural Normandy and easily accessible from Paris by train, Giverny attracted diverse figures of the cultural avant-garde. Among these were certainly some of America's most progressive talents and intellectuals, who hoped they could imbibe the aesthetic inspiration that manifested itself in the brilliant canvases of Monet, then the leading figure of modern art. One of these Americans was Theodore Butler, who had been studying art in the academic tradition at the Parisian schools and gaining recognition at the Salons. Undoubtedly, Butler must have

Ill. 2-9. View of the Eiffel Tower at the time of the Universal Exposition, 1889. Photograph. R.H. Love Galleries Archives, Chicago.

heard about Monet's presence in Giverny from Wendel or from Butler's Salon masters such as Carolus-Duran. Influenced by the juste-milieu painters and the synthesis of Puvis de Chavannes's art, Butler had been exploring new approaches in his work. He was anxious to take a closer look at impressionism.[21] Consumed with creative urges and striving to advance beyond his debonair lifestyle in Paris, Butler took the train with Wendel in Paris and arrived in Giverny where they checked in at the Hotel Baudy on 20 May 1888.

In the summer of 1889 Lilla Cabot Perry vacationed in Giverny with her husband Thomas Sergeant Perry, a former professor of English literature at Harvard.[22] Little more than an art student, Lilla was introduced to Monet along with her husband and a sculptor friend who had obtained a letter of introduction to the master. Lilla was immediately taken with the famous painter and wrote to her American friends that "here was a very great artist only just beginning to be known, whose pictures could be bought from his studio in Giverny for the sum of

$500."[23] That first summer of 1889 kindled a friendship between Lilla and Monet that led the Perrys to purchase a house adjacent to Monet's (see map of Giverny, ill. 2-2). The Perrys were to return to Giverny for ten consecutive summers. Here, Lilla became one of the few artists, especially American, to develop a strong friendship with Monet. She was also one of the few who enjoyed the master's advice on painting. Eventually Lilla Cabot Perry became one of America's leading female impressionists, owing, most scholars would very likely contend, to Claude Monet's influence. However, when the Perrys' first summer visit came to an end and Lilla brought home a Monet canvas that a friend from Boston had purchased, Lilla was astonished to find that "hardly any one liked it, the one exception being John La Farge."[24]

While the American pioneers in Giverny prepared themselves to paint impressionistically, Parisians were preparing themselves for the great Universal Exposition of 1889, a world's fair unlike any observed before. The great event marked the centenary of the French Revolution. At this time, the citizens of France could well afford to be proud: the year seemed to symbolize France's international leadership in many areas, especially in culture. The exposition area covered nearly 250 acres, and guidebooks reported that it would take visitors ten to twenty days to "see" the extravaganza. A feature of the fair was a reconstructed Bastille, a kind of exposition within an exposition, in which a complex array of amusements would provide endless hours of entertainment. Visitors would be able to see "enchanted fountains with colored-light projections"; take in special shows at the Théâtre des Variétés; browse in shops, old-fashioned cabarets, and boutiques, and haggle over prices with merchants dressed in historic costumes. The writer-cartoonist Fernand Bac reported that he felt "reborn to a new world," a man brimming with the "magic of the new times by ingenious sorcerers."[25] For children, there would be the fascinating Pays des Fées (fairyland), but the display that was expected to attract the most attention was the Galerie des Machines, a unique place for sixteen thousand mechanized curiosities. Before the show opened, the well-known critic J. K. Huysmans reported that visitors go out "stupefied."[26] Planners were most excited about the Esplanade des Invalides, an amazing, even exotic playground where examples of strange architecture from all over the world could be seen.

Cleaned and made beautiful for the spectacular year-long event, the complex interior of Paris had been transformed. At the hub of activity on the Champ de Mars, the newly built Eiffel Tower rose in great majesty or loomed in arrogant ugliness, depending on who described it (ill. 2-9). With a seventy-five-mile view from the top levels, the iron structure would be a fascinating place for drinking and dining. Also in this area was the huge building that housed an art exhibition intended to display the best productions of the Salon masters ever witnessed by foreigners and a few works of the juste-milieu group. The various independents mounted their own shows. The United States was well represented in the exposition, with 252 artists displaying 565 works. One of the reasons behind such a good representation of American art at the exposition was the effort put forth a year earlier by expatriates. They had elected a committee to ensure that the work of their American constituents would be adequately shown. At this large and prestigious event, the works of a surprising number of relatively progressive American artists were also exhibited — painters like Otto Bacher, Edward H. Barnard, Frank W. Benson, Childe Hassam, William Merritt Chase, Robert Vonnoh, Thomas Wilmer Dewing, and numerous others who would one day become impressionists. If a few of their friends were in Giverny learning how to paint like Monet, hundreds more were in Paris struggling for recognition at the Salon. The opportunity to show their work at the Universal Exposition was a wonderful plus to the expatriates, but most of these artists had their sights set on long-range goals of becoming known as masters in Paris; if an artist could achieve that, he would be a master anywhere.

As Parisians were making preparations to receive an onslaught of world visitors, far away in Eastern Europe Louis Ritman drew his first breath. Louis was born on Sunday, 5 January 1889, in Kamenets-Podolsky, Russia, to Solomon and Rebecca Ritman. Having lived in the city for several years, the Ritmans were established members of the considerably large local Jewish community. The area encompassing Kamenets-Podolsky, part of the medieval duchy of Volhynia and Podolia, contained a rich cultural heritage of Jewish folk art, as documented and described by later scholars and researchers.[27] Moreover, the synagogues of the region contained a wealth of examples of folk art, which later inspired such artists as El Lissitzky.[28] The specifics of the Ritman family's regard for and response to local culture are unknown, but it is said that the children were encouraged to read, to study art when possible, and to learn Hebrew traditions.

Meanwhile, as Russia moved closer to France by concluding the Franco-Russian Alliance, Tsar Alexander III continued to repress internal liberal movements. At the same time, the tsar embarked on an intensive policy of industrialization (heavily financed by French loans) and increased exportation of agricultural products and raw materials. Problems continued, however, and soon Russia would experience its great yearlong famine in the countryside and tremendous unrest among its growing

Ill. 2-10. The beach at Dinard on the north coast of Brittany was one of several resort areas frequented by American expatriates. Maurice Prendergast painted at Dinard in the late 1890s. R.H. Love Galleries Archives, Chicago.

numbers of industrial workers in the cities. Anxious for reforms, the workers turned to political radicalism, and the constant proletarian turmoil in Kamenets-Podolsky may have provided a strong incentive to the Ritman family to seek their fortunes in America.

Of course, there was much more that beckoned the Ritmans to the new land across the Atlantic. More than twenty years had passed since the United States resolved its great internal conflict by war. Industry was booming and the nation was expanding westward. Not only to a family in Russia but to most continental Europeans and even to the British, America seemed free and accessible, wide open to all possibilities, a wild and exotic place where cowboys rode in off the range to mingle with the city folks. Over the years, as the United States moved westward, this image had been exploited in countless publications. It was magnified as never before, however, when Buffalo Bill brought his Wild West show to Europe. Boasting 200 cowboys, cowgirls, and Indians, 150 horses, and 20 buffaloes, the show included realistic reenactments of chases and fights straight from the "Far West." During its run at Neuilly in France, the Wild West show competed very well with the Universal Exposition in Paris. In 1889, the people of France learned a great deal about the people of faraway lands, but they learned more about Americans than about anyone else. For the most part, Europeans could not be blamed for thinking the worst and the best of the United States — to them it was a vast underdeveloped nation in desperate need of talented and enthusiastic Europeans. Nowhere in Europe were Americans more self-conscious than they were in Paris, even though the exposition underlined the very best about their young country across the Atlantic.

During Louis Ritman's adolescence in the 1890s,

impressionism spread rapidly throughout all of Europe and America. Although the actual movement had already been eclipsed by more avant-garde styles like neo-impressionism under the aegis of Paul Signac and a watered-down synthetism under the Nabis, the style of impressionism was still the most influential aesthetic produced anywhere in the Western world. Monet's style had reached every country in Europe and many areas in other continents. While liberal-minded artists in New York were slowly switching to the style, however, most of the Americans in Giverny had already adopted its features in their imagery. A few of the pioneer group had gone to other places, but of those who still worked there, a certain few were especially analytical of Monet's style. Some of the best were John Leslie Breck, Theodore Earl Butler, Guy Rose, Howard (Peggy) Hart, Theodore Robinson, and Lilla Cabot Perry. With most lining up to the right of Monet's pictorial doctrines, these American converts to impressionism distanced themselves to positions where they felt comfortable in their quests to arrive at their own styles.

During the late 1880s, Monet's finances had so improved that by November of 1890, he was able to purchase the estate he had been renting for the past seven years. Although he had been cultivating his now-famous garden, he had not yet made an image of it on canvas. The greenhouses that Robinson found so interesting were still a couple of years away, but Monet was becoming increasingly interested in flowers as an art subject. From 1890 onward, the Baudys routinely installed more artists' studios inside and outside. An urgent need for expansion developed because of the growing stream of visitors from Paris. Americans, many of whom visited out of curiosity's sake, dominated the guest list at the Hotel Baudy.[29] Writing in the summer of 1890, Kate Kinsella revealed that the Baudy group maintained a "queer household." She reported: "Mr. Robinson sits at the head of the table. I next on his left. . . and then an entire family, sisters and mother of a [California] painter called [Guy] Rose."[30] The Baudys remained gracious hosts, frequently allowing their hotel to be used for costume parties and masked balls. Music was provided by the multitalented guests, and the dining room walls were used for painting as substitutes for canvases. By this time, Hotel Baudy served as a home away from home for aspiring expatriate artists, and Giverny had become the leading art colony in France, especially for Americans who had established their headquarters in Paris (ill. 2-10). "With Barbizon practically abandoned, its [Giverny's] only rival was Pont-Aven, a once sleepy village in Brittany which Gauguin had turned into an active art colony. It was not as dominated by Americans as Giverny, but

serious and talented artists like Thomas A. Harrison, Charles "Shorty" Lazar, Arthur W. Dow, Childe Hassam, Cecilia Beaux, and many others helped to make the Pension Gloanec at Pont-Aven almost as crowded as the Hotel Baudy."[31] Without a doubt, Pont-Aven was well known to Americans as an art colony about the time Monet moved to Giverny: Blanche Willis Howard's novel *Guenn, A Wave on the Breton Coast* (Boston, 1883), had popularized the place among American art students a

Ill. 2-11. Theodore Robinson. *The Wedding March.* 1892. Oil on canvas, 22 x 26 inches. Terra Museum of American Art. Daniel J. Terra Collection.

good deal prior to Gauguin's period of activity there, "but even Gauguin's loud activities could not draw them to Pont-Aven as Monet's quiet, even aloof presence brought them to Giverny."[32] Notwithstanding his common-law marriage to Alice Hoschedé, Monet pursued a serious, productive life at Giverny. This existence was considerably more appealing to American artists, whose puritanical traditions still lingered behind facades of Parisian bohemianism, than was Gauguin's romantic, antiestablishment lifestyle on a faraway island. Gauguin's motivations were too far left of the genteel tradition to suit most Americans, even the most progressive souls.

Since the American group first came to Giverny, Monet had become far less receptive to them, and he had been downright intolerant of John Leslie Breck's courtship of one of the Hoschedé daughters.[33] Another young American whose amorous advances toward a second Hoschedé daughter had infuriated Monet was Theodore Butler. This talented painter from Columbus, Ohio, had learned to imitate Monet's landscapes and had converted to impressionism by the fall of 1891 (pl. 2-1; 2-2). Shortly thereafter, he began secretly courting Suzanne Hoschedé, Monet's favorite model. When Monet learned of their romance in the early spring of 1892, he was painting the cathedral in Rouen and wrote an angry letter to Alice Hoschedé, demanding an immediate end to Butler's courtship. He even threatened to sell the estate and leave Giverny. After several weeks of family trauma, however, Monet agreed to the marriage.[34] Although he doubted Butler's sincerity, Monet thought it proper to marry Alice Hoschedé before he gave away Suzanne. The Butler wedding took place that summer of 1892 in a Giverny church, an event which Theodore Robinson recorded on canvas (ill. 2-11). With these family matters resolved, Monet settled down, resumed his painting routine, and soon thereafter purchased a strip of land adjacent to his property between the railroad and the Ru River.[35] Here he planned to excavate a pond that would derive its water from the slow moving stream.

Meanwhile, soon after his marriage to Suzanne, Butler plunged into a highly productive and most innovative period of his career. With the birth of two children, Jimmy and Lilly, Butler was inspired to develop post-impressionistic tendencies in his work which were far ahead of his times. In addition to his artistic endeavors, he headed the publication of an informal periodical entitled *Le Courrier Innocent* which was intended for the art colony at Giverny. Dawson Dawson-Watson, Thomas Buford Meteyard, and Bertrand Goodhue were among other contributors to the publication. The literary side of the magazine included poems by the Illinois poet Richard Hovey and the Canadian poet and journalist Bliss Carmen, who eventually came to reside in the United States.[36] In its spirit, the *Courrier Innocent* promoted the ideas of a creative, unencumbered, and idyllic existence of an artist in Giverny, a lifestyle which Louis Ritman would value highly in years to come when he discovered the charms of the village.

Notes

1. For a discussion of the relationship, see Richard H. Love, *Theodore Earl Butler: Emergence from Monet's Shadow* (Chicago: Haase-Mumm Publishing Co., Inc., 1985),chap. 9. See also Daniel Wildenstein, *Claude Monet* (Paris-Lausanne: La Bibliothèque des Arts, 1974-1979), vol. III.

2. Wildenstein, *Claude Monet,* vol. II, p. 17, and Claude Monet to Paul Durand-Ruel, letter 348, n. 168.

3. Ibid. See also Claude Monet to Paul Durand-Ruel, letter 349, n. 170.

4. Daniel Wildenstein, *Monet's Giverny* (New York: The Metropolitan Museum of Art, 1978), p. 18.

5. Paul Durand-Ruel, quoted from Wildenstein, *Monet's Giverny*, p. 19.

6. Wildenstein, *Claude Monet*, vol. II, p. 50. Reference is made here to Jean-Pierre Hoschedé's reminiscences. The result of Suzanne's poses were several fine canvases, one of which is *Femme à l'Ombreille Tournée vers la Droite (Lady with a Parasol)*, 1886.

7. A signed and dated picture from 1886, known as *Girl with Turkeys* (Sheldon Art Gallery, Lincoln, NE), would seem to confirm Wendel's presence in Giverny at this time.

   See also the discussion provided by Elizabeth de Veer and Richard J. Boyle in *Sunlight and Shadow: The Life and Art of Willard L. Metcalf* (New York: Abbeville Press, 1987), pp. 41-45.

8. According to de Veer, Metcalf recorded a "bird's egg find at Giverny in 1885," and this event may have occurred during a stop in Giverny when Metcalf was on his way to visit the painter Paul Coquand at Fourges.

9. Claire Joyes states that Metcalf came upon Giverny and contacted Mrs. Baudy in 1886. At this time Mrs. Baudy and her husband, Lucien, had only recently established their store-café. The couple lived in a cottage in another part of the village. While Lucien worked as a sewing machine salesman, Mrs. Baudy operated the establishment. See Claire Joyes, "Giverny's Meeting House: The Hotel Baudy," in David Sellin, *Americans in Brittany and Normandy, 1860-1910* (Phoenix, AZ: Phoenix Art Museum, 1982), pp. 97-102.

10. On 6 May 1887, William Blair Bruce wrote from Paris to his mother in Canada that he intended "to go to the sea shore with a small party of Americans." See Joann Murray, *Letters Home: 1859-1906: The Letters of William Blair Bruce* (Moonbeam, Ontario, Canada: Penumbra Press, 1982), p. 122.

11. In spite of Bruce's count of six men, the actual number is difficult to ascertain. Traditionally, the group included Bruce, Metcalf, Wendel, Ritter, Taylor, Breck, and Robinson, seven in all. Indeed, there may have been a much larger number later that summer and fall of 1887. Ibid., pp. 123-125.

12. Louis Ritter was born in Cincinnati in 1854 and studied art there at the McMicken School of Design in 1873 and 1874. Later he was listed as lithographer. Eventually Ritter went to Munich, where he became one of the "Duveneck boys." He was in Florence with Duveneck. Dejected over harsh criticism leveled at a group show he had arranged in Cincinnati, Ritter moved his studio to Boston.

13. Limetz is just south of Giverny and east of the Seine River. This branch of the Epte is one of two; the northern stream runs along the outskirts of Giverny after branching off from another stream to the east.

14. Edward Breck, "Something More of Giverny," *Boston Evening Transcript*, 9 March 1895.

15. The existence of this photo is recorded by Joyes in "Giverny's Meeting House," p. 101.

16. William Blair Bruce to his mother, 3 October 1887, *Letters Home*, p. 125.

17. "Boston Art and Artists," *The Art Amateur*, 17, no. 5 (October 1887), p. 93.

18. John I. H. Baur, *Theodore Robinson, 1852-1896* (Brooklyn, NY: The Brooklyn Museum, 1946), p. 26.

19. Dawson Dawson-Watson, "The Real Story of Giverny," appendix in Eliot Clark, *Theodore Robinson: His Life and Art* (Chicago: R. H. Love Galleries, 1980), pp. 65-68. This account was given by Dawson Dawson-Watson to Eliot Clark. Excluding Breck's report, Dawson-Watson's account remains unconfirmed by any other memoirs or documents emanating from the other pioneer artists. As told to Dawson-Watson by John Leslie Breck, the story was repeated in 1929 (forty years after the event) to the author, Eliot Clark, whose manuscript was published fifty years later. When interviewed by Richard Love in 1978-79, Eliot Clark was anxious to have Dawson-Watson's story published. Taped interviews, Eliot C. Clark to Richard H. Love, 1978-79, R. H. Love Galleries Archives, Chicago.

20. Dawson-Watson, pp. 66-67.

21. Love, *Theodore Earl Butler: Emergence from Monet's Shadow*, pp. 63-64.

22. For an overview, see Stuart P. Feld, *Lilla Cabot Perry: A Retrospective Exhibition,* exhibition catalog (New York: Hirschl & Adler Galleries, Inc., 1969). See also A. J. Philpott, *Boston Sunday Globe*, 29 October 1933.

23. Lilla Cabot Perry, "Reminiscences of Claude Monet from 1889-1909," *The American Magazine of Art*, no. 3 (March 1927), p. 119.

24. Ibid.

25. *Bulletin officiel de l'Exposition universelle de 1889*, 7 August 1889, p. 2. See also Lucien Biart, *Mes promenades à travers l'Exposition souvenir de 1889* (Paris: A. Flennuyer, 1890), p. 4.

26. J. K. Huysmans, *Revue de l'Exposition universelle de 1889*, May 1888, p.18.

27. For example, it was S. Ansky who led the Jewish Ethnographic Expedition into the towns and villages of the area in 1912. See Avram Kampf, *Jewish Experience in the Art of the Twentieth Century* (South Hadley, MA: Bergin & Garvey Publishers, Inc., 1984), pp. 17-18.

28. Ibid., pp. 18-19. El Lissitzky explored the art and architecture of the area in 1916 under the auspices of the Jewish Ethnographic Expedition.

29. Love, *Theodore Earl Butler: Emergence from Monet's Shadow*, p. 92.

30. Kate Kinsella to Philip Hale, 14 July 1890. Philip Leslie Hale Papers, Microfilm Roll D98, Archives of American Art, Smithsonian Institution, Washington, DC.

31. For an interesting discussion of the topic, see Frederick C. Moffatt, *Arthur Wesley Dow (1857-1922)* (Washington, DC: Smithsonian Institution, 1977).

32. Love, p. 92.

33. Jean-Marie Toulgouat to Richard H. Love, 24 November 1984, tape recording, transcript, R. H. Love Galleries Archives, Chicago.

34. For an in-depth discussion, see Love, "Theodore and Suzanne," in *Theodore Earl Butler: Emergence from Monet's Shadow* , pp. 102-116.

35. A kind of secondary branch of the Seine, the Ru River ran nearly adjacent to the railroad near Giverny. Outlining the northern border of the small area known as the Plains of the Ajoux , the Ru River actually junctioned with the northern branch of the Epte, also a branch of the Seine.

36. Richard, Hovey, "La-Bas," *Le Courier Innocent*, no. 6 (1897).

CHAPTER THREE:
THE CHICAGO ART COMMUNITY

In spite of its humble beginnings, the Chicago art scene had evolved cultural establishments of great complexity before the Ritmans settled in the city. In truth, the city had concerned itself with serious art matters for over half of the past century. Although the art exhibition at the 1855 Illinois State Fair, which was held in Chicago, included a relatively large number of entries, the work was for the most part that of amateurs. For that reason, the Chicago Exhibition of Fine Arts, presented in the spring of 1859, is usually considered the first important professional art show in Chicago. Nearly 370 works were on display and 12,000 tickets were sold. The profit was sufficient to commission a sculpture from Leonard Volk, the local master who had been sent to Europe by Stephen A. Douglas to learn his skill. Soon the Chicago Art Union was formed, and later in 1859, the group sponsored its first art exhibition in Hesler's Photograph Gallery.[1] In the 1860s a number of art societies and art unions were active in Chicago. Although many of the works shown in the sponsored exhibitions were European imports, some pictures came from the hands of Thomas Cole, Eastman Johnson, Albert Bierstadt, and other New York painters.

During the Civil War, Chicago was one of the northern cities that hosted the Sanitary Commission fairs. The premier exhibition, which was held in the McVickers Building, attracted 25,000 visitors in only two weeks, and by far the most popular picture in the show was Bierstadt's large oil entitled *Rocky Mountains* . In the post–Civil War years, when Chicago was little more than a rapidly expanding frontier city, Chicagoans still enjoyed one of the nation's earliest pictorial displays — the panorama . There remained a few panorama buildings where visitors could see inspiring works such as Charles McEvoy's *The Hibernicon* (1869), and in the 1870s reviewers were fascinated with panoramas depicting scenes of the Civil War. During the 1871 Chicago fire, Charles Peck's huge panorama (2,400 yards of canvas) of cities and towns in California was rescued and put into storage.[2] Panoramas continued to inspire Chicagoans until the turn of the century.

Art was preceded by music and literature in Chicago, but the traditional works on canvas known as easel pictures were also well received in the second half of the nineteenth century. When Chicago was little more than a sprawling prairie town on the shores of Lake Michigan, its first mayor, William Butler Ogden (ill. 3-1), entertained Daniel Webster and Ralph Waldo Emerson in his home, but he also persuaded the portraitist G. P. A. Healy to settle in Chicago. The Healy family was an instant success in Chicago's burgeoning cultural circles, and the artist enjoyed outstanding patronage.[3] In a very short time,

Ill. 3-1. William Butler Ogden, first mayor of Chicago. R.H. Love Galleries Archives, Chicago.

Healy "fell in love with the new city in all its uneven progress, its primitiveness, and boastful Americanism."[4] Two of Healy's portraits—the only American paintings in Newberry's collection—were lost when the great home of Walter H. Newberry was consumed by the Chicago fire.

Assessing the Chicago art community in 1870, George P. Upton reported that for thirty years local auctions and private dealers had promoted thousands of "atrocious daubs" imported from Eastern picture factories.[5] As Chicago grew, numerous picture dealers satisfied the voracious appetites of wealthy collectors, even though many buyers thought they would find better works in New York and Europe. Ureah Crosby had included an art gallery filled with excellent art in his famous Opera House, but nearly all of Crosby's art was lost in the Chicago fire. The Jevne & Almini Gallery sold many "home pictures," during and after World War I.

Chicago, being unable to provide local artists with as many opportunities as New York did, boasted fewer painters than its eastern counterpart. While a number of painters did maintain studios in Chicago, they often traveled far and wide to find suitable subjects. Of these, the first and foremost was probably Samuel Marsden Brooks, originally from Middlesex, England. Brooks and the painter Thomas H. Stevenson (ill. 3-2) worked on certain canvases together as they traveled throughout the country. Martin J. Heade, the famous painter of salt marshes and hummingbirds, worked for a brief period in Chicago in 1854, but he eventually settled in New York. Heade exhibited at the 1859 show, but he described Chicago as "that grimy and wicked city."[6] Other traveling painters who made Chicago their base of operations included Henry C. Ford, Henry A. Elkins, and James F. Gookins, who displayed landscapes they had worked up from sketches made on trips to Denver.[7] Some of their pictures were published in *Harper's Weekly*.[8] Elkins's painting of Mount Shasta was shown at the Philadelphia Centennial, and at least one critic found that it compared favorably with the work of Bierstadt.[9]

Neither Gookins nor Elkins could live from the sale of pictures alone, so they supplemented their incomes by writing and teaching. Gookins had studied in Europe and worked for some time as an illustrator for *Harper's Weekly*. A gregarious and engaging personality, Gookins was very active in the early Chicago art community, serving on exhibition committees and working tirelessly as a founder of the Chicago Academy of Design, which would later become the Art Institute of Chicago. Elkins, also a founding member of the Chicago Academy of Design, was an eccentric individual who sported long hair and wore strange clothes. Elkins was one of the organizers of the Vincennes Gallery, a private club for artists that had gallery space open to the public. He contributed much to Chicago's early art community, but most of its constituents thought of him as a rather strange personality, a true bohemian.

Over the years, other enthusiasts of the fine arts emerged in Chicago as the art community expanded rapidly. Indeed, in 1876, when the nation looked to the great Centennial Exposition in Philadelphia for direction, Chicago made substantial progress in expanding its post-fire art community. During the winter, the Associated Artists of Chicago organized a series of successful auctions. The art offered in these sales was juried, and works were sold without price reserves.[10] Several distinct art circles already existed in the city, and each made every effort to outdo the others in promoting local art. All of the Chicago hierarchy was in agreement, however, that Leonard W. Volk's new casting of his statue of Stephen

A. Douglas, "The Little Giant," was an outstanding presentment of the great orator.[11] At the same time, the art community was anxiously awaiting the completion of the new building for the Chicago Academy of Design that would replace the one lost in the great holocaust.

Ill. 3-2. Thomas H. Stevenson. *Untitled*. 1859. Oil on canvas, 29 x 39¾ inches. Private Collection. Courtesy R.H. Love Galleries, Inc., Chicago.

The period of the late 1890s marked the beginning of even a local bohemian group in Chicago. Showing real concern, one editorial described these writers, artists, musicians, and the like as "a class well worthy of study. . . . Chicago has several fine specimens of the people we mean, and will have many more with every passing year."[12] Indeed, from these years onward, Chicago's art community established itself with zeal; its members organized various art societies, encouraged collectors, wrote art columns, taught art, founded the Art Institute from its predecessor, the Chicago Academy of Design, and planned the amazing World's Columbian Exposition.[13] For several decades Chicago prided itself on the support of several prestigious cultural leaders and collectors like Charles L. Hutchinson, Mrs. Potter Palmer, Martin Ryerson (ill. 3-3), Charles T. Yerkes, Henry Field, Edward B. Butler, and others.[14] Although the art community in Chicago was neither as large nor as sophisticated as the one in New York, sometimes it surged with greater enthusiasm. Occasionally, for example, attendance at the Art Institute of Chicago exceeded that recorded at the Metropolitan Museum of Art.[15] Furthermore, owing not only to its relative youth but also to its location in the heart of the nation's agricultural-industrial community, Chicago possessed cultural leaders who were especially determined to lessen the city's potential for a

reputation of provinciality and who sought to inflate its image of cosmopolitanism. Indeed, they were anxious to eliminate the memories of Madame Ambre, the French singer who, in 1879, brought the first example of impressionism to America. Madame Ambre, escorted by her manager, Gaston de Beauplan, had come to New York and Boston for engagements with Colonel Mapleson's Italian Opera Company. The singer, who had posed for Manet, agreed to show his *Shooting of Maximillian* (Kunsthalle, Mannheim) in the American cities she visited because the Paris authorities had not allowed it to be exhibited publicly. After the showing had only a limited success in New York and was a failure in Boston, Ambre's manager abandoned plans to show Manet's work in Chicago because he thought it was no more than a city of "lard, Jews, and swine."[16] The two returned to France with Manet's picture.

One way in which the cultural leaders of Chicago attempted to bolster their city's image was by importing outstanding examples of European art for private collections and for the Art Institute. For example, during the late 1880s, when young American expatriates were first congregating in Giverny, the Chicago patrons Charles L. Hutchinson and Martin A. Ryerson followed the lead of New Yorker W. T. Blodgett, in traveling to Italy to purchase everything that was left of Prince Demidoff's collection of old masters for the Art Institute—paintings by Rubens, Hals, Ostade, Rembrandt, and others.[17] Even the uneducated and opinionated Charles T. Yerkes used his fortune to gather a collection that included works by Rembrandt, Rubens, Hals, Corot, Reynolds, and Botticelli—and eventually sold it for more than $700,000. In 1893, slightly less traditional art came to grace the galleries of the Art Institute with the donation of Henry Field's important collection that included the work of numerous French Barbizon masters.[18]

The most devoted collector and enthusiast of avant-garde art was the multitalented lawyer Arthur Jerome Eddy. Until the turn of the century, Eddy's most interesting foray into modern art had been his trip to Paris to sit for a portrait by Whistler, a painting that would one day become part of the permanent collection at the Art Institute of Chicago. Eddy's activity in contemporary art was just beginning, and the whole art community gossiped about his obsession with things modern. Another important, albeit forgotten, collector whose tastes ran somewhat contrary to Chicago's fashion was James Ellsworth, who bought pictures painted in America by Americans. Ellsworth had only one work in his collection that met the popular Chicago trend—Rembrandt's *Portrait of a Man* —although he also owned Chinese porcelain. His American collection was relatively modern in that it included works by William Merritt Chase, William Morris Hunt, Albert Pinkham Ryder, and Winslow Homer.[19]

Works from the walls of collectors such as Yerkes, Butler, Hutchinson, and others came to the Art Institute gradually over the years. The most important donation was the impressionist collection that Bertha Honoré Palmer had acquired through the guidance of Mary Cassatt and especially of Sara Hallowell. The latter became a very important figure in selecting the art work that was to be shown at the World's Columbian Exposition in 1893. Like Louisine Havemeyer, Palmer started her collection with a pastel by Degas, receiving extensive advice from Hallowell. Without the Palmers, Chicago would not have come to know and embrace impressionism as quickly as it did. Theirs was one of America's premier collections of impressionism, and owing to her credibility in art circles, Mrs. Palmer laid down the rules by which Chicago culture guided itself in the 1880s and 1890s.

Sara Tyson Hallowell had been active on Chicago's art scene for over twenty-five years. She came to the city from Philadelphia with her mother and became secretary of the art department of the recently organized Interstate Industrial Exposition of Chicago. Since then Miss Hallowell had become the guiding light in the Chicago art community by bringing to the city exemplary works by

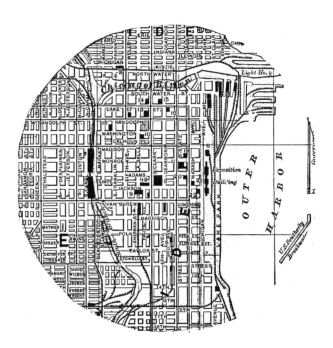

Ill. 3-4. Map of downtown Chicago, showing the location of the Interstate Industrial Exposition, 1890. R.H. Love Galleries Archives, Chicago.

Ill. 3-3. Martin A. Ryerson and Claude Monet in the garden at Giverny. Photograph. Courtesy the Art Institute of Chicago.

front-line American painters.[20] As early as 1885, a New York art critic, Montague Marks, reported: "Largely due to the personal efforts of that extremely intelligent and energetic lady, Chicago this year has anticipated New York, Boston, and Philadelphia in exhibiting the important American pictures from the last [Paris] Salon." He exclaimed, "Bravo, Chicago! and particularly bravo, Miss Sara Hallowell!"[21]

Even prior to the display of French art at the World's Columbian Exposition in 1893, Hallowell brought first-rate examples of impressionism to Chicago via the 1890 Interstate Industrial Exposition (map, ill. 3-4). In booths surrounded by machinery and agricultural exhibits, she boldly displayed six Monets, four Pissarros, and a Degas, that had been loaned by Paul Durand-Ruel. Actually, it was at this interstate show that Potter and Bertha Palmer became interested in impressionism. With her enthusiasm sufficiently aroused, Bertha Palmer visited Monet in Giverny in 1891. The trip was followed by extensive acquisitions of Monet's works by the Palmers in the same year, in 1892, and later. By the turn of the century, the Palmers had already established a large collection of impressionism. Sara Hallowell and Mary Cassatt were still active as art consultants for the Art Institute, even though they had to contend with male consultants assigned by the administration. Hallowell frequently traveled back and forth between Chicago and Paris. She corresponded extensively with the director of the Art Institute, William M. R. French, a person with whom she did not always see eye to eye. For the most part, Miss Hallowell's missions were fully sanctioned by the Institute and rather complicated. For example, in the spring of 1900, Director French wrote to her in Paris, "The trustees voted to let you continue the work this year." He explained what was hoped for: "I do not know what the state of things in Paris is this year with regard to the Salons, but of course you know all about it and will proceed to get us the pictures. We should be glad to make the collection even more marked than usual . . . .We are making an effort to build the fourth side of our building. The preparation of the two galleries, No. 41 and 42, assigned to the Nickerson collection, with mosaic and marble is in progress. I hope you will keep your eyes open for notable things, American and foreign, which may be secured for us next season. We should be glad of something striking enough to arrest popular attention."[22]

The contribution of Judge Lambert Tree and his wife (daughter of H. H. Magie) was different from that of their collector friends, but in some ways even more impor-

Ill. 3-5. Doorway of the Tree Studio Building. Photograph. R.H. Love Galleries Archives, Chicago.

tant.[23] When Judge Tree was a diplomat, he and his wife became quite familiar with Europe and developed a special fondness for Paris. Accordingly, they had come to understand the need for artists to work in low-cost studio space. Determined to provide this necessity for Chicago artists, they sacrificed the stable and paddock area of their property, the west half of one full city block that was bounded on the north and south by Ontario and Ohio streets respectively, only one block from the lavish home of Henry J. Willing, one of Marshall Field's jun-

Ill. 3-6. Detail: doorway of the Tree Studio Building. Photograph. R.H. Love Galleries Archives, Chicago.

ior partners.[24] Designed by Henry Ives Cobb, the impressive Tree mansion, facing east onto Wabash, was described as "brick gabled" and "full of beautiful things brought from abroad."[25] The rest of the property was devoted to a U-shaped building designed for artists by the Parfett Brothers of Brooklyn and erected in 1894. Called the Tree Studio Building, the structure reflected modern architectural trends: it was constructed of a steel skeleton covered with brick. Designed for small shops, the lower State Street facade was of cast iron and the second story had large casement windows. Artists could reach their studios through the two main entrances on Ohio and Ontario streets. Both entrances gave access to the large garden between the Tree mansion (now the Medinah Temple) and the rear of the studios and led to stairways to second-floor studios, each of which contained a skylight projected to catch northern light. Elaborately carved limestone doorways were reported to contain the portrait likenesses of Judge and Mrs. Tree (ill. 3-5; 3-6). Almost immediately, the Tree Studios became an amazingly productive watering place for Chicago artists.

From its inception, the permanent collection of the Art Institute had exerted a strong influence on its students. Historically, academic art had always been the first and foremost consideration of the Chicago Academy of Design and then the Art Institute hierarchy. As the influence of the French international style spread to Chicago, teachers of the antique classes at the Art Institute took advantage of the ample supply of plaster casts (more than 500), which they used to prepare students for study from a live model. A variety of academic courses beckoned young aspiring students, and new classes were frequently added. These ranged from cartooning to commercial design, decorative arts, history, and even children's classes. Hired as drawing cards, many well-known artist-teachers who had been trained in Europe were imported from the East Coast.

It was with this kind of artistic and cultural environment that Lawton S. Parker, the talented farm youth from Kearney, Nebraska, had to deal when he unexpectedly won an art prize and came to study at the Art Institute of Chicago. In 1886, Dr. W. S. Gray, editor of the *Interior*, a religious newspaper published in Kearney, had arranged an amateur drawing competition that called for the best rendition of country life by a student without art school training. Acting as judges were Dr. Gray, John H. Vanderpoel, instuctor at the Art Institute of Chicago, and Cyrus Hall McCormick, son of the inventor of the reaping machine. Lawton Parker was awarded the first prize, and his father was urged by the jury to send his son to study at the Art Institute of Chicago.[26] With his father acceding, Parker began his studies under Vanderpoel in the fall of 1886.[27] Interestingly, this was the year in which Durand-Ruel's show of French impressionists in New York marked a turning point for the movement and relative acceptance for the aesthetic.

Rapidly progressing through the academic curriculum, Parker received a medal from the School of the Art Institute at the end of his first year. Parker's extraordinary performance at the school aroused more than a casual interest of the leading members of the staff—Director William M. R. French and sculptor Lorado Taft (ill. 3-7).[28] Little did French realize at the time that this talented and ambitious student would one day become his professional nemesis. Absorbing new knowledge, Parker soon felt restless within the confines of the rather traditional academic policies of the Art Institute. As one of the leading progressives in the Chicago art community, Parker came to view Director French as his chief antagonist.

Nearly all of the administrative decisions of the Art Institute, including the hiring and firing of teachers, were made by French. Being a member of a very art-conscious family, he knew the art industry quite well. He was the brother of Daniel Chester French, the famous American sculptor from Massachusetts, who had studied under the masters J. Q. A. Ward and William Rimmer, from whom he learned anatomy. It was D. C. French who was commissioned by the towns of Concord and Lexington to sculpt the famous *Minute Man*. In Chicago, D. C. French was especially famous for his *Statue of the Republic*, a huge gold-leafed colossus that stood in front of the triumphal arch created for the World's Fair.[29] His Americanism was seen in another large bronze known as *Statue of Plenty*. Probably the best known American

sculptor of his time, French also made the monumental likeness of Abraham Lincoln for the memorial in Washington, DC. D. C. French's extraordinary technical skill and quest for the inner qualities of his subject made him an outstanding representative of nineteenth-century academic art, and his brother William espoused many of the same ideas in his role as director of the Art Institute. In fact, it was in 1900, after Lawton Parker had gained

Ill. 3-7. Lorado Taft in his studio. Photograph. Chicago Historical Society.

artistic reputation in Paris that Director W. M. R. French engaged his services to obtain for the Art Institute the cast of the equestrian statue of George Washington executed by his brother D. C. French—this famous sculpture had been exhibited in the Pavilion of the American Building at the great Paris Universal Exposition of 1900.[30]

A graduate of Harvard, William M. R. French had made his way from secretary to director of the Art Institute of Chicago. He was also a lecturer on "artistic anatomy," having shared his teaching assignments in the 1890s with fellow instructors like Charles Francis Browne, John H. Vanderpoel, Frederick Freer, and Enella Benedict. At this time the foremost instructor was Oliver Dennett Grover, a native of Illinois who had trained at the old Chicago Academy of Design and in Europe. The local master Lorado Taft, heir apparent to Leonard Volk, taught and lectured in sculpture while William Le Baron Jenney, Louis Sullivan, and a few others taught architecture. William M. R. French knew most of the important individuals in the Chicago art community quite well and maintained friendly relations with them. Although he made every attempt to posture himself as a far-sighted liberal, an administrator tolerant of innovation and progress, French's behind-the-scenes maneuverings reveal his political perspicacity and unswerving conservatism. His methods of directorship were autocratic at times and always self-protective, regardless of the consequences. Yet Bill French, as he was known to some, was also a shrewd diplomat, one who got the job done; for that reason, he had the unremitting support of most of the Art Institute trustees.

Traditionally, artists from a large area surrounding Chicago had been assured of a place to show at the annual "Chicago Artists" exhibition hosted by the Art Institute. There were also other places to exhibit, including the quarters of various art and social groups—such as the Palette and Chisel Club, Union League Club, Calumet Club, Municipal Art League of Chicago, and the Chicago Society of Artists. The well-publicized annual Chicago artists show drew the largest number of entrants, but no organization proved as effective in its purported ecumenical purpose as the Central Art Association, still guided by the principles laid down by art community leaders like Hamlin Garland and Lorado Taft.[31]

A far less formal group, which included Garland and had no membership rules, was the "cult of poverty and jollity," the bohemians who met at several "chaotic" clubs.[32] Competing fiercely, the Bohemian Club and the Cypher Club catered to essentially the same crowd, and they did so by creating an ambience of *la vie de bohême.* Gallons of beer and thick smoke from "strong black pipes" contributed to the atmosphere of these meeting places for Chicago's intellectual and artistic crowd. The other side, the genteel and frequently wealthy majority of the art community, was shocked to learn that ladies frequented the Cypher Club unescorted; indeed, some observers thought that these obviously slackened morals were no less than the lingering residuals of the World's Fair days. Many residents remembered the anti-establishment antics of Eugene Field, who would have been a great contributor to Chicago's bohemian milieu had he not been so ill in recent years. Purposefully imitating the *Café du Dôme* in the Latin Quarter of Paris, the bohemian clubs of Chicago contributed a great deal to the proselytization of "respectable" artists, writers, and poets to the quite less genteel, Parisian bohemian type.

In addition to the many influences to which a struggling talent was subjected in these unique environments, a kind of guide to the lifestyle of the Chicago Latin Quarter soon appeared in *Under the Skylights,* a book by Henry Blake Fuller.[33] If occasionally some confusion arose as to the proper attire or behavior of a true bohe-

Ill. 3-8. A scene of Bohemian life in an etching from a design by Montader appearing in Henri Murger's book *The Bohemians of the Latin Quarter.*

mian of Latin Quarter style, a young artist or writer could consult Fuller's book if he had no copy of *The Bohemians of the Latin Quarter (Scènes de la vie de Bohême)* by Henri Murger.[34] Indeed, many a Chicago artist was inspired by various passages from Murger's work (ill. 3-8):

> Schaunard was living at Montmartre. It was necessary to go right through Paris. This peregrination was one most dangerous to Rodolphe.
> "Today" said he, "the streets are paved with creditors.". . . After a two hours' walk he got to Schaunard's.
> "Ah, its you," said the latter.
> "Yes; I have come to ask you for some breakfast."
> "Ah, my dear fellow, you come at the wrong time. My mistress has just arrived. . . ."

"Marcel was then residing in the Rue de Bréda. Rodolphe found him in a very downcast mood, contemplating his great picture that was to represent the passage of the Red Sea."[35]

When it was published during the World's Columbian Exposition, Fuller's other work, *The Cliff Dwellers,* had also made an impact on Chicagoans. Another publication that promoted bohemianism in Chicago, and elsewhere for that matter, was *The Chap-Book,* which first appeared in 1894, even prior to James Gibbons Huneker's *M'lle New York* and the *Cypher,* the short-lived weekly published by the Cypher Club. If images of the expatriate life in Montparnasse lay dormant in the mind's eye of young artists, these visions were sure to be aroused as they read the stories, essays, and poetry in *The Chap-Book* by authors such as Stéphane Mallarmé, T. B. Aldrich, Paul Verlaine, and others. Issues of the *Yellow Ghost* from London also prompted Chicago artists to yearn for the bohemian life in Europe. Conversations with Mallarmé in Degas's studio or heated discussions in the Café du Dôme about the vicissitudes of symbolism, synthetism, or neo-impressionism were the fantasies that dominated the imagination of the would-be expatriates. In the late 1890s, "impressions" of *la vie de bohème* inspired Chicago painters almost as much as the art they saw in art publications. By the turn of the century, the bohemian life in Chicago was well established; indeed, though it occasionally produced scandalous gossip, bohemianism formed an inextricable part of the local art community.

Notes

1. For this important event, a special lottery was organized, to which 800 visitors responded by purchasing tickets at $1 each. As a result, 47 works, including paintings and sculpture, were distributed. See Esther Sparks, "A Biographical Dictionary of Painters and Sculptors in Illinois, 1808-1945," Ph. D. diss., Northwestern University, 1971, vol. 1, p. 72.

2. Charles Peck (1827-1900) left his home in Vermont, California, to find gold, and during his long trek he made sketches of various places he visited. These he used as the basis for his huge rolled painting *Panorama of California* , depicting 38 cities and towns. Peck was the first secretary of the Chicago Academy of Design.

3. For an interesting discussion of Healy's first meeting and continued relationship with W. B. Ogden, "the Railroad King," see Marie de Mare, *G. P. A. Healy: American Artist* (New York: David McKay Co., Inc., 1954), pp. 175-184.

4. Ibid., p. 180.

5. George P. Upton, "Art in Chicago," *Western Monthly,* IV, (December 1870).

6. For the most authoritative text on Heade, see Theodore E. Stebbins, *The Life and Works of Martin Johnson Heade* (New Haven, CT: Yale University Press, 1975), pp. 13-14; quoted from Didymous (Heade's pen name), "Little Sunny Spots," *Forest and Stream,* 21 (December 1895), p. 534.

7. Sparks, vol. 1, p. 4.

8. Robert Taft, *Artists and Illustrators of the Old West, 1850-1900* (New York: Scribner's, 1953), p. 55.

9. A. T. Andreas, *History of Chicago from the Earliest Period to the Present Time,* (Chicago, 1884-86), vol. III, p. 491.

10. "Art in Chicago," *The Art Journal,* May 1876, p. 160.

11. This bronze is a full figure sculpture of the great orator who was the northern Democratic nominee for president in 1860. Best remembered for his stunning debates with Lincoln, Douglas served as an outstanding Illinois and United States legislator. It was in a temporary frame building called the Wigwam in Chicago that the Republican convention was held in 1860 and nominated Lincoln. Douglas's last speech was delivered in Chicago in May 1861. The sculpture stands atop a large round column and monument at the Douglas gravesite. Leonard Volk executed the statue of Douglas at the request of the State of Illinois.

12. The Chicago newspaper *Post* used the term "Bohemians," but concerned itself mostly with writers rather than artists. For a comprehensive study of Chicago bohemianism, see Albert Perry, *Garrets and Pretenders: A History of Bohemianism in America* (New York: Dover Publications, Inc., 1960), pp. 175-211.

13. Gardner C. Teall, "Our Western Painters: What Chicago Is Doing toward the Development of a Vital National Spirit in American Art," *The Craftsman,* XV (1908), pp. 139-153. See also Ida M. Condit, "Art Conditions in Chicago and other Western Cities," *Brush and Pencil,* 4 (1899), pp. 7-11.

14. Frederick A. Sweet, "Great Chicago Collections," *Apollo,* 84 (1966), pp. 190-228.

15. In the 1895-96 season, the Art Institute recorded 680,706 visitors, while the Metropolitan counted only 526,488. See Leslie Goldstein, "Art in Chicago and the World's Columbian Exposition of 1893," Master's thesis, The University of Iowa, 1970, p. 50. See also Eugenia Remelin Whitridge, "Art in Chicago: The Structure of the Art World in a Metropolitan Community, " Ph. D. dissertation, University of Chicago, 1946, p. 79.

16. Hans Huth, "Impressionism Comes to America," *Gazette des Beaux-Arts*, Series 6, vol. 29 (April 1946), pp. 225-252.

17. Sparks, vol. 1.

18. The Field Collection did not formally become a part of the Art Institute holdings for several years. See *Art Institute of Chicago Report*, 5 June 1895, p. 37. See also *Chicago Tribune*, 4 March 1894, p. 27.

19. Lucy B. Monroe, "Art In Chicago," *The New England Magazine*, New Series, VI (1892), pp. 427-28.

20. Jeanne Madeline Weimann, *The Fair Women* (Chicago: Academy Chicago, 1981), pp. 104-5.

21. Montague Marks, *Art Amateur*, 1885.

22. W. M. R. French to Miss Sara Hallowell, Chicago, 29 March 1900, Director WMRF, Letter Book, General Correspondence, Archives of the Art Institute of Chicago, Chicago.

23. For a comprehensive discussion of the Tree Studio Building, see Donald James Anderson, "Those Haunting Trees," *Inland Architect*, 25, no. 5 (June 1981), pp. 4-11.

24. Ibid.

25. Thomas E. Tallmadge, *Architecture in Old Chicago* (Chicago: University of Chicago Press, 1941), p. 87: quoted from Mary Drummond in Kirkland, *Chicago's Yesterdays*, p. 131.

26. Maude Marston Burrows, comp., "Lawton Parker, Artist," Lawton Parker File, R. H. Love Galleries Archives, Chicago, p. 4.

27. Ibid.

28. Ibid., p. 3.

29. The statue, which measured 65 feet by 100 feet including the base, was the largest sculpture ever made in America at that time. The *Republic* statue and the *Triumph of Columbia* were destroyed the night of 8 January 1894 when the monumental quadriga by the lagoon went up in flames. A half-sized replacement statue of the *Republic* now stands in Jackson Park, its pedestal designed by the artist-architect Henry Bacon. Critics found it less effective, no longer in its original setting near the lagoon. See James L. Riedy, *Chicago Sculpture* (Urbana, IL: University of Illinois Press, 1981), pp. 27-30. See also Charles H. Caffin, *American Masters of Sculpture* (Garden City, NY: Doubleday, Page & Co., 1903), p. 65.

30. For details of Director French's arrangements with Parker, see W. M. R. French to Lawton Parker, Chicago, 2 November 1900, Director WMRF, Letter Book, November 1, 1900 — May 31, 1901, Correspondence, Archives of the Art Institute of Chicago, Chicago.

31. Lorado Zadoc Taft was another native of Illinois. Born in Elmwood, Peoria County, Illinois, on 29 April 1860, he died on 30 October 1936. Taft studied at the University of Illinois, where his father was a professor of geology. Later he was a student at the Ecole des Beaux-Arts in Paris under Duncan, Jean-Marie Bonnassieux, and Emile Thomas. In addition to executing his many important sculptural commissions, Taft wrote the *History of American Sculpture* and *Modern Tendencies in Sculpture*. He taught at the Art Institute from 1886 until 1906 and lectured there until 1929. See Robert H. Moulton, "Lorado Taft: Dean of Chicago Sculpture," *Art and Archaeology*, XII (1921), pp. 243-252.

32. Parry, p. 179.

33. Henry Blake Fuller was born in Chicago on 9 January 1857 and died on 28 July 1929. As a novelist, Fuller adopted the pseudonym Stanton Page. Under that name, he wrote *Chevalier of Pensieri-Vani* in 1890 and *The Chatelaine of La Trinité* two years later. After *The Cliff Dwellers,* Fuller wrote *With the Procession,* and *Under the Skylights*; the latter was published in 1901.

34. Reference is made here to the 1883 English translation of Henri Murger's *The Bohemians of the Latin Quarter (Scènes de la vie de Boheme),* published by Vizetelly & Company in London. This edition contains reproductions of "scenes," etched from works by Pierre M. A. Montader, which provides the reader with excellent illustrations of bohemian dress and lifestyle.

35. Ibid., p. 111-12.

CHAPTER FOUR:
THE IMPACT OF THE WORLD'S COLUMBIAN EXPOSITION AND OF HAMLIN GARLAND ON IMPRESSIONISM

In 1893, the year of the World's Columbian Exposition, Louis Ritman was a three-year-old child, living with his parents in Kamenets-Podolsky, Russia. His father, Solomon, worked as a weaver-designer in a local clothing company, and the family had little opportunity to come in contact with Western European culture. Thousands of miles away in Chicago, however, the whole American cultural community was preparing for the fifteenth and largest yet of the world's fairs of the second half of the nineteenth century. From the first, this fair was intended to be a great event that would open the floodgates of the American art community to the onrushing tide of European art and culture. Mostly, Americans loved what was old and time-tested, as it were, in European art. The Exposition managers made every attempt to embrace tradition in both architecture and art, but they also intended to prove that America was modern, liberal in thought, and receptive to new trends!

The idea for a "Columbian Exhibition" went back as far as the 1880s, when the federal government announced that one of the great urban centers of the United States would host an exposition to commemorate the 400th anniversary of Columbus's discovery of the New World. In 1886, a group of businessmen who wanted the show to be held in Washington, DC, had founded an organization to work toward that end. As the idea blossomed

in the minds of other city leaders, Chicagoans joined the front ranks of those who were most interested in hosting a world fair. In July 1889, the Chicago City Council instructed Mayor DeWitt Cregier to appoint a committee of 250 leading citizens to make efforts to bring the fair to Chicago. The project was scrutinized by both the New York and the Chicago press, but by the late summer of 1889, there was little doubt that the "Columbian" would take place either in New York or in Chicago but not in Washington. The battle to host the show became downright vicious in the press. While New Yorkers considered Chicago quite beneath the enormity of the project, writers of editorials in the *Chicago Tribune* flatly stated that New York was not patriotic, or even truly American, and that the "prominent citizen" of New York was a "partially civilized hog." New Yorkers countered with the charge that Chicago lacked both culture and tradition, and that visiting foreigners would not want to travel so far inland. It was evident during this period that even New York artists like James Carroll Beckwith watched the artistic growth in Chicago and the Midwest with a jealous eye. The following entry from Beckwith's diary amply illustrates the point: "This morning I wrote an article for the catalog of the Academy spring exhibition and chose for my subject the importance of retaining New York as the art capital of the country which I think is pertinent

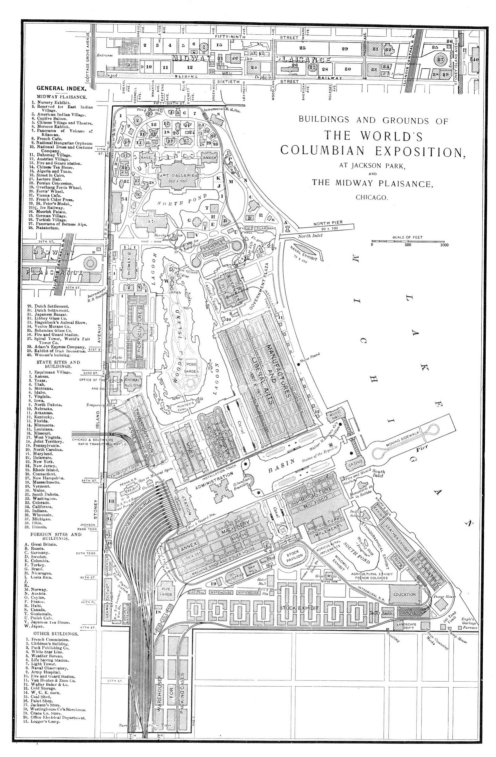

Ill. 4-1. Map of the World's Columbian Exposition of 1893, Chicago. R.H. Love Galleries Archives, Chicago.

in view of the big art bequests they are getting in Cleveland and Chicago."[1]

Finally an executive committee headed by Lyman J. Gage, vice president of the First National Bank of Chicago, proved its fund-raising capabilities while others, including Myra Bradwell of the Women's Department, established lobbying headquarters in Washington, DC. In January 1890, the Quadro-Centennial Committee of the Senate heard arguments on potential sites for the fair; Chicago representatives included Mayor Cregier and Thomas B. Bryan (executive manager of the 1865 Northwestern Sanity Fair), who stated that "the West" demanded that Chicago host the Fair.[2] In February, Chicago won its bid—but not without a great deal of political support from much of the Midwest. Those with even a modicum of political clout became supporters of the fair. Even a Board of Lady Managers was put into place.[3] On 25 April 1890, President Benjamin Harrison signed an act providing that Chicago would host an international exhibition of arts, industries, manufactures, and the products of the soil, mine, and sea," a show which would be known as the World's Columbian Exposition.[4] Mayor Cregier saw it as the greatest single achievement of his five-term reign. Soon the Exposition would run full speed on funds raised by a corporation that issued 5 million dollars of stock, which was matched by the State of Illinois.

During the planning period, there were some jaundiced New Yorkers who insisted that Chicago could not make the project a success because the city had no cultural product to offer—only "beans, pigs and wind." Some predicted it would become only a "cattle show." From the very first, however, the Chicago planners intended the exhibition to be a cultural marvel, an opportunity for Chicago to demonstrate as never before the superior skills of its famous architects. Because so many leading participants bragged openly about the project, Chicago became known as the "windy city."[5] Soon intense intracity rivalry developed between factions in the North, South, and West sides as they competed to host the exposition. Chicago swelled with activity as Frederick Law Olmsted, planner of Central Park in New York, and Henry Codman consulted with Daniel Burnham and John Root (creators of the Rookery and Monadnock buildings) to prepare Jackson and Washington parks on the south side for the fair. Located near the lakeshore, these areas were quite suitable for the construction of canals, lagoons, and formal pools (map, ill. 4-1).[6] With Root at his side, Chief of Construction D. H. Burnham reported that "about the end of November, 1890. . . the Exposition [officials] adopted a general plan, roughly and hastily drawn on brown paper [Root always had "pencil in hand"] to the scale of one hundred feet to the inch, as the basis for the final plan of the grounds."[7] Ever since he had seen the Paris Universal Exposition of 1889, John Root had dreamed of making a superior exposition site in Chicago. He was a tireless worker who wanted the exposition to reflect the virtues of the Midwest, but he also pushed to see that great architects from New York, Boston, and Kansas City were invited to participate.[8] Having driven himself to the point of exhaustion, Root became quite ill in early January 1891 and died a few days later, just as his dreams for Chicago's great fair were coming to fruition. In a later biography, his sister-in-law, Harriet Monroe, one of Chicago's most highly regarded art critics, wrote of Root's hopes: "He wished to offer to the older nations a proof of new forces, new ideals, not yet developed and completed, but full of power and prophetic charm. He wished to express our militant democracy as he felt it."[9] Had Root lived, he would have had a better opportunity than most planners to express his artistic dreams, but Root's enthusiasm about Chicago and the Midwest was shared by most of the culture makers of the city. Indeed, one night after a performance of *Jeanne d'Arc*, even world travelers like Sarah Bernhardt proclaimed "Chicago is the pulse of America."

Burnham called a meeting of all the World's Fair architects, prophesying that it would be "memorable in the annals of architecture."[10] When the group met in Chicago in 1891, Burnham told them that although "the city of Chicago was one of the greatest centers of power in finance, commerce, and manufactures, our cultivation in higher and more refined interests, and especially regarding the fine arts, was denied." He also pointed out that in spite of this problem, "there existed. . . . strong and growing appreciation of these interests, and that this feeling would not be satisfied with merely the extent and abundance of the Exposition." Burnham assured his designers that they "would be strongly supported by the people in an endeavor to attain a superior result in the fine arts themselves."[11] Burnham recalled that at another meeting, in which the grounds and buildings committees joined the architects, the great sculptor Augustus St. Gaudens, who had said very little, came to him, took him by both hands, and said, "Look here old fellow, do you realize that this is the greatest meeting of artists since the 15th century."[12] The weighty potential of the gathering was subsequently manifested in the production of these gifted men.

Even prior to the opening of the exposition, local art galleries did their best to take advantage of the art mood it generated. Culture mongers from many parts of the nation came to Chicago. Even the Collier Gallery of London rented gallery spaces in Sullivan's Auditorium Build-

Ill. 4-2. Albert Fleury. *Wabash Avenue*. Oil on canvas,
9¾ x 13 inches. Private Collection.

ing to show portraits by Dutch and French masters.[13]
The Auditorium Building itself — successfully decorated
by the French expatriate artist Albert Fleury, who had
done a whole series of paintings of Chicago scenes (ill.
4-2) — was a potential source of attraction to visitors of
the fair. The press, too, devoted a lot of space to art,
although one critic thought that the commercial galleries should show much better work.[14] Shows were
presented by art clubs, by artists in their studios, and by
private collectors in their homes, all in the spirit of the
World's Fair. Most Chicagoans were enthusiastic about
their new roles in contributing to the cultural betterment
of the city.

In 1892, the Chicago Society of Artists held a special
exhibition for the purpose of honoring artists from other
cities who were working on various projects of the fair.
Many important artists came from cities like Cincinnati,
Philadelphia, Boston, and Saint Louis, but, of course,
the largest and most ambitious delegation came from
New York City.[15] The selection of art from New York
began in January 1893; William Merritt Chase, Frederick Dielman, and others arranged to ship the entries to
Chicago. From over 2,000 works submitted to the New
York selection jury, 1,349 were accepted; of these, 324
were oil paintings.[16] Later, in its report to the Board of
General Managers, the New York art bureau stated: "New
York City, as the art center of America, furnishes the
standard for the rest of the country, and the notable victory gained at the Chicago Exposition is a direct
acknowledgement of the superiority of New York and
New York artists." Most Chicagoans were aware that their
city had been lagging substantially behind New York City
in cultural matters, but they also knew that for the years

of 1892 and 1893 Chicago was the leading art capital of
the world. All in all, Chicago became an art-conscious
city in a short time.[17]

Once the great Chicago architect and teacher William
Le Baron Jenney had recommended that instead of con-
structing a group of buildings on a site, the builders of
the fair should erect a magnificent "White City" on carefully designed grounds that should be twice the size of
the Philadelphia Centennial Park. For the most part, the
plan had been accepted by the local board of directors,
most of whom were businessmen. They too preferred the
so-called classical look, neoclassicism put forth as never
before. Once actualized via Burnham and his group, the
great White City would also prove to the world that traditional European architecture could be built (even temporarily) in America and, indeed, that Chicago could
reflect the cultural splendor of Mother Europe.[18]

The magnificent Art Palace was to be one of the central features, but the show planners also hoped to emphasize the aesthetic integration of all architecture,
decoration, and landscaping (ill. 4-3).[19] Another impor-

Ill. 4-3. The Palace of Mechanic Arts and Electricity. World's
Columbian Exposition of 1893, Chicago. R.H. Love Galleries
Archives, Chicago.

tant ingredient would be the Woman's Building, a project emanating from the Board of Lady Managers — and
a structure the completion of which would prove to be
no simple task from beginning to end (ill. 4-4). The
Women's Building project was guided in its entirety by
Mrs. Potter Palmer. She commissioned large, nonimpressionistic murals by Mary F. MacMonnies (*Primitive
Women*) and Mary Cassatt (*Modern Woman*).[20] In other
buildings, J. Alden Weir and Robert Reid would paint

Ill. 4-4. Interior view of the Women's Building. World's Columbian Exposition of 1893, Chicago. R.H. Love Galleries Archives, Chicago.

murals that bore no trace of impressionism either, but these ambitious projects were to inspire a new interest in American mural production.

The architecture of the great White City, considered retardataire instead of progressive by Frank Lloyd Wright, was nonetheless, a sight to behold (ill. 4-5). Indeed, the style prompted critical response around the world. A major part of the complex was still intact when the Ritman family arrived nearly a decade later. Many distinguished planners and thinkers came to Chicago to create an unprecedented amalgam of industry and art, which in turn provided an unprecedented forum for architects, designers, engineers, artisans, and artists of the Western world (ills. 4-6, 4-7, 4-8). All of these crosscurrents laid much of the foundation upon which young Louis Ritman would build his art in the future.

Although many commentators claimed that the leading figures of the event harbored considerable male prejudice, numerous women played extremely important roles in the organization of the exposition, especially at management levels.[21] Mrs. Bertha M. Honoré Palmer served as the tireless President of the Board of Lady Managers (ill. 4-9); in fact, to many followers who saw the Fair project as a symbol of feminine emancipation, she became a kind of goddess. The name Board of Lady Managers, given by the United States Congress, was not what Susan B. Anthony and her suffragettes had in mind, and many observers thought it was demeaning. Sarah Hallowell, one of the most knowledgeable people about art in Chicago, was offered the position of director of the Department of Fine Arts of the exposition, but for various reasons she turned it down. Halsey C. Ives, Director of the Museum of Fine Arts in Saint Louis, was then appointed to the directorship (see ill. 4-10).

There is no question but that in 1893 Americans, more specifically Chicagoans, intended to upstage the famous Philadelphia Centennial Exposition of 1876 and the Paris Universal Exposition of 1878. Americans especially hoped to demonstrate that progress had been made in native art since the Philadelphia Centennial. Director Ives hoped to show not only the world's best art but also a wide variety of paintings that were "not yet handled by the French dealers."[22] Although France led all of the Western Hemisphere in the production of art, Ives, Burnham, St. Gaudens, and other exposition authorities were anxious to create an unprecedented forum for "world art." Accordingly, Ives visited many foreign countries, setting up art conferences to bring the best European art to Chicago. He reported that "the result of these efforts may be measured by the applications for space in the Art Department, coming as they did from every country which had been visited. In nearly every case the space applied for far exceeded that which it was possible to grant."[23] The total wall space for pictures in art galleries

Ill. 4-5. Fine Arts Building. World's Columbian Exposition of 1893, Chicago. R.H. Love Galleries Archives, Chicago.

and courts amounted to 205,000 square feet, of which 35,000 feet were designated for the United States section (ill. 4-11). "When we consider the amount of space this represents as compared with that granted to foreign countries in our own exhibition of 1876, and realize that it is more than double the space occupied by foreign countries in that exhibition," Ives said, "those who were familiar with the vast collection of pictures brought together there may form some conception of the great extent of the present collections."[24] At the 1889 Paris Exposition,

Ill. 4-6. Interior View: 1892 construction of the Manufactures and Liberal Arts Building, in preparation for the World's Columbian Exposition of 1893, Chicago. R.H. Love Galleries Archives, Chicago.

discouraging, but not to the student who ponders on the environments and conditions of American life. Having the instincts and modes of life of many nationalities, it should not seem strange that our art possesses the peculiarities of each."[27] Ives knew well the routine that had been followed by American artists for a couple of generations: he pointed out that American "students early in life seek the masters of foreign schools, imbibe their sentiments and technical qualities, and reproduce them in their own work a second, third, or fourth removed from the original. It is not an unusual thing to hear pessimistic expressions as to the probability of there ever being an 'American school.'"[28] This art-learning process was the foundation of American art upon which Ritman's future teachers and subsequently Ritman himself would build their imagery. For example, it was at the time of the

the French section of the art show had covered over 90,000 square feet; the French applied for the same amount in Chicago, but they were allocated only one-third the space. The entire Eastern Annex was turned over for the French section, and over 1,100 pieces of art were exhibited. When the exhibition had been assembled, some observers said the French show in Chicago was no more than a mirror of the Paris Salons since Gérôme headed the selections jury with the assistance of Puvis de Chavannes.[25] As a result, no examples of impressionism were included in the official French section, an obvious cultural prejudice that was likened to a cultural Dreyfus affair—an injustice that needed correction.

The paintings shown in the United States section had all been executed after the Philadelphia Centennial. Nearly 1,500 works had been submitted to the selection jury. The American show was billed as a "Retrospective Exhibit of American Painting."[26] The executive committee consisted of Thomas B. Clarke, John La Farge, and John F. Weir. After the paintings were selected, the influence of foreign styles became obvious. "Among the various art sections in the three pavilions," Ives reported, "nowhere is found greater variety of subject and technical treatment than in the United States galleries." He continued: "In walking through these galleries we find on one side works possessing the technical qualities of the French school; on the other, German; then again may be seen pictures that evidently were influenced by the Dutch school—echoes, in fact, of every master and of every school that we have known in our time." Ives was careful to point out that "to many persons this fact might be

Ill. 4-7. The Ferris Wheel. World's Columbian Exposition of 1893, Chicago. R.H. Love Galleries Archives, Chicago.

World's Columbian Exposition that Frederick Frieseke began his studies at the Art Institute of Chicago, while Richard Miller attended the Saint Louis School of Fine Arts. Lawton Parker, who would one day exert the greatest influence on Ritman, had already graduated with high honors from the Art Institute of Chicago, studied in Paris, and was exhibiting work at the World's Fair.

French impressionism was especially obvious in the American section of the exposition. One impressionistic picture that commanded a great deal of attention was entitled *In the Orchard* , an entry from Boston by Edmund Tarbell. The work of Tarbell's associate Frank Benson, who submitted *Girl in a Red Shawl* (1890, Museum of Fine Arts, Boston, MA), was also admired. Childe Hassam's conservatively impressionistic *Grand Prix Day* , executed in 1887 (Museum of Fine Arts, Boston, MA), was praised, as were several snow scenes by

Ill. 4-8. Interior Detail: Fine Arts Building, sculpture wing with central view of *The Angel of Death and the Sculptor,* by Daniel C. French. World's Columbian Exposition of 1893, Chicago. R. H. Love Galleries Archives, Chicago.

John H. Twachtman. In his superb chapter on the World's Columbian Exposition, William Gerdts points out that "it would be easy to overestimate" the amount of American impressionism shown in the American section since there were those who "chose to show more conservative works or to emphasize the variety of their art rather than its modernity."[29] Among these, of course, were a number of early converts to impressionism, like Vonnoh, who showed conservative images, and Lilla Cabot Perry, in whose canvases little influence from her time with Monet in Giverny was evident.

As never before, however, the exposition demonstrated America's interest in impressionism, a greater interest in fact than the French themselves were willing to show. Not only were impressionistic paintings shown in the official American section, while none were shown in the official French section, but the Fine Arts Board of the exposition corrected the injustice by providing a disguised but very successful forum for the new aesthetic in a special "Loan Collection of Foreign Works from Private Galleries in the United States." For this decidedly pro-French show, works by Monet, Renoir, Pissarro, Sisley, Manet, Degas, and many others were loaned by progressive collectors like Albert Spencer, Alexander Cassatt, the Havemeyers, and the Palmers. Even though they were only a small part of the Loan Collection, the impressionistic canvases stood apart from others like stars shining on a dark night. Included also were some outstanding works by artists such as as Carolus-Duran, J. F. Millet, J. B. C. Corot, Fritz von Uhde, Georges Michel, Rosa Bonheur, and other European greats, from collectors like the late Henry Marquand and Cornelius Vanderbilt.

In evaluating the great art-historical significance of the World's Columbian Exposition of 1893, Daniel Wildenstein, the noted French art historian, explained that "Chicago definitely represented for the participants of the exposition a major development of the end of the nineteenth century, with its entirely new art-viewing public and its enormous wealth available for all kinds of bold experimentation."[30] Pelting the French art world for lack of foresight, Wildenstein concluded: "The French officialdom did not understand this reality. Befuddled by their madcap race for medals and grossly misjudging the continent [America], they [the French] gauged that the awards jury did not offer the necessary guarantees and declared their section a nonjuried [*hors concours*] event. It looked like the situation at the Palace of Industry in the days of Cabanel and Count Nieuwerkerke."[31]

Yet, the impact of impressionism was felt by every visitor — it was a new and influential art movement that made its mark at the exposition, and the mark would prove to be indelible. Monet's works were featured and frequently discussed, since the impressionists were displayed in splendid fashion as never before. To most visitors it seemed that the French aesthetic was becoming fashionable even in Chicago; it was known that only a year earlier, Mrs. Potter Palmer had purchased twenty-two canvases by Monet. The movement was soundly criticized by a few ultraconservative critics, but for the most part, the impressionists were praised for their innovation and their cheery canvases, whose bright colors seemed to capture magical qualities of sunshine. Finally, a large seg-

Ill. 4-9. Bertha Honoré Palmer, a leader in the Chicago art world. R.H. Love Galleries Archives, Chicago.

its "growth" as "an idea in painting must not be confounded with a mere vogue." He concluded: "It is evolutionary, if not destructive, in the eyes of the old-school painters, at least. To the younger men it assumes almost as much importance as the law of gravity." Aware of the need to educate his readers, Garland reported that the impressionists "strive to represent in color an instantaneous effect." He explained: "Every degree of the progress of the sun makes a new picture. They follow the most splendid and alluring phases of nature, putting forth almost superhuman effort to catch impressions."[34] Hoping that an explanation of technique would augment the viewers' appreciation of the new aesthetic, the author elaborated: "The impressionist . . . paints with nature's colors,— red, blue, and yellow; and he places them fearlessly on the canvas side by side. . . . This placing . . . gives a crispness and brilliancy, and a peculiar vibratory quality. . . . it must be admitted that too many impressionists have painted as if the blue shadow were the only distinguishing sign of the difference between the new and the old." Garland reported that he, too, had to learn impressionism before he could *see* it: "I got my first idea of colored shadows from reading one of Herbert Spencer's essays ten years ago. I then came to see blue and grapecolor in the shadows on the snow. . . . I came to see that shadows falling upon yellow sand were violet, and the shadows of vivid sunlight falling on the white of a macademized street were blue, like the shadows on snows. . . . In this world stone-walls were no longer cold gray, they were warm purple. . . . And so the landscape grew radiant year by year, until at last no painter's impression surpassed my world in beauty."[35]

Such acute sensitivity and raw courage made Garland's brief chapter on impressionism in *Crumbling Idols* an extremely important contribution to the history of the aesthetic; yet art historians seldom mention the text as the first "defense" and critical promotion of *American* impressionism. Moreover, scholars fail to point out that Garland was the first critic to champion American impressionism over its French precursor— Garland saw impressionism as a manner of painting, an idea in art manifested in a general style with certain obvious characteristics which, when applied to local subjects, could produce a decidedly "American" look. Ironically, unlike the cosmopolitan expatriates Cassatt, Sargent, Whistler, La Farge, or Hunt, who came to know the aesthetic firsthand, Garland did not "discover" impressionism or come in direct contact with the movement in Paris; instead, he first saw it in some paintings by the American convert and fellow Givernyite John Leslie Breck that Lilla Cabot Perry brought home to Boston from Giverny. Garland also came to know something of the movement through his

ment of the public agreed with the critics who found something good in impressionism, in contrast with the previous reactions. As a matter of fact, the art shown in the exposition inspired Hamlin Garland to write his now-famous chapter "Impressionism," which first appeared in a small collection of essays entitled *Crumbling Idols* in 1894. John Rewald has called Garland's unprecedented thesis the "first all-out defense of the movement to be written in English."[32]

Garland was convinced that "every competent observer" who visited the art exhibition "was probably made aware of the immense growth of impressionistic or open-air painting."[33] Continuing, he speculated that "if the Exposition had been held five years ago [1888, the year, by the way, that Parker graduated from the Art Institute of Chicago], scarcely a trace of the blue-shadow idea would have been seen outside the work of Claude Monet, Pissarro, and a few others." Implying the strength of impressionism as a movement, Garland pointed out that

Ill. 4-10. Halsey C. Ives, director of the Department of Fine Arts. World's Columbian Exposition of 1893, Chicago. R.H. Love Galleries Archives, Chicago.

friendship with John Joseph Enneking in Boston. Garland was intelligent and very sensitive to trends in literature and art. Although self-educated in New England, he remained a proud native of Wisconsin who clung to his "Middle Border" heritage, hoping, like Walt Whitman before him, that he might discover a profound American art. If he was unable to find something specifically unique in American painting, then at least he should find "veritism," a harmonious, moral, and positivist *realism*, which could be depicted by the American impressionist who intuitively applied his skills to native scenes.[36] Like William Dean Howells (also a Midwesterner), Garland believed that the artist was obliged to seek "truth" in realism, and the artist's impression was "real" only if it presented the finer side of American life. In this way, Garland reasoned, realism, veritism, and Americanism meant "practically the same thing."[37]

To Garland, impressionism was simply a new way of painting, the origin of which he gave to the French, but one which was as viable in Midwestern America as it was in Giverny. "As I write this," Garland informed his readers, "I have just come in from a bee-hunt over Wis-consin hills, amid splendors which would make Monet seem low-keyed." In 1893, few American critics would dare compare the talent of a native innovator with that of a Monet, but Garland stated courageously that "only Enneking and some few others of the American artists . . . have touched the degree of brilliancy and sparkle of color which was in the world to-day. . . . Everywhere amid the red and orange and crimson were lilac and steel-blue shadows, giving depth and vigor and buoyancy which Corot never saw (or never painted)." Continuing, Garland put forth his "settled conviction that art, to be vital, must be local in its subject; its universal appeal must be in its working out,—in the way it is done." Then Garland stepped out on a cultural limb by implying that expatriate impressionists might stay abroad too long, for "dependence upon the English or French groups is alike fatal."

Obviously, young Louis Ritman in Russia could not yet be interested in Garland's treatise, but his future mentors were as each came in contact with the World's Columbian Exposition. When Garland turned his discussion to figurative subjects, in his own indirect way, he did, in fact, help form the foundation upon which Ritman's art would be built. The critic declared: "The impressionist paints portraits and groups, but paints them as he sees them . . . . He never sees human flesh unrelated in its color, it is always affected by other colors . . . . Observe some of the portraits by [Dennis Miller] Bunker, by. . . Mrs. [Lilla Cabot] Perry, or the figures in firelight by [Frank] Benson or [Edmund] Tarbell, and you find them all subtle studies of the interplay of color."[38] Louis Ritman's response to Garland in art would not be seen for yet another twenty years, but now we see that Ritman came to understand Garland's meaning inside and out.

Ill. 4-11. Interior Detail, Art Gallery: United States, section no. 3. World's Columbian Exposition of 1893, Chicago. R.H. Love Galleries Archives, Chicago.

Like Howells's, Garland's demand for something good, for harmony, or "veritism" as he put it, was reflective of the *genteel tradition* in American life, which, at the time of the World's Columbian Exposition, was synonymous with American art, especially figurative impressionism, the kind young Ritman would perfect. As Garland reminded his readers, "the impressionist . . . takes fresh, vital themes . . . . The impressionist is a buoyant and cheerful painter. He loves the open air, and the mid-day sun." Finally Garland prepared the specific critical defense for impressionism that set the precedent for future American critics, and he also pointed out that a need for change existed, and that idols in art were crumbling under the impact of impressionism as it forged ahead, gathering converts along the way: "The iconoclast is a necessity. He it is who breaks out of the hopeless circle of traditional authority . . . . The impressionist is unquestionably an iconoclast, and the friends of the dead painters are properly alarmed. Here, as everywhere, there are the two parties, — the one standing for the old, the other welcoming the new . . . . To a man educated in the school of Munich, the pictures . . . of the Giverney [sic] group of Frenchmen and all other pictures with blue and purple shadows, are a shock. They are not merely variants, they are flags of anarchy . . . . If they are right, then all the rest are wrong. By contrast the old is slain . . . . Let the critic who thinks this is a vogue or fad, this impressionist view of nature, beware. It is a discovery, born of clearer vision and more careful study . . . . The dead must give way to the living. It may be sad, but it is the inexorable law, and the veritist and the impressionist will try to submit gracefully to the method of the iconoclasts who shall come when they in their turn are old and sad."[39]

So it was that the World's Columbian Exposition virtually opened the floodgates to impressionism. At no time did Americans embrace impressionism with as much energetic optimism as they did in the decade of the 1890s, years that witnessed the conversion of many academicians to the broken-color technique — if not fully, at least in part. Proselytization was most obvious in large urban centers, especially New York, Philadelphia, and Boston. In Chicago, where the exposition presented impressionism as never before, the French aesthetic became vogue. Local artists were so inspired during and after the exposition that they organized an informal group known as the *Vibrant Club*. The members of this enthusiastic society were devoted to the promotion of impressionism. Constituents met weekly over dinner at the Restaurant des Champs-Elysèes on Michigan Avenue, where they pledged their "allegiance to the new school" and discussed their progress as painters of "spots and iridescent color

or modelling."[40] Artists with strong connections at the Art Institute were less dramatic in their conversion to the French style, but the influence was obvious in each new exhibition.

As one might expect, Garland, who had moved from Wisconsin to Chicago, continued his avid interest in impressionism, but he was determined that it be applied to the American scene. Even more specifically he longed for a Midwestern impressionism. Much of his enthusiasm was productively channeled into a Chicago-based organization known as the Central Art Association .[41] Garland became president of this rather pro-impressionist clan in March 1894 and contributed to its monthly publication, *Arts for America*. The members of the Central Art Association sought to broaden their overall cultural horizons, but painting constituted one of the most important spheres of action for the group, with Garland remaining its chief force for quite some time.

In response to the Seventh Annual Exhibition of American Paintings, held at the Art Institute of Chicago in October 1894, the year after the World's Fair, the Central Art Association published a small brochure entitled *Impressions on Impressionism*.[42] The authors of this publication — written as an "informal" discussion among three anonymous visitors to the exhibition — were identified only as "*A Critical Triumvirate* ," a novelist, a painter, and a sculptor. Most scholars agree that these reviewers were Hamlin Garland, Charles Francis Browne, and Lorado Taft, all important figures in the Chicago art community. Composed as a three-part dialog, the criticism bore distinct similarities to Louis Leroy's already famous "walk-and-talk" review of the first group exhibition of impressionists at Nadar's in Paris twenty years earlier. Unlike Leroy and his friends, however, Garland was a champion of the movement, not a destroyer. In spite of their sincerity about impressionism, Garland and his associates made no effort to identify themselves, merely explaining in the brief introduction that they were "self-appointed" and did not take themselves "too seriously." In typical Midwestern fashion, the group (committee) pointed out that their criticism was "kindly meant" and it was "not intended to be final — merely suggestive." In referring to a landscape by J. Appleton Brown, the critics stated:

NOVELIST: He seems to have felt the influence of the open air method. That certainly seems keyed higher than usual. It's very sweet and sunny; too sweet, perhaps.
CONSERVATIVE PAINTER: Yes, it's too pretty.
SCULPTOR: I like it, but I'm always a little sus-

picious of the "fake" in his work. See his snow scene up yonder. They keep them at Siegel & Cooper's at 99 cents, with mica sprinkled on for frost effects.[43]

As the triumvirate continued its review, a fourth visitor known only as an "Enthusiastic Westerner" (meaning one living west of the east coast states) entered the discussion and commented on a painting by Frederick Freer, a prominent local artist: "The only trouble with him," the Westerner stated, "is that he has been catering too long to the ignorant down-east trade where 'finish' is everything." He continued: "(With exaltation.) 'That may be all right for New York, but for Chicago, the home of art—' "[44]

The critical triumvirate went on to discuss the work of Robert Vonnoh, Louis Dessar, Charles C. Curran, Edmund Tarbell, Charles Davis, Theodore Robinson, and others. About the work of Frank Benson, Garland wrote: "Ah! There's Benson's picture. . . . See the simplicity of his method. That hand and arm is painted with three broad strokes of the brush, but it takes genius to do that."[45] Charles F. Browne, the "conservative" painter, responded to Garland's high regard for Benson's work: "Steady—steady," Browne said, "now hold up a bit. Benson is a good painter and a splendid fellow as well, but don't put on your praises as some of us put on paint, in chunks. . . . In color it is delicate. . . but I don't believe he needs to fill her hands with vermillion and cadmium to represent fire reflection. The quantity of paint is objectionable. . . it's too painty."[46] Browne's spirited response to Garland's analysis of figurative subjects was typical of the times. In the post-Exposition era, the Chicago art community was more concerned with figurative impressionism than with landscapes. This was the tradition that Louis Ritman would come to know.

In discussing Theodore Robinson (ill. 4-12), Garland wrote that he was "another masterly painter, but he has not selected an interesting subject." He continued: "Like [T. C.] Steele and Herter and Benson he conceals his means and gives us only the effect."[47] Every member of the triumvirate was concerned with the resolution of technique to subject. In discussing one of the works with another visitor, an anonymous "Eminent Painter," Taft posed the following question: "Now supposing that garden had been painted by a pupil of yours, what would you tell him about it—how would you go to work to improve it?" The eminent painter replied that he would tell his student "that such an amount of detail took away all charm, that an *impression* of the scene is really far truer than all of the actual facts."[48]

Like most critics of his generation, Garland was

Ill. 4-12. Theodore Robinson. *Summer Hillside, Giverny.* Oil on canvas, 18 x 24 inches. Private Collection. Courtesy R. H. Love Galleries, Inc., Chicago.

extremely concerned with the quality of the subject matter in art, especially in impressionism, since he felt the subject should express the quality he called "veritism," which was as evident to him in Wisconsin, Illinois, or Indiana, as it was in Giverny or Pont-Aven. One must keep in mind the historical context of Garland's view of impressionism: the aesthetic was relatively new; the future generations that would place Monet and his Giverny subjects on a plateau beyond reproach had not yet done so. Therefore, in the early 1890s Garland saw impressionism as a vibrant new style that was as viable in America as it was anywhere. Garland and his friends were unaware that in time the promoters of impressionism would convince most Americans that the true impressionism emanated only from France. Accordingly, as the group finished its review, a few were overheard: It's good. It's American. Nothing but a fad. They're on the right track.

Although he had no way of knowing the impact of his opinion, Garland was setting the stage for Louis Ritman and countless other latter-day impressionists, especially Midwesterners, when he stated: "What I miss in the whole Exhibition I miss in American art—and that is the drama of American life. It is all so far removed from human interest. I'd like to see more figures in sunlight—not exactly like Tarbell's—but characteristic American scenes, dainty figures."[49] "What pleases me about the Exposition," Garland reported, "is that while the principle of impressionism is almost everywhere, it is finding individual expression. Henri and Herter, and Steele, and Tarbell and Vonnoh, and Robinson all have a different touch—they are gaining mastery of an individual technique. This shows we're pulling out of the imitative stage. There are very few pictures here with Monet's brushstroke imitated in them. The next step is to do interesting American themes and do it naturally."[50]

Garland was very sincere about finding impressionists who could paint American themes "naturally," and he hoped they would be Midwesterners. Probably with this in mind, in November 1894 he sent a copy of *Impressions on Impressionism* to an impressionist he admired greatly, a fellow native of Wisconsin and a Giverny expatriate, Theodore Robinson. Robinson, who was still reaching for something in America that was as significant as what he had found in Giverny, described the review as "witty and sensible and suggestive—the sort of thing that ought to do good." He wrote in his diary in December that he liked "its freedom from heaviness, dogmatism—and a number of good things are said, pour et contre."[51]

Before Garland found veritism in the work of French or East Coast impressionists, he had discovered it in the canvases of Midwestern artists, ironically not those of his beloved Wisconsin or Chicago, but in the work of a few painters from nearby Indiana. Although they concentrated on landscape subjects, these painters—William Forsyth, John Ottis Adams (ill. 4-13), and Theodore C.

Ill. 4-13. J. Ottis Adams. *Sycamores, All in Yellow Clad.* Oil on canvas, 20 x 30 inches. Courtesy ACA Galleries, New York.

Steele—had studied in Munich and with the American expatriate J. Frank Currier in Schleissheim, Germany. A fourth, Otto Stark, had trained in Paris. Most of these artists had been in Europe nearly a decade earlier, however, and by the time Garland saw their work at the art show of the World's Columbian Exposition, their painting showed the strong influence of impressionism. This was true especially of the work of T. C. Steele, to which he had referred in *Crumbling Idols*. These painters were considered regionalists because they remained in Indi-

anapolis and rural Indiana, but they were also seen as surprisingly progressive and quite reflective of the growing trend of avant-garde art in the Midwest.[52] Indeed, these Indiana landscapists—discovered far from Paris in the American wilderness—were Garland's answer to veritism: later he would come to call them the "Hoosier School" of American impressionists. They depicted the rolling Indiana farmland around Brookville, with its Whitewater River, or Vernon, with its several nearby creeks. Accordingly, it was not difficult for Garland to rationalize that as a subject for an impressionistic painting, Vernon, France, with its nearby Seine and Epte, was not intrinsically superior to Vernon, Indiana, with its nearby streams. Steele and his friends were confident of themselves as painters, and Garland made them feel still more confident as impressionists. Even before he championed them, the group had published *Modern Art*, a magazine described by Gerdts as "the finest, best-designed publication on art in this country (in the 1890s)."[53] Here, they promoted impressionism through positive reviews (including those on the Exposition of 1893) and articles on the topic by Forsyth, Steele, and Stark.[54]

It seems that of all the members of the Hoosier group, T. C. Steele was the most professorial in his attempts to educate the public on "impressionalism," the term he used to refer to the aesthetic in an 1893 article.[55] He pointed out that the landscapist might find colors mixed on his palette "dull and lifeless compared with nature's living tones," so he could remedy the problem by putting "the colors side by side upon the canvas, unmixed . . . . in this he . . . . attains to a brilliancy of light and a vibration of color that is many times nearer that of nature."[56] Steele went on to explain that this method of painting (broken color) was the "peculiarity of the impressionists that is so much criticized by the public, for it breaks at once with those smooth conventions, insipid prettiness and surface finish that count for so much with the uneducated eye." "But it will be conceded," Steele wrote, that the impressionists "have given us pictures of nature with a power of illusion that no other painters have ever attained."[57]

All in all, at this point in the history of American impressionism, the Hoosier School was the leading group of impressionists in the nation. The upshot of it was that when Hamlin Garland saw an exhibition of their work at the Dennison Hotel in Indianapolis in 1894, he invited them to loan the show to the Central Art Association in Chicago.[58] Under these auspices, the Hoosier Group exhibition was hung in December 1894 in Lorado Taft's studio, then located in the Chicago Athenaeum. The show prompted another impromptu review by the Critical Triumvirate, two of whom (Garland and Taft) had organized the exhibition. Entitled *Five Hoosier Painters*, the pamphlet was published by the Central Art Association.[59] The anonymous reviewers reported that the Hoosier impressionists had been "isolated from their fellow artists, they were surrounded by apparently the most unpromising material, yet they set themselves to their thankless task."[60]

Garland and his friends agreed that the Hoosier show demonstrated "the power of the artist's eye to find floods of color, graceful forms and interesting composition everywhere."[61] Charles F. Browne, the "Conservative Painter," saw the Hoosiers as "conservatively impressionistic," while the sculptor Taft thought they "had selected the better part of impressionism."[62] Although canvases by these Indiana artists had been shown at the World's Columbian Exposition, the show mounted by the Central Art Association was actually the national première for the Hoosier Group. Not only was the exhibition successful, but it also proved the validity of Garland's premise that impressionism was actually veritism and was as viable when done in Vernon, Indiana, as in Vernon, France. Furthermore, the exhibition pushed a small devoted band of Midwesterners to the forefront of American impressionism. Almost immediately, other Chicago critics began to agree with Garland that the Hoosier Group was producing "an indigenous art."[63] At the national level, a reviewer for *Art Amateur* concluded that T. C. Steele was a member "of the impressionist school, and deals in the glorification of the commonplace Indiana landscape."[64]

Garland knew that he had discovered an important regionalist group, and he did everything in his power to promote their art. Only a couple of weeks after their group show at Taft's studio, most of the Hoosiers contributed paintings to the joint exhibition of the Palette and Chisel Club and the Cosmopolitan Art Club in Chicago. Held in January 1895, the joint show inspired a good deal of positive critical attention. Garland wrote the introduction to the exhibition catalog. Determined to convince the art community that the Midwest was as good a place to create impressionism as France, he stated: "Monet makes Giverny. Giverny does not make Monet."[65] With total conviction, Garland stressed local over European subjects when he wrote: "The light floods the Kankakee marshes as well as the meadows and wil-

Ill. 4-14. Will H. Low. Photograph. R.H. Love Galleries Archives, Chicago.

lows of Giverny. The Muscatatuk [River] has its subtleties of color as well as L'Orse."[66] Garland believed that an observer like Will H. Low (ill. 4-14) could have been describing rural Illinois or Indiana as well as Giverny when he wrote that: "between the village and the larger river winds a small stream. . . with pleasantly shaded banks enclosed between broad meadows gracefully bordered by long lines of poplars. Its greatest charm lies in the atmospheric conditions over the lowlands, where the moisture from the rivers, imprisoned through the night by the valleys bordering hills, dissolve before the sun and bathe the landscape in an iridescent flood of vaporous hues."[67]

Notes

1. James Carroll Beckwith Diary, Roll No. 800, no frame no., Archives of American Art, Smithsonian Institution, Washington, DC.

2. Thomas Barbour Bryan from Alexandria, Virginia, graduated from Harvard in 1849 and after a few years in Cincinnati, established a law practice in 1853 in Chicago. Bryan was involved in Illinois real estate, but especially so in Chicago. An eloquent speaker, he devoted a good deal of his time during the Civil War to recruitment of Union forces. In 1865, he became the executive manager of the Northwestern Sanitary Fair of 1865 which was centered in a large building in Dearborn Park. Bryan was exceedingly vocal in his promotion of the World's Columbian Exposition, subsequently serving as its vice president.

3. For a comprehensive study of women's role at the World's Columbian Exposition, see Jeanne Madeline Weimann, *The Fair Women* (Chicago: Academy Chicago, 1981).

4. It was at this time that the Chicago Fair Corporation was established. The large organization held a meeting at the lakefront and chose forty-five directors. Lyman Gage was elected president, and Thomas B. Bryan and Potter Palmer were elected first and second vice president, respectively. Ten committees controlled finance, grounds, buildings, fine arts, transportation, and more. Two months later, it was decided that the Fair would not be called the "World's Exposition of 1892," but the "World's Columbian Exposition."

5. This appellation arose from the pontification of Charles A. Dana, editor of the *New York Sun,* who stated: "Don't pay any attention to the nonsensical claims of that 'Windy City.'"

6. In the planning stages, several sites had been chosen by Olmsted and Co. The Lake Front Park site downtown was abandoned, and Jackson Park and Washington Park were connected by the Midway Plaisance. For an in-depth discussion, see D. H. Burnham, "The World's Columbian Exposition: The Plan of the Builders," in *The Art of the World Illustrated in the Paintings, Statuary, and Architecture of the World's Columbian Exposition*, ed. Ripley Hitchcock (New York: D. Appleton and Co., 1896), Vol. I,, pp. ᴵ·VI. In spite of his fame in New York, Olmsted was no foreigner to Chicago, for as early as 1868 he had planned the town of Riverside on Chicago's west side. Later he was engaged by the South Park Commissioners (of Chicago) to improve recreational facilities.

7. Ibid., p. II.

8. Root sent invitations to R. M. Hunt, McKim, Mead & White, and George B. Post of New York; to Peabody and Stearns of Boston; and to Van Brunt and Howe of Kansas City. They were to design buildings that would circle the Court of Honor.

9. Harriet Monroe, *John Wellborn Root: A Study of His Life and Work* (New York, 1896), facsimile edition (Park Forest, IL: Prairie School Press, 1966).

10. On their first day in Chicago, the architects met with Burnham for breakfast. Burnham recalled that "they were filled with enthusiasm." Quoted from Thomas S. Hines, *Burnham of Chicago, Architect and Planner* (Chicago: The University of Chicago Press, 1974), p. 88.

11. Burnham, p. II.

12. Hines, p. 90.

13. *Chicago Tribune*, 18 January 1891, p. 29.

14. *Chicago Tribune*, 24 March 1889, p. 32.

15. Auspices for New York City were provided by an "art bureau for the State of New York." Members for this bureau consisted of committees of sculptors, painters, and architects. After a preliminary meeting at the Century Club in October 1892, a formal group was organized on 21 December, and J. Q. A. Ward was elected chief of the art bureau. "It was decided to hold a preliminary competition in New York City and to send to the fair [in Chicago] such works only as should in the opinion of the committee possess recognizable merit." The painting committee consisted of William Merritt Chase, Eastman Johnson, H. Bolton Jones, R. Swain Gifford, and Frank D. Millet. See "Report on the Fine Arts Exhibit," *Report of the Board of General Managers of the Exhibit of the State of New York at the World's Columbian Exposition* (Albany, NY: James B. Lyon, State Printer, 1894), p. 379.

16. Ibid., p. 380.

17. For a comprehensive study, see Leslie S. Goldstein, *Art in Chicago and The World's Columbian Exposition of 1893*, Master's thesis, University of Iowa, May 1970.

18. Henry Van Brundt, "Architecture at the World's Columbian Exposition, *Century Magazine*, 44 (1892), pp. 81-89.

19. M. G. Van Rensselaer, "Artistic Triumph of the Fair Builders," *Forum,* 14 (1892), pp. 535-541.

20. Ellen M. Henrotin, "An Outsider's View of the Woman's Exhibit," *The Cosmopolitan*, XV (1893), pp. 560-66.

21. Weimann.

22. Julien Ralph, ed., *Harper's Chicago and the World's Fair*, (New York: Harper and Brothers, Publishers, 1893), p. 191.

23. Halsey C. Ives, 'The Department of Fine Arts," in *The Art of the World, Illustrated in the Paintings, Statuary, and Architecture of the World's Columbian Exposition,* p. VIII.

24. Ibid., p. X.

25. Theodore Stanton, "Europe at the World's Fair—The French Section," *North American Review*, 156 (1893), pp. 241-46.

26. For a comprehensive study of the topic, see Elizabeth Brown, "American Paintings and Sculpture in the Fine Arts Building of the World's Columbian Exposition, Chicago, 1893," Ph.D. diss., University of Kansas, 1976.

27. Halsey Ives, pp. XVII-XVIII.

28. Ibid.

29. William Gerdts, *American Impressionism* (New York: Abbeville Press, 1984), p. 141.

30. Daniel Wildenstein, *Claude Monet: Biographie et catalogue raisonné*, Vol. III, *1887-1898, Peintures* (Lausanne-Paris: La Bibliothèque des Arts, 1979), p. 55.

31. Ibid.

32. John Rewald, *The History of Impressionism* (New York: The Museum of Modern Art, 1961), p. 610, n. 38.

33. His first and only major contribution to literary theory, Garland's *Crumbling Idols* was once described by a reviewer for the *Atlantic Monthly* as a "little book on literary topics." Significant portions of several chapters had appeared in articles in the *Arena* (Boston) and the *Forum* (New York) magazines, while chapter IX on impressionism was written in 1893 when Garland came to Chicago. Garland cited Eugène Véron's *Aesthetics*, trans. W. H. Armstrong (London, 1879), as a major source for his work. For an excellent overview of the topic, see Jane Johnson, "Introduction," in Hamlin Garland, *Crumbling Idols* (Cambridge, MA: The Belknap Press of Harvard University Press, 1960), pp. ix-xxviii; see also Jesse Goldstein, "Two Literary Radicals: Garland and Markham in Chicago, 1893," *American Literature*, XVII, 2 (May 1945), p. 160.

34. Garland, *Crumbling Idols*, pp. 97-98. Although he did not actually refer to Monet here, in this brief paragraph it is likely that Garland's "instantaneous effect," the "progress of the sun," and the "alluring phases of nature" refer to Monet's recently coined term (1891) *instantaneity (l'instantanéité)*. Attempting to achieve this special quality, Monet painted a series of haystacks en plein air under varying light conditions at different times of the day. See Rewald, pp. 562-63.

35. Garland, *Crumbling Idols*, pp. 100-03. Herbert Spencer, an English philosopher and theorist, was born at Derby on 27 April 1820 and died at Brighton on 8 December 1903. Having abandoned engineering, Spencer devoted his career to philosophy and literature. In this new capacity he first authored a series of letters to the *Nonconformist* (1842) and published his *Principles of Psychology* in 1855, a treatise based on principles of evolution, prior to Darwin's *Origin of Species*. Exactly which essays influenced Garland is unknown, but Spencer did visit America in 1882, when he

delivered several lectures. He also published a series known as "A System of Synthetic Philosophy."

36. The term "veritism" as used by Garland was inextricably tied to realism and the traditional American values in literature as applied to art. For a discussion of Garland's use of the term, see Jane Johnson, "Introduction," in *Crumbling Idols*, pp. xxi-xxiii.

37. Garland, *Roadside Meetings* (New York: The Macmillan Co., 1930), pp. 252-53.

38. Garland, *Crumbling Idols*, p. 104.

39. Ibid., pp. 105, 109-10.

40. *Chicago Tribune*, 20 August 1893, p. 31.

41. Records show that the Central Art Association of America was organized by Mrs. T. Vernette Morse in March 1894, and that its first meeting was held at the Art Institute of Chicago two months later. By 1898, the organization counted "about 3,000 members scattered throughout the United States." Ten departments, ranging from painting to house decoration, pursued their separate activities. An annual congress was held in October. See Florence N. Levy, ed., *American Art Annual, 1898* (New York: The Macmillan Co., 1899), p. 164.

42. A Critical Triumvirate [assumed authors: Hamlin Garland, Lorado Taft, Charles Francis Browne], *Impressions on Impressionism* (Chicago: The Central Art Association, 1894). On page V of the pamphlet, an anonymous writer [Garland?] explains: "The idea came to the Committee while publicly discussing the pictures in the present art exhibition. . . . The judgments are off-hand and the talk informal."

43. Ibid., p. 2.

44. Ibid., p. 4.

45. Ibid., p. 10.

46. Ibid., pp. 10-11.

47. Ibid., p. 11.

48. Ibid., p. 16.

49. Ibid., p. 22.

50. Ibid., p. 23.

51. Robinson Diary, Frick Art Reference Library, 1894.

52. For a comprehensive study of the Indiana Impressionists, see Judith Vale Newton, *The Hoosier Group: Five American Painters* (Indianapolis, IN: Eckert Publications, 1985). See also Selma N. Steele and Wilbur D. Peat, *House of the Singing Winds*, pp. 38-46, 175-192.

53. Gerdts, p. 147.

54. See issues of *Modern Art* (a very rare publication), ranging from T. C. Steele's "Impressionism," in vol. 1 (Winter

1893) to Stark's "The Evolution of Impressionism," in vol. 3 (Spring 1895), pp. 53-56.

55. J. M. Bowles, "Impressionalism," *Modern Art* (Winter 1893).

56. Ibid.

57. Ibid.

58. The première Indiana exhibition at the Dennison Hotel was sponsored by the Indianapolis Art Association.

59. In addition to T. C. Steele, Otto Stark, and William Forsyth, there was Richard Gruelle from Indianapolis and J. Ottis Adams, another native Hoosier. See Newton, *The Hoosier Group*, "J. Ottis Adams," pp. 87-110.

60. A Critical Triumvirate (assumed authors: Hamlin Garland, Charles F. Browne, Lorado Taft), *Five Hoosier Painters* (Chicago: Central Art Association, 1894).

61. This statement reflects Garland's theory of veritism in painting, since these artists proved their abilities to perceive and record "impressions" of nature's finer qualities, just as in literary impressionism the author demonstrated veritism that could be defined as "the truthful statement of an individual impression corrected by reference to the fact," in the painter's case, "by reference to" nature's facts. See Hamlin Garland, "Productive Conditions of American Literature," *Forum*, XVII (August 1894), p. 690.

62. "Critical Triumvirate," *Five Hoosier Painters*.

63. Harriet Monroe, "Chicago Letter," *Critic*, no. 22 (29 December 1894), p. 450.

64. *Art Amateur*, no. 32 (March 1895), p. 107.

65. Hamlin Garland, "Art Conditions in Chicago," introduction in *Catalogue, United Annual Exhibition of the Palette Club and the Cosmopolitan Art Club*, exhibition catalog (Chicago: The Art Institute, 1895).

66. In his comparison of the "Kankakee marshlands" to the Giverny area, Garland was referring to the area about sixty miles south of Chicago where the Kankakee River crosses the Indiana-Illinois state line between Shelby, Indiana, and Momence, Illinois. In his comparison of the Muscatatuck with l'Oise, Garland referred to one of T. C. Steele's favorite painting spots in southern Indiana, the Muscatatuck River, south of Vernon.

67. Will H. Low, *A Chronicle of Friendships, 1873-1900* (New York: Charles Scribner's Sons, 1908), pp. 446-47.

CHAPTER FIVE:
SETTING THE STAGE FOR RITMAN —
THE EXPANSION OF IMPRESSIONISM

Not everyone was as sympathetic to impressionism as Hamlin Garland. As late as the turn of the century there were numerous diehard stalwarts of academicism in America, ranging from artists at the National Academy of Design in New York City, such as Edwin H. Blashfield and Kenyon Cox (ill. 5-1), to art critics, such as Arthur Hoeber. "If under the new conditions, we get color," Hoeber wrote, "it is at the expense of composition; if we are blinded with brilliant sunshine, we look in vain for qualities of careful draughtsmanship; if there is suggested the sparkle and the vibrancy of nature, then we are bothered by spots of crude color, awkward brushwork, and unpleasant prominence of pigment. In short, the fin-de-siècle men present their one new true note at the expense of many other unharmonious ones."[1]

The spread of impressionism was irreversible, however. For all of its drawbacks, impressionism displayed an attractive imagery and an optimistic mood. Impressionism had already become an American movement unto itself in those years, winning the admiration of artists and public alike.[2] In their aggressive, if not audacious manner, Americans led the world in the pursuit and promotion of impressionism. In fact, as early as 1893, when Garland wrote *Crumbling Idols*, the American market was already so important to the French artists that Pissarro feared for the well-being of his constituents when

the American economic recession dragged down sales.[3] Still later in the decade, certain concerned Frenchmen worried that wealthy Americans like Mrs. Palmer or Mrs. Havemeyer would take all the great impressionist works to America.[4] According to H. Wayne Morgan, "the American art world treated the early impressionists as part of a larger wave of 'modernism' which had fascinated them since the 1860s." He points out that in addition to its being a new way of painting, impressionism "was a new way of perceiving old things, offering fresh insights into familiar landscapes, city views, and personalities." Morgan concludes: "It also captured the sense of change that permeated modern life. And it could make that change orderly and secure in an essentially cheerful art comprehensible to everyone."[5]

As the aesthetic was interpreted by American painters, it took on many interesting twists within the larger parameters originally set by the French in both landscape and genre. Even with the best of intentions, however, American impressionists, especially those who worked in their homeland, could not bring themselves to expand the aesthetic as far as their French counterparts had done. Theirs was a recapitulation of the stereotypical broken-color technique, an overt style change that allied them with contemporary modernism but with nothing much beyond. As a matter of fact, some observers were not

Ill. 5-1. Kenyon Cox. Photograph. R. H. Love Galleries Archives, Chicago.

overly concerned about the radicalism inherent in impressionism if it induced no greater deviation from academicism than the broken-color technique: "We are inclined to think," a writer for the *Nation* stated, "that there were heroes before Agamemnon, and that the art of the past will not necessarily tumble into oblivion because of the discovery that three primary colors, placed side by side, give more of the physical sensation of light than does a bit of white paint."[6] Nonetheless, the style was pervasive, and in spite of warnings that impressionism promoted disregard for discipline and skill, the look of Monet not only triumphed over some harsh criticism, but it also became America's most highly regarded art movement.

In the early 1890s Childe Hassam (ill. 5-2), Ernest Lawson (ill. 5-3), and a few other friends followed John H. Twachtman's advice and painted in and around the Connecticut towns of Cos Cob and Branchville. Solon Borglum and Hamilton Hamilton began working in the

nearby Silvermine area. Donelson Hoopes goes so far as to describe this general region near "the shoreline of Connecticut" as a "kind of Giverny in America."[7] The fact that the area was quite rural and not far from New York gave Cos Cob some resemblance to the relationship between Paris and Giverny, but the similarity ended there. The Cos Cob School of Art that Hassam occasionally mentioned probably began in 1890 and consisted mostly of Twachtman's and J. Alden Weir's students from their winter classes at the Art Students League. In addition to the Giverny pioneer Theodore Robinson, there were a few nonimpressionists like Albert P. Ryder and writers like Lincoln Steffens and Willa Cather who were drawn to the art colony, which, in its special way, seemed to evoke the mood of "the spirit of place," a quality that they all tried to capture in describing "the local and the specific."[8] The outcome of it was that whether American artists worked in their native land or in Giverny, they came to look upon certain rural areas not only as places to escape from the clamor and confusion of the big city but also as places that contributed to their inner consciousness and to their artistic development. Just as Robinson had been aware of the importance of his being in Paris to his career but had nonetheless been anxious to return to rural Giverny, Twachtman in New York confessed: "I am caught in the meshes of this den of iniquity . . . . I wish . . . I could row ashore and go back to Cos Cob."[9]

The American impressionists were about a decade behind their French counterparts, owing first to the fact that they had had to learn the style from the original innovators, and second to the fact that they were generally more conservative in their application of the new style. A few rare individuals like Theodore Butler in Giverny fully assimilated Monet's formula and by 1894 had expanded it so daringly in terms of color, execution, and subject that he had arrived at a radically post-impressionistic style (ill. 5-4). Other artists, like Hassam, learned the features of impressionism and clung steadfastly to its prescribed boundaries. Someone like Mark Fisher in England never fully assimilated the style, while Garland's friend Enneking vacillated between tonalism and impressionism. Of course, there were also progressives like Robert Vonnoh, Eugene Vail, J. Alden Weir, and even Theodore Robinson, who waged war with themselves to liberalize their palettes and brushwork.

Some of the Midwestern artists who would later teach impressionism to Louis Ritman progressed at a slightly slower pace in their discovery and assimilation of the French style. The most influential of these was Lawton Parker (ill. 5-5), the career of whom it will be instructive to discuss briefly. Parker had completed his studies at the Art Institute when he reached Paris in 1888, the same year

Ill. 5-2. Childe Hassam. Photograph. R. H. Love Galleries Archives, Chicago.

that Butler arrived in Giverny. Parker passed the entrance requirements and enrolled at the Ecole des Beaux-Arts, where he met the rigors of the nineteenth-century Salon style head on. Lured by progressive painting, Parker also joined the student ranks of the private but highly competitive Julian Academy, where he sketched from live models and worked on outside assignments that involved independent study in museums and art galleries. In Paris Parker was subject to numerous contrasting influences, ranging from Jules Bastien-Lepage's plein-air painting and Jean Bernard's juste-milieu manner to Claude Monet's impressionism. By 1890, Parker had absorbed enough for a while and returned to America.

In New York City, Parker enrolled at the Art Students League, where he benefited from the critique of William Merritt Chase and John La Farge. At this time Chase and other distinguished painters were falling under the influence of impressionism; and like them, Parker was learning to assimilate certain telltale features of the style. His canvases were meeting with approval, showing as they did a certain progressive Salon style. Parker traveled back to the Midwest, and in 1892 – one year before Richard Miller came to study art at that institution – he accepted an instructor's position at the Saint Louis School of Fine Arts. Halsey C. Ives was head of the school at the time. In 1893, Parker assumed a more lucrative post as director of fine arts at Beloit College in Wisconsin. Two years later he resumed his studies at the Art Students League in New York, and in 1896 he won the John Chandler European Scholarship, amounting to $5,000, which enabled him to return to Paris.

Parker went back to intensive studies at the Ecole des Beaux-Arts and the Julian Academy in Paris, working under Gérôme, Laurens, and Constant. Soon he received a school prize for portraiture and was promoted to the rank of *hors concours*. In 1897, Gérôme announced that Parker had been awarded the prestigious Studio Prize, the highest distinction available to a foreign student. Albert Besnard, a French painter of great distinction, invited Parker to assist him in the mural decoration of the Cazin hospital at Berck. Besnard's ideas were in sympathy with impressionism and influenced Parker's handling of portraiture. During this period Parker also received training and advice from the then famous James A. M. Whistler. Rapidly gaining admiration for his work among French Salon masters, Parker made friends with Gérôme, Constant, Carolus Duran, Charles Cottet, and Lucien Simon. In the 1890s Cottet attracted national attention in France and exhibited with other impressionists at the avant-garde Le Barc de Boutteville Galleries in Paris, where the American Theodore Butler had gained acceptance with his advanced post-impressionist paintings. Lucien Simon also had established a reputation as a portraitist, so Parker's association with Cottet, Simon, and others enabled him not only to move with ease in the French art circles but also to present his growing expertise on art and artists more convincingly when he returned to the New York and Chicago art world. Thus it was that back home, Parker's recommendations began to carry weight, a consequence that became a crucial factor in Ritman's life.

Another important influence in Ritman's career was Frederick Frieseke (ill. 5-6), who enrolled at the Art Institute of Chicago in 1893, when the World's Columbian Exposition was dazzling the city, and studied there until 1896. We have seen that during these post-exposition years impressionism became a strong movement in Chicago. Frieseke, however, was mainly concerned with the Salon style, and moved from Chicago to New York for additional training at the Art Students League. He stayed there until 1897. With a strong academic background in draftsmanship, Frieseke made his living by drawing cartoons for the *New York Times* and other dailies in the late 1890s. In letters to his future wife, Sarah Ann O'Bryan, he complained, however, about the hardships he experienced in attempting to support himself in this manner. In 1898, having received some money from his father to cover traveling expenses, Frieseke sailed for Paris.

If Lawton Parker succeeded in acquiring painting techniques from developing a close association with atelier masters, Richard Miller from Saint Louis rammed his way into the academic world of Paris through his technique and sheer stamina for work (ill. 5-7). In 1898, Miller enrolled in the Julian Academy, where he studied under the academic masters Jean-Paul Laurens and Benjamin Constant. Although Miller restricted himself to charcoal drawings at the Academy in order to keep his expenses

Ill. 5-4. Theodore Earl Butler. *Jimmy in a Garden.* 1894. Oil on canvas, 26 x 32 inches. Private Collection. Courtesy R. H. Love Galleries, Chicago.

Ill. 5-3. Ernest Lawson. Photograph. R. H. Love Galleries Archives, Chicago

down, his work was soon held up as a model for both French and American students. According to one writer, Miller's "early work was in quiet grays." Executing his images rapidly but carefully, so as to render properly the *caractère* of the figure, Miller achieved a successful blending of verisimilitude and plasticity of form. The praise Miller received from French instructors resulted in his giving private lessons to students from wealthy families. In addition, Miller contracted for an illustration job with a London publishing house in 1900.

While Ritman's future mentors were learning about impressionism, the style changed radically in France. The mid- to late 1890s witnessed the birth of new movements that had been conceived earlier. Since the death of Georges Seurat in 1891, the baton of neo-impressionism had been carried by his very capable friend, the painter theorist Paul Signac. Born in 1863, the year Delacroix died, Signac had from early on been peripherally attached to the impressionist movement; but as a leader of the neo-impressionist movement, he was convinced that impressionists depended inordinately on instinct and impulse. Since 1884, Signac had been a founding member of the Society of Independent Artists and had become a close friend of the literary symbolist Félix Fénéon, who had proclaimed several years earlier that "Monet's renown increases but his talent does not seem to have developed since the Etretat series."[10] During the decade of the 1890s, Signac guided the neo-impressionist movement to a position of strength and influence. In 1892 Signac discovered Saint Tropez and for many years returned annually to paint there—quiet Giverny, far from a coastline, did not interest him; moreover, Signac could not have shared a position of leadership with Monet. In chapter IV of his book *From Eugène Delacroix to Neo-Impressionism*, published in 1899, Signac boasted: "One can say that generally speaking, a Neo-Impressionist work is more harmonious than an Impressionist one, one of the reasons being that because of the way contrasts are always observed, there is more harmony in the detail." Continuing his comparison, which at first reading smacks of Garland's veritism, Signac tried to convince his readers that there "is also greater harmony in the general effect, and a kind of 'moral harmony' too because the composition is based on aesthetic principles and the language of Colors." He concluded: "Impressionism has none of this." Implying his group's debt to the original innovators, Signac continued: "Far be it from me to compare the merits of these two generations of painters; the Impressionists were supreme artists who achieved the splendid task they set themselves; the Neo-Impressionists are still in the process of discovery and realize the immense amount of work that remains to be done."

Ill. 5-5. Lawton Parker. Photograph. R. H. Love Galleries Archives, Chicago.

After Gauguin (ill. 5-8) had stretched impressionism even beyond the limits reached by Van Gogh, in an effort to arrive at what Gauguin and Emile Bernard termed *synthetism,* he inspired a younger group (roughly contemporaneous with the American pioneer painters in Giverny), who, calling themselves the Nabis (a Hebrew term meaning "prophets"), became the leaders of the avant-garde in Paris during the decade of the 1890s. Gauguin referred to himself as an impressionist for quite some time after he had abandoned the formula, but his followers, the Nabis, demanded a separatist role. The work

Ill. 5-6. Frederick Carl Frieseke. Photograph. R. H. Love Galleries Archives, Chicago.

of the Nabis, among whom were artists such as Paul Sérusier, Ambroise Vuillard, and Pierre Bonnard, differed from that of the impressionists not only in terms of style but also in color and content. A large part of their subject matter contained figurative elements, the incorporation of which owed something to a combination of influences, ranging from Manet to Degas to Puvis de Chavannes to Bernard and Gauguin. In the 1890s, the imagery of the Nabis was far different from anything like the figurative works of Monet, Renoir, or Pissarro. The

Nabis's deviation from both impressionism and synthetism was obvious to critics and the public alike when their paintings were shown at the Fourth Le Barc de Boutteville Exhibition in Paris in April 1893.[11] With his gallery situated on the rue Le Pelletier, the art dealer Le Barc presented an impressive show consisting of 146 works by 24 artists—impressionists, symbolists, neo-impressionists, synthetists, and, of course, the Nabis. Ironically, the show was billed as a collective event and called the "Impressionist and Symbolist Painters," a catchall title through which only the most discerning eyes could see. In this way, Le Barc's efforts reflected those of many constituents of the Parisian art community who sought to present an image of unity among otherwise disparate factions, the members of some of which promoted not only artistic anarchy, but the sociopolitical kind as well.[12]

Meanwhile, back in America during the post-World's Columbian Exposition years, Theodore Robinson had become exceedingly distraught over his lack of progress as an impressionist. Struggling as never before with his art and suffering from illness, the artist died quite unexpectedly in the spring of 1896 at his cousin's place in New York. Robinson had been absent from Giverny since 1892 and for the past few years had worked in Greenwich, Cos Cob, and Haverstraw, New York, and even in Townshead, Vermont. Robinson was the first member of the Giverny pioneer group to die. The milieu of that art colony, however, had expanded and changed since he had guided the group at the Hotel Baudy in the late 1880s.

At the very end of the following year of 1897, when Louis Ritman was nearing his ninth birthday in Russia, several artists, firmly committed to impressionism, met at The Players Club of New York to discuss a double-headed plan to withdraw from the Society of American Artists and to form an independent association known as The Ten (American Painters).[13] It was in January 1898 that the *New York Times* first informed its readers of the formation of the new group: "The seceding artists grew dissatisfied with their membership in a large body which is governed by form and tradition, and having sympathetic tastes in a certain direction in art [impressionism], they had withdrawn from the Society of American Artists to work together in accordance with those tastes."[14] When the elitist society was officially organized in the early spring of 1898, it included Childe Hassam, John Henry Twachtman, J. Alden Weir, Frank Weston Benson, Willard Metcalf, Edmund Charles Tarbell, Robert Reid, Joseph Rodefer De Camp, Edward Simmons, and Thomas Wilmer Dewing, reflecting therefore a New York and Boston constituency.[15] Some time earlier, Tarbell had written to Chase, a future member of

the group, referring to the Society of American Artists as the "Society of Mediocrity." Of the members of The Ten, which E. P. Richardson called "a kind of academy of American Impressionism," at least one-half—De Camp, Metcalf, Simmons, Dewing, and Weir—were exceedingly reticent in their devotion to the impressionist

Ill. 5-7. Richard Miller. *Along the River, Sunset.* Oil on academy board, 12 x 16 inches. Private Collection. Courtesy R. H. Love Galleries, Chicago.

mode.[16] However, the voluntary alliance of these painters with figures such as Hassam, Twachtman, and Tarbell thrust them immediately into the foremost rank of impressionists in America. It is noteworthy that Metcalf was the only member of The Ten who had also been a member of the Giverny pioneer group (ill. 5-9).

On 31 March 1898, Paul Durand-Ruel held the first of many exhibitions for The Ten in his New York facilities. Durand-Ruel was the champion of impressionism, who had introduced it to America over a dozen years earlier, so this show was a further confirmation to the public that the group was allied with the movement. During the preceding dozen years or so, Durand-Ruel's track record in New York had been excellent. He was always anxious to show the work of American impressionists. For example, the exhibition prior to the première of The Ten was a solo show of paintings, pastels, and etchings by Mary Cassatt (ill. 5-10). The Havemeyers had loaned several works to the show, and critics had praised Cassatt's work in general. A reproduction of a painting by the "impressionist from Pennsylvania" appeared on the cover of the spring issue of the *Art Amateur*.[17]

With the advent of The Ten, impressionism was in the hands of some of America's leading masters, artists who had paid their debts to the academic tradition, graduated to the avant-garde, and helped propel it to a plateau of high regard. In fact, by the turn of the century there was nothing very radical about impressionist art, especially when it was compared with imagery created by Gauguin or the Nabis, Europe's leading post-impressionists. Because impressionism was finally in vogue, it began to dominate the walls of local and national exhibitions everywhere.

For the most part, impressionist subjects fell into two basic categories – landscape and figurative. But no matter what "real life" subject was depicted, however, the image was usually optimistic about life in general. Impressionism was seldom sad and nearly always happy. Indeed, H. Wayne Morgan tells us that whether French or American, impressionism "depicted many informal activities such as dancing, picnicking, boating, and outings in the park, yet it remained stylish."[18] Morgan further notes: "Treatments of smoke, of steam and fog, of water reflections, and of changing light and foliage, were equally exciting," because they reflected flux, such as that in the movement itself and in Western society: "Impressionism's general concern with motion and change in optimistic settings made it attractive to the industrial age. And it promised refinement and enjoyment through art to a widening range of people who had hitherto found art forbidding or threatening."[19] As far as the artists, the makers of impressionism, were concerned, they all adhered to the unwritten credo that in spite of observed hardships, they would seek the bright side of their own environments, whether these were American or European. Typifying the collective attitude of most of his constituents, Childe Hassam said that he believed "the man who will go down to posterity is the man who paints his own time and the scenes of everyday life around him."[20] In their pictures, impressionist artists focused on the "smiling aspects of life," qualities which Garland's associate, William Dean Howells, the dean of American literature, and others thought to be the essence of good American art and literature.[21] It should also be mentioned that Howells and Garland were acutely aware of the ironic contrast between the lifestyles of certain impressionists and the subjects they depicted. At one time, for example, Howells detested the term "bohemia" and the whole image of bohemianism. His mood had mellowed somewhat by 1893, the year Garland wrote *Crumbling Idols* and *The Coast of Bohemia;* nonetheless, Howells worked diligently to show that bohemianism was nothing more than a long-lived fad, frequently an affectation assimilated by certain wealthy individuals who wished to hobnob with artists and intellectuals. This behavior, he believed, had little to do with the intrinsic qualities of the "good life" depicted by artists like Tarbell, Chase, or Has-

Ill. 5-8. Paul Gauguin in the early 1890s. Photograph. R.H. Love Galleries Archives, Chicago.

sam, and in future years by younger men like Ritman.

The studios of Dewing, Tarbell, De Camp, Benson, Philip Hale, Weir, Potthast, Helen Turner, Charles Curran, William Paxton, J. Carroll Beckwith, Reid, Chase, and many others were, in fact, filled with images that actually represented impressionistic slices of the genteel tradition. Their works depicted beautiful women, picnics with children, models in gardens, wives and daughters captured unawares in quiet interiors where nearby windows subtly or strikingly illuminated their frequently intimate surroundings and much more that showed an untrammeled, if not leisurely life. These same healthy young ladies were also depicted out of doors, their frilly white and slightly diaphanous dresses bathed in brilliant summer sunshine and softly blown by a gentle breeze (ill. 5-11). Painters who succeeded in conveying the message that their feminine lovelies lived in a white-washed environment, which protected them from the coarse elements of the world, much as their lace-trimmed parasols protected them from harsh weather elements, were successful since their pictures reflected the nineteenth-century concept of the "good life" or a holiday mood by which most artists hoped to mirror their own existences.

American painters, like their French counterparts— although a bit more reserved—produced images of the women in their lives. The ladies were shown in similar surroundings. Monet, for example, who drew far less well than Degas or Renoir, painted his first wife, Camille, and later Suzanne Hoschedé on a small knoll, silhouetted against a bright blue sky. Showing attractive women in leisurely genre was also characteristic of many French impressionists and late nineteenth-century painters in general. Consequently, American critics could see that such a special kind of genre was wonderfully blended in canvases done by American expatriates in Giverny—in these, the French and American ideas of beauty were commingled via impressionism in the late 1890s, and the result pleased many on both sides of the Atlantic, but it was somewhat different from Garland's vision at the time of the World's Columbian Exposition.

As the art colony at Giverny grew in the 1890s, so did the number of American impressionist figure painters who worked there. Of the original American pioneer group, only a few remained—Theodore Butler, William (Peggy) Hart, Guy Rose, and Lilla Cabot Perry; many

Ill. 5-10. Mary Cassatt. *Mother and Child*. Oil on canvas, 36¼ x 29 inches. The Metropolitan Museum of Art. George A. Hearn Fund, 1909.

others came and went. Soon after his marriage, Butler had sacrificed his Monet-style landscapes for a radical post-impressionistic genre style. He began his "baby-bathing" series as early as 1893 and continued until the death of his wife, Suzanne, seven years later (ill. 5-12). Monet's influence on Lilla Cabot Perry resulted in some outstanding landscapes (pl. 5-1;5-2), but she also applied her conservative broken-color technique to figurative subjects. During the decade of the 1890s, various other artists who posed models indoors and outdoors came to Giverny and went back to other parts of Europe or America.

By 1900, the Giverny colony included Frederick Frieseke, a painter who had felt the influence of Garland and others when he studied at the Art Institute of Chicago, and who had already come to specialize in the depiction of women in both garden and interior settings. Indeed, even in 1900, Frieseke's subject mode, which the French critics referred to as *intimisme*, might have been included by Garland in the larger framework of veritism. Although he arrived in Giverny for his first summer visit more than a dozen years after the pioneer group, Frieseke eventually purchased a home near Monet's and became a leading American spokesman for the Giverny art

Ill. 5-9. Willard L. Metcalf. *The Pool*. 1904. Oil on canvas, 36 x 36 inches. Private Collection. Courtesy R. H. Love Galleries, Chicago.

colony. Whether out of loyalty to the spirit of the independent movement or simply to distance himself from the academicians, Frieseke described himself as a "self-taught" painter. This was certainly not the case. After his time in Chicago and New York, Frieseke went to Paris, where he worked under Benjamin Constant and Jean-Paul Laurens at the Julian Academy. It is also possible that he spent a brief period with Whistler at his Carmen Academy in Paris. In any instance, it was in the French capital that he gravitated to impressionism and

Ill. 5-12. Theodore Earl Butler. *Jimmy Butler and His Dog*. 1895. Oil on canvas, 42 x 34½ inches. Mr. and Mrs. James P. Liautaud Collection.

Ill. 5-11. Lawton Parker. *Woman in a Garden*. Oil on canvas, 24 x 24 inches. Private Collection. Courtesy R. H. Love Galleries, Chicago.

in the process became especially fond of the art of Henri Fantin-Latour and Renoir.[22] Frieseke's work was soon accepted for exhibition at the Paris Salons – from that point onward, his career rocketed. It took very little time for him to develop his style, characterized basically by a high-key palette and a skillful rendering of pigment. He assimilated impressionism so well that the French critic Pierre Bandin described him as an American "impregnated" by the French school. Frieseke placed his feminine subjects equally well in sunlit gardens or in various interior settings. Soon he became a reputed master of an American type of *intimisme*. From early on Frieseke had enjoyed the patronage of the wealthy American art enthusiast Rodman Wanamaker, president of the American Art Association of Paris. Despite his insistence upon

being labeled a self-taught painter, Frieseke was elected an associate member of the *Société Nationale des Beaux-Arts*. In the years to come, Frieseke would play a major role in Louis Ritman's Giverny experiences.

Giverny became home to another American expatriate, Guy Rose. Born in Gabriel, California, Rose had studied under a Chicago painter, Emil Carlsen, at the California School of Design. In Paris Rose also trained under Jules Lefebvre, Benjamin Constant, and Henri Lucien Doucet (ill. 5-13). When at the age of twenty-three he first signed the guest register at Hotel Baudy in 1891 – two years after Lilla Cabot Perry had arrived – Rose was more a landscapist than an intimist. He had come and gone several times during the 1890s, but for a couple of years after the turn of the century, he and his new wife Ethel had lived in a house they had purchased in the village. Although lead poisoning, reportedly contracted from white oil paint, had prevented him from making many pictures, he was recuperating and hoped to stretch some canvases again.

Around 1900, Lawton Parker, who traveled routinely back and forth between Chicago, New York, and Paris, was just learning of Giverny. An amazingly ambitious

Ill. 5-13. Lucien Doucet. R. H. Love Galleries Archives, Chicago.

ate group from Giverny; in this regard, their names would become synonymous with expatriate American impressionism, and their ideas would influence young Ritman.

Regardless of their sophistication, American artists in Giverny received their impetus from the art community of Paris. The great city of lights was only a short ride away by rail, and a real and implied connection existed between Paris and Giverny because of the waterway of the Seine. As a result, the painters who worked in Giverny were actually on a kind of annual sabbatical from Paris, "the distributing centre of art" at that time.[24] Married artists like Frieseke and Miller brought their wives to live with them in Giverny, while bachelors like Parker stayed for a few weeks or for the summer and returned to Paris, or even traveled back and forth several times in the course of the summer. The subject matter and style of nearly all of the American expatriates in Giverny were those of the mainstream art of Paris. Being foreigners, the American artists actually worked more diligently at their professions than their French counterparts. Although their paintings were

individual, Parker had only recently served as president of William Merritt Chase's New York School of Art, but now back in Paris he was pursuing his career again at the Salon. Although a relatively significant number of American expatriates had studied at the Art Institute of Chicago, Parker was one of the few who considered himself a Chicago painter. He did so in spite of the fact that he spent as much time in Paris and New York as in Chicago; accordingly, on account of his burgeoning reputation in the international art community, he enjoyed a celebrity status in the Midwest. At the turn of the century Parker wielded great influence in the Chicago art community, especially at its nucleus, the Art Institute, where he served as a kind of liaison (in addition to Sara Hallowell) with the Paris art community.[23] In a few years Parker would play an important role in the life of Louis Ritman, who was now braving the cold Russian winter to learn how to draw.

Another American who worked in Giverny for a short time was the highly skilled and ambitious painter Richard E. Miller (ill. 5-14), from the Midwest. Miller had studied at the Saint Louis School of Fine Art and at the Julian Academy and then had become an instructor at the Colarossi Academy in Paris. Rapidly learning to paint like an impressionist and like Frieseke, Miller preferred the intimist mode (pl. 5-3). Soon Miller and Frieseke would become known as the leaders of the American expatri-

Ill. 5-14. Richard Miller. Photograph. R. H. Love Galleries Archives, Chicago.

created for the French art industry, the expatriates were usually passed over at award time. The prejudice which certain French officials displayed toward Americans in trade and diplomatic relations had been particularly evident since the years of the American Civil War as reported by French visitors to America such as Jean-Jacques Ampère and Ernest Duvergier de Hauranne, heirs apparent of Alexis de Tocqueville.[25] In art circles, anti-American sentiment had deepened in recent years among French critics like Charles Morice, and the attitude had become increasingly evident to artists and other members of the American art community, whether they produced their art in a colony like Giverny, or in Paris. Even the usually liberal American critic Charles Caffin noted the prejudice "There is quite a showing by Franco-Americans, and they have been given every advantage of good positions on the walls [of the Salons], yet, the jury have passed them by in awarding gold medals; discovering more interest and individuality in the pictures of the painters who work in their own country."[26]

Notes

1. Arthur H. Hoeber, "The Art of the Month," *Bookman*, 9 (April 1899), pp. 137-145.

2. Hans Huth, "Impressionism Comes to America," *Gazette des Beaux-Arts*, 29 April 1946, pp. 225-252.

3. John Rewald, ed., and Lionel Abel, trans., *Camille Pissarro: Letters to His Son Lucien* (New York: Pantheon Books, Inc., 1943).

4. Harrison C. White and Cynthia A. White, *Canvases and Careers* (New York: John Wiley & Sons, Inc., 1965), pp. 128-29.

5. H. Wayne Morgan, *New Muses: Art in American Culture, 1865-1920* (Norman, OK: University of Oklahoma Press, 1978), pp. 125-26.

6. Anonymous (possibly William A. Coffin and Kenyon Cox), "Fine Arts: The Society of American Artists," *Nation*, 50 (8 May 1890), p. 382.

7. Donelson F. Hoopes, *The American Impressionists* (New York: Watson-Guptill Publications, 1972), p. 16.

8. Charles Eldredge, "Connecticut Impressionists: The Spirit of Place," *Art in America*, 62, no. 5 (September-October 1974), p. 84.

9. John Henry Twachtman to Josephine Holly, New York, 28 January 1902. See John Douglass Hale, "The Life and Creative Development of John Henry Twachtman," Ph.D. diss., Ohio State University, 1957, pp. 135-36.

10. Félix Fénéon, *La Revue Indépendante*, July 1888.

11. The exhibition catalog *Impressionist and Symbolist Painters,* published by Le Barc de Boutteville Gallery, included a preface by Camille Mauclair, a symbolist writer.

12. Eugenia W. Herbert, *The Artist and Social Reform: France and Belgium, 1885-1898* (New Haven, CT: Yale University Press, 1961).

13. Patricia Pierce, *The Ten* (Concord, NH: Rumford Press, 1976); see also William H. Gerdts, *American Impressionism* (New York: Abbeville Press, 1984).

14. *New York Times*, 9 January 1898.

15. Trevor Fairbrother, *The Bostonians: Painters of an Elegant Age, 1870-1930* (Boston, MA: Northeastern University Press, 1986).

16. E. P. Richardson, *Painting in America: From 1602 to Present* (New York: Thomas Y. Crowell Co., 1965), p. 306.

17. Frances Weitzenhoffer, *The Havemeyers: Impressionism Comes to America* (New York: Harry N. Abrams, Inc., 1986), p. 130.

18. Morgan, p. 132.

19. Ibid.

20. A. E. Ives, "Mr. Childe Hassam on Painting Street Scenes," *Art Amateur*, 27 October 1892, pp. 116-17.

21. In recent scholarship, it was Richard T. Boyle who first related the genteel tradition to the American impressionist movement in *American Impressionism* (Boston, MA: New York Graphic Society, 1974).

22. For an interesting study on Frieseke, see Allen S. Weller, "Frederick Carl Frieseke: The Opinions of an American Impressionist," *The Art Journal*, XXVII, no. 2 (Winter 1968-69).

23. W. M. R. French to Lawton Parker, Chicago, 2 November 1900, Director WMRF, Letter Book, November 1, 1900 – May 31, 1901, General Correspondence, Art Institute of Chicago Archives, p. 6. Parker corresponded with Art Institute Director W. M. R. French on various projects, but the official representative of the Art Institute in Paris was Sara Hallowell, a professional paid by the institute trustees. See W. M. R. French to Sara Hallowell, Paris, 29 March 1900,

Director WMRF, Letter Book, December 27, 1899–October 26, 1900, p. 463.

24. Charles Caffin, "The Art and Influence of Paris To-Day," *Artist*, 29 October 1900, p. iii.

25. Jean-Jacques Ampère, son of the French physicist André Marie Ampère, was professor of literature at the College de France. After his stay in America, Ampère published his report in 1855, but later editions were published in the 1860s and as late as 1874. Duvergier de Hauranne was a French journalist who wrote on America during the Civil War. His article appeared in the *Revue des Deux Mondes*.

26. Caffin, p. iv.

CHAPTER SIX:
A NEW CENTURY IN THE LAND OF HOPE

This is the rejoicing city that dwelt carelessly, that said in her heart, I *am*, and *there* is none beside me.

Zephaniah 2:15

During the late 1890s, the Ritman family in Kamenets-Podolsky knew next to nothing about the impressionist movement in Paris or New York or Chicago. Neither was it aware of the expansive art colonies in Giverny or New England. The Ritmans had heard stories of opportunities in the New World, but they had no firsthand knowledge of actual life there, let alone of art. At the turn of the century, Louis was only ten but nearing puberty; by Hebrew tradition he would soon be a man. Realizing his responsibilities, Louis studied diligently and even took a passing interest in his father's weaving-designing career. Even at this early age, apparently, Louis demonstrated some aptitude for art each week. He trudged through the snow to Hebrew School; he also took drawing lessons from a local teacher, but he had little opportunity to develop his talent. The Ritman family was convinced that young Louis would become an artist one day because he was obsessed with drawing and made pictures on every available surface.

Some time earlier, Solomon and Rebecca Ritman had allowed their second eldest daughter, Molly, to travel to America. Long after the trip, her younger brother Maurice wrote a fascinating story of her emigration from Kamenets-Podolsky to Chicago: "Molly was very young and adventurous by nature. On hearing of an aunt who had passage for [her] husband and daughter and that her husband had changed his mind about going to America, Molly saw an opportunity to step in. She cajoled and pleaded with her aunt to let her use her uncle's ticket. With great persistence, she obtained her aunt's consent and her parents' blessing. Dressed as a male and using her uncle's name, Molly crossed the ocean. By youthful cunning and maneuvering, she eluded close examinations and entered the land of promise. Soon she was able to obtain employment, and, after a period of time, she had accumulated sufficient funds to send for the rest of her family."[1] At this time, the United States was admitting thousands of European immigrants.

Anticipating a wonderful new life in America, the Ritmans left Russia with their five sons some time around the turn of the century. Although Rebecca was pregnant, they traveled overland to the Black Sea port of Odessa, where they boarded a ship for New York. The long crossing was arduous because they sailed in the lowest possible class of accommodations. During the difficult voyage across the Atlantic, Rebecca suffered a miscarriage, a traumatic event for the otherwise optimistic family. Like all immigrants, the Ritmans were obliged to enter America via the facilities at Ellis Island, where Bartholdi's huge Statue of Liberty on Bedloe's Island had already been holding her lamp for the masses for nearly fifteen years. Still weak from her ordeal on board, Rebecca

Ill. 6-1. Hester Street, New York, around 1900. Photograph. R. H. Love Galleries Archives, Chicago.

feared that she would not pass inspection by the immigration authorities. Solomon was successful in drawing attention away from his wife's condition by feigning illness himself, and the entire Ritman clan cleared the official examination at Ellis Island. The Ritmans were but one family in a huge wave of Eastern European immigrants; each day new arrivals swelled the already large Jewish community in New York. Indeed, on the Lower East Side, one could only inch one's way along Hester Street; the thoroughfare overflowed with immigrant merchants (see ill. 6-1).

Exactly how long the Ritmans remained in New York is unknown, but eventually they made their way to Chicago to meet Molly.[2] In Chicago, they had friends who would help them get settled. Even with their help, adjusting to life in this bustling new city was a challenge. Soon, however, they found temporary quarters on the near south side of the city. In spite of their difficulties, the Ritmans had symbolically entered a new Jerusalem, a promised land of hope and opportunity, a place where every member of the family could enjoy freedom and

demonstrate his or her talents to the fullest. Furthermore, they entered Chicago at the dawn of a new century, a time when the future looked bright to everyone, especially to European immigrants who came in quest of fame and fortune.

As the year 1900 drew to a close, newspapers lauded the remarkable achievements of the passing century and prophesied unthinkable progress for the future. One farsighted writer predicted that "such a vulgar thing as a horse will never be seen upon the down-town streets of the city," while another thought that the city could eventually become the "free and sovereign state of Chicago, an autonomous area covering 1600 square miles with 10 million citizens."[3] The well-known architect James J. Egan foresaw that Chicago's skyline would soon be dominated by what he called "super structures," some as high as sixty stories. He went on to predict that elevators would run solely by electricity, that coal would no longer be used as heating fuel, and that wooden tenements would be a thing of the past.[4]

Having spent their first Chanukah in the United States

(ill. 6-2), the Ritmans joined thousands of immigrants on that Monday night of 31 December 1900 in hailing in the new century. "A heavy snow blanketed the ground that afternoon, and temperatures dipped to the low teens. But the New Year's celebration would be something special . . . . Even in the tenement districts the poor found time to celebrate. They put candles in their windows because they believed that the coming century would be something good, if not for them, then for their children."[5] Mayor Carter B. Harrison (ill. 6-3), Jr., then in his second term, announced to the public that he had imposed a law banning saloons to be open past midnight, but behind closed doors he told Police Chief Joseph Kipley to "let the boys have a good time." The Loop pulsated with celebrants from every walk of life. Even at State and Madison streets, people drank gin and fired pistols into the air. In the rest of the Loop and on tugboats in the lake, earsplitting noises greeted the new century. In striking contrast, religious services were held at the Chicago Colisseum: William Penn Nixon read inspirational messages sent by Clara Barton, William McKinley, and William Jennings Bryan. Great women of Chicago made their impact on the event: social leaders like Mrs. George M. Pullman and Mrs. Robert R. McCormick were in the crowd, a very serious Chicago crowd.

On the North Side, far from the Ritmans' humble new surroundings, the Nickersons entertained scores of important guests in their mansion on Erie street. Fireplaces were blazing and a small stringed orchestra played appropriate selections as fine ladies and gentlemen admired the paintings hung in nearly every room. The ballroom of Potter Palmer's "castle" was comfortably

Ill. 6-2. The Solomon Ritman family after their arrival in Chicago. Louis Ritman is standing at the far right (top row). His mother Rebecca is in the center, with her arm resting on Solomon's shoulder. Photograph. Courtesy Maurice Ritman.

HARRISON HAS THE GRIP.

Courtesy *Chicago Herald and Examiner* (*Times-Herald*).

Cartoon by Charles Lederer.

Ill. 6-3. Carter H. Harrison, Jr., mayor of Chicago. R. H. Love Galleries Archives, Chicago.

anyone else in the city, she sought the best — from society to civic responsibility to clothing to jewels to furniture to art.

Another kind of art crowd gathered at the Bohemian Club and at Mary Evelyn Chisholm's Cypher Club: novelists, poets, all with "glib tongues and pens, abounded here." Also present were artists, painters, and sculptors — as well as critics and other enlightened people who wrote about the creativity of others. Many times on that last night of the century, Miss Chisholm rang the cowbell to restore order, but to no avail. The Cypherites were ready for a new century; some even twirled like Isadora Duncan, who had begun her dance career among fellow bohemians in Chicago.

Mrs. Martha E. Holden, or "Amber" as she was known, had been the "dynamo" of the Bohemian Club until her unexpected death in 1896, but memories of her bohemianism and the impact of her lifestyle itself were poignant topics of conversation: "On the eve of the twentieth century, the pillars of Chicago society were getting nervous. They did not like the fact that Amber's cluster lingered in the city. There was talk of well-bred women degenerating into smoking and illegitimate sex lives. The pillars were alarmed and blamed it all on the demoralizing effect of the World's Fair . . . . the artists and writers of Chicago began to colonize the vacant territory of the grandeur that was the World's Fair. But they did not claim the grandeur itself, only its fringes. Not the palaces, but the buildings of drabber frame and purpose were now rented . . . vacant stores, former photo shops, ex-restaurants. These buildings, with a minimum of altera-

Ill. 6-4. The Palmer residence in Chicago, known otherwise as the "Castle." Photograph. R. H. Love Galleries Archives, Chicago.

filled with 175 guests who intended to make major contributions to Chicago in the coming century. Few in Chicago had imagined a residence as magnificent as the Nickersons', but the Palmers in their opulent castle, with its many interior styles designed by Henry Ives Cobb, symbolized the Gilded Age and Chicago's high society (ill. 6-4). Their castle contained the first Louis XVI Salon in Chicago. Referring to herself as "the nation's hostess and the nation's servant," Bertha Honoré Palmer was known as Chicago's most knowledgeable collector of French impressionism.[6] Gentlemen and ladies alike admired her taste and her willingness to step beyond the constrictive boundaries of tradition. Since the World's Columbian Exposition, Mrs. Palmer had been the undisputed leader of Chicago's cultural life. More than

tions, made picturesque studios. Did the Chicago intellectuals learn living in vacant stores from the American Gypsies, or did the Gypsies learn it from the Chicago intellectuals?"[7]

The new century had barely begun when a number of people who had made important contributions to the old one died. In Chicago, on 6 January 1901, Philip Armour, developer of the city's famous stockyards, died at the age of sixty-eight. In the art community, great American painters died—Hudson River School masters like Frederick E. Church and Jasper Cropsey—and the deaths of others like William H. Beard, William L. Sonntag, and W. S. Haseltine were considered great losses. Across the Atlantic, a great era ended on 22 February with the death of eighty-two-year-old Queen Victoria at Cowes, on the Isle of Wight. In her rule of over half a century, the queen had presided over the vast expansion of the British Empire and even reigned as empress of India. Her son, the Prince of Wales, who was at her deathbed, would soon become King Edward VII and embark on an amazing reign of his own. Only a few days later, the great composer Giuseppe Verdi, who had dominated Italian opera for nearly sixty years, died in Milan.

Almost immediately after his arrival in Chicago at the turn of the century, Solomon Ritman had resumed his career: he began to work as a designer-tailor for Hart, Schaffner, and Marx, a company that specialized in making men's suits. At this time in his life, Solomon was not interested in entrepreneurships, only in a steady job. His position was not a high-salaried one, but it provided security and sustenance for his tightly knit family, who spoke almost no English—only Yiddish, Russian, and some German. Chicago was drastically different from Kamenets-Podolsky, but each member of the Ritman family was determined to have a good life in his or her adopted land. As the oldest male, Louis had the added responsibility of helping his father provide funds for the family in whatever way he was able. Indeed, when Louis became old enough to work, he was expected to find a part-time job; and plenty of jobs were available for children in the sprawling, dirty Central Manufacturing District, not far from their home.

In the early years of the century, Chicago, as a relatively young city, was dynamic and exciting, but it was also very large and difficult to control. On the one hand, the city was very cosmopolitan; on the other, it was crude and confusing. Chicago's constant growth, its insatiable appetite for industrial and commercial progress, and its surprising willingness to embrace modernity brought admiration from all parts of the world. Yet, for all of its dynamism, there was also an inordinate amount of polit-

Ill. 6-5. A street of merchants in the Levee section of Chicago around 1900. Photograph. R. H. Love Galleries Archives, Chicago.

ical corruption, vice, and downright evil which threatened the welfare of every citizen.

Most low life existed in the Levee areas (ill. 6-5), one of which began in the Loop, actually within view of the prestigious Union League Club (ill. 6-6). This section of the Levee was truly a den of iniquity, which had run rampant since the time preceding the World's Columbian Exposition; no one seemed to remember how it got started. At the Customs House Place Levee, one could find gamblers, pickpockets, opium peddlers, pimps, and anyone who wanted to make a fast, dishonest dollar. All of the vice operations were controlled by a few Levee bosses, among whom stood out Carrie Watson, who saw to it that the important names in Chicago's society were well cared for, and Vina Fields, a huge black madam, who was known as a kind of female Robin Hood because of her efforts to feed the poor with her ill-gotten profits.

Many aldermen were known as "boodlers" because they accepted bribes. Several of Chicago's wealthy elite were known to have successfully evaded taxes. One if these was Charles T. Yerkes, an ex-con millionaire businessman and art enthusiast whose collection was once described as the best in the century.[8] When the Ritmans arrived, Yerkes no longer lived in Chicago, but memories of his years of corruption were indelible in the minds of local politicians and society leaders. Apparently there had been little that was honest about Yerkes. Norman Mark writes that he was "Chicago's ultimate corrupter at a time when almost everyone in the City Council and local government was ready, willing and anxious to be bought."[9] There was also John "Bathhouse" Coughlin, the Irish hotshot who dressed like a dandy and added swashbuckling politics to the city council—he made no excuses about paying for votes. By the time the Ritmans arrived, one Michael "Hinky Dink" Kenna, a small but amazingly tough Irish saloon owner, had already become known as one of Chicago's most powerful politicians. Kenna had reached the top rank by selling and giving booze to the right people, who ranged from members of the newly arrived huddled masses to certain influential friends. Together, Coughlin and Kenna designed and built the now-famous Chicago political machine.

A small Jewish immigrant boy like the young Louis Ritman, who had mostly art on his mind, would have had little opportunity to become involved with the gangs of

Ill. 6-7. Urban ghetto in the area of Louis Ritman's home in Chicago. Photograph. R. H. Love Galleries Archives, Chicago.

Ill. 6-6. Union League Club Building, Chicago. R. H. Love Galleries Archives, Chicago.

young hooligans who grew up to become the backbone of Chicago's elite crime system. The once young tough Dennis "The Duke" Cooney, for example, worked his way up in the vice ranks and virtually directed the police from his Rex Café at 2138 South State Street. Cooney—known as Kenna's bagman—told officers when to arrest and when to "look the other way." Later, the Duke put his skills to better service under Al Capone. Open vice was not only condoned but actually sanctioned. Well-intended citizens' vigilante committees, especially from the First and Second wards, made ongoing attempts to reform and rehabilitate the Levee; but internal dissension in the committees and control of the police by the machine bosses prevented any real progress from being made in the first few years of the new century.

In spite of the complexity of their new environment, the Ritmans were attempting to become Chicagoans. They finally settled into permanent quarters at 371 West Fourteenth Street, a so-called ghetto area northwest of the South Side Levee. Their small neighborhood was predominantly Jewish (ill. 6-7). Not many blocks away, ironically, was the fashionable Prairie Avenue section (ill. 6-8) bounded by Sixteenth Street, Calumet, Indiana, and Michigan avenues. A novelist's interpretation of the ideals and moods prevailing in Chicago's high society clustering in this area at the time may be gleaned in Arthur Meeker's book *Prairie Avenue*[10]. Indeed, the Ritmans

Ill. 6-8. A section of the fashionable Prairie Avenue in Chicago around the turn of the century. R. H. Love Galleries Archives, Chicago.

lived all too close to the vice district, which was also threatening the peace, serenity, and luxury of the Prairie Avenue area. Society leaders like the Fields, Palmers, and others were horrified that their way of life, their insulated community, was permanently disrupted by the spreading tentacles of the vice district. The vigilante committee could do very little because so many police officers were controlled by bosses and had connections with politicians.

Each day scores of new faces stepped off the train at Dearborn Station in search of new opportunities in Chicago. Not all of these newcomers were so fortunate as young Louis Ritman, who had a concerned family to encourage, guide, and support him. Many immigrant youths found out all too quickly that treasures were not very abundant on State Street or LaSalle Street or Michigan Avenue, and sought them at the Levee.

Notes

1. Maurice Ritman, "My Brother Louis Ritman," unpublished manuscript, Chicago, August 1987, p. 1, R. H. Love Galleries Archives, Chicago.

2. The exact date of the Ritmans' departure from New York for Chicago and their method of travel is unknown, although Maurice Ritman assumes their trip was made by rail.

3. Anonymous, quoted from Richard Lindberg, *Chicago Ragtime: Another Look at Chicago, 1880-1920* (South Bend, IN: Icarus Press, 1985), p. 115.

4. Ibid.

5. Ibid., p. 114.

6. Aline B. Saarinen, *The Proud Possessors* (New York: Random House, 1968), pp. 4-5. See also Lucy B. Monroe, "Art in Chicago," *The New England Magazine*, VI (1892), pp. 410-432.

7. Albert Parry, *Garrets and Pretenders: A History of Bohemianism in America* (New York: Dover Publications, Inc., 1960).

8. Leslie S. Goldstein, "Art in Chicago and the World's Columbian Exposition of 1893," Master's thesis, The University of Iowa, 1970.

9. Norman Mark, *Mayors, Madams & Madmen* (Chicago: Chicago Review Press, 1979), pp. 104-5.

10. Arthur Meeker, *Prairie Avenue* (New York: Alfred A. Knopf, 1949).

CHAPTER SEVEN: GENESIS FOR RITMAN IN CHICAGO AND CHANGES ELSEWHERE

It would hardly have been possible for young Louis Ritman to miss impressionism in Chicago. We do not know whether it took him a month or a year or a longer period of time to get a glimpse of the Chicago art scene, but we do know that he looked at art a great deal. Inevitably, then, he would have noticed paintings in which objects were blurred and shadows were purple. He would have seen that the artists had covered these canvases with many touches of different colors laid on side by side. Louis could not have known, of course, that this method of paint application was called broken color—the main feature of impressionism. Nevertheless, the eleven-year-old Louis now lived in a progressive, dynamic metropolis which, in spite of its corruption and vice, had warmly welcomed and embraced the trendy cultural move from academic art to impressionism for about a decade. Chicago did it with ease, much in the way it accomplished other cultural innovations like the skyscrapers he saw mushrooming from the streets every day.

In the Ritman household, "every member of the little flock did enough work to set about earning a living in the strange land" that was now home.[1] Louis, the oldest boy, was still in school, but it became necessary for him to find at least a part-time job. Public school was difficult for him because he was not fluent in English, but he persevered in spite of his heavy Yiddish accent. After only a

short time, however, Louis discovered that he could communicate on a different plane: by making pictures on paper. Louis's first formal art experience in the United States took place in an evening class at Jane Addams's Hull House, Chicago's unique social settlement (ill. 7-1).[2] His family recognized his potential for art in the

Ill. 7-1. Jane Addams's Hull House, located at 800 South Halsted Street, Chicago. Photograph. R. H. Love Galleries Archives, Chicago.

prodigious drawing talent he had demonstrated for several years and saw to it that he attended the special art classes at Hull House given every Wednesday evening at seven thirty. Located at 800 South Halsted, the settlement was not too far from the Ritmans' residence, but it lay within the general parameters of the Levee area, and Louis was cautioned by his parents and teachers to be careful in going there. The Ritmans could afford the lessons, since the course fee was only fifty cents, but it is possible that Louis attended free of charge.[3] In the *Hull House Bulletin*, Louis's class was listed as a "drawing class." The special "studio" in which it was held was "crowded" with twenty students. In the so-called daylight classes, in which there was a model, the maximum class size was "twelve or thirteen" students, since the west end of the room could not be used.[4] In later years, a "poll tax of fifteen cents was put into a saucer-pour honor," which produced a "slight excess every year."[5] We have no insight into Louis's performance at Hull House, for he left no youthful diary or later memoirs that might have provided one.

Ill. 7-3. Jane Addams as she appeared in 1902, founder of Hull House and Chicago's leader in organizing educational and cultural opportunities for the disadvantaged. Photograph. R. H. Love Galleries Archives, Chicago.

Ill. 7-2. Hull House: entrance to school facilities, Chicago. Photograph. R. H. Love Galleries Archives, Chicago.

This settlement house was unique, not only in Chicago, but also in the United States (see ill. 7-2). In the minds of most of those who lived and studied in Hull House, the experience remained indelible. The reminiscences of the writer Francis Hackett, who was slightly older than Louis and who went there a bit later, might give us some idea of Louis's first impressions: "Here on the ash-heap of Chicago was a blossom of something besides success. The [Hull] House was saturated in the perfume of the stockyards to make it sweet. A trolley-line ran by its bedroom windows to make it musical. It was thronged with Jews and Greeks and Italians and soulful visitors to make it restful. It was inhabited by high-strung residents to make it easy. But it was the first place in all America where there came to me a sense of the intention of democracy, the first place where I found a flame by which the melting pot melts." Much in the way Louis must have imagined what his time at Hull House would be like, Hackett reported that he had "heard queer words about it." He elaborated: "The ruling class spoke of 'Unsettlement workers' with animosity, the socialists of a mealy-mouthed compromise. Yet in that strange haven of clear humanitarian faith I discovered what I suppose I had been seeking—the knowledge that America had a soul" (ill. 7-3).[6]

Whether they sought America's soul or some other hidden quality, immigrants who professed reform through anarchism had been considered enemies of the American government by Chicagoans since the awful days of the Haymarket riots nearly fifteen years earlier. Even after the anarchists involved in the Haymarket calamity were hanged—in spite of pleas for amnesty from thousands, ranging from George Bernard Shaw to Potter Palmer— Chicago continued to produce an anarchist movement. There were many militant anarchists in the city, no small percentage of whom met secretly and communicated through a crude but burgeoning national network.

Rumors ran rampant at Hull House on Saturday, 7 September 1901, the day after President William McKinley had been shot while attending the World Exposition at Buffalo, New York. The president was not killed but gravely injured by one Leon Czolgosz, a so-called follower of Emma Goldman, the Russian immigrant and former anarchist whose liberal views inspired many Americans nationwide, including a number of artists. Czolgosz had recently visited Abraham Isaak, Sr., at 515 Carroll Avenue. As publisher of a radical paper known as *Free Society*, Isaak had widely publicized his views on anarchism, so he and several friends were arrested at his home that Saturday. Complicity was not proven, and the charges were dropped. President McKinley died far away a week later. At 3:32 P.M. Saturday, 14 September 1901, Theodore Roosevelt was sworn in as president of the United States by Judge John R. Hazel of the U.S. District Court.

During the week that America waited anxiously for the recovery of President McKinley, the art community was shocked by the unexpected death of the French painter Henri de Toulouse-Lautrec.[7] The young master died at the age of 36, already recognized as a great interpreter of bohemian Montmartre.[8] Descended from a wealthy aristocratic family, Toulouse-Lautrec focused on entertainers such as Jane Avril and Louise Weber, better known as "La Goulue." His first poster known as "Moulin Rouge-La Goulue," had been published only a decade earlier. Chicago newspapers carried brief notices of the artist's death, but they were all but lost in the wake of news about McKinley's condition.

Earlier that year, in Paris, artists, critics, collectors, and dealers had buzzed with excitement about the forthcoming exhibition of Van Gogh's work at the prestigious Bernheim-Jeune Gallery. Still painting with a dark palette, Matisse visited the Van Gogh show, where André Derain introduced him to Maurice de Vlaminck. Always excited about art, the enthusiastic Vlaminck reported later that "on that day I loved Van Gogh more than I loved my father."[9] Monet was in London again to record on canvas his impressions of the Houses of Parliament. This year was no different from others in that the Salon des Indépendants prompted a good deal of comment from Claude Roger Marx, Charles Morice, Louis Vauxcelles, and other critics. The usual questions and answers about the changing art scene entered the columns as did the usual praise for the Nabis—Vuillard, Sérusier, Vollard, and Bonnard. For all of the success of the Nabis, however, the ever-inquisitive French art dealer Ambroise Vollard presented another young talent that summer, a Spaniard known as Pablo Ruiz Picasso. The art critic Gustave Coquiot wrote the catalog preface, and fifteen works were sold even before the show opened. In the *Revue Blanche*, art critic Felicien Fagus reported that Picasso was "the brilliant newcomer."[10]

Back in America, another quaint and rather elitist art colony had been gathering new members in Old Lyme, Connecticut. The American tonalist Henry Ward Ranger had discovered the place a few years earlier, but after the turn of the century, many highly regarded impressionists were drawn there, artists like Hassam and Metcalf. Twachtman spent a great deal of time at the Holley House, near Cos Cob (ill. 7-4).[11] Gloucester, Mass-

Ill. 7-4. John Henry Twachtman. *Winter Scene.* Oil on canvas, 29½ x 29½ inches. Private Collection. Courtesy R. H. Love Galleries, Chicago.

Ill. 7-5. Enella Benedict, art instructor of Louis Ritman at Hull House. Photograph. R. H. Love Galleries Archives, Chicago.

achusetts, another booming New England art colony, had also been attracting impressionists, including some of those who painted in Old Lyme. There was a difference between Old Lyme and Gloucester: Old Lyme had been colonized by a rather selective, if not elitist, group of artists; Gloucester, presenting itself as a picturesque location, attracted anyone and everyone who could put a brush to canvas. Scenes of Gloucester Harbor were showing up more regularly in New York exhibitions, and occasionally one would be seen in the Midwest.

In Chicago, Louis Ritman and others of his age who attended the Wednesday evening classes at Hull House absorbed the fundamentals of drawing taught by Miss Enella Benedict (ill. 7-5), a talented painter who was also an instructor at the Art Institute of Chicago and exhibited there. There was probably little conversation between teacher and pupil: Louis was naturally shy and Miss Benedict had the reputation of keeping "her hands busy" and

her "tongue silent." Nevertheless, Miss Benedict did teach Louis the fundamentals of drawing, and if she expounded at all about her own background, the boy would have learned that in spite of her formality and "effacing dress, like a Holbein painting," Miss Benedict had studied at the Art Students League of New York and under Lefebvre, Constant, and Laurens at the Julian Academy in Paris. She recognized Louis's talent immediately. It was as obvious to her as to his other teachers that this boy was substantially more capable with a drawing pencil than with a writing pencil and books. Even at this point young Louis took his sketch class very seriously. Tradition has it that he drew all sorts of objects, but in class these usually involved various forms of still life. He also drew portrait heads, as they were called. Actually, outside of class he drew anything he had time to record with pencil or charcoal—only a scant few of these early drawings are still in existence.

Had the Ritmans been able to afford it, they could have sent Louis to the School of the Art Institute of Chicago, which had made great strides. Like most administrators at the institute, Director W. M. R. French was anxious to have not only reliable teachers like Miss Benedict but also well-known personalities who had received their training in Europe and maintained strong ties with leading members of the European art community, especially those in Paris. John H. Vanderpoel was an extremely capable and reliable teacher, but he was an academic master who had strong reservations about the merit of the French impressionists.

The instructor who made the greatest impact at the Art Institute after William Merritt Chase's short-lived tenure was Lawton Parker, a former student of Vanderpoel at the institute. Not yet thirty, Parker had already accomplished a great deal. When he worked under Albert Besnard in Paris, Parker had come to know many influential members of both the French and American art communities. As an expatriate he had established the Parker Academy in Paris and directed it for a short time. In 1901 he accepted a teaching position at the Art Institute of Chicago, where he attempted to incorporate many of the liberal practices he had learned in Paris and elsewhere. His ideas were frequently too radical to suit Director W. M. R. French, and soon friction developed between the two men. Although French was firmly entrenched in his director's role, he was only too aware of Parker's outstanding reputation as a painter and teacher. French was also sensitive to Parker's wide-ranging influence in Europe and America. Parker was an enterprising individual. Like that of all his teaching and administrative jobs, his tenure at the Institute was short-lived;

although French wanted him to teach until March 1902, Parker resigned in January of that year.[12] As usual, Parker was anxious to get back to Europe to paint and to join the annual Salon crowd. To the Paris Salon that spring he submitted a stunning full-length *Portrait of Mrs. W.,* a painting which was well displayed "on the line" and which received considerable critical praise.

Having recorded two full years of history, the twentieth century continued its momentum into 1902, a year of energetic optimism that overshadowed less fortunate events in America. In January 1902 the founding of the Carnegie Institute to promote research in the humanities and sciences was announced. The following month witnessed the death of the famous and wealthy Charles Lewis Tiffany at the age of 90 and the birth of Charles Lindbergh, who would one day make the first transatlantic flight. That spring, thousands of miners went out on strike in Pennsylvania. In June, Congress passed Senator Spooner's bill authorizing President Theodore Roosevelt to pay $40 million for the rights to build a canal across the Panamanian isthmus to connect the two oceans. In July, Chicagoans were fascinated by the news that the Twentieth Century Limited (ill. 7-6) had set a rail-

Ill. 7-6. Twentieth Century Limited departing LaSalle Street Station around the turn of the century, Chicago. Courtesy Fred G. Korth. Chicago Historical Society.

road speed record by covering a 481-mile stretch from New York to Chicago on the Lake Shore and Michigan Southern Road at the rate of "over a mile a minute." In August, the federal government passed strict game laws to protect the American bison from extinction.

That same month, the news of John Henry Twachtman's death in Gloucester, Massachusetts, received little public attention. Nearly a pauper when he died, Twachtman left a studio stacked with unsigned canvases

Ill. 7-7. Open-air painting class at the School of the Art Institute of Chicago. Photograph. R. H. Love Galleries Archives, Chicago.

and a wife and children in desperate need of funds. Friends made every effort to assist them, but the tragic reality was that one of America's most talented and most intellectual impressionists had died at the young age of forty-nine.[13] In later years, the painter-art writer Eliot Clark wrote of him: "Twachtman was an impressionist and as such he was a follower rather than an imitator of a movement." Continuing, Clark pointed out: "If the general viewpoint is of foreign origin, Twachtman makes a very personal use of it . . . . Monet has a more colorful palette; a more vigorous and exuberant expression as he was in physique likewise more robust."[14]

Also in the fall of 1902, newspapers in Chicago, New York, and other large cities carried lead articles on the career of Emile Zola, the controversial French novelist and critic who had died of asphyxiation in his Paris home. Of course, Zola's demise was of special concern to the international art community on account of his involvement with the evolution of impressionism, his defense of it, and his subsequent attacks on it, but the end of his career was also of interest to the public at large because of his great defense of Captain Afred Dreyfus, the Jewish military officer accused of spying for Germany.

Louis Ritman had not met Parker before the latter left Chicago early in 1902; he was probably unaware that Parker won a bronze medal earlier that spring at the Paris Salon. Soon, however, young Louis would find that Parker was a dynamic individual who thrived on competition — nothing less than a gold medal satisfied him, but to young admiring Chicago students like Louis, and even to the Art Institute hierarchy, Parker's success at the Salon was significant (ill. 7-7). Accordingly, some time that summer, while Parker was in Paris, French's Assistant Director N. C. Carpenter "engaged" him to teach at the Art Institute again the following winter term.[15] Students were anxious to work under Parker, but his return was somewhat problematic for French, inasmuch as plans had already been made to have the long-time expatriate Will H. Low teach that term.[16] Nonetheless, Parker was the kind of artist who attracted students, so French was willing to "experiment" for a "couple of months," hoping to "establish for the time separate *ateliers* for each master entirely under his control, admitting however, only full life students."[17] In a revealing letter to Caroline D. Wade, an instructor at the institute, French discussed the current teacher situation: "Our object is to keep the school fully up to the latest ideas of the art world." He pointed out that "we are all growning [sic] old, and I, as the oldest of the lot, am especially anxious lest we fall too much into routine." French admitted: "None of our advanced teachers have had the opportunity of studying in the foreign schools, or even visiting foreign countries, for quite a good many years and under our system our younger men [teachers] upon their return . . . get no chance at the life students at all. At this time French had no reservation in stating that "Parker has some ideas and is certainly as well informed as any man living with regard to the Paris school and their relations to the American schools."[18]

Indeed, Parker had many ideas about teaching art, a good number of which he had clearly outlined in an article written just prior to the time he was to return from Paris to teach at the Art Institute. His numerous teaching experiences had made him bitter about certain common shortcomings in the typical American system, but someone as sensitive as W. M. R. French might easily have taken Parker's following critical analysis as a clear indictment of him and the School of the Art Institute: 'To-day art education is a sort of corporation arrangement. The student, instead of being apprenticed to a master, usually has his education mapped out by the layman, and the artist instructor is only a hired servant in some large institution, which takes most of his time and gives him little to say in its control."[19] Parker's wide teaching experience on both sides of the Atlantic gave him ample justification in stating that there was "a vast difference in the methods of our American schools as compared with those of Paris." He detailed: "The principal advantage in Europe is the privilege of coming into close relationship with the old masters, or before these old master[s] are understood, with the men who are best able to interpret them . . . . The French masters have always lived with the fine old paintings, and the fact that simple methods of the old masters can be more easily explained by them should make Paris the art center for the student." Continuing his analysis, Parker explained:

"There are many weak features in our methods of instruction which are harmful to the beginner. One is caused by the difference in conditions under which American and foreign art schools have been developed. Another is the conceit of the home school and the advice given to the student who proposes to go abroad. The American school," Parker wrote, "has a system of its own production, not based on the old schools of Europe. It has been shaped in its growth by the methods of a financially successful institution, controlled by students whose experience does not extend beyond its own walls . . . . Happily there are one or two large schools which are free from this influence; notably one in Philadelphia. There the influence of one artist, William M. Chase, has been of great value, and the American nation and the American artist owe a deep debt of gratitude to this pioneer of artistic training of the highest order." Embittered but optimistic about the future, Parker stated that "the American undoubtedly has by nature all the qualities that will make him win in any field, including art, if he is given a chance."[20]

Parker's article was published in October 1902, at just the time he was supposed to resume his tenure at the Art Institute of Chicago. As Parker might have expected, French was infuriated by his article. Earlier that summer he had been willing to give Parker a relatively free hand at the school, but the article made him angry and defensive. To make matters worse, when Parker returned, he decided not to resume teaching at the institute but instead to assist in the establishment of a private school of art, one in which some of his own ideas could be incorporated, one which eliminated long arduous study from antique casts, and one which was similar to his own in Paris. Officially established on 6 October 1902 by Carl N. Werntz (ill. 7-8), the Chicago Academy of Fine Arts set up its teaching facilities in the Fine Arts Building, just north of Louis Sullivan's Auditorium Building on Michigan Avenue.

Starting classes with only 18 students, Werntz and several other dedicated teachers, including the former Art Institute instructor Oliver D. Grover, were thrilled that Parker had left the institute to join the academy faculty. Anxious for reform in art education, this idealistic group adopted Parker's ideas immediately. Both Parker and his constituents knew that he was Chicago's most prominent artist, and they were anxious to exploit his reputation for the good of the academy. Theirs was an idealized mission devoted to the betterment of young students like Louis Ritman, and they assumed that the press would support their efforts. After all, the academy was "the outgrowth of a conviction that the time is at hand for the establish-

Ill. 7-8. Carl N. Werntz, director of the Chicago Academy of Fine Arts. R. H. Love Galleries Archives, Chicago.

ment of an art school where more freedom is allowed students both in the selection of studies and the time devoted to them, than is allowed in the more conservative schools where the system of courses and graduation prevails . . . . drawing should not be from casts but from life."[21] Beginning with the first concours, and in the European tradition, the best studies from life were pinned up on the wall. Lawton Parker's ideas were exploited at the new academy, and were soon to figure prominently in the life of Louis Ritman.

Another school of art, known as the Art Academy of Chicago and located at 46 Jackson Boulevard, had already been in operation for six years, but it was not particularly progressive. Established by J. Francis Smith, a disgruntled Chicago artist who patterned his school after

the Julian Academy in Paris, the Art Academy opened with seven students in cramped quarters at 300 Wabash Avenue, only a couple of blocks from the Art Institute. Smith's Art Academy employed the tonalist painter Chauncy F. Ryder, Antonin Sterba, and a few others who professed the French manner of teaching. Some time later an art writer reported that Lawton Parker found "much of the spirit of the French schools [at the Chicago Art Academy] and that it [was] like a little bit of Paris set down in Chicago," but at this time, the winter season of 1902-03, all attention was focused away from Smith's school to the new Academy of Fine Arts under the guidance of Lawton Parker.[22]

Meanwhile, the highly publicized Chicago Fifteenth Annual Art Exhibition was held at the Art Institute of Chicago in the latter part of 1902. A writer for *Brush and Pencil* described it as "the most interesting display offered by this institution in recent years," but he also reported that none of the important expatriate stars like William Merritt Chase, Alfred Maurer, Henry O. Tanner, Cecilia

Ill. 7-9. Walter McEwen. Photograph. R. H. Love Galleries Archives, Chicago.

Beaux, or John Alexander had sent canvases to the show.[23] The exhibition contained 524 oil paintings, more than ever before. Of these, 65 had been selected from the two Paris Salons and sent to Chicago by Sara Hallowell, the institute's agent in France. Other works came from New York, Philadelphia, Boston, Cincinnati, and of course, Chicago. Waving a flag of cultural patriotism, the critic James Ford Buell pointed out that "the pictures selected by the juries in this country were this year, as they usually have been, superior on the average to those forwarded by Miss Hallowell from Paris." He pointed out, however, that she probably had "to take what she can get, and that the better canvases shown by American artists in Paris Salons do not thus find their way to Chicago."[24] One work receiving a great deal of attention and local praise was Lawton Parker's *Portrait of Mrs. W.*, a full-length Sargentesque depiction of an elegant lady posed by a desk in front of a mirror. In this painting, which had been seen in the Paris Salon, the artist presented an interesting front and back views of the subject. The device of showing the subject's reflection in the mirror was certainly not unique to Parker; it had been commonly used by fin-de-siècle European and American painters. In fact, the exhibition included a similar work in which a female subject was posed looking into the mirror: *A Woman of the Empire* by Walter McEwen, a native Chicagoan and confirmed expatriate (ill. 7-9). While the subjects of these two very genteel images were similar, Parker's painting was less academic; the awards jury, nonetheless, preferred McEwen's work and sent him the highly coveted $500 Harris award. Buell wrote in his long review of the show: "that the Harris prize was wisely bestowed would doubtless be the opinion of the rank and file of visitors." He pointed out, however, that "many competent judges . . . would prefer to have seen the prize go to Parker or [Karl] Buehr."[25]

Notes

1. H. Effa Webster, "Paris Lauds Chicago Boy—Ghetto Artist Wins Honor," unidentified newspaper clipping of the *Chicago Examiner*.

2. For a history of Jane Addams's Hull House, see Allen F. Davis and Mary Lynn McCree, eds., *Eighty Years at Hull House* (Chicago: Quadrangle Books, 1969).

3. "Hull House Classes," *Hull-House Bulletin*, VI, no. 1 (Mid-Winter, 1903-4), pp. 2-3. In some instances, exception was made for especially talented children, and the fees were waived.

4. Enella Benedict to Jane Addams, 13 August [1931], Pentwater, MI, Jane Addams Papers, Series 1, Supplement, Swarthmore College Peace Collection, Swarthmore, PA.

5. Ibid.

6. Francis Hackett (1893-1962) came to America from Ireland in 1906, when he found Hull House. He was therefore about five or six years older than Ritman. His descriptions of Hull House depict the institution during its most important period. See Francis Hackett, "Hull House—A Souvenir," *Survey* 1 (June 1925), pp. 275-79.

7. M. G. Dorter, *Toulouse-Lautrec et son oeuvre* (New York: Collectors Editions, 1971).

8. Philippe Jullian, *Montmartre*, trans. Anne Carter (New York: E. P. Dutton, 1977).

9. Maurice de Vlaminck, *Dangerous Corner* (London: Elek Books, 1961), p. 147.

10. William Rubin, ed., *Pablo Picasso: A Retrospective*, exhibition catalog (New York: The Museum of Modern Art, 1980), p. 29.

11. *Twachtman in Gloucester: His Last Years*, exhibition catalog (New York: Ira Spanierman Gallery, 1987).

12. W. M. R. French to Lawton Parker, Chicago, 30 January 1902, Director WMRF, Letter Book, January 3, 1902—October 25, 1902, General Correspondence, Art Institute of Chicago Archives, Chicago.

13. Eliot Clark, *John Twachtman* (New York: Frederick Fairchild Sherman, 1924), pp. 71-72.

14. Ibid.

15. W. M. R. French to Caroline D. Wade, Glendale, MA, 16 July 1902, Director WMRF, Letter Book, January 3, 1902-October 25, 1902, p. 675.

16. Born in Albany in 1853, Will Hicock Low studied at the Ecole des Beaux-Arts under Gérôme and Carolus-Duran. The recipient of numerous awards, Low won a medal at the World's Columbian Exposition. He had also been friendly with Theodore Robinson and visited Giverny early. His book, *A Chronicle of Friendships*, provides extensive information on his generation of American painters, sculptors, and other culture makers.

17. W. M. R. French to Caroline D. Wade, Glendale, MA, 16 July 1902, Director WMRF, Letter Book, January 3, 1902-October 25, 1902, General Correspondence, p. 676.

18. Ibid., p. 675.

19. Lawton S. Parker, "Another View of Art Study in Paris," *Brush and Pencil,* XI, no. 1 (October 1902), pp. 11-15; note that the article was signed and dated "Paris, September 1, 1902."

20. Ibid., p. 15.

21. "The Chicago Academy of Fine Arts," *The Sketch Book*, III, no. 8 (April 1904), p. 265.

22. Irma Thompson, "The Art Academy of Chicago," *The Sketch Book*, III, no. 7 (March 1904), p. 214.

23. James Ford Buell, "Chicago's Fifteenth Annual Art Exhibition," *Brush and Pencil*, XI, no. 1 (October 1902), p. 298.

24. Ibid., p. 299.

25. Ibid., p. 302.

CHAPTER EIGHT: RITMAN'S EARLY ART TRAINING IN CHICAGO

Few jobs were available in Chicago to a young immigrant boy whose best talent was for drawing. Some time late in 1902 or early 1903, nonetheless, Louis Ritman "drifted into a sign painter's shop and got a job."[1] After a brief period he had become a little more skillful and found new employment with a different enterprise, the Thomas Cusack Company, a maker of signs.[2] Most of the employees of this small firm came from Irish or German ethnic backgrounds. Louis's fellow workers admired his youthful talent and escalated his apprenticeship time. Now a so-called painter of letters, albeit little more than an apprentice, Louis made seven dollars each day— welcome funds that he contributed in full to his parents; some reports claim that he was the sole support of the family at this time. At Cusack's shop it was not long before Louis's wish to become an artist, a painter of pictures instead of letters, was well known to his fellow workers. Of course, Louis had not been hired to make pictures, a situation that probably frustrated him; however, the discipline he derived from sign layout and lettering as well as the skill he achieved in handling a brush served as an important step in his development as an artist. Louis was determined to make pictures eventually, and with this purpose in mind, he continued his classes under Miss Benedict at Hull House and practiced on his own, making small sketches of the people and things around him.

Small-boned and only about five feet tall, Louis was also very quiet, a trait his employers appreciated because he spent his time working at the sign boards instead of talking. Helping his parents shoulder the responsibilities of the family, Louis worked long hours each day and had little time for himself except when he attended his art classes at Hull House.

The Cusack Sign Company was not just another commercial enterprise. Its owner, Thomas Cusack, had been an alderman of the Chicago City Council, the legislative body of the mushrooming metropolis, during its most colorful period in the 1890s, when affairs relating to the World's Columbian Exposition and matters concerning gambling and vice operations were debated and voted upon with equal glee and intensity. Cusack was one of the leading alderman representing the reform forces of Carter Henry Harrison the Elder, the Democratic mayor of Chicago at the time of the World's Columbian Exposition. Just a few days before the closing of the exposition on 28 October 1893, Harrison was assassinated by Eugene Prendergast, who had been defeated in his efforts to become city corporation counsel. Apparently even after the death of Harrison the Elder, Cusack remained in the camp of his son, Harrison the Younger, who represented the live-and-let-live faction of the Democratic party in Chicago.

Ill. 8-1. Carter Henry Harrison, the Younger, mayor of Chicago. R. H. Love Galleries Archives, Chicago.

cigar box, a forthright presentation that subsequently resulted in a raise and his dual promotion to picture illustrator and master craftsman.[7] No longer a mere dabbler in paint, Louis was now expected to make pictures to order. In this sense, then, he began his professional career as an illustrator at the age of fourteen (ill. 8-2).

In 1903, the Art Institute presented its Chicago Artists Exhibition, a show that was dominated by salon style art and impressionism. The press had its usual praise for local artists like Karl Buehr, Pauline Palmer, and others, while the bohemian group at the Cypher Club argued over the qualities of French poetry and painting. In the meantime, Lawton Parker's tenure at the Chicago Academy of Fine Arts had been amazingly successful. As Werntz and others at the academy had anticipated, Parker's reputation magnetized Chicago hopefuls to the school. Many Art Institute students were anxious to rid themselves of the many required hours of drawing from casts, while others simply wanted to learn from someone as famous as Parker. The already strained relationship

Ill. 8-2. Louis Ritman with his foreman, John McInerney, viewing a painting in the studio. Photograph. Courtesy Maurice Ritman.

Thus, it was not very surprising that when Carter Henry Harrison the Younger was running for his fourth term as mayor of Chicago in 1903 (ill. 8-1), his campaign forces turned to Cusack's sign enterprises with an urgent project:[3] to increase their candidate's visibility, the mayor's election committee "wanted his portrait painted on a banner."[4] Louis was busy at Cusack's on the hot day in 1903 on which the election committee made its appearance. From several accounts of the episode, John McInerney, the shop foreman, "said that it couldn't be done." It was apparently then that the young Ritman "who [normally] was . . . very quiet, spoke up and said 'I can do it,' which he did in half a day. He received about $4 for it and the firm got $100."[5] After this portrait demonstration, Louis's fellow workers were even more impressed with his artistic skills. In fact, McInerney, himself an amateur artist, "saw in Louis what he perceived to be innate talent."[6] Encouraged, young Louis showed his foreman a portrait he had executed on the top of a

between Parker and Art Institute Director French was considerably aggravated when some of the institute's most promising students left the school to study at the academy. Parker's work was included again in the Paris Salon, but he remained in Chicago until late spring, hoping to bolster the first term of the academy. He made plans with Werntz and others to return to the Academy to teach the following November after his annual sojourn in Europe.

During the summer of 1903, Parker devoted much time to painting in Holland. He also went to Giverny, where he stayed briefly before leaving with Guy Rose, Alson Skinner Clark, and Frederick Frieseke on a painting trip to Brittany. Exactly how long they stayed in places like Le Pouldu, Quimper, and Finistère is unknown, but it seems that the sweet nectar of Giverny and its colorful gardens called them back in time to execute some local canvases. After his return to Paris, Parker reestablished his school of art which, like his efforts in Chicago, yielded surprising results. However, since he had already made definite plans to return to America, he arranged with his friends, the French artists Charles Cottet and Lucien J. Simon, to continue its operation in Paris during his absence the following season. Meanwhile in Chicago, Director French wrote an article on art education, which was published in the July issue of the *Sketch Book*. In an obvious rebuttal to the recent pronouncements by the Chicago Academy of Fine Arts, French stated clearly that at the Art Institute, "not all students are admitted at once to regular life study." Making implicit reference to the two academies, he told his readers: "Some private schools make it their boast that all students study from the life and that the study of the antique is not required. Such schools are open to the suspicion of sacrificing thoroughness to the object of attracting students for it may be doubted whether there is a regularly organized independent school of art in the world which finds this method advantageous." French went on to explain that the Art Institute had successfully adopted the "atelier and concours" system.[8]

Parker had intended to come back to Chicago in November of 1903 to teach at the Academy of Fine Arts and to begin a commissioned portrait of the Chicago collector and Art Institute trustee Martin H. Ryerson. Werntz and his fellow academy constituents were anxious for Parker's return. During his absence, the academy had grown to such an extent that Werntz took new quarters on the top floor of the building at 338 Wabash. Here they arranged for a large center space with skylights and classrooms for portraiture, nude studies, illustration, miniature painting, design, composition, sculpture and more — there were even lunchroom facilities. Besides the Academy of Fine Arts, the Bohemia Guild and some private studios were located in the 338 Wabash Building. All in all, the place was the talk of the Chicago art community. The Bohemia Guild was a kind of early Bauhaus group devoted to bringing art and industrial design together.[9] Actually, the goals of the Bohemia Guild had originated in the late nineteenth-century Arts and Crafts movement. Known as the Chicago Arts and Crafts Society, this group had officially come into existence on 22 October 1897 at a meeting at Hull House and had been exceedingly active in Chicago ever since. Hoping to counter the ubiquitous industrial age canons of Victoriana, and to inspire latent folk art talents and a subsequent American style, the Arts and Crafts community in Chicago became a highly visible and active force in early twentieth-century America. The credo of the original society was continued: "Nothing is too insignificant to merit the labor of an artist, and the artistic temperament can express itself in any material." So it was that the Chicago Arts and Crafts movement became well known for its rebellion against the so-called Eastern Style, especially, for example, in the furniture of a local designer like Isaac Scott.[10] Of course, Frank Lloyd Wright, an outspoken Midwesterner and founding member of the society, designed simplistic furniture within the Arts and Crafts mode that functioned harmoniously with his Prairie School style of architecture, but he also argued that the machine was capable of mass-producing quality goods.[11] Soon, Hull House became the foremost center for the Arts and Crafts movement in Chicago. The art gallery at Hull House had been designed by the Pond brothers, and its reproductions of works by the great masters were specifically intended to inspire young artists like Ritman who sought a career in high art. Many of the members of the Bohemia Guild had been inspired over the years by the craft shops at Hull House, which, under the guidance of Ellen Gates Starr, produced a wide variety of work ranging from woodcarving to bookbinding. Starr was convinced that in encouraging young men like Ritman to exercise their creative minds and make use of their hands, she had provided healthy competition to the saloons, cheap concert halls, and "museums of anatomy." At this time, Hull House emphasized its Labor Museum, which had been in operation about three years. Intended to show how craft had evolved through the machine age, the museum was also designed to restore dignity to the laborer and to focus on his ethnic craft traditions.

Although the Bohemia Guild was the distinct product of the Arts and Crafts movement in Chicago, it was quite different from Hull House and unique unto itself. In fact, it was a by-product of the Industrial Art League, which had been organized a few years earlier by Oscar Lovell Triggs, an English professor at the University of Chicago. The president of the League was Frank Lowden, George Pullman's son-in-law, and the vice president was Rabbi Emil Hirsch. Together, these men inspired the group to establish art libraries, to provide instruction in arts and crafts, and to organize the Bohemia Guild. Unfortunately, not everyone was pleased with the Loop location of the guild. Accordingly, alternative suburban groups were being organized, such as the Longwood Art Industry, set up by George L. Schreiber in an old church, and the South Park Workshop on Kimbark Avenue in Hyde Park. Indeed, the Arts and Crafts movement exerted considerable influence on the Chicago art community in general. It fostered, even demanded, excellence in technique, the craft side of making art, which was the kind of discipline Parker and other teachers expected from their students. That was also the kind of instruction Louis Ritman received at Hull House.

In anticipation of Parker's return to Chicago, a special play was written and rehearsed, and a gala reception was

Ill. 8-3. F. Luis Mora. Photograph. R. H. Love Galleries Archives, Chicago.

planned in his honor. Everyone was convinced that Parker's presence would guarantee many new students and new levels of achievements at the Chicago Academy of Fine Arts. Alas, however, the local star of fine arts did not return to the academy; instead, he accepted a position at William Merritt Chase's New York School of Art, then presided over by Robert Henri. Parker, who took over F. Luis Mora's classes (ill. 8-3) while the latter worked on the upcoming Saint Louis World's Fair, had been offered a better deal by either Henri or Chase, but the group at the Chicago academy was devastated by his absence. Putting it mildly, the writer of an article in the January 1904 issue of the *Sketchbook* reported that his failure to return to Chicago must have been "somewhat of a disappointment to those art students of Chicago who were led to believe that Mr. Parker intended to open classes at the Academy of Fine Arts." The writer continued that "the students of the New York School of Art are overjoyed to have Mr. Parker with them."[12]

Although Parker was absent for the 1903-4 season, the Chicago Academy of Fine Arts functioned routinely because it boasted several other well-credentialed teachers, men like Ralph Clarkson, Oliver D. Grover, and Wellington J. Reynolds. Whether at the New York School of Art or Chicago's Academy of Fine Arts, Parker was better suited to a private school environment in which he could be a leader. At the Art Institute, French was Parker's superior, but at the academy, Parker was the guiding light. At the New York School of Art, Parker was quite willing to be secondary to Chase, whom he admired as a teacher. His earlier acceptance of the principalship of the academy was just one more point of contention between him and French. To make matters worse, Werntz's aggressive, entrepreneur-like attitude also irritated French. Nonetheless, even during his absence, Parker was considered one of the most important painters the Chicago art community had ever produced.

In 1904, Chicago generated amazing commercial, industrial, and political activity. Louis's portrait banner of Carter Harrison had contributed at least a little to the latter's success at the polls. In charge again, Harrison made overt gestures toward Levee reform, but encroachment on the wealthy Prairie Avenue district by the vice lords was almost certain. Even in the short time the Ritman family had lived in Chicago, the city's population had grown; huge new buildings seemed to shoot up overnight, and the Loop swelled with shoppers and the ever-dominant business crowd. The intersection of State and Madison streets was called "the busiest corner in the world" (ill. 8-4); cable cars, horse-drawn carriages, and noisy automobiles vied for precious space as they passed

Ill. 8-4. Intersection of State and Madison Streets at the turn of the century, Chicago. Chicago Historical Society.

Louis Sullivan's beautiful cast-iron facade of the Carson, Pirie, & Scott store. Although Mrs. Ritman had little extra money to spend on her children, she took pleasure in browsing occasionally in big, fancy department stores like Marshall Field's or the Fair. Each day huge crowds of shoppers descended upon the famous Siegel-Cooper Company Store on State Street. Built by Levi Z. Leiter, the building was considered a prime example of "good taste, munificence, and wisdom."[13] It provided fifteen acres of floor space on eight stories, and customers were moved about by twelve elevators. Considered the largest retail establishment in the world, the Siegel-Cooper stood in glaring contrast with the run-down buildings of the sweatshops of the garment district. Solomon Ritman could see these sweatshops as he worked under better conditions at Hart, Schaffner, and Marx.

Louis, with little time to waste, spent most of his extra hours at Hull House. Here Miss Benedict and others took an interest in his artistic progress, while many other boys his age loitered for countless hours in penny parlors, nickel theaters, and arcades. Adults could go to the Seaato, the Grand Palace, and Little White City, the exotic building where Little Egypt had danced in the window for passers-by.

Surely Louis was not aware of his presence, but it was at this time that the French writer Jules Huret came to Chicago to observe American culture. Ironically, one of the places he chose to observe was Hinky Dink Kenna's saloon, the Workingman's Exchange. Another writer, Francis Cheney Bennett, who was also studying Chicago cultural life at this time, visited the Art Institute. With a much greater sensitivity than Huret's to the relationship of the Art Institute to Chicago's art scene, Bennett reported: "Of necessity, the history of art in Chicago is practically the history of art in Illinois."[14] Bennett was correct in assuming that the history of art in Illinois had traditionally centered around Chicago where dedicated career art teachers such as O. D. Grover, Lorado Taft, Enella Benedict, Wellington J. Reynolds, Carl N. Werntz, and John Vanderpoel faced hopeful students emerging from an American no-nonsense society. Quite unlike Louis Ritman, most of these students reflected a basic Midwestern mentality, that is, a far greater concern for the practical things of life than for art. Consequently, those who were proselytized to art came to realize the limitations of the art industry in the Midwest. To be sure, in art Chicago stood head and shoulders above any other area west of the Hudson, with Cincinnati and Saint Louis close behind. In general, however, art educators like Lawton Parker or William Merritt Chase, both Midwesterners, waged an uphill struggle in their attempts to teach art to the Midwestern audience from agricultural communities. The job of these educators, wrote Esther Sparks in her study on art in Illinois, was not that "of convincing an art-minded public that the traditional way was not necessarily the best. Their's was the task of elementary education of building respect for their profession. Their craftsmanship, their amalgamation of foreign and native tastes filled an important role for their time and place."[15]

As he continued his classes under Miss Benedict and became more aware of the burgeoning art community around him, Louis increasingly favored subjects with a figurative content in paintings, something promoted by Benedict and many other art instructors in Chicago. Even so, Louis and other students could not help but notice the inordinately large ratio of landscapes to portraits and genre subjects in local exhibitions. This unbalanced preference for landscapes was not only the result of the Midwest's lingering love for the nineteenth-century landscape tradition in the Midwest but also of the continuing trend of impressionism in Chicago, so much of which was landscape-oriented.

Well-known and respected landscapists such as T. C.

Steele from Indiana or John F. Stacey from Chicago, produced many good works that helped to keep the landscape tradition alive in the Midwest. Stacey was vice president of the Arts Club of Chicago and with his wife, Anna, a pillar of the art community who participated regularly in local events. After a period of art studies at the State Normal School in Boston, Stacey had taught drawing in Pittsfield and North Adams, Massachusetts, and then worked under Lefebvre and Boulanger at the Julian Academy in Paris. He had been director of the Kansas City Art School before coming to Chicago to teach at the R. T. Crane Manual Training School. Strictly a landscapist, Stacey took sketching trips to France as well as to Mystic, Connecticut, where he executed many "Yankee" scenes (ill. 8-5). One of these, *Overlooking the Valley of the Mystic* , had been purchased a couple of years earlier by the Union League Club of Chicago.

Ill. 8-5. John F. Stacey. *Corn Shocks*. Oil on canvas, 15 x 18 inches. Private Collection. Courtesy R. H. Love Galleries, Chicago.

Stacey's wife, Anna, had studied at the Pritchard School Institute in Missouri and then at the Kansas City Art School where John Stacey was teaching. They married and came to Chicago, where Anna continued her studies at the Art Institute of Chicago. Only two years earlier in 1902, she won the Martin B. Cahn prize for *Village at Twilight* and received the Best of Show award for a painting entitled *Florence*. Anna Lee Stacey was admired locally, owing to her ability to paint both figures and landscapes, and frequently combined the two specialties.

Louis, along with his friends, admired landscapists such as John and Anna Lee Stacey, but he found nature less magnetic than people as a topic. In spite, then, of its considerable influence on fellow students, landscape painting by its numerous Chicago talents did not truly interest Louis; he preferred, instead, to depict the human figure. Indeed, Louis, who had come from a village in Russia and who was now a city boy, knew nothing of the country; furthermore, he had received his first art training from a figure painter at Hull House, where the only concern was for humanity.

There is a very remote possibility that Louis had an opportunity to visit the 1904 Saint Louis International Exposition, a huge show that had generated much talk. After five years of planning and building, the exposition opened officially at noon on April 30, when President Roosevelt pressed a golden button in Washington. In Saint Louis, Secretary of War William H. Taft represented the president in the ceremonies of the show, in which the stressed themes were education and American ingenuity. Here, then, just beyond the southernmost boundary of Illinois, a great number of outstanding examples of contemporary art were on view. Halsey C. Ives, who had been instrumental at the Chicago World's Fair, headed the art department at the Saint Louis exposition (ill. 8-6). Many Chicago painters exhibited at the event, and won several awards. The Art Institute was represented by several of its teachers and many of its graduates. Vanderpoel showed *Little Miss Moffett* . The Chicago Academy of Fine Arts, was represented by Lawton Parker, who received one of the highest awards, a silver medal. Parker's friend Alson Skinner Clark won a bronze medal for a painting entitled *Snowstorm*. Special travel rates were available for Chicagoans who wanted to visit the exposition. Thus, it would have been a simple matter for Louis to travel from Chicago to Saint Louis by rail. Considering the Ritman family's financial situation, however, it is not likely that Louis visited the Exposition. If he did not, the only examples of contemporary art he saw that year were works displayed in local Chicago exhibits.

Louis was learning something about the latest trends in art, but he also studied various art publications, not the least of which were *Scribner's Magazine, Harper's*, and local reviews like the *Sketch Book* and *Brush and Pencil*. Chicago newspapers devoted a lot less attention to art than to political or sports events—the Socialist Party's nomination of Eugene Debs for president, for example, or the first perfect game in baseball pitched by Cy Young of Boston—but they published reviews of local exhibitions.

These reviews by local critics, which were not always

signed, were more informational than critical. Sometimes the newspaper featured full pages of reproductions separated by fanciful art nouveau borders and arabesques. All in all, the city publications, including the bohemian magazines, provided a generally well-rounded overview of local, national, and even European art. Louis would have had an opportunity to see any of the local publications or the *New York Times*, which never failed to present critical opinions of American or European art. Indeed, an article such as Charles De Kay's "French and American Impressionists" might easily have reached him and other students in Miss Benedict's class. Louis was

Ill. 8-6. View from the Cascade Terrace, overlooking the Palace of Education and Social Economy, St. Louis World's Fair. R. H. Love Galleries Archives, Chicago.

considerably more interested in painting than in reading, but the viewpoint of a critic like De Kay might have taken his eyes off the model. With tongue in cheek, De Kay pointed out that "in the academical schools the good boys and docile girls who imitate their masters cleverly are pushed forward, get prizes, and are started on the road to financial success."[16] Making specific reference to impressionism, De Kay reported: "what impresses one in the Frenchmen and the Americans is the fundamental similarity of their efforts . . . . they do not carry their work to a high finish, but leave it at a certain point . . . . by doing this they openly advertise that the public they hope to interest is one so familiar with pictures that half a sentence is as well understood as a paragraph."

An article like De Kay's, which served as a kind of critical thesis for the comparison and contrast of French and American impressionism, might have inspired Louis or any mature artist to maintain his individuality in learn-

ing French impressionism. However, there were other, less optimistic articles brought home each year by returning expatriates like Lawton Parker, Karl Buehr, or Sara Hallowell. The articles most demeaning to Americans were usually written by French critics whose anti-American attitudes would have dampened the hopes of any American artist who aspired to paint like Monet or Bonnard. It is not likely that Louis ever saw the review written by Charles Morice and published in *Mercure de France*, but the article certainly came to the attention of Parker and other Midwestern members of the American milieu at Giverny. Morice had ridiculed all American art productivity and then focused on Frieseke and even Whistler. Making specific reference to the recent Salons of 1904 in Paris, Morice bellowed: "Is it for Americans? Well, I would like to tell you sir . . . . what a mess we see in American painting."[17] Vehemently disagreeing with a pro-American writer like Urbain Gohier, who had predicted that Americans would "have an art in less than fifty years" because "they work, they search, they apply themselves," Morice told his readers that "one does not 'become' an artist, a creator either collectively or individually." He concluded: "The Americans may conquer the world, buy out our museums, call our artists to help and dine them, but I do not expect a spontaneous generation of artistic genius to arise from the past or from the present in New York or Chicago."[18] Admitting that Americans worked very hard and "very skillfully, too skillfully," Moriced asked, "but what have they added? We are already glutted with American paintings . . . the Salon des Artistes Francais [Paris Salon] is a colony of the new world . . . It is the 'nonsense of ourselves,' it's the aping of our aesthetics, of our schools, of our works, that America sends back to us . . . it is from real artists that the Americans pry their secrets." When Morice finished with generalities, he pointed out specific artists who personified America's artistic inferiority — in this instance, a prominent Giverny expatriate, Frederick Frieseke: "Here you will . . . say to me: Frieseke . . . yes, the feminine nude by Mr. Frieseke, *Devant la glace (Before the Mirror)* is a pleasant work, almost beautiful and exceptionally sensual...but you will have to tell me in what sense these talents signify an ethnic essence...at least a new contribution coming from afar." Finally Morice took aim at the greatest of all expatriates, Whistler, in stating that "even in his case, let us not forget that [he] was a student of our painters . . . he came to us seeking instruction and the whole French school is partly in the masterworks of which America prides itself so exclusively with a little ingratitude."

Elsewhere in the world, events were taking place which would affect Louis Ritman indirectly. The year 1904 began with political upheavals at different levels of many societies in the world. The art community in Paris, which would soon explode with controversy, anxiety, and anger, may have been merely a microcosm of the world's sociopolitical turmoil. For example, irreversible conflict loomed heavily in parts of Russia, though not in Kamenets-Podolsky. Acting directly on orders from Tsar Nicholas II, police in St. Petersburg gunned down a priest, who was leading a peaceful workers' demonstration and many of the participants. Not long afterward, news of that event, known as "Bloody Sunday," spawned other riots in Russia. Later, Nikolai Lenin's return to Russia from exile sparked more skirmishes. The pervasive mood of anxiety and fear that crept over Europe came to be felt even in large American cities, especially in New York and Chicago, where sizable concentrations of European ethnic groups lived close together.

At first, newcomers like the Ritmans may have been oblivious of the opposing forces, which frequently remained latent, representing a potential danger to the American "good life"; by 1904, however, they were painfully aware of European hot spots, especially those in the Austro-Hungarian Empire and Russia. In Chicago and elsewhere, considerable antagonism existed between business and labor. The United States seemed to be thriving; but for all of its progress, the country's well-being was threatened by an impasse between these two giants. Led by Eugene Debs, the Socialists made a loud voice in Chicago, pointing out the problems between labor and business. One segment of the labor force, which aggressively organized itself and would one day appeal to men like Solomon Ritman in Chicago, was the Industrial Workers of the World (IWW), a group that openly criticized the American Federation of Labor for cooperating with big business. These issues were beginning to reverberate loudly through most levels of the American socioeconomic system.

In New York art circles, pressure developed among various liberal-minded artists to identify themselves closer with the masses (the so-called proletariat) and to assist them by supporting their causes. As a result, it would not be long before the followers of the former impressionist Robert Henri would arbitrarily fuse their viewpoints on "art, politics, and social reform." As in France, anarchy was in the air in terms of both art and politics, and frequently membership in the two camps overlapped. The local political issues that prompted the formation of Robert Henri's circle in New York differed from those in Paris, but in both cities the artists sought immediate changes in art and society. No longer willing to abide by the pronouncements of the hierarchy of government or culture, artists in Paris and New York, including some in Chicago, wanted to replace the worn-out sociocultural machinery of the nineteenth century with brand-new models, symbolically reflective of the progress displayed in both science and industry at the recent world fairs. The key word was reform, at almost any cost, even "anarchy if it brought results."[19]

Louis Ritman was far more interested in learning how to draw figures convincingly than in Chicago's sociopolitical groups. He was beginning to learn about art and the way in which he might one day actually play a role in its complex industry. From the practical standpoint, however, he was only a student. He used charcoal extremely well and even experimented with paint, an endeavor in fine art that was facilitated by his job as an illustrator at Cusack's. Nevertheless, the facilities and classes offered at Hull House were quite limited; therefore, both his foreman McInerney and Miss Benedict urged him to seek more advanced training. Miss Benedict suggested that the best place for Louis at this time would be the Art Institute, where she herself had once been a student and where she was now an art instructor. Although it had not been possible for him to study at the Art Institute earlier, urged by McInerney and Benedict, Louis hoped to attend evening classes in 1905. He was already obsessed with art — there were not many who discouraged him — and he made every effort to see it and to learn more about it: at this time, his art had nothing whatsoever to do with social upheavals or politics.

Notes

1. Maude I. G. Oliver, "Gossip of the Artists," *Chicago Sunday Herald*, 27 December 1914.

2. Thomas Cusack, born in Ireland in 1858, immigrated with his parents to the United States when he was only three years old. After losing his parents, he came to Chicago in 1863 and started his sign-painting business in 1875. A member of the board of education in 1891-98, Cusack was elected to the 56th Congress, serving from 1899 to 1901. During World War I, President Wilson appointed Cusack to a com-

mission of seven to manage war information. Cusack had his offices at 2900 Straus Building in Chicago and was a member of prestigious sports clubs. He sold out his business and retired in 1924. Albert Nelson Marquis, comp. and ed., *Who's Who in Chicago: The Book of Chicagoans: A Biographical Dictionary of Leading Living Men and Women of the City of Chicago and Environs, 1926* (Chicago: A. N. Marquis & Co., 1926), p. 217.

3. For an interesting account of this important and influential Chicagoan, see Carter H. Harrison, *Stormy Years* (New York: The Bobbs-Merrill Co., 1935).

4. Oliver, "Gossip of the Artists."

5. Ibid.

6. Maurice Ritman, interview with Richard Love, August 1987, R. H. Love Galleries Archives, p. 2.

7. At least one of these early cigar box top portraits is extant. The author examined one, which appeared to be authentic, in August 1987. Richard Love to Bruce C. Bachman, memo, R. H. Love Galleries Archives, Chicago.

8. As far as the School of the Art Institute was concerned, Director French explained that their new so-called atelier and concours system was similar to that followed by schools in Paris: "Under this plan each master has an atelier or studio consisting of one or more classes made up of students who become his pupils by their own choice and who may pass to any other teacher at the end of the month. A concours or competitive examination is held at the end of each month in which the studies are arranged upon the wall in the order of merit and a record is kept. This gives freedom both to teacher and student and is capable of indefinite expansion." See M. D. R. [sic], French, "The Art School of the Art Institute of Chicago," *Sketch Book*, II, no. 6 (July 1903), p. 8.

9. In the Bohemia Guild at 338 Wabash, there were quite a number of workshops whose artisans specialized in bookbinding (Gertrude Stiles), leather work (Amelia Ceuter), pottery (Edith Freeman), and more. The guild was attempting to organize an apprentice system "for the training of artistic craftsmen." See "Gossip of the Ateliers: Being Sundry Notes of Interest Picked up in Studios and Art Schools," *Sketchbook*, III, no. 2 (October 1903), p. 61.

10. Scott designed and produced a kind of local variation of the British Eastlake style of furniture. He was commissioned to design furnishings for the John J. Glessner's mansion on Prairie Avenue, which was designed by H. H. Richardson.

11. The text of Wright's already famous 1901 address, "The Art and Craft of the Machine," was published in the exhibition catalog of the Fourteenth Annual Exhibit of the Chicago Architecture Club.

12. "New York School of Art," *Sketchbook*, III (January 1904), p. 143.

13. Levi Zeigler Leiter (1834-1904) arrived in Chicago at the age of 20 and worked in the wholesale and retail business until 1865, when he and Marshall Field purchased controlling stock in Potter Palmer's business. Selling his share to Field in 1881, Leiter spent the rest of his life in his amazing library, tending to his vast real estate holdings.

14. Francis Cheney Bennett, ed., *History of Music and Art in Illinois* (Société Universelle Lyrique, 1904), p. 11.

15. Esther Sparks, "A Biographical Dictionary of Painters and Sculptors in Illinois, 1808-1945," Ph.D. diss., Northwestern University, 1971, Vol. I, pp. 102-3.

16. Charles De Kay, "French and American Impressionists," *New York Times*, 31 January 1904, p. 23.

17. Charles Morice, "Les Salons de la Nationale et des Français," *Mercure de France*, June 1904, pp. 686-705.

18. Ibid., p. 693.

19. Richard H. Love, *Theodore Earl Butler: Emergence from Monet's Shadow* (Chicago: Haase-Mumm Publishing Co., 1985), p. 250.

CHAPTER NINE:
A STRUGGLE FOR CULTURAL ALTERNATIVES

After seeing the show of Foreign and American pictures at the Fine Arts Building in New York in 1905, the critic Russell Sturgis, while praising the exhibition in general, complained that there were "no canvases which might give the last word of what we call impressionism." He lamented further that "of the American group the limitations were equally notable."[1] Whether in New York, Boston, Philadelphia, or Chicago, critics, artists, dealers, and collectors strove to comprehend the full meaning of impressionism. If it failed to dominate an exhibition, critics pointed out that the selection evidenced a lack of modernity, and the public was disappointed. To all but a few staunch academicists, and even these were declining in numbers daily, Monet had become the leading master of the Western art world.

In 1905, while Louis painted signs at Cusack's and sat in the Hull House drawing classes in Chicago, impressionism gave birth to its last offspring in one painful event in France; to the initiated, pregnancy had been very apparent during the last few months. Labor seemed imminent in Paris at the Salon des Indépendants, a show that swelled with brilliantly colored canvases. Though many of these works obviously represented cases of the latest aesthetic trends, others seemed very unusual, very different indeed from the prevalent examples of neo-impressionism that Signac promoted. The most obvious of these came from the easels of the *coloristes* — Henri Matisse's group soon to be dubbed *Les Fauves*. The colorists stood out because their pictures had been hung together — as if they were given a group show. The reason for this was that Signac had placed Matisse in charge of the all-important hanging committee after their summer spent together at Saint Tropez. The caustic and usually anti-American critic Charles Morice considered the colorist works a departure from both impressionism and the Nabi style, but he stopped short of giving the trend a title, calling it instead another movement of "something else."[2] The influential critic Louis Vauxcelles also praised the group, prophetically calling them the "masters of tomorrow."

In spite of its apparent labor, Paris did not deliver Fauvism until later that fall at the now famous 1905 Salon d'Automne. Here, Matisse's avant-garde circle exhibited new canvases, which looked garish and strange even by the standards of impressionism. These paintings prompted most visitors to accuse Matisse of having "gone too far!" Many critics agreed with the public and even stated that the pictures were reflective of anarchism, a growing movement in France with which Vlaminck and a few others in Matisse's circle had been associated. These paintings were so radical, so brightly colored, and so lacking in fidelity to nature, that Louis Vauxcelles, who had praised the colorists at the Indépendants show only months earlier, now referred to them as *Les Fauves*, the Wild Beasts.[3]

About the same time in New York, Lawton Parker's friend John Sloan made a small etching entitled *Fifth Avenue Critics*. In this biting social comment, Sloan reflected Robert Henri's ideas about art and also demonstrated outstanding draftsmanship, the kind admired by Louis Ritman in Chicago. While Louis might have been influenced by Sloan's draftmanship, he would have rejected his satirical subject matter. The urban realism created by Sloan and other members of Henri's group in New York (excluding Parker) was vastly different from that produced in Chicago. Ritman was fast becoming an urban artist, but unlike Parker's friend Sloan or any of his Philadelphia artist-reporter constituents, Ritman wanted to produce a Chicago-style realism. Louis wanted to make pictures like Parker's — striking portraits and carefully planned genre that featured women engaged in pleasant activities of American life. He was not interested in cynical satire or downtrodden slum dwellers.

Ritman's skills were far more advanced than those of his fellow students at Hull House, owing especially to his ability to paint, something most of them had not been allowed to try. Nonetheless, Miss Benedict was convinced that Louis still needed extensive training from the live model. Since he had clearly advanced well beyond the level of drawing offered at the Hull House, she urged him to enroll in the life class at the Art Institute of Chicago. It is possible that Ritman also had heard a lot about the institute from his friend Clara Kretzinger who preceded him there as a student. Exactly how Louis approached his parents with the idea of studying at the institute is unknown, but they supported his wish to progress in art. In fact, Maurice Ritman reports that his parents were very proud of Louis's talents. They may have been a bit mystified by his art, given that he was the only one on either side of the family for generations who had demonstrated such innate skill, but they were anxious for him to proceed to the Art Institute.[4] The next hurdle standing in his path to the institute was his position with Cusack's. After a discussion with McInerney, the shop foreman, Louis was told that classes would pose no problem at Cusack's so long as he was still able to put in a full day's work. Cusack's earlier service as member of the Board of Education of Chicago may have influenced company policies in this regard. So it was that with the assistance of family, friends, and Miss Benedict in the summer of 1905, sixteen-year-old Louis Ritman submitted his hard-earned portfolio to the review board at the Art Institute of Chicago and was accepted to the evening life class beginning in October. The administration at the institute made

Ill. 9-1. Samantha Littlefield Huntley. *Portrait of John H. Vanderpoel.* Oil on canvas, 25 x 17 inches. Beverly Art Center, Chicago.

every effort to limit each life class to thirty-five students.[5] Louis's tuition was fifty cents a week for three evenings, or six dollars for twelve weeks. He was given the opportunity to choose the master under whom he wished to study. On 2 October 1905 he began instruction under the institute master John H. Vanderpoel (ill. 9-1). Although the evening students were sometimes less advanced than the day students, they were in general more serious-minded about their pursuits. Louis found himself at a higher level of achievement almost immediately; he skipped the antique probationary period and was placed in the academic class. At this time, the life class had been operating under the "atelier and concours" system for a couple of years. This system consisted of a highly procedural manner of instruction, derived from the French schools, and it fostered competition.

If Vanderpoel was a highly talented instructor, he had students with great artistic potential. In the Art Institute enrollment records for the fall of 1905, besides Ritman's, another name was of great significance for the future development of American art—Georgia O'Keeffe. She also matriculated at the school and studied under Vanderpoel during the fall of 1905 and spring of 1906.[6] Information is sparse on student contacts and we do not know whether Ritman and O'Keeffe were aware of each other's presence. A few minds like theirs, however, could have raised the general level of training for the whole group studying under Vanderpoel.

This great teacher made the discipline of draftsmanship the sum and substance of his fine art instruction. Although he was born in Holland in 1857, Vanderpoel had figured prominently on the Chicago art scene for many years, both as a teacher and as a mainstay of the art community. At the Chicago Academy of Design, Vanderpoel had taken instruction from Herman Hanstein, Christian F. Schwerdt, Laurence Earle, Henry F. Spread, and the pioneer Chicago painter- teacher-poet and art critic from Indiana, James F. Gookins.[7] Although Vanderpoel promoted the strict academic side of art, he was well aware of other more modern styles. He had witnessed the evolution of impressionism in both Europe and America, since he had also been a student at the Julian Academy under Gustave Boulanger and Jules J. Lefebvre, both influential professors who drummed the merits of draftsmanship into the minds of their students. Vanderpoel had acquired his experience in Paris many years earlier, but drawing eventually became the primary ingredient in his teaching philosophy in Chicago because he too professed Ingres's dictum he found posted over the door at the Julian Academy: *Le dessin est la probité de l'art* ("Drawing is the integrity of art"). To Louis Ritman and scores of students before him, Vanderpoel preached and demonstrated that the practice of drawing was a good deal more than credo (ill. 9-2)— it was practice. In 1903, two years before Ritman met him, Vanderpoel had written a series of articles on art and anatomy, illustrated with his own outstanding figure studies, for the *Sketch Book*. These were later reorganized and published as *The Human Figure*.[8]

In every way, Vanderpoel was a solid, dependable member of the Art Institute hierarchy; in contemporary terms, he was a "team player." Although he was not officially a member of the administration as was W. M. R. French or Newton H. Carpenter, he might as well have been, since he coordinated his activities carefully with the director and other institute powers. A family man, Vanderpoel was married to Henrietta Van Vlissingen, who unswervingly supported his art career. Their son Robert attended Tilden Technical School and would go on to study at the University of Chicago.[9] Working diligently in the hope that his contribution would be valuable and long-lasting, John Vanderpoel was content to live in Chicago,

Ill. 9-2. John Vanderpoel. *Untitled*. Private Collection. Courtesy R. H. Love Galleries, Chicago.

expounding on the ideas and practices of academic art to youths like Ritman.

In this regard, Vanderpoel's raison d'être was the antithesis of Lawton Parker's, for if Vanderpoel was an organization man, Parker was the opposite, a fiercely competitive individual who thrived on challenge, innovation, travel, and interaction with other progressive members of the international art community. Nevertheless, in his role as both a former student and a one-time faculty colleague of Vanderpoel's, Parker admired his former teacher for his skill, sincerity, and devotion to art education.

Conversely, Parker did not admire W. M. R. French, who had combated him openly and had refused to invite him to faculty meetings during his tenure as a part-time teacher at the Art Institute, yet assured him repeatedly that "we are not at all afraid of a change and are open to any good ideas."[10] Although it irritated French, he knew that Parker's opinion and services were sought by many figures in the art world of Chicago. French could do very little to dissuade these mutual associates from dealing with Parker because the latter's reputation was growing by leaps and bounds on both sides of the Atlan-

Pl. 2-1. Claude Monet. *Spring in Giverny*. Oil on canvas, 25¹¹⁄₁₆ x 32 inches. Sterling and Francine Clark Institute, Williamstown, Massachusetts.

Pl. 2-2. Theodore Earl Butler. *New Road, Giverny*. 1902. Oil on canvas, 25½ x 32 inches. Private Collection. Courtesy R.H. Love Galleries, Chicago.

Pl. 5-1. Claude Monet. *Haystack at Sunset, near Giverny.* 1891. Oil on canvas, 28¾ x 36¼ inches. Museum of Fine Arts, Boston. Julia Cheney Edwards Collection. Bequest of Robert J. Edwards in memory of his mother.

Pl. 5-2. Lilla Cabot Perry. *Haystacks.* Ca. 1896. Oil on canvas, 25¾ x 32 inches. Private Collection. Courtesy R. H. Love Galleries, Chicago.

Pl. 5-3. Richard Miller. *Interior*. Ca. 1910. Oil on panel, 24 x 26 inches. Private Collection. Courtesy R. H. Love Galleries, Chicago.

Pl. 4-1. Charles Francis Browne. *Indiana Autumn*. 1897. Oil on canvas, 16 x 24 inches. Collection of Dan and Nancy Schneider. Courtesy R.H. Love Galleries, Chicago.

Pl. 9-1. Alson Skinner Clark. *Brittany Landscape*. Oil on canvas, 25 x 31 inches. Private Collection. Courtesy R. H. Love Galleries, Chicago.

Pl. 10-1. Ada Shulz. *Picking Flowers*. Oil on canvas, 16 x 20 inches. Private Collection. Courtesy R. H. Love Galleries, Chicago.

Pl. 10-3. William Merritt Chase. *Red Roofs of Bristol.* Oil on canvas, 20 x 30 inches. Private Collection. Courtesy R. H. Love Galleries, Chicago.

Pl. 11-1. Julian Alden Weir. *Autumn Landscape.* Pastel and pencil on board, 11⅛ x 15¼ inches. Private Collection. Courtesy R. H. Love Galleries, Chicago.

Pl. 10-2. Lawton Parker. *April Afternoon*. Oil on canvas, 25 x 31 inches. Private Collection. Courtesy R. H. Love Galleries, Chicago.

Pl. 12-1. Richard Miller. *Lady Reading.* Oil on canvas, 34 x 36 inches. Private Collection. Courtesy R. H. Love Galleries, Chicago.

Pl. 12-2. Frederick Carl Frieseke. *Lady in a Garden*. Ca. 1912. Oil on canvas, 31 x 26½ inches. Terra Museum of American Art. Daniel J. Terra Collection.

tic. French's best method of keeping Parker at bay was to distance him from the institute by enlisting the counsel of other highly respected individuals. For example, in early 1905 there had been some talk of Parker's selecting a group of pictures from the Paris Salon for an exhibition at the Art Institute. That spring, French wrote to Sara Hallowell, reporting that he "saw [Walter] McEwen the other day," and that "he [McEwen] thinks our Paris business is managed as well as anybodies [sic], better than Philadelphia's for instance." Director French also mentioned that the institute had "a young teacher in Paris named Allen E. Philbrick." "It has occurred to me," French explained, "to ask Philbrick [not Parker] to examine the works in the Salons and make a note of those he would like to see invited to Chicago . . . and let you confer with each other on the subject."[11] Unknown to French, however, Parker had already made arrangements with other administrators at the Art Institute, so it was the latter's selection of works by Salon artists that was shipped to Chicago in the spring of 1905 in spite of the director's attempts to preclude his efforts. Later that summer French admitted to Hallowell that he had felt obliged to accept Parker's selection since he "was in some danger of the suspicion that [he] was influenced by. . . personal disagreements with Parker." He wrote: "It is far from my intentions to injure Parker in any way. I am only trying to protect myself against his uncertainties."[12]

Louis Ritman was still too young and inexperienced to understand politics, too naive to know that the Art Institute promoted some students over others regardless of talent. French and others of the Institute hierarchy were determined to promote Philbrick because he had been an excellent student-teacher and had abided by every rule; he was a cooperative individual who they believed should one day return to Chicago to continue in their footsteps. Accordingly, French had already mentioned his name in a letter sent off to Paris earlier that spring of 1905, this one to Mary Cassatt, at 16 rue Lafitte. His letter was in answer to Cassatt's of the previous December, in which she had informed him and the institute that it would be "impossible" for her to accept the prestigious N. W. Harris Prize of $500 awarded her by the Art Institute. The award had been given for an oil, *Caress*, one of four pictures loaned by the Durand-Ruel Gallery "under the proviso that they were not [to] be in competitions for any awards."[13] This was the first time Cassatt's work had been shown at the Art Institute, and it was praised by critics and public alike. Lena M. McCauley reported to *Chicago Tribune* readers that Cassatt's children were "affectionately and tenderly considered" (ill. 9-3).[14] The great impressionist from Philadelphia explained to French (as though he were unaware of the fact) that she

"was one of the original 'Independents' who founded a society where there was to be no jury, no medals, no awards." She reiterated that "none of us [impressionists] have sent to any official exhibitions and have stuck to the original tenets." Miss Cassatt recommended that the prize money be given "to some young artist to whom it might be of greatest use." In his answer of 1 March, French stated that he "was not surprised" that she had declined

Ill. 9-3. Mary Cassatt. *Baby John Asleep Sucking His Thumb.* Ca. 1910. Pastel on paper, 26 x 21⅞ inches. Private Collection. Courtesy R. H. Love Galleries, Chicago.

the Harris Prize. He suggested that "Allen Philbrick, who we hope has in him the making of an artist" be given the Harris money for "another year of study abroad."[15]

The feud between French and Parker was to grow more intense over the next few months. Of course, young students at the Art Institute school heard rumors of their squabbles, but they were affected only in the most indirect ways. One day, however, Louis would get to know Parker very well, and many of their ideas would become similar. Earlier in the spring of 1905, Parker had been in Paris, where he met with Sara Hallowell and other friends. He also exhibited the portrait he had painted of Martin Ryerson, vice president of the Art Institute. The painting received considerable local promotion. By late summer Parker resumed his activities in Chicago. He lived in Evanston, a suburb just north of the city and the home of Northwestern University. He was still anxious to maintain ties with the Art Institute but found his way blocked at every turn by Director French. Even when Parker's highly praised portrait of Ryerson, "a reading of character," was returned to the institute from the Paris Salon with a bill for 18.85 francs, Director French informed the senders that "Mr. Lawton Parker is in no way connected with the Art Institute."[16] He also let them know that the portrait was the property of the University of Chicago, not his institution, and that Parker "has not been in very friendly relations with the Art Institute of late." It is doubtful that French's actions were effective in alienating Parker from the local art community, since he enjoyed the friendships of so many of its trustees and well-placed members. One of these was Alson Skinner Clark, the wealthy Chicago artist, with whom he painted in Brittany (pl. 9-1) and Giverny, and who had recently returned to the city. Clark had just rented quarters in the Tree Studio Building where he was taking portrait commissions and painting local street scenes.

In the fall of 1905, Louis Ritman was sixteen years old. He worked about ten hours a day at the Thomas Cusack Company and refined his art skills in the evening in front of the live model at the Art Institute. The number of regular day students amounted to over 600; and Louis's night class constituents, fewer than 500. Director French was very proud of his school, calling it "one of the most comprehensive in the world" and "the largest in America."[17] Under Vanderpoel, Louis attended his anatomy lectures, worked from various models, nude and costumed, and studied portraiture. He concentrated on the human form, both the head and figure, analyzing each part of the body. For charcoal studies he usually worked on large sheets of paper. From his instructor, Louis gained immeasurable insight into technique. He learned to render form by tone and by line, practicing each discipline separately until he could combine the two methods to create a convincing figure that pleased his instructors. Louis's parents still needed his paycheck; by studying in the evenings, he was able both to pursue his art and to continue working at Cusack's to help his family. Louis's maturity amazed the adults who observed him pursue his activities quite undaunted by his station in life. His parents and siblings were industrious and ambitious, but they still lived on Fourteenth Street, in a very poor, albeit productive Jewish section of the city. Indeed, Louis was the exact opposite of Daniel Schaffner, a fellow student from his neighborhood at the School of the Art Institute; Schaffner was continually in trou-

ble and had recently faced threats of expulsion from the school and even arrest on account of his repeated offenses.

Working each day at his art, Louis progressed rapidly in the winter season of 1905-6. He made many sketches in charcoal and continued his experiments in painting. Even from this early time, he was fiercely committed to the figure as his favorite subject. In spite of his progress, however, Louis was anxious to do more; he was inspired by constant stories about other art centers, cities like Boston, where Tarbell and Benson worked, and Philadelphia, where Eakins had taught and Chase was teaching, and, of course, New York, where Parker had worked with Robert Henri, who still promoted unpretentious "American" subjects. Louis was especially interested in the gossip he heard about J. Alden Weir, Childe Hassam, and other members of The Ten, who received so much praise for their high-keyed canvases with purple shadows. Encouraged by his instructors at the Art Institute, Louis tried diligently to save a few dollars for travel expenses, so that he might see those places in the East where he planned to study with someone like Tarbell or Chase.

If it was really true that one could stand quietly in a farmer's field in Kankakee County and hear the corn grow on a hot June day, one could also stand in Chicago's Loop that summer of 1906 and see the skyscrapers grow. The whole city seemed to pulsate with energy and activity. There were constant labor problems and threats and rumors of scandals in high places, but the city was doing its best to become an international center for cultural achievements. Leaders of every rank hoped to be recognized for his or her contribution to Chicago's reputation as one of the nation's most highly respected cities of opportunity. Obvious efforts were made to bolster its image. The Chicago School of architecture was already famous, and Frank Lloyd Wright was making innovative strides in residential architecture with his "prairie style houses." The design of Owen P. Aldis's Monadnock building on West Jackson Boulevard, in which the walls bore the weight of the structure, had already been made obsolete by more modern steel-framed structures like the Fair Store and later the Home Insurance Building. No city in the world was boasting more innovation in architecture than Chicago.

Unfortunately, in the domain of fine arts Chicago established a considerably less progressive and innovative record than in architecture. Even New York critics admitted that Chicago enjoyed the leadership in modern architecture; its great buildings had risen from the ashes of the Chicago fire like a never-ending regeneration of new phoenixes. Builders and architects came from all parts of the Western world to see great structures by master architects like William LeBaron Jenney, Dankmar Adler, Louis Sullivan, H. Ives Cobb, Henry Hobson Richardson, and the firms of D. H. Burnham and J. W. Root, the great designers of the World's Fair complex. Each day new board fences were hastily nailed up to protect curious passers-by from cavernous basements that were being dug by steam shovels and teams of horses. All over the bulging Loop great tiers of scaffolds clung to the sides of strange cagelike iron skeletons that awaited their skins of brick or cut limestone from downstate Indiana. The Loop, Chicago's noisy, thriving center of operations, was truly an incredible sight to behold, an amazingly dynamic nucleus of human activity which had increased tremendously since the Englishman C. B. Berry described it twenty-five years earlier: "The feature of Chicago is its marvelous energy," he reported and concluded: "America is energetic, but Chicago is in a fever. It does not rest one moment, but goes on, on—ever ceaselessly ahead—to buying, and selling, and getting gain. Everything is rapid, everything is keen. There are hardly any idlers on the streets. Everyone has an object in immediate view—and is walking fast to reach it."[18]

It may have been that way in the Loop, the exciting, throbbing part of the city viewed by visitors, but there were many other sections of the city—the ethnic ghetto area, where the Ritman family lived; the Central Manufacturing, District with its frame dwellings, its squalor and rats and smell, its perpetual danger, and its perennial unemployed; and to be sure, the Levee, where criminals and pimps scraped away what they could from Chicago's filthy underbelly. Whiskey Row on South State Street had been closed down by Police Chief John Collins for several months. Of course, some of the nickelodeons remained, and there was always bustling activity in the white slave trade. In recent years, the latter had become a big business run by Levee bosses like whoremasters Baptista Pizza, Leona Garrity, and the husband-and-wife team Maurice and Julia Van Bever.[19] Misinterpreting, perhaps, the image striven for by city leaders a year earlier, Bud White ignored the presence of Chicago gambling-squad detectives when he set his gambling boat into operation outside city jurisdiction on Lake Michigan; by the summer of 1906, however, competitors had ruined his monopoly and launched a gamblers' war. Honest and law-abiding businessmen were also in abundance as they supported various reform measures and attempted to back honest politicians. Chicago was expanding at a rate faster than it could be properly controlled. The whole nation had watched Chicago since the World's Fair and still watched the city as it gained prestige and made unprecedented progress in countless commercial, industrial, social, and cultural endeavors.

Chicago always "busted its buttons" with pride; to its own citizens, the city seemed capable of nearly any undertaking, commercial or otherwise. The city even hosted an All-Chicago World Series in baseball: on 14 October 1906, the Sox beat the Cubs to become the world champions.

In some ways, the unprecedented expansion of Chicago was deplorable because it was so difficult to manage. In terms of the local art community, however, expansion meant progress. It also increased the potential of Chicago's becoming a cultural alternative to New York City, a dream cherished by men like Martin Ryerson, Owen P. Aldis, and Potter Palmer, originally from New York State. As the influence of Chicago art spread, the suburbs became more sophisticated. Several suburban art societies had come into existence, but few were like the one in Park Ridge, which was stimulated by the presence of artists such as Albert Krehbiel, Walter Marshall Clute, Adam Emory Albright, and the architect William F. McCaughley. Excluding these few pockets of extraordinary art activity, most of the serious art endeavors centered around the Art Institute. Even these dedicated suburban artists were strongly tied to the Chicago art community. For example, in addition to his alliance with the Park Ridge organization, Albright had been a successful exhibitor at the Art Institute, a frequent jury member, and a generous contributor to its functions. In fact, at the annual Chicago Artists Exhibition of 1906 at the institute, he was awarded second place. In a letter to fellow administrator N. H. Carpenter, Director French reported: "The excitement in the Exhibition of Chicago Artists continues . . . . Mr. Albright was second in the number of votes and would have taken the medal if there had not been a number of proxies sent in which [Ralph] Clarkson yielded . . . . Albright was furious because of the proxies. I am told [H. Leon] Roecker got some votes and not true expressions of opinion."[20]

Supported as it was by the bulwark of Chicago's political, social, and business leaders and directed by the everprotective W. M. R. French, the Art Institute faced little competition; even the once relatively autonomous Municipal Art League cooperated in joint ventures. In terms of art instruction, too, only a few alternatives existed to the decidedly conservative policies of the School of the Art Institute. Once again, directives on procedures were handed down by Director French, who maintained strict regimen and rejected the ideas of a progressive teacher like Lawton Parker. Clinging to nineteenth-century traditions in art education, French and his counterparts in other schools of the Western world were reluctant to face the radical changes in doctrine and practice that constantly radiated from the revolutionary world of modern art that confronted them. Culture was in flux, but directors like French or President Frederick Dielman of the National Academy of Design in New York were cautious in initiating changes too quickly in their art school policies. Indeed, even Robert Henri was moving a bit too fast for William Merritt Chase as he directed the master's New York School of Art. Soon Dielman was to tell his fellow academicians that "legitimate and intelligent criticism of our policy and methods, publicly expressed, we must be prepared to hear and regard, particularly when they reflect sentiments current among the body of our fellow artists."[21] Motivated by similarly good intentions, French saw himself as a tolerant administrator, but he was, nonetheless, a conservative aristocrat who resisted change, a fact confirmed by his ongoing dialog with Howard Pyle, the great teacher from Wilmington, Delaware: "I shall be very glad indeed to receive some kind of a sketch of your idea of how art education ought to be conducted . . . I am seriously contemplating adopting such suggestions as commend themselves to me in our school." Even to someone as devoted to tradition as Pyle, French reiterated: "My way is not to make the violent revolutions [as Henri was doing] but to introduce new ideas quietly."[22]

So it was that an art student like Ritman, who knew very little about trends in art or differences in art education, innocently accepted his American academic discipline and was molded by its traditions. Certainly there were many advantages to this kind of art instruction, the most important being the emphasis placed on draftsmanship, which was disciplined through repetitious practice, a workable and time-proven system that produced many skilled masters of the human figure, especially in the Midwest. On the other hand, fidelity to nature was being challenged at every turn in Paris, by some artists in New York, and a scant few in Chicago, so a program such as that maintained by W. M. R. French and his colleagues at the Institute was actually old-fashioned. Since the Art Institute held a firm grip on art education in Chicago, if not the whole Midwest, little opportunity existed for the struggling art student to be subjected to modern ideas or even to learn alternative viewpoints without going to New York or, better yet, to Paris.

What, if any, were the alternatives for Ritman in Chicago? There was the Art Students League of Chicago which was based on its counterpart in New York, but played a much smaller, less visible, and generally less active role in the local art community. Traditionally, the annual exhibitions of the league took place at the Art Institute in the spring.[23] Although costume balls and quaint teas formed part of its programs, the league was not progressive in its art functions and amounted to no

more than a poorly disguised appendage of the Art Institute. The Art Students League was actually an affiliate of the Municipal Art League of Chicago and remained inextricably tied to the Art Institute, whose students made up most of its membership rolls.

Another alternative for Ritman was the Chicago Academy of Fine Arts. The academy served as a kind of Julian Academy of Chicago, while the Art Institute stood as the counterpart of the Ecole des Beaux-Arts, replete with bureaucracy and old-fashioned teaching methods. Carl N. Werntz, the founder of the Chicago Academy of Fine Arts, was a native of Illinois and a former student at the Art Institute. Ironically, he had never trained at the Julian Academy, although he maintained numerous contacts in Paris. A painter and cartoonist, Werntz was a former student of J. H. Vanderpoel and Frederick Freer. Apparently he had also taken criticism from Lawton Parker and Richard Miller and had exhibited at the spring and autumn salons in Paris, at the Royal Academy in London, and at the National Academy of Design in New York. Summarily, one concluded that Werntz possessed ample credentials and experience to organize an art school in Chicago.

The Chicago Academy of Fine Arts enrolled nearly 600 students and hired 15 teachers, including Werntz. Following the methodology used in Paris, Werntz and his teachers concentrated on drawing from life as the basis of study in the atelier and concours system at the academy, but unlike the School of the Art Institute, the academy eliminated the requirement of elementary study from casts. This was a radical move on the part of the academy, since it virtually eliminated the elementary discipline considered the foundation practice for all art students by the Art Institute. Therefore, during its short existence, the academy became relatively competitive with the School of the Art Institute. In terms of the variety of courses offered by the academy, students could choose from painting and composition, cartooning, design, anatomy (taught by an M.D.), nude and portrait painting, miniature painting, illustration, watercolor, sketch class, pottery, and more, even business ethics of art.[24] Although the academy listed an impressive number of instructors on its staff, not all of them boasted impressive credentials. In addition to highly trained and respected masters like Oliver Dennett Grover, Wellington J. Reynolds, Harry Townsend, and William Penhallow Henderson, there were lesser names like William A. Hartman, instructor of interior design, Ezra Winters, instructor of the Saturday sketch class, and Jessica Fergus, teacher of school methods.

For four years Werntz had proven to be an exceptionally capable businessman, organizer, and promoter, having guided the academy to an enrollment of several hundred students; clearly the academy stood out as the best alternative to the School of the Art Institute. In fact, the academy became so successful that at one point Werntz entered into negotiations to sell it to the Art Institute. For reasons that are unclear, the sale was not consummated, and the existing adversarial relationship between Werntz and the institute worsened. The result was that Werntz was even more determined to make the academy a highly visible art school which would openly compete for Art Institute students, who were already working in crowded conditions. Relentlessly pursuing his goal, Werntz took advantage of every opportunity to lure students from the Art Institute. For the most part, he followed ordinary rules of aggressive business competition, offering smaller classes, better individual attention, lower tuition, an inordinate number of scholarships, and a legitimate art gallery for "the sale of pictures by American artists and of craft work."[25] At one time, however, Werntz became involved in a controversy regarding the sale or unauthorized use of the Art Institute's student mailing list.[26]

As the Chicago Academy of Fine Arts expanded, Werntz made every effort to increase the credibility of his institution by hiring better instructors and by cultivating relations with important personalities in the art communities of New York and Paris with whom he might establish alliances. Apparently he had written to, or contacted in some way (perhaps through Parker), the master innovator Alphonse Mucha (ill. 9-4), asking him to teach or lecture at his academy in 1906.[27] Of course, Mucha's presence at the academy would have been an impressive coup for Werntz in his competition with the School of the Art Institute. However, Director French learned of Werntz's negotiations with Mucha and attempted to dissuade the master by offering an alternative position at the School of the Art Institute. In a February 1906 letter to an associate, French reported that he had written to Mucha in Paris the previous fall and "received no answer."[28] He explained that he did "not like to do things merely out of competition with Werntz's school." Attempting to show his willingness to cooperate, French speculated that "it would probably answer all our purposes if Mucha would lecture or do something at the Art Institute, even if he went to the other school, but," he continued, "I presume Werntz will attempt to make an exclusive contract with him." Obviously, with all the facilities of the Art Institute at his disposal, French was able to make a far more attractive position available to Mucha, so he added: "I think there is no doubt that we would be glad to have Mucha come here and teach and exhibit next season."[29]

Another personality Werntz contacted was the French

Ill. 9-4. Alphonse Mucha in his studio in Paris. Photograph. R.H. Love Galleries Archives, Chicago.

art dealer Durand-Ruel. Once nearly bankrupt for his support of the impressionists, Durand-Ruel had had many contacts with Hallowell, Mrs. Palmer, and other Chicagoans over the years. Now he was hailed as the pioneer champion of the impressionist movement in France and America. Knowing little about Werntz the cartoonist or his Chicago Academy of Fine Arts, Durand-Ruel had written to French about a year earlier, seeking his opinion of Werntz. The following is an excerpt of French's response of March 1906, offering a brief overview of his competition: "The Chicago Academy of Fine Arts is a private school of drawing and painting, which appears to be getting along pretty well, and of which Mr. Werntz is the manager . . . . The Academy of Fine Arts does not include any artists of considerable standing, except Mr. W. P. Henderson, though Mr. Norton and Mr. Reynolds are highly respectable men, formerly students here. Our policy has been to treat this other school with politeness, and we furnish tickets of admission to our galleries to their students. Mr. Werntz, however, has made things rather disagreeable by denouncing our school as an old fogey affair by stationing men with circulars at our doors, and by possessing himself of our lists of students addresses by underhanded means. I thought at first the school could not last a great while, but it now seems, as I said above, to be going on pretty well. Mr. Werntz tried at one time to sell out to us. I do not see how their backing could be of any great value."[30]

Meanwhile, the art world outside Chicago moved to new creative efforts as sociopolitical changes throughout the nation became more evident with each passing day of 1906. Some of these shifts affected the art community only indirectly; in other instances, important members of America's art network were directly involved. "The men with the muckrakes are often indispensable to the well-being of society," said President Roosevelt in a highly publicized address to the Gridiron Club in Washington, DC, on 14 April 1906, "but only if they know when to stop raking the muck and look upward . . . to the crown of worthy endeavor." Implicit in his comment was a reference to a similar passage in *Pilgrim's Progress* (1689) by John Bunyon, and his meaning stirred up a good deal of reaction from the press, but very little in comparison with that produced by the tragedy that occurred four days later. At 5:13 A.M. on Wednesday, 18 April, the citizens of San Francisco were thrown from their beds by the worst earthquake ever to hit an American city. The ensuing three-day fire destroyed a major portion of San Francisco, killing over 450 people and leaving another 250,000 homeless. Outstanding examples of architecture and art were lost in the holocaust. Around this time, the junior senator Robert M. LaFollette from Wisconsin gave a three-day speech in the Senate, which prompted comment on railroad rates from Alexander Johnston Cassatt, president of the Pennsylvania Railroad and the brother of Mary Cassatt.[31] Excavation of the Panama Canal began. *Mother Earth*, a social protest magazine, was founded by the anarchist Emma Goldman and Alexander Berkman, both of whom would soon have a great impact on American art. Released from prison after having served time for an attempted assasination of the great art collector Henry Clay Frick, Berkman had made his name well known to the national art community.[32] At the end of June, another great leader in the American art community was attacked, only this time the perpetrator succeeded: while watching a play on the roof of Madison Square Garden, which he had designed, Stanford White, the famous architect and prominent member of New York's high society, was shot to death by Harry K. Thaw, a member of a wealthy Pittsburgh family and the brother of the Countess of Yarmouth.[33] Apparently the murder was premeditated and the result of Thaw's "intense jealousy and brooding over the alleged wronging of Mr. Thaw's wife by Mr. White years ago when she was Evelyn Nesbit, an artist's model."[34] Soon the clubhouse at 120 Madison Avenue that Stanford White had designed for New York's Colony Club (founded by J. P. Morgan's sister Anne Morgan and others) would be completed. At the same time the highly successful retailer and art collector Benjamin Altman was

Ill. 9-5. Wellington J . Reynolds. Photograph. R. H. Love Galleries Archives, Chicago.

moving his department store from its location at Sixth Avenue and Eighteenth Street, where it had stood since 1865, to Fifth Avenue at Thirty-fourth Street. Altman's collection was already well known to the New York art community, but it contained little American art.[35]

In Chicago, Werntz's aggressive recruiting procedures were successful in luring Louis Ritman away from the School of the Art Institute to the Chicago Academy of Fine Arts. It is possible that Louis received a special scholarship for evening study since class tuitions ranged from fifteen to one hundred dollars per season, a prohibitive fee for the Ritman family.[36] No doubt Louis was anxious to study figure painting with Wellington J. Reynolds (ill. 9-5), a highly respected teacher, but he probably hoped to study under Parker as well. Few instructors professed academic methodology with greater commitment than Reynolds, and with good reason, for he had been trained according to its traditions in Europe and America. Records show that Reynolds had studied at the Royal

Academy and at the Hollósy Academy, both located in Munich, the capital of Bavaria. The Munich Academy followed a traditional academic regimen, but its faculty members and students formed more experimental groups like the Wilhelm Leibl circle, which emphasized brushwork and skillful expression inspired by Frans Hals.[37] Numerous other artist constituents who had since become impressionists had studied at the Munich Academy, earlier men from the Midwest like Frank Duveneck, J. H. Twachtman, William Merritt Chase, Joseph R. De Camp, Otto Bacher, Theodore C. Steele, and many more; some of these well-known painters knew Reynolds and respected his art and teaching abilities. Reynolds's former teacher, Simon Hollósy (1857-1918), was the leading member of an innovative group of Hungarian painters at the Munich Academy at the end of the nineteenth century. Dissatisfied with the traditional approach of the academy, Hollósy had set up his private school in Munich, which stressed Jules Bastien-Lepage's precepts of plein-air painting. Possessed of persuasive and artistic talents, Hollósy attracted not only a Hungarian but also an international following with his group, of which Reynolds also became a member (ill. 9-6).[38]

As much as Louis may have wished to, it was impossible for him to attend the Chicago Academy of Fine Arts full time because the Ritman family needed the paycheck provided by his sign-painting job at Thomas Cusack's. With some weekend exceptions, Louis attended the evening classes at the academy. He still lived with his parents at 371 West Fourteenth Street. It was at this time that his brother and future biographer Maurice was born. Maurice would also become a skillful painter.[39]

Before long, Louis became one of Reynolds's favorite students. What Louis liked about Reynolds was that he explained techniques, procedures, the "hands on" processes of painting, and ideas about subjects and compositions. Reynolds showed Louis how to arrange his palette, how to lay in a wash on a bare canvas, and how to hold the brush. The master spent many hours professing art principles and instructing his young pupil in both figure and portrait painting. Reynolds's own style was an interesting blend of the painterly Munich School tradition and the French international style. In this regard, his work was quite similar to that of William Merritt Chase. If Reynolds could be said to belong to any group, he might be characterized as a member of the American juste milieu. His style of painting was typical of the times, and his genteel-tradition subjects were basically generated out of the fin-de-siècle concern for the good life. In his works he frequently depicted an attractive woman engaged in some leisurely activity. Reynolds was straightforward in his preferences, saying openly that he preferred

"to paint young women."[40] He explained that "they enter more perfectly into the spirit of picture making." Reynolds elaborated: "They [women] are willing to agree with my arrangements and follow in imagination the thought which I suggest. When I have become acquainted with my subject the surroundings seem to shape themselves about her as if by magic. I have discovered her easiest attitude and unconsciously the background and various

Ill. 9-6. Wellington J. Reynolds. *Dutch Girl in a Landscape*. Oil on canvas, 20 x 30 inches. R. H. Love Galleries, Chicago.

effects adapted to the impression that she has made rise before my imagination." Not only to young Ritman, but to everyone who took the time to analyze his work, Reynolds's imagery was allied to this narrow but distinct segment of the genteel tradition in art. His pictures were considered to be very American; they could have been painted in New York, Boston, or Chicago. One local critic implied as much in his references to other masters from those cities who made imagery like Reynolds's: "Those who remember a portrait of a lady in a yellow robe by Mr. Frank Benson recognize a similar illumination of 'sweetness and light.'" He pointed out that it was "to the sunny qualities of Edmund C. Tarbell and Frank Benson that Mr. Reynolds pays deference though there is still sufficient distinction to make a contrast . . . .Among his gentlewomen none have that 'intensity of eagerness'. . . . Their composure is of a contented adjustment with life as they find it."[41]

Reynolds's raison d'être appealed to Louis. Reynolds was a proud and self-confident man. He knew that his art was as well conceived and executed as the works of many better-known constituents, and he imparted much of his art philosophy to Louis. As Louis analyzed works by masters from other cities, these images seemed to manifest the credo put forth by Reynolds. Soon, Louis had assimilated Reynolds's style. After he had sketched in the rudimentary form of his subject in charcoal on canvas, Louis worked up his figure from a wash sketch in oil as Reynolds had taught him. He finished his figure with large, fully loaded brushes in a manner that smacked of Reynolds's Hollósy-Munich school style. Like his master's art, Louis's work revealed keen draftsmanship and skilled manipulation of fat pigment, but the finished image looked as though it had been accomplished spontaneously, perhaps even in one sitting.

No better example by Ritman exists from the time than the portrait he executed of his teacher, a likeness entitled simply *Wellington J. Reynolds* (ill. 9-7). The Ritmans had allocated a small space in their house on Fourteenth Street for Louis to paint in. Reynolds agreed to come there and sit for his portrait. A dapper personality, Louis's self-confident master posed in a typical artist's portrait style of the time, in a proud, jaunty position, as we might expect from a Whistler, Chase, or John La Farge. The portrait of Reynolds, the earliest extant (full-fledged) painting by Louis Ritman, was executed in 1906, when he was only seventeen years old.[42] The somber palette and striking brushwork reveal the influence not only of his teacher but also of William Merritt Chase in a rather elliptical way, since the painting style of the New York master was still strongly felt in Chicago. A typical vertical portrait canvas, the likeness of Reynolds was executed as no mere sketch, although it shows remarkable spontaneity and directness — as if Louis had been taught by Chase or Carolus-Duran instead of the sitter. As taught by Reynolds, the figure's tonal contrasts were first achieved, and then the portrait was worked in stages until the finished image appeared spontaneous, revealing as it does Ritman's prodigious skill by most standards. So we see the painting as a fine example of portraiture, but considering Ritman's age at the time of execution, it is nothing short of remarkable. Expanding his talent with brushes, Louis continued his evening studies at the Chicago Academy of Fine Arts and, with Reynolds's help, began executing easel pictures for the forthcoming spring exhibition season.

As exemplified by the transfer of Ritman and others from the School of the Art Institute to the academy, Director W. M. R. French was justified in fearing the potential of Werntz's entrepreneurial prowess. He was also justified in his anxiety over Werntz's continued alliance with Lawton Parker, whom he described that fall as one who "has the ear of the people most influential in the Art Institute."[43] Reacting to gossip as usual, a couple of months later French wrote a friend in Paris that Parker

Ill. 9-7. Louis Ritman. *Portrait of Wellington J. Reynolds.* 1906-7. Oil on canvas, 36 x 29 inches. The David and Alfred Smart Gallery, University of Chicago. Gift of the Estate of Louis Ritman, in memory of Wellington J. Reynolds.

had hoped "to be made a teacher in the school and aspires I am told, to the general directorship of the Art Institute."[44]

Not only did Parker have the ear of the Art Institute hierarchy, but he was also admired by students like Ritman and by other mature artists like Reynolds. One of these artists was Alson Skinner Clark, whose wealthy Chicago banking family had provided him with art training at the Art Institute, under Chase in New York, under Whistler, and at various other ateliers in Paris.[45] Apparently it was when Parker was teaching at the Chase School of Art in 1896 that Clark first met Parker, but by 1906 they had made many mutual friends in France and America. These included Frederick Frieseke and his wife Sadie, with whom Clark and his wife, Medora, had spent time in Paris and Giverny.[46] For the Annual Exhibition of American Artists, held at the Art Institute in October 1906, Clark chose to submit, not one of his impressionistic scenes, but a rather dark depiction of Chicago's State Street bridge in the winter, entitled *The Coffee House.* Clark's picture had a certain look of Robert Henri, not

Monet, but the image was praised by local critics, and the awards committee granted Clark the Martin B. Cahn Prize. Like his friend Parker, Clark traveled extensively between Chicago, New York, and Paris, and he, too, had the ear of many influential members of the local art community. Ritman would meet Clark later.

In 1907, Ritman had no way of knowing more about art than what he had learned from various members of the Chicago art community; he certainly knew little about Giverny. His enlightenment, as it were, came from stories and gossip he heard from teachers and students at the academy and from newspapers or periodicals. He read publications like the *Art Amateur, International Studio,* and the *Sketch Book* or *Brush and Pencil,* or the *Cow Bell.* These diverse "art sheets" provided excellent coverage of general trends, including even some news about art events other than exhibitions; but whether in Chicago or New York, students had little direct knowledge of the actual art industry or its foreign art colonies. Academy students were encouraged to read these publications, and Ritman was anxious to see them because they provided a great deal of information about faraway art communities.

In Chicago, Louis had no way of knowing, as Parker did, that in Giverny the master Monet was beginning on the second large series of *Paysages d'Eau* paintings. Only considerably later would Louis discover that some French critics found Monet's pictures overly decorative and lacking in profundity. Former Art Institute students like Parker, his friend Frieseke, and Buehr were glad to work near Monet, and although they were impressionists, they followed their own career paths, only a slim branch of which led toward Chicago. Parker, Rose, Miller, Perry, or the newcomer Edmund W. Greacen shipped their works to exhibitions in Chicago, indeed, all over America, as well as to the salons in Europe. Also, they all knew that in spite of their efforts to satisfy the American appetite for art, even the best shows in Chicago, Boston, Philadelphia, and New York were considered second-rate, compared with the salons in Paris.

When young Ritman overheard discussions about Paris, its famous salons, its bohemian areas and about Monet and Giverny, he could only hazily envision an expatriate artist's life in France. It would take several years for him to reach Giverny and experience the artistic ambience that existed there as nowhere else. Ritman was yet too young to appreciate the fascinating lifestyle that Edmund Greacen and his wife were just discovering in Giverny as they set up housekeeping in a cottage not far from Monet's. Indeed, like most of those who orbited around Monet, Greacen would seldom visit the master, but he would come to admire him. Greacen described

Monet as a "handsome, rugged, grey-bearded man with a keen blue eye, constantly smoking cigarettes that seemed about to disappear in his great beard and set it in flames." He described Giverny as a place of "outward contrasts and inward harmony," quoting a French visitor who had been amazed at all the bearded men drinking and arguing at the Hotel Baudy. The Frenchman noted the scene where *"un grand diable jouait de vieux airs américains que tout le monde reprenait a tue-tête"* ("a huge character played nostalgic American tunes, which everybody else in the place took up in accompaniment at the top of their voices").[47] American artists who had lived in Paris and Giverny could not adequately convey their experiences; they could only attempt to inspire young artists like Ritman, the boundaries of whose art experiences were strictly limited to Chicago.

Chicago's greatest competition was New York, where the National Academy of Design held its Eighty-Second Annual Exhibition in the spring of 1907, the first to be presented after the union of the Society of American Artists and the National Academy. As usual, a large catalog appeared and ample attempts followed to promote the show locally. The event was treated with lukewarm interest in the New York press, however, and few sales took place.[48] Angered over the response of the local press, Academy President Dielman queried: "Is it anything less than unblushing impudence that emboldens any newspaper writer on art and miscellaneous topics to set his individual judgement against that of thirty professional painters and sculptors [the jury] and to represent that body as incompetent, ignorant, or jealous and afraid to encourage new genius?"[49]

A surprisingly large number of expatriates had ceased sending their work to the National Academy shows in New York, concentrating instead on outlets in Europe. Like Parker, though, most of them maintained strong ties with friends in America. Chicago expatriates wrote to French, Reynolds, Vanderpoel, Parker, and many other associates at the Chicago Academy of Fine Arts and the Art Institute, informing them of the latest gossip and trends. Indeed, admirable attempts on the part of numerous Chicagoans, artists and otherwise, helped to maintain good communications with the expatriate art community in Paris. In addition to an official representative like Sara Hallowell, certain trustees of the Art Institute, like Hutchinson or Ryerson, spent a good deal of time commuting between Chicago and Paris.

Lawton Parker was one of the most traveled expatriates, but there were other Chicagoans, like Walter McEwen and the sculptor George Gray Barnard, who had been away from Chicago for many years. Once a struggling bohemian expatriate, Barnard left Kankakee,

Illinois, to study sculpture in Chicago and then in Paris. In order to support himself and to purchase costly materials, he found and sold medieval artifacts. Later he was highly praised by Rodin and won numerous high honors, including the coveted Gold Medal at the Paris Salon.[50] Like other Chicago artists, Barnard stayed in occasional contact with the Art Institute. At this time, he was waiting for an answer from Director French, who was enthusiastic about the "beautiful Gothic cloister" Barnard had offered to the Art Institute at a price of $15,000.[51]

Even as an isolated evening art student in Chicago, Ritman heard of the recently nicknamed *Fauves,* whose radical pictures had been seen in the *cage centrale, Salle VII* (main showroom, Hall 7), of the Salon d'Automne in Paris a couple of years earlier. Since then the growing movement had been refined and expanded by the Matisse circle, gathering around it a new group of avant-garde critics, not the least of whom was Guillaume Apollinaire. Therefore, by 1907 the term *Fauvism* was nearly as well known in the progressive Chicago art community as *impressionism.* Just as fauvism had been born with little warning, it died in the same way. For the most part, fauvism as a viable movement would play itself out that year, and Ritman would not come into real contact with it until later.

In spite of its untimely death, fauvism remained curiously influential and firmly established Matisse as the new leader of modern art. Numerous American critics thought that he had some strong competition from Pablo Picasso, a young Spaniard, about eight years older than Ritman. In April and May of 1907, Picasso was working on a painting now known as *Les Demoiselles d'Avignon* (Museum of Modern Art, New York). Only a few people had seen it at the opening of the Salon des Indépendants. Although Picasso's picture featured young women and may have been worked up from an allegorical theme, it implied a brothel nonetheless, and it was stylistically far different from anything Ritman could have ever seen in Chicago (ill. 9-8). Furthermore, he would not have been impressed with Picasso's picture. Nor would he have cared for the Fauves' recent work. As a protégé of Reynolds and a product of the conservative Chicago art-education community, young Ritman would have agreed with the French critic Vauxcelles who wrote in *Gil Blas* that fauvism had gone too far in ignoring all pictorial conventions except for the "nice outline" of the central motif.

As the spring exhibition season in Paris brought forth its comparisons and contrasts, so did the one in Chicago. What happened at the Art Institute Spring Salon of 1907 made little impact on the international art community

relative to that made by the Paris salons, but Chicagoans were impressed with the productivity of the past season. Actually, some local critics thought they recognized a certain progressive trend in all the impressionism they saw exhibited; others found little innovation, only routine purple shadows and "bad drawing."

As usual, the first and most important show of contemporary art in 1907 was the Eleventh Annual Chicago Artists' Exhibition, held in January and February as a joint venture by the Art Institute and the Municipal Art League. For years, the show committee had welcomed artists from a large surrounding area, and it was no different this season. According to records, the exhibition included "works in various media by 122 artists, 79 men, and 43 women."[52] Over 280 works were selected, from 818 submitted, by an elected jury of painters and sculptors. In retrospect, we see that the jury consisted of some of the best-known artists working in Chicago at the time: among the painters were Adam Emory Albright, Charles Francis Browne, Pauline Palmer, and John H. Vanderpoel; among the sculptors, Leonard Crunelle and Lorado Taft. Exactly how many works Louis Ritman submitted to the jury is unknown, but his catalog entry number 217, entitled *Indian Head*, was accepted for exhibition with a price listed of $40. Because artists were ranked alphabetically, Wellington J. Reynolds's work appeared in the catalog near Ritman's; there were four of his paintings, one of which seems to have been inspired by Sargent since it was entitled *Portrait of Mrs. X.*

After the close of the Chicago Artists' Exhibition, only a week went by before Ritman's work was shown to the Chicago art community again, this time at the Thirteenth

Ill. 9-8. The Trocadero Palace where Pablo Picasso was inspired by African sculpture at an ethnographic show in 1907. R. H. Love Galleries Archives, Chicago.

Annual Exhibition of the Art Students League of Chicago. The show opened on 1 March 1907, at the Art Institute and closed toward the end of the month. Following in Reynolds's footsteps, Ritman submitted only portraits, four of them in fact, including one of himself and another of his father, Solomon Ritman.[53] Out of the 165 works shown at the exhibition, only 7 were sold for an aggregate amount of $92.[54] Very little is known of Ritman's activity in the Art Students League of Chicago, but one must assume that his role was rather passive since records support little more than his participation in exhibitions. Since the late 1890s, the league exhibitions had been tightly bound to the Art Institute. Award winners at the 1907 show included well-known locals such as Karl Buehr, Lucy Hartrath, Lawton Parker, and Joseph Birren.

A perpetual need for funds existed at the Art Institute, and no one knew its financial condition better than Director French. Wealthy benefactors like the Palmers, Ryersons, Harrises, Goodmans, Hutchinsons, and a few others were usually quite generous, and it was no secret that their financial support formed the backbone of the institution. These were dynamic businessmen and financiers who knew how to make money, multiply it, manage it, save it, and give it. Frequently their wives were equally active in related matters. Because of their roles as trustees of the Art Institute, the opinions of these dynamic community leaders were highly regarded by William French and other institute administrators, even when it came to art matters. When the local and national economies flourished, so did the Art Institute because it was well supported by both the trustees and the public at large. With Chicago situated in the center of the nation and its production resting primarily on an agricultural-industrial base, Chicago's economy remained surprisingly autonomous and stable even in the face of national economic storms. Nevertheless, Director French, the trustees, the local art instructor, the merchant of art supplies, Ritman's foreman at Cusack's, and nearly everyone else in Chicago had real reason for concern about the future when on 13 March in 1907 prices on the New York Stock Exchange suddenly collapsed. Among the many explanations offered as to why the crash occurred, was the inordinate drain on the money supply caused by the Russo-Japanese War of 1905 and by the rebuilding of San Francisco following the earthquake. All in all, however, it seemed that this time Chicagoans faced an economic crisis along with all other Americans. Young Ritman knew very little about the grim details, but he remembered hearing predictions about "depression times again, like it was before the Fair."[55]

Ill. 9-9. Louis Ritman as a young student painting in his studio. Photograph. Courtesy of the Ritman Estate.

Meanwhile, the American art community would be affected directly or indirectly by the complex socioeconomic conditions that prevailed in 1907. Soon a Franco-Japanese treaty would be signed which guaranteed both France and Japan an "open door" access. President Theodore Roosevelt showed grave concern for the problem of anti-Japanese agitation on the West Coast, much of which was being fostered by labor unions that were hostile toward Japanese laborers. It was also at this time that the French newspaper *Le Matin* promoted the first long-distance motorcar race from Peking to Paris. On the other side of the English Channel, Britain's Cunard Line was preparing the huge S. S. *Lusitania* for her maiden voyage in September.[56] In America the United Press was founded to compete with the Associated Press, and Rube Goldberg began as a cartoonist for the *New York Evening Journal*. In Washington, DC, the Union Station, designed by Chicago architect Daniel Burnham, was nearing completion. Modeled on the Baths of Diocletian and the Arch of Constantine in Rome, the structure prompted a good deal of critical comment. Another Chicagoan, the trial lawyer Clarence S. Darrow, was preparing his defense of "Big Bill" Haywood, who, as leader of the Western Federation of Miners, was accused of complicity in the murder of former Idaho Governor Frank R. Stennenberg. Many Chicagoans had no use for Darrow, but he was known as a person who cared about "the little guy."

During the entire year of 1907, Ritman strove harder than ever before to master the elusive qualities of the pictorial conventions he had been taught over the years. Working his canvas up from the direct charcoal sketch, he laid in the basic planes of the figural forms and any surrounding objects with thin color washes (ill. 9-9); in this way tonal values were established early in the painting procedure. For several years already he had practiced painting still lifes and interiors in an attempt to place his portraits and occasional genre subjects into more interesting surroundings. It was Wellington Reynolds who had insisted that his subjects be depicted in the proper pictorial environment: "In no place in life," he told his student, "is man or woman disassociated from the tell-tale arrangement of clothes or the equally potent testimony of their haunts." Reynolds pointed out to Louis and others that "the portrait head against an empty background is outside of nature's plan of doing things. Mirrors and vases of flowers, books or drapery, lovely woman in her boudoir or the scholar in his library give color and meaning."[57] Actually, Louis paid little attention to the scholar in his library, but the rest of Reynolds's dictum served as an inflexible rule in the making of his imagery for at least the next twenty-five years. It was as though Reynolds had forced his young student to sign an irrevocable contract to pursue his imagery as outlined above, including the repetitious employment of singular motifs such as the mirror or vase of flowers. In many ways, from this point on, Louis's direction in art was permanently set, and he would not deviate from it under any circumstances. By this time, also, it was no more or less difficult for him to work up a "tea service" or a reflection in a mirror from the delicate hues of a turpentine wash on canvas than it was to use the same process in achieving a convincing nude form or a full-length portrait of a fashionably dressed lady. Reynolds convinced his young student that a truly successful painter was capable of combining technique, draftsmanship, and expression. The master believed in the subjective, a special quality allied to an artistic imagination without which art failed in its purpose. For young Ritman the problem was neither a misunderstanding of Reynolds's credo, nor a lack of technical skill, but rather a need for diversity; his choice of subjects became limited, repetitious, and routine, regardless of how he altered the settings. Ritman found that the Chicago art reservoir contained little variety, and that his own art began to look the same as everyone else's. It was time for a new experience, but none seemed imminent. Even at this point in his life, Ritman's greatest asset was his ambition, his drive to continually seek a higher plateau of achievement. He had little doubt but that he could stand on the next rung, although he was not always sure about how to reach for it.

Unable to find sufficient time for a more sustained effort in solving his painting problems, Louis felt hemmed in. He was ready to advance, but working at Cusack's during the day allowed only a few precious evening hours for study at the Chicago Academy of Fine Arts. It became impossible to set aside time for the arcades or baseball with friends. Time existed only for work and art; if he was unsure about that routine, his family reminded him of his responsibilities. Reynolds and others were anxious to help, but they also realized how important it was for Louis to help support his family. Like Louis, Solomon Ritman worked long hours each day. Having progressed beyond the rank of ordinary tailor, he now worked with unique suit fabrics, designing and marking them for patterns. Solomon also cut special decorative embroidered fabrics that were made for wholesalers. On occasion, Louis would express his admiration for some of the fabrics he saw his father work on at home. He also watched him make pencil designs for fabric patterns.[58]

Early in 1907, a solution appeared to Louis's plight: Lawton Parker, who had not been principal of Werntz's Chicago Academy of Fine Arts for over three years now, was "called in to judge a concours for a year's tuition at the Academy." Werntz, Reynolds, Parker, and others on the staff of the Academy had been convinced that concours, especially those which carried scholarship awards, not only motivated students but also prepared them for the rigors of the grueling competition they would face in the professional world of fine art, specifically in New York and Europe. Perhaps no one championed the credo of competition more than did Lawton Parker, who had lamented earlier that "competition—the keynote of the whole question [of teaching art]—is generally disregarded." Moreover, Parker, who had spent two separate stints at the Ecole des Beaux-Arts and at the Julian Academy, believed strongly in "the atelier system, where each professor can have the absolute direction of his own classes, and where competition is made for the basis of advancement."[59] Unfortunately for Louis, Parker would not be teaching at the academy, since he had already agreed to resume instruction with Robert Henri at William Merritt Chase's School of Art in New York. Parker's move followed French's consistent refusal to hire him as a teacher at the School of the Art Institute.

Louis submitted pictures to the academy competition exhibition, and Parker awarded him the tuition scholarship. This award was not only a high achievement in itself, but it would also result in a significant change in Louis's life. Also, for the first time, Louis Ritman came to the attention of Lawton Parker, a famous artist as far as the winner was concerned.

Notes

1. Russell Sturgis, "The Recent Comparative Exhibition of Native and Foreign Art," *Scribner's Magazine*, XXXVII, no. 2 (February 1905), p. 253.

2. Charles Morice, *Mercure de France*, 15 April 1905.

3. The bibliography for this topic, the Fauves, is voluminous. Nonetheless, one relatively recent publication exploring the whole scope of the movement is Marcel Giry, *Fauvism: Origins and Development* (New York: Alpine Fine Arts, 1982); see also Charles Chasse, *Les Fauves et leur temps* (Lausanne-Paris: Bibliothèque des Arts, 1963); Bernard Dorival, "Fauves: The Wild Beasts Tamed," *Art News Annual,* 1952-53; and Henri Dorra, "The Wild Beasts: Fauvism and Its Affinities at the Museum of Modern Art," *Art Journal*, XXXVI, I (Fall 1976).

4. Maurice Ritman, interview with Richard Love, September 1987, R. H. Love Galleries Archives, Chicago.

5. Art Institute of Chicago, *Catalogue of Students 1905-06*, Louis Ritman: Evening Class, life, p. 159.

6. Jack Cowart and Juan Hamilton, *Georgia O'Keeffe: Art and Letters*, exhibition catalog (Washington, DC: National Gallery of Art, 1987), p. 291.

7. The Chicago Academy of Design, where Vanderpoel studied, was not the institution which Ritman later attended. Several trustees of the Chicago Academy of Design resigned and formed the Chicago Academy of Fine Arts in 1879. In 1882 the name of the Chicago Academy of Fine Arts was changed to the Art Institute of Chicago. It was about this time that the Chicago Academy of Design ceased to exist, but its collection had been purchased by the new academy led by George Armour, Levi Z. Leiter, Charles L. Hutchinson, and Marshall Field. Ritman, however, studied at the Chicago Academy of Fine Arts, which was founded by Carl N. Werntz in 1902.

8. John H. Vanderpoel, *The Human Figure* (Chicago: The Inland Printer Co., 1907). Nearly all of the original drawings used by Vanderpoel in this series and in the other publications form part of the permanent collection of the Beverly Arts Center in Chicago.

9. Robert P. Vanderpoel was born in Chicago on 10 January 1894. He graduated from Wendell Phillips High School and received a Ph.D. from the University of Chicago in 1916. In the 1920s, he served as financial editor of the *Chicago Daily Journal*.

10. With reference to French's refusing to invite Parker to faculty meetings, see W. M. R. French to Lawton Parker, Chicago, 6 December 1902, Director WMRF, Letter Book, October 26, 1902 – July 7, 1903, General Correspondence, Art Institute of Chicago Archives, Chicago, pp. 188, 360.

11. W. M. R. French to Sara Hallowell, Paris, 4 March 1905, Director WMRF, Letter Book, November 5, 1904-March 29, 1905, p. 634.

12. W. M. R. French to Sara Hallowell, 28 August 1905, Director WMRF, Letter Book, March 30, 1905-August 29, 1905, p. 735.

13. Mary Cassatt to W. M. R. French, 4 December 1904, quoted in Frederick A. Sweet, *Miss Mary Cassatt: Impressionist from Pennsylvania* (Norman, OK: University of Oklahoma Press, 1966), p. 168.

14. Lena M. McCauley, *Chicago Tribune*, 22 October 1904.

15. W. M. R. French to Mary Cassatt, Paris, 1 March 1905, Director WMRF, Letter Book, November 5, 1904-March 29, 1905, p. 601.

16. W. M. R. French to George W. Wheatley & Co., Paris, 16 August 1906, Director WMRF, Letter Book, May 8, 1906-December 7, 1906, p. 669.

17. W. M. R. French, "The Art School of the Art Institute of Chicago," *The Sketch Book*, II, no. 6 (July 1903), p. 7.

18. C. B. Berry, *Chicago* (1892), quoted in Harold M. Mayer and Richard C. Wade, *Chicago: Growth of a Metropolis* (Chicago: The University of Chicago Press, 1969), p. 134.

19. According to Wiley J. Phillips, chairman of the White Slave Traffic Committee, no less than 278 girls under the age of 15 were rescued from Levee houses of prostitution during a two-month period in 1907. Apparently Chicago was the headquarters of the illegal slave traffic.

20. W. M. R. French to N. H. Carpenter, Chicago, 14 February 1906, Director WMRF, Letter Book, August 29, 1905-May 7, 1906, p. 670.

21. Frederick Dielman, quoted in Eliot Clark, *History of the National Academy of Design, 1825-1953* (New York: Columbia University Press, 1954), p. 163.

22. W. M. R. French to Howard Pyle, Wilmington, DE, 10 July 1905, Director WMRF, Letter Book, March 30, 1905-August 29, 1905, p. 479.

23. For a comprehensive discussion of the Art Students League of Chicago, see Martha S. Baker, "The Art Students League," *Brush & Pencil*, 1, no. 3 (December 1897), pp. 61-77.

24. Florence N. Levy, ed., *American Art Annual 1905-1906* (New York: American Art Annual, Inc., 1905), p. 292.

25. Levy, *American Art Annual, 1910-1911* (New York: American Art Annual, Inc., 1911), vol. VIII, pp. 48-49.

26. The Art Institute had lent its student list to the business offices of the *Sketch Book*. Allegedly, an employee of this periodical sold the list to the manager of the Academy of Fine Arts. The academy used the list to mail "confidential circulars" to all the students of the Art Institute. W. M. R. French to F. C. Bartlett, May 26, 1905, Chicago, Director WMRF, Letter Book, March 30, 1905-August 29, 1905, p. 250.

27. Alphonse Marie Mucha was born in Ivancice, Czechoslovakia, in 1860 and died in 1939. An illustrator and theatrical designer, Mucha scored his first success by creating posters that advertised Sarah Bernhardt and her roles.

28. W. M. R. French to Frederick Richardson, Bronxville, New York, 10 February 1906, Director WMRF, Letter Book, August 29, 1905-May 7, 1906, p. 657.

29. Ibid.

30. Ibid., W. M. R. French to Durand-Ruel, March 1906, Chicago.

31. Born in Pittsburgh on 8 December 1839, A. J. Cassatt was trained as a civil engineer and served with the Pennsylvania Railroad System from 1861 to 1906. He died on 28 December 1906.

32. Berkman's prison sentence stemmed from an attempt on Frick's life during the Homestead Strike of 1892.

33. Stanford White (1853-1906) was born in New York, the son of Richard G. White. Gatrill J. Richardson was the architectural firm White worked with until about 1872. After 1880, he collaborated closely with Charles F. McKim and W. R. Mead to form the firm McKim, Meade & White. Applying different styles, White designed luxurious homes, churches, clubs, and a few larger buildings. He was famous for the decorative features he created for wealthy clients. White was an exceedingly visible member of the progressive side of the New York art community.

34. *New York Herald*, 27 June 1906.

35. After Altman's death in 1913, his $20 million collection would be bequeathed to the Metropolitan Museum of Art. It contained Chinese enamels and porcelains and paintings by Botticelli, Filippo Lippi, Holbein, Rembrandt, and others. For the so-called modern pictures, which were mostly French, see *Bulletin of the Metropolitan Museum of Art,* IX, no. 12 (December 1914), pp. 252-56.

36. Werntz offered scholarships and monthly cash prizes. There were special classes for public school pupils. Class fees ranged from two dollars to fifteen dollars per month. See Levy, *American Art Annual, 1905-06*, p. 293.

37. For an interesting discussion of this topic, see Michael Quick and Eberhard Ruhmer, *Munich & American Realism in the 19th Century*, exhibition catalog (Sacramento, CA: E. B. Crocker Art Gallery, 1978).

38. Hollósy's Hungarian compatriots established a summer art school at Nagybanya in Transylvania, a province of Hungary at the time. This summer school was the equivalent of an American New England art colony and marked the origins of modernism in Hungarian art. See Antal Kampis, *The History of Art in Hungary*, trans. Lily Halapy (Budapest, Hungary: Corvina Press, 1966), pp. 289-90.

39. For information regarding Maurice Ritman's activity in the art community, see Louise Dunn Yochim, *Role and Impact: The Chicago Society of Artists* (Chicago: Chicago Society of Artists, 1979).

40. Reynolds, quoted in L. C. McCauley, "Wellington J. Reynolds — Painter," *The Sketch Book*, V, no. 7 (May 1906), p. 336.

41. Ibid., p. 334.

42. This work is a finished oil-on-canvas portrait intended for display. Extant small oil sketches are "cigar box top" studies, not finished major works.

43. W. M. R. French to Mr. Sammons, Chicago, 28 August 1906, Director WMRF, Letter Book, May 8, 1906-December 7, 1906, p. 406.

44. Ibid., W. M. R. French to Caroline D. Wade, Paris, 26 October 1906, p. 752.

45. Jean Stern, *Alson S. Clark* (Los Angeles, CA: Petersen Publishing Co., 1983). This study is based on the biography of Clark by his wife, Medora Clark.

46. Clark and Frieseke traded similar portraits of their wives as wedding gifts in France. A. S. Clark and Atta Medora McMullin were married in Watertown in 1902. Frieseke and Sarah Ann O'Bryan were married in 1905.

47. Elizabeth Greacen Knudsen, *Edmund W. Greacen, NA: American Impressionist, 1876-1949: A Biography*, exhibition catalog (Jacksonville, FL: The Cummer Gallery, 1972), p. 9.

48. Sales yielded $12,050 from the exhibition. See Eliot Clark, *History of the National Academy of Design, 1825-1953*, p. 162.

49. Ibid., p. 163.

50. For more on Barnard's achievements, see Harold E. Dickson, "Barnard's Sculptures for the Pennsylvania Capitol," *The Art Quarterly*, XXII, no. 2 (Summer 1959), pp. 127-147.

51. This is the now-famous Saint Guilhem Cloister, which, after Art Institute Trustee Hutchinson decided against its acquisition, was purchased for the Metropolitan Museum of Art and is now enclosed in a large structure on the Hudson River in Fort Tryon Park in New York. See W. M. R. French to D. C. French, Chicago, 12 December 1906, Director WMRF, Letter Book, December 7, 1906-August 2, 1907, pp. 27-28. See also Harold E. Dickson, "The Origin of the 'Cloisters,'" *The Art Quarterly*, XXVIII, no. 4 (1965), pp. 253-274.

52. The Art Institute of Chicago, *Catalogue of an Exhibition of Works by Chicago Artists*, January 29-February 24, 1907.

53. The Art Students League of Chicago, *Thirteenth Annual Exhibition Catalogue,* 1-24 March 1907. Ritman's catalog entries were listed as numbers 116 through 119. The portrait of Solomon Ritman is unknown since it is no longer extant and photographs have been lost.

54. Ibid.

55. Maurice Ritman, interview with Richard Love, September 1987.

56. The *Lusitania* was the largest liner that had been built until that time; she weighed 31,550 tons and measured 790 feet in length, had 4 screw propellers, and could carry 2,000 passengers and a crew of 600.

57. McCauley, "Wellington J. Reynolds — Painter," p. 337.

58. Maurice Ritman, interview with Richard Love , September 1987.

59. Mrs. George, "Lawton Parker, Artist," an unpublished compilation of facts about Lawton Parker, derived from various newspaper clippings, p. 4, R. H. Love Galleries Archives, Chicago.

CHAPTER TEN:
A PASSION FOR EXCELLENCE

Ritman's multiple commitments had resulted in a "real struggle for an artistic career."[1] The scholarship award at the Chicago Academy of Fine Arts meant that he had to give up his job at Cusack's and concentrate on his studies: "Although he was the chief support of the family, his parents willingly made the sacrifice of allowing him to attend the day classes at the Academy, thus giving up his position as a street sign painter" and, of course, his income. The opportunity may have looked promising to Louis and his parents, but apparently his leaving Cusack's was considered foolhardy by other people close to him: "Such recklessness thought the busybodies, who felt they knew him sufficiently well to inform him that his success in obtaining the scholarship had gone to his head a bit. Why give up a seven-dollars-a-day job for the possibility of some day becoming an artist? For a sensitive lad such criticism is none too easy to take and but for the loyal faith in him, which his own parents had, young Ritman might have lost courage."[2]

Out of necessity, Louis had learned to be practical in his pursuit of an art career. He once said that "it is more important to be an artist than to look like one."[3] Louis knew only too well that there were no rich uncles, no trusts, no nestegg funds that could keep him in front of an easel instead of a signboard. He was painfully aware that if he was to succeed, he would have to make the most

of his year at the academy; there would be no second opportunity. Under these circumstances he was probably a good deal better off at Werntz's academy than at the Art Institute, because the smaller academy classes allowed Reynolds and other instructors to spend more time with each individual, and because Werntz's insistence on pragmatism about the commercial aspects of fine art in his school spelled rapid advance in studies. Ritman and other students who had no time for pedantics were impressed with Werntz's promise that the academy would always cut "out frills, [keep] its feet on the ground, and [make] its classes as much like real professional life as possible."[4]

From the start, Louis "showed genius that amazed the instructors" at the academy. It appears that his prodigious talent and reserved manner also impressed other students. Among Louis's admirers was Rebecca Kruttschnitt, a painter herself and later a writer of some local reputation. Rebecca was one of the four children of E. Minna Koch and Julius Kruttschnitt, a wealthy Jewish family. It is not known whether Louis and Rebecca were more than good friends, but it is reported that she helped him obtain portrait commissions, possibly through her father's many connections in Chicago as vice president of the Union Pacific Railroad and Ore Shore Line Railroad.[5] An older individual who became an ardent promoter of young Ritman was Peter C. Stohr, an associate of Julius Kruttschnitt's at Ore Shore Line Railroad. Both Stohr and Kruttschnitt are said to have recommended Louis for portrait commissions while he was still at the academy. Apparently they also helped him sell landscapes (none have been located), thus providing much needed funds to continue his studies at the academy. In setting prices for his portrait commissions, Louis received advice from Reynolds and perhaps even Parker, both of whom had clients sit for them at their studios in the Tree Studio Building on State Street. Of course, Louis could not get prices that compared with those commanded by Parker, Reynolds, and other professionals, such as Ralph Clarkson at the Fine Arts Building and Frederick Freer on Ontario Street. Occasionally, these artists charged as much as $1,000 for a finished likeness; other artists charged as little as $100. Louis's prices are unknown.[6]

Those who were present at the grand opening of the thousand-room Plaza Hotel in New York on 1 October might have assumed that the American economy had recovered and that all was well. Just the opposite was true, however, as seen in the panic of October 1907, which was brought on by rash speculation, overdrawn credit, and the lack of a federal banking system. Many business leaders across the nation, including some who were involved with the Art Institute, called President Roosevelt their "chief panic-maker." The president countered by saying that the problem was not simply national in scope and warned certain "malefactors of great wealth," who he believed were attempting to discredit him and his sound policies. To certain trustees of the Art Institute, the panic was alarming; but to young Ritman, who was willing to paint a portrait for a very reasonable fee, the crash was of little consequence. The young artist had no way of knowing that Roosevelt had called the ailing J. Pierpont Morgan out of semiretirement in Richmond to New York to straighten out the crooked economy. Financial leaders everywhere, including the Secretary of the Treasury George Courtelyon, bowed to Morgan's expertise.

In November 1907 many American newspapers ran stories about the Wright Brothers of Dayton who claimed that they had flown more than 24 miles. In a report to the Aero Club, the Wright brothers stated: "Even in the existing state of the art, it is easy to design a practical and durable flyer that will carry operator and fuel for a flight of more than 500 miles at fifty miles an hour." As the world concerned itself with flight and "aeroplanes," J. P. Morgan virtually became the financial dictator of the United States.

In Chicago, under Reynolds's watchful eye, Ritman worked during the winter of 1907-8, executing canvases for the following spring season. It was his first year of full-time productivity. He worked on numerous canvases;

unfortunately, however, nearly all of these are unlocated and known only through family records and scant titular references in catalogs. In the past, Louis had profited from words of encouragement coming not only from Reynolds but occasionally from Lawton Parker. For the past several months, however, Parker had been in Europe and, more recently, at the New York School of Art, which had changed so drastically under Robert Henri's guidance that its founder, William Merritt Chase, decided to resign and return to the Art Students League in New York City.[7] Parker's views of the controversial situation are unknown, but he knew that Chase could not tolerate Henri's anarchistic teaching methodology. At the time of his departure, Chase told a reporter that he feared someone would "mistake violence for strength."[8] Parker, who had fought French's "old fogey" ways at the Art Institute, probably aligned himself a bit less with Chase than with Henri, who said that the older master was jealous and "bitter about the way the students of the school have flocked to my classes."[9] Apparently, Parker would have preferred to teach at the School of the Art Institute; thus, the chief reason for his teaching in New York was French's continuous refusal to hire him at the institute.

Earlier in 1907 Reynolds took Ritman to visit Parker at his spacious studio, located down the hall from his own in the Tree Studio Building. Parker seldom stayed in the Tree Studio complex very long at one time, but Frederick Freer and Pauline Palmer had maintained studios there since the first years of its existence, and Reynolds had been there since 1897; his corner studio, which looked west on State Street and north on Ontario Street, was number 28 at the top of the north stairs (see axonometric ill. 10-1). It was larger than most, but all of the second-floor studios on the west side had twelve-foot-high ceilings and wood-burning fireplaces.[10] Situated in the hallway wall near each studio door was a recessed, lockable display box for the presentation of the tenant's art. This method of showing allowed prospective clients to see at least one example of each artist's work as they strolled through the hall. Because many nonartists visited the building — for portrait sittings, for meeting an artist, or for some other business matter — a sign was posted in the hall: "In Consideration of Visitors all models are required to wear a garment when leaving the studio to walk to the bathroom." Because there had always been many painters in the Tree Studios, the building continued to serve as a kind of informal gathering spot — Parker's and Reynolds's studios always had visitors. Artists felt very comfortable at Tree Studios; they knew that it was really their own building even though they paid rent. Any of them could recall many a pleasant winter afternoon spent painting with a friend near a crackling fire while the falling snow

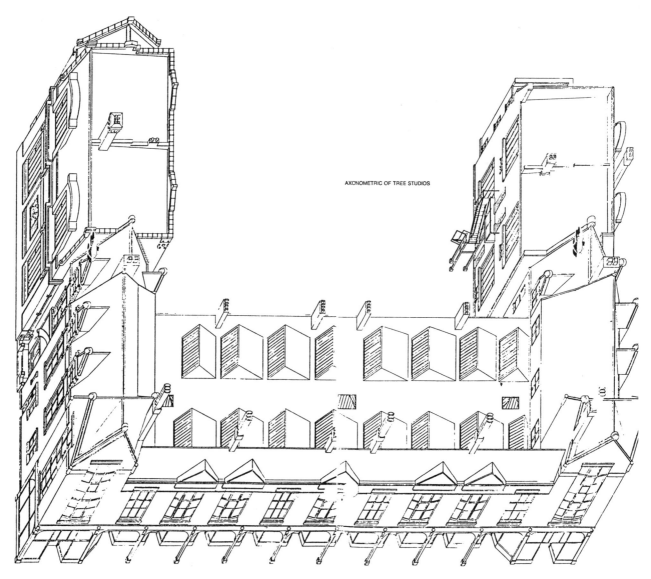

AXCNOMETRIC OF TREE STUDIOS

Ill. 10-1. Axonometric view of the Tree Studio Building, Chicago. R. H. Love Galleries Archives, Chicago.

cushioned the sound of horses' hooves on the street below. In the summer, the enclosed courtyard (ill. 10-2) behind the studios was a delightful area for lunch or for simply sitting and chatting while the busy city rumbled on outside. When the weather permitted, Ritman, Reynolds, and other artists often sat on the stone benches and discussed art.

In the spring of 1907 Parker had suggested to Hutchinson and several other trustees at the Art Institute that a group of pictures by French artists be selected each year from the Paris Salon for a Chicago exhibition. Because Parker and French were still adversaries as far as exhibi-

tions at the Art Institute were concerned, there was little cooperation, so the plan crumbled. Parker was irate, telling friends privately that he wanted nothing more to do with French or the Art Institute of Chicago. Of course, the situation irritated French; however, later that fall he had little choice but to write to trustee N. W. Harris in Lake Geneva, Wisconsin, requesting Parker's recent portrait of Harris for the Annual Exhibition of American Paintings.[11] Trustee Hutchinson, who was usually impressed with Parker, as were most of the other trustees, suggested that French also borrow Parker's portrait of M. A. Ryerson for the show. French did so, and in both

Ill. 10-2. Enclosed courtyard in the back of the Tree Studio Building, Chicago. Photograph. R. H. Love Galleries Archives, Chicago.

good."[15] Most artists at the Tree Studios, including Ritman, sided with Parker.

On 4 February 1908, the Art Institute and the Municipal Art League presented its Twelfth Annual Exhibition of "Works by Chicago Artists." This time the selection jury consisted of artists outside the Art Institute hierarchy—in fact, even the ever-present John Vanderpoel was not a member. On the other hand, Louis's teacher Wellington J. Reynolds was on the jury, as was the impressionist John F. ("Long John") Stacey and Adolph R. Shulz.[16] The balance of the jury consisted of F. C. Bartlett, W. M. Clute, and Edgar S. Cameron. The exhibition reflected the collective opinion of these relatively "outside" artists, who were even more discriminating than previous juries: out of nearly 1,000 entries, they selected only one-third—330 to be exact. Louis, one of the 121 artists who submitted work to the exhibition—and certainly one of the youngest—entered one painting entitled *Girl in Brown* , a typical subject for a Reynolds student.

More than Ritman himself, Reynolds perceived the potential of his young student's extraordinary skill in art. Actually, the presence of a prodigious talent like Louis's was an asset to both Reynolds and the Chicago Academy of Fine Arts. Indeed, if the school and the teacher could attract students like Louis Ritman, they would have little difficulty appealing to less talented ones. Nonetheless, it was also important that Louis make progress, and everyone interested in his career agreed that his next step should be to study elsewhere, probably on the East Coast. Some suggested New York; others Philadelphia or perhaps Boston. Louis was eager to study in the East, but without a scholarship, such a goal would be unattainable: it was difficult enough to study full-time in Chicago, let alone to find funds with which to travel. Louis was only too aware of his own predicament, but he was also very determined to succeed. At Reynolds's and Parker's urging, then, he submitted his work in a scholarship competition at the Pennsylvania Academy of the Fine Arts in Philadelphia, where William Merritt Chase was still a resident professor. There was little else Ritman could do if he really intended to study in an East Coast art school, since the small amount of money he had saved would not be enough for full tuition and expenses. Moreover, he had learned the value of competition from Parker, Reynolds, and others at the academy, so that competing for a scholarship was quite in line with everything he had been taught about getting along in the art world. Perhaps even more exciting was the wonderful possibility of his studying under the great William Merritt Chase in Philadelphia (ill. 10-3).[17]

During the late spring and early summer of 1908, Chicago swirled with activities surrounding the National

instances pointed out that the portraits would not be submitted to the jury.[12] In November, French wrote to Parker that he had "the pleasure of informing [him] that the Cahn Prize of $100 for the best painting in the Annual Exhibition by a Chicago painter has been awarded to you for your picture entitled, 'Portrait of Mr. M.A. Ryerson.'"[13] French made every effort to thwart Parker's relationship with trustees of the Art Institute, but the artist was simply too highly regarded. Indeed, French was even instructed to ask Parker if he still wished to mount a one-man show at the Art Institute.[14] The whole Chicago art community, including Ritman, knew how angry Parker was with French and the institute; indeed, he was even upset with Chicago! Before the turn of the year, Assistant Director N. H. Carpenter, not French, wrote to Parker in New York, asking whether he wanted "to be considered a Chicago artist" for exhibition purposes. Carpenter explained that "some of the artists [at the institute] say that you told them you were leaving the city for

Republican Convention. For over a year Charles Evans Hughes of New York had been considered a front-runner for the presidential nomination, but in recent months, President Roosevelt had backed his secretary of war William Howard Taft. Louis was far more immersed in art than in politics, but he and most Chicagoans could not help but be impressed with the excitement the convention brought to the city. After weeks of preparation, the convention was assembled. On the morning of 18 June, nomination speeches began. When the parades, cheers, flag-waving speeches, and constant deal making was over, the delegates chose William H. Taft as their candidate for the fall election. From Oyster Bay, President Roosevelt would soon write to Taft, "You are now the leader and there must be nothing that looks like self-depreciation or undue subordination of yourself."[18]

It was during the Republican Convention of 1908 that Louis learned that he had been awarded the William L. Elkins tuition scholarship to the Pennsylvania Academy of the Fine Arts in Philadelphia.[19] With this exciting news, Louis became even more keen about studying there. He even thought it might be possible to work under Chase during what he had learned would be the master's last term in Philadelphia in 1908-9. Officially, Louis was not scheduled to begin classes until October. This gave him an opportunity to gather more funds, which would allow him to go to Philadelphia ahead of time to arrange for lodging and to visit the academy. He also planned to visit Boston and, if possible, New York. With this idea in mind, he recruited Norbert Heerman, who had been his fellow student at the Art Institute, to join him on his tour. Heerman was from a wealthy family, and may have lent his friend some money to make the trip, or Ritman may have received a loan from the Kruttschnitts or C. P. Stohr. Louis and Norbert were inexperienced but wildly enthusiastic. The plan to move to Philadelphia was the next and largest step thus far in Louis's pursuit of an art career. To study in Philadelphia meant that he had to sacrifice the security of family life and warm friendships at the Art Institute and at the Chicago Academy of Fine Arts for a commitment to the risky quest of art. Even at this early age Louis probably realized that in time he could easily join the ranks of local hopefuls whose pictures had dominated — and would continue to dominate — Chicago exhibitions and go no further. He did not want to become another "local artist," however; he wanted to become a great American painter who would enjoy the recognition from the international art community since this was the career for which his teachers had been preparing him. Louis wanted to be an artist like Chase, McEwen, Parker, Frieseke, Miller, and many others from the Midwest who never severed their

Ill. 10-3. William Merritt Chase. Photograph. R. H. Love Galleries Archives, Chicago.

ties to Chicago but had expanded their professional activities far beyond its restrictive boundaries.

The fine arts community of Chicago, for all of its efforts to project an image of progressiveness, had become a *milieu retardataire* when its accomplishments were compared with those in the sister arts of theater, literature, architecture, and now even motion pictures. Unlike the great innovators in other fields who found adequate local support for their productions, Chicago painters and sculptors were obliged to go to Europe to find success. Although Chicago artists could find conditions that were somewhat better in New York, but eventually, even the most determined patriot made his way across the Atlantic to join the burgeoning American expatriate crowd in Europe. Indeed, in his last presidential address to the National Academy of Design less than a decade earlier, Thomas Wood had lamented the foremost cause of expatriation when he said: "The large sums paid in this country to foreign painters . . . and the meagre support given to our own artists by Americans, is rather discouraging to American art." In spite of the bleak outlook, Wood tried to look ahead to Ritman's day, urging his fellow artists to "hope and pray that the patriotism of this country may in time extend even to the Art of our own land."[20] So it was that at this time Chicago could support writers like Floyd Dell, Upton Sinclair, and Witter Bynner; architects like Frank Lloyd Wright; theaters like the Garrick and the Cliff Dwellers; and even pioneer motion-picture makers like William Selig and George Spoor, but the city could not support a William Merritt Chase, Frederick Frieseke, Lawton Parker, or even a Louis Ritman, for that matter.[21]

It is no wonder that Louis hoped to study under William Merritt Chase. In spite of the recent controversy generated by his run-in with Henri, the master's gilt-edged reputation as a teacher had been indelibly impressed upon the Chicago art community since his solo show and his teaching stint with Frank Duveneck (ill. 10-4) at the Art Institute of Chicago in 1897. At that time Chase had taken a leave of absence from the Pennsylvania Academy to set up the exhibition and to teach in Chicago. Chicagoans, including Potter Palmer, who added five works to the show, were unanimous in their high appreciation of Chase's work. One enthusiastic critic went so far as to say that his presence "instilled new life and vigor into the art interests of the West."[22] Students in Philadelphia complained so vehemently about his absence, however, that Chase returned to the Pennsylvania Academy after only one session at the Art Institute.[23] In addition to the fact that Chase was actually a Hoosier and maintained many lifelong friendships in Chicago, both Reynolds and Vanderpoel were his fans and encouraged Louis to study under him. Of course, Parker believed Chase to be nothing less than one of America's great masters, an opinion he imparted frequently to others.

Even if Louis were not to study under Chase, matriculation at the Pennsylvania Academy would be excellent: the institution was one of the nation's foremost promoters of American impressionism, the only art Louis admired almost as much as he did academic painting. The majority of the 500 pictures in the One Hundred Third Annual Exhibition, held at the academy a couple of months earlier in 1908, had shown greater or lesser influences of impressionism. The coveted Temple Gold Medal had been awarded to Frank W. Benson for his *Portrait of My Three Daughters*, an outstanding example of figurative impressionism. Later that spring, the Pennsylvania Academy presented the annual exhibition of works by The Ten. By this time, J. H. Twachtman's place in this elitist society of American impressionists had been filled by Chase. Paintings that would soon be purchased for the permanent collection included some superb examples of impressionism by former members of the Giverny group: *Twin Birches* by Willard Metcalf, *The Crimson Rambler* by Philip L. Hale, and *Winter at Ipswich* by Theodore

Wendel.[24] Meanwhile, Chase was in Florence, Italy, where he was working on a self-portrait for the Uffizi Gallery.

Back in Chicago, it became quite apparent to W. M. R. French that the School of the Art Institute was in need of a well-known and highly respected teacher, not necessarily one of Chase's caliber but a leading figure in the American art community, hopefully an expatriate from Paris. Under no circumstances would he hire Parker, but he did favor one of the Giverny expatriates or their like. French's chief instructor, John H. Vanderpoel, had been residing in Montparnasse at 72 rue Notre Dame des Champs for quite some time, so French enlisted his assistance in his search for a teacher: "I want very much," he wrote, "to get hold of some good man to cooperate with you and strengthen our painting from the nude."[25] Continuing, French reported: "I hear you think greatly of Mr. [Richard] Miller. Will you please ask him if he would consider coming to Chicago and enlisting in our school. Of course I do not expect a man like him to give

Ill. 10-4. Frank Duveneck. Photograph. R. H. Love Galleries Archives, Chicago.

anything like his whole time to the school, but I believe a really good painter could accomplish something very fine here." Referring to various talents, French reminded Vanderpoel that the School of the Art Institute had "students sufficiently advanced to profit by the best instruction." As director, he was only too aware that the loss of students like Ritman would continue without a well-known master of figure painting. "We have nobody," he wrote, "corresponding to Tarbell, Benson, Chase, and Miss Beaux as teachers. I want to attach some strong man to us and bring the school up on this side . . . . I believe it is true in America as it is in Paris that a man's reputation is much increased by his students — for example, Tarbell and Chase."

Regardless of French's good intentions to hire a major impressionist like Miller who specialized in figure subjects, the fact remained that at that moment he had no one of the rank he sought. Actually, French's request was born out of a certain naiveté, since a highly successful expatriate such as Miller would have been foolish to trade his place in the bright limelight of the Parisian art scene for a teaching spot in Chicago — especially after Parker had told him about his experiences with French. Indeed, it had always been difficult to lure a highly successful painter from New York or Paris to teach in Chicago. Therefore, to many observers it seemed logical that Parker, who was very active in New York, Paris, and Giverny, and who considered Chicago his home, should be offered

Ill. 10-5. Old Dearborn Street Station at the turn of the century, Chicago. Chicago Historical Society.

Ill. 10-6. Edmund Charles Tarbell. *In the Orchard.* Oil on canvas, 60¼ x 65 inches. Private Collection. Courtesy Vose Galleries, Boston.

the teaching job. But alas, French would not hear of it! He looked elsewhere for his "strong man." Thus, Ritman and motivated students like him continued to look elsewhere for advanced study in figure painting.

In the summer of 1908, with high goals in mind and expectations of a great experience ahead of them, Louis and Norbert boarded a train at Dearborn Station (ill. 10-5) and made their way to Philadelphia. Their first activities in the city are vague. It seems that they may have stayed with friends. Because classes did not begin until October, they apparently took the opportunity to tour both Boston and New York.

It is said that in Boston, Louis and Norbert visited the Museum of Fine Arts, where the influential impressionists and members of The Ten reigned supreme in their promotion of figurative subjects done in an impressionistic style. Since his first major impressionist canvas, *In the Orchard* (ill. 10-6), made a hit at the World's Columbian Exposition in Chicago in 1893, Tarbell had continued to interpret the genteel tradition in his art, specifically via the depiction of lovely young women engaged in leisurely activities.[26] Although he was considered more a citizen of the world than of Boston, John Singer Sargent also figured as an influential force in the promotion of figure subjects in Boston because he visited and worked there from time to time. Directly and indirectly, Boston was connected with the history of American impressionism. Seven members of The Ten had been born in Massachusetts and regarded Boston as a kind of home base. With the exception of Hassam, all of the Boston group were known as figurative painters; Edward Simmons's impressionism was a watered-down type since he spent more time making murals than painting easel pictures. In his comprehensive analysis of the Boston art scene of the period, Trevor Fairbrother points out further: "The New York members [of The Ten] had close ties with Boston: Dewing and Hassam had been born there, and Metcalf, Reid, and Simmons had studied at the Museum School. Moreover, their annual exhibition traveled to the St. Botolph Club in Boston in 1900, 1902, and 1905."[27]

Ritman knew and admired the work of some of these men, but he would not be one of them. Virtually scores of students in Boston had absorbed lessons that taught them mainstream figurative impressionism with a long-lasting Bostonian flavor, usually seasoned with Tarbell and Benson. Over and over again they carefully designed compositions featuring attractive young ladies in both indoor and outdoor settings, pictures which essentially showed the artists' so-called good life (pl. 10-1). If Ritman and Heerman spent much time in Boston, they may have seen works by some of these Tarbellites. At that time, painters like Gretchen Rogers, William Paxton, Joseph Rodefer De Camp (a member of The Ten), Edward Wilbur Dean Hamilton, Ernest Major, and many others were very busy producing respectable images of American gentility (ill. 10-7). What appealed to Ritman about these pictures was that they were essentially the same in character as those produced by his Chicago mentors, Reynolds and Parker (pl. 10-2).

Louis and Norbert reached New York quite some time after the very successful exhibition of Henri's group, called "The Eight," at Macbeth's Gallery. Parker, who had taught with Henri (ill. 10-8) so many times at the New York School of Art, had already told Ritman a good deal about the ideas of this group. As revolutionary to American art as the Fauves' show at the Salon d'Automne was to French, the exhibition of The Eight had drawn huge crowds when it opened in February: the show had been planned for months, and long before it opened, critics had expressed pro and con opinions.[28] Parker was teaching at Henri's New York School of Art at the time the show of The Eight was being planned and promoted, but he was not one of the group in spirit, since his brand of imagery was more closely allied with that of William Merritt Chase (pl. 10-3). Like the Fauves, Henri's Ash Can painters were determined to be different from the impressionists. Their work, however, was not remotely similar to that of the Fauves, except for being, in the opinion of some commentators, radical and even anarchistic. In fact, The Eight's "vulgar" imagery was made from a formula diametrically opposed to the tenets of impressionism:

Ill. 10-7. Lilla Cabot Perry. *Lady at a Tea Table.* Oil on canvas, 45 x 34½ inches. Private Collection. Courtesy R. H. Love Galleries, Chicago.

their scenes were not always sunbathed, their downtrodden masses did not engage in leisurely activities mirroring the good life, their palettes were frequently not high-keyed, and they did not employ the broken-color technique. Actually, the Ash Can formula was quite antithetical to impressionism, and its practitioners openly admitted as much when their viewpoint was published in James Huneker's paper, the *New York Sun*: "We often are called devotees of the ugly," said one spokesman. Hoping to clarify their purpose, he pointed out that "the trouble with a lot of artists, so-called, is that they draw an arbitrary line across God's work and say: 'In this half of His works He has been successful, but over here in the shadows and the misery of life, the seamy side, He has failed.' We mustn't paint the seamy side. It's vulgar. Your portraits, for instance, must be only of the rich . . . Ever notice the gold chain in those pretty portraits? That's part of the formula."[29] The Ash Can group wanted nothing to do with the "formula," since it was inextricably bound to the academic and impressionist traditions—which they found shallow, pretty, and detached from the realities of true American life. Henri and followers like John Sloan were convinced that the proper goal for the artist was to extol "the dignity of life, the humor, the humanity, the kindness" of the ordinary folk, whether they were urban or otherwise.[30]

Consequently, Henri's group reacted against a good deal more than the mere style or decorative prettiness of impressionism. They had been sensitive to and suspicious of nearly any kind of fin-de-siècle painting that was based on some vision of idyllic and pleasant existence characteristic of the genteel vision. Actually, in this regard, they aimed more at the academicians than at the impressionists, in that the latter had already won the war with the former. Devoted to even more radical principles, however, Henri gathered his Young Turks into ranks considerably to the left of the battle-fatigued impressionists, since the Ash Can School stood for "truth" instead of beauty, "life" instead of art, and "real" instead of artificial. Henri was quick to denounce "art for art's sake." Nevertheless, in spite of their much-publicized collective stance, The Eight was not wholly united in its rejection of impressionism or even the academic mode. Members like Glackens, Lawson, and frequently Luks painted pictures that owed a great deal to impressionism. Indeed, Lawson, whose palette has been described as one of "crushed jewels", learned to exploit broken color to its fullest. The fact that Lawson occasionally concentrated on trains was not unique since after Turner both Monet and Theodore Butler set the precedent for such subject matter in impressionism. In later years, Glackens stripped himself of individuality by copying both the style and the subject matter of Renoir. Luks executed various impressionistic canvases (ill. 10-9); and A. B. Davies painted Arcadian subjects directly from the textbooks of European academicism, while maintaining an alliance with the brutal Ash Can School.

To greater or lesser degrees, certain members of the Ash Can group like John Sloan, George Bellows, George Luks, and even Henri himself were associated with the American socialist and anarchistic movements.[31] By this time, Henri maintained close contacts with the anarchist Emma Goldman. For him, it was better to "amass knowledge than money." Later he would teach at Emma Goldman's radical Ferrer Center School.[32] Henri's influence was amazingly effective on his followers. In fact, Sloan once reported that "we thought we were attacking the capitalistic system so long as we put an ash can in a drawing." In his important work, *Art and Politics*, Richard Fitzgerald wrote: "In practice, politics and esthetics were not complementary."[33] The Chicago writer and artist Art Young agreed that usually "literary editors were on one side . . . and artists on the other."[34] At bohemian-style social gatherings in New York, they all discussed the

Ill. 10-8. Robert Henri. Photograph. R. H. Love Galleries Archives, Chicago.

pertinent issues of politics and art. "Most of the time, these intellectuals drew optimistic conclusions about the future and foresaw the day when art itself would help bring about a socialist revolution and a classless society."[35] Several artists tried diligently to see that the political persuasions of the Ash Can group were reflected in their art (especially Henri, Bellows, and Sloan), but others like Lawson, Glackens, and sometimes Luks leaned closely to the unidealized and nonpolitical mode of impressionism. Parker knew all of this as a result of his close association with Henri and his circle, but he rejected the Ash Can dogma in his own art. He was, arguably, probably the only Chicago painter who could have effectively imported Henri's philosophy into the city; consequently, in Chicago there was no movement in art that was equivalent to realism in literature. That fact is ironic, since much of what came from the Chicago realistic movement in literature was allied to its counterpart art movement in New York's Ash Can group.

If Louis and Norbert saw works by the Ash Can painters at Macbeth Gallery in New York City, Louis, at least, remained as uninfluenced as Parker had been. Instead Louis preferred Chase's subjects and his style, examples of which he would also have seen at Macbeth's. Ritman must have looked forward to the possibility of spending some time with the master, for those who studied under him remembered the experience for life. James Daugherty, for example, remembered Chase as a painter with an "immense capacity for inspiring enthusiasm;" and like so many others, he had been thrilled by Chase's "dazzling brushwork" when he demonstrated for the class.[36] It was common knowledge that Chase actually enjoyed sharing the secrets of his methodology with his students, although he was also renowned for his firm but cordial manner. That was the kind of teaching that inspired Ritman, since he had experienced a similar kind of discipline under Reynolds, who was also an admirer of Chase.

At the Pennsylvania Academy of the Fine Arts, the study of the human figure had reigned supreme since the days of Thomas Eakins more than twenty years earlier. Thus, for Ritman, studying there was a logical step after his Chicago training. After Eakins's controversial departure from the academy, several accomplished painters had attempted to take over its leadership. Thomas Anshutz, a highly regarded Philadelphia artist, made inroads at the school. Robert Henri, John Sloan, William Glackens, George Luks, and Everett Shinn developed practices and ideas there which served as the artistic mortar that bound them together in their struggle to revolutionize the kind of painting Ritman wanted to master.

Heerman either remained in New York or went back shortly after he and Ritman returned to Philadelphia. In any instance, Louis's funds were nearly depleted when he started the life class at the academy.[37] His anxiety over his dwindling reserves was usually mitigated by thoughts of his studies as he walked north on Broad Street and entered the academy each morning. The Philadelphia academy was one of the most unusual nineteenth-century buildings in the city, and Ritman enjoyed being in that unique building which provided a forum for unique persons. Surely to Ritman, as to everyone who visited it, the Pennsylvania Academy was built on aesthetic holy ground. Three years earlier, at its one-hundredth anniversary, William Merritt Chase referred to it as "the most important art institution in America."[38] At the academy tradition was extremely important. In addition to what he learned in his daily class work, Louis could learn a great deal from the excellent collection of the Academy, just as he had done at the Art Institute—only here he found more, much more. He admired great figurative

works, like *Turkish Page* (1876) by Frank Duveneck and the classic masterpiece known as *Ariadne Asleep on the Island of Naxos* (c. 1809-14) by John Vanderlyn, famous paintings by Charles Willson Peale and his talented family members, and, of course, a number of great works by Thomas Eakins. Ritman was especially enamored of Eakins's draftsmanship as he studied his figures. Ritman's schedule kept him busy, to say the least, but during his free time he visited other places like the Free Library or the Pennsylvania Museum, which stayed open on Sunday afternoons. Philadelphia was very different from Chicago—older, more traditional. Faced with the contrast, Ritman began to explore this comparatively quiet and orderly environment.

Ill. 10-9. George Benjamin Luks. *Madison Square*. Oil on panel, 38⅛ x 44⅜ inches. Private Collection. Courtesy R. H. Love Galleries, Chicago.

We know that Ritman had conversations with Chase and took his valuable words to heart.[39] However, the young man had little opportunity to study with the master because he returned to Chicago after less than two months work in Philadelphia. Extant documents provide no apparent reason for his sudden departure, only a brief note at the bottom of his enrollment card indicates that "circumstances compelled him to leave in November [1908]."[40] Ritman had no reserves when he came to Philadelphia, so "compelling circumstances" probably amounted to a lack of funds. This sudden turn of events dashed his hopes temporarily! He had had every intention of completing his term under Chase in Philadelphia and possibly even joining his famous summer sojourn to Europe. He was especially eager to go to France because Chase had suggested that he study there as soon as possible. It was not possible; in fact, he had no choice but to return to Chicago. Although Ritman had made new acquaintances during his short-lived stay in Philadelphia, he left the academy with no prior notice.

The big news not only in Chicago but all over the nation was the election of William H. Taft as president of the United States. Republican Vice President Theodore Roosevelt had become president when McKinley was assassinated in 1901 and was reelected in 1904. The 1908 election made it clear that the American people preferred to continue with a Republican administration under Taft, who had promised to lower tariffs.[41] Chicago's political machinery ran under its own steam while architects Daniel Burnham, chief architect of the World's Columbian Exposition, and Edward Bennett were putting their final touches to the "Plan of Chicago," a program of planned growth which would incorporate transportation facilities, park systems, and lakefront preservation.[42]

The Chicago art community had been quite active during Louis's short absence. Ironically, Macbeth's exhibition of The Eight had been presented at the Art Institute. The show had generated some controversy but nothing in comparison with the reaction in New York to their vulgar scenes. Ritman missed the show in both New York and Chicago, but he had seen a few examples of the group's work during his sojourn. He had also learned that in spite of Vanderpoel's approaches in Paris, Richard Miller had turned down W. M. R. French's offer of a teaching position at the Art Institute.

Almost immediately upon his return from Philadelphia, Ritman made special arrangements to rent a studio at the Chicago Academy of Fine Arts.[43] Reynolds, his former teacher, agreed to critique his productions. The young artist did not yet consider himself a full-fledged professional for three basic reasons: first, he was aware of his lack of exhibition credentials; second, he had no dealer representation; third, he had not yet studied in Europe, an experience that each and every teacher had told him was imperative for the serious American artist of his generation. With his funds exhausted, Louis had to start his career somewhere, and Chicago was the most logical place. In any case, Chicago was his home. Having visited the three greatest art capitals of America, Ritman knew Chicago's shortcomings, but the city was a friendly place and, like him, exuded energy and confidence. Living with his parents at 371 West Fourteenth Street, Ritman soon established himself in his new studio on the top floor of the academy on Wabash Avenue. Here he hoped to execute a few portrait commissions and continue his figurative subjects. Realizing the impropriety of his sudden departure from the Pennsylvania Academy, on 20 November 1908 he penned the following letter to Charles F. Ramsey, curator of schools at the academy:

> My dear Sir:
> I take this opportunity to apologize [sic] to you it was simply due to my negligence that I didn't bid you good bye I shall never forget the kindness you have shown me and I apreciate [sic] it very much, I hope some time the opportunity will [present] itself that I will be able to recipricate [sic]. I have a studio of my own in Chicago now and I paint all the time and Mr. Reynolds criticizes me and I also expect to exhibit at the Chicago Artist Exhibit. Hoping this letter finds you in the best of health with regards to Mr. Tresk [sic: John E. D. Trask, manager of the Pennsylvania Academy of the Fine Arts] and everybody I remain your most sincere friend Louis Ritman
> P. S. if ever you find time to write I shall be delighted to hear from you my address Chicago Academy of Fine Arts. Chicago Ill.[44]

A portrait commission or two may have emanated from Ritman's studio during the winter of 1908-9. He worked diligently at becoming a professional, seeking the advice of experienced friends like Reynolds, Vanderpoel, and Lawton Parker when the latter was in Chicago. All of them urged him to save funds to study in Europe. To this end Ritman could only obtain as many portrait commissions as possible and hope to sell a canvas to some interested party who had seen his work in an exhibition. Each day he arrived at the studio around eight o'clock. Even then, tall buildings surrounded his studio at 338 Wabash, so light was at a premium in the winter months, when the sun rose late and set early. Louis maintained a neat and orderly space, arranging it in such a way that he could work at his easel comfortably but also continue on other pictures that were stacked around him in various stages of finish. In addition, he prepared other surfaces, intending to use them for smaller oil sketches. Thus, each day, beginning sometimes in mid-morning, Ritman worked at his easel — usually with no live female model — painting portraits of his friends, a few contrived landscapes, and certain compositions derived from earlier charcoal life drawings. At other times, he shared the fee for a live model with another artist in the building. He could always depend on Reynolds to provide advice and encouragement.

In January of 1909, when it was time to submit canvases to the Thirteenth Annual Chicago Artists Exhibition, Ritman discovered that he had few to enter. He chose two works that were atypical, in that they were portraits of males. One was the striking likeness of Reynolds, previously discussed; the other, a portrait of his friend Norbert Heerman.[45] The makeup of the selection jury differed substantially from that of the previous year: once again the jury included John Vanderpoel, Lorado Taft, and Adam Emory Albright, but it also featured some younger, more progressive blood in the names of Louis Betts, the impressionist Wilson Irvine, and the ever-present former member of the Critical Triumvirate, Charles Francis Browne. Most of Ritman's close friends were impressed with his portrait of Heerman. Reynolds even suggested that it was good enough to enter in the Paris Salon.

In spite of his efforts to earn a living from his art, Ritman was simply too poor to hire a model to come regularly to his studio. Occasionally he was able to work with Reynolds but found it very difficult to set up a temporary easel at someone else's studio. To solve his dilemma, and to collect more life studies for a portfolio that he could eventually take to France, Ritman signed up in February 1909 for the morning life class supervised by Vanderpoel. In preparing a portfolio for a master at the Ecole des Beaux-Arts, there was no teacher better suited to guide Ritman to that school than Vanderpoel. He was the Art Institute's equivalent of Thomas Eakins, and over the years he had prepared many students, including Lawton Parker, for higher study in Europe. In order to be able to study privately under Reynolds and register officially in Vanderpoel's class, Ritman was obliged to obtain permission from the institute by submitting a "written petition to the board of teachers."[46] During the past few months, Ritman had subjected himself to several different instructors, each of whom was as opinionated as he was expected to be; but this kind of diversity in philosophy and technique was what the young artist sought, since he intended to be a master himself.

At the Art Institute, trusting that refining his skills before a live model would help him succeed in the concours of the Ecole des Beaux-Arts, Ritman once again joined scores of other (mostly older) aspiring artists, who usually demonstrated considerably less talent than he. A few of Ritman's more capable constituents such as Leo Blake, Charles Dahlgreen, Frederick M. Grant, and others, would also go on to contribute excellent work to local and national exhibitions. Few of his fellow students, however, could render the figure from life with such effortless grace as Ritman. At the time of his arrival, Louis was considered one of Vanderpoel's most advanced students. Having worked under Reynolds for so long and having already completed a fully preparatory curriculum,

Ritman was one of the "very advanced students" who projected well from their "separate life class" instruction.[47] Following the tradition of the atelier system, Vanderpoel provided concours, which were described in the official catalog as student competitions in which the individuals "whose work gets the highest numbers are given their choice of position in the next pose." The concours not only motivated the students to compete but also gave them an opportunity "to see what qualities their Master values most highly."[48] Accordingly, the professor exhibited the most exemplary works, singling them out for special attention under the heading of H.M., or honorable mention. For Ritman, who had been a consistent winner in concours over the years, the inscription "H.M." after his name had become commonplace. It was no different during the spring of 1909: at least once during every month's grading period from February through June, Vanderpoel chose Ritman's work for honorable mention.[49] At his level of advancement, Ritman worked for the most part on his own. During that season of 1909, the master regarded the paintings that Ritman executed for his criticism so highly that he awarded him the greatly coveted Class Honorable Mention, a prize usually reserved for Institute graduates for a life study head (portrait).

Louis took a studio near Reynolds's in the Tree Studio Building. Self-disciplined to a pauperlike budget, Ritman would not have been able to take the studio had it not been for some portrait commissions and perhaps some assistance from an unknown benefactor.[50] At Tree Studios, requests for space always exceeded what was available; moreover, it was somewhat of an honor to have a studio in the building that had housed so many well-known Chicago artists for so many years. Entering through the arched north doors on the Ontario street side, Ritman climbed one short flight of wide stairs, at the top of which was Reynolds's studio, number 28, and then, turning left, he walked down the hall to number 10, his own. His, like Reynolds's, looked west onto State Street and, like all the other west studios, had a fireplace. The studio had become available at a time when he was expecting to go to Europe, but the facilities were a welcome asset in his production of paintings. Here, he painted portraits, and when he could afford a model, or borrow or share one, her form was illuminated by light from the projecting ceiling skylights. The same sign warning her to wear a garment when walking to the washroom was still posted in the hall, and the same atmosphere of artistic activity prevailed. Although he was still considered a student—and looked more like a boy than a man—young Ritman stood out as one of the most promising artists at Tree Studios.

Owing to his youth and willingness to work for less than his constituents did, Ritman received several portrait commissions. In fact, he and Arvid Nyholm , who worked down the hall in Tree Studios, were two "young artists" whom Director French recommended to the wealthy Art Institute trustee Arthur T. Aldis for portraits.[51] Aldis was one of the most liberal members of the institute hierarchy, and a commission from this financial wizard would have served as an important credential in Ritman's dossier.[52]

Determined to prepare an outstanding portfolio to take to Paris, Ritman took no time off that summer of 1909; instead, he painted from early morning until darkness in the evening, sometimes with no time out for lunch. It was

Ill. 10-10. Louis Ritman. *Study of a Woman in a Hat.* Location unknown. Photograph courtesy of R. H. Love Galleries Archives, Chicago.

all accomplished with Reynolds's criticism at his new studio, where from July through September Ritman also continued to refine his skills at draftsmanship after working in the charcoal life class at the Art Institute. In this class he made no paintings, only charcoal studies from the live nude. These highly academic works on paper would serve as proof of his talent in applying for concours at the Ecole in Paris. Finished studies from this stint were final demonstrations of his skill in life class. They were even more important than letters of introduction from

Vanderpoel, Parker, and Reynolds — he would have to prove himself again at concours time. Until then, he could rest assured that his charcoals were excellent, not only in Vanderpoel's judgment, but even in that of the local critic Maude I. G. Oliver, who went so far as to reproduce one of his drawings in an article on student work from the Art Institute in the September issue of *International Studio* (ill. 10-10).[53] In this charming portrait study of a young woman wearing a large-brimmed hat, we see Ritman skillfully manipulating both tone and line. He signed his drawing "L Ritman" and inscribed Vanderpoel's name beneath it to indicate unmistakably that it had been executed under the master's guidance. For the rest of his life, Ritman would honor the memory of his time with Vanderpoel — he considered himself a "Vanderpoel student."[54]

Louis finished the charcoal life class with flying colors. After the end of the summer term on 18 September 1909, twenty years would go by before Louis officially participated in classes at the Art Institute of Chicago again. Ritman did not graduate from the Art Institute. While he had attended the institute twice over a five-year period, his actual study time there had amounted to less than a year and a half. Nonetheless, the training he had received at Hull House, the Art Institute, and the Chicago Academy of Fine Arts provided all the foundation necessary to study in Paris. Ritman made it known to others that he was ready to climb to the next rung on the ladder of success, and all of his admiring teachers agreed.

An artist of lesser ambition would have been more than satisfied with Louis's level of achievement. Louis, however, told his family that as far as he was concerned, he had not yet really begun because he had not yet worked in Europe. Obsessed with the lure of the Continent — especially Paris — he saved as never before, every nickel, every quarter; he sold pictures and cut expenses where possible, hoping to have enough funds to live and work in France. Now that he had an impressive collection of works to present to a master at the Ecole, and letters of introduction from Parker, Vanderpoel, and Reynolds, he prepared to sail for France just in time to take the difficult Ecole concours that began in late October and ran into the following month. It was important to arrive in time for the October concours, in which the work was done from life — in the next concours in April, the work was done from casts (antique). He could not afford to take a step backward in his precarious career plan. His future looked bright, but the tasks before him were intimidating to say the least. With help from a few friends, who had agreed to submit pictures to local exhibitions in his absence, Louis and his friend Norbert Heerman prepared to leave in September.

It must have been in Chicago during the summer of 1909 that Ritman and Lawton Parker had discussed contemporary art as they perceived it. Parker more than anyone else, Ritman was convinced, could give him the best advice about his career direction: Parker had spent many years in Europe, including some in Giverny; in recent years he had achieved international status. Thus his advice would have weighed heavily on the young artist when he "told him that he had real talent, and that he ought to go to Paris." Narrating the incident in later years, Parker reported: "He [Ritman] told me he had no money." Parker had responded with a quip: " 'Well, the walking is good,' I said, merely intending to pass it off as a joke, until something could be done for him." According to the report, "three months later Mr. Parker went to Paris. Almost the first person he met was Louis Ritman. 'I took your advice and walked,' the young artist said."[55]

Obviously, it was not solely at Parker's urging that Ritman had been prompted to move to France; in fact, he had planned to do so since his first days at Hull House, but had no opportunity. Exactly how he gathered enough funds to cross the Atlantic is unknown. Extant records and letters provide no explanation other than the fact that he lived frugally and saved until he had enough money for the trip and some extra for living expenses. He may also have been assisted by Heerman or an admiring patron, although no such person is mentioned in records or biographical sketches. Be that as it may, in September 1909 Louis Ritman and his friend Norbert Heerman once again boarded a train at Dearborn Station; this time they were going to New York, where they would sail for Europe. At the age of twenty, Ritman left Chicago a decade after he had arrived there with his parents.

Notes

1. Maude I. G. Oliver, "Gossip of the Artists," *Chicago Sunday Herald*, 27 December 1914.

2. Lawton Parker File, R. H. Love Galleries Archives, Chicago.

3. Maurice Ritman, interview with Richard Love, August 1987, R. H. Love Galleries Archives, Chicago.

4. Effa Webster, "Paris Lauds Chicago Boy," *Chicago Examiner*, unidentified clipping.

5. Albert Nelson Marquis, comp. and ed., *The Book of Chicagoans* (Chicago: Albert Nelson Marquis, 1911), p. 400.

6. Regarding prices for portraits by these artists, see W. M. R. French to an unidentified person at the Green Club, Chicago, 6 September 1906, Director WMRF, Letter Book, May 8, 1906-December 7, 1906, General Correspondence, Art Institute of Chicago Archives, Chicago, p. 464.

7. Ronald G. Pisano, *A Leading Spirit in American Art — William Merritt Chase 1849-1916* (Seattle, WA: Henry Art Gallery, University of Washington, 1983), p. 97.

8. "William M. Chase Forced Out of New York Art School: Triumph for the 'New Movement' led by Robert Henri," *New York American*, 20 November 1907, p. 3.

9. William Innes Homer, *Robert Henri and His Circle* (Ithaca, NY: Cornell University Press, 1969), p. 106.

10. Donald James Anderson, "Those Haunting Trees," *Inland Architect*, 25, no. 5 (June 1981), p. 8.

11. W. M. R. French to N. W. Harris, Chicago, 27 September 1907, Director WMRF, Letter Book, August 3, 1907-January 25, 1908, p. 348.

12. Ibid., W. M. R. French to Martin A. Ryerson, Chicago, 27 September 1907, p. 347.

13. Ibid., W. M. R. French to Lawton S. Parker, Chicago, 16 November 1907, p. 666.

14. Ibid., W. M. R. French to Lawton S. Parker, Chicago, 17 September 1907, p. 280.

15. Ibid., N. H. Carpenter to Lawton S. Parker, New York, 6 November 1907, p. 609.

16. Adolph R. Shulz was an accomplished landscapist. He was born in Nashville, Indiana, in 1869 and died in Delavan, Wisconsin, at the age of 94. He studied in Paris at the Julian Academy and in Munich. He won many awards in the Midwest as a member of local art societies. His wife, Ada Shulz, was an exceedingly accomplished master of the genteel tradition, posing attractive females in out-of-door settings (see pl. 10-1).

17. Maurice Ritman, interview with Richard Love, August 1987, R. H. Love Galleries, Chicago.

18. Theodore Roosevelt to William Howard Taft, 21 July 1908 in Henry F. Pringle, *The Life and Times of William Howard Taft: A Biography* (New York: Farrar & Rinehart, Inc., 1939), vol. I, p. 358.

19. Academy enrollment records: Louis Ritman, the Archives of the Pennsylvania Academy of the Fine Arts, October/November 1908. Vytautas Babusis to Charles Leibold, Registrar, 1987, Pennsylvania Academy of the Fine Arts, Philadelphia, PA.

20. Thomas Waterman Wood quoted in Eliot Clark, *History of the National Academy of Design, 1825-1953* (New York: Columbia University Press, 1954), p. 161.

21. It was exactly at this time that William Selig built his first motion picture studio in Chicago. George K. Spoor, a native of Highland Park, Illinois, pioneered motion pictures by devising a lamp to illuminate images of pictures on a wall. He sold his Kinodrome machines to Vaudeville theaters and formed the National Film Printing Company. Selig, also a Chicagoan, had begun selling his Selig Stand and Camera and projector, the Selig Polyscope, by 1896, but he also began making commercial films and sold them to vaudeville houses. In 1907, Bronco Billy Anderson, a partner of Spoor's at Essanay's, starred as a cowboy actor. See Perry Duis, "Chicago and the Movies," *Chicago Creating New Traditions*, (Chicago: Chicago Historical Society, 1976), pp. 91-93.

22. "William Merritt Chase: His Life and Work," *Arts for America* , no. 7 (December 1897), p. 200.

23. Pisano, *William Merritt Chase, 1849-1916.*

24. Florence Levy, comp., *American Art Annual, 1910-11* (New York: The Macmillan Co., 1912), pp. 219-220.

25. W. M. R. French to John H. Vanderpoel, Chicago, 27 April 1908, Director WMRF, Letter Book, January 25, 1908-July 9, 1908, p. 548.

26. For an overview of the impressionist period in Boston, see Trevor Fairbrother, *The Bostonians: Painters of an Elegant Age, 1870-1930* (Boston, MA: Northeastern University Press, 1986), pp. 50-64.

27. Ibid., p. 58.

28. For a comprehensive discussion of The Eight as they orbited around their leader, see Homer, pp. 126-164.

29. "Eight Independent Painters to Give an Exhibition of Their Own Next Winter," *New York Sun*, 15 May 1907.

30. Robert Henri, The *Art Spirit*, comp. Margery Ryerson (Philadelphia, PA: J. B. Lippincott Co., 1939), p. 148.

31. For an interesting discussion of the topic, see Annette Cox, *Art-as-Politics: The Abstract Expressionist Avant-Garde and Society* (Ann Arbor, MI: UMI Research Press, 1982), pp. 19-21.

32. Founded later in 1910 by Emma Goldman and a few supporters, the Modern School of the Ferrer Center in New York was named in honor of Francesco Ferrer Guardia, the Spanish anarchist who was found guilty of conspiring against the clergy and state in his radical educational system. George Bellows would also teach at the Ferrer Center School.

33. Richard Fitzgerald, *Art and Politcs* (Westport, CT: Greenwood Press, 1973), p. 27.

34. Ibid.

35. Cox, p. 21.

36. James Daugherty, interview with Ronald J. Pisano, quoted in Pisano, p. 108.

37. Maurice Ritman, interview with Richard Love, September 1987.

38. Richard J. Boyle in the preface to Frank H. Goodyear, Jr., et al., *In This Academy: The Pennsylvania Academy of the Fine Arts, 1805-1976* (Philadelphia, PA: The Pennsylvania Academy of the Fine Arts, 1976), p. 7.

39. The brief contents of their discussions are unknown, but the artist revealed to his biographer, Maurice Ritman, that Chase "had given him good advice."

40. Student enrollment record for Louis Ritman, Pennsylvania Academy of the Fine Arts, no. 133.

41. "William Howard Taft: Defense of a High Tariff," excerpted speech given by Taft at Winona, Minnesota, 17 September 1909. See *The Annals of America, 1905-1915*, vol. 13 (Chicago: Encyclopaedia Britannica), pp. 176-180.

42. Daniel Burnham and Edward Bennett, *Plan of Chicago* (Chicago, 1909).

43. Ritman may also have had another studio elsewhere at this time, but it has been difficult to ascertain its location.

44. Louis Ritman to Charles T. Ramsey, Curator of Schools, Pennsylvania Academy of the Fine Arts, Philadelphia. Letter is dated 20 November 1908 and inscribed "Chicago." Pennsylvania Academy of the Fine Arts Archives, Philadelphia, PA.

45. In the official catalog for the Thirteenth Annual Works by Chicago Artists show of 1909, Ritman's entry number 251 lists the title of Heerman's portrait as *Portrait of N. Hermani,* with Heerman's name misspelled as "Hermani." The artist's name is also misspelled as "Rittman, Louis."

46. *The Art Institute of Chicago School Catalog, 1908-09*, "Course of Instruction and Regulation, Class IV, Life," p. 26.

47. Ibid.

48. Ibid.

49. Student record card (1908-9) for Louis Ritman, Art Institute of Chicago Archives, Chicago.

50. At this time some funds were reaching Ritman, but family records yield no evidence of sources. Maurice Ritman, interview with Richard Love, September 1987, R. H. Love Galleries Archives, Chicago.

51. W. M. R. French to Arthur T. Aldis, Chicago, 16 December 1910, Director WMRF, Letter Book, June 20, 1910-February 8, 1911, p. 700. This text will show that Ritman had already been in Paris for quite some time when French made his recommendation. French was obviously impressed with Ritman's talents but quite unaware of his absence.

52. Whether a portrait was ever executed or even discussed is unknown, since no evidence of such a canvas is extant. Only French's recommendation is on record.

53. Maude I. G. Oliver, "Work of School of the Art Institute, Chicago," *International Studio* (September 1909), pp. LXXVIII-LXXIX.

54. Maurice Ritman, interview with Richard Love, September 1987.

55. Parker, quoted from an unidentified newspaper clipping, "Former Poor Art Student Wins Victory in Chicago," c. 1915, Ritman Scrapbook, R. H. Love Galleries Archives, Chicago.

CHAPTER ELEVEN: SALON, SALON . . . ENTERING THE HALLOWED HALLS

It is said that Ritman reached Paris with "$30 to pay for his art education."[1] With such limited funds, finding a suitable residence could have been a frustrating experience had it not been for the help of Lawton Parker, a good friend and mentor away from home. Parker immediately took him to the Latin Quarter, where American expatriates had been gathering for nearly a century. Although American artists lived in various sections of Paris, by far the most popular area for them was Montparnasse in the Latin Quarter (ill. 11-1). Since the sixteenth century when students from various colleges congregated on nearby slopes and summits to read poetry and discuss art, the name of Montparnasse had become synonymous with haven for artists and intellectuals. Long before confronting it, a would-be expatriate could learn about the Latin Quarter from scores of artists who had returned to America's metropolitan centers with stories about life there. For years, too, numerous articles had appeared in the press about the strange "bohemian" lifestyle in the Latin Quarter. Some of these reports were quite detailed. One such account that Ritman could easily have come across in a local art magazine was "Art Student Life in Paris," written by Bertha F. Beale, a former student at the Art Institute of Chicago.[2] After reading similar articles and firsthand accounts, a student such as Ritman might feel a bit more confident about his initial

stages of expatriate life in Paris (ill. 11-2). However, when Ritman arrived there, he reported years later, he was overawed and frightened by the strange new environment.[3] It was Europe again but far different from his memories of Kamenets-Podolsky. Apparently it was so unique that he could muster little from his Chicago experience to apply to his new lifestyle. Navigation was confusing for the first few days, but he and Heerman quickly learned to make their way in the amazingly complex city.

The boulevard du Montparnasse (ill. 11-3), running in an east-west direction, formed a large and busy traffic artery intersected by numerous other thoroughfares, including the boulevard Raspail, which was nearing completion when Ritman and Heerman came to Montparnasse. This was the area in which the young men hoped to find a place to live. Where they stayed those first nights is unknown, but it is possible that like many others before them, they found rooms at the dilapidated Hôtel Saint-André des Arts. Located on the street bearing the same name, the hotel was known as a "dingy" place even before Ritman and Heerman came there, but it was cheap and well known as a kind of meeting place for male art students, especially Americans. The Hotel Saint-André was within walking distance of the Louvre, the Luxembourg gardens, art schools, the Sorbonne, the University of France, the Panthéon, the Notre Dame, the Madeleine,

Ill. 11-1. A panoramic view of Paris around the turn of the century, with the Eiffel Tower looming in the distance. R. H. Love Galleries Archives, Chicago.

the Grand Opéra, the Bon Marché, restaurants, and many other places that might interest an art student. Whether they stayed at a hotel or in a studio apartment, it would be advantageous for them to live in the Latin Quarter where they could survive on an extremely low budget, walk to their destination, and mingle with the art crowd. Before beginning to look for permanent quarters, Ritman and Heerman had to take their passports to the prefect of police and register so that they could study lawfully in Paris. Registration papers served as official identification for foreigners in the city.

Parker helped Ritman and Heerman find quarters at 15 rue Delambre (ill. 11-4), not far from where the street junctioned with the boulevard du Montparnasse and the boulevard Raspail. Nearby was the art school of the Grande Chaumière, where they found themselves in the midst of the bohemian art section of Paris. Their studio apartment, with a small skylight and a place to store canvases, was not far from the former residence of the most trend-setting bohemian of them all, the American master James A. M. Whistler. Ritman's place was also near the former residence of the American sculptor Jo Davidson, who had come there about a year earlier. When Ritman and Heerman took the studio, the painter Abel Warshawsky, who was soon to become their friend, occupied the Jo Davidson studio, and there were many other residents of note. Long before he developed any new friendships in Paris, Ritman visited Clara Kretzinger, his artist friend from Chicago. As in the case of her studies at the School of the Art Institute of Chicago, Clara had preceded Ritman to Paris by a short interval, eventually to gain recognition as both an artist and a social figure. Actually, if one were to compose a list of the American expatriates who lived or had lived near Ritman and Heer-

man's studio when they settled in Montparnasse, it would read like a Who's Who of American culture.[4] The Latin Quarter was rather run-down in comparison with the Champs Elysées, but it was a far cry from the Levee in Chicago.

Once settled, Ritman was ready to resume his art career. Armed with letters of introduction and an impressive portfolio, he enlisted Parker's help to learn about concours procedures at the Ecole des Beaux-Arts. He was anxious to become a student at the old bastion of academic art, but in case he was not accepted, Ritman needed a place to work. With that in mind, he enrolled in the famous Julian Academy on the rue du Dragon, just off the rue des Saints-Pères. Here he arranged to study under Jean-Paul Laurens (ill. 11-5) and Tony Robert-Fleury. In this amazing place, Ritman joined the tradition of countless Americans before him who had competed with their French counterparts on the road to professionalism and acceptance by the Salon hierarchy. Lawton Parker had been able to tell him a good deal about the Ecole because he had been a student there himself, but Parker had also attended the Julian Academy, as had nearly all of Ritman's teachers, so the agenda, even the place, seemed familiar. Like everyone else, Louis scrambled for easel space to sketch the standing live model and accepted outside assignments, which required independent study in museums and galleries.

As John Rewald has pointed out, in the strict sense of the term, "the Académie Julian was not an 'academy' at

Ill. 11-2. Daniel Putnam Brinley. *Boulevard Montparnasse.* 1907. Oil on canvas, 26 x 32 inches. Private Collection. Courtesy R. H. Love Galleries, Chicago.

Ill. 11-3. A view of the boulevard du Montparnasse in Paris. The Café de la Rotonde is on the right side of the street and the Café du Dôme on the left. Rue Delambre branches off to the left. R.H. Love Galleries Archives, Chicago.

all but merely an art school which furnished models and not too close supervision of its pupils work."[5] Actually, the Julian Academy was a highly successful private business, organized in the last quarter of the nineteenth century and run by Rodolphe Julian, who had himself studied under Alexandre Cabanel. Two generations after Vanderpoel had studied there, the American George Biddle described the place as a "cold, filthy, uninviting firetrap."[6] Parker, Reynolds, and many other American art teachers recommended it as an alternative to the Ecole. Thus, in spite of its crowded, noisy environment, which had been frequently aggravated by practical jokes (*blagues*) since the period of the rise of impressionism, more Americans studied at the Julian Academy than at any other art school in Europe.

Like any other *nouveau* ("beginner"), Ritman had not been in class long before he learned about the blagues and jeers, "Ah! le voilà!" ("Ah! There he is!") Yet, even as small as he was, Ritman was not overwhelmed by the French pranksters, because American students enjoyed a reputation for countering with their fists. Virtually hundreds of American painters had walked through the doors of the Julian Academy, above which were the inscriptions: "*Le dessin est la probité de l'art*" ("Drawing

is the integrity of art") and "*Cherchez le caractère dans la nature*" ("Seek the essence of things within nature"). The already very aged master Tony Robert-Fleury, the specialist in history and genre, had long been a favorite with many American students at Julian's, and so he was with Ritman. Professor Fleury was a *sociétaire* at the Salon.

As Ritman was making his rounds of Paris, putting in time at the Julian Academy and waiting for the concours at the Ecole des Beaux-Arts, his art was being exhibited in Chicago: on 19 October 1909 the Art Institute presented its Twenty-Second Annual Exhibition of oil paintings and sculpture by American artists, a prestigious exhibition open to all American artists regardless of where they lived.[7] The selection jury was as political as any other large national show because it included members from the board of trustees of the Art Institute, men like R. Hall McCormick, Martin A. Ryerson, and Charles L. Hutchinson, whose high positions in city life rather than professional expertise assured them of votes in selecting works for exhibition. The jury committee of artists included painters and sculptors like Adam Emory Albright, Louis Betts, Harry M. Wolcott, and Lorado Taft. One woman, Nellie I. Walker, was elected as a voting jury member. Exactly how many canvases Louis had intended to submit before he left is unknown, but the jury accepted two of his pictures for exhibition, a painting called *In the Studio,* the whereabouts of which is unknown, and a likeness of himself, listed officially as *Portrait of the Artist.* Other contemporaries whose work was listed on the same catalog page with Ritman's were Frederick Remington, with a painting entitled *Fired On*; Chauncey Ryder, the American Barbizon painter, with an oil entitled *The Clearing*; Morton L. Schamberg, from Philadelphia, with *The Surfside* and *In the Park*; and the expatriate impressionist Elmer Schofield (he worked at Saint Ives, Cornwall, England), with *Old Mills on the Somme,* lent by the Art Association of Indianapolis. All in all, the exhibition was highly praised by local critics. It reflected mainstream art in America, much in the way that other national shows did in New York, Philadelphia, or Boston. Ironically, Ritman participated in his first major national exhibition in absentia.

Finally, toward the end of October, it was time for him to try the entrance concours at the Ecole des Beaux-Arts. Situated for decades at the Quai Malaquais, between the rue Bonaparte and the rue des Saints-Pères, this hallowed hall of art served as the official school for all serious artists who intended to become master painters — in no way could it be likened to any private art academy, French or American. Actually, it had begun on very narrow principles, but in 1863 the Ecole expanded its curriculum, offering for the first time classes in perspective, history, and anatomy. Students were given the opportunity to specialize in architecture, painting, sculpture, and engraving; they accomplished it by working in the atelier of a master who gave routine criticism; thus originated the atelier-concours system that most Americans held in such high esteem.

Many Americans studied at the Ecole des Beaux-Arts, but only a few stayed long. For example, J. Alden Weir (pl. 11-1), a leading member of The Ten, worked under the famous Salon master Jean-Léon Gérôme (ill. 11-6) six days a week from October until July with great perseverance.[8] In his superb study on French painting, Albert Boime points out that "atelier life . . . exerted enormous pressure on the average art student."[9] Parker had worked long hours under Gérôme until he won the *Prix d'atelier* (Studio Prize). Thirty years earlier, Kenyon Cox had described his instructor Gérôme as a "tall and thin" man, "erect and soldierly, with gray hair and large gray moustache, a small head, hook nose, and sharp eye." Cox noted that Gérôme's stark exterior belied his inner character: "He [Gérôme] looks like a rigid disciplinarian . . . . In spite of this he is in fact a singularly kindhearted man."[10]

Ill. 11-4. Rue Delambre with a view toward the boulevard du Montparnasse. R. H. Love Galleries Archives, Chicago.

A student knew that upon admission to an atelier, he was in effect beginning preparation for the coveted *Prix de Rome,* the most important award any academic painter could receive. In this grueling competition, however, "favouritism and nepotism were rampant, and often consideration of seniority outweighed those of merit."[11] To make it worse, as foreign students, neither Ritman nor any other American was eligible for the Prix de Rome, but all other concours were open. The *concours des places*, for which he had applied and which would determine whether he would be admitted to the Ecole, had to be repeated each term. Some individuals passed the first time, others tried several times, while still others failed after having studied a few terms at the Ecole. Although Professeur Léon Bonnat was a favorite among American students because he spoke English, Ritman submitted his drawings to Professeur Adolphe Déchenaud, who was very impressed with his work. At the same time, Ritman took the concours that included other subjects such as architecture and anatomy. When the official announcement was made, Ritman was elated to learn that he had been accepted into the atelier of Adolphe Déchenaud, a former student of Jules Joseph Lefebvre, Gustave Boulanger (ill. 11-7), and Benjamin Constant (ill. 11-8). Master Déchenaud had been a multiple Prix de Rome

Ill. 11-5. Jean-Paul Laurens. R. H. Love Galleries Archives, Chicago.

winner (1891 and 1894), then became *sociétaire* of the Salon des Artistes Français, and was recently appointed Knight of the Legion of Honor. Passing the concours in such a short time constituted an outstanding accomplishment for Ritman, and more important, it enabled the young Chicagoan to make official entry into the ranks of the Ecole.

Tuition at the Ecole, even for a foreign student like Ritman, was free, with the exception of a fee of about seven dollars for an easel, brushes, and other supplies. The art curriculum at the Ecole was focused on an extremely structured drawing regimen, actually based on the tradition of the old Académie Royale de Peinture et Sculpture (abolished in 1793), in which painting was considered, in essence, drawing. Ritman's drawings provided entrance into the *département de peinture* (department of painting). At the old Academy, the genesis of painting instruction had come from the great neoclassicist Jacques Louis David, who dropped in occasionally to criticize the work of students as they painted primarily on their own. In the second half of the nineteenth century before the rise to prominence of Léon Bonnat, the most sought-after professor for Americans at the Ecole had been Jean-Léon Gérôme, the great champion of academia. Gérôme had

died before Ritman's arrival in Paris, but the latter was quite satisfied with having become a student member of the Déchenaud atelier. The master was one of the most influential academicians at the Salon. If his work pleased Déchenaud, Ritman would have an opportunity to have a canvas accepted at the Paris Salon.

Ill. 11-6. Jean-Léon Gérome. R. H. Love Galleries Archives, Chicago.

Ritman's initial period at the Ecole may have been difficult. At the time, he was neither proficient in French nor was his English flawless. Of slight build, he may have been obliged to tolerate the *blagues* played on atelier initiates, as he had been obliged to do at the Julian Academy. Nevertheless, Ritman was surprisingly mature for his age, and since he had enrolled in Déchenaud's class to learn how to make art, he accepted the situation for the traditional period of initiation.[12] If later he himself participated in the practical jokes, the action was easily justified; in the words of Boime, "the 'serious' craft of Academic painting required an apprenticeship tolerable only in a ritualized context permitting periodic outbursts of unconstrained behavior."[13]

From a personal standpoint, Ritman concerned himself mostly with painting because he was far more interested in technique than in theory, although he was expected to attend lectures on anatomy, in which actual skeletons and cadavers (unidentified bodies from the

Ill. 11-7. Gustave Boulanger. R. H. Love Galleries Archives, Chicago.

about Paris. In addition to his formal painting studies, Louis spent considerable time in the Louvre, where the *conservateur des musées* gave him permission to copy from the masters. Louis formally submitted the number of a picture he wished to study and received special permission to set his easel up in front of it. Certain masters, like Rubens, Hals, and Velásquez, were more popular than others, so it was sometimes difficult to obtain a good position in front of a painting.

During the 1909-10 winter season, the Paris art scene was electrified with nervous energy. Controversy raged over new art ideas, and the Latin Quarter was jammed with personalities who strove to don the garb of bohemian citizenry. The Montparnasse area, where Ritman, Heerman, and most of the expatriate art milieu congregated, had changed considerably since the American dandy James A. M. Whistler had lived nearby and helped set the trend for the bohemian lifestyle that became so prevalent.[16] By the time Ritman and his friend moved to the Latin Quarter, it was common to dress the part of a struggling artist or poet, or some other creative individual devoted to the artistic expression *"la vie de Bohême."* As previously discussed, the bohemian lifestyle of Paris had

morgue) were used for illustration. There were also lectures on costume, in which models had draperies arranged on them to illustrate various surface changes of the material. Additional art source materials were available to students in the Ecole library.[14]

Ritman's chief goal in Paris was to do well at the Ecole and to eventually succeed at the salons, but there were many times during those first few weeks when he thought his task was too great. He quickly learned the importance of friends in a place so far from home. In Chicago he had had the love and support of his family, but in Paris he had only Dutchie Heerman, with whom he could not share his innermost fears and anxieties. Although the challenge excited him, there were times that he lay in bed on the verge of tears, asking himself over and over why he had risked so much to chase the elusive dream of becoming an accomplished artist in Paris.[15] At times he thought "it was impossible" to succeed; at others, he wanted to go back to Chicago to follow a less difficult path.

Exceedingly few documents remain through which one might trace Ritman's activities during his first year in Paris. One must assume that initially his time was completely absorbed by his study schedule and orientation

Ill. 11-8. Benjamin Constant. R. H. Love Galleries Archives, Chicago.

been imitated in Chicago; thus, while this way of life was not a shocking discovery to Ritman, the original version was different from what he had seen back home. By 1910, *la vie de Bohême* was commonplace in Paris, even expected, though also quite different from Murger's mid-nineteenth-century depictions of it. Indeed, to many observers, the so-called bohemian life was still viable, but it resembled more a fashionable affectation than real experience; to others, it was a lingering social phenomenon. Indeed, while Ritman was still living with his family in Russia, the French writer Francisque Sarcey had written in the *Cosmopolitan Magazine*: "I do not know whether in your country [America] Bohemia is known. I see no mention of it in the notes which Mr. Paul Bourget made on his journey in America. Your minds are, doubtless, too clear and precise, and your spirit of initiative too strong to allow your young men from twenty-two to twenty-eight years of age to waste their time lounging in so-called literary cafés, awaiting a fame that rarely comes to any but the industrious, or pursuing that wild, elusive animal known as the dollar bill. Poor and gay, they can console themselves for all the wretchedness of their precarious life by a bon-mot, a witty prank, or—although such lax morals may shock you — by one of those fleeting passions whose sudden joys are moistened by quickly-forgotten tears . . . . Murger's Bohemia is a thing of the past. Men of my age remember it, some with melancholy tenderness, others with a mistrust that has never been overcome . . . . I now think that it does an artist no harm to go through Bohemia, but he should guard against the peril of staying there too long. For when one has only traversed it in the days of youth and beginnings, he is apt to gain a broader mind and a freer and more lively fancy . . . . I have lacked that indescribable alertness which is so pleasing to our Parisian public, and which can only be acquired by a rapid voyage through that bright and sacred region of artistic lounging."[17] The bohemian lifestyle appealed very much to Dutchie, Ritman's tall, slim roommate, who would soon be known as one of the bohemian dandies of the Latin Quarter.

Ritman was neither attracted to nor offended by the bohemian way, but being obsessed with the goal of gaining admission to the spring Salon, he had little time to get involved. To this end, he worked long hours. Evenings were welcome, though, because they gave him an opportunity to meet with artist friends at favorite café-bars. Here he experienced the bohemia that everyone thought to be an indispensable part of the expatriate life in Paris. Occasionally, he and Dutchie enjoyed a good meal, including wine, for about twenty-five cents at the Procop or Bouillone Georges on the rue Mazarin.[18] There was also the Restaurant de la Garde, where a simi-

Ill. 11-9. Robert Henri. *Café Du Dôme*. Oil on canvas, 26 x 32 inches. Private Collection. Courtesy R.H. Love Galleries, Chicago.

lar budget would cover wine and a four-course meal—the tip of one *grand sou* (two cents) was expected for the waiter. The favorite haunt, however, was the now famous Café du Dôme (ill. 11-9), located near Ritman and Heerman's studio apartment at the corner of the rue Delambre and the boulevard du Montparnasse. At that time it was owned by Mr. and Mrs. Berger—Madame Berger tended the cashier's desk behind the bar. Many American artists, poets, and writers have sketched, painted, and described the café. Perhaps the most interesting image—ironically a written one—is that of Ritman's friend Abel Warshawsky, the American impressionist, who described the café as it was at the time when Ritman first visited it. "There was the usual zinc counter," he wrote, "across which drinks would be served direct to standing customers who could thus avoid the tip to the waiter, and a couple of rooms with small marble tables, somewhat dilapidated black leather sofas, and a 'billiard' . . . . The fact is that the Dôme made no efforts to please or attract customers. The *consommations* were neither better nor cheaper than those served by its rival establishments."[19]

When Ritman and Heerman first visited the Café du Dôme, the waiters were André and Eugène, both of whom were conversant in art and enjoyed the friendship of many Americans.[20] In cold weather, especially, the leather bench behind the billiard table was filled with artists whose funds were so low that they could not afford food, a drink, or even a billiard game unless it was offered by a benevolent friend. Ritman seldom had enough money for himself, let alone enough to lend for gambling at billiards. According to most reports, there was little overt abuse of liquor—the Dôme offered coffee, beer, and soda water. As in Chicago, Ritman saw a good deal of poker being played, important games upon which a new portable easel or a month's rent might depend. Ritman did not play poker at the Dôme. Unlike the shootouts in the gambling episodes of America's Wild West, no violent outbursts rocked the Dôme, but there were financial casualties among the young expatriates who lost funds supplied from home for living expenses.

Other cafés, such as the Brasserie Dumesnil and Lavenue's, offered better service, but aside from a meal here or there, Ritman, Dutchie, and their friends preferred to spend most of their free time at the Dôme. Even the American Art Club, with its excellent facilities, had difficulty luring young artists from the Café du Dôme. Warshawsky explains that when the Art Club was "compared with the Dôme, where absolute and untrammeled liberty prevailed, the restrictions of club rules and club etiquette, and a certain cliquiness among the more prominent artists frequenting the club, were further deterrents in the eyes of the young men." Warshawsky continued: "At the Dôme there existed not even an artistic Aristocracy. Students rubbed shoulders and hobnobbed on equal terms with celebrities, and a good storyteller or billiard player was of as much consequence in this little Dôme world as the man who had painted the picture of the year."[21] In the circle Ritman became acquainted with, there were good-natured accomplished artists like Warshawsky who were willing to discuss art in general, the art scene in Paris, and sometimes life as such. Two artists from the Midwest whom Ritman came to know through Parker at the Dôme were Frederick Frieseke and Richard Miller. These already well known painters told him about their work in Giverny.[22] To Ritman and others like him, the whole nucleus of American impressionism appeared to be centered at the Dôme.

By the time of Ritman's arrival in Paris, Parker, Frieseke, and Miller had become regulars at the Café du Dôme. Frieseke and Miller frequently stopped at the café to fortify themselves with a drink before dinner time. Miller always wore a Stetson hat. He was an ardent billiard player and a keen observer of the characters and life around him. The artists Max Bohm and Robert Mac-Cameron, a Chicagoan, formed a little group with Frieseke and Miller. Led by MacCameron, these expatriates advised the younger set of artists from America, even visiting them in their studios or residences.[23] In this way, the Midwestern expatriates who frequented the Café du Dôme became a close group.

Louis Ritman and Norbert Heerman, along with other rising expatriates such as Morgan Russell and Huntington Wright, were among the younger generation of Americans who became habitués of the Café du Dôme.[24] If these young artists could not always afford a sumptuous dinner, a more prosperous colleague would foot the bill. If the colleague did not show up on time and the meal had already been consumed, as happened once to Ritman and Warshawsky, the management of the café was very understanding about delayed payments. Meanwhile, as in the days of the early impressionists, when Edouard Manet and his Batignolles group met at the Café Guerbois, discussions (sometimes arguments) and wine flowed freely at the Café du Dôme. As Monet remembered in an interview with Thiébault-Sisson (a critic who would soon compliment Ritman), the gatherings resulted in a "perpetual clash of opinions [which] kept our wits sharpened [and] they encouraged us with stores of enthusiasm."[25] When an evening at the Café du Dôme had run its course, a visit to a friend's studio provided relaxation to conclude the activities of the day. At his studio, Warshawsky, a talented boxer, featured regular workouts that attracted such diverse personalities as Leo Stein, the collector of works by Matisse and Picasso; Walter Pach, artist and art critic; and Louis Ritman, Norbert Heerman, and Richard Miller.[26]

A significant difference existed between the time of the Café Guerbois and the time of the Café du Dôme, namely, neither Ritman nor older artists like Parker or Frieseke were obliged to suffer for their art as Monet had done a quarter of a century earlier. Like the French master, the younger generation of artists expected of themselves the same high quality of work; now, however, they were openly praised by artists for their common use of broken color. If they, too, struggled, it was not because of their avant-garde aesthetic but rather because of their trying to make a living as artists.

When the time came that Ritman submitted his canvases to the salons, he was not an artistic rebel: he was listed as a student of Déchenaud, a *sociétaire* of the Paris Salon; and even Ritman's brief study under Robert-Fleury was found worthy of mention. Thus, Ritman's work was traditional and contained no fuel for controversy. Under these rather advantageous circumstances, the Paris Salon jury was generally receptive to work like Ritman's, which at this time owed nothing to the pioneer efforts of Monet, Van Gogh, Seurat, Whistler, Sargent, Cassatt, and a few other French and American champions of the antiacademic independent movement.

Back in Chicago, Ritman's work was seen again at the Fourteenth Annual Chicago Artists Exhibition, which opened on Tuesday afternoon, 4 January 1910. The pictures displayed had been chosen by a jury that included Reynolds, Bartlett, and the impressionist Alfred Juergens. Only one painting by Ritman—listed simply as *Portrait*

Ill. 11-10. Salon jurors in the midst of deliberations. A rope was used to prevent damage to paintings in case of heated arguments. R. H. Love Galleries Archives, Chicago.

—was shown, but it was chosen for a full-page reproduction in the exhibition catalog, truly a fine honor for the young expatriate. If the picture still exists, its location is unknown. Judging from photographs, however, we see that it was an exemplary work: employing a typical nineteenth-century format, Ritman positioned his lovely young woman model fully clothed against a dark nondescript background in much the way he had done when he executed his earlier portrait of Reynolds. By this time, however, Ritman's technique was more highly developed, and his skill in rendering the textures of flesh and drapery seemed to rival that of older, more experienced artists.

As the winter of 1910 turned to spring, Ritman's talents burst forth even more than he could have imagined in Chicago. Under Déchenaud, the young man sensed that he was nearing professionalism; his master must have agreed, since he allowed him to prepare paintings for the forthcoming Paris Salon jury. Of course, Ritman was advised that it was highly unlikely that his work would be accepted; but the young Chicagoan was anxious to try—after all, the purpose of his being in Paris was to have his work shown at the Salon, the world's greatest forum for contemporary art. Although he was especially proud of a portrait of his roommate Dutchie Heerman, Ritman worked on other pictures, hoping that one or more of them might please the sophisticated Salon jury, which was made up of members of the Société des

Artistes Français. Because the painting has since been lost and no photographs of it are extant, we are unsure whether this portrait of Heerman was the same one that was shown a year earlier at the Annual Chicago Artists Exhibition or a new and more ambitious work executed under the guidance of Déchenaud. Assuming the latter case to be true—since it is unlikely that either Fleury or Déchenaud would sponsor a work produced under another master (especially a foreign one)—we can expect that Ritman's portrait of Heerman was similar, at least in style, to the female portrait that he had shown in Chicago, in January of 1910.

According to tradition, pictures for Salon jurying were to be delivered to the Grand Palais des Beaux-Arts by 20 March. Whether Ritman retouched his entries up to the last minute, as did most of his constituents, is not known, but he delivered his pictures on time. However, nothing Ritman had ever witnessed in Chicago could have prepared him for the experience of submitting his work to the Salon. He was one of scores of artists, models, teachers, and art enthusiasts who congregated en masse at the entryway to the Palais as workers moved pictures of every dimension into the hallowed halls. Bewildered gendarmes did their best to control the jeering but jovial mob. The loud and boisterous event had become a tradition, a very special day, no different for Ritman than for Will H. Low, who recalled that everyone there was "intent on taking part in the joyous ceremony, which marked the termination of their labours for the exhibition of the year." Low described the mood of the crowd: "Spectators lined the steps and the landing . . . . At times eight or ten perspiring workmen would bear an enormous canvas . . . but one and all of these canvases, subjected to the criticism of a lawless band, would elicit some comment, shouted so that all could hear, that more or less critically characterized the picture, then being conveyed to its final judgment before the regularly constituted jury." Low continued: "A majority of these critics had work of their own in the mass, and, when one could single it out borne in the slow moving procession up the stairway, ears were strained to discover in the jeering comment some murmur of admiration. The pupils of various masters essayed to provoke applause as the work of their teacher would be carried by, applause which would be as quickly drowned in the cat calls and groans of the adherents of rival schools."[27]

After his work was deposited at the Palais, Ritman waited for nearly another six weeks — a time described by Low as "torturing suspense, until an official notification brought the glad tidings" — before learning that his portrait of Dutchie Heerman had been accepted by the Salon jury (ill. 11-10).[28] This was truly an extraordinary accomplishment for anyone who had worked in Paris for only a few short months. Finally the all-important date arrived — 1 May 1910. This day, known as the *vernissage* (varnishing day), was reserved not only for competing artists like Ritman but for "all the nobilities of art, letters, and the drama, supported by those who make up the 'Tout Paris.'"[29]

Ritman was one of the many artists who wandered from gallery to gallery in the Palais, looking for their work. A few disgruntled artists, he noticed, were trying to rehang their pictures for better positioning, although such a practice was strictly against the rules. Ritman's memories of his Salon debut must have been quite like those of Low. "It is a thrilling experience to seek for the first time, among the thousands of pictures which line the walls of this great exhibition, your maiden effort," wrote Low. "You first search feverishly through the pages of the catalogue, to make assurance doubly sure, and at last you find the entry."[30] In Ritman's case, the entry read as follows: "*No. 1594, Portrait de M. Norbert Heerman.*" The following notation was on the same catalog page: "Ritman [Louis], né en Amérique, élève de MM. Tony Robert-Fleury et Déchenaud — Rue Delambre, 15."[31] Low further details the reactions of a neophyte to the Salon: "Guided by the letters which designate the various rooms, you search in those which bear the initial of your name and, at last, there, on the second row, a strangely

shrunken frame encloses a gruesome work which you are forced to recognize, with painful emotion, as the picture that, in its bright new frame, looming large in your small studio, and fresh in its newly applied colour some six weeks ago, you modestly believed to be 'not so bad.'"[32] In a brief article on the Salon *vernissage*, one critic found only a few American portraits worthy of consideration: works by Henry S. Hubbell, Max Bohm, and a few other Americans. Ritman's name was not among those mentioned. His portrait won no award, not even honorable mention, but it had been included in the prestigious Paris Salon, triumph enough for an initiate.

Ill. 11-11. Michael and Sarah Stein, Henri Matisse, Allan Stein, and Hans Purman in the apartment of Michael and Sarah Stein, 58 rue Madame, Paris, late 1907. The Baltimore Museum of Art. The Cone Archives.

In the spring of 1910, after the excitement of the Paris Salon, Ritman and his friends had a little more time to spend at the cafés in Montparnasse and at the American Art Club. Each day Dutchie Heerman assimilated more of the bohemian role, while both Heerman and Ritman made the acquaintance of many interesting personalities at the Dôme. A few of these were Walter Pach, Patrick Henry Bruce, Max Weber, and other American members of Matisse's school at the Lycée Victor Durvy on the boulevard des Invalides.

Although the event of their meeting is not clear, Ritman also came to know Leo Stein, who already owned works by Picasso and Matisse (ill. 11-11). Indeed, it was back in 1905 that Leo and Gertrude Stein "entered deci-

Ill. 11-12. Frederick Carl Frieseke. *Lady Trying on a Hat*. 1909. Oil on canvas, 63¾ x 51 inches. Courtesy Art Institute of Chicago. Walter A. Schulze Memorial Collection.

longer. Work as conservative as Ritman's would not have entered Leo's collection, but in some ways it was considerably closer to his idea of good art than were Picasso's radical experiments from this time onward. Later Ritman and Stein would get to know each other better, but for now theirs was only a passing acquaintance.

Ritman was not interested in Stein's Matisse. Indeed, he was satisfied with expanding the academic mode he was learning from Déchenaud by loosening his brushwork somewhat and brightening his palette. Of course, this slow evolution of style toward impressionism had nothing to do with Matisse's circle: it was prompted by artists like Parker and Frieseke (ill. 11-12), with whom Ritman visited occasionally. Apparently both of these men came to Ritman's studio-apartment one day from the Dôme.[36] Frieseke and Parker did not stay in Paris past the spring Salon; in fact, they were in Giverny long before the so-called summer season began and recommended that Ritman join them there.

Ritman's exact whereabouts during the spring of 1910 are vague. On the other hand, we know that he and Heerman spent many hours with their friends at the Café du Dôme and other favorite local spots. The two of them, and sometimes others, walked to the nearby American Express to check the mail in the hope of finding a letter from the family, an artist friend, or a former teacher, or even receiving one with a bank draft that could be quickly

sively into the world of twentieth-century art . . . at a moment of crisis — the furor generated by the exhibition of Matisse's *Woman with the Hat*."[33] Leon Katz explains that the purchase of this work "marked the beginning of the Steins' major influence as collectors and publicizers of the most advanced art being produced in Paris at the time." Katz also points out that there is "no doubt that in the voyage of brother and sister toward the center of the then current revolution in painting, it was Leo who steered the course."[34] Ritman was in Paris during the last year or so of the "heroic" years of Analytic Cubism, when Gertrude was chiefly concerned with her huge novel *The Making of Americans*, but the young Chicagoan did not meet her at this time, and soon Gertrude and Leo would take different aesthetic paths.[35] In 1910, Leo had not purchased a Matisse work for a couple of years, and he was then buying his last painting from Picasso, which he said he got only to settle his account with the artist, to whom he had advanced funds. At this time Leo and Gertrude's collection was a joint endeavor, but as his sister followed Picasso more deeply into Cubism, their opinions divided. Leo simply did not believe in the ongoing saga of Cubism and could not support the movement any

Ill. 11-13. The Café of La Coupole, a favorite watering place of expatriate artists. R. H. Love Galleries Archives, Chicago.

cashed. Also, as they got to know Paris better, they tried other cafés, especially La Coupole (ill. 11-13), Le Select, or La Rotonde. Here, in addition to the constant rehash of art at the Salon, there was talk aplenty about current art events—the Fauves' show, for example, or Albert Marquet's solo show that opened on the first of May at the Galerie Druet, only to be followed by a similar one for Henri Charles Manguin at the end of the month.

Ill. 11-14. Giverny as it appeared during a period of floods. Copyright Jean-Marie Toulgouat, reproduction interdite.

Although most conversation in these cafés centered around art, other topics surfaced occasionally. For example, rumors and gossip of a different sort circulated when

the French submarine *Pluvoise* sank outside Calais harbor after being hit by a ferryboat. Ritman's friends and American expatriates all over Paris were shocked, and many wanted to help. Shortly afterwards in June, the New York Metropolitan Opera Company gave a benefit performance at the Opéra in Paris for the survivors of the *Pluvoise*.

Apparently, Ritman and Heerman left Paris for some time that summer. It is said that they visited various well-known painting haunts like the Forest of Fontainebleau, Grez, and other picturesque locations south of Paris. If they had traveled north of Paris to Giverny, their sojourn would have been difficult. Earlier that spring, the Seine and the Epte had flooded and all of Giverny and the surrounding territory had been endangered. Some members of the American pioneer group remained in Giverny, and one of them, Theodore Earl Butler, painted several views of the flood. Never before had Giverny been so threatened by nature. Armed with box cameras, many citizens took snapshots, which now provide striking visual records of the destructive waters as they rose over the riverbanks (ill. 11-14).

Notes

1. Parker, quoted from an unidentified newspaper clipping, "Former Poor Art Student Wins Victory in Chicago," c. 1915, Ritman Scrapbook, R. H. Love Galleries Archives, Chicago.

2. Bertha F. Beale, "Art Student Life in Paris," Part I, *The Sketch Book* (October 1904), pp. 56-58, and Part II, *The Sketch Book* (June 1905), pp. 251-52.

3. Maurice Ritman, interview with Richard Love, September 1987, R. H. Love Galleries Archives, Chicago.

4. See Brian N. Morton, *Americans in Paris* (Ann Arbor, MI: The Olivia & Hill Press, 1984).

5. John Rewald, *Post-Impressionism from Van Gogh to Gauguin* (New York: The Museum of Modern Art, 1956), p. 272. See also Maurice Denis, "Gauguin, ses amis, l'école de Pont-Aven et l'Académie Julian," *Gazette des Beaux-Arts*, Paris, n.d. See also William Rothenstein, *Men and Memories: A History of the Arts, 1872-1900*, vol. 1 (New York: Tudor Publishing Co., 1931), pp. 36-50.

6. George Biddle, *An American Artist's Story* (Boston, MA: Little, Brown and Co., 1939), p. 125.

7. The Art Institute of Chicago, *Catalogue of the Twenty-second Annual Exhibition of Oil Paintings and Sculpture by American Artists, 19 October to 28 November 1909*. Ritman's work is listed on page 33.

8. Doreen Bolger Burke, *J. Alden Weir: An American Impressionist* (New York: Cornwall Books, 1983), pp. 41-42.

9. Albert Boime, *The Academy & French Painting in the Nineteenth Century* (London: Phaidon Press, Ltd., 1971), p. 50.

10. H. Wayne Morgan, ed. *An American Art Student in Paris: The Letters of Kenyon Cox, 1877-1882* (Kent, OH: Kent State University Press, 1986), p. 161.

11. Ibid.

12. For an interesting discussion of the topic, see Charles Henry White, "Student Humor in Paris," *The Sketch Book*, III, no. 2 (October 1903).

13. Boime, p. 50.

14. The library was available to any student who produced a letter of introduction from the American ambassador. Letters were usually obtained prior to sailing for Europe or at the time of arrival at the American Embassy in Paris. See Beale, p. 58.

15. Maurice Ritman, interview with Richard Love, September 1987.

16. For a discussion of Whistler's role, see Roy McMullen, *Victorian Outsider: A Biography of J. A. M. Whistler* (New York: E. P. Dutton & Co., Inc., 1973), chap. IV.

17. Francisque Sarcey, "Murger and Bohemia," *The Cosmopolitan Magazine*, XX, no. 4 (February 1896), pp. 332-33.

18. Maurice Ritman, interview with Richard Love, September 1987.

19. Abel G. Warshawsky, *The Memories of an American Impressionist* (Kent, OH: The Kent State University Press, 1980), p. 107.

20. Ibid., p. 108.

21. Ibid.

22. Maurice Ritman, interview with Richard Love, September 1987.

23. Warshawsky, pp. 109-11.

24. Ibid., p. 111.

25. Claude Monet to Thiébault-Sisson, *Le Temps*, 27 November 1900; quoted in English in Rewald, *History of Impressionism* (New York: The Museum of Modern Art, 1973), p. 197.

26. Warshawsky, p. 116.

27. Will H. Low, *A Chronicle of Friendships, 1873-1900* (New York: Charles Scribner's Sons, 1908), p. 168.

28. *Exposition annuelle des Beaux-Arts, Salon de 1910* (Paris: Société des Artistes Français, 1910).

29. Low, p. 169.

30. Ibid.

31. *Exposition Annuelle des Beaux-Arts: Salon de 1910.*

32. Low, p. 169-170.

33. Leon Katz, "Matisse, Picasso, and Gertrude Stein" in *Four Americans in Paris: The Collections of Gertrude Stein and Her Family,* exhibition catalog (New York: Museum of Modern Art, 1970), p. 51.

34. Ibid.

35. Gertrude Stein's *The Making of Americans* was first serialized in the *Transatlantic Review* (April-December 1924). One year later, it was published as a book by Contact Editions in Paris. Stein's notes and studies for the manuscript are in the Collection of American Literature, Beinecke Rare Book and Manuscript Library, Yale University.

36. Maurice Ritman, interview with Richard Love, September 1987.

CHAPTER TWELVE:
THE ACADEMICIST ROUTINE

Had it not been for the upcoming Salon d'Automne (Fall Salon), Ritman might have spent a little less time in front of the easel during the early summer of 1910. Considering the fact that his work had already been accepted to the Spring Salon, and that he was allowed several entries (the limit of four had not yet been established), the works for the Salon d'Automne had to be submitted early that summer, so Ritman must have worked as hard then as he had during the winter season, when he was preparing for the Spring Salon. In the minds of most younger artists, the Fall Salon was almost as important as the one held in spring; actually, the Fall Salon was a good deal more reflective of new trends than the earlier exhibition. That summer Ritman was notified that his work had been accepted by the Salon d'Automne jury, a group of artists who had a liberal reputation. With this announcement came the realization that his work would be seen in the same forum in which Fauvism had been unveiled five years earlier. As with the Spring Salon, a vernissage marked the opening of the Salon d'Automne, which ran from 1 October until 5 November. Many Americans attended the exhibition, which was held at the Grand Palais on the Champs Elysées. Conversation abounded about the competition between Matisse and Picasso and about Cubism in general. Many viewers expressed concern about the impact of Cubism on other

work at the Salon, but the controversy and fever-pitch excitement of the Fauvist years had died down.

Along with Ritman's, the work of many other American painters appeared at the Fall Salon of 1910. One of these was the Giverny pioneer Theodore Butler, who had been elected that year to the position of *sociétaire,* a status roughly equivalent to an associate membership in the National Academy of Design in New York. Nothing indicates that Ritman met Butler at the Fall Salon, though both attended, as did many mutual acquaintances from Giverny like Frieseke, Miller, and Parker. Here, Ritman had an opportunity to discuss the show and other art matters with his Giverny friends. He probably learned of the irritation of the Giverny artists over the rumor that W. M. R. French of the Art Institute of Chicago did not consider the American expatriates in France good painters. One is tempted to believe that it was Parker who informed both Miller and Frieseke of French's prejudices and even told them of derogatory comments made behind closed doors. In any instance, French would soon write an apologetic letter to Miller, hoping that it would "relieve" him "of all idea that [he had] been speaking ill of the American group in France." Director French explained that he had "a high opinion" of Miller's art. "You will remember," he wrote, "my desire that you should come and teach in the Art Institute . . . . I assure you that I entertain no such strange opinions as that the Americans in France do not paint well."[1] French wrote a similar letter to Frieseke, hoping that it would dispel any ideas the artist may have had about his prejudice toward him or any other expatriate in France.

Ritman's acceptance into the Salon d'Automne, certainly the most avant-garde French annual, was most gratifying, yet the young man belonged to no avant-garde Parisian art society, nor was his art characteristic of Cubism or any other radical modern trend. One doesn't know whether Ritman entertained notions about submitting work to the Salon des Indépendants, an exhibition that had traditionally been sponsored by the Société des Artistes Indépendants.[2] Founded by leading modernists, such as Odilon Redon, Georges Seurat, Paul Signac, and others, the Salon des Indépendants was installed in the Pavillon de la Ville de Paris at least a full month ahead of the Paris Salon as a deliberate rival attraction. In recent years, however, the once very avant-garde Indépendants' Salon had become a kind of annual showplace for Signac's band of latter-day neo-impressionists, Matisse's Fauves, the Nabis, and other French cliques. Ritman may have set his top priority on adjudication by the juried salons or simply felt no desire to exhibit at the stereotypical Indépendants' Salon. In any instance, he did not submit his work to that special exhibition. Instead, to gain appropriate exposure, he carefully placed his paintings in the salons that openly rewarded his kind of imagery, namely, academic work with distinct elements of impressionism—which, albeit old-fashioned, was still by far the most influential modern art mode in Paris.

More than ever before, pluralism in art prevailed in Paris: numerous legitimate art movements (some were merely trendy) existed side by side while the older ones were still being examined with respectful interest. Earlier that year, for example, the whole Paris art community buzzed with excitement about the exhibition of Toulouse-Lautrec's paintings and lithographs at the Musée des Arts Décoratifs in the Louvre. At about the same time, Bernheim-Jeune presented a one-man show for Matisse. Ritman's work was more accomplished than that of many long-time impressionists, but compared with the work of Matisse, Braque, Picasso, or other members of the avant-garde, it was ultraconservative. By and large, "the international art community [most of whose leaders were in Paris] was convinced as never before that the painter, the poet, the musician, the writer, the critic (who usually considered his opinion creative) and even the public had finally purged itself of useless tradition and worn-out doctrine to stand upright and 'unfettered' at the threshold of the twentieth century, a bright, new modern era in which man was encouraged and in fact, expected to

Ill. 12-1. John Singer Sargent in his studio on the rue Berthier in Paris. His controversial painting of Madame Gautreau hangs on the wall behind him. R.H. Love Galleries Archives, Chicago.

drop the old for the new."[3] Ritman's study at the Ecole was old-fashioned in that it followed tradition, but along with his previous academic training, he used it to provide a solid foundation for the impressionism he hoped to master. In his imagery, he was determined to focus on figurative subjects just as French and American masters, like Degas, Renoir, Cassatt, Tarbell, Chase, Reynolds, and now even Bonnard, had done before him.

During the winter of 1910-11, Ritman and Heerman moved to another studio apartment in Montparnasse, this one somewhat larger. It was located at 85 Notre-Dame-des-Champs, not far from the former residences of the American sculptor Augustus Saint-Gaudens, John Singer Sargent (ill. 12-1), J. Carroll Beckwith, Whistler, and the future apartments of F. Scott Fitzgerald and Ezra Pound. Only a few doors away, at number 72, Vanderpoel had had his quarters just a couple of years earlier. Now the American sculptress Malvina Hoffman worked on the second floor of number 72 in her first "north light studio," replete with two flights of squeaking stairs. She described it as "a stage setting worthy of a scene in La Boheme." Soon she would receive a commission to make the likeness of the American ambassador to France, Robert Bacon. It had been over thirty years since John Singer Sargent worked in the number 73 studio. It was there that he received his first important commission provided by Edouard Pailleron, the wealthy French playwright. Next door to Ritman's place, at number 86 (ill. 12-2), was the top-floor studio that had once belonged to the great American master—James A. McNeill Whistler. Here, up the twisting stairway, Whistler had brought the multitalented, self-proclaimed Chicago champion of anything avant-garde, Arthur Jerome Eddy, to have his portrait painted. From the unique vantage point of this studio, Whistler and his wealthy sitter could see the Luxembourg Gardens. Ritman and Heerman had heard many fascinating stories about Eddy, who was still one of the leading members of the Chicago art community. Eddy's experiences with Whistler had occurred over fifteen years earlier though, so Ritman had no opportunity to know him now — except at a great distance. In this fascinating area of Parisian bohemia, Ritman and Heerman were very near 70 rue Notre-Dame-des-Champs, the place which one Reverend Van Winkle had converted to a reading room for Americans, usually writers, artists, and other creative residents of the Latin Quarter. Here, everyone, artist or otherwise, was welcome for a small membership fee of three francs, which provided a key admitting him or her to reading rooms, the adjoining library, scheduled demonstrations in art and music, and discussions in science and literature. In future years, the poet Ezra Pound occupied the space. Ritman and Heerman lived on a street lined with studios, the occupants of which had already or would become some of the greatest American contributors to culture.

Ritman spent the next grueling months of the 1910-11 winter in preparation for a suitable salon composition. The most important task was the execution of the picture, but he couldn't have a canvas stretched until he had arrived at an acceptable composition. Most critics at the time shared the opinion that "the lacking quality that one feels in the artistic education of Paris — and regrettably, not Paris only — is composition."[4] Sensitive especially to the American figure painters in Paris, one critic lamented that "the model is worshipped to the exclusion of greater selection and self-expression. That composition cannot be taught may be true; still, it can be helped and the average student made the keener-sighted."[5]

Ritman's routine at the Ecole would not have been significantly different from that of many Americans who were fortunate (at times it seemed unfortunate) enough to study there. In fact, because he came to Paris during the years when the academic power and influence of the Ecole was waning, Ritman's path was far less strewn with rocks than were those of American predecessors like Thomas Eakins, Edwin Blashfield, or J. Alden Weir, who had had to buck the powerful headwinds of nineteenth-century academic dominance in art.[6] Ritman's regimen at the Ecole was far more complex than anything he could have imagined when he was in Chicago. Nevertheless, he found that he was achieving much more and with less criticism — progress he attributed more to the milieu in which he worked than to his professors. Recently Louis had had the added opinion of Fernand Cormon, a highly respected academician who had been successful since his own student days under Cabanel and Eugène Fromentin.

Ill. 12-2. James McNeill Whistler examining a proof of etchings in his studio at 86, rue Notre-Dame de Champs in Paris. R.H. Love Galleries Archives, Chicago.

Specializing in history paintings derived from J. L. David's neoclassical tradition, Cormon had enjoyed great acclaim for religious works such as *Jesus Christ Resurrects Jaires' Daughter* and *Cain*, for which he had won the cross of the Legion of Honor. Of course, Cormon was also a professor at the Ecole des Beaux-Arts and a member of the Institute of France, so Ritman considered it a high honor to study under him. Unfortunately, Cormon spent very little time in front of the young Chicagoan's work, but every word of advice was a nugget of aesthetic gold to Ritman.

Ritman's many labored preparatory *académies* (drawings) at the Ecole des Beaux-Arts prepared him to render acceptable figure studies for a rather elaborate composition that he intended to call *La Toilette*. It was not a history picture, as Gérôme might have expected from Eakins or Parker, but a perfectly acceptable academic subject for his professors Cormon and Déchenaud and, more importantly, for an academic jury. A Prix de Rome winner himself, Déchenaud was a thorough and demanding professor who encouraged his students to compete, but he was really no different from Cormon and others of the Ecole hierarchy who visited the so-called atelier once or twice a week and then left the students to work out their own minor problems. Following the tradition of the Ecole, Ritman could not have submitted a painting to the salon without having made painstaking preparatory drawings of his subjects in singular poses as well as other distinctive plans for a composition. In these he was expected to present harmonic resolutions of aesthetic problems (such as conflicts in foreshortening or surface textural clashes or balance of organic and geometric) in achieving the nebulous but commonly referred to quality of *disegno* (or in French, *dessin*). There can be no doubt that young Ritman suffered many doubts about

Ill. 12-3. Louis Ritman. *La Toilette*. Location unknown. Photograph courtesy of the family of Louis Ritman.

his chances during this long and tedious winter of preparation for a suitable salon entry, but inspired by his recent success, he persevered.

Not surprisingly, the final composition of *La Toilette* reflects an eclectic array of influences derived from Ritman's several years of study (ill. 12-3). Generally speaking, the style of his painting is academic but it smacks of the American genteel tradition: it follows the pictorial formula set forth earlier by Reynolds who called for "mirrors and vases of flowers, books or drapery, lovely woman in her boudoir."[7] Thus, we see a well-planned academic composition whose subject is in strict conformity with the teachings of Reynolds. In composing his picture, Ritman came up with an interesting blend of pictorial precedents, beginning, perhaps, with Titian and ending with Déchenaud. Stylistically, we notice the lingering influence of Reynolds and Parker as well as hints of Carolus-Duran, John Singer Sargent, and William Merritt Chase. Thus, we see that while Ritman's painting contains elements derived from diverse sources, it is also an accomplished example of fin-de-siècle formula imagery. A large initial tour de force, his picture demonstrated his knowledge of the salon formula and his obvious alliance to the French and American academic milieu; but with a brighter palette and some broken color, it could easily have been converted into an impressionistic mode.

Officially entitled *La Toilette* , as intended, Ritman's picture reveals two women: one is fully draped and seated in profile at the left; the other is a nude standing with her back to the viewer but frontally revealed in a huge framed mirror that takes up most of the wall. There is nothing particularly innovative about the overall scheme of his composition, since Ritman had been exploring similar examples for several years, but the arrangement of figures and objects is pleasing, even successful in a traditional manner. Now that he was in Paris, Ritman observed countless variations on his theme — even from the hand of Frieseke, who was preparing a similar work for the Champ de Mars Salon. This kind of pictorial format harked back to virtually scores of European precedents. The most obvious of these were set by Jan Vermeer, who frequently posed a seated and a standing figure together in a small and presumably private but implicit proscenium-like area. Such scenes are severely limited in depth by a rear wall, upon which a rectangular shape tends to balance other less strictly geometric objects and forms in the room. Generally speaking, *La Toilette* would also have been a fine picture to show in Boston, where Sargent, Tarbell (ill. 12-4), De Camp, Benson (ill. 12-5), and Paxton (ill. 12-6) created many interior scenes of women engaged in intimate leisure activities. While the overall parameters of his subject were similar to those of

Ill. 12-4. Edmund C. Tarbell, *New England Interior.* Oil on canvas, 30⅛ x 25⅛ inches. Museum of Fine Arts, Boston. Gift of Mrs. Eugene C. Epplinger.

the Boston painters, the front and back views of the nude would have shocked the local brahmins unless the shock may have been somewhat mitigated by a classical title. Moreover, Ritman now worked to please a Parisian audience, avid salon goers who were no longer shocked by nudity in secular settings, as they had been when Manet submitted his radical images.

Ostensibly following in the footsteps of Ingres, Gérôme, or Cabanel, Ritman made no overt attempt to create a subtle iconographic scheme beyond that implied in the simplistic title, exploiting as he did the subject's use of mirror. On the other hand, we might speculate on whether we are not privy to more than an intimate scene? Is this subject not similar to Titian's complex yet pictorial expositions of vanity and self-indulgence? Narcissistically captivated by her own mortal beauty, each woman is unaware of the other's presence as she prepares herself in an obviously opulent environment, in which fine objects expand the ambience of luxury. Thus, we speculate, keeping in mind Ritman's indelible artistic background, whether his ambitious yet derivative scene is no more than a shallow nineteenth-century tour de force reflecting the American genteel tradition or a highly sophisticated image, with an iconography that was inspired by the great

European masters. The answer is not immediately apparent. We know, however, that Ritman was determined to prove himself as an academician, that he read about art a great deal, and that he visited museums regularly. For example, in the Louvre he could have been inspired by Titian's *Portrait d'Une Femme à Sa Toilette,* in which the iconography very obviously centers on the themes of vanity, fleeting mortal beauty, and death.[8] Taking our speculation somewhat further, we recognize that in other European paintings, such as Gerard Honthorst's *Vanitas,* the incorporation of mirrors into their compositions symbolized these issues of life in the way that mirrors did in the sonnets of Shakespeare:

> Look in thy glass, and tell the face thou viewest
> Or who is he so fond will be the tomb
> Of his self-love, to stop posterity?[9]

Ritman's focus on the relation of his subject to the mirror is not proof that he intended to create a *Vanitas* iconography in his *Toilette* scene. Yet the mirror device was one with which he had been familiar with since his earliest student days in Chicago, and which he exploited regularly at this time, having taken it not so discreetly from the history of European art that surrounded him. At the Ecole, the production of academic art was justifiably his goal; this kind of iconography, whether subtle or obvious, was common even in his day. Furthermore, at the Ecole Ritman was obliged to attend lectures on art history, and these could easily have inspired him to design a modern composition incorporating old symbols. Then, too, he may have heard words to the effect of those of Erwin Panofsky: "Small wonder that the mirror—that awe-inspiring device which could symbolize self-awareness as well as self-indulgence, and was credited with magic powers from times immemorial—was the standard attribute not only of Prudence and Truth but also of Vanity—in the sense of being inordinately pleased with oneself as well as in the more terrible sense of the Preacher's 'Vanity of vanities; all is vanity.' "[10]

Ritman finished his picture in time for the salon jury reception in March. The same rowdy crowd made its appearance on the steps of the Palais as porters brought the pictures from the vans to the huge entry doors of the exhibition hall. Commonly, several thousand pictures were submitted, yet exhibition space existed for less than one-half or even one-third of them if the number was unusually large. Although his work had been accepted there a year earlier, Ritman waited anxiously for jury results for nearly six weeks. As usual, time dragged on in spite of his busy spring routine. He was even more concerned this year than last because *La Toilette* was a larger and much more important-looking work, one which he thought might have a better chance of advantageous display and possibly even an award. "Nevertheless," he was warned, "a large picture attracts more scrutiny." Ritman felt as though he stood at the brink of success, but he was still overawed by the scope of the salon and its political machinations. Some of the stories he had heard about salon politics made him wonder if his efforts were worth

Ill. 12-5. Frank Benson. *The Black Hat*. 1904. Oil on canvas, 40 x 32 inches. Museum of Art, Rhode Island School of Design. Gift of Walter Callander, Henry D. Sharpe, Howard L. Clark, William Gammell and Isaac C. Bates.

the emotional pressure. From the time he had been a youngster in Enella Benedict's sketch class at the Hull House, he had been coached on the qualities that would make a picture win an award; on top of that, he was being coached by two of the salon's most influential masters, but these considerations did not relieve his anxiety. The idea that fruition in the profession of fine art was measured by one's victories at the Paris Salon had been so firmly implanted in his motivational makeup that he had every intention of succeeding with *La Toilette*. When selections were announced early that spring of 1911, Ritman discovered not only that *La Toilette* had been

accepted but that another work of his, entitled simply *Portrait*, was also going to be hung.[11] At the risk of underestimating Louis's reaction to having his first major work included in the famous Paris Salon, we may assume that he was thrilled!

There was the usual pomp and circumstance at the opening of this One Hundred Twenty-Ninth Annual Paris Salon some weeks later. Once again, the exhibition was held at the Grand Palais des Beaux-Arts, and it was as much a social as an art event, where fashionable men and women spent most of their time looking at each other instead of at the art (ill. 12-7). Nevertheless, it was the Salon, it was spring, it was Paris, and young Ritman finally realized that he was climbing the ladder of success much faster than even his most ardent supporters in Chicago had expected. At the moment, visitors and artists alike realized that they were participating in the making of art history: everyone knew that the eyes of the art world focused first on the Paris spring salons, and that the viewers formed part of the grand event. Visitors were anxious to obtain the official catalogs which served as souvenirs for most and valuable records for others. When Ritman read a copy of the catalog, he found that his paintings were noted as entries 1598 and 1599, and that he was listed as a painter born in America, a student of Tony Robert-Fleury, Cormon, and Déchenaud.[12]

Claude Roger-Marx, the chauvinistic publisher, editor, and self-styled critic of *La Chronique* was present at the vernissage.[13] Like most of his French constituents, Roger-Marx found that when he compared landscapes by foreign artists with those by French artists, the latter demonstrated "graceful charm" and they dealt with "the soil of their country, maintaining a relationship which leads them to a closer and more intimate communion." He postulated in conclusion: "These differences seem to grow less as far as figural and genre painting is concerned. I believe it is . . . the dominance which the Parisian studios have managed to maintain in the shaping of talents from abroad." Making implicit reference to the Giverny expatriates, Marx ranked *Ritman* with Miller and Parker: "An important colony of American artists attend the studios [of Parisian training]; in their minds they blend the French lessons with the memory of 'Whistlerian' arrangements and a pronounced taste for the exploration of boudoir scenes, picturesque and amusing but evincing insufficient variety in the long run."[14] Writing for the *Gazette des Beaux-Arts*, René Jean failed to mention Ritman's picture, but he singled out a similar work by Miller which also featured "two women, richly adorned, closeted in a room, where one of them admires, in front of the *Toilette*, the erudite art which presided at her hairdressing session."[15]

His work having received significant praise from influential French critics in three major salons in Paris, Ritman knew that he was rapidly rising as one of the bright stars in the American expatriate milieu, especially in his relationship to the Giverny group. He gained a little more recognition when the famous critic for *Le Temps*, Thiébault-Sisson, thought *La Toilette* worthy of mention and wrote "of the American Ritman who exhibited a rather fascinating portrait of a young woman (de l'Américain Ritman [who exhibited] un portrait assez séduisant de jeune femme)."[16] Although he received no medal, Ritman's accomplishment was stellar for a twenty-two-year-old immigrant painter from Chicago.

Back in Chicago, the Ritman family was elated when it learned of Louis's acceptance to the salon. The success was made even more palatable when a local paper ran a feature article on him: "Across the sea, in Paris, a Chicago lad, Louis Ritman is in the limelight of popular acclaim as an artist and skillful painter—a genius in the translation of themes and a draughtsman wonderfully attuned in technique," reported H. Effa Webster. "How did it happen that a Chicago youth of 20 [incorrect age] accomplished two paintings that were accepted and hung in the Paris Salon with a consequence of sudden fame for the modestly alien student in the Latin Quarter? Here is the answer, and you'll find ambition and industry and romance in it." Again reporting an incorrect date, Webster continued: "Less than three years ago, the Ritman family came from Russia to Chicago and found an abiding place in our West side ghetto. Forthwith, every member of the little flock old enough to work set about earning a living in the strange land. Louis Ritman, hardly 17, was clever with pencil and brush and loved to dabble in paint pots, so somehow, he drifted into a sign painter's shop and got a job. In due course, he aspired to develop into an artisan of high degree."[17]

Without a doubt, a large part of Ritman's youthful achievement was the result of prodigious talent, but it was also the product of hundreds of hours of carefully disciplined study and an unusually mature mind. It is true that Louis was as much a part of the young bohemian milieu as were most of his fellow expatriates—excepting perhaps his roommate, Dutchie Heerman—but the rather superficial, even amoral lifestyle did not distract him to the degree of mitigating his productivity. One must conclude, then, that Ritman was more stimulated by the potential of his career momentum than by the magnetic but shallow social alliances that resulted in the downfall of many young American expatriates.

In later years, a friend who was with Ritman at this time reported that "after a year or two in Paris, many a talented lad has returned to his home with no benefit from his stay abroad, and only an acquired habit of drinking, gambling, and loafing in cafés."[18] Ritman's devotion to academic discipline and to a goal in high art was similar to that of many former expatriates. In this regard, Ritman was like his mentor, Lawton Parker, who had also put his time in at the Ecole and built his style on the academic tradition, following a methodology far different from that of Whistler, who thumbed his nose at everything academic, disciplined, and traditional. In any case, the result of the widely disparate expatriate careers of Parker and Whistler was the same—outstanding fine art produced early in their expatriate careers. Ritman sought the same result, provided it could be achieved with dignity.

Having achieved a measure of recognition from the

Ill. 12-6. William Paxton. *Sylvia.* 1908. Oil on canvas, 49 x 39 inches. Butler Institute of American Art.

salons in Paris, Ritman was ready to pursue other goals. His recent successes created better opportunities for exhibiting in various national shows in the United States, especially at the annual shows of the National Academy of Design in New York. He hoped, too, that his work might attract the attention of a gallery in New York or Chicago, since commercial representation at home would furnish new funds to extend his stay in Paris. Therefore, he reasoned, if he pursued his art by following the academic procedure, he would almost be guaranteed future successes and patrons who would invest in his career. With such an optimistic prospect, Ritman intended to work even harder for the forthcoming salons. At the same time, he wondered about the world of the independent painters, men like Miller and Frieseke, who could follow the path hacked out by the impressionists and yet find acceptance and reward at the salons.

Notwithstanding his latest achievements, Ritman was not fully convinced that the salon style or its routine was the right direction for him. Working each day in the city where impressionism was born, he had come to respect the aesthetic, the waning but highly respected impressionist movement, and the latter-day generation of American impressionist painters. Yet, in spite of its magnetic lure, the path of the independents seemed risky and insecure; moreover, Ritman realized that it was imperative for him to succeed at the Salon. Repeatedly he had been taught the value of the Ecole education and of painting in an acceptable style. Alas, perhaps alliance with the independents, even the conservative impressionists, would have to be sacrificed for recognition by the traditional art establishment. On the other hand, he felt constrained and not as innovative as he might feel if he did not pursue impressionism as others urged. Certainly he would have no problem learning its salient features, since he had Parker, Miller, and Frieseke to guide him. There were also scores of fine examples of impressionism to study in Paris, so Ritman could experiment with the broken-color technique while continuing to prepare canvases for salon shows. Recently it seemed that he saw more impressionism than academicism.

The problem for Ritman was to figure out how he should respond to his temptation to become an impressionist. He asked himself over and over how he might best proceed, since most of the original innovators were already in their sixties, no longer in Paris, and unwilling to accept students. The most obvious solution was to forget about working under a French impressionist and take the advice given repeatedly by Parker, Frieseke, and Miller—namely, to go to Giverny where they worked in serenity near Monet. Here, surrounded by the color of his gardens and the mists of the Epte and the Seine,

Monet hid himself and refused to take students, especially American expatriates. Yet everyone knew that the American milieu in Giverny consisted mostly of confirmed impressionists who were anxious to add a young member as talented as Ritman to their ranks. Although in years past Monet had consistently demonstrated prejudice against Americans, he eventually made an exception to his rule of no students by counseling his son-in-law,

Ill. 12-7. The Grand Palais des Beaux-Arts. R. H. Love Galleries Archives, Chicago.

Theodore Butler. He had also given advice to Lilla Cabot Perry, one of the few American pioneers who had stayed in Giverny until recently.[19] Only years later would the art world learn just how close Perry had been to Monet and what a great debt her early productions owed to his instruction. In describing that first summer of 1889 in Giverny, Perry recalled that she "was a student in the Paris studios at that time and had shown at the Salon for the first time that spring." With the exception of Theodore Robinson and Theodore Butler, Perry was one of the few American artists who was granted entry to Monet's studio. On one of these occasions, she recalled: "There were two pictures on the walls of his studio which I particularly liked." She went on to report that "they were of his stepdaughter [Suzanne Hoschedé Butler] in a white dress, a green veil floating in the breeze under a sunshade, on the brow of a hill against the sky."[20]

Although Monet had already ceased his production of figurative works, owing to his all-too-frequent lack of success with them, he recognized the abilities of others to incorporate the fully draped female within an otherwise full-blown impressionistic scene. In fact, judging from Perry's recollections, Monet may have given momentum to the tradition of painting young women posed in out-of-doors settings in Giverny. He subsequently encouraged Butler in this direction and also told

Perry that her "forte was 'plein air' figures out of doors." Surely his advice to Theodore Robinson was similar even before he instructed Perry to "remember that every leaf on the tree is as important as the features of your model." Prophesying Picasso's mannerism, Monet continued: "I should like just for once to see you put her mouth under one eye instead of under her nose!"[21] Monet's concept was to be realized in the history of art, but Perry was interested only in impressionism, reiterating that Monet "never took any pupils, but he would have made a most inspiring master if he had been willing to teach."[22]

As he moved about Paris, Ritman undoubtedly heard innumerable rumors and stories about Monet and the Americans who worked near him in Giverny. Of course, the best information he could have unearthed came from a nearby source, the Giverny group itself, some of whom frequented the Café du Dôme in the winter seasons. Among the most reliable expatriates on Giverny were those Ritman had come to know, Frieseke, Miller, and Parker, who balanced their time between Paris and Giverny, with Parker making annual trips to Chicago and New York. Numerous other second-generation American impressionists inhabited the village, accomplished painters like the Chicagoan Karl Buehr, Edmund Greacen, and George Oberteuffer. Even if he had not liked the art of his mentors—Frieseke, Miller, and Parker—Ritman would have been obliged to respect their advice in consideration of their impressive credentials. All three had won numerous awards in the salons, and Miller had even been made Knight of the Legion of Honor several years earlier. Furthermore, they were well known not only in France but in the United States as well. The New York critic E. A. Taylor stated: "Frieseke, like Miller cannot complain of want of appreciation; for artists who are still in their spring-time of energy the success of both is quite phenomenal." Taylor reminded his readers that "in following Miller and Frieseke's work through its many phases one can undoubtedly trace influences of the time, but added to that their own personality, which as it grew, increased their knowledge and receptive faculty; these are the means by which the seeker acquires dexterity and capability, two qualities which are necessary to the artist, and which both men possess to a marked degree." (pl. 12-1).[23]

Like Frieseke and Miller, Ritman wanted recognition

and financial security. After all, he could not forget the rave reviews his Giverny friends had received from the New York critics when their paintings were shown at the Madison Art Gallery only a few months earlier: "A group of Americans living abroad (who call themselves the Giverny Group) are having an exhibition . . . . These are Lawton Parker, Frederick Frieseke, Richard Miller and Guy Rose. These intensely modern young men are better known abroad than in their own country . . . . They are not afraid to put a figure right out in the glaring light and paint it."[24] Another critic reported: "These brothers of the brush are often seen walking arm in arm in the streets of the French capital ordering in the same cafés. They paint in much the same style, usually using brilliant colors and employing a high key. Also they like to limn parasols with the light shining on them—gay parasols in gardens, held at bewitching angles by pretty young women. Three of these painters, Messrs. Miller, Frieseke, and Parker, have contributed *In a Garden*." (pl. 12-2).[25] Yet another critic reminded his readers that "it would be easy to praise too highly these summer glories seen against the pallor of the current exhibitions, but they certainly contribute a joyous note to the rather colorless art of this big, indifferent town. They are not the last cry of French art by any means. All the artists represented are Americans who appear to be in good and regular standing in the Paris Salons."[26]

Thus, to whatever degree Giverny beckoned him on account of Monet's presence, Ritman was just as lured by the achievements of Parker, Frieseke, Miller, and other members of the American expatriate milieu, who spent their summers in Giverny and their winters in Paris and found enthusiastic response for their Giverny productions wherever they were shown. Like any other young and enthusiastic expatriate, Ritman needed recognition from the salons, but he also needed a fuller share in the glittering American experience, which was dominated by two basic factions—the Matisse followers who were gravitating to Gertrude Stein in Paris, and the impressionists who were based near Monet in Giverny. There were peripheral groups—well-meaning associates whose motivations were as viable as any other—but Ritman was not interested in these; he was still a Chicago expatriate, still magnetized by the dreams of his early youth.

Notes

1. W. M. R. French to Richard H. Miller, Chicago, 29 November 1910, Director WMRF, Letter Book, Art Institute of Chicago Archives, Chicago.

2. An official forum for the Société des Artistes Indépendants (Society of Independent Artists), the Salon des Indépendants was founded in 1884 for the purpose of showing art with no jury. A number of painters organized the society as a result of having been rejected from the Paris Salon, the official forum of the Société des Artistes Français (Society of French Artists).

3. Richard H. Love, *Theodore Earl Butler: Emergence from Monet's Shadow* (Chicago: Haase-Mumm Publishing Co., 1985), pp. 330-31.

4. E. A. Taylor, "The American Colony of Artists in Paris," *International Studio*, XLIII, no. 172 (June 1911), p. 263.

5. Ibid., pp. 263-64.

6. For a study on American students, see H. Barbara Weinberg, "Nineteenth Century American Painters at the Ecole des Beaux-Arts," *American Art Journal*, 13 (Autumn 1981), pp. 66-84.

7. Lena C. McCauley, "Wellington J. Reynolds—Painter," *The Sketch Book*, V, no. 7 (May 1906), p. 337.

8. Reference is made to Titian's *Vanitas* (c. 1515) in the Pinakothek in Munich. See Erwin Panofsky, *Problems in Titian* (New York: New York University Press, 1969), pp. 92-94.

9. William Shakespeare, Sonnet Number 3, quoted from *Love Poems and Sonnets of William Shakespeare* (Garden City, NY: Doubleday & Co., Inc., 1957), p. 10.

10. Panofsky, p. 93.

11. *Exposition annuelle des Beaux-Arts: Salon de 1911* (Paris: Société des Artistes Français, 1911).

12. Ibid.

13. Claude Roger-Marx, "Varnishing Day at the Salon of the Société des Artistes Français," *La Chronique des Arts et de la Curiosité*, no. 17 (29 April 1911), p. 132.

14. Ibid.

15. ". . . deux femmes parées richement dans la chambre close, où l'une d'elles admire, devant la *Toilette*, l'art savant qui présida à l'ordonnance de sa coiffure." René Jean, "Les Salons de 1911: Le Salon de la Société des Artistes Français," *Gazette des Beaux-Arts*, vol. 2 (1911), p. 420.

16. Thiébault-Sisson, *Le Temps*, 29 April 1911.

17. H. Effa Webster, "Paris Lauds Chicago Boy—Ghetto Artist Wins Honor," *The Chicago Examiner*, unidentified newspaper clipping.

18. G. Warshawsky, *The Memories of an American Impressionist*, ed. Ben L. Basham (Kent, OH: The Kent State University Press, 1980), p. 109.

19. Lilla Cabot Perry and her husband lived in their Giverny house near Monet from not long after their arrival in 1889 until 1909.

20. Lilla Cabot Perry went on to explain that Monet showed her a large repaired tear in one of them. The master explained that he had put his foot through it because he had been dissatisfied with his progress on it. Perhaps the tale is correct, but it smacks of a temper tantrum in response to Suzanne's romance with Theodore Butler. Suzanne had been Monet's favorite model at the time she met Butler. For an in-depth discussion of the family relationship, see R. Love, Chap. 11. See also Lilla Cabot Perry, "Reminiscences of Claude Monet from 1889 to 1909," *The American Magazine of Art*, XVII, no. 3 (March 1927), p. 120.

21. Perry, p. 120.

22. Ibid.

23. Taylor, p. 270.

24. *New York Telegraph*, 21 December 1910.

25. *New York Herald*, 21 December 1910.

26. *New York Times*, 25 December 1910.

CHAPTER THIRTEEN:
AN INTIMIST SURGE

It was probably with one of his American friends that Ritman first visited Giverny in the late spring or early summer of 1911. Still devoted to the goal of winning recognition at the salons, he also hoped to expand his perception by experimenting with Monet's broken-color style.

Like everyone before him, Ritman went to the sleepy Normandy village by train. He left no written record of his first impressions, but since very little about the place had changed over the years, one can assume that an earlier description provided by Will H. Low will serve as a relatively accurate substitute: "Giverny, as a hamlet struggling along an unshaded road, offers at first glance little that is picturesque. Through the valley which it dominates runs the Seine, and between the village and the larger river winds a small stream, the Epte, with pleasantly shaded banks enclosed between broad meadows gracefully bordered by long lines of poplars. Its greatest charm lies in the atmospheric conditions over the lowlands, where the moisture from the rivers, imprisoned through the night by the valleys bordering hills, dissolve before the sun and bathe the landscape in an iridescent flood of vaporous hues, of which Monet in his transcripts has portrayed the charm—a beauty which escaped most of the anxious neophytes who were . . . 'camping on his trail.'"[1] Ritman was not a neophyte, but as far as impres-

sionism was concerned, he had to expand a good deal of his academic training to assimilate the style. He was fortunate in this regard to have friends in Giverny who had done so before him—to them he was a kind of apprentice.

All newcomers in Giverny stayed at the Hotel Baudy (ill. 13-1), the wonderfully charming inn that was still well managed by Angelina Ledoyen Baudy. Ritman was neat and clean-shaven, an artist who presented a far different appearance from that of Willard Metcalf, the first American artist to seek lodging there exactly a quarter of a century earlier. Although the Hotel Baudy had been set up primarily for artists, a variety of personalities were boarding there when Ritman first signed the guest register. Whether Heerman accompanied him is unknown, but it was not long before Ritman became acquainted with other hotel guests. Like so many others before him, Ritman became enchanted with Giverny (ill. 13-2), which, more than any other place, seemed to possess a potent magic power to captivate Americans (ill. 13-3). The village of Vernon, where Robinson, Butler, and others had painted, was nearby. Pierre Bonnard was living in its tiny suburb of Vernonnet, when Ritman came to Giverny.

The time spent in Giverny during the summer of 1911 was a truly eye-opening experience for Ritman. Parker had returned to Chicago earlier in the spring, but Frieseke and Miller felt more generous with their time. Alson Skin-

Ill. 13-1. Louis Ritman with his model [Mimi?], at the Hotel Baudy, Giverny. Photograph. Courtesy Maurice Ritman.

ner Clark and his wife were also in Giverny. Because this Midwestern group knew a good deal about Parker's trouble with Director French at the Art Institute, a lively conversation would often ensue about the state of art in Chicago. The topic gained momentum when certain important members (usually trustees) of the Art Institute visited or contacted an artist in the Giverny group. Such was the case earlier that spring when an art committee consisting of George F. Porter, Ralph Poole, and Robert Allerton came to Frieseke's studio. As its representative, Porter subsequently wrote to French in Chicago, recommending that he send an official letter to Frieseke asking him to send pictures they liked. "If you wish," Porter continued, "I will also be very glad to write Mr. Frieseke, as I know him personally."[2]

During the same sweltering July of 1911 in Chicago at the Art Institute, Lawton Parker exercised his political prowess to exclude French from an impromptu meeting that included Ritman's former teacher, Enella Benedict. They voted to include Parker's salon picture entitled *The Souvenir* in the works to be sent from Paris. Having been informed of their decision, French wrote to Sara Hallowell in Paris, asking her to put the painting with the rest of her selection. As if she were oblivious to their continual disagreements, French explained: "My relations with Mr. Parker became somewhat strained some years ago and I am careful to treat him as well as other people."[3] Only a few days later, as Ritman was trying to discover the secrets of impressionism in Frieseke's garden, Director French wrote to Hallowell again, telling her that Trustee Ryerson had returned from Paris with a personal checklist of his favored paintings from those she had selected from the salon. Among the many he had chosen were Parker's *The Souvenir* and *Premier Chagrin,* Miller's *La Toilette,* Karl Buehr's *Repetition,* Max Bohm's *Mère et Enfants,* and Ritman's *Portrait.*[4]

While Ritman's art thus was receiving greater recognition from the cultural leaders of Chicago in 1911, other events in the city and in the Western world were signifying the beginnings of both major scourges and blessings for the twentieth century. Most of these events were soon to effect significant changes in Ritman's life. The burning question of Serbian unification in the Balkans reverberated in Chicago. Since the Ritmans enjoyed the friendship of the Serbians, Ritman and his Midwestern friends soon learned of the unrest in Chicago's large Serbian community. Trouble stemmed from the controversy surrounding the Black Hand secret society, which had been reuniting Serbs living in the Austrian and Ottoman empires with their relatives in Serbia and whose slogan was *Unedinjene ili Smrt* ("Unity or Death").

Ill. 13-2. Louis Ritman with his model [Mimi?] in Giverny. Photograph. Courtesy Maurice Ritman.

It seemed to some Chicagoans that the American art world was sprinting at a pace equivalent to that of technology, but the latter usually received larger headlines in the press. In Chicago rumors circulated about the forthcoming deluxe railroad service to Los Angeles on the Santa Fe. This weekly, sixty-three-hour passenger run, it was said, would offer an amazing variety of services, including a barbershop, library, stenographer, daily market reports, and, of course, the Fred Harvey dining cars and the Pullman sleeping cars, the latter of which were manufactured in the vast and famous Pullman complex on the city's South Side.

Not only to Chicagoans but also to urban dwellers throughout the entire Western world, each day brought inventive new transportation services. In Chicago, New York, London, and Paris, fewer horse-drawn vehicles were found on the crowded streets; in fact, it was at this time that the last horse-drawn bus was taken out of service by the London General Omnibus Company. In Chicago, traffic usually moved at a snail's pace because of the competition between horse-drawn and motor vehicles. Ritman's parents did not own an automobile.

Ill. 13-3. Louis Ritman. *View of Giverny.* Oil on canvas, 26 x 32 inches. Private Collection. Courtesy R. H. Love Galleries, Chicago.

In May 1911, about 180 miles south of Chicago, auto enthusiasts were thrilled to witness the first Indianapolis 500 motorcar race, in which a Marmon Wasp won with an average of 75 miles per hour. In art, Indianapolis and Muncie still boasted of their pioneer impressionists — Theodore C. Steele, J. Ottis Adams, Otto Stark (who had recently moved to Norwalk), and William Forsyth. They all remained active in the Chicago art community but were not as highly visible as they had been in the days of the World's Fair in 1893, when Hamlin Garland championed their art.[5] North of Chicago in Spring Green, Wisconsin, Frank Lloyd Wright completed Taliesin East. Without a doubt, Frank Lloyd Wright was fast becoming one of the leading architects in the United States, and Chicagoans were fascinated by his avant-garde residential architecture as he built homes in and around the greater Chicago area. As usual, Chicago served as a kind of nucleus for most of the serious art activity in the Midwest while peripheral areas made stellar contributions from time to time.

As if he were aware of the limitations that future events might impose on his time, Ritman hurried back to Paris

as soon as his canvases in Giverny were transportable. He had been inspired by the American group at the Hotel Baudy and by the pictures they made in and around Giverny, but once back in Paris, he was ready for a different challenge — that of preparing another major canvas for the Salon. Ritman needed desperately to succeed in the Salon: he needed a medal to prove his talents to himself and to others in Chicago. Once again, he consulted Professor Déchenaud regarding his plans to show at the Salon, but he also requested criticism from Henri Paul Royer, *sociétaire hors concours* with the Société des Artistes Français. Royer was a highly respected salon master, a former student of Jules Lefebvre and a winner of the Prix Nationale, but he was somewhat more liberal in his teaching than were other academicians. Royer was versatile, in that he painted both landscapes and portraits, but his specialty was genre. Ritman was interested in both his subject matter and his technical dexterity. The impressionism with which Ritman had been experimenting had to be sacrificed for the time being as he concentrated once again on the characteristics of academic imagery. To this end he worked long hours in his Montparnasse studio. In the evenings he renewed his acquaintanceships at the Café du Dôme.

In the arrangement of his compositions, Ritman deviated little from his quasi-salon formula; but in his choice of subject matter, his Giverny experience seems to have solidified his preference for fully draped female figures posed in intimate modern-day Vermeeresque settings. When it was possible, he tried to pose his model in such a way that light from a nearby window would cast interesting patterns on her figure and on the surrounding objects in the room, as Reynolds had taught him. In these works the influences are obvious, since they range from Reynolds to Renoir, Chase, Parker, Miller, and Frieseke; however, the general pictorial format was just as popular among academic artists. We see that in terms of pictorial content, the greatest influence in his work at this time was *intimisme*, the kind exhibited by the Giverny impressionists and the similar French mode: the depiction of an attractive young female in an intimate setting, frequently indoors (pl. 13-1). Art-historically, the genesis of intimism occurred in Holland, then became popular in France, and finally proliferated on both sides of the Atlantic for several decades.

In the winter of 1911-12, Ritman had not yet become a true Francophile, but he was in Paris at the end of *la belle époque*, the art of which often featured lovely young women in small, happy gatherings and in quiet intimate settings.[6] An artistic product of fin de siècle, the fashion of feminine loveliness magnetized Ritman, as he had already proved in **La Toilette**. Little has been written

Ill. 13-4. Louis Ritman. *Before the Ball*. Location unknown. Photograph. Courtesy of the Louis Ritman family.

ous art statements, thus appreciated by the critics and public alike. To American philosophers like George Santayana, however, these paintings represented insubstantial reflections of life, shallow symbols in art of the genteel tradition, which he thought "avoided the reality of life."[8]

In spite of what was said about intimism in elitist intellectual and cultural circles, first the American group in Giverny and now Ritman continued to explore and exploit it. Ritman demonstrated his predilection for that kind of genre of intimism in the picture he prepared in the winter of 1911-12 for the forthcoming Spring Salon. Capitalizing on his success with *La Toilette*, Ritman designed a similar scene, which he called *Before the Ball* (ill. 13-4). Except for stylistic differences, his large vertical image might have been painted by Parker or Miller. Once again the composition includes two women — one seated at the left, the other standing at the right. This time, however, the standing figure faces forward as she communicates with the other subject, and her back is reflected in the mirror. Once again, we are made privy to a private scene: two young women are obviously concerned with their appearances as they primp before a festive event. As in *La Toilette*, the objects in the room indicate wealth and opulent surroundings. Ostensibly, the scene is an intimate and quite informal one, but in terms of pictorial design, it is a formula composition, manifesting balance of form, space, and texture. Whether Royer or Déchenaud had much influence on Ritman's composition is unknown, but the final design includes an interesting and sensible variety of room elements that serve as integrating motifs. Apparently no subtle iconography was intended here: both subjects ignore the single mirror at the back of the room. On the other hand, do these sophisticated ladies only pretend to ignore vanitas? In this painting, Ritman demonstrates considerable skill in draftsmanship and brushwork but very little imagination. This picture proves that Ritman, in spite of his youth, was already a master technician, working surface textures with the convincing skill of an older painter. Nonetheless, *Before the Ball* is little more than another artistic tour de force and a prime example of the shallow iconography that Santayana considered typical of the American genteel tradition and a lingering expatriate slice of the French juste milieu.

Certainly Ritman made no conscious effort to create pictorial insipidity, but his work reflected insubstantial, albeit mainstream academic taste trends, and he had been guided every step of the way to paint in that mode. He succeeded in this regard, but in retrospect we judge that the work was not innovative, not progressive, not avant-garde, and thus mediocre.

Ritman and Heerman were not part of the first group

about the American kind of intimism that emerged from the *belle époque*, since it is related to, but is quite different from, the famous French art usually associated with the period, namely that of exuberant fetes; entertainment at places like Maxim's or the Chat Noir; laughter, music, dancing, wine, absinthe, and *la vie bohéme* , depicted by artists like Toulouse-Lautrec, Jules Chéret, Renoir, and others. American intimism was by contrast quiet, reserved, and above all, discreet, never outside the parameters of the genteel tradition.

Especially since his first sojourn to Giverny, Ritman had homologized more American intimism. In that unique French village, this mode had manifested itself as a pictorial fad, which, as a kind of by-product of the more moderate French *juste milieu*, was assimilated to greater or lesser degrees by newcomer American painters like Ritman.[7] In this special environment, intimate subjects were presented in good taste, and these images were seri-

of American expatriates to study in Paris, nor were they the first to become homesick or lonely for the camaraderie of fellow Americans. As early as 1890, A. A. Anderson had recognized the need for "an agreeable headquarters and a common meeting-ground for . . . young men as have not forgotten their Americanism nor lost their desire for American news, American faces, and some features of the life they left at home."[9] Anderson was interested only in intiating the organization, hoping that eventually the club would stand on its own as a smooth-running society. He discovered the perfect place to serve this purpose as he walked "along the Boulevard du Montparnasse one day in April . . . . He found an old wall and he looked over it." Thinking of the future, Anderson mentally transformed the "long, narrow building whose entire first floor was below the level of the street," and which had been "half ruined and abandoned," into a suitable meeting place for the homesick American art students. Within a few weeks the building was restored and its interior remodeled into an attractive, invitin(place. Having adopted a nine-year lease, Anderson funded the entire renovation of the building; however, he did not wish to participate in the operations of the organization, known as the American Art Association of Paris, and relegated its running to the association of students who made up its initial membership. After some time, Rodman L. Wanamaker, the wealthy art enthusiast from Philadelphia, was elected president.[10] Soon many American art students joined the club. As Anderson had hoped, they met to share conversation about art and their lives, about games and food, and about home. Rooms had various functions: one served as a gallery; another, a library; and still another, a reading-room that was a "low, cozy, and nicely heated [room] in winter, and . . . a favorite lounging-place during dark, bad weather, when it is next to impossible to work for want of light."[11]

At the time of the inauguration of the American Art Association in 1890, Whitelaw Reid, the American ambassador to France, estimated that there were about 1,500 American art students in Paris. Even though this estimate may have been somewhat exaggerated, American artists formed the largest group of expatriates by the 1890s. According to statistics compiled by Lois Fink, 640 American artists participated in the annual exhibitions of the French salons during the most active period of artistic productivity in the 1890s. Ambassador Reid also speculated that most of the expatriate art students were concentrated "within a mile or two" of the American Art Association's club quarters at 131, boulevard du Montparnasse.[12]

By 1911, the premises of the club had become inadequate for its burgeoning membership, thus forcing the association to relocate its quarters to rue Joseph Bara at boulevard Raspail, not far from Ritman's apartment. The presidency of the organization still belonged to Rodman Wanamaker (Frieseke's close friend and patron), through whose benevolent efforts the new site became more useful. As before, it included a well-stocked library and parlor, but now also a restaurant, a small garden, and even an athletic room. The bulletin board always remained a point of attraction because mail was posted there. In her descriptive text on Henry Ossawa Tanner, who was a member of the club when Ritman joined it, Marcia M. Mathews points out that "the American Art Club [Association] was not only a pleasant place to spend leisure hours, but one where he [Tanner] could keep au courant of happenings in Paris and meet some important members of the American art colony."[13] Visitors were obliged to ring a bell for entry, but the club was kept open late to allow a homesick artist an opportunity to talk things over with another American artist-friend.

Although women were not allowed to become members of the American Art Association, they had an equivalent organization known as the Home Club. Here, as at the association, American women students were treated to lectures, concerts, and teas. They also had library facilities and a quiet place to read and write letters, but most importantly, they had a place where their "home-sick" hearts were "rejoiced by the chatter of fifteen or twenty American girls."[14]

For men there was also the French Club, or *cercle* as it was called, and the Anglo-Saxon Club, but these were exclusive organizations and would not have been open to artists, especially if they were Jewish. So it was that Ritman belonged to the American Art Association of Paris. Even though it was a long way from Chicago, many Midwesterners could be found there who shared his interests and goals and even certain memories of Chicago. In fact, the first reopening exhibition at the association, which took place in the spring of 1912, was arranged by Walter Griffin, Richard Miller, and Parke C. Dougherty, but it included work by Midwesterners like Alson Skinner Clark, Frieseke, Oberteuffer, Karl Buehr, and, of course, Louis Ritman. A critic writing for *International Studio* praised the association and its new spring exhibition and reported that "the work was markedly characteristic of American art in Paris." He stated flatly that "there was nothing outrageously modern or foggily dull, brilliancy of colour and naturalism being the dominant features." He suggested, however, that "a welcome addition of a little more unconventionality would have filled a felt void and completed the lacking note." He found that "Mr. Miller was well represented . . . . That he is a strong personality with an influence was distinctly evident by the adaptation of his subjects and methods which have been unblushingly appropriated by other painters and are recognizable in their work."[15] All in all, the American Art Association of Paris played an important role in the life of Louis Ritman and many of his expatriate comrades.

Ill. 13-5. Guillaume Apollinaire, the influential art critic who shaped the ideas of the art world in Paris after meeting Picasso in 1904. R. H. Love Galleries Archives, Chicago.

As the 1912 spring exhibition season evolved, gossip proliferated about the mounting influence of the Cubists and about the future of art in general.[16] The so-called modern art movement was fractured into a number of camps which spread their tentacles to both sides of the Atlantic via a trunk system from Paris to New York. There were many high-powered promoters of modernism in Paris, men like Daniel-Henry Kahnweiler and Guillaume Apollinaire (ill. 13-5), but their American counterparts, individuals like Gertrude Stein (ill. 13-6), Walter Pach, and others, were exceedingly instrumental in maintaining its momentum as an international movement.[17] Of course, no one in America was as devoted to modernism as were Alfred Stieglitz and his group. Also, just as the Stein apartment served as a convenient and welcome meeting ground for modernists in Paris, the apartment of the avid collector Walter C. Arensberg on West Sixty-seventh Street served as a kind of informal forum for modern poets, painters, and thinkers in New York.[18] Through these few very influential promoters, Cubism and other modern styles came to the attention of leaders of the Chicago art community. Along with the very liberal collector Arthur Jerome Eddy and a couple of farsighted Art Institute trustees, W. M. R. French had "considered" the work of the modernists for exhibition in Chicago. In a February letter to Hallowell in Paris, French revealed that it had occasionally crossed his mind "that a small collection of works by the post-impressionists or Cubists might be found interesting here, if it were possible to procure them without in a manner endorsing them." French made it clear that "they are not yet taken at all seriously in America, and I should scarcely think they would damage our students. We have always been willing to give audiences to heresies and advanced ideas. Of course we would never exhibit some of the subjects they offer."[19] Hallowell's response to French about the Cubists was negative, and in March French replied: "I suppose what you say about the 'Cubistes' etc., to be entirely true, but of course they excite a good deal of interest in art circles here as they have in Paris."[20]

Except through his close relationship with Parker, Ritman had no way of knowing about the many inside maneuvers of the trustees at the Art Institute. Politicking, nevertheless, was going on in that hallowed hall, and most of it involved French, who was usually very sensitive to the influence of outsiders—especially artists who "had the ear" of influential members of the international art community. For example, about a year earlier, Willard Metcalf, a Giverny pioneer and Parker's acquaintance, suggested that the Art Institute present a solo show of his work. Later French wrote to Hallowell that Metcalf's "friends are so powerful that I arranged for [his show] in March [1912]."[21] Also concerned over his troubles with Parker, French arranged for a solo show of Parker's work as well. It was also slated for March, but the exhibitions did not conflict because Metcalf's paintings were primarily impressionistic landscapes, while Parker's were impressionistic figure works.

Ill. 13-6. Gertrude Stein. Photograph. Yale Collection of American Literature, Beinecke Rare Book and Manuscript Library, Yale University.

Officially recognized as a student of Déchenaud and Royer, 23-year-old Ritman sent several works to Paris Salon jury that March of 1912. As usual he joined in the crowd that stood by at the entrance of the Palais as the procession of paintings moved by and then returned to his studio to wait for the jury results. He would not know the results for several weeks, but that allowed him plenty of time to finish other pictures.

In Chicago, newspapers ran article after article about Pancho Villa, Mexican President Huerta, and worsening relations between America and Mexico. Most Chicagoans were more concerned with current global and local issues than with art, but the same newspapers carried glowing reviews of Parker's solo show that was seen at the Art Institute from 5 to 27 March 1912. Thirty-three works were mounted, including several important portraits and a number of Giverny pictures such as *Summer Sun Spots, The Bather, A Windy Sky — Giverny, Awaiting the Garden Party,* and *The Orange Parasol,* an oil destined to become well-known (pl. 13-2). In the foreword to the exhibition catalog, the writer, identified only as "W," reported that "the canvases exhibited by Mr. Parker present him in a new and interesting light for they show the departure of one hitherto known as a portrait painter into an impressionism of a rather new sort." The reviewer went on to explain that while Monet's impressionism "was the illustration of a theory," Parker "has approached some of the more intimate aspects of nature . . . together with his fellow Luminists, he has painted the nude figure out-of-doors in every variety of sunlight and shade, and his flesh tones, like those of his foliage . . . are modified in wide variety by their environment."[22]

Back in Paris, Ritman was busy in front of his easel. Although he was anxious to prove himself at the upcom-

ing salon, his less ambitious easel pictures showed increasing influences of the intimism he saw in Giverny. At this point, he did not imitate Frieseke, Miller, or Parker, but an amalgamated influence is evident. One example is *Nude in Chair* (ill. 13-7), a rectangular oil probably done some time in the 1911-12 winter season in Paris. The attractive model is completely nude and positioned on a leather chair with her back to the viewer. Drapery on the chair and at the window adds textural variety to the otherwise simplistic scene. The model's pronounced curvilinear form contrasts harmoniously with the numerous vertical lines that make up most of the balance of the image. No obvious broken color is used here, revealing Ritman's reluctance to present his intimism in a typically impressionistic way, but the subject and setting are those of his Giverny friends (ill. 13-8).

During these early spring days of 1912, Ritman was notified that two of his paintings had been accepted —

Ill. 13-7. Louis Ritman. *Nude in Chair.* Oil on canvas, 31¾ x 31¾ inches. Location unknown. Photograph. Courtesy Christie's.

an oil known as *Portrait de l'artiste et son modèle (Portrait of the Artist and his Model)* and his large complex work, *Femmes parées pour le bal masqué (Before the Ball).*

The Salon was large and impressive as usual — the *vernissage* took place on Wednesday, 1 May 1912. All of the right people — indeed, those who made up the "Tout Paris," as Will H. Low said — gathered again "to do hom-

Ill. 13-8. Richard Miller. *Nude*. Oil on canvas, 30 x 34 inches. Private Collection. Courtesy R. H. Love Galleries, Chicago.

age to the arts, before the doors of the Salon [were] opened to the general public."[23] In the official salon catalog, Ritman's pictures were entered as numbers 1589 and 1590, and he was listed as a student of Fleury, Déchenaud, and Henri Royer. Ritman's older expatriate friends from Giverny were well represented, especially Parker, who had recently returned from Chicago. To most visitors there seemed to be no lessening of emphasis on impressionism in spite of the growing interest in more modern trends. As far as academicism in art was concerned, there were plenty who believed that it would never be replaced by "ugly art."

In the following couple of days, every art critic in Paris published his views on the salon. One of these, the venerable Claude Roger-Marx, observed that the influence of impressionism was quite apparent in the show. He reminded his readers that as far back as 1884, "Zola said [with regard to Monet] that 'little by little he pulled our salons from the black kitchen of bitumen and brightened them up with a flash of sunlight.' " Continuing along this line, Marx pointed out that "American artists . . . yield to it [Monet's influence] when they treat intimate or genre scenes, delighting as Mr. Miller and his disciples do, in running the shimmering light on the epidermis of the flesh, the shiny surface of cloth, and the pallor of silvery foliage."[24] No one questioned Ritman's being a disciple of Miller, although his salon entry was comparatively conservative, and he had not yet learned to make flesh shimmer in light.

Because many critics in America preferred intimism to Ash Can or Cubist types, the pictures Ritman submitted

to salon exhibitions were occasionally reproduced with captions in Chicago and New York newspapers, and sometimes the works were discussed briefly in the accompanying art columns. Even then, in the field of fine art, name recognition was important, although Ritman was not as skilled at promoting himself as were his friends Parker, Miller, and Frieseke. Ritman had come to understand the value of newspaper coverage wherever it could be generated. None compared, however, with the *New York Times*, where **Before the Ball** was reproduced in large format in the picture section on Sunday, 5 May 1912. Serious members of Chicago's art community, like Director French and a few artists and critics who read the Sunday *Times,* were impressed with Ritman's burgeoning reputation.

In his painting **Before the Ball**, Ritman followed a mainstream art trend if we are to believe the analysis of an anonymous *New York Times* reviewer who reported to his readers that "the nude as a subject of pictorial art is going out." He explained: "This is the impression forced on one by the sight of this year's Salon paintings, of which there are just upon two thousand. The undressed human body, which has for so long been considered in Europe the highest form of painting, is out of fashion . . . . It is significant that among the American work, which ranks exceedingly high this year in quality and quantity, there is hardly a single nude." Referring not only to Ritman but to many other American expatriates, the writer was optimistic about the future of the art: "Following the success won by Americans at the Beaux-Arts Salon, nothing could be more encouraging than the showing made by natives of the United States at this Salon." Uninhibited about making comparisons, this patriotic writer informed his readers that "not only does their work hold its own easily with any other, but some of the best canvases displayed are from American hands."[25] The reviewer went on to include Ritman in a long list of American painters, some well-known Salon regulars like J. Carroll Beckwith, Frederick Bridgman, George Brown, Max Bohm, Charles Warren Eaton, Richard Miller, Frank Boggs, Preston Dickinson, and several lesser-known artists, including one of Ritman's Chicago friends, Karl Buehr. It is reported that the Salon included over eighty works by American painters. The *Times* critic found "conservatism" to be "the distinguishing characteristic of the forty-odd galleries of paintings in the Salon."

Before the Ball is an outstanding example of Ritman's so-called salon style. Like some works of the earlier French juste-milieu group, the painting demonstrates Ritman's ability to mix the proper ingredients of academicism with certain telltale features of impressionism. No doubt Ritman was fully aware that when judged by modernist standards this art was conservative. His work bore no resemblance to that generated by certain acquaintances who had gravitated to the Stein circle. It took little analysis to see that it was in striking contrast with the paintings recently created by Max Weber, another young American Jew.

Weber, also the son of a tailor, was born in Bialystock, Russia, and had immigrated with his family to Brooklyn. While there were certain similarities in their backgrounds, Ritman and Weber had traveled very different paths to their art. After an inspiring term under Arthur Wesley Dow, Weber taught for two years and then went to Europe, where he studied at the Julian Academy under Jean Paul Laurens before falling under the influence of Cézanne and Matisse.[26] Only about a year before Ritman came to Paris, Weber had returned to New York, where he became one of the circle of the avant-garde painters who orbited around the art dealer Alfred Stieglitz. Stieglitz featured the work of his young associates in a group exhibition, called "Younger American Painters," which was hailed by many moderns as the signal of a new art movement. With regard to the show, the art writer E. A. Taylor reminded his readers: "The modern movement that is so much afoot in Paris just now is producing in the older generation a rousing effect that is distinctly for its good, and amongst the American colony it is decidedly manifest."[27] The set of principles that motivated the avant-garde group was far different from the ideas that dominated Ritman's mental process in producing art.

Ritman had had opportunities to meet some of the New York avant-garde artists at one time or another at various artists' haunts, exhibitions, or other events in Paris because the group found a major source of inspiration in the Gertrude Stein circle. It is known that he spent time with Walter Pach, Edward Steichen, Leo Stein, and Alfred Maurer. In the conversations of this group, the work of Picasso, the most avant-garde artist in Paris, was thoroughly analyzed because it had been shown at Stieglitz's "291," Little Galleries of the Photo-Secession in New York. A bystander like Ritman would probably have agreed with Jerome Meyers (who lived then not far from him in Montparnasse) that "the American art world in the years preceding 1913 was a landscape before an impending storm."[28] Meyers, who was never an expatriate, resented "the claims for French art made by its dealers, to the unjust detriment of our [America's] own work, even of the highest grade."[29] Like Ritman, Meyers was sensitive to the plurality that prevailed in art of Paris: "There were many groups of artists, with conflicting points of view, who felt a distinction between American

art work and the higher-classed foreign work . . . . Childe Hassam was an artist of might. Redfield was scooping up honors. The exhibitions of the 'Eight' were artistic events of note; and on the outskirts, Max Weber and others were growling against the [National] Academy [of Design]. Europe and America were still fairly good neighbors in art and the stage was well set for the greatest French invasion that was ever to descend upon us."[30]

Ill. 13-9. Gare Saint-Lazare around the turn of the century, Paris. Photograph. R. H. Love Galleries Archives, Chicago.

Pluralism in and of itself was problem enough for those who were embroiled in the sorting out of art. Regardless of their pragmatism and objectivity, they knew that something unusual was about to happen. Even to the dilettantes the flux was obvious, but to a critic like Benjamin de Casseres, it was ominous. In the pages of Stieglitz's *Camera Work* at this time, Casseres questioned whether the strong-hearted optimism that had once unified pioneer Americans in their zest for exploration and change had not faded.[31] Years later, H. Wayne Morgan would point out that "the new painters and their friends still saw the artist as a finder of special truth, now seeking the first principles, designs, and forces that underlay 'reality.' " Morgan would ask whether "a generation that needed the comforts of that reality" could "afford the quest?"[32]

Ritman was uninterested in the quest for first principles as he saw it pursued in Paris. He did not wish to be among "the young painters who would now seek notoriety, shortcuts to fame and fortune."[33] Therefore, in spite of avant-garde influences in Paris, the Giverny experience lingered with Ritman. Having been unable to forget Reynolds's pictorial formula, in recent years Ritman had become so inspired by painters in Giverny who concentrated on intimism that he felt it necessary to return to Monet's Norman village. A few years earlier, Ritman's friends Abel Warshawsky and Samuel Halpert had actually hiked all the way to Giverny. In the spring of 1912,

Pl. 13-1. Lawton Parker. *Day Dreams*. Oil on canvas, 40 x 36 inches. Private Collection. Courtesy R. H. Love Galleries, Chicago.

Pl. 13-3. Louis Ritman. *Lily Garden*. Oil on canvas, 32 x 32 inches. Private Collection. Courtesy R. H. Love Galleries, Chicago.

Pl. 13-4. Frederick Carl Frieseke. *Wind and Sun*. Oil on canvas, 32⅛ x 25¾ inches. Private Collection. Courtesy R. H. Love Galleries, Chicago.

Pl. 13-5. Theodore Earl Butler. *Spruce, Poplars and Rainbow.* Oil on canvas. 25½ x 31¾ inches. Warren P. Snyder Collection. Courtesy R. H. Love Galleries, Chicago.

Pl. 13-6. Lawton Parker. *Woman in a Boat*. Oil on canvas, 30 x 24 inches. David Ramus Fine Art.

Pl. 15-1. Charles Webster Hawthorne. *Le Peignoir Rosé*. Ca. 1912. Oil on canvas, 35 ¼ x 31 ½ inches. Private Collection. Courtesy R. H. Love Galleries, Chicago.

Pl. 15-2. Lawton Parker. *Spring Blossoms*. Oil on canvas, 30 x 24 inches. Private Collection. Courtesy R. H. Love Galleries, Chicago.

however, Ritman boarded the train at Gare Saint-Lazare in Paris (ill. 13-9), rode leisurely for about an hour until he reached Mantes, then rode the rest of the way along the Seine to Vernon, the village nestled in a valley only about three miles from Giverny. At Vernon he loaded up a horse-drawn wagon with art paraphernalia and set out for Giverny.

In his fascinating article on Giverny, Pierre Toulgouat related that "the cabbies of Vernon were so used to Americans that they recognized them on sight: they knew their dress and their slightly bewildered look when set down in a strange town in the provinces." Surely Ritman was easily recognized as an American artist. "Hardly anyone got off the train," Toulgouat reported, "before he was shepherded into one or another conveyance and rushed off to Giverny."[34] Once in town, Ritman unloaded his painting gear at the Hotel Baudy, signed the register, and renewed old acquaintances.

There was access through the village on two curving, albeit parallel streets, route Basse and route du Roi, which were "tied together by a network of narrow alleys, each just large enough for a farm wagon to trundle through." Toulgouat described the village as follows: "The houses are of stone, stucco-covered, and since the town is pre-eminently a farming town—and since in France, by a custom that dates from the turbulent Middle Ages, farmers live in the security of town and drive out daily to work in their fields—most houses have a kind of walled barnyard with a grange and poultry shed, all forming part of the property. It's a small town, a quiet town, a peaceful town. There is a church, of solid but unremarkable Norman architecture, and a massively built, once-ecclesiastical structure, the Ferme de la Dîme, or Tithe Farm, where the monks of a now ruined monastery, just outside of town, used to collect their tithings from the peasants."[35]

Ritman truly liked the village—so different from Chicago, Philadelphia, and Paris; its quaint rural quietude and its friendly milieu attracted him as much as the art experience. So enamored was he of the area that he decided to follow the lead of Parker and others by renting one of the charming stone farmhouses, replete with a walled barnyard. The task was easier contemplated than accomplished, since most of the houses had already been let to artists, writers, and wealthy dilettantes. One old farmhouse, called the *Hameau*, had been turned into an art school, which its director, Miss Wheeler, had organized primarily for American girls. Actually, the village was bursting at its seams with aspiring young women artists, as it had been since the early days when Will H. Low observed that at Hotel Baudy alone there "were thirty painter-esses of various ages; and if there were four or five paintermen present they were so outnumbered, and virtually in the shade, that my memory is equally shadowed as to their personality."[36] According to Low, it was Theodore Robinson who "owned partial responsibility for the feminine invasion, as he had unguardedly recommended the place to one or two young women painters in Paris."[37] Regardless of the much higher ratio of women to men, at age twenty-three Ritman was a confirmed bachelor—not the bohemian bon vivant that his friend Heerman was, but a devoted artist to whom dating was quite secondary to art. Moreover, to Ritman marriage was a very serious matter, a responsibility he could not yet accept: he needed to be able to offer financial security before entering into holy matrimony. Indeed, at this point he was far more interested in renting one of the quaint Giverny cottages and converting it into a working studio than in setting it up for a wife.

Ill. 13-10. Frederick Carl Frieseke. *The Yellow Room.* Oil on canvas, 32¼ x 29 inches. Indianapolis Museum of Art. Presented to the Art Association by James E. Roberts.

As he searched for a house in Giverny, Ritman stayed at the Hotel Baudy and took his place with others at the table d'hôte. Having been patronized mostly by Americans over the years, the hotel had become somewhat Americanized, a fact lamented by some observers and preferred by others. Frequently the expatriates conversed in English. Try as they might to look French, some telltale garment or social behavior gave away their American background. Even the food had become Americanized in an evolution of cuisine that started early in the history of Giverny as an art colony. The painter Will H. Low recalled that at his first meal at Hotel Baudy, "Boston baked beans" were served! Seeing the unusual menu more as a rude attempt on the part of the Americans to impose their tastes on Mrs. Baudy than as a simple business gesture on her part to please the majority of her foreign guests, the artist reported: "Poor patient Madame Baudy had concocted, under the direction of one of her guests, a *version Française* of this dish at which the codfish in the State House above the Common would have blushed, but the presence of its pretense at her board was sufficient evidence that the Philistines possessed the land."[38]

Although Low's first visit to Giverny had preceded Ritman's by twenty years, Low's reaction was typical of "the attitude of most American expatriates who went to France not only to learn and work, but also to imbibe all things of a superior cultural climate. Once there, they judged everything French a good deal better than everything American, even the food at the village inn. But if some of the expatriates occasionally interrupted their cultural routine to cling to a bit of Yankee custom, dress, or cuisine, they, especially those who went to Giverny, were anxious to purge themselves of their old ways in art."[39]

Louis Ritman proved to be no exception: his style was so academic, so old-fashioned that in order to remain a viable contributor to mainstream art, he needed to take a giant step forward. Although he had exiled himself to a sleepy Norman village far from Paris, he knew he was not far removed from knowledge of current events, trends, and gossip. Actually, ever since the early years, Giverny had been "a sort of outpost of Montparnasse when on the café terrasse [of Hotel Baudy] of a week end, you might see the same faces and hear the same talk you had seen and heard, through the week, on the terrasses of the Dôme, the Rotonde and the Select in Paris."[40] Indeed, at Madame Baudy's table d'hôte or over a billiard game or in a friend's studio, a fascinating variety of conversation was often in progress. The topics ranged from current events in America to matters concerning art, especially the latter now that modernism threatened not only the salon style but also impressionism and even Fauvism. While some observers perceived avant-gardism to be continued evidence of Old World decadence, others agreed with the New York critic Royal Cortissoz, who considered the modernistic painters no more than "misguided experimentalists, wallowing in error."[41] Many critics of Cubism and other avant-garde movements had reduced contemporary imagery to "ugly pictures," while only a few months before Ritman arrived, the slightly more liberal critics like Frank Mather had warned that contem-

porary art might degenerate to imagery generated from the "vivid isolated vision."[42]

Even the once anti-impressionist Kenyon Cox (who had taught the previous year at the Art Institute of Chicago) feared that modernism threatened to eclipse the French aesthetic, clearly the semblance of "reality" in the art of the time. Cox voiced the opinions of many in Giverny when he told an interviewer in New York that modernism demonstrated an abandonment of technical discipline and refinement which was acquired via the processes of tradition in art.[43]

Cox taught in Chicago after Ritman's departure for Paris, but the young artist was not one of those who forsook rules in art, since he thrived on draftsmanship and other artistic disciplinary skills. Accordingly in Giverny, the lingering bastion of romantic impressionism, where Monet personified the aesthetic, Ritman heard few discussions in which Fauvism and Cubism were praised. Hence, he could ask questions about the principles and techniques of impressionism. In spite of warnings about simplifying impressionism into a kind of formula of a "purple cow eating blue grass against a green sky," there had been and would continue to be open and frank discussion about how to paint impressionistically. This was objective analysis of impressionism's subjectivity. In addition to news from home or Paris gossip about Monet, impressionism had been the main topic of discussion since the pioneer days in Giverny, when the "conversation was largely technical about 'colour values,' 'vibration,' 'decomposition of tones,' 'the orange light and the purple shadow.' "[44] Ritman, who looked not to Monet but to Parker, Miller, and Frieseke as he sought to incorporate the general features of impressionism into intimism, might well have given a good deal of thought to Mather's recent warning about his kind of art: "The danger is lest blondness degenerate into the generalized pink bloom of Boucher, or attenuate itself more acceptably in the nacreous greys of Fragonard."[45]

Very few canvases by Ritman from the summer of 1912 are extant. One unsigned experimental work emanating from this time is a square painting known as *Lily Garden*, which was most likely executed in Frieseke's walled garden (pl. 13-3). It is obvious that Ritman was struggling with the technical side of impressionism. We also see that he was attempting to emulate Frieseke's manner of execution (pl. 13-4), with limited success. Allowing the primed canvas to show through an amazingly complex pattern of brushstrokes, Ritman applied fat and thin pigment in juxtaposed dabs. From the foreground to the limited backdrop of dense foliage, Ritman's wedgelike strokes are consistent in shape and direction, like a mosaic. In spite of this typical impressionistic feature, the artist did not succeed in achieving the sought-after quality of color vibration, mainly because he had not yet discovered the secret of true broken color. In *Lily Garden* there is no chromatic variation, thus no scintillation. Save the rather poorly executed model in the middleground, the whole scene is rendered in a nearly monochromatic repetition of green tones — here and there we find strokes of deep purple heightened with white. As if to emphasize the model, Ritman surrounded her with white flowers, the shapes of which were achieved with heavy impasto dabs of pigment. Although he attempted to depict a bright summer day, his scene is devoid of sunshine, and the contrast between the treatment of the figure and of the foliage is inharmonious. The sprinkling can in the foreground is rendered with the same nonimpressionistic brushwork that we find in the figure. All in all, it is obvious that this is one of Ritman's first attempts to create imagery based on Frieseke's well-known subjects. One must assume that since he left his production unsigned, Ritman was aware of his shortcomings.

In Giverny, Ritman lived near artists who embraced many of his ideologies, as old-fashioned as they were. Here, he found artists who worked as he did. Although he was a young and adventuresome artist, seeking the highest rung of artistic achievement, Ritman was not one of the Matisse-Stieglitz group and apparently did not wish to be. From the older pioneer expatriates like Butler (pl. 13-5) to the second generation like Frieseke (ill. 13-10), to the youngest like himself, the artists in Giverny, as nowhere else, demonstrated a mutual interest in impressionism, especially scenes of women in sunlit gardens, but Ritman had yet to prove himself in this regard. Perhaps more than anyone else, it had been Frieseke who popularized the brilliant garden images in the Paris salons. Ritman and the others admired his devotion to that limited environment better than the critic René Jean. Reviewing Frieseke's work in the Champ de Mars Salon, Jean had written: "Mr. Frieseke loves intimism: plein-air intimism with roses in the garden, intimism of bright pictures where the feminine silhouette is in harmony and engaged in some pleasant task, all this beauty that our eyes can catch."[46] So it was that nearly all the painters who came to Giverny, especially the Americans, wanted to produce an example of impressionistic intimism like Frieseke's.

The proof that Ritman was no exception is another unsigned oil, known as *Woman with Watering Can* (ill. 13-11). Obviously employing the same model in almost the same setting as that in *Lily Garden* , Ritman produced a canvas nearly smothered in colorful blooms. Again, the attractive young woman stands in profile as she sprinkles

Ill. 13-11. Louis Ritman. *Woman With Watering Can.* Location unknown. Photograph. Courtesy of Christie's.

the luxuriant flowers in which she walks knee-deep. Again, we find a great disparity between the execution of the small figure in the middle ground and the execution of the masses of blooms. Unlike the form of the woman, the flowers were created by juxtaposing innumerable shinglelike strokes of pigment. Ritman's overall transition from the brushy salon style to the pronounced impasto of impressionism was not easily accomplished. It is obvious that he was quite capable of producing Frieseke's unyielding mass of flowers as well as any impressionist — summarily, he had learned the technique of producing a typical Giverny-type flower garden in the manner of Frieseke or any other Monet disciple — but when it came to inserting a figure into the mass of broken-color dabs, he was reluctant to treat the figure in a similar manner. Apparently young Ritman had simply spent too many hours learning how to paint the figure, especially a female one, to abandon his salon manner overnight.

A painting that demonstrates a much better resolution of the problem of the figure in a garden setting than those previously discussed, is a work known as *An Improvised Flower Basket* (ill. 13-12). Here, the subject still stands in the middle ground as she devotes her attention to the flowers before her, but in this instance the composition is not dominated by an impenetrable mass of flowers covering most of the picture surface but rather consists of an interesting design formed by a path with a chair, a wide border of flowers from which the woman fills her hat, a sun-dappled lawn, and a tree-lined background. Pictorially, the viewer stands at the left on the receding path and seems to be beckoned by the empty chair, while the attractive young woman stands to the right and is separated from us by a row of blooming flowers that recede at a somewhat oblique angle to the picture plane. The bright patterned effect created on the lawn by the sunlight filtering through nearby trees is a motif Ritman would use frequently in years to come. The figure of the woman is more harmoniously integrated into this multitextured scene than in other works from this period because her dress also shows a patterned fabric, and it is sun-dappled like the lawn; the figure is executed with a more sophisticated brushwork, which tends to serve as a convenient transition from the lawn to the flowers—indeed, in this way she stands as a subtle vertical element between these areas and as such is an understated focal point. This is one of Ritman's best early garden scenes.

Lawton Parker was no less influenced in this direction than Ritman, who shared his studio occasionally. At times they worked together en plein air (pl. 13-6), but Ritman seemed to prefer posing his model indoors. In one instance during the summer of 1912, Parker had no choice when a downpour and several rainy days forced him and his model to work in the studio. The result was an unusually large canvas depicting a nude. From the beginning sketch, the composition took on a certain "look of success." Parker devoted considerable time to the work that summer—although he wanted it to have a "spontaneous" quality, as befitted any good example of impressionism. Ritman admired his mentor's canvas a great deal.

Basically Giverny was not different from what it had been at the time Metcalf first requested room and board of Madame Baudy, although many more artists lived there now. The artists came there to learn how to become impressionists, and Ritman was no exception. Everyone in Giverny knew that these days Monet was concentrating on his water-lily paintings, some of which the master had burned because they fell short of his standard of quality. Struggling American artists were amazed that the art-buying public (including several American collectors) was eagerly awaiting the finished ones as Durand-Ruel made them available in highly publicized exhibitions.[47] Still inspired by his own beautiful water-lily ponds and the voluminous critical praise heaped upon his last exhibition, Monet worked ceremoniously in his garden, lining up several easels in a row to enable him to capture variations in daylight. Later he carefully refined his images, reworking subtle nuances after he had "vigorously" dashed them off "in one afternoon." The result was unanimous critical acclaim, typified by that of Jean-Louis Vandoyer: "None of the earlier series [haystacks, for example] . . . can, in our opinion, compare with these fabulous Water Landscapes, which are holding spring captive in the Durand-Ruel Gallery." Continuing the nineteenth-century fad of synaesthetics, Vandoyer proclaimed that in these canvases, "more than ever before, painting approaches music and poetry."[48]

Ill. 13-12. Louis Ritman. *An Improvised Flower Basket*. Oil on canvas, 36¼ x 36¼ inches. Location unknown. Photograph. Courtesy of Christie's.

Working occasionally in Frieseke's walled garden, Ritman heard a lot of the gossip about Monet's water-lily pictures, but he caught only glimpses of the master working on them, and he knew nothing of his personal life. In 1912, about the only American privy to Monet's private everyday life was Theodore Butler, who would not have shared secrets with a casual acquaintance like Ritman. In spite of his wealth and success, Monet's autumnal years yielded their share of trauma. For example, only a year earlier, when Ritman first came to Giverny, Monet's wife, Alice Hoschedé Monet died. Monet's stepdaughter Marthe (Butler's second wife), the Butler grandchildren, and Blanche Hoschedé Monet spent a great deal of time with the master, consoling him in his loss. In July 1912, when Ritman was painting and settling into his newly rented house, a Paris physician discovered cataracts on Monet's eyes. Notwithstanding the trauma, Monet was relieved, for he had been convinced that he was going blind.

Ritman spent most of his time in Giverny, but occasionally he and friends went to nearby Vernon, where Abel Warshawsky and Samuel Halpert had painted a few years earlier. This was also a charming village with an old stone bridge, houses like those in Giverny, and the Hotel du Soleil d'Or, whose owners were pleased to provide artists lodging and full board, including wine, beer, or cider, for about twenty dollars a month.[49] Giverny

Ill. 13-13. Louis Ritman. *Mimi on a Summer Morning.* Oil on canvas, 36 x 29 inches. Private Collection. Courtesy R. H. Love Galleries, Chicago.

boasted many more guest artists each summer, but Vernon frequently provided rooms for artists who had found no lodging in the more famous village. The area was not populated exclusively by Americans by any means; the French artist Pierre Bonnard lived in *Ma Roulotte*, a cottage he had purchased in Vernonnet. Bonnard visited Monet on occasion, and there he came to know Theodore Butler quite well, but it is doubtful that Ritman met him. By 1912, Bonnard's synthetism had taken on a new look: his special intimism manifested the bright colors of Monet's palette, as Butler's had for nearly two decades. Like Ritman, Bonnard was Jewish, and the two had ample opportunity to become acquainted through mutual friends, but there is no record of a relationship.

As Ritman continued his assimilation of impressionism in Giverny during the summer of 1912, he came to understand more of the aesthetic. Nonetheless, he was still walking a tightrope between the salon style and impressionism. Perhaps his relatively unsuccessful garden scene had prompted him to bring his model indoors. He was accustomed to working indoors anyway, so that posing her by an open window would not only align him with the Giverny intimist pictorial format but also allow him to exploit the effects of the bright summer sunlight.

One painting from this time which demonstrates Ritman's transition from the academic manner to impressionism, is a vertical canvas entitled *Mimi on a Summer Morning* (ill. 13-13). Here, we find the same model as before, posed in profile in the middle ground of the pictorial field. Dressing for the day's activities, Mimi has raised one foot to the wicker chair on which her clothing is arranged as she adjusts her corset. Obviously, this is an intimate boudoir scene: standing just to the left of an open window, the subject is engaged in the same kind of private feminine toilette that we saw in earlier salon imagery; now, however, we see a single figure strategically centralized, as we might expect to find in the Giverny productions of Parker, Miller, or Frieseke. Typically, Ritman has created an extremely limited space, relieved only by the open window; the window, however, provides very little extra dimension, since another vista-blocking wall exists only a few yards away. Here we see the genesis of Ritman's favorite Giverny intimist pictorial device: *a feminine figure is positioned in a shallow space between the viewer and a wall, which runs parallel to the picture plane and in which there is an open window that opens out onto a space severely limited by a leafy garden wall.* Using this device, Ritman carefully emphasizes the figure as the focal point of the scene by subtly contrasting her curvilinear form with the simple shapes of the surrounding objects, which, except for the wicker chair and garments, are basically geometric. Save the foreshortened window casement frames that project into the room, Ritman's design yields few angles; the most obvious one is formed by the wicker chair that is rounded in form, but it is carefully positioned at an oblique angle to the picture plane.

Stylistically, in *Mimi* Ritman has shown little reservation in extending his salon style by employing impressionistic brushstrokes to describe the garden wall, the colorful compote of flowers, and the tabletop—forms and surfaces that are limited to the range of sunlight. He renders everything else in the picture, outside of the direct illumination, in his usual academic manner. Ritman was unable to unify all pictorial elements via an impressionistic technique in the way that Monet had counseled Lilla Cabot Perry, leading us to conclude that *Mimi* exemplifies his transition from the salon style to an impressionistic brand of intimism.

Notes

1. Will H. Low, *A Chronicle of Friendships* (New York: Charles Scribner's Sons, 1948), pp. 446-47.

2. W. M. R. French to Sara Hallowell, Chicago, 7 July 1911, Director WMRF, Letter Book, February 8, 1911-August 9, 1911, General Correspondence, Art Institute of Chicago Archives, Chicago, p. 771. French quotes George F. Porter from a letter received by French earlier.

3. Ibid.,W. M. R. French to Sara Hallowell, Chicago, 5 July 1911, p. 762.

4. Ibid.,W. M. R. French to Sara Hallowell, Chicago, 13 July 1911, p. 799.

5. Judith Vale Newton, *The Hoosier Group: Five American Painters* (Indianapolis, IN: Eckert Publications, 1985).

6. The phrase *la belle époque* has become especially popular among historians since World War II. The term refers specifically, however, to the three decades in France prior to World War I, although it was not commonly used at that time since the French did not equate this period with a time of extraordinary harmony and beauty. For a study of the period, see Charles Rearick, *Pleasures of the Belle Epoque* (New Haven, CT: Yale University Press, 1985). See also Willy Haas, *Die Belle Epoque* (Munich: Verlag Kurt Desch, 1967), and Raymond Rudorff, *Belle Epoque: Paris in the Nineties* (London: Hamilton Publishing Co., 1972).

7. In this context, the *juste milieu* comprises those French painters who "deliberately applied the techniques of the impressionists to the drawing style of the Academy." Their subjects were "anecdotal scenes of middle class life . . . Box at the Opera, At the Racetrack." For a comprehensive discussion of this group, see Carol M. Osborne, et al. *The Impressionists and the Salon (1874-1886)*, exhibition catalog (Los Angeles, CA: Los Angeles County Museum of Art, 1974).

8. It was at this time that Santayana delivered his famous address at the University of California entitled "The Genteel Tradition in American Philosophy." In his speech, he contended basically that the arts in America preferred the never-never land of the abstract.

9. Speech given by the Honorable Whitelaw Reid, the American ambassador to France, on the opening night of the American Artists Association of Paris, May 1890. Speech quoted in E. H. Wuerpel, "American Artists' Association of Paris," *The Cosmpolitan Magazine*, XX, no. 4 (February 1896), pp. 402-409.

10. Rodman Lewis Wanamaker was born in Philadelphia on 13 February 1863 and died in Atlantic City, New Jersey, on 9 March 1928. An American merchant and art patron, Wanamaker did everything in his power to create good will among the ranks of the American expatriate community in Paris.

11. Wuerpel, p. 405.

12. Billy Klüver and Julie Martin, *Ki Ki's Paris: Artists and Lovers 1900-1930*, (New York: Harry N. Abrams, Inc., Publishers, 1989), p.21. Also see p. 212 for statistics on American artists in Paris compiled by Lois Fink.

13. Marcia M. Mathews, *Henry Ossawa Tanner, American Artist* (Chicago: The University of Chicago Press, 1969), p. 61.

14. Bertha F. Beale, "Art-Student Life in Paris," *The Sketch Book*, IV, no. 2 (October 1904), p. 57.

15. "Studio Talk," *International Studio*, LV, no. 228 (April 1912), pp. 222-23.

16. By 1912, the theory of Analytical Cubism manifested itself in a fully mature style. Guillaume Apollinaire expostulated a great deal over the theories of the movement in various periodicals. Soon the door to Synthetic Cubism was open, and finally the union of color (as an abstract entity) with the forms of Cubism made it possible to arrive at another idea, championed by Robert Delaunay and termed *orphism* by Apollinaire. For a general discussion, see Werner Haftmann, *Painting in the Twentieth Century* (New York: Frederick A. Praeger Publishers, 1965), vol. 1, p. 102.

17. Gertrude's brother, Leo Stein, who had been a major promoter of modernism via Matisse and later Picasso, had come to reject Cubism. Turning his back on the movement, he left Gertrude to champion it on her own.

18. Alfred Kreymborg, *Troubadour: An American Autobiography* (New York: American Century, 1957), p. 128.

19. W. M. R. French to Sara Hallowell, Chicago, 3 February 1912, Director WMRF, Letter Book, December 8, 1911-April 18, 1912, p. 484.

20. Ibid., W. M. R. French to Sara Hallowell, Chicago, 12 March 1912, p. 513.

21. Ibid., W. M. R. French to Sara Hallowell, Chicago, 8 February 1912, p. 730.

22. *Paintings by Lawton Parker Exhibited at The Art Institute of Chicago, March 5 to March 27, 1912,* exhibition catalog (Chicago: The Art Institute of Chicago, 1912).

23. Low, p. 169.

24. Claude Roger-Marx, "Le Vernissage du Salon de la Société des Artistes Français," La *Chronique des Arts et de la Curiosité*, no. 18 (4 May 1912), p. 140.

25. "American's Work Superb," *New York Times*, 1 May 1912.

26. Max Weber, "The Reminiscences of Max Weber," unpublished manuscript in the Weber Collection, Oral History Research Office, Columbia University, New York, NY. See also Holger Cahill, *Max Weber* (New York: Downtown Galleries, 1930).

27. Taylor, p. 273.

28. Jerome Meyers, *Artist in Manhattan* (New York: American Artists Group, Inc., 1940), p. 32.

29. Ibid., p. 23.

30. Ibid., p. 32.

31. Benjamin de Casseres, "The Unconscious in Art," *Camera Work*, 36 (October 1911), p. 17.

32. H. Wayne Morgan, *New Muses: Art in American Culture, 1865-1920* (Norman, OK: University of Oklahoma Press, 1978), p. 157.

33. Ibid.

34. Pierre Toulgouat, "Skylights in Normandy," *Holiday* (August 1948), p. 66.

35. Ibid., p. 68.

36. Low, p. 448.

37. Ibid.

38. Ibid., p. 447-48.

39. Richard H. Love, *Theodore Earl Butler: Emergence from Monet's Shadow* (Chicago: Haase-Mumm Publishing Co., 1985), p. 114.

40. Pierre Toulgouat, p. 66.

41. Royal Cortissoz, *New York Tribune*, February 17, 23, 1913.

42. Frank J. Mather, Jr., "The Present State of Art," *Nation*, 93 (4 December 1911), pp. 584-87.

43. "Interview with Kenyon Cox," *New York Times*, 16 March 1913, Part VI, p. 1. See also Kenyon Cox to Allyn Cox, 16 April 1912, Cox Papers, Avery Architecture Library, Columbia University, New York City.

44. Low, pp. 448-49.

45. Mather, pp. 584-87.

46. René Jean, "Les Salons de 1911: La Société Nationale des Beaux-Arts," *Gazette des Beaux-Arts*, 2 (1911), p. 364.

47. Robert Gordon and Andrew Forge, *Monet* (New York: Harry N. Abrams, Inc., Publishers, 1983), pp. 223-38.

48. Jean-Louis Vandoyer, *La Chronique des Arts et de la Curiosité*, 15 May 1909, p. 159.

49. Abel G. Warshawsky, *The Memories of an American Impressionist* (Kent, OH: Kent State University Press, 1980), p. 162.

CHAPTER FOURTEEN: A CONSERVATIVE CHICAGO HOSTS A REVOLUTIONARY SHOW

With a number of quasi-impressionistic canvases on hand, Ritman returned to Paris from Giverny in the fall of 1912 and soon settled into a new studio at 59 Avenue de Saxe. Parker usually left early for New York and then for Chicago, but this year he went to Paris. Frieseke stayed in Giverny later than the others, but Miller and his wife returned to Paris, as did most of the other summertime painters.

The winters in Paris were never as treacherous as they were in Chicago, but like other artists, Ritman had to arrange for a supply of coal and other provisions to hold him over the winter season. Like most of his friends, he purchased his art supplies from Maison Lefebvre Foinet, a family-run shop on rue Vavin off boulevard Montparnasse. Canvases came from Paul Foinet Fils at 21 rue Bréa. The Foinet family was cordial not only to Ritman but also to most other American artists. Over the years the Foinets had dealt with Whistler, Sargent, Chase, Frieseke, and many lesser-knowns like Ritman, who lived in the Latin Quarter during their expatriate careers. The Foinets enjoyed an enviable reputation: most of the American artists were convinced that their pigments were better than the machine-made oils that came from the wholesalers. "In the back of the shop," a friend of Ritman's remembered, "one could see the workmen grinding the colors by hand on the long marble-topped tables."

Members of "the Foinet family . . . were proud of the quality and durability of their wares," he wrote, and "were continually experimenting in mixtures that would not darken or fade."[1] In addition to purchasing art supplies from the Foinets, Ritman also had them package and ship his pictures to Chicago. When he or his expatriate friends were low on funds, it was not unusual for Papa Foinet to extend credit for art supplies, for he believed that "a young painter should be able to work continuously and not be hampered by lack of materials."[2] Without Papa Foinet's credit and encouragement, Louis Ritman and many of his friends would have found it very difficult at times to paint in Paris.

During the summer of 1912, Ritman had been consumed with artistic experiments in Giverny and submitted nothing to the 1912 Salon d'Automne. This year the show contained enough Cubism to make it controversial. Picasso, whose studio was at 242 boulevard Raspail, was now flattening forms in his late Analytic Cubism and making a transition to Synthetic Cubism. Ritman had many friends among the progressive American painters in Montparnasse, so it is quite possible that he and one of his more liberal artist comrades attended the Salon of *La Section d'Or* at the Galerie de la Boétie. If so, they would have immediately noticed that much of the work shown was by such painters as Jacques Villon, Marcel

Duchamp, and Albert Gleizes, all of whom manifested the influence of Cubism, but that strangely neither Picasso nor Braque were represented.

In view of Ritman's friendship with Alfred Maurer and others in the circle of the expatriate avant-garde, it seems unlikely that Ritman would not have heard of the European project undertaken by Walt Kuhn as secretary of the Association of American Painters and Sculptors (AAPS). Parker's friend A. B. Davies, once a member of Henri's Ash Can group and then president of the association, had suggested to Kuhn that he organize a show of impressive modern art like that presented at the Sonderbund exhibition in Cologne. Kuhn was immediately inspired to see the Cologne exhibit.[3] Leaving New York in September, Kuhn saw the Sonderbund show only on its last day, but the idea of a similar event in New York gained momentum. By the time he came to Paris, Kuhn had already been to Holland, Munich, and Berlin, gathering works to be shipped across the Atlantic.[4] In later years, Kuhn reported that as his trek continued, "things got more and more exciting."[5] He recalled that he and a couple of other acquaintances of Ritman's, Alfy Maurer and Walter Pach, "went from collection to collection, from gallery to gallery, with constantly growing success. Talk spread in Paris." Kuhn reported that Jo Davidson (who had lived near Ritman on the rue Notre-Dame des Champs) had introduced him to the Chicago real estate magnate Arthur T. Aldis, who played an influential role at the Art Institute. Aldis asked that the exhibition be sent to Chicago after it ended in New York, an idea that Director French said he had entertained for a number of months. Parker, Ritman, and others from their group learned of the arrangement, so that it subsequently became common gossip in Paris and Giverny. Shortly, Davies joined Kuhn and Pach in Paris on their curatorial quests for modern art that would form the nucleus of the soon-to-be-famous New York Armory Show. Just as Ritman was establishing himself in new quarters in November, Kuhn and Davies returned to New York, leaving Walter Pach to handle matters in Paris. Before they sailed for home, Kuhn and Davies visited another exhibition of modern art organized by Roger Fry at the Grafton Gallery in London. Later the results of their European mission would have a great impact on the art community of Ritman's hometown.

Ritman spent the whole winter season of 1912-13 in his Paris studio (ill. 14-1). In addition to putting finishing touches on a considerable number of canvases from Giverny for the spring exhibition season, he started a few new paintings. His friend Parker was retouching the large canvas of the nude that he had executed earlier that summer in Giverny. He had already entitled the painting *La*

Ill. 14-1. A Paris Studio. R. H. Love Galleries Archives, Chicago.

Paresse and planned to enter it in the forthcoming Paris Salon.

It was an amazingly busy time in Paris, and the art community was constantly embroiled in controversy, much in the manner of the European political community. There was a great deal of art to see in Paris. Exhibitions mounted by commercial galleries had become hot topics for critics in recent years, and the 1912-13 season was no exception. Ritman visited, for example, the annual group show at Galerie E. Druet, featuring the work of Maurice Denis, Henri Lebasque, Aristide Maillol, Odilon Redon, Sérusier, Valtat, and others. Ritman left no record of his reaction to the show, but it is known that he preferred Vuillard to the other Nabis. By January, he had made substantial progress in changing his style to impressionism, but he also prepared new works — a nude, which was considerably less ambitious than Parker's large canvas, and a work he called *Le Matin (Morning)*. Both of these paintings were intended for the Paris Spring Salon.

Letters that Ritman received later in the winter from friends in New York City and Chicago contained descriptions of an art controversy beside which even the Fauve debut of a few years earlier paled. The highly publicized Armory Show had opened in New York in mid-February 1913, and the whole American art community became embroiled in a battle royal of aesthetic preferences. The exhibition was not simply a showing of the latest trends in international art but also a forum of modernism for the American public. Organizers soon learned that they were dealing with a public that was concerned about the social and moral implications of modern art. "Proponents saw it as liberating and expansive. But opponents quickly equated it with social, political, and economic turbulence. The last great artistic innovation, impressionism, had emphasized motion and change, but remained basically optimistic. The new modernism seemed to contain a threatening tone in praising condensed imagery, symbols, and the unknown."[6] The public had expected the exhibition to be controversial because it featured the most avant-garde modern European art; it was huge, intimidating, and quite unlike anything "even dreamed of before."[7]

In some ways, the Armory Show was a chronological arrangement of modern art. It included work by early innovators like Courbet, Corot, Puvis de Chavannes, Manet, Degas, Signac, and Seurat, some of whom still inspired Ritman. In the category known as "romanticists," Delacroix, Daumier, Renoir, and Redon were represented. There were the Nabis and the Fauves and the sculpture by Alexander Archipenko and Constantin Brancusi. Conspicuously absent were the Italian Futurists and the German Expressionists. Controversy surrounded Marcel Duchamp's *Nude Descending a Staircase* and works by Brancusi, Picasso, Braque, and other "radical" Europeans.[8] Some viewers interpreted these works as the cultural manifestation of Old World decadence, while others regarded the artists as "cousins to the anarchists in politics."[9] The exhibition also included works by a number of so-called radical American modernists, artists like Maurer, Marsden Hartley, Morton L. Schamberg, Patrick Henry Bruce, Arthur B. Carles, and Morgan Russell, among others. On the other hand, the Armory Show failed to include work by some very modern American painters. For example, two of Stieglitz's best, Georgia O'Keeffe and Arthur Dove, were not seen, nor was John Covert (still in Paris) or Man Ray, both of the Walter C. Arensberg milieu. Also strikingly absent were the soon-to-be synchromist Stanton Macdonald Wright and another Ritman acquaintance in Paris, Arthur B. Frost. In retrospect, we see that the American modernists were poorly represented, compared with their European counterparts.

Ritman's work was not shown, but ample space had been allotted to American impressionist friends, including some of the Giverny pioneers like Theodore Robinson and Theodore Butler. To say that the show caused shock waves felt throughout the American art community is to understate the effect of the event that opened at the Sixty-ninth Regiment Armory in New York on 17 February 1913 and subsequently traveled on to Chicago and Boston. Kuhn, Davies, and other organizers knew the show was revolutionary—they had even appropriated the green pine tree symbol of the American Revolution. The show drew thousands of visitors, even former President Theodore Roosevelt. It also prompted responses from art critics as never before: Kenyon Cox, the conservative, was convinced that the "real meaning of this Cubist movement is nothing else than the total destruction of the art of painting."[10] The well-known critic Royal Cortissoz stated flatly that whether "Post-Impressionist, Cubist, or Futurist, however they may be designated, their cue is to turn the world upside down."[11]

As a young academician-turned-impressionist who knew a number of both the organizers of and the exhibitors at the Armory Show, Ritman probably had mixed emotions about the controversy, yet in Paris he was for the most part isolated from it. If his own youth prompted him to admire or even empathize with other young innovators, like Stanton Macdonald Wright, or acquaintances like Alfy Maurer and A. B. Frost, Ritman was probably more in agreement with the reflections of Parker's friend, Jerome Myers: "Our land of opportunity was thrown wide open to foreign art, unrestricted and triumphant, more than ever before, our great country had become a colony; more than ever before, we had become provincials."[12] Art writer Milton W. Brown summarized a contemporary article which offered the academic viewpoint: "It [the article] contended that the deliberate turning of modernists toward the ugly was a menace to the development of art and the retention of high and pure ideals . . . . the human form was the perfection of beauty and to distort either nature or humanity was to desecrate the noblest work of God. Modern art, in stooping to vulgarity, was pulling down the ancient temple of art."[13]

Before the Armory Show was over in New York on 15 March 1913, Walt Kuhn had persuaded the Irish lawyer John Quinn to spend over $5,000 for works by Derain, Duchamp, Pascin, and other French artists.[14] Walter C. Arensberg purchased Duchamp's bewildering picture *Nu descendant un escalier (Nude Descending a Staircase no. 2*, Philadelphia Museum of Art). Later, Duchamp explained that "the idea of the Nude came from a drawing which I had made in 1911 to illustrate Jules La Forgue's poem *Encore à cet astre*.[15] Arensberg was courageous in his purchase of the work since in spite of its seriousness, the image had become the laughing stock of the public and of much of the press.

No sooner were these purchases made than another lawyer, Arthur Jerome Eddy of Chicago, also spent nearly five thousand dollars for eighteen paintings and seven lithographs, some of which were radical by anyone's standards.[16] Owing to his humble beginnings, Ritman had no opportunity to meet someone as important as Arthur J. Eddy, a close friend of Mayor Harrison's and a prominent figure of Chicago's social elite. An author on corporate law, art critic and collector, wine connoisseur, expert in cuisine, orator, innovator, dancer, fencer, sportsman, and angler, Eddy was described as one "who excelled in too many lines of activities for his own good."[17] Eddy's abilities as a collector were second to few: he had purchased Manet's *Philosopher* (1865, Jamot and Wildenstein, no. 111, Art Institute of Chicago) long before most Americans had ever heard of the artist. When he commissioned Whistler to paint his portrait, as previously mentioned, Eddy went to the master's Paris studio and the picture was finished on time; Whistler's continual retouching, however, delayed its arrival in Chicago for over a year.[18] Eddy had been so taken by his "Whistler experience" that he had written a sensitive study on the master, *Recollections and Impressions of James A. McNeill Whistler*, about two years before Ritman started his art lessons at Hull House. In 1904 the Eddy portrait was shown in Boston; from that time until he rushed to New York to purchase works from the Armory Show, Arthur J. Eddy had played quite an active role in the Chicago art community and become extremely well known on the international art scene. On the other hand, he eschewed provinciality, tending instead toward the avant-garde from the time he had commissioned Whistler to his purchase of Gleize's *Man on the Balcony*. Although he had always sought out the avant-garde, after his Armory Show purchases Eddy was nearly obsessed with the cause of modernism. Once again, his inspiration resulted in a heartfelt treatise, soon to become a book entitled *Cubists and Post-Impressionists*. Eddy's sensitivity to and keen insight into modernism resulted in one of America's first studies of the movement. Typically optimistic about the future of art, Eddy prophesied that "America . . . will absorb all that is good in the extreme modern movement and reject what is bad."[19] Milton Brown described Eddy's writing as an "exciting mixture of idealism, faith, evidence, and argument [which] reads like the impassioned plea of a defense attorney for the life of his client."[20] Indeed, it was important to the "life" of Cubism and other modern movements because most American artists wanted to paint like impressionists — like Monet or Renoir or Frieseke or even Ritman — not like Picasso, at least not yet. Eddy, on the other hand, was aware of the plight of all new movements as was his New York counterpart, John Quinn, who wrote to a friend at this time: "After studying the works of the Cubists and Futurists, it makes it hard to stomach the sweetness, the prettiness and the sentiment of some of the other work."[21] As an upright Chicago leader, Eddy walked shoulder to shoulder with the members of high society, most of whom were confused by his cultural antics. He shocked constituents with the art in his office and enjoyed

doing that. Subsequent proof of Eddy's fascination with the avant-garde was his purchase of several paintings by Wassily Kandinsky, some of the first in America and now the property of the Art Institute of Chicago. Ritman, whose work was of the kind that Quinn found "hard to stomach," learned of Eddy's Armory Show purchases later when he was in Giverny.

Another important figure from the Chicago art community, whom Ritman had seen only from a distance, was the ever-influential trustee of the Art Institute, Arthur T. Aldis. Aldis was somewhat more forward-thinking than other members of the exhibition committee who joined him on the New York sojourn to visit the Armory Show. He had met Kuhn earlier in Paris and was anxious to have the Armory Show come to Chicago. At that time the committee wanted American works to be limited to those by members of the Association (of American Painters and Sculptors), and unlike Aldis, they were not yet as convinced that the show would be good for their city. After some calculated diplomatic pressure Aldis persuaded most of the trustees to sponsor the show, but a few staunch conservatives, along with Director French, opposed the project. In his revealing study of the Armory Show, Milton W. Brown points out that "French, without being openly antagonistic, dragged his feet and anything else available during all negotiations."[22] Eventually the board ignored French's numerous reasons for scrapping the plan, and once the preliminaries were set in place, the director "carried on negotiations with the Association as punctiliously and correctly as was to be expected."[23]

To assure that preparations ran well, Aldis maintained close contact with Walt Kuhn, and French wrote to Gutzon Borglum requesting his assistance. It had not been until December 1912 that French officially requested the Armory Show for the Art Institute, and in January he went to New York to discuss the project with A. B. Davies and Kuhn. French was quite aware that he was involved in a cultural revolution, although he had little choice but to proceed since official sanction had come from the trustees. Similar arrangements for a Boston show, sponsored by the Copley Society, prompted Aldis to remind Kuhn that Chicago assumed a priority status, and that the institute trustees expected nothing less than a complete exhibition.[24] Surprisingly, French informed Davies that the institute was anxious to have not the most conservative works but the most avant-garde examples of the modern European section. As the show drew closer, however, French prepared to slip out of Chicago on a vacation trip; accordingly, he turned the whole project over to the Institute Secretary Newton H. Carpenter, secretary of the Art Institute, who was eager to handle it.

Only a few days before the opening, nearly 634 works were still on a train en route to Chicago. Aldis, Eddy, and other trustees worried that the exhibition could not be installed in time. Frederick Gregg, the publicity manager of the Association of American Painters and Sculptors, arrived early and held a press conference on 19 March, which revealed that Chicago was expecting a strange and wonderful event. It was about this time that Director French and his wife quietly boarded a train for California, leaving Chicago's presentation of the Armory Show to subordinates. Just as the armory had been in New York, the Art Institute was specially decorated, and the exhibition was carefully installed.

Offering distinct contrasts were two other shows held at the Art Institute, an exhibition of works by members of the Watercolor Society, and a solo show of works by Pauline Palmer. There was also an exhibition of the Horticultural Society, but the group made it clear that none of its floral arrangements could be used in the Cubist show area.

With its enthusiasm fueled by New York's response to the Armory Show, the Chicago press, armed to the teeth, was lying in ambush for the association's radical display of artistic anarchism. Controversy over the show had been strong enough in New York, but many observers expected it to be even worse in Chicago, where trouble had already been brewing over the display of a painting that a few ladies found "lewd and indecent." Only a few days earlier, after the women had complained to Detective Hersch of the Police Censor Bureau, the owners of Jackson and Semmelmayer's photographic shop were forced to remove a copy of **September Morn** by the French painter Paul Chabas (a Medal of Honor winner at the Paris Salon of 1912).[25] On Sunday, 23 March, the day before the opening of the Armory exhibition, the Chicago *Sunday Record Herald* devoted a full page to the show headlining an article by Herman Landon entitled "Hark! Hark! The Critics Bark! The Cubists Are Coming!" Landon pointed out that this exhibition went a long way to make "Insanity Profitable."[26]

The Armory Show opened in Chicago on 24 March and closed on 16 April 1913. From the day of the opening, the guns of the Chicago critics blazed at any moving target, the most obvious of which was Marcel Duchamp's *Nude Descending a Staircase*. One newspaper reported that "Cube Art Staggers Institute Members," all of whom dressed for the opening as if it were a high-society ball.[27] Adding to the excitement was the presence of various important members of the Association of American Painters and Sculptors from New York, who were generally quite gracious and informative in fielding questions from a curious and sometimes hostile press and public. One reporter observed that Walt Kuhn "bore the brunt of the battle and bore it bravely."[28] The same writer overheard someone declaim: "And you call that art . . . ? But I see neither a nude nor a staircase . . . Ravings on canvas of an inane mind . . . . And all the time Mr. Kuhn was saying: You see, it is the idea the artist wishes to convey . . . . The highest expression of art is that which appeals to the most limited circle of patrons."[29] In later years Kuhn wrote that he and other representatives of the Association of American Painters and Sculptors had been met by "a most formidable array of scribes. The echoes of the New York press had done their work, evidently Chicago was not to be fooled."[30] When the opening festivities were over that Monday, a liberal reporter for the *Chicago Evening Post* suggested that the city "ought to give 'the greatest exhibition of insurgent art ever held' a fair hearing and a serious consideration." The writer explained: "We have heard it attacked in New York as a crazy, revolutionary, impudent circus, and we have shown a preliminary disposition to receive it in a spirit of humorous hostility."[31] Arthur Eddy found nothing humorous about the Armory Show, but he vacillated about giving it full support. For several days rumors circulated that he intended to side with the conservatives by publicly denouncing the foreign degenerate artists; but after the show opened, he aligned himself with the association and even attempted to make a diagram outlining Duchamp's nude in a reproduction in the *Chicago Daily Tribune*.[32] In a lengthy caption, the *Tribune* article instructed: "Place a piece of paper over the left three-fourths of the picture . . . Her head is located about one inch from the upper border of the picture."[33] Obviously offended by Chicago's response to the show, Kuhn wrote to a friend: "Last night was the opening reception, they charged a dollar a head admission to come in and see the 'circus' as they called it." He reported that "all the artistic lights in town are lecturing on cubism. Carpenter is all right and we pull fine with him . . . . Chicago ought to run up to 200,000 attendance . . . . Guess we'll pull out O.K . . . . I shall be god-damned glad to get through here and back to N.Y."[34] Although the show attracted more visitors in Chicago, it had the same effect of stirring the ire of the conservatives as it did in New York. Quoting scripture, a member of Hamlin Garland's original "Critical Triumvirate," Charles Francis Browne, told a women's club in Evanston that "the body is the temple of God and the cubists have profaned the temple." The Reverend Simiron Gilbert wrote a letter of protest to the offices of the Art Institute of Chicago; and the highly respected critic H. Effa Webster stated flatly that "this pollution is materialized in several paintings of the nude; portrayals that unite in an insult to the great, self-respecting public of Chicago."[35] The continued barrage of complaints about the moral issue of the show actually brought a brief "investigation" on the part of the Senatorial Vice Commission, which had already been actively investigating the Levee's white slave trade. Few visitors were ambivalent about the exhibition, but as one observer reported, "more than once the critic has been asked 'not to take sides' — as if the pen of a modest writer could have any weight whatever in so momentous a question as this." She wanted to convince her readers that "these paintings do not need a gallery tour. They speak, swear, blaspheme, or plead for themselves, as one chooses to listen or to look. The viewing public does all these things — therefore why not learn by taking notes."[36] That is exactly what the public chose to do — not always with a sincere motivation, however. Only a couple of days after the opening a satirical entertainment took place: "Employees of the institute, art students, alumni, artists, architects, and university professors" joined in a special " 'Futurist Party' given by the Chicago Artists club . . . . Each was dressed in a futurist costume. There were imitation futurist pictures on the walls . . . . Dr. Alfred Emerson, archaeologist and Chicago university professor, made a Cubist speech. His wife played a futurist sonata, 'Running Water,' by Revel . . . . Twelve stalwart Indians, with all their feathers and paint, and dressed in what were made to look like cube-gowns . . . entered the hall and marched around the place with war whoops."[37] During the party, both Charles Francis Browne and Pauline Palmer, whose solo show had become a convenient alternative attraction at the Institute, gave short and "mildly sarcastic" speeches on the Armory Show. Kuhn was pleased with the visitor turnout, but he feared that the show would "leave but a scant impression upon the development of Chicago art." He added that "this applies to the 'high as well as the low brows.' The very sponsors with the possible exception of Aldis look upon this thing in the usual 'Porky' parvenue manner."[38] Convinced that they should try to educate the comparatively backward Chicago art community, Kuhn and Gregg published a small catalog entitled *For and Against*, the intended purpose of which was to present pro and con opinions that had already been published.[39] The pamphlet consisted of reprints of various statements and articles.

The plan to convert the public and the press to at least a modicum of appreciation for modernism was relatively successful, for as the show continued, various critics and observers demonstrated greater tolerance. Arthur Eddy actually purchased more work from the show, and the *Tribune* critic Harriet Monroe wrote an article that was headlined by her editor "Cubist Art a Protest against Narrow Conservatism." In the essay, Monroe reported that she had viewed the show earlier in New York and recommended it for Chicago. She also pointed out that "the exhibition represents certain phases of European art . . . recognized abroad by critics and students and . . . have enthusiastic admirers among well-known connoisseurs. Under these circumstances, why should we not acquaint ourselves with the facts, learn what is going on?"[40]

Kuhn called Harriet Monroe at the *Chicago Daily Tribune* an ally, but in spite of her professed liberal attitude, she had insisted earlier that Matisse had not always been successful in his "search for significant form," especially in a painting such as *The Blue Woman*.[41] On another occasion, she could not resist describing Matisse's paintings as "the most hideous monstrosities ever perpetrated in the name of long suffering art."[42] Such a harsh response to the radical Europeans was actually a blessing in disguise to certain American moderns, for as the ubiquitous critic George B. Zug pointed out, "if the exhibition of paintings by progressive Americans . . . had come to us at any other time it would have created a sensation." Zug referred not to Childe Hassam or A. P. Ryder, whose works were also there, but to artists such as Leon Kroll, one "to be reckoned with in the future."[43] Other, less radical art was shown in Chicago during the run of the Armory Show. Maude I. G. Oliver reported on exhibitions at Anderson's, O'Brien's, Young's, and Moulton and Ricketts galleries. She also commented on Pauline Palmer's solo show at the Art Institute, claiming that it had been "marked by almost phenomenal success."[44] Palmer's exhibition was succeeded by a solo show for Frieseke, which opened on 8 April, when the Armory Show was still in full swing. Chicago critics responded more favorably to the images of Ritman's friend than they did to Marcel Duchamp's works. As a matter of fact, the public appreciated most intimist pictures, although they had come out for curiosity's sake to see the Armory Show. Yet there were some purchases of the so-called ugly art: the architect Maniere Dawson, urged on by his friend Arthur Eddy, bought a version of Duchamp's nude; the liberal critic Harriet Monroe bought a lithograph by Odilon Redon; and John Quinn purchased a Gauguin print. In summary, however, there were relatively few sales of important works.

As the Armory Show drew to a close in Chicago, attendance slackened, but not before an unprecedented flow of visitors on the last weekend. In spite of making some converts, the show still prompted hostile reaction, not so much from the public at large as from the conservative Art Institute teachers and their students, whom Kuhn described as "a lot of rowdy rough-necks." Hoping to close the show with a bang, on 16 April students had planned to hang Brancusi, Matisse, and Walter Pach in effigy, but certain members of the Chicago Art Students League declined to involve themselves in the demonstration. Moreover, when Elmer MacRae, a stalwart of the American Painters and Sculptors Association, heard of the mischief, he complained vehemently to acting director N. H. Carpenter. Nevertheless, in spite of an injunction against the demonstration, students convicted one *Henri Hairmatress* of many crimes at a trial. To eliminate him as a threat to the art community, they sentenced Hairmatress to death, beat him, stabbed him, and dragged his "corpse" with glee in front of curious Michigan Avenue bystanders. The rowdy crowd showed their dislike of avant-garde European art by burning copies of Matisse's paintings while they joined in a kind of ritualistic spring dance over their desecrated symbols. Most observers were confused or amused, but one high-up member of the institute "praised the students for their display of sanity," while others found their actions shameful.[45] It should have come as no surprise that the revolutionary show would cause such a violent reaction. Fanned by the winds of journalistic rabble-rousing, the public was aroused, shocked, insulted, and angered. In spite of it all, the Chicago phase of the Armory Show ended as a bloodless cultural revolution, and Kuhn dismissed the problems associated with it as "just clean fun."[46] Several Chicago artists sent letters about the event to their artist friends in Paris and Giverny. Frieseke's solo show, which remained hanging as the Armory Show moved on to Boston, even drew some compliments.

Once the Armory Show had taken America by storm with radical works produced mostly by French artists, American expatriate camps in Paris reverberated with nervous energy. The event was mainstream news there, proving more definitely than ever before that Paris, the mecca of modern art, was truly the art capital of the world. There was no doubt in the minds of most American expatriate artists that if the art was generated in a Parisian source, it would succeed in America. And once again the mainspring of American expatriation was wound tight in anticipation of running for many years. For his own good, an artist should live and work in Paris, where great art, traditional or avant-garde, was produced.

Notes

1. Abel Warshawsky, *The Memories of an American Impressionist* (Kent, OH: The Kent State University Press, 1980), p. 162.

2. Ibid.

3. The Sonderbund exhibition, held in Cologne, Germany, in 1912, was the first exhaustive retrospective exhibition dealing with the development of modern art. The show embraced practically an encyclopedic array of European moderns, with Van Gogh in the lead, followed by Cézanne, Munch, Signac, and other French, Swiss, Dutch, and English painters. The Blaue Reiter group from Munich and the rebellious New Secession from Berlin were also there. The Sonderbund show demonstrated that the antinaturalist trend engulfed all of Europe, especially Germany, and was not just the idiosyncracy of a few individual artists. The foundations of the future artistic explosion in Weimar Germany were rapidly taking shape. See Werner Haftmann, *Painting in the Twentieth Century*, vol. I, *An Analysis of the Artists and Their Work* (New York: Frederick A. Praeger, 1965), pp. 58, 129.

4. Milton W. Brown, *The Story of the Armory Show*, 2d ed. (New York: Abbeville Press, Publishers, 1988). See also Lloyd Goodrich, *Pioneers of Modern Art in America: The Decade of the Armory Show, 1910-1920* (New York: Frederick A. Praeger, 1963).

5. Walt Kuhn, "The Story of the Armory Show," in *The Armory Show, International Exhibition of Modern Art, 1913*, vol. III, *Contemporary and Retrospective Documents* (New York: Arno Press, 1972), p. 10.

6. H. Wayne Morgan, *New Muses: Art in American Culture, 1865-1920* (Norman, OK: University of Oklahoma Press, 1978), p. 162.

7. "The Greatest Exhibition of Insurgent Art Ever Held," *Current Opinion*, no. 54 (March 1913), pp. 230-32.

8. *New York Times*, 23 February 1913, part VI, p. 15.

9. *New York Times*, 16 March 1913.

10. Kenyon Cox, "The 'Modern' Spirit in Art," *Harper's Weekly*, LVII (15 March 1913), p. 10.

11. Royal Cortissoz, "The Post-Impressionist Illusion," *Century*, LXXXV, (April 1913), p. 813.

12. Jerome Myers, *Artist in Manhattan* (New York: American Artists Group, Inc., 1940), p. 36.

13. "Frightfulness in Art," *American Magazine of Art*, VII (April 1917), pp. 244-45.

14. For data regarding the Quinn collection, see *John Quinn, 1870-1925, Collection of Paintings, Water Colors, Drawings and Sculpture* (Huntington, NY: Pidgeon Hill Press, 1926).

15. Marcel Duchamp, quoted from *Marcel Duchamp*, exhibition catalog (Chicago: The Art Institute of Chicago), p. 13. This famous work in the Philadelphia Museum of Art is not to be confused with the other version by Duchamp with the same title that was purchased by Quinn, only a study for the large painting.

16. Arthur Jerome Eddy (1859-1920), was a prominent Chicago lawyer, writer, and collector. Most of Eddy's art collection is now at the Art Institute of Chicago.

17. For a brief but interesting description of Eddy, see Carter H. Harrison, *Growing up with Chicago* (Chicago: Ralph Fletcher Seymour, 1944), pp. 188-89.

18. The portrait of Eddy has been known as **Arrangement in Flesh Color and Brown: Portrait of Arthur J. Eddy** (oil on canvas, signed with butterfly, and inscribed on the reverse). The work is now owned by the Art Institute of Chicago.

19. Arthur Jerome Eddy, *Cubists and Post-Impressionists* (Chicago: A. C. McClurg & Co., 1914), p. 3.

20. Milton W. Brown, *American Painting from the Armory Show to the Depression* (Princeton, NJ: Princeton University Press, 1972), p. 95.

21. John Quinn to George W. Russell, 2 March, 1913; quoted from B. L. Reid, *The Man from New York: John Quinn and His Friends* (New York: Oxford University Press, 1968), p. 151.

22. Brown, *The Story of the Armory Show*, p. 188.

23. Ibid., p. 189.

24. Ibid., pp. 190-91. Brown points out that Aldis was worried about Director French's reluctance to have the show in Chicago. Aldis suggested that the association, not French, select works for the Chicago show. Kuhn reassured Aldis that French was "in the hands of Davies . . . if anyone could handle the director, Davies was the man." Kuhn sent Aldis a copy of the show contract in February 1913. The show fee was $2,500 and the Art Institute was also to pay for all insurance and transportation (net receipts would be shared between Chicago and the Association of American Painters and Sculptors). After continued negotiations, Kuhn advised Quinn, the association's legal counsel, that "Chicago accepts all conditions"—this was not until 5 March 1913, ibid., p. 192.

25. The court convened on the issue on 21 March 1913. The copy of Paul Chabas's "lewd lady" painting was brought before a distinguished panel of clerical, educational, and art authorities. After roughly 30 minutes of deliberation, the painting was vindicated. Panel members recommended that the police concern themselves with more pertinent issues. See Sparks, "Winds of Chicago," p. 143.

26. Herman Landon, "Hark! Hark! The Critics Bark! The Cubists Are Coming!" *Sunday Record Herald* (Chicago), 23 March 1912, p. 2.

27. *Inter Ocean*, Tuesday, 25 March 1913, p.5.

28. Ibid.

29. Ibid.

30. Kuhn, p. 20.

31. "Fair Play for Insurgent Art," *Chicago Evening Post*, 24 March 1913, p. 6.

32. *Chicago Daily Tribune*, "Here She Is: White Outline Shows 'Nude Descending a Staircase,'" Monday, 24 March 1913, p. 5. As late as Wednesday, 26 March, the *Tribune* reported that "Arthur J. Eddy will follow tomorrow afternoon with a verbal bombardment of the cubists and futurists in particular." "Chicago Artist Starts Revolt," p. 15.

33. Ibid.

34. Letter from Walt Kuhn to Elmer MacRae; quoted from Brown, *The Story of the Armory Show*, p. 203.

35. H. Effa Webster, *Chicago Examiner*, 1 April 1913.

36. Lena C. McCauley, "Art and Artists," *Chicago Evening Post*, 27 March 1913, p. 8.

37. "Artists Give Cubist Play," *Chicago Daily Tribune*, 27 March 1913.

38. Kuhn to A. B. Davies, quoted from Brown, *The Story of the Armory Show,* p. 208.

39. This small brochure was nicknamed the "Red Pamphlet" owing to its color. Out of the 5,000 copies, the association sold over 1,500 at 25 cents per issue.

40. Harriet Monroe, "Cubist Art a Protest against Narrow Conservatism," *Chicago Sunday Tribune*, 8 April 1913, p. 11.

41. Harriet Monroe, "Art Exhibition Opens in Chicago," *Chicago Tribune*, 25 March 1913.

42. Harriet Monroe, *Chicago Tribune*, also quoted in "Literature and Art," *Chicago Opinion*, LIV (April 1913), p. 316.

43. George B. Zug, "Among the Art Galleries," *Inter Ocean*, 6 April 1913, p. 5.

44. Maude I. G. Oliver, "Of Art and Artists," *Sunday Record-Herald* (Chicago) 6 April 1913.

45. Brown, *The Story of the Armory Show*, p. 210.

46. Kuhn, "The Story of the Armory Show," p. 21.

CHAPTER FIFTEEN: RITMAN IN THE POWERHOUSE OF GIVERNY

Since Ritman's studio time was limited by the few daylight hours available in the winter, he worked feverishly to prepare for the spring exhibition season of 1913 (pl. 15-1). The salons were still important forums, but in view of his new alliance with the Giverny impressionists, Ritman also wanted to experiment in his urban studio with the broken-color technique. He finished some canvases for shipment to American shows, one of which was the upcoming 108th Annual at the Pennsylvania Academy of the Fine Arts. He also sent a painting to Chicago.

In March 1913, just before the Armory show opened in his hometown, Ritman took pictures to the Paris Salon jury. This time he paid little attention to the mass of onlookers, artists, models, and dilettantes who stood by making their usual comments and catcalls as porters carried works of art to their place of judgment. He had not lost his enthusiasm for the grand old event, but recently he had come to believe that his success depended less on the salons than on his self-promotion as an expatriate impressionist. Nonetheless, like others who needed salon recognition, he waited patiently for the results, as he always did. Several weeks later he learned that two works, *Nue* and *Le Matin*, had been accepted to the 1913 Paris Salon. He also heard that Parker had submitted his *La Paresse*, the large and striking depiction of a reclining and exceedingly sensual nude that he had begun painting the

previous summer when a shower forced him indoors. Most visitors who had seen the painting exclaimed that it was "masterful." Many commented that by and large, it represented his best work thus far, and Ritman had stood in awe, not daring to compare it with his own work. Undoubtedly, Parker's picture would fetch some kind of award, notwithstanding the fact that the work came from the hand of an American from Nebraska.

Finally, on that great day of the first of May, *le vernissage du Salon de la Société des Artistes Français* (the varnishing of the Salon of the Society of French Artists), took place. As in years past, Ritman hoped for an award, if nothing more than an honorable mention. He was confident of the quality of his imagery, and if politics were factored into the system, he had even greater hope after reviewing the governing board of the society, for the secretaries Déchenaud and Royer had been his teachers. Paul Chabas, whose picture had recently been banned from the window of a Chicago photography shop, was also a board member of the *société*. On the other hand, there were so many pictures, indeed, so many good pictures, that Ritman dared not set his hopes too high.[1]

As customary, the Grand Palais was crammed with thousands of paintings, and once again, Ritman joined the throng of artist-participants who rushed eagerly through the galleries to see whether their work had been well displayed. The large catalog indicated that Ritman had been born in Chicago; that he studied under Tony Robert-Fleury, Déchenaud, and H. Royer; and that he resided at 59 Avenue de Saxe in Paris.[2]

Ritman won no award for his pictures! He was disappointed, as one might expect, for his original goal had been to score at the Salon. He was elated, however, when he learned that two of his teachers had won awards: Parker won the coveted Gold Medal, and Déchenaud was awarded the Grand Medal of Honor. Most viewers had expected Parker's *La Paresse* to win an award, but no one, not even he, had expected the Gold Medal; no American had received a comparable award in years. Parker's great triumph was the talk of the Paris art community. Before long, however, Sara Hallowell would write to French in Chicago explaining that Parker's Gold Medal actually corresponded to a second-place medal as a result of the recent revision of awards.[3] She was careful to point out, however, that "apart from all this, Lawton Parker's picture of this year is admirable. It is the first work that I invited [to Chicago] from this [Paris] Salon — and this long before there was any suggestion of a medal. It is a life-sized nude — a woman — and sufficiently academic to satisfy the demands of the 'old school.' "[4]

Substantial critical acclaim greeted Parker's effort, but very little came Ritman's way. In reviewing the Salon for *La Chronique des Arts*, critic Roger-Marx wrote that "the moment is not here yet to examine all the results arising from a more exacting study of the phenomena of light." Referring to both Ritman and Lawton Parker, he stated that "in the case of paintings of nudes, the overall effect has been advantageous."[5]

After the Salon of the Société des Artistes Français in 1913, Ritman went back to Giverny. Once again he made no effort to submit his work to the Champ de Mars Salon. Back in Giverny, he joined an optimistic American milieu consisting primarily of already successful impressionists who hoped their paintings would create as much excitement as Parker's had. Most of the expatriates were still inspired by Monet's presence, but they actually derived a greater sense of pride from Parker's triumph, Ritman's productions, and their own forthright existence, since their mentor had already received more than his share of praise. They were very much aware of their reputation in the international art community as a relatively conservative group that provided distinct images for the French and American markets. Their success and camaraderie generated a special kind of expatriate-art-colony spirit, which never reached those who remained in Paris. Although some very reclusive individuals resided in Giverny, nearly everyone was welcomed into the group. Unlike the initiates at the Julian Academy or the Ecole,

an American freshman was not subjected to the *blague* in Giverny.

Even for nonguests, local activities in Giverny gravitated toward the Hotel Baudy, where "the dining room walls were covered with paintings, some of them gifts, others left as pledges for unpaid bills."[6] Living in his own cottage, Ritman was no longer a guest at the Baudys', although he joined its expatriate milieu frequently and in time would also contribute an image to the dining room walls. There had been a certain tradition in painting the dining room walls at the Baudys': before Ritman came to Giverny, the English painter William Rothenstein, who had been brought to the hotel by a Yankee friend, remembered the "billiard room whose white plastered walls [had] tempted" the guests.[7] Over the years, most of the artists' faces in Giverny had changed, but their routine had not: in the tradition of plein-air paintings, artists still gathered their collapsible easels and set them up in the surrounding "fields where white umbrellas opened out like mushrooms."[8]

From spring onward, the village and its environs turned into a beehive of artistic activity. Even before the cherry blossoms came out, painters braved the unpredictable spring weather to work en plein air. A mood of excitement, anticipation, and genuinely good-natured competition pervaded the area — and there was always optimism, arising from the hope that the next picture would be somewhat better than the one before. While Giverny had become a kind of American outpost, the village remained very French and basically unchanged. Much as they did in the mid-1880s, painters arose early in the morning to share breakfast at Madame Baudy's and rush off into the countryside to work until noon. They were loaded with painting gear, and the morning dew made their shoes and trouser legs wet; but they soon found a suitable location since the nearby Epte, the small groves of trees, the open glens and hills, and the plowed fields were all within walking distance. The warm morning sun dried their clothes in due course. Frequently accompanied by another artist, a model or both, they brought lunches so that they would not have to trek back to the Baudys'.

On their sketching trips the Giverny painters, following Monet's lead, took along several canvases or academy boards, which allowed them to change scenes at will. Academy boards with wet paint were slipped into a grooved box fitted with a handle. Larger stretched canvases were difficult to carry, especially on windy days, so frequently only one image was begun. In the spring, the weather determined the number of works done al fresco, but during the warm days of summer, when the sun arched directly overhead and the days were long — sometimes too long for one outing — in the bucolic environs of Giverny the Americans made numerous outstanding images in which they focused upon the beauty of feminine grace in a natural setting. These were magical days, ebbing by quietly, harmoniously, in an idyllic place; some artists caught glimpses of the magic, put it on canvas, and brought it back to the real world for others to see. The routine of the expatriate artist in Giverny was as close to living fiction as one could imagine. This charming existence, contrasted with *la vie bohème* in Paris, proliferated stories (published and otherwise) that made a life like Ritman's seem quite enviable to folks back home.

Ritman settled into a comfortable working routine, the product of which revealed a decisive move from his brushy, brightly colored salon style to a manner which incorporated many more of the distinctive features of impressionism. At first glance, one might assume that the change in Ritman's art resulted from his proximity to Monet — the direct influence, as it were, of the master himself — or perhaps from Ritman's vicarious assimilation of the master's style. Such was not the case, however, since the young American received no guidance from Monet, not even an audience with him. Instead, the change came about as a result of Ritman's own inherent tendencies toward the style — as seen in a higher-key palette, a greater awareness of light, a limited incorporation of broken color — and as a result of the direct influence of a number of Givernyites who happened to be from the Midwest — Parker, Miller, and Frieseke. The pioneer expatriate Theodore Butler from Columbus, Ohio, had returned to New York to complete another artist's commission, so that Ritman had no opportunity to spend time with him this summer. Other Chicago artists sojourned in Giverny, men like Karl Buehr and Karl Anderson, and, of course, the village played host to numerous Americans who spent only a couple of weeks, imbibing the quaint charm and beauty of the place.

Ritman's raison d'être synchronized with the serene village, with its leafy walls, its worn paths and colorful gardens, its friendly townsfolk, its misty mornings and bright sunshine, its quietude and simplicity, its bucolic beauty — all of it was a kind of Brigadoon made for an artist; to Ritman and his friends, Giverny was the perfect place for an impressionist to live and work. Conservative Americans, and maybe Midwesterners even more so, found the area especially comfortable because of its rural environment. Like Midwesterners, the citizens of Giverny led routine lives and were quite disciplined, even pragmatic — sometimes too much so in the opinion of Monet. Giverny was no place for the artist who loved the urban environment exclusively; it was no place for a Nebraskan like Robert Henri, but it was a utopia for a

Nebraskan like Parker as long as he could get back to the city (Paris, New York, or Chicago) when he pleased. In Giverny, there were outside toilets, mud, pigs, honeybees, cherry blossoms, farmers, cows, vinyards, horse-drawn wagons, wooden fences, and country breakfasts — life in this village was quite unlike anything one experienced in Montparnasse, excepting, of course, the comradeship of the American expatriates.

In many ways, Parker had been a guiding light to Ritman, who had become fiercely loyal to his mentor in recent times. In spite of the rumors about Parker's conflicts, he had never failed Ritman. Moreover, Parker had succeeded as an artist; he had just received what Ritman longed for — a gold medal from the Paris Salon. During the summer of 1913, Ritman joined in numerous discussions about *La Paresse*; everyone agreed that the work contained qualities that had never appeared before in Parker's painting. An American critic would later report that in the picture there was a "subtle use of colour, a harmony in lavender, and in the play of light from before and behind, as it falls on face and figure."[9] Just as Chicago was becoming increasingly proud of Ritman, the American art community restored his teacher's reputation as a culture hero. In spite of Director French's efforts to keep him at bay, Ritman's mentor had become a celebrity. In Parker's home state, officials at the University of Nebraska in Lincoln were considering awarding an honorary doctorate degree to their favorite son artist.

Ritman maintained excellent relations with Frieseke. Although Frieseke was fifteen years his senior, the difference in age meant plenty in terms of experience to guide the younger man. Frieseke was impressed with Ritman's outstanding ability to draw with a brush, but he knew that Ritman needed help with color, something for which Frieseke had always been praised. He also helped Ritman to become more selective in his compositions, pointing out especially the need to properly arrange the settings in which he posed his figures.[10] It was probably Frieseke who urged Ritman to limit the depth of space by placing his model in front of a wall, be it an interior or garden scene. Of course, Frieseke was an expert at painting his lovely women en plein air in a walled garden, a decorative lovely spot bursting with foliage and color. His American friends liked this colorful section of Giverny with its profusion of flowers almost as much as they liked Monet's garden: it had served as the background for models posed by Parker (pl. 15-2), Edmund Greacen, Karl Buehr, Richard Miller, and now Ritman. Making an exception to his rule of taking few or no pupils, Frieseke gave Ritman a good deal of friendly assistance, while his beautiful garden provided a further advantage to the younger artist.

Although Ritman enjoyed the friendship of many American expatriates in France, it seems that he gravitated more easily to those with a Chicago or Midwest connection. In the larger sense, there was apparently greater camaraderie among the expatriates from the Midwest than has hitherto been accounted for in the history of American impressionism. In Paris, the American Art Association, sponsored by Frieseke's patron Rodman Wanamaker, had served as a meeting ground for Ritman, Parker, Frieseke, Greacen, Buehr, and other Midwestern expatriates. A close professional brotherhood also existed among the members of other art colonies, such as the one in Trépied (near Etaples), where the *Société Artistique de Picardie* (Art Association of Picardy) functioned as a gathering place for a number of Midwesterners.[11] Like Giverny, Trépied was a small village, only about 25 houses, in fact; but it was a kind of minisuburb of Paris-Plage, a popular seaside resort. The society had sponsored its first show nearly a decade earlier under the guidance of Max Bohm, an expatriate from Cleveland.[12] Called a romantic impressionist, Bohm had studied at the Julian Academy and exhibited yearly in the Paris salons, residing in Etaples where he painted and taught. Henry O. Tanner, whose work had been shown quite successfully in Chicago a couple of years earlier, was also a staunch member of the *société*.[13] In his nearby studio, Tanner had received a visit this year from the artist-critic Clara MacChesney, who described the studio as "an ideal workroom, being high-ceilinged, spacious and having the least possible furniture, utterly free from masses of useless studio stuff and paraphernalia . . . . In this simply furnished room he often poses his models."[14] At this time, members of the Art Association of Picardy like Bohm, Tanner, and Roy Brown (born in Decatur, Illinois and engaged as an illustrator for the *Chicago Tribune* during Ritman's early student years) were preparing invitations to their annual show, which included names such as Albert Besnard, Alfy Maurer, Walter Griffin, Walter MacEwen, Frederick Frieseke, and others, but not Ritman, who had not yet visited Trépied. Like Monet before him, Theodore Butler had spent several summers on the Normandy coast, and Lawton Parker had also worked in the Dieppe and Trépied areas. Ritman's association with members of this expatriate group had developed in Paris.

Like Bonnard, the French intimist who painted in nearby Vernonnet, the American painters in Giverny did not rationalize about their status as intimists. They were proud artists who specialized in capturing the special ambience of an attractive woman engaged in leisurely or intimate activities. Unlike Bonnard, whose intimist pictures so frequently focused upon the nude and carried subtle erotic messages, Frieseke, Parker, Miller, and other

Americans usually produced more conservative images, even when the subjects were nude. Of course, some were convinced that Parker's last salon award winner disqualified him from this generalization, since his subject conveyed distinct erotic overtones. Revealing, nonetheless, the lingering influences of America's puritanical tradition, the American intimists in Giverny portrayed the nude in what most observers believed to be good taste: frequently, their models were only partially nude and posed in a boudoir setting; seldom was there any suggestion of eroticism in their works.

William H. Gerdts notes that the rising interest in the nude as a theme in American painting around the turn of the century still had to face antagonistic forces. He summarized the situation as follows: "On the one hand, puritanical opposition to the theme remained never far from sight, and charges of vulgarity, coarseness, and immorality were continually thrust at painters of the undraped figure. On the other hand, no sooner did the artists trained in Munich and Paris exert their right to portray the nude than charges of artificiality were brought against them."[15] The art of the Ash Can School had successfully countered the idealized and sentimental depictions of nudes. Although the growing number of life classes in the United States brought more freedom and led to a more frank depiction of the nude; in many instances, the public considered the nude as a taboo subject matter — a fact that had been recently confirmed in Chicago, where a photographer was forced to remove the Chabas nude from his shop window.

Ritman, on the other hand, was a relative newcomer to the conservative American tastes in art; and after Parker's success, he was somewhat more willing than his expatriate friends to imply eroticism in his nudes. By the early summer of 1913, he was busy producing a new kind of imagery, sometimes centered on the partial nude, at other times on the fully undraped model, but always in good taste, as one might expect from an American Givernyite. Because he had already assimilated the so-called Giverny style of American intimism, Ritman eventually produced a number of outstanding canvases featuring the nude in both indoor and outdoor settings.

Although the facade of Giverny had altered only slightly since the early days of the art colony, the relationship of the village with the sophisticated international art community gave it a certain aesthetic egalitarianism. Indeed, over the years the little village had witnessed an amazing array of celebrities. Many of them had come to visit Monet, but others simply wanted to know what was so special about this place in the country — personalities like the great statesman Clemenceau, the art dealers Paul Durand-Ruel and the Bernheims (of the Galerie

Bernheim-Jeune), the sculptor Auguste Rodin, the publisher Thadée Natanson, and many others of burgeoning or declining fame from various strata of culture and politics. For example, in the summer of 1913, the American vocalist Marguerite Namara was driven by Ritman's place when she visited Monet and "insisted upon singing" for him "beside the pond." In her revealing study on Monet's years at Giverny, Claire Joyes explained that Ms. Namara's performance "involved the not inconsiderable feat of transporting Theodore Butler's piano from the rue du Colombier to the water garden."[16] After the performance, Monet posed with the singer for a photo taken by the French playwright and actor Sasha Guitry, who had recently finished *La Prise de Bery-op-Zoom*. Sometimes celebrities (artists and otherwise) rented cottages in Giverny simply to breathe its apparently rich aesthetic air. Most of these were painters, however, and "sky-light windows appeared in the weathered slate roofs" of a number of cottages. The streets kept the same look, as did the trees, worn paths, and fences, so that in the eye of the visitor who had been away for a long time, the village had actually changed very little. Monet's grandson-in-law Pierre Toulgouat remembered that "for a time, the little village took on some aspects of a summer 'art colony' in America." However, "there was something in the bland, peaceful, simply Norman atmosphere that kept it from succumbing completely."[17]

One of the most striking works from Ritman's sojourn of the summer of 1913 is an oil known as ***Dormitory Breakfast*** or ***Mimi at Breakfast*** (ill. 15-1). Instead of the typical two figures seen in his Salon pictures, we now find only one: an attractive young woman seated on the seat-ledge of an open window that reveals a backdrop of brilliant foliage. Apparently lost in thought, Mimi stares into a cup of tea that she is preparing to raise to her lips. We are privy to this quiet, intimate scene, but a closer approach is prevented by the breakfast table positioned between us and the subject. In spite of the fact that Ritman has depicted an interior scene, he has also achieved some of the effect of a plein-air picture by providing a view of the out-of-doors, thus access to another spatial dimension. The juxtaposition of a portrait figure with a window-framed distant vista is an age-old artistic device; therefore, in an attempt to accentuate a modern impressionistic look, Ritman severely limited the outdoor space with a leafy, curtainlike backdrop executed in the bold broken-color technique. Parker had used the same setting in many of his Giverny works. Ritman's indoor-outdoor resolution provides a sense of privacy in spite of the open window, but it also typifies the basic pictorial formula to which he routinely adhered in Giverny. Here and frequently hereafter, Ritman silhouettes his subject against

Ill. 15-1. Louis Ritman. *Dormitory Breakfast* or *Mimi at Breakfast*. 1913. Oil on canvas, 36 x 36 inches. University of Nebraska Art Galleries, Sheldon Art Gallery, Lincoln, Nebraska. I.M. Hall Collection.

a decoratively papered wall or a curtainlike wall of foliage, either of which provides a colorful backdrop to a private scene.

Another impressionist quality in this picture is the way Ritman has captured the effects of atmosphere and light. In this breakfast scene, we sense that a gentle morning breeze, warmed by a summer sun, wafts through the open window and softly caresses Mimi as she loses herself in recent memories. Backlighted by sunshine, her gowned form is softly silhouetted against a framed background, a portraitlike device that emphasizes the focal point in the composition.

If Ritman intended any subtle secular iconography, one might find it in the table setting: conforming to the lingering tradition of Victorian decorum, Ritman provides not two, but three places at the table, thereby dispelling any symbolic implication of a single overnight guest. However, the propriety suggested in an artist's work was not always truly reflective of the artist's own social behavior. So it was with Ritman, since his model Mimi lived with him at his studio cottage and there shared many breakfasts (ill. 15-2).

In ***Dormitory Breakfast*** and other works from this period, Ritman demonstrated a sophisticated, albeit conservative assimilation of impressionism. Obviously the new intimist milieu at Giverny provided fuel for a new imagery, the aesthetic embers for which had been glowing for several years.

Fascinated with his new pictorial formula, Ritman was determined to exploit it to its fullest potential. Accordingly, at about the same time he executed the breakfast pictures, he also painted *Early Morning* (pl. 15-3). Once again the scene is set in the morning hours, but this time he has captured a moment even more private than any he has painted before. His lovely feminine subject is seated near an open window, stealing a few precious moments

Ill. 15-2. Ritman's model [Mimi?] seated at an outdoor table, Giverny. Photograph. Courtesy Maurice Ritman.

in the fresh morning air. Unaware of our intrusion on her privacy, Mimi is partially undressed as she languishes in the midst of her morning toilette. Her dress and hat are laid out on the nearby wicker chair. In his simple yet masterfully designed composition, Ritman deftly balances a few forms, textures, and patterns. Arranged for the sake of pictorial harmony, all the physical elements in this small room imply the quality of softness; contrasts between the elements are achieved mainly through variations in texture and color. Of course, this ensemble of yielding surfaces enhances the already obvious feminine ambience of the scene.

Taking Ritman's place as he stood at his easel, the viewer is confronted with an extremely shallow picture space, limited as it is by a backdroplike wall. In contrast, both the figure and the wicker chair project into the viewer's space at an oblique angle to the picture plane. It is instructive to note that while the subject's body and legs are positioned at one angle, her head is turned at the opposite angle to view the scene out of doors.

One of the most striking features of this picture is the effect of light: the figure is bathed in a warm summer luminance, which justifies the artist's high-key palette; in other areas, light is absorbed and no highlights are evident. Harmonically orchestrated, light flows evenly and softly in this pictorial environment. One is also confronted with an inordinate number of material (cloth) surfaces, which provide a wonderful interplay of brightly colored patterns. We should not be surprised at the artist's predilection for such material, since his father had been a designer of textiles for as long as Louis could remember. Louis had frequently seen him mark and cut bolts of decorative material for garments.

In *Early Morning*, Ritman excelled in drawing with a brush, a technique he had practiced since his first years with Reynolds in Chicago. Using a wide variety of bristle brushes fully loaded with pigment from a high-keyed palette, Ritman did not juxtapose small strokes of contrasting hue to arrive at a typical broken-color style. Instead, he employed a combination of sweeping elongated strokes and smaller wedgelike dabs to create repetitious patterned areas. The result is a harmonious balance of blues, pinks, lavenders, and yellows—delicate colors that are sensitively combined in keeping with the general mood of his extremely intimate scene.

This is not yet pure impressionism. Although *Early Morning* is an outstanding example of American intimism as it evolved from Chicago to Giverny, the palette and brushwork are quite different from Monet's or Frieseke's. A careful comparison of styles shows that Ritman was still more influenced by Parker than by any other of the Midwestern expatriates in Giverny. Indeed, what one critic wrote about Parker might be applied to Ritman as well: the artist, reported the critic, "could not rest content with being a mere portrait painter, and hence his move a few years ago to Giverny and his rush of enthusiasm for painting the figure, draped and nude, out of doors."[18] The critic pointed out that "it is a somewhat new kind of impressionism which has been practiced in recent years at Giverny by Parker and other Americans [in this case, Ritman]. For although the little village on the Seine is the home of Monet, the founder of impressionism, this American movement in Giverny is not connected with that great master, and differs somewhat in method from his." Continuing his discussion, the critic observed that the artist "does not see nature in the way of the French impressionists, he does not adopt their method of painting in broken colour. To him nature in her lights, hues, forms and various appearances is fused and blended into a gracious and harmonious whole. He, therefore, prepares his colours on the palette, matching his greens to those of nature, his blues to her blues; and his results justify his methods. For while rendering warm sunlight, cool shadows and the brilliant hues of foliage and flowers, he also suggests the luminosity of nature and the softening influence of the atmosphere."[19]

Another relatively large Ritman canvas (32 x 40 inches) from the summer of 1913 is signed and dated at the lower left and entitled *Pink and Blue* (pl. 15-4). Focusing again on the typical intimist theme, the artist has posed a young woman at a table near an open window. Here, we notice that Ritman's composition is a good deal more geometric than others: half of a rectangular table implies projection beyond the picture plane, as does the window. The right casement sash projects at an angle toward the viewer. Seated in a frontal position with her back against a papered wall, the subject occupies the whole right side of the scene. As in the breakfast picture, the artist arranges an interesting table setting — a teapot, a bowl of fruit, and a vase of flowers — all illuminated by the bright summer sunshine that finds its way through the blinded window behind. The flowers, the fruit, and subject are the only strictly organic forms in the composition, and they all serve well as balancing contrasts in an otherwise severe composition consisting of flat planes relieved only by decorative patterns. The subject's facial expression is ambiguous — is she happy or sad? In either instance, as in *Early Morning*, she is introspective — lost as it were, in her own thoughts.

It was not only the candid depiction of a young woman lost in reverie which came to be a favorite theme for Ritman but also the general compositional format like the one he used in *Pink and Blue* and in works yet to be discussed: the female subject seated against a wall or backdrop, with a table projecting from her into the viewer's space. Although there are similar works by both Parker and Frieseke, one must assume that all three artists were influenced by precedent examples from Degas.[20] For example, although the theme of the French master's already famous oil *In a Café (The Absinthe Drinker)* (c. 1875/76) was different from Ritman's favorite theme, the overall composition could have served as an inspiration to him or to his mentors because it had been in the Louvre since 1911.[21] Degas depicts a young woman and her companion seated in a bar at night; a drink is on the table in front of the young woman who stares ahead in a drunken stupor. In contrast, in a picture entitled *A Pensive Moment* (pl. 15-5), Ritman depicts a young woman seated on an open window ledge in the morning, apparently lost in thought as she examines a small Japanese sugar bowl. In Ritman's *Dormitory Breakfast*, Mimi, quite unlike Degas's drab model, is colorfully draped and silhouetted against the familiar leafy garden backdrop, with her form highlighted by bright sunlight. Farther inside the room, light continues its magic as it illumines and reflects every object it touches, especially the table (which projects toward the viewer) and its colorful objects — a vase of flowers, a Japanese tea service, and a compote filled with fresh fruit. As in *Pink and Blue*, both casement sashes are open and Mimi's back is reflected (as in earlier mirror pictures) in the right pane, while light filters through the diaphanous curtain on the left as it moves softly in the summer breeze. Indeed, while Ritman's picture probably owes a certain debt to Degas's compositional genius, the similarity ends there. Unlike Degas's dark, moody, and artificially lit scene depicting a woman gazing into space, Ritman's scene is bright, colorful, optimistic, and focused on an attractive and healthy young woman who is probably beginning her day with tea, not ending it with absinthe. Accordingly, Ritman's imagery, executed in a foreign land and as conservative as it was, is, nonetheless, far more typically American than French, given its relative place in the history of art. There is no doubt that in order to understand Ritman's imagery, we must look for diverse French influences and specific American ones, whether these emanate from Wellington J. Reynolds, Lawton Parker, Degas, Renoir, Monet, Vuillard, or Bonnard. And so it was that young Ritman had already arrived at an unmistakable American kind of impressionism, a Givernyesque intimism far more allied to the work of Parker and Frieseke than to that of Monet and Degas.

Though altered somewhat, another similar work from this summer of 1913 is an oil known as *Early Morning Sunshine* (pl. 15-6). Like *A Pensive Moment* and *Dormitory Breakfast*, this painting is a fine example of Ritman's morningtime intimism. In this work, the viewer is presented with a candid glimpse of Mimi soon after she has awakened. The room seems to cling to its nighttime coolness, while the sun makes its bold passage through the open window where Mimi sits entranced by her memories, the loveliness of the new day, or perhaps nothing more than a butterfly spreading its wings in the warmth of the sunlight. Ritman's observation of light and its effect on local color is exemplary. His draftsmanship is without flaw, especially as he brushes in Mimi's very feminine features and hands. The ubiquitous green table and its carefully arranged top is still in this composition, but it is relegated to a lesser position to the left of the window and shaded somewhat from the light which begins to penetrate the sheer curtains. Softening form, Ritman creates a sophisticated ensemble of light and color, utilizing a single figure, posed as typically as one might expect from an American intimist working in Giverny.

Also emanating from this period is a striking picture known as *Morning Tea* (ill. 15-3). This painting bears no signature, perhaps because Ritman considered it unfinished. Supporting this deduction is the fact that at a later date, he used the reverse side of the canvas for an image known as *Before the Masquerade (The Yellow Couch)*. [22] In *Morning Tea*, Ritman has moved his lovely model from the table to the nearby wicker chair. Still lost in reverie, Mimi stares out of the window as she holds a cup of tea on her lap. The influence of Miller is apparent in the subject, the setting, and the general ambience, but the accurate draftsmanship and brushy style is Ritman's. The model's partially nude torso, as in *Early Morning Sunshine*, is bathed in brilliant morning sunshine; a teapot, cup, and saucer are positioned at the left corner of the composition. In viewing the original canvas, one derives considerable insight into Ritman's skillful technique: certain unfinished sections reveal the evolutionary stages of production. The area of the raised arm seems lost in form-diffusing sunlight, but upon closer inspection we discover that the brushwork was halted abruptly. Had Ritman simply chosen not to continue the image? Why was his work unfinished? Nonetheless, its strong relationship to other morning pictures is quite obvious, and it presents a fine example of his spontaneity.

A painting that is quite similar to *Morning Tea,* and one which the artist finished in every way, including affixing his signature at the lower right, is his masterful composition *Repose in the Garden* (pl. 15-7). In this work, Ritman excels in presenting the quintessential example of Givernyesque American intimism. Without a doubt, this is the kind of image that would soon prompt critics to rank the young man with his older Giverny mentors. Posed as she was for *Morning Tea*, Ritman's subject

Ill. 15-3. Louis Ritman. *Morning Tea*. Oil on canvas, 32 x 32 inches. Private Collection. Courtesy R. H. Love Galleries, Chicago.

relaxes nude, her voluptuous body partially draped. Although the setting is out-of-doors, the scene is very private; indeed, the model seems protected from intruding eyes by a leafy cocoon. Since the subject fills up most of the picture space, there is little room for surrounding space or related objects, one exception being the still life at the lower center of the composition. We get only a glimpse of the table top and its arrangement of luscious summer fruit and the ubiquitous Japanese fan. Here, Ritman has demonstrated with great skill his ability to render textures, nearly all of them soft and organic but delightfully varied in surface properties. All textures are mitigated by the lovely soft flesh of Mimi's feminine form as each gentle curve is reflected by other undulating arabesques with which the artist subtly sensualizes his image. No longer lost in reverie, this beauty lies sleeping in the warm gentle breeze, which, like the soft beams of sunlight, filters through the protective trees and bushes that surround her. Could *Repose in the Garden* be a contemporary depiction of Sleeping Beauty portrayed with the delicate hues of impressionism? A more plausible deduction is that Ritman, Parker, Frieseke, and others simply found this kind of subject interesting and successful in exhibitions, especially in France.

Ritman's brushwork is as refined as his subject; even Frieseke's skill in manipulating pigment would soon fall short of Ritman's. Like both Parker and Miller, Ritman is careful to render the flesh of his nude in a different manner from all the other elements; he has employed the impressionist broken-color technique for the rest of his picture surface. In summary, the canvas known as **Repose in the Garden** is not only a consummate example of Ritman's art, but it is also one of the finest examples of American intimism to emanate from Giverny.

Ritman was totally devoted to the Giverny art experience. He was also committed to its pleasant lifestyle, which was different from anything he had known in the major metropolitan centers in which he had learned to be an artist. Art was paramount in Giverny, for most of its foreign guests were concerned only with making art, and the majority of its citizens had learned to coexist with these artists. To put it simply, in Giverny the members of Ritman's rather conservative group were as removed from the dynamics of the metropolitan art centers as they wanted to be. They knew that their rural exile insulated them from the fast moving and radical shifts in art trends, at least for a while. In 1913, Ritman, like his Giverny friends, could ignore all such events as the Armory Show and their side issues while he continued to develop his intimism.

Ritman's friend Parker tried to do the same, but it was more difficult for him to remain disinterested this summer, since his picture had won the gold medal at the Salon. At this time he was attempting to make arrangements to have the painting sent to Chicago for the annual fall show of American artists. At about the same time, Sara Hallowell was also arranging to crate and ship to Chicago other pictures that she had selected from the salons. In the course of the Armory Show, the Chicago art community had seen intimism by Pauline Palmer and Frieseke, but after the event Chicagoans remained eager to see some more non-avant-garde art, especially the expatriate works from the salons, and more than any other, Parker's gold medal winner, **La Paresse**, or **Idleness**, as it was known. From the salons, Hallowell had also chosen works by Frieseke, Bohm, McEwen, and Miller.

As never before, art was becoming important to Americans, especially in New York and Chicago. Paintings were still not the investment commodity they were in Paris, as Renoir had complained, but they were becoming important products, especially in the post–Armory Show days. Whether they were shown at the National Academy of Design or the Art Institute of Chicago, exemplary works of the Giverny group were in demand by an increasingly sophisticated art audience, which had demonstrated its preference for scenes of rural Normandy over scenes of rural Illinois or Indiana — and over blue nudes by Matisse, for that matter. Ritman and his mentors were quite aware of the preferences of American collectors and made every

effort to comply with their tastes, but none of them ever hoped to attract the attention of Henry C. Frick, who announced in May that he had paid $235,000 for Holbein's portrait of Oliver Cromwell.[23]

As never before, France was closely bound to the English-speaking world, especially to the United States via its large expatriate group. Various factions of the French populace did not appreciate the presence of so many English-speaking foreigners in Paris, and certain individuals demonstrated downright hostility and prejudice. On the other hand, many Americans and Britons had to a greater or lesser degree become Francophiles and actually sided with the French in a mutual display of a "sociocultural superiority complex which made residents feel that they were the trend setters and that the tourists were benighted provincials trying to get in on their cosmopolitan act."[24] All too many talented Anglo-American expatriates tended to decrease the number of places available in the cultural spotlight; yet, when one finally succeeded, like Whistler or John Singer Sargent, France was quite willing to adopt them as their own, pointing out that their art was the result of European training and thus ruling out any American factors in their success stories. Indeed, earlier that spring all of France mourned with Isadora Duncan after she lost her young daughter and son when her limousine plunged off a bridge into the Seine. Claude Debussy was so moved by the tragedy that he went to her studio and stood in silence and then played his "Danse Macabre" at her piano. In spite of the prejudice that seemed so blatant to some expatriates, good will prevailed. In June 1913 the mood of sincere cooperation was underlined when French President Poincaré received a warm welcome in London. At a lavish state dinner, King George predicted a "glorious future" for France.

Ritman may have missed some of the summer events in Paris, but he was quite content to stay in Giverny. Here, he produced a large square canvas (36 x 36 inches) known as **The Boudoir** (pl. 15-8). Comparing this composition with **Early Morning**, we see at first glance that he has changed very little: the bed is positioned parallel with the backdroplike wall, and the same wicker chair, draped with a dress and hat, is placed at an oblique angle to the picture plane. Now the subject is completely nude, and we are reminded of the figure he depicted in the salon work **La Toilette** ; in this instance, however, the young woman raises her arms above her head to fix her hair, a pose the artist would use several times in years to come. The room has no window — there is no chance here of bringing the outside inside, but we must remember that his model is completely nude; thus, the room should be completely private.

Much of the same textural contrasts and color patterns are evident here as in *Early Morning,* but in both pictures we are especially aware of Ritman's outstanding ability to harmonize these paramount pictorial ingredients. In *The Boudoir,* he also employs the same skillful brushwork, manipulating his bright pigment effortlessly to create a complex, even busy ensemble of otherwise flat, two-dimensional surfaces. Here pigment is applied in both fat and thin strokes, all of which range from squarish to wedgelike and from elongated diagonals to sweeping arabesques, but the artist stops short of the typical broken-color style he saw in the work of his neighbor Claude Monet. Once again, Ritman's outstanding ability to draw with a brush is seen in the development of the figure. Also quite evident is the form-softening penumbralike outline (ranging from violet to variations of green), used to isolate the figure from its colorful kaleidoscopic environment; this is a direct influence from Parker and to some extent of Miller.[25] In spite of its similarity to *Early Morning,* Ritman's *The Boudoir* evokes a noticeably different mood in the viewer; in both paintings, the artist has captured his subject unawares, but in *Boudoir* the subject is not seated and she is not daydreaming; instead, she is standing, actually busy as she dresses to start the day's activities. All in all, *Boudoir* is a superb example of Ritman's restrained assimilation of impressionism and his application of the technique to a common theme.

Like his mentors, Ritman executed some of his canvases al fresco, at times wandering in the nearby environs of Giverny to set up his easel. When depicting nude subjects, however, he usually worked within the confines of his walled backyard. One canvas that emanates from this setting is the well-known oil entitled *Sun Kissed Nude* (pl. 15-9). Here we find a full nude seated on a decorative coverlet under a shade tree. Again we see the influence of Parker in both the composition and style. The ground plane, which has been rendered in a rhythmic system of evenly spaced vertical strokes, tilts upward out of the picture area. This very impressionistic tapestrylike plane, which serves as a pictorial background for the subjects, has been rendered in broken color—here we find a painterly manner much unlike the style used for the deftly rendered nude. Achieved with an exceedingly skillful manipulation of high-key pigment, the lovely pink and lavender body of the nude is dappled with Renoiresque spots of sunlight that have filtered down from the foliage above, but there is no hint of juxtaposed strokes of contrasting color. Though the artist has presented a candid view of this lovely model, she turns her head discreetly. Ritman's *Sun Kissed Nude* stands as a superb

example of his early single-figure, plein-air works, exemplifying his contribution to the American intimist movement in Giverny. Perhaps more than any other picture in Ritman's oeuvre, this work has inspired the greatest praise and critical attention over the years.

For the most part, the content of Ritman's pictures, their general format, and theme had revolved around the intimist mode (pl. 15-10). Summarily, we see that his work remained consistent during the 1913 painting season. One more masterful example is a painting known as *The Blue Sash* (pl. 15-11), a square canvas (36 x 36 inches) signed typically "L. RITMAN" at the lower right. Although he chose another interior scene and positioned his model in front of an open window, there is no reference here to the boudoir theme; furthermore, there is no implication of morning in this depiction of a lovely young woman. For the first time the subject is cognizant of the viewer's space; in fact, we actually make eye contact with her. Positioned in profile, the model turns her head slightly and assumes a very feminine pose—but is she posed? Is this narcissism? Might she be posing before a mirror and admiring herself? In any case, she now wears the dress we have seen draped across the wicker chair in the bedroom, and she has a blue sash tied around her waist. Superbly executed, a vase of flowers on the table is intensified in colorful translucency as brilliant sunshine pervades the room.

Ritman has excelled in his observation and expression of light. Extending the parameters of his usual artistic license, he intensifies its luminous qualities by presenting fascinating pictorial examples of reflection, refraction, and absorption. Color is taken from a very high-keyed palette, but in certain areas it seems to manifest a unique glow, an alluring Milleresque pearlescent quality in the model's flesh tones. The feminine subject is the most frontal form in the shallow depth of field, which is once again limited by a wall, albeit one opened by the window area. An interesting contrast of canon shapes is provided by the juxtaposition of the rectangular window and the circular table surface, both of which function well in this way to emphasize the model's organic form. In *The Blue Sash* Ritman presented an attractive woman, someone whose beguiling smile suggests a knowledge of something more than we can ever know; indeed, like Leonardo da Vinci, Ritman has painted more than a mere portrait; it is obvious that he knew his model quite well, and that he made a special likeness of a special person; this is Mimi, the model with whom Ritman shared his cottage in Giverny.

Since Ritman maintained close contacts with Frieseke, Greacen, Buehr, Miller, Parker, and various other artist guests who stayed at the Hotel Baudy, he became a devoted member of the permanent Giverny group. In the fall of 1913, Ritman intended to return to Paris as was the practice of the other painters in Giverny. This was the time to reestablish oneself on the Paris art scene and to prepare canvases for the following spring season.

Notes

1. Maurice Ritman, interview with Richard Love, September 1987, R. H. Love Galleries Archives, Chicago.

2. The official salon catalog for 1913 lists his entries as number 1542, *Nue*, and number 1543, **Le Matin**.

3. Hallowell's letter to French in which she discussed the revision of salon awards as it pertained to Parker is long and complex. Reference is made to French's quoting of Hallowell's letter. See W. M. R. French to Miss Mabel Packard, Chicago, 6 February 1914, Director WMRF, Letter Book, December 22, 1913-April 18, 1914, General Correspondence, Art Institute of Chicago Archives, Chicago, pp. 416-18.

4. Ibid., p. 418.

5. Claude Roger-Marx, "Le Vernissage du Salon de la Société des Artistes français," *La Chronique des Arts et de la Curiosité*, May 1913, p. 140.

6. Claire Joyes, *Monet at Giverny* (New York: The Two Continents Publishing Group, Ltd., Mathews Miller Dunbar, 1976), p. 26.

7. William Rothenstein, *Men and Memories: A History of the Arts 1872-1922* (New York: Tudor Publishing Co., 1931), vol. 1, p. 49.

8. Joyes, *Monet at Giverny*, p. 26.

9. Breed Zug, "The Art of Lawton Parker," *International Studio*, LVII, no. 226 (December 1915), p. XLIII.

10. Maurice Ritman, interview with Richard Love, September 1987.

11. The *Société Artistique de Picardie* was a local organization made up primarily of American expatriates who lived in the Etaples area. An annual show was mounted in the late summer season.

12. Max Bohm was born in Cleveland, Ohio, on 21 January 1868 and died on 19 September 1923 in Provincetown, Massachusetts. After four years of training at the Cleveland Art School, he went to Paris in 1887, where he studied under Benjamin Constant, Jules Lefebvre, and Jean-Paul Laurens at the Julian Academy. He was usually quite successful at the Paris Salon. He married Zella Newcomb of Minneapolis and became an influential member of the art colony at Trépied. He served as president of the Société Artistique de Picardie.

13. For an interesting biography of this important black American expatriate, see Marcia M. Mathews, *Henry Ossawa Tanner, American Artist* (Chicago: The University of Chicago Press, 1969).

14. Clara T. MacChesney, "A Poet-Painter of Palestine," *International Studio*, L, no. 197 (July 1913), p. XI.

15. For a comprehensive study of the nude in American art, see William H. Gerdts, *The Great American Nude* (New York: Praeger Publishers, 1974).

16. Joyes, *Monet at Giverny*, p. 39.

17. Pierre Toulgouat, "Skylights in Normandy," trans. Robert M. Coates, *Holiday*, August 1948, p. 69.

18. George Breed Zug, "The Art of Lawton Parker," *International Studio*, LVII, no. 226 (December 1915), p. XLII.

19. Ibid.

20. Beginning as early as 1869 (**Sulking**, Metropolitan Museum of Art, New York), Degas produced pictures in which the subject is seated in a very shallow space, usually against a backdroplike wall and behind a table which separates him or her from the viewer. We are also reminded of **Woman with a Bandage** (1872/73, Detroit Institute of Arts), **Mme Jeantaud Before a Mirror** (c. 1875, Musée d'Orsay), **Uncle and Niece** (c. 1876, The Art Institute of Chicago), and others.

21. The subject of Degas's painting is Ellen Andrée and his artist friend Marcellin Desboutin. The place and circumstance depicted in this work is also quite different from those surrounding Ritman's genre. Yet, we see a young woman seated in front of a wall (note the rectangular shapes behind), with tables projecting into the viewer's space; seated in a darkened café, the subject stares into space as if she were drunk, while Ritman's subject sips breakfast tea or coffee in bright

daylight. Degas's picture was entered into the Louvre in 1911 after the 1908 bequest by Comte Isaac de Camondo. See Jean Sutherland Boggs, et al, *Degas* (New York: The Metropolitan Museum of Art, 1988), pp. 287-88.

22. An earlier catalog contributed to by this author lists his double-sided canvas as entries no. 6 and 6a, and titled **Before the Masquerade (The Yellow Couch)** and **Morning Tea** . In that catalog the erroneous date of 1916-17 was suggested. See Richard Love, *The Paintings of Louis Ritman* (Chicago: Signature Galleries, 1975), p. 35.

23. *The Frick Collection, An Illustrated Catalogue*, vol. I, *Paintings* (New York: The Frick Collection, 1968), pp. 234-39.

24. Tony Allan, *The Glamour Years: Paris 1919-40* (New York: Gallery Books, 1977), p. 10.

25. The comparison is most evident in works from the period. The best source is Parker's solo show of the preceding year at the Art Institute of Chicago.

CHAPTER SIXTEEN:
SUNSPOTS AND SIMPLICITY

After an amazingly productive summer in Giverny, Ritman returned to Paris for the winter of 1913-14. The city was as dynamic as it was when he had left it, and most of his friends had returned from their various sojourns in Europe. As usual, his lifestyle changed drastically once he was back in Paris. In cafés and other meeting places, he heard the rumors of impending war. He also listened to news about art exhibitions in New York and Chicago and the recurrent gossip about the Armory Show. Outside of art discussions, there was a good deal of talk about the new United States income tax law; arguments about the "New York" world series between the Athletics and the Giants; and wonderment over the joining of the Atlantic and Pacific Oceans when President Wilson officially opened the Panama Canal. The Paris edition of the *New York Herald* carried articles about the Triple Alliance between Germany, Austria-Hungary, and Italy, and in November it ran headlines on Pancho Villa's capture of Juarez and his intent to take all of northern Mexico. Letters from Chicago reported that in December Charles Moyer, president of the Miners Union, had been shot and dragged through the streets. More important to Ritman and his friends, however, was the announcement that after a two-year theft episode, Leonardo's *Mona Lisa* had been returned to the Louvre.

Working diligently in his Paris studio, Ritman spent much of his time putting the finishing touches on pictures that he was going to send out for exhibition. At least one of these was crated by Foinet's and shipped to Chicago for a spring show. In the meantime, the annual exhibition of American paintings was shown at the Art Institute of Chicago in October. Sarah Hallowell had selected most of the expatriate works from the spring salons in Paris. Parker, who had been in New York in September, failed to get *La Paresse* to the Art Institute in time for the awards competition. Consequently, the best of show prizes went to Edward Redfield—although Director French had hoped it would go to Gari Melchers.[1] An unusually small canvas by Frieseke, which Hallowell had selected, was shown, as was a work by Miller. When Parker's painting finally arrived, it was centered on a wall in Gallery number 50, facing a picture by Gari Melchers. In a letter to Hallowell, French complained that it had cost the institute ninety dollars to get Parker's masterpiece to Chicago, but that "it excites a good deal of admiration especially among the artists."[2]

About the same time, Parker's friend Alson Skinner Clark returned to Chicago from an exhaustive painting trip to the Panama Canal (ill. 16-1). The canvases he had produced there were mounted in a solo show at O'Brien Galleries in November (ill. 16-2). The exhibition attracted much attention including that of John E. D. Trask, direc-

Ill. 16-1. Alson Skinner Clark and Medora Clark in Culebra Cut, Panama Canal, 1913. Photograph. Courtesy Petersen Galleries, Beverly Hills.

tor of the Department of Fine Arts for the forthcoming Panama-Pacific Exposition in San Francisco, who requested a special showing of certain works for the event.

In Paris, Ritman painted every day and frequented various spots where other artists congregated. He spent time at friends' studios, the Café du Dôme, and the club quarters of the American Art Association. Hardly a day went by that he did not visit a museum or a gallery; he and a few friends took time to visit the *Mona Lisa* after it had been returned to the Louvre. At one of their informal gatherings, probably some time in late 1913 or early 1914, Ritman and several fellow members of the American Association of Painters and Sculptors decided to collectively paint a portrait of their constituent Walter Griffin.[3] The caper was intended only as amusement, but an account of it appeared in a Chicago newspaper. An anonymous reporter wrote that the portrait had been "done at a smoker in thirty-five minutes by seven of his colleagues in Paris' Latin Quarter," observing that "the colony of American artists [in Paris] does its share in contributing to the gaiety of the Latin Quarter." Continuing the report on Ritman's circle, the writer informed his readers that "nowhere do Americans exhibit more readily the national trait of adaptability than in this picturesque region of the French capital, where they have their own cafés, their own little neighborhoods, their own social organizations. Prominent among them is the American Art Association in the rue Joseph Bara within whose comfortable clubrooms most of the artists and a good many of the writers of the American colony meet. Over its door sits enthroned a spirit of kindly good humor and none who enter may escape this contagious influence." In describing the procedure taken in painting the Griffin portrait, he explained that all seven of the con-

tributors "used the same palette and brushes and each in turn [painted] five minutes. The first daub was swished upon the canvas at 9:15 by Louis Ritman, who formerly was a pupil at the Chicago Art Institute. The last daub was added scarcely half an hour later by H. O. Tanner, a painter of religious pictures."[4]

Although he wrote few letters home, Ritman regularly received correspondence from others.[5] In addition to his family, there were those at the Art Institute and at the Chicago Academy of Fine Arts, who kept him abreast of the local events, sometimes art-related, sometimes not. Having been absent from Chicago for several years, he scarcely knew the inside of the Chicago art circle. Learning only through gossip of his friends' activities, he certainly was unfamiliar with the many changes that had occurred at the Chicago Academy and the Art Institute.

Carl Werntz still ran the Chicago Academy with undaunted optimism, but many of the teachers whom Ritman had known were no longer on the staff. The 1913-14 faculty included George Brehm, the illustrator, Frederick V. Poole, the English portraitist and figure painter, A. Laurence Erickson, a painter and illustrator, and many

Ill. 16-2. Alson Skinner Clark. *Work Trains, Miraflores.* 1913. Oil on canvas, 25½ x 31½ inches. Private Collection. Courtesy R. H. Love Galleries, Chicago.

others, but it did not include Wellington J. Reynolds who was making preparations to teach at the Art Institute of Chicago. To some contemporary observers it seemed that Werntz's academy tended more each year toward the commercial side of art and away from fine art. If so, Reynolds could not have remained at the academy, for few who knew him well could have forgotten that he looked upon his profession as a noble, uncompromising profession.

He once explained that "the majority of people prefer decorative paintings . . . portraits with pictorial effects . . . .. as my mission lies in the ways of imaginative treatment . . . I see beauty in suggestive art and in tones rather than in abundant color."[6] It is true that Reynolds was closer in spirit to Sargent and Chase than to Monet and Renoir, but it is also true that Reynolds's influence on Ritman was indelible. Even after Ritman had spent several years in Paris and Giverny, the imprint of Reynolds's teaching still remained greater than the impact of Monet's influence.

In the early spring of 1914, Ritman submitted no work to the Old Salon of the Société des Artistes Français. No longer did the young Chicagoan look to Déchenaud and the official French Salon as his only measure of success. After three years of faithful service to the academic system, Ritman had been received but not rewarded, so he joined the ranks of the American independents. This was a different road from the one he had intended to travel, but it headed in the direction of success. Possessing no experience in promoting his own work, he received ample advice from friends, especially the Giverny group. These artists knew much more than he did about working in Paris during the winter season. Young independents were advised to follow a certain routine.

This year, however, the threat of war hung over the city, and one's future in the Paris art community became a secondary topic of conversation. Actually, the outward face of Paris seemed no different from what it had been for the last couple of years, but a mood of anxiety, a certain sense of impending doom, was in the air. In anticipation of war, Great Britain had increased its military budget in March, and soon afterwards French Defense Minister Joseph Noulens also requested a large increase for the military. Letters home repeated the rumors of war, and some of the artists with whom Ritman spent time in the Café du Dôme were already making plans to return to New York. Ritman was not ready to sail back since he had not yet completed enough work for a one-man show in Chicago — or anywhere else for that matter. Parker had been back to the United States several times, as had Karl Buehr and others; but Ritman, usually low on funds, was determined to stay in France until he had at least forty canvases to ship home.[7] Accordingly, he made arrangements to hire a model, so that he could begin some new canvases, and during the rest of the time, he planned to finish various works he had brought back from Giverny. His studio was crammed with canvases, some with no more than images sketched in; occasionally, he would restretch a canvas and paint on the other side if the first image seemed unsuccessful. He worked from early morning until lunch and concluded his painting activities about four o'clock in the afternoon before spring lengthened the daylight hours.

From letters and from friends, Ritman learned that the annual exhibition of American paintings at the Art Institute of Chicago had seemed to calm the fears raised by the city's controversial encounter with the Armory Show. He also learned that very little had changed at the institute: Director French guided it each day as a steady dependable ship through the rough seas of contemporary art. A few months earlier, French had written Sara Hallowell, who was living in Moret-sur-Loing, that in his opinion the selection she had sent from the salons was "the best . . . we have had from Paris in late years."[8] In April he wrote her another letter, with the information that Arthur Aldis and Abram Poole were traveling together in Europe. "Their chief errand as regards the Art Institute," he explained, "is to arrange for an exhibition of pictures from Germany, but our Art Committee suggested to them that if they found pictures in the Salon or elsewhere...for our Autumn exhibition, they might communicate with you."[9] Chicago had a large and influential German community, and the leading members of the Art Institute apparently made an effort to follow President Wilson's policy of neutrality. In matters of art, however, they leaned increasingly toward France. Of course, Chicago's preference for French art over all other, including American, was not a recent tendency. At this time, however, sponsoring institutions in the United States could face problems in its choice of exhibitions to be imported from Europe to Chicago or any American city. Conversely, in showing the work of someone as famous as Mary Cassatt demonstrated no bias, especially since she was considered by most as much French as American. In his letter to Hallowell, Director French quoted Aldis as writing that he [Aldis] and Poole had already arranged "for a small but very good collection" of Mary Cassatt's pictures. "We hope," Aldis confided to French, "to do this through Mrs. Havemeyer."[10]

French made every effort to stimulate art activity in Chicago, but his approaches were conservative. Usually much more progressive creativity was visible in other branches of the Chicago cultural community than in the art circle. For example, there was always a lot of avant-garde activity on the literary scene. Floyd Dell and George Cram Cook had recently fled to Greenwich Village to work on the *Masses* magazine, but Edgar Lee Masters and Carl Sandburg were still in Chicago, and so were Maxwell Bodenheim and Ben Hecht who worked diligently to promote their "art for art's sake" credo.[11] Determined to contribute something significant to American literature, both Hecht and Bodenheim were at the center of Chicago's bohemia, lending rumors of scandal to their creative dossiers. Both men were about five years younger than Ritman and about that far behind him in their respective careers. Soon Bodenheim and the most avant-garde artist of Chicago, Stanislaus Szukalski, would found the Vagabonds Club, located in Szukalski's studio on the top floor of the Kimball Building. There was also the Questioners, where art debates were the chief topic of conversation. Locally, nearly everyone had heard of the sculptor Lou Wall Moore, whose fame rested not on her sculpture, but on her dancing, since she reinterpreted Isadora Duncan. Lou was referred to as "the soul of Chicago," "the Princess of Bohemia," and Bodenheim called her "Princess Lou." It is doubtful that Ritman ever met her; he only heard rumors.[12] All in all, Chicago knew a good deal more about Paris than Paris knew about Chicago. That, however, was the way it was supposed to be in the spring of 1914, when most people were still convinced that the only important art came from the City of Lights across the Atlantic where all the expatriates lived.

When Ritman returned to Giverny in the spring of 1914, rumors of war dominated the conversations at Hotel Baudy: Albania had already called for general mobilization and threatened war with Greece. Ritman also learned of the recent death of Jean Monet, the master's son, at the age of forty-seven. It was said that for quite some time Jean had suffered from an unknown disorder of the central nervous system, but no one at the Baudys' really knew any details and fewer still understood the traumatic effect his death produced on Monet and his son's wife, Blanche. The threat of international war and the local tragedy cast a pall over the small group in Giverny.

More bad news reached Giverny from Chicago in the spring of 1914: Ritman and his friends were surprised to learn that in the last week of May, Art Institute Director W. M. R. French had become alarmingly ill and was taken to Saint Luke's Presbyterian Hospital.[13] An immediate operation revealed cancer and French declined rapidly. With his family at his side, French died on Wednesday, 3 June 1914. The body lay in state in Fullerton Hall at the Art Institute and two services were held for French, one especially for students and employees of the institute.[14] Many impressive eulogies were presented, and newspapers published long accounts of his career accomplishments. Newton H. Carpenter, once again made acting director of the institute, stated that "it was due chiefly to [French's] efforts . . . that the Art Institute was more than a cold storage place for pictures."[15] French had only contributed indirectly to the New York art world, but his years of service in Chicago were highly regarded by leaders on the East Coast. The writer of a note of appreci-

ation published in the *New York Times* called him "a great art leader" and reminded his readers that "when William M. R. French entered Chicago's School and Museum of Art less than forty years ago the fine arts were regarded by the rough-barked Chicagoans as effeminate and exotic: not nearly so valuable, for instance, as the beef industry that was making their city famous." Making the inevitable comparison, the *Times* writer reported that "last year, Director French saw his museum attended by more people than crowded the Metropolitan Museum in this city . . . Mr. French not only used exquisite judgement in the acquisition of art objects for Chicago, but he preached his aesthetic ideals throughout the country. The art school connected with the Chicago Art Institute became one of the largest in the world and its pupils became in turn missionaries of the gospel of taste and appreciation."[16]

In spite of the atmosphere of gloom in Giverny, the expatriate group were fascinated by the news that Rodman Wanamaker, the president of the American Art Association, had conducted a successful test flight of the flying boat *America*. Also, the constituents of Ritman's milieu were sufficiently optimistic about art to generate a number of outstanding paintings. Like his enthusiastic friends, Ritman hoped for a full, productive summer in the sleepy Norman village. To this end he and his model took up residence in his studio-cottage and started the spring-summer season.

At the urging of Frieseke or Parker or both—or because of nothing more, perhaps, than the general influence of others—Ritman began producing more scenes al fresco. These were still genre works in which he focused on a single figure, specifically an attractive young woman, but distinct variations appeared within the overall compositional design. In addition, there were obvious degrees of success and failure in Ritman's resolve to integrate his subject into a typical Givernyesque garden scene. Although the general direction of his intimism was altered slightly, the main features of his pictorial formula remained intact. In some of these plein-air works, the figure takes up even more of the picture format; but in other examples from the same period, the model is relegated to a lesser role and woven almost imperceptibly into a tapestry-like background. There is no question but that his style became increasingly influenced by Monet via Frieseke, with the latter urging Ritman to concentrate on a more typical broken-color technique. Frieseke and others of the American intimist circle admitted that they had been influenced indirectly in their palettes and techniques by Monet, but that they also owed a certain debt to Renoir in terms of their subject matter.[17]

One painting from this time that reveals the gradual

evolution of Ritman's style is a brightly colored, broadly brushed work known as *Girl with a Fan* (pl. 16-1). In still another square format, the image consists of a single seated figure near a table, but in this case the setting is out of doors. In the Giverny tradition, Ritman has painted it en plein air, posing his model in a colorful garden—as Frieseke demonstrated—working up his composition from a bare canvas. In *Girl with a Fan*, a foliate backdrop limits the distance behind the sitter and emphasizes the decorative, two-dimensional quality of the picture. Seated in profile, the model takes up nearly all of the frontal picture plane. The upper-right spandrel consists of the table top and a vase of large flowers. Obvious is the fact that Ritman's painting is filled from top to bottom with a fascinating variety of brushwork, which ranges from shinglelike strokes to elongated ones that serve to outline form. Adding to the overall pattern quality of the painting are the bright spots of sunlight that have filtered through the trees above to dapple the figure and her immediate area, as they did in Renoir's *The Swing* (Musée d'Orsay, Paris, Galerie du Jeu de Paume), executed nearly forty years earlier. Ritman's brushwork is a good deal less sketchy than Renoir's was, and the plasticity of his model's figure is more pronounced; but the older master's cool-toned palette of the mid-1870s and even his subjects and settings are at least an indirect influence in these early Ritman paintings from Giverny. Although he focused on a single figure posed en plein air in only a few works, Renoir frequently exploited the sunspot device in ambitious multifigured compositions like *Ball at the Moulin de la Galette* (1876, Musée d'Orsay, Paris), a painting which Ritman, Frieseke, and others knew well because it was one of the Gustave Caillebotte bequest of 1894. By the time Ritman had experimented with sunspots—whether on his own or under Frieseke's influence—the device was already well known to the French art community. In 1877, however, the art critic G. Vasay, who wrote for *L'Evénement*, was shocked when he first saw Renoir's sunspots in *Ball at the Moulin de la Galette* and complained that "the sunlight effects are combined in such a bizarre fashion that they look like spots of grease on the model's clothes."[18] At about the same time, the great anti-impressionist critic Louis Leroy wrote in the pages of *Le Charivari* that he was offended by Renoir's "violent" blue. Over the years, however, the way was paved for Ritman's sunlight experiments by the appreciation of critics such as Ch. Flor o'Squarr (a pseudonym), who, in retrospect, could have been describing a work by Ritman as well as one by Renoir: "The harsh daylight is filtered through the greenery, sets the blonde hair and pink cheeks of the girls aglow, and makes their

ribbons sparkle. The Joyful light fills every corner of the canvas and even the shadows reflect it."[19]

In *Girl with a Fan*, the sitter is unaware of our presence as she glances wistfully to the left and cools herself with the paper fan she holds in her right hand. In every way, this is summer in Giverny and Ritman has made every effort to capture its qualities. We are reminded indeed of paintings by Frieseke, Parker, Miller, Buehr, Anderson and others, but few were executed with such skill in draftsmanship and composition. Parker also made good use of Renoir's sunspot device.

Perhaps it was a rainy day when Ritman painted a smaller easel picture entitled *The Letter* (pl. 16-2), because it is an interior scene and the light is relatively dull when compared with that in other works. Here we find a single figure standing at a table. Not far behind the subject, a wall threatens to severely limit the depth of field, but as in the works of Degas, Ritman provides an open door that leads to another room, much in the way that in earlier works he provided an open window with a view to a nearby garden.[20] In every way, the work is an outstanding example of compositional balance and harmony. Just as in other works he focused on the decorative, in this work Ritman has reached the opposite pole of simplicity.

There is also a story in *The Letter*. Absorbed by the import of the correspondence she has received, the subject stands erect and motionless. The rigid pipe folds of her dress—the same dress that she has worn in many earlier works—resemble those found in a Greek caryatid. In this work the forms are not as soft as they were in earlier ones. The light is not as intense. The subtle variations of color tone are exemplary, however, and the brushwork is skillful. It is apparent that Ritman has utilized a rather repetitious system of narrow vertical and horizontal strokes in rendering this rather solemn scene. All in all, *The Letter* is an example of Ritman's justemilieu imagery.

The long hot days of the summer of 1914 brought no relief as Ritman worked furiously to complete enough pictures to send to Chicago. He composed the works he painted in his studio-cottage simply, instructing his model to stand or sit here or there and arranging peripheral interior elements accordingly. This summer, however, it seems that he felt more comfortable than ever working en plein air; he and his model went to various picturesque areas to set up his easel— for nude subjects, he posed her within the privacy of his walled-in backyard. The area surrounding Ritman's cottage was not large, but it was shady and very handy. The wall that so frequently served as a convenient backdrop was covered with rich green vine

Pl. 15-3. Louis Ritman. *Early Morning*. Oil on canvas, 36 x 35 inches. Terra Museum of American Art. Daniel J. Terra Collection.

Pl. 15-4. Louis Ritman. *Pink and Blue*. 1913. Oil on canvas, 32 x 40 inches. Private Collection. Courtesy R. H. Love Galleries, Chicago.

Pl. 15-5. Louis Ritman. *A Pensive Moment*. Oil on canvas, 36½ x 36¼ inches. Courtesy Spanierman Gallery, New York.

Pl. 15-6. Louis Ritman. *Early Morning Sunshine* or *At the Window, Giverny*. Oil on canvas, 36 x 29¼ inches. Courtesy Spanierman Gallery, New York.

Pl. 15-7. Louis Ritman. *Repose in the Garden*. Oil on canvas, 36 x 36 inches. Private Collection. Courtesy R. H. Love Galleries, Chicago.

Pl. 15-8. Louis Ritman. *The Boudoir*. Ca. 1913. Oil on canvas, 36 x 36 inches. Private Collection. Courtesy R. H. Love Galleries, Chicago.

Pl. 15-9. Louis Ritman. *Sun Kissed Nude*. Oil on canvas, 31 x 31 inches. Oshkosh Public Museum, Oshkosh, Wisconsin.

Pl. 15-10. Louis Ritman. *By the Brook*. Oil on canvas, 36⅜ x 28⅝ inches. Private Collection. Courtesy R. H. Love Galleries, Chicago.

foliage. One work probably emanating from this back-yard area is a large oil (32 x 40 inches) entitled *Quietude* (pl. 16-3). Here the viewer looks down on a reclining nude from the waist up. The intended iconography is simple: this genteel genre scene suggests that the day is very hot, and that the attractive young woman has found a secluded spot under a shade tree and removed her blouse to get some relief from the hot summer air and the blazing sun. A parasol lies nearby, and the subject languidly moves the still air with the same delicate fan that was used in an earlier work. A simplistically arranged still life, rendered in large bold patches of blues, greens, and violets, is almost lost in the overwhelming patterns surrounding it. If his arrangement of these simplistic canon forms (variations of the sphere) is a bit ordinary, Ritman's colorful treatment is dynamic. Separated from its subject format, this utilitarian ensemble could function abstractly. Much the same may be said about the expressive brushwork that fills the upper left spandrel of the picture; taken alone, this rich pigment surface even prophesies certain aspects of abstract expressionism (pl. 16-4). The figure lies flat on the ground, an amazing tapestrylike surface rises swiftly out of the top of the picture area. The overall palette is quite cool, and the brushwork is outstanding: the kaleidoscopic juxtaposition of bright blue, red, and green pigments has been achieved with consummate skill. Moreover, as in *Girl with a Fan*, Ritman has exploited the Renoiresque sunspot treatment, as had Parker and Frieseke in similar works.

Before Ritman finished many more canvases, the threat of war loomed larger on the European horizon. Actually, World War I had already begun at the end of July, when Austria-Hungary (the core of the Hapsburg Empire) declared war on Serbia. One day later Russia mobilized over a million troops. Soon other European countries followed suit in accordance with existing alliances. From the summer of 1914 onward, no fewer than eighteen declarations of war would transform Europe into a checkerboard of military skirmishes. Ritman and his many expatriate friends were very sensitive, of course, to news of the daily expansion of the war, while Americans across the Atlantic were as yet basically unaware of its potential. In the words of Charles Seymour, in the United States "not one in ten thousand felt more than an ordinary thrill of interest on the morning of June 29, 1914, when they read that the Archduke Franz Ferdinand of Austria had been assassinated." He reflects that not even "a month later, when it became obvious that the resulting crisis was to precipitate another war in the Balkans, did most Americans realize that the world was hovering on the brink of momentus events."[21]

Like Ritman, Frieseke was painting in Giverny at the end of July when France declared general mobilization. For Frieseke the situation was far more precarious because his wife, Sarah, was in her final stages of pregnancy in Paris (under doctor's care), and mobilization could prevent him from getting there quickly. Determined to be with his wife, Frieseke bid Ritman and others adieu and made his way to Giverny's little white depot, where he hoped to catch the last train carrying civilians back to Paris. On the basis of his reminiscences, his daughter, Frances, later wrote that "there were a few moments to spare and he looked at the river where the trout were rising [Frieseke loved trout fishing] then entered Madame Honette's kitchen to buy his ticket."[22] Endowed with a voice shrill enough to compete with a train whistle, Madame Honette not only sold tickets and flagged the train at the unscheduled Giverny stop, but she was also the proprietress of a comfortable little nook in the depot which catered to travelers. "A ticket for Paris?" screeched Madame Honette, "Why, don't you know sir? I wondered how you could be so calm, walking in here just as though those dirty Germans were not doing their best to cut our poor boy's throats."[23] Continuing her tirade, Honette told Frieseke, "The men are being mobilized and sent to the German frontier and there is going to be a war; but we will beat those pigs, we will beat them and France will hold up her head once more."[24] If the American painters in Giverny had insulated themselves somewhat from the harsh realities of the impending war, when Frieseke boarded the train and rode to Paris, the chilling effects of change were already obvious: the train was "filled with shouting men" as Frieseke "climbed the steps of an overflowing compartment." He had "no need of a book to shorten the trip. One could not look at the countryside gliding past, heart-rendingly peaceful under the red sunset sky, with the little farm houses modestly and neatly framed by thorne hedges, without seeing old men carrying heavy loads and little boys reaching up on tiptoe to bolt barn doors and women watching the trains, their arms weighted with pails of milk or bundles of fodder, their faces hot under disheveled hair. The men were gone and the work must be done."[25]

In Paris, Frieseke made his way to his apartment just off boulevard Raspail. It was a drab building located in a section of the city that bustled with merchants and craftsmen. The food situation was exacerbated by the closing of stores and banks following street riots against merchants of German descent. On 3 August 1914, the day after Sarah had given birth to a daughter, Germany declared war on France. Frieseke wrote to his New York dealer William Macbeth: "We are provisioned for a six months' siege. I couldn't stand leaving Paris after the years I have lived there."[26]

Soon war engulfed Europe; there were counterattacks by Serbia and Great Britain, and eventually even Japan became involved. In August, the most important conflict was the battle of Tannenberg in East Prussia, which resulted in the sound defeat of a large Russian army whose generals had hoped to relieve pressure on the French. War had become an oppressive reality, and by fall it had made a grave impact on the minds of the French. Still, for those artists who remained in Giverny, including Ritman and some of his friends, the war did not yet affect the daily picture-making activities. In one way it actually increased their productivity since several artists became more anxious than ever to paint a few more Givernyesque scenes to send home. Indeed, they rationalized, if the war subsequently moved west to engulf Giverny, they would be unable to return in the spring. Others simply had no intention of returning to France until the war was over: Europe's conflict was not their concern. For still others, the fight was as much theirs as it would have been had the United States Congress declared war.

Ritman was one of those who needed to paint as many pictures as possible to take back with him to America. With this purpose in mind, he worked diligently from early morning until late afternoon, when the light became less intense and the shadows lengthened. One of his most successful works from that fall is a painting known as *Sunspots: Arranging Flowers* (pl. 16-5). For this composition, Ritman chose one of Foinet's square canvases (36¼ x 36¼ inches) and positioned it on an easel in his backyard. For this brilliant record of a warm fall day in Giverny, Ritman worked en plein air, as he had many times before, but this time his efforts yielded unprecedented results.

It is possible that Ritman was inspired by Degas's uncanny exploitation of the table as a supportive pictorial motif in contemporary genre, but in any instance, Ritman's composition is unique in both its contrast and balance. Taking up the whole lower right of the picture, the table top is pushed forward into the picture plane not only to provide a surface for the display of fresh fruit and flowers but to serve as a severe geometric contrast to the otherwise predominant organic elements of the composition. As if standing, the viewer looks down on a scene in which the subject is quite unaware of anyone else's presence as she touches the delicate flower arrangement. As usual, she is placed against a view-limiting backdrop, this time a curving a row of shrubbery in Ritman's walled-in space. The shrubbery serves as a believable balancing element to the square table at the bottom of the picture. A

sense of seclusion is notable, and the Renoiresque sunspots that dapple the area suggest that the space is surrounded by trees through which the sunlight emerges. Taking his pigment from a very high-keyed palette, Ritman employs a rather limited broken-color technique and one which makes no sacrifice of object properties. Here, no forms are lost in shimmering sunlight, but the artist has concentrated upon the effects of a warm autumn day.

By mid-August 1914, it was apparent even to the most uninformed bystanders that France desperately needed the military assistance of England and other allies if the German invasion was to be checked. The American expatriates in Paris and outlying art colonies such as Giverny felt a great empathy with the French patriots who were rallying to the call "Aux armes, citoyens! La Patrie est en danger!" Across the Atlantic, however, the Americans were not eager to become involved in Europe's spreading internal conflict, so President Wilson and Congress maintained a strict policy of neutrality. On 19 August, Wilson told the American people: "I suppose that every thoughtful man in America has asked himself, during these last troubled weeks, what influence the European war may exert upon the United States...." "Every man," he urged, "who really loves America will act and speak in the true spirit of neutrality, which is the spirit of impartiality and fairness and friendliness to all concerned...The people of the United States are drawn from many nations, and chiefly from the nations now at war.... I venture, therefore, my fellow-countrymen, to speak a solemn word of warning to you against that deepest, most subtle, most essential breach of neutrality which may spring up out of partisanship, out of passionately taking sides."[27]

Having spent nearly five years in France, Ritman could not help taking sides. He and his expatriate friends loved Giverny nearly as much as their own hometowns, and in some ways even more for different reasons. Indeed, when someone like Madame Baudy, who had served as a mother to many young men and women artists away from home, was being threatened by German invaders, that fact instilled a mood of protective patriotism in numerous expatriates.

At this point, however, any stouthearted artist living in Giverny could continue his routine with virtually no interruption. Indeed, Ritman worked at his easel every day. A painting which may emanate from this time is an oil known as *Sun Spots and Shadows* (pl. 16-6).[28] Originally executed as a larger composition, including an infant in the green chair at the right, today the image consists of two women having tea in a garden. As the composition exists, it reveals the influence of Richard Miller, but the draftsmanship and execution are distinctly Ritman's and resemble another work known simply as *Mother and Child* .[29] Exactly why or who painted out the infant in this attractive canvas is unknown, but Ritman's spontaneous handling of light and color was handsomely achieved. The brightly patterned parasol was a motif borrowed from both Miller and Frieseke, but Ritman places it in such a way that it did not decoratively consume the figures as we have seen in the works of his older mentors. The two models were also borrowed from his friends — probably Miller — since neither one was Mimi, or another young woman was posed for Ritman at this time. In summary, we see that although *Sun Spots and Shadows* stands out as a bold and colorful work, it is also a relatively unusual image in Ritman's oeuvre and seems to owe a great deal to the influence of his fellow Givernyite, Richard Miller.

In Paris, Frieseke faced the dilemma of either staying in the city with his wife and infant Frances, where they were comparatively safe, or returning to Giverny, where he could finish many canvases for the new season. Some American friends urged him to take his family back to America "by any means available," but Frieseke was a true Francophile, so he decided to stay in Paris and to go back to Giverny as soon as possible. Indeed, it was a trying time for some of his French friends, who, haunted by the memories of the Franco-Prussian War of 1871, expected a siege of Paris. Madame Lefebvre, the wife of Frieseke's art-supply dealer, provided "siege" provisions: macaroni and tomato puree that would last for at least a year.

To Ritman's family and friends in Chicago, as to most Americans, Giverny was no more than a village somewhere in faraway France; even Paris seemed distant, very distant. The only views of war activity were those seen in grainy black and white photographs reproduced in newspapers, since in theaters *Movietone* newsreels were as yet nonexistent. Instead, "crowds gazed upon the bulletin boards and tried to picture the steady advance of German field-gray through the streets of Liège, asked their neighbors what were these French 75's, and endeavored to locate Mons and Verdun on inadequate maps. Interest could not be more intense, but it was the interest of the moving-picture devotee . . . . It was a tremendous show and we were the spectators."[30]

When the predicted invasion finally became a reality and its full force was felt on French soil, the advance came as no surprise to France or to America, since French General Joseph Joffre's year-old plan for defense at the Marne River and a swift counteroffensive was well known. Fortunately for the artists in Giverny, the battles were expected to take place at a considerable distance to the east and north of them and Paris, so they continued to paint but not without anxiety. Implementing their Schlieffen Plan, the Germans launched an offensive against France through Belgium. Paris newspapers carried headlines reporting first the capture of Liège and then the occupation of Brussels by German troops on 20 August. At the same time, General Joffre ordered his forces over the Vosges Mountains into Alsace, an area that had been controlled by Germany since 1871. Both the French and German military chiefs expected the worst at the Marne line east of Paris.

With such destructive battles raging around them, Ritman and other expatriates lingering in Giverny could no longer remain oblivious to the war. Like Frieseke, several other artists left Giverny that summer and fall to tie up loose ends in Paris and book passage to New York. Needing more canvases for his Chicago debut, Ritman continued to paint in Giverny, where it was still relatively quiet. Also, like Frieseke, he was convinced that no place was equal to Giverny for producing intimism, so he intended to work in the fall beauty of the Norman village as long as possible. He worked harder than ever before to finish canvases, although he also began new ones optimistically. As the days went by, however, he, too, began making arrangements to return to Paris and then to America.

Meanwhile, at the Hotel Baudy, everyone expected to hear cannon blasts soon. Unable to repulse the advance of the German First Army, the French had fallen back to within thirty miles of Paris. Joining Joffre's Allied forces, Field Marshal Sir John French brought his British Expeditionary Force to the Marne line, and by early September the Germans had begun to withdraw. After continued clashes along a front that stretched from Verdun in the east to Noyon in the west (about seventy-five miles northeast of Giverny), the first battle of the Marne was over, but the French had won no major triumph, because they had not shattered the German lines as expected; in fact, their successful counterattacks simply ensured that the war would escalate and last a long time. When the frontline northeast of Paris stabilized somewhat in September of 1914, Frieseke returned to Giverny to paint. His wife and the new baby had remained in Paris where house servants and better medical care were available. Upon his return, Frieseke reported to Ritman that the Montparnasse section of Paris where they had lived was deserted because so much of the male working population was at the front. Amazingly, he said, Paris was a quiet place to raise families for the time being.

In the meantime, many other Americans left Giverny for Paris, where they could settle for the winter or arrange for passage back to New York. Although Frieseke had returned to work, Ritman, like many of his friends, no longer wished to remain in France. The decision to leave

Giverny was easier for him, a bachelor who had no ties, than it was for his friend Frieseke, who had lived there for more than a decade.

In spite of the apparent exodus, a few of Ritman's Midwestern friends remained in Paris. One of these was George Oberteuffer, who lived with his wife in Montparnasse, not far from Frieseke's place and Ritman's first residence. Trouble was apparent to everyone, however, and according to Warshawsky, "there was uneasiness among the foreigners, who suddenly began to feel themselves undesirable intruders in a domestic drama." Warshawsky related that "the uneasiness became positive panic when suddenly foreign money lost its prestige and the dollar dropped by a fifth." To many of his compatriots, including Ritman, "that was sufficient warning that it was time for all good Americans to return to their own country."[31]

Finally, in late September of 1914, Ritman gathered and packed most of his belongings, including the paintings he had executed during the summer, and purchased tickets at Giverny's little white depot for a one-way trip to Paris. Since mobilization, troops had taken first priority, but he made his way to Paris, and once there, he spent time making arrangements to leave for New York. Ritman had Foinet's ship forty canvases, painting materials, and personal belongings to Chicago, his eventual destination. He met many expatriate friends at that time, most of whom were also planning to return home for the duration of the war. It seemed certain that Paris was on the brink of invasion; during the first week of September, the French capital was officially moved from Paris to Bordeaux. It was an unhappy but timely opportunity for Ritman to return to his hometown after a longer-than-anticipated absence of five years.

Frieseke was back in Paris with his family in October 1914, and Ritman probably visited them there before he left for the coast to sail home. The war was always foremost in their discussions, but both artists were also quite concerned about getting their work to San Francisco for the forthcoming Panama-Pacific Exposition. Writing from Paris to his dealer Macbeth in New York City, Frieseke explained that he was sending him a large canvas by the steamship *Chicago*, which was departing on 14 October and would arrive on 23 November. It is possible that Ritman sent his entries (three canvases) to the exposition at the same time and on the same liner, since there was no jurying in Paris as had been planned, and all expatriate works had to be juried in New York before being shipped to San Francisco.[32]

Always anxious to see exhibitions, Ritman visited Galerie Levesque before he left. The paintings of Bryson Burroughs and Ernest Lawson were being featured in a show entitled *Première Exposition d'Art Moderne*

Ill. 16-3. Louis Ritman. *Déjeuner.* Location unknown. Photograph. R. H. Love Galleries Archives, Chicago.

Américain.[33] Interestingly, the catalog text was written by two sympathizers of the avant-garde, Léonce Bénédite and André Degarrois. Of course, this so-called première of American modernism was problematic since it did not feature Stanton MacDonald Wright, Arthur Dove, and other abstractionists, but two relatively conservative painters. Ernest Lawson was really more an impressionist than an Ash Can painter. On the other hand, there was some justification for including Bryson Burroughs, whose paintings were academic, but whose curatorial ideas were quite liberal. It was Burroughs who was still withstanding the rebuff of many colleagues at the Metropolitan Museum of Art for his recent purchase of Cézanne's *La Colline des Pauvres* from the Armory Show for its permanent collection.[34]

Just before he returned to the United States, Ritman also submitted works to the large annual Anglo-American Exposition to be held at Shepherd's Bush in London during the fall of 1914. The fine arts section of the exposition contained separate subsections, notably, the American and the American-British. There were also the American-French section and some lesser subdivisions. Writing from a biased British viewpoint, the critic for the *International Studio* insisted that the art history of the United States had been too short for the development of "any peculiarly national attributes."[35] However, taking note of the heavy influx of American artists into Paris, the critic argued that sometimes in works submitted to the salons, the expatriates outdid the Parisians with their own Parisian approach. Organized by Hugo Reisinger, a noted American collector of impressionist works, the London exposition included five galleries for resident American artists. Visitors saw works by stellar impressionists such as Childe Hassam, William Merritt Chase, Edward W. Redfield, and Emil Carlsen. Also exhibiting were W. Elmer Schofield, Thomas Wilmer Dewing, Cecilia Beaux, and others. The British-American section took up four galleries and included works by Sargent, Joseph Pennell, Mark Fisher, Edwin Austin Abbey, and etchings and lithographs by Whistler.

In reviewing the entries hung in the two galleries devoted to American artists who were residents of France, the writer for the *International Studio* singled out the canvases of certain Giverny painters, namely Ritman,

Ill. 16-4. Louis Ritman. *Freshly Picked Flowers.* Ca. 1914. Oil on canvas, 30¾ x 31⅞ inches. Location unknown. Photograph. Courtesy of Christie's.

Miller, and Frieseke, in the same context. Ritman's painting, entitled *Déjeuner* (ill. 16-3), showed a young woman arranging flowers in a vase that had been carefully placed on a breakfast table. The scene was typical for Ritman, but it was painted outdoors, with a lush impressionistic foliage providing the background. The brushwork was characteristically varied. The critic defined Ritman's *Déjeuner* as "a work in which the problem of figure painting in sunlight is treated with marked success."[36] Although he alluded to the influence of Miller, the reviewer lauded the impressionistic light and color effects in Ritman's work: "The artist has achieved a composition, happy alike in colour and design, in which the whole is as it were tremulous with morning sunlight and the promise of a glorious unclouded day."[37] Indeed, Ritman's figure in the American Givernyesque style is treated quite differently from the manner in which the American expatriate Daniel Ridgeway Knight painted his out-of-doors figures in the plein-air style of Bastien-LePage. In Ritman's work, bright sunlight refracts and reflects on varied surfaces on a cloudless European day, producing a fascinating intermingling of bright local color and highlights, while in a similar work by Knight, the same sunlight from a cloudy grey day cannot intermingle, but reveals plain modulated surfaces, soft and solid, each maintaining its own distinct physical quality.

Ritman was aware of his skill in painting the figure *al fresco*, but when he was particularly successful with a composition, such as *Déjeuner,* he was not above using it again as in *Freshly Picked Flowers.* In this instance, we find the same figure dressed and posed almost identically as she arranges flowers in a vase on a table, but this time the model is seen indoors, probably in Ritman's own cottage (ill. 16-4). We still see the figure silhouetted against a leafy backdrop but, owing to the placement of the figure indoors, sunlight emanating from the familiar open sashes is directional and limited, as though the figure were backlighted. Moreover, Ritman's design is more balanced and harmonious in *Freshly Picked Flowers,* since he introduces a complex arrangement of rectangular shapes, not found in the otherwise allover organic picture. Which picture was executed first is unknown, but, in spite of the similarity of their subject, the composition, color, and effect of light is so different that each stands on its own as a distinct and exceedingly successful image.

Notes

1. W. M. R. French to Sara Hallowell, Chicago, 22 November 1913, Director WMRF, Letter Book, August 11, 1913-December 30, 1913, General Correspondence, Archives of the Art Institute of Chicago, p. 732.

2. Ibid.

3. Walter Griffin was born in 1861 in Portland, Maine, and studied in Paris under Jean Paul Laurens and Raphael Collin. He had developed the impressionist style by about 1907, when he began to paint in Old Lyme, Connecticut, in association with Childe Hassam, William L. Metcalf, William Singer, Jr., and others. Griffin's best works originated in the years that followed. He logged several years of travel and independent study in Europe before he returned to the United States on a more permanent basis in 1915 and died in 1935 in Stroudwater, Maine.

4. *Chicago Daily News*, February 1914.

5. R. H. Love Galleries Archives, Chicago (restricted use).

6. L. C. McCauley, "Wellington J. Reynolds, Painter," *The Sketchbook*, V, no. 7 (May 1906), p. 337.

7. Maurice Ritman, interview with Richard Love, September 1987, R. H. Love Galleries Archives, Chicago.

8. W. M. R. French to Sara Hallowell, Chicago, 22 November 1913, Director WMRF, Letter Book, p. 732.

9. W. M. R. French to Sara Hallowell, Chicago, 14 April 1914, Director WMRF, Letter Book, December 22, 1913-April 18, 1914, p. 985.

10. Ibid.

11. Born in New York in 1894, Ben Hecht attended high school in Racine, Wisconsin, until he came to Chicago to become a newspaper reporter. At this time, Hecht was beginning his job on the staff of the *Chicago Daily News*. Later he would found and publish the *Chicago Literary Times*. Maxwell Bodenheim came to Chicago from Mississippi, where he was born in 1895. Bodenheim did not write *Minna and Myself* until 1918.

12. Albert Parry, *Garrets and Pretenders: A History of Bohemianism in America* (New York: Dover Publications, Inc., 1960), pp. 192-95.

13. "William M. R. French Sinking," *Chicago Daily Tribune*, 2 June 1914, sec. I, p. 1.

14. "Students at French Funeral," *Chicago Daily Tribune*, 5 June 1914.

15. "French Funeral Set for Tomorrow," *Chicago Daily Tribune*, 4 June 1914, Sec. I, p. 2.

16. "A Great Art Leader," *New York Times*, 6 June 1914, p. 8.

17. Maurice Ritman, interview with Richard H. Love, June 1987, R. H. Love Galleries Archives, Chicago.

18. Anne Distel, *Renoir*, exhibition catalog (London: Arts Council of Great Britain, 1985), p. 210.

19. Ibid., p. 211.

20. For more on this topic, see Theodore Reff, *Degas: The Artist's Mind* (New York: Harper & Row, 1976), pp. 90-146.

21. Charles Seymour, *Woodrow Wilson and the World War* (New Haven, CT: Yale University Press, 1921), p. 27.

22. Frederick C. Frieseke (1874-1939), Reminiscences, Writings, Price Lists, Frances Frieseke, "It's Only the Cannon," Roll No. N737, frames 0017-0018, Archives of American Art, Smithsonian Institution, Washington, DC.

23. Ibid.

24. Ibid., Frame 0018.

25. Ibid.

26. Allen S. Weller, "Frederick Carl Frieseke: The Opinions of an American Impressionist," *The Art Journal*, XXVII, no. 2 (Winter.1968-69), p. 161.

27. President Woodrow Wilson, Address to the American People, "American Neutrality," 19 August 1914, *President Wilson's Great Speeches and Other History Making Documents* (Chicago: Stanton and Van Vliet Co., 1917-18), pp. 43-44.

28. This title may not be the one given the picture by Ritman, since the canvas has a rather bizarre history. Although originally the painting was somewhat wider than now (39½ x 25½ inches), several inches of the right side of the canvas were overpainted, cut down, and wrapped around the stretcher bars. Exactly how much of the composition has been lost in this process is unknown, since photographs of it are not extant, but the strip of canvas that has recently been cut away and the part that has been overpainted reveal a third figure, an infant. It should also be noted that Ritman always signed his pictures at the lower right or left; thus one must assume that the original signature was cut off within the strip and the new signature, "Louis Ritman" (a rare inscription), added farther left below the area where the infant was painted out. There is no proof that Ritman painted out the infant, restretched the canvas, and resigned it; however, there is no doubt that the original work is from the hand of Louis Ritman. There is also no doubt that the mother and child subject was unusual for Ritman, the intimist, since we find it in only one other known work, entitled *Mother and Child* (see note below).

29. See Folsom Galleries exhibition catalog, ill. 16-3. Since Ritman was unmarried and devoted to childless compositions

featuring attractive young women, the employment of children in this imagery was less practical for him than it was for Frieseke, whose children were close at hand. Moreover, since neither *Sun Spots and Shadows* nor *Mother and Child* were painted from Ritman's regular models, one must assume that he set up his easel in the garden of either Frieseke or Miller where a model and child (son or daughter?) were already posed. Ritman's *Sun Spots and Shadows* resembles a signed work by Miller known as *Afternoon Tea*, c. 1910 (39½ x 32 inches), in which similar models posed in a similar way. Not only is Ritman's composition strikingly like Miller's, but it also retains the identical furniture.

30. Seymour, pp. 27-28.

31. Abel G. Warshawsky, *Memories of an American Impressionist,* ed. Ben L. Bassham (Kent, OH: Kent State University Press, 1980), p. 170.

32. We are not sure how Ritman shipped his pictures to New York to be juried for the San Francisco exposition, but since he was leaving Paris about this time, it seems quite possible that his entries were sent with Frieseke's. Moreover, he was shipping another large group of paintings to Chicago. These too may have been crated and sent on the liner *Chicago* on 14 October 1914. For an interesting letter to Macbeth from Frieseke, dated 6 October 1914, in Paris at 64 rue du Cherche Midi, see Macbeth Gallery Papers, 1911-1933; Microfilm Roll No. NMc46, Frame 0541, Archives of American Art, Smithsonian Institution, Washington, DC.

33. The "Première Exposition d'Art Moderne Américain: Bryson Burroughs Ernest Lawson" was held from 3 July to 1 October 1914 at Galerie Levesque & Cie, 109 Faubourg Saint-Honoré in Paris. The catalogs, with text by Léonce Bénédite and André Degarrois, are exceedingly rare, since only a few were printed.

34. Bryson Burroughs, curator, Department of Paintings at the Metropolitan Museum of Art, had been a student at the Art Students League and also a student of Luc Olivier Merson. He would soon have a canvas, entitled *Consolation of Ariadne*, in the Metropolitan Museum of Art, which he signed and dated 1915. The canvas was purchased by the (George) Hearn Fund in 1918. The Cézanne, entitled *La Colline des Pauvres (The Poorhouse on the Hill)* (25 x 32 inches), was purchased by Burroughs with the Wolfe Fund.

35. A. R., "American Art at the Anglo-American Exposition," *International Studio*, LIII, no. 212 (October 1914), p. 298.

36. Ibid.

37. Ibid.

CHAPTER SEVENTEEN: OLD TIES RE-ESTABLISHED

About the middle of November 1914, having set his affairs in order in Paris, Ritman sailed for the United States. Once he had arrived in New York, he decided to spend some time there before returning to Chicago, but the extent of his activities remains unclear. No duty was owed on his forty pictures when they came through customs, so they were forwarded to Chicago.[1] In New York Ritman renewed various acquaintances and visited art galleries and museums. He probably saw the exhibition at the Montross Gallery, 550 Fifth Avenue, billed as Opening Exhibition, Season 1914-1915. As at the Macbeth Galleries, Montross showed leading American artists, and the gallery was well known for its competitiveness. This was the kind of gallery that Ritman hoped would represent him soon. He saw another exhibition in which "a number of" paintings by Wellington J. Reynolds, his former instructor at the Art Institute of Chicago, were included. Even by Ritman's standards, Reynolds's work was relatively conservative; nonetheless, Ritman was very impressed with his former teacher's canvases and decided then and there to urge him to submit them to the 1915 Paris Salon if the war conditions permitted.[2]

By the late fall of 1914, France was totally embroiled in war. Ritman fully intended to return to Giverny after the conflict, but for now America remained neutral, and he thought he might have an opportunity to work and

reestablish himself in his hometown and perhaps even in New York. Back in Chicago, most of the Ritman family met Louis at the Dearborn Street Station. It was a joyous event for the family, for they had not seen their now successful son and brother for five years. Although he was still small and thin, Louis looked aged, according to most family members. Maurice, the youngest of the Ritman children and Louis's future biographer, was only eight; Louis did not remember his "baby brother" who would later play such an important role in his career.[3] It was evident immediately that the Ritman family had made nearly as much progress as Chicago itself. During Louis's absence, his father, Solomon Ritman, had resigned from Hart, Schaffner & Marx to take a position with Koplowitz & Mattenberg, an embroidery and stamping company at 600 Blue Island Avenue.[4] The firm continued to prosper and a couple of years before Louis returned, his father had become a partner in the business, which was renamed Mattenberg & Ritman. Although the Ritmans still lived at 1049 West Fourteenth Street, their financial condition had improved since the young artist left for Paris, and the entire family faced the future with optimism.

During Louis Ritman's absence, the face of Chicago had taken on impressive new dimensions as the city expanded. Outwardly there had been great progress, but some aspects of the city never seemed to improve. Louis's extraordinary talent had magically propelled him to a plateau of distinct honor in the art world, but for many friends whom he had left behind, life was still drudgery—consisting of long days of hard work that yielded little reward. Allied to the elder Ritman's profession, virtually thousands of seamstresses, tailors, and other garment workers forced themselves through hour after hour, day after day, in rowlike workshops on the east side of Wells Street (then Fifth Avenue), just north of Madison Street. The memories returned vividly to Louis; and he also knew that this area of human depravation was located only a block or so away from the huge and opulent La Salle Hotel, which, now catering to the rich, had been completed a few years earlier under the direction of Holabird and Roche, Chicago's most prominent architectural firm. Another new sight and bittersweet sign of progress was the congestion caused by trucks and automobiles. Now artists transported their pictures via Brinkmann's Express or some other short-haul company, but the delivery trucks still competed for space with horsedrawn vehicles on the busy streets. When Ritman arrived, motor vehicles had already made even a greater impact on the city than they had at the time an earlier observer reported: "Probably never before has a popular mechanical invention had such a potent influence in diverting the development of a pertinent style of architecture as has the automobile in transmuting Michigan Boulevard in the city of Chicago, from a residence to a business street."[5]

Ritman had not forgotten the Central Manufacturing District, one of the most successful sections of town, albeit a blight on the city. This area was now served by the huge Chicago Junction Railway, on whose tracks passed all freight moving in or out of the stockyards, Packingtown, or the district. The Central Manufacturing District encompassed a miserable conglomeration of squalid tenement houses, which provided a constant supply of laborers, including children, who were eager to work for the very low wages. Some of the workers had been Louis's boyhood friends. Remembering his days at Hull House, Ritman understood only too well what manufacturers meant when they recently boasted that the area was "easily accessible on a five cent fare from thickly populated section, where live the laboring classes . . . . the men employed in the packing houses all have large families, and prefer that their children shall find employment within walking distance of their homes."[6]

Ritman must have been amazed at the transformation of the Loop skyline in Chicago. So many new skyscrapers had arisen that he found it difficult to recognize previously well-known buildings. Moreover, the changes that were occurring on nearby Lake Shore Drive represented

a kind of microcosm of the whole city, a place that Ritman had to get to know all over again.

After only a short time, Ritman's crate of pictures arrived in Chicago. Once settled, he lost no time to forge ahead in the local art community. To do this, he consulted with Lawton Parker, who as a celebrity, had enjoyed a good press even when he was in Paris and Giverny. Parker's one-man show at the Art Institute a couple of years earlier and his salon gold medal added to his Chicago reputation. Some Chicagoans knew that he had recently received an honorary doctorate from the University of Nebraska, which was an unusually distinctive honor for an artist.[7] While he bowed to Parker's experience, Ritman, a comparatively reserved young artist, may not have always agreed with his rather outspoken manner. Only recently, Parker "blew his stack" when his gold medal picture, *La Paresse (Idleness)* —which had been accepted by the international jury—was "quietly removed" from the galleries of the Carnegie International Exhibition by Director John Wesley Beatty and "excluded from the official catalogue" because Beatty did not "think the public sufficiently enlightened in art to accept the work properly."[8] The painting had already been shown at the Art Institute and at the Pennsylvania Academy of the Fine Arts. Parker, Ritman, and others in Chicago were gratified to learn that it was reinstated in the exhibition after the committee of the Carnegie had viewed the picture in Wunderly Galleries (a private gallery).[9]

Parker undoubtedly advised his protégé to enter a competition for Chicago artists that was being sponsored by the city; according to one newspaper account, Ritman had arrived "just in time" to submit his work, but "he was one of more than 300 who entered."[10] Having made the extra effort to enter the contest, Ritman was amply rewarded: his painting, entitled *Hollyhocks*, was the first of thirteen to be "purchased for a permanent city art collection." Ritman shared the budget of $2,500 with twelve other purchase award winners. Local newspapers gave the contest extensive coverage. Thus, as a result of the competition, Ritman achieved nearly instant recognition soon after his return to Chicago. One observer reported that for Ritman, the sale of *Hollyhocks* was "the first artistic recognition won in his native city."[11]

To help Ritman gain greater exposure of his work in Chicago, Parker encouraged him to hold an exhibition in his own small studio at 19 East Pearson Street in December 1914. Although Parker's studio space made for very crowded conditions, the local art community expressed a lively interest in Ritman's show even before it opened. About a week prior to the opening, an unknown reporter, with a somewhat limited knowledge of contemporary art, was quite helpful, nonetheless, in writing a short notice of the show. Hoping to pique his readers' interest, he inquired: "Do you know what a 'pointist' [pointillist] is? It is certain you do not unless you are familiar with the crisp, expressive lingo of the French art student." Explaining the term, he related that "one who uses short brush strokes of broken color in painting is a 'pointist.' " Apparently the reporter was confused about Ritman's work or did not understand the difference between the *pointillist*, or neo-impressionist style of someone like Signac, and the older so-called romantic style, soon to be shown by Ritman. The critic referred to Ritman's pictures as "all out-of-door studies, full of life and color and realism—not of the post-impressionists, but vivid, modern in the best sense."[12]

Chicago newspapers published various biographical sketches with accounts of the young artist's meteoric success. Typical was the report written by Maude I. G. Oliver, art critic for the *Chicago Sunday Herald*: "About forty canvases, perhaps three-fourths of which have been produced within the last two years, are delighting their limited audience in the studio of Lawton Parker."[13] Making it clear that the show was hampered by small quarters, Oliver stated clearly that "the verdict of all who viewed" the pictures was "that they should have a more central location."[14] Informing those who knew nothing about the artist, she wrote: "Louis Ritman, a young Russian Pole whose privations and struggles in the name of art have been, to say the least, picturesque, if not plucky, is the modest author of this assemblage. Fresh, vivid impressionistic records, all of them, these vital notes— now sunny, now veiled in a 'gray day' seriousness— contain each a graceful accent in the demure charm of a young girl."[15]

Oliver went on to describe several paintings, enticing her readers with explications that might have referred to the work of Frieseke, Parker, or nearly any Giverny intimist: "A luxurious growth of garden flowers appears between the house and the walk and a woman stoops to gather a bouquet forgetful of the open parasol beside her." Describing other works, she continued: " 'Reflected Color' is the title belonging to the nude seated out of doors in a Morris chair asleep. The painting of flesh in this example is most remarkable, every plane reflecting some tint in the surrounding nature. The red hair, even, catches the colors about it. Another nude, in this case an interior, is presented by the title 'The Kimonos.' Painted in the same Giverny room wherein Lawton Parker executed his 'La Parosse' [sic], one is not surprised to discover many similar tints in the lavendar [sic] flesh tones. Between the warm over-head light and the cool light from the green outside the window, there is a subtle modification of all local color that is most pleasing." There was

a great deal to report about the bright new local star, so Oliver offered a prophetic review of his career: "Being still a very young man, having accomplished so much that is refreshing and able already and having the promise from an artist friend of three years' further European study as soon as the war is over, Louis Ritman is certain to be harkened to as one who has something original to tell. He has already spent six years in Paris and his history up to this time is more than interesting . . . . Mr. Parker points out with quite paternal pride to the first canvas that the young man painted, which the Giverny group felt was 'different.' Since then his strides have been noticeable."[16]

Apparently, Ritman's art was rapidly noticed by numerous influential members of the local art community. During the month of January, he met many people who complimented him on his show and offered him suggestions about how to proceed with his career in Chicago. The most advantageous opportunity presented itself in January, however, when he was tentatively offered a solo show at the Art Institute. Perhaps it was the combination of published praise for his art and complaints about the cramped space in Parker's studio that had prompted the officials of the institute to consider a show for their former student, or perhaps it was at the strong urging of someone like Parker or Maude Oliver that they did so. In any instance, during this time numerous individuals in Chicago's art community, not the least of whom were members of the art press, exerted unanimous pressure for a solo show. In this way, Ritman's exhibition became a kind of local cause célèbre. Typical was an article in the *Chicago Herald*:

> Whether Chicago will be given an opportunity to see the brilliant canvases that Louis Ritman has brought home—the first of his six years in Paris —rests entirely upon the generosity of his confreres, the artists of Chicago. The trustees of the Art Institute, who are keenly interested in his work, will give Mr. Ritman a room for a one- man show during the entire month of March provided the Chicago Society of Artists whose annual exhibition will run through the same period, does not object. The only other time the trustees can offer adequate space would be the week preceding the opening of the Chicago artists' show. To go to the expense of framing and the trouble of hanging for an exhibition lasting only one week Mr. Ritman does not consider worthwhile. The matter will come up before the directors of the Chicago Society of Artists this evening [1 February 1915]. It is probable that, in view of the fact that the space

allotted Mr. Ritman will not in any way inter-
fere with or curtail the space given the Chicago
show, the directors will agree to the proposition
of the trustees. From the point of view of the
public, a one-man show will add much to the
interest of the Chicago artists' exhibition. Mr.
Ritman brings to his work a splendid sense of
color, as well as thorough knowledge of technique. He works preferably out of doors and his
pictures are full of sunlight and a buoyant
youthfulness. To those who have seen them [at
Parker's studio] it will be a real regret if the
general public is denied an opportunity to know
and appreciate them.[17]

Although no dates were set, even negotiations for such
an event signaled great progress. After the directors of the
Chicago Society of Artists voted to cooperate, Ritman's
show became a real event, a dream that had come true.
Conscious of the fact that Reynolds had never received
a solo exhibition at the Art Institute, and that Parker had
received his first one only a year or so earlier, Ritman realized that the show was an enviable achievement for an artist who had emerged from the so-called local ghetto.[18]
Soon arrangements for Ritman's exhibition were made
with N. H. Carpenter, still acting director of the Art Institute. The opening was planned for 22 February 1915, and
Ritman's paintings were brought to the institute. His
friends and former teachers were elated. Arrangements
were made to have his pictures framed for the show.

Although certain factions of the Art Institute and Carl
Werntz's Chicago Academy of Fine Arts still harbored
bitter feelings toward each other, their issues were of no
real concern to Ritman, who still had good friends at both
institutions. At the academy, the British portraitist
Frederick V. Poole had taken over the painting classes
from Wellington J. Reynolds, who had been at the Art
Institute for the past few months. The academic procedures professed daily by both Reynolds and Vanderpoel
were still highly regarded by the board of trustees at the
institute and by local artists, but both men were clearly
members of the old school.

On 25 January 1915, Ritman received a letter regarding his forthcoming show from C. H. Burkholder, director pro tempore of the Institute:

"I do not believe that Mr. Carpenter realized that February 22 is a holiday, and that we could not put up your
exhibition until the morning of the twenty-third." Carpenter explained, however, that "one man can hang as
rapidly as an artist can lay out the walls. I believe we could

continue the exhibition until the morning of the first
which would run it over Sunday . . . as you say, the
period is short."[19]

Ill. 17-1. Frederick Fursman. *In the Woods.* Oil on canvas, 32 x 41
inches. Private Collection. Courtesy R. H. Love Galleries, Chicago.

Some time in the last week of January, Ritman received
an invitation to attend a special "Artists' Dinner" that was
being sponsored by the Palette and Chisel Club and the
Press Club of Chicago on Friday evening, 5 February. The
event was to honor the prominent Western artist Charles
M. Russell. Russell was not the only painter of the American West who had ties in Chicago; indeed, the city had
served as a base for many painters who considered themselves Western artists. Even the great Frederick Remington, who had died a few years earlier, showed his work
at the O'Brien Gallery in Chicago. The evening was not
intended as a gathering for Western artists, but that
unique faction of the American art community was well
represented in the persons of Victor Higgins and Walter
Ufer. Other artists invited were Lawton Parker, Wilson
Irvine, A. F. Brooks, Jerome S. Blum, Roy Brown, J.
Jeffrey Grant, George Senseney, L. O. Griffith, Joseph
Kleitsch, F. F. Fursman (ill. 17-1), and several more. Prior
to the dinner, one of Chicago's newspapers reported that
"among those who will speak at the dinner are Messrs.
Parker and Senseney, Louis Ritman . . . [and others]."[20]
Focusing on Senseney, the reporter stated that like Ritman, Senseney had "left Paris when the war began." "The
artist," he continued, had "selected Chicago as his home
and the scene of his future activities" because he believed
that the city was "'more plastic' than New York and less
saturated with European ideas."

All the right people came to the Friday night dinner at the Press Club, and all were anxious to hear Charlie Russell speak. "Just to make Mr. Russell feel at home," reported a writer for *The Cow Bell*, the official monthly publication of the Palette and Chisel Club, "the Club, at vast expense, had imported from Montana the celebrated 'Hot Dog Bar.' "[21] In the Chicago bohemian tradition, a dancer known as Yvonne entertained the group. After the guest of honor's remarks, however, "a conversational 'battle royal' took place with the entire mob on the job."[22] The clash was pertinent to art community observers, and it was interesting copy for numerous members of the press who also stood by. A local paper known as *ART* reported: "Another shot was fired yesterday in the feud between factions of Chicago artists, who are at odds over the Municipal Art League's method of selecting prize winning paintings." According to the article, the shot "came in the form of a statement by Louis Ritman, one of the partners who protested against 'pink tea' juries of club women and asked for juries of artists instead. Mr. Ritman took issue with Victoria [sic] Higgins, one of the faction satisfied with the present method and who charged that the protestants were 'disappointed and disgruntled.'"[23]

" 'War in art means progress,' said Mr. Ritman, 'and what Mr. [Victor] Higgins and his fellow members of the Palette and Chisel Club call war really means progress. When he refers to us as disappointed and disgruntled, because of our not receiving prizes, I want to say that three of our number received honors from the exhibition. Three others are not even exhibitors.' As for Mr. Higgins accusing Lawton Parker of being dissatisfied over his failure to divert the purchase prize to a protégé of his, Louis Ritman, I can but say that I had no $200 pictures to go into the competition for purchase prizes. We do not accuse Mr. Higgins and his friends of being disgruntled. It is none of their affair if we choose to refrain from exhibiting under the auspices of the [Municipal] Art League."

Directing his comments specifically to the jurying process, Ritman stressed that "the artists have never protested against the League's selecting the pictures it purchased for exhibition in the Art Institute, but only against the appointment of juries to award prizes. The present method misleads the public." To the obvious discomfort of certain mutual acquaintances, Higgins and Ritman argued from their respective positions as artists, the former defending the traditional jury process, the latter calling for its abolishment. On a further issue, the article reported that "Mr. Ritman also referred to the purchase by the League of one of Mr. Higgins' own paintings when the latter was a member of the jury award."[24]

Most of the artists and interested bystanders agreed with Ritman that the awards selection jury should be composed of professionals and not members of women's clubs. Several months prior to the eruption at the Press Club dinner, a local newspaper editorialized:

Hostilities opened in the local world of artists by the protests of a number of painters against the awards of the Municipal Art League ought to be welcomed by everyone who wishes to see the arts flourish and Chicago something better than the biggest town in America. The vision of Mr. Lawton Parker at the head of his rebels storming the Art Institute over the prostrate forms of President Hutchinson and the trustees is not necessarily one which should horrify the discerning city patriot. One the contrary, until we can care enough for an art to make war for it, if our pacifist friends will pardon the military metaphor, it will derive very little sustenance from prize awards, although the favored artists and their worthy families may. This is an issue which ought to be faced, not shirked for the sake of peace or on the theory that somehow indiscriminating rewards will stimulate a general artistic activity in which merit may be left to look out for itself.[25]

The Palette and Chisel Club dinner at the Press Club had turned out to be the best local forum on contemporary Chicago art that the city had witnessed in many years (ill. 17-2). That two distinct factions were active and accounted for was an obviously healthy sign of an active art community. Because Ritman had left Chicago as a mere struggling prodigy, his views on art had been neither heard before nor invited, but now that he had returned triumphant, a tested expatriate, his opinion had become valuable. Ironically, while in Paris he was allied through his art with the conservative American expatriate camp, in Chicago he was thrust into the liberal camp, even before his solo exhibition, by his remarks equating "war in art" with "progress." Formerly a quiet, hardworking, and unassuming lad, Ritman had returned from Europe with ideas of his own about reform, and to make matters worse, he was General Parker's most trusted colonel. In his summary of the Press Club dinner, a reporter had written: "A. F. Brooks, veteran painter, talked of the old days, and was followed by Victor Higgins and Wilson Irvine of the Municipal Art Commission: then Lawton Parker, Louis Ritman, and others." He continued:

Ill. 17-2. Hosts and guests at the Artists' Dinner sponsored by the Palette and Chisel Club and the Press Club in Chicago on February 5, 1915. Victor Higgins (bottom row, first from left), Lawton Parker (second row, second from left), and Louis Ritman (second row, third from left) were the principal speakers representing opposing views on art policies. Palette and Chisel Club Archives, Chicago.

"Trouble threatened for a moment as the radicals gnashed their teeth at the conservatives; but it all blew over."[26]

It is highly probable that although Ritman was well-liked at the Art Institute, his close relationship with Parker would have jeopardized his chances for a show if French had still been director. Indeed, French had been well known for his policy of including women's clubs in the art jury and selection process at the Art Institute, the tradition attacked by Ritman and Parker. Parker had reasserted himself in the city, however, and Ritman profited from his mentor's burgeoning reputation—French was no longer an adversary with whom he had to deal. Among Parker's recent gains was his appointment to the position of first vice president of the Arts Club of Chicago, then headquartered at 408 South Michigan Avenue. One of the goals of this group was to "promote the mutual acquaintance of art lovers and art workers."[27]

Karl Buehr was another friend who had been in Giverny with Ritman and was now back in Chicago. Buehr was not only finding ample opportunities in Chicago, but had recently accepted the position of vice president of the Chicago Society of Artists; Adam Emory Albright was its president, and Victor Higgins, its secretary. Higgins, with whom Ritman had argued publicly, also sat on the board of the prestigious Commission for Encouragement of Local Art. The president of this commission was Wilson Irvine, a very conservative local impressionist whom Ritman had come to know better after the Press Club dinner.[28] Although the commission had just been established by a city ordinance about two months earlier, it promised to be an influential group, guided as it was by board members like the liberal collector Arthur J. Eddy, William O. Goodman, and Frank G. Logan (vice president of the Art Institute of Chicago).

There was a good chance that Ritman's work would be selected for the city's permanent collection because this group was "empowered to select and purchase paintings, sculpture, and other works of art produced by residents of Chicago and to place them in City buildings."[29] Works that would soon be purchased by the commission included *Morning at Kasba, Tangiers* by Walter Ufer, and *Hills of Belvedere* by John Stacey.

At the suggestion of Parker and a few others, Ritman joined the Artists Guild, an organization that met at the Fine Arts Building, just south of the Art Institute on the west side of Michigan Avenue. For Ritman, a professional artist, the entrance fee was twenty-five dollars. It was an excellent group to belong to, since the guild maintained an exhibition gallery as well as a bureau of information, and frequently sponsored lectures. It also organized annual competitions, but Ritman had just missed the 1914 annual.

Ritman's solo show at the Art Institute was inspiring lively interest even before it opened, and it was assuming a much greater significance than the impromptu exhibition set up in Parker's studio. One enthusiastic writer who had actually gone with a companion to see Ritman as he worked in Parker's Pearson Street studio reported: "We mounted another flight of stairs and landed in the studios of the painters [Ritman and Parker]." The men "first visited Mr. Rittman [sic], who was preparing for his one-man exhibit at the Institute." The writer explained: "It was a new experience for some of us to see pictures before they are hung; to meet the artist and hear him tell about them."[30]

Ritman was receiving much more attention than he did in Paris as Chicago newspapers carried reminders of his show.[31] Finally, on Tuesday, 23 February 1915, Louis Ritman opened his first official one-artist exhibition, complete with a tea, at the Art Institute. As for any important solo show, the institute prepared a catalog of the works shown. The catalog was no more than a brochure, and the biography was slightly inaccurate and exceedingly brief, but the titles of all nineteen pictures were listed.[32] The painting known as *Sun Kissed* was lent by the great Art Institute supporter W. O. Goodman, who had apparently purchased the work prior to the show.[33]

The exhibition opened on a typical bleak winter day. The weather, however, was a far lesser deterrent to a successful opening than was the Chicago Democratic primary, which, among many contests, featured the mayoral race between former Mayor Carter H. Harrison, whose portrait Louis had painted on a banner a dozen years earlier, and Robert M. Sweitzer. In spite of the competition from the primary, Ritman's show attracted a surprising number of visitors. Parker, Reynolds, and other

associates and acquaintances attended the opening. In fact, one observer reported that the opening-day guests included "many fellow members of Mr. Ritman's craft, and the genuine expression of pleasure from this fraternity was a feature of the occasion quite in keeping with the joyous character of the display."[34] Most critics commented that the show was truly a great achievement for the twenty-five-year-old artist, but even more visitors were pleased that his nineteen French canvases could now be properly seen by the entire Chicago art community. Indeed, some important cultural leaders attended the opening tea, women like Mmes. John Alden Carpenter, Robert G. McGann, Frederick Clay Bartlett, and W. O. Goodman, whose husband had purchased *Sun Kissed*.

In their roles as cultural leaders, these society women were courteously enthusiastic; they complimented Ritman on his art and made every effort to make him feel comfortable. However, they had another cause for celebration that day: the Chicago electoral primary was the first election in which women had been allowed to vote. Some of them had already cast their ballots before they attended Ritman's opening. The results would not be known until later that night. Many other interested viewers were present at Ritman's opening, a wonderful event that was covered to a greater or lesser extent by most of the local newspapers in spite of the hotly contested races in the Democratic primary.[35]

The fact that Ritman was a Jew was well known to most of the institute hierarchy, but it did not prejudice his exhibition. In fact, his religion, his Russian origin, and his humble beginnings seemed to prove the viability of the American dream, something honorable, and in this case more important than anti-Semitism. Moreover, Lawton Parker, Vanderpoel, and other leading members of the local art community liked and respected Ritman a great deal. In describing Ritman's work, one unidentified critic wrote that "the floods of sunshine that stream from the young artist's pictures made visitors to the room to-day exclaim with delight, as they declared the scenes were an antidote to the dismal weather of the city outside." The local art writer Inez Travers visited the exhibition and observed that "in spite of the bad weather, the gallery given over to the exhibition of paintings by Louis Ritman, which opened at the Art Institute yesterday, contained a satisfying number of visitors by 1 o'clock." She continued: "By 1:30 it was crowded with a more or less hurried throng who curtailed the lunch hour by half in favor of art. Mr. Ritman's pictures are a blaze of color and a riot of bloom. On a dull, chill February day a rather painful stretch of the imagination and an assiduous brushing of memory are required to believe that he found his models in the realms of reality . . . .He paints women more knowingly and truthfully than he does flowers. 'The Yellow Jacket' is a buoyant glimpse of youth . . . . She is cleverly posed against a green shutterlike screen through which the golden sunlight filters."[36]

In France Ritman had heard about the controversy which arose over the removal of Chabas's picture of a nude from a local photographer's window in Chicago. He was also quite aware of the controversy surrounding Parker's *La Paresse.* Among the forty canvases Ritman had shipped from Paris, there were a number of nudes, and several of these were included in the Art Institute show. If he harbored any anxiety over the public's response to these paintings, it was dispelled when Travers wrote that his nudes too, were "really beautiful, delicately treated, and artistically posed." Referring to the nude that had been bought by Goodman, Travers wrote: " 'Sun Kissed' is without a doubt the best thing in the collection. It is the figure of a slender girl reclining under the thick boughs of a tree. Her rather colorful skin is flecked beautifully with sunshine and shadow."[37]

At the end of the first day of the show, Ritman was more encouraged about his future than he had been in months. Conversely, when Carter Harrison and his brother Preston walked home from City Hall that night, their futures looked dismal: Harrison had been defeated by Bob Sweitzer, largely as the result of a two-to-one "thumbs down" vote by Chicago women, undoubtedly some of whom had attended Ritman's opening. Harrison's defeat was a kind of litmus test for women's suffrage. Accordingly, the election upset was big news everywhere since it owed so much to the women's vote. The *New York Evening Star* stated flatly that "the first result of suffrage in Illinois seems to be that Chicago has lost the Carter Harrison habit." The *Kansas City Journal* made the statement that "Carter Harrison and Theodore Roosevelt haven't much in common politically, but they ought to be able to get together on the proposition that a pitcher may go to the well once too often." Many other cynical editorials appeared in newspapers across the country as the nation reflected upon Harrison's raw defeat at the hands of Chicago women.

The women, however, did not defeat Harrison without substantial behind-the-scenes support, ironically the result of infighting between Mayor Harrison and his former First Ward allies, Bathhouse John Coughlin and Hinky Dink Kenna. For many months County Judge Owens had spearheaded a movement within the Democratic Party to reform Chicago by dumping The Bath and Hinky Dink. Thus, when Charles Wheeler, the political reporter of the *Chicago Tribune,* had interviewed Mayor Harrison some months earlier about his old First Ward cronies, Harrison had replied: "Coughlin and Kenna are through unless they will support Judge Owens and the entire Democratic slate . . .. Coughlin and Kenna must go. I have reached the final conclusion that my ideas on the vice question have been wrong."[38] Mayor Harrison's reform measures came too late, however; the public had no faith that he had disassociated himself from the First Ward Levee bosses; and now on the opposite team, Coughlin and Kenna turned their vote-getting vehicle in another direction. So it was that Sweitzer received over six times as many votes as Harrison. The coalition between the mayor and the lords of the Levee was over, and finally, it seemed that the days of the Levee were also numbered. Sweitzer, however, was opposed by a tower of a man, the likeable Republican Big Bill Thompson, the ex-football star and former ranch cook who would prove to be unstoppable.

In striking contrast to Harrison's failure, Ritman's debut was a huge success. He and his work impressed the Chicago art community in general, and the Art Institute hierarchy in particular. At every opportunity, Acting Director N. H. Carpenter and his assistant C. H. Burkholder praised the young artist's work. For example, in a letter written to a director of the Terre Haute (Indiana) Art Association, Burkholder discussed a group exhibition that the Art Institute planned to send for a loan exhibition: "We will send you . . . paintings . . . by Peyraud, Irvine, Higgins, Fleury, and Parker." Burkholder confirmed that "Parker has promised that he will select a fine painting by Louis Ritman. Ritman has an exhibition opening at the Art Institute today, and his canvases are very attractive. I wish it were possible to transport the collection to your city. Mr. Ritman is a young man who has been working [words faded] at Giverny, and his paintings savor greatly of the style of Miller, Buehr, Parker, Frieseke, etc."[39]

As Ritman's show continued its very short run, critics unanimously agreed that the artist had demonstrated that he was Chicago's best new talent. An anonymous critic headlined his brief review "Ritman's Sunlit Gardens." With no reservations, he stated: "Mr. Ritman is interested chiefly in out-of-door painting, and some charming transcripts of sunlight are shown in his many variations of the garden subjects that he likes so well to paint." Associating Ritman with the known Giverny milieu, the critic continued: "He is a very close follower of the style of Frieseke in choice of subjects, in handling and color. His color schemes are usually in cooler greens and blues with just enough warm pink to give life."[40]

Any inhibitions or anxieties that Ritman may have suffered prior to the show must have evaporated rapidly as accolades continued to fill the art pages of local newspapers. One of the most complimentary pieces was written by the respected critic Lena M. McCauley for the *Chicago Evening Post*:

> Louis Ritman . . . should burnish his shield of courage and turn his face to the East when the voice of approval tells him that he is on the way . . . . in painting, as in poetry, music or any other craft, be it the vocation of artist or artisan, the very greatest good that can come to the young worker is to know that he is on the way. After this the secret of success will be unraveled as he goes on, avoids the blind alley of self-satisfaction, and escapes the dangerous labyrinth of walking in a circle because he can do a certain thing well . . . . So brilliantly sunny, so pretty, so cleverly done are the nineteen canvases brought from abroad by Mr. Rittman [sic] that they dazzle the eyes . . . What will his seniors say if the enthusiasts suggest that Mr. Ritman has surpassed them all in sun spots, light rays playing between shadows, radiance of midday in the garden?[41]

McCauley reported to the potential visitor that they would see "charming studies of women in gardens, at the tea tables out of doors . . . not nymphs or farces, but models posed where the sunlight plays upon the pearly flesh and the painter is put to the test of drawing the human figure, that enigma of subtle grace . . . Each is a charming etude, not from Mr. Ritman's Russian inheritance, however, but suggested by the chanson in France and played in a key only possible in a walled garden."[42]

Five years had gone by since Ritman's work had been seen at the annual Chicago Artists show. This spring the exhibition was scheduled to be seen at the Art Institute from 9 through 31 March 1915.[43] During Ritman's absence, the annual show had actually generated greater attention from the press than in earlier years. Ritman was eager to have a second forum for his work on the heels of his one-man show. Before he and other artists delivered their work to the Art Institute, however, the members of the Municipal Art League announced to the press that they were officially protesting the manner in which prizes were awarded, and that they intended to boycott the show unless procedures were changed. Obviously this move was the result of the controversial Palette and Chisel Club dinner at the Chicago Press Club a month earlier. One newspaper heading read: "Artists Rebel at 'Layman' Jury of Club Women."[44] The article reported that "the Art Institute faces a secession of a number of Chicago's best known artists . . . .The artists are demanding the

right to elect jurors who award the prizes at the annual exhibition . . . . The following letter will be sent to the trustees of the Art Institute today . . . . For many years it has been your practice at the annual exhibition of the works of Chicago artists to permit the award of prizes to be made by representatives of the women's clubs of Chicago constituting the Municipal Art League. It has long been our opinion that this method was undignified, unjust and indeed farcical. Prizes given in this manner carry no presumption of merit to the works they decorate, and the neglect of meritorious works does an injustice to the authors as well as to the public . . . . For these reasons we beg leave to announce our decision to refrain from sending our pictures to this exhibition until these prizes shall be awarded in a traditional manner." The article listed the names of the fifteen persons who had signed the letter. At the top of the list was Lawton Parker and then other associates like Reynolds, W. P. Henderson, Karl Buehr, Alson Skinner Clark, Walter Ufer, and, of course, Louis Ritman, who had been one of the most vocal spokesmen on the issue. A representative for the women in the Municipal Art League said that she thought the boycott was "a foolish step." After further debate, however, and a change in policy, the Chicago Artists show took place.

Wellington J. Reynolds, now an instructor at the Art Institute, showed only one painting, a canvas entitled ***The Green Parasol***; Parker, the chief painting instructor at the Academy of Fine Arts submitted a work known as ***Irene***. A few artists declined to exhibit. Ritman was given space for no less than five paintings; all of these were typical, but apparently none of the works from his one-man show was included. After seeing these works, visitors recognized Ritman's growth as a Chicago painter, but they could also see that he had followed in Parker's footsteps to become a full-fledged member of the Giverny expatriates.

As the result of Burkholder's suggestion, apparently, a small selection of pictures from those that Ritman had exhibited at the Art Institute was shipped to Terre Haute for a show at the public library.[45] Once again, the exhibit was short, lasting only until the latter part of March. No sooner had the canvases been returned to the institute, however, than a few of them were requested by the Park Ridge Art Association for inclusion in a memorial exhibition for the late Walter Marshall Clute, a highly respected Chicago artist. The exhibition was planned for 12 through 19 April. In a March letter to Ritman, N. H. Carpenter assured the artist that his "pictures [would] be hung by our men, individually lighted, and properly insured."[46] Later that month, Ritman's ***Dormitory Breakfast*** was crated and shipped with paintings by Lucy

Pl. 15-11. Louis Ritman. *The Blue Sash*. Oil on canvas, 36 x 36 inches. Private Collection. Courtesy R. H. Love Galleries, Chicago.

Pl. 16-1. Louis Ritman. *Girl with a Fan.* 1914. Oil on canvas, 36 x 36 inches. Private Collection. Courtesy R. H. Love Galleries, Chicago.

Pl. 16-2. Louis Ritman. *The Letter*. Ca. 1914. Oil on canvas, 25½ x 25½ inches. Private Collection. Courtesy R. H. Love Galleries, Chicago.

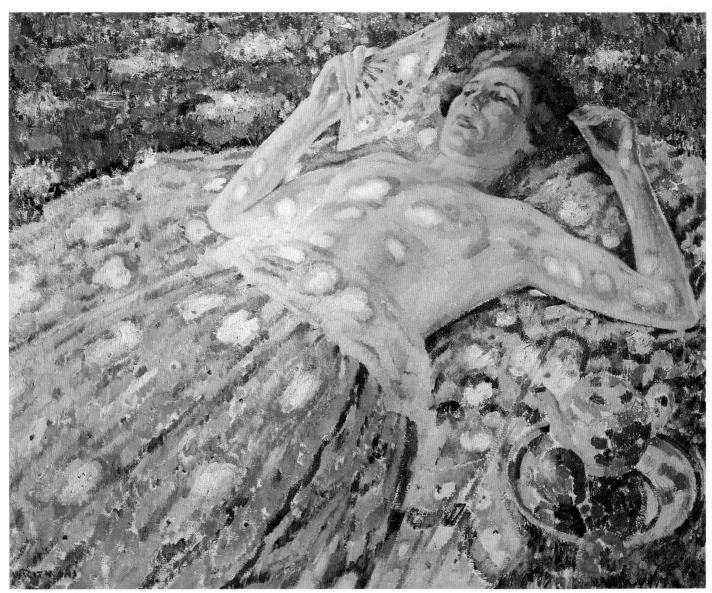

Pl. 16-3. Louis Ritman. *Quietude*. Ca. 1916. Oil on canvas, 32 x 40 inches. Private Collection. Courtesy R. H. Love Galleries, Chicago.

Pl. 16-4. Louis Ritman. Detail: *Quietude*.

Pl. 16-5. Louis Ritman. *Sun Spots: Arranging Flowers*. Oil on canvas, 36 x 36 inches. Private Collection. Courtesy R. H. Love Galleries, Chicago.

Pl. 16-6. Louis Ritman. *Sun Spots and Shadows.* Ca. 1913-1914. Oil on canvas, 39½ x 25½ inches. Edward and Deborah Pollack Fine Art.

Pl. 18-1. Louis Ritman. *Quiet Afternoon*. 1915. Oil on canvas, 31½ x 38¹⁵⁄₁₆ inches. Phoenix Art Museum. Gift of Mr. Maurice Ritman.

Hartrath, Irvine, Higgins, and others for a group show at the Art Association of La Crosse, Wisconsin. Burkholder explained later in a letter to the association that he had secured special reduced prices from the contributing artists so that "the Association will have an opportunity of clearing expenses."[47] Prices ranged from $200 for Hallberg's *The Wave* to $500 for Ritman's *Dormitory Breakfast*, the highest priced canvas in the small show.

Young Ritman's paintings were in high demand. In April 1915, at about the same time as the Park Ridge show, another selection from the original forty works was exhibited at the John Herron Art Institute in Indianapolis. The directors of that institute must have considered it fitting that the works of Ritman, a former expatriate from Giverny, be exhibited in conjunction with those of the French artist Odilon Redon.[48] If the citizens of Indianapolis had been unaware of the vast differences between the images of these two men who got their inspirations in France, they certainly discovered the striking contrast immediately upon viewing the show. Not only were Redon's strange visionary images unrelated to impressionism, but they were also quite unrelated to the natural world, which Ritman tried to depict.

During the show, William Merritt Chase, Ritman's former teacher and a resident of Indianapolis, visited the Herron Institute on his return to New York from Saint Louis, where he had served on a jury for the artists guild. A local critic interviewed Chase while he was in Indianapolis, reporting that the master had no use for "modern tendencies in art."[49] Making explicit reference to Redon, Chase commented on the exhibits at the Herron: "The moderns are divided into two classes—those that never have done good work, but seek notoriety and those who do mediocre work and deliberately changed their manner of expression also to attract attention." The writer went on to report that "the exhibition of impressionistic paintings by Louis Ritman in the east gallery attracted Mr. Chase much more. He said, however, that he did not believe the effect of pure color, and sunshine would be as lasting as the impressionists hoped." Continuing, the critic pointed out that Ritman "worked his way up from the humblest social conditions," and that "he paints in the same style and coloring as F. C. Frieseke, with whom he has worked in Frieseke's delightful old garden, where flowers run riot and a fish pond still exists that was there years ago." Referring to Frieseke—and not Chase, who apparently did not remember Ritman's exceedingly short stint in Philadelphia—the writer stated that "Ritman's aim, like that of his teacher, is to depict foliage in brilliant sunlight. Figures, flowers and garden furniture take their places as spots of color . . . . Ritman's work stands up very well with the examples of

Frieseke's already shown here . . . . These two artists choose for their subjects women attired in organdies and garden hats and with parasols, which by this time both artists have learned to draw astonishingly well. The women are gathering flowers, sewing, reading, or busy at the tea table, all very delightful and femininely alluring."[50]

Less than a week after the close of the Ritman-Redon show in Indianapolis, banner headlines reported that the Cunard steamship *Lusitania,* one of the largest and swiftest passenger ships ever launched, was torpedoed and sunk by a German submarine off the coast of Ireland. Counted among the victims were 102 Americans, a fact that shocked and outraged not only Chicagoans but people all over the United States. Angered citizens called for an immediate cessation of neutrality and even the declaration of war, but President Wilson urged the people to remain calm and insisted that the country maintain its official policies. Regardless of the position of the American government, however, the *Lusitania* tragedy set a precedent that made passenger travel across the Atlantic perilous, even on American vessels, which, as ships of a neutral country, were supposed to be able to sail unhampered. Ritman had intended to return to France, but now more than ever, he and other former expatriates were concerned about their own safety in making the trip.

Later in the spring of 1915, Ritman learned that the work he had submitted to the Panama-Pacific International Exposition in San Francisco had been awarded a silver medal.[51] This coveted prize, received by few others, especially an artist of his age, was of greater significance than any award he could have attained in Chicago. In the making of his career, Ritman could not have had better credentials than a prize from this prestigious and highly competitive international forum. The Panama-Pacific was at that time the largest and most highly publicized art exhibition in the world. This fair served as a convenient and timely alternative to any exposition that might have taken place in Europe had it not been totally involved in war. The exposition "celebrated two events, the rebuilding of San Francisco after the catastrophic earthquake and fire of 1906, and the opening of the Panama Canal and consequent enormous reduction in distance of San Francisco, by sea, from Europe."[52] The art exhibition was filled to overflowing with American paintings, including Ritman's, that had been inspired by several decades of dominant French influences. Officials of the exposition were so impressed by the gallant attempts of the French to participate in spite of adverse wartime conditions "that after the close of the exhibition they rebuilt the French pavilion in permanent materials as a memorial of their effort."[53]

The huge and impressive Exposition transformed the scene in San Francisco with millions of visitors. Moreover, the art exhibition displayed hundreds of pictures. These included perhaps the greatest number of works by American impressionists that had ever been assembled. The Panama-Pacific International was not simply a large forum for contemporary impressionism like Ritman's; it was organized in such a way that one could review the whole history of the impressionist movement in America: crowding the walls were works by pioneer impressionists like Theodore Robinson (gone from Giverny over 20 years and deceased; 9 of his works were shown), Robert Vonnoh, Mark Fisher, James A. M. Whistler (deceased for twelve years; 25 works shown), Mary Cassatt (only 3 works), Willard Metcalf, Theodore Butler (only 3 works), Lilla Cabot Perry, J. H. Twachtman (deceased 13 years;19 works), J. Alden Weir, John Singer Sargent (13 works), Childe Hassam (38 works), and William Merritt Chase, who had recently taught a summer class at Carmel-by-the-Sea and actually received a special gallery for his work at the exposition (32 works). The only Chicago painter to be given a whole gallery was the expatriate Alson Skinner Clark, whose Panama Canal scenes had been requested by the exposition art director John E. D. Trask. Not all of the critics shared Trask's enthusiasm for the repetitious subjects, although Clark was awarded bronze medal for his efforts. In his usual forthright manner, Eugene Neuhaus stated: "Alson Skinner Clark has been given the privilege of almost an entire gallery, without any other justification than historical interest in his shallow Panama scenes, devoid of any quality. They are illustrations — that is all."[54] Characteristically caustic, Neuhaus wrote: "Gifford Beal disappoints in some superficial paintings of commonplace subject," and "Here is Frederich [sic] Frieseke, our expatriated American, with his fascinating boudoir scenes." He described Frieseke's paintings as "very high in key and full of detail . . . . Frieseke's clear, joyous art is typically modern, and expresses the best tendency of our day." Of a Ritman painting, he wrote: "Very much in the style of the Frieseke, Rittman's [sic] 'Early Morning in the Garden' is easily taken for the art of his fascinating neighbor, but it should be recognized as the work of another kindred spirit."

Focusing his official catalog essay on the achievements of the American impressionists, art writer J. Nilsen Laurvik maintained that the influence of the French had been "a stimulating and beneficial tonic." He singled out parties like J. Alden Weir and the Giverny pioneer Willard Metcalf, Ernest Lawson, and a few others as having been "most intoxicated by this aesthetic nectar."[55] Laurvik stated that "all of these men owe much of what is most vital and lasting in their work to their intelligent application of lessons taught by the Impressionists. Of these, Childe Hassam is perhaps the most brilliant exemplar in this country of the ideas and practices of Monet."[56]

Laurvik was not the only art writer of the time to assess the weight of impressionism. An exhibition as large as the Panama-Pacific Exposition simply underscored the obvious: that impressionism was by far and away still the most dominant aesthetic in the Western hemisphere. Louis Weinberg, writing for *The New Republic*, felt compelled to analyze the current state of the movement: "Impressionism in art is something more than a method of painting," he said. "Impressionism has a broader significance and a truer one than is expressed in the technical formula of its painter disciples, with their broken color tones, their purer palette, their interest in values, in luminous shadows and in vibrating light . . . . Impressionism as a technique is a means of recording the transitory nature of phenomena and the fluidity of motion . . . as painters, as writers, as musicians, impressionists . . . are craftsmen recording the flitting sensations of an ever changing world . . . . But this is not alone a description of the art of our times: it is the very essence of our lives . . . . most things are enveloped in the vibrating atmosphere of doubt — light the rationalists call it. In our social life, in our industrial life, in our political and in our very religious life, all is change . . . . The railroad, the telephone, the telegraph, the linotype machine, the steamship, the phonograph and 'the movies' all contribute to the rush of changing impressions, to the bewildering multiplicity of effects. What time is there for revery, imagination or principle in the life of the modern city dweller? His newspaper furnishes numberless thrills each hour . . . . His very excursions and vacations are not given to idling or play . . . . The dominance of impressionism in our art is the outcome of this life."[57]

Weinberg's ideas about "current impressionism" were intuitive; but while his thesis accounted for much of what was seen in contemporary exhibitions, it was not a wholly accurate description of Ritman's work. Ritman and his Giverny expatriate friends had made a specialty of depicting "revery, imagination," and "idling or play." Theirs was not the French kind of impressionism from which Weinberg drew his inspiration; it was a special American type that had been popularized by a few Midwesterners who worked in Giverny.

Nearly every prominent Chicago painter was represented at the San Francisco exposition, and Lawton Parker won the coveted Medal of Honor. In light of the importance of the event and Ritman's own achievement there, one must assume that the young artist had wished to attend, perhaps with Parker. But alas, no letters, no family memoirs, no expended train tickets indicate that he made the trip from Chicago to San Francisco. Nonetheless, the two pictures that Ritman submitted were in every way typical of his Giverny productions; one was entitled *Early Morning in a Garden*; the other, *Déjeuner*.[58]

Ill. 17-3. Louis Ritman. *Déjeuner.* Location unknown. Photograph. R. H. Love Galleries Archives, Chicago.

Many paintings, including works by the Giverny group, were reproduced in the official catalog of the Panama-Pacific show. Among these reproductions we find a large oil known as *Summer,* by Frieseke; the famous *La Paresse,* by Parker; *Nude,* by Miller, and *Déjeuner,* by Ritman (ill. 17-3). In Ritman's outstanding canvas, two young women are shown seated out of doors at a linen-covered luncheon table. The composition is arranged in such a way that the two subjects are seated in line at an oblique angle to the picture plane. Probably executed in the summer of 1913, the image consists of a foreground figure holding a hat in her left hand and a fan in the other, while the subject across the table shades herself with a parasol as she reads. At first glance, the composition is simply two attractive young women seated leisurely on a summer afternoon, but more careful analysis reveals a compositional masterpiece: femininity in form is subtly underscored as the image abounds with a carefully balanced group of overlapping circles, some of which

actually outline spherical forms and others are implied (see diagram, ill. 17-4). There are few surface varieties in this picture — flesh, drapery, still life, and grass — an abundance of rich textures is achieved through Ritman's skillful brushwork. *Déjeuner* is one of the artist's most successful works. At the exposition, it pleased critics and public alike and prompted the Panama-Pacific jury to

Ill. 17-4. Diagram. Louis Ritman. *Déjeuner.* R. H. Love Galleries Archives, Chicago.

award Ritman a silver medal.

Even as a devoted expatriate anxious to return to France, Ritman could not have missed the amazing change that came over Chicago politics with Big Bill Thompson's mayoral takeover. The change had to do with the players, however, not the game. Ritman had gained some indirect knowledge of the game when he worked at Cusack's, where politics was nearly as important as the job at hand. In recent months Bathhouse John and Hinky Dink had reasserted their control over the First Ward, which lay near the Ritman home, but all else had been taken over by Big Bill — he needed no more middlemen to maintain vice. In the words of Wendt and Kogan, "the crooks guffawed and set up their gambling outfits, the men of the red lights sighed in relief and looked for the keys to the rusty padlocks, and Carter Harrison began to interest himself in the war in Europe."[59]

In spite of Thompson's corruption, business and industry prospered as never before, and Chicago expanded in every way. New buildings and improvement projects dotted the city like a checkerboard; one of the most noticeable was the Iron Street project, whose multistoried incubator buildings made the area usable again. More attractive areas, like the Loop or Hyde Park, teemed with human activity as citizens rushed from early morning until late at night in pursuit of business, industry, education, or culture. One place that catered to artists, writers, and the bohemian lot in general was the Players' Work Shop, a club that had been founded by Lou Wall Moore and Maxwell Bodenheim. Conversation at the Shop frequently centered on Stanislaus Szukalski, the sculptor, whom Hecht described as one resembling "a feline Madonna." Szukalski's face," he said, was "alive with the careful cruelty of an obsolete Jesuit;" others

called him "the greatest living artist."[60] None of Ritman's circle paid much attention to Szukalski and his enthusiastic supporters. Whether Ritman frequented any of these clubs that were fashioned after the Parisian cafés of the Latin Quarter is unknown, but many of his artist friends were regular visitors. Just as in Montparnasse, however, these noisy smoke-filled rooms were the perfect forums for talk about Picasso, Rodin, Nietzsche, Sherwood Anderson, Monet, Ben Hecht, Mallarmé, Cubism, Stieglitz, and, of course, Szukalski and the young erstwhile expatriate Louis Ritman. In spite of such attempts, however, the bohemian haunts in Chicago remained a far cry from those in Montparnasse, and artists like Ritman who had frequented those in Paris found little inspiration in Chicago.

Notes

1. As previously noted, perhaps his entries to the San Francisco Panama-Pacific Exposition were sent with Frieseke's and were handled by either Ritman himself or Macbeth, who saw to it that Frieseke's work reached the jury in New York.

2. Maurice Ritman, interview with Richard Love, Chicago, September 1987, R. H. Love Galleries Archives, Chicago.

3. Maurice Ritman, interview with Richard Love, Chicago, June 1987.

4. Reuben H. Donnelley, *The Lakeside Annual Directory of the City of Chicago* (Chicago, 1912), p. 1184.

5. *Architectural Record*, 1910.

6. From *The Central Manufacturing District*, (1915), quoted in Harold M. Mayer and Richard C. Wade, *Chicago: Growth of a Metropolis* (Chicago: University of Chicago Press, 1969), p. 235.

7. Inasmuch as Parker was considered a Chicago artist, various local newspapers mentioned the artist's honor, but in some of the art sections, reporters had been reminding readers of the award for quite some time: "Recognition, by the way, came to Mr. Parker last season from his own native state of Nebraska in the conferring upon him of the degree of doctor of fine art." See *Chicago Herald*, 14 January 1915.

8. Unknown source, quoted from Jane Clapp, *Art Censorship* (Metuchen, NJ: The Scarecrow Press, 1972), p. 196.

9. Ibid., p. 126.

10. "Former Poor Art Student Wins Victory in Chicago," unidentified newspaper clipping.

11. Ibid.

12. One of Ritman's canvases, entitled *Tea in the Garden* , was reproduced in Section II, Literature and Art, *Chicago Sunday Herald*, 10 January 1915, p. 7.

13. Maude I. G. Oliver, "Gossip of the Artists," *Chicago Sunday Herald*, 27 December 1914.

14. Parker's studio on East Pearson was located on the Near North Side of Chicago, but it was a full ten blocks away from the Art Institute located at 200 South Michigan Avenue, at Adams Street.

15. Oliver.

16. Ibid.

17. "The Fine Arts," *Chicago Herald*, 1 February 1915, p. 10.

18. According to Maurice Ritman, the artist's brother and biographer, Louis was sensitive to his relatively meteoric rise to success in Chicago's art scene. Reportedly, Louis was concerned that his older constituents remain his mentors, and not become his competitors. Maurice Ritman, interview with Richard H. Love, Chicago, June 1987.

19. C. H. Burkholder to Louis Ritman, Chicago, 25 January 1915, Director [Pro Tem] NHC [Newton H. Carpenter] Letter Book, October 17, 1914-April 18, 1915, General Correspondence, Art Institute of Chicago Archives, p. 659.

20. "Chicago's Art Advance to be Told at Dinner," unidentified newspaper clipping, Palette and Chisel Club Log Book, 1906-1915, vol. 2, no. 2, p. 105, Special Collection, Newberry Library, Chicago.

21. "A Tale of a Night for the Actives," *The Cow Bell*, 4, no. 3 (March 1, 1915), p. 2.

22. Ibid.

23. "Art,"unidentified newspaper clipping, Palette and Chisel Club Log Book, 1906-1915, vol. 2, p. 100.

24. Ibid.

25. "Art Awards and Art," unidentified newspaper clipping, c. 27 October 1914.

26. "A Tale of a Night for the Actives."

27. Florence N. Levy, ed., *American Art Annual, 1916* (Washington, DC: The American Federation of Arts, 1916), vol. XIII, p. 95.

28. Wilson Henry Irvine (1867-1936) was born in Byron, Illinois, and studied at the Art Institute of Chicago. First exposed to impressionism at the World's Columbian Exposition of 1893, he traveled and studied in Western Europe after the turn of the century. A crisp delineation of form and lacy intermingling strokes of pure or mixed pigment mark his impressionist mode. He played a leading role in the Chicago art world, including the Palette and Chisel Club, the Cliff Dwellers, and the Chicago Arts Club. By 1918 Irvine had resettled permanently at the art colony of Old Lyme in Connecticut, where he excelled in rendering hazy landscapes. Here, he made friends with other impressionists such as Guy Wiggins, Robert Vonnoh, and Bruce Crane.

29. Levy, *American Art Annual*, 1916, p. 97.

30. Unidentified newspaper clipping, Ritman scrapbook, R. H. Love Galleries Archives, Chicago.

31. "The Fine Arts," *Chicago Herald*, 22 February 1915.

32. Art Institute of Chicago, *Exhibition of Paintings by Louis Ritman, February 23 to March 9, 1915*, exhibition catalog. The brief biography was printed as follows: "Louis Ritman. Born in Odessa, Russia. Studied at the Art Institute of Chicago and at the Beaux-Arts, Paris. Exhibited at the Art Institute of Chicago, The Pennsylvania Academy of the Fine Arts, and at the Salon, Paris. Address, 19 E. Pearson Street, Chicago."

33. The painting entitled *Sun Kissed* was included in the 1987 exhibition and is discussed on page 206 and reproduced as pl. 15-9.

34. "The Fine Arts," *Chicago Herald*, 25 February 1915, p. 10.

35. The *Chicago Herald* noted that in addition to Ritman's solo show, the Art Institute also featured an exhibition of "Etchings by European Masters from The Clarence Buckingham Collection," *Chicago Herald*, 1 March 1915, p. 10.

36. Inez Travers, "Art," unidentified newspaper clipping dated on reverse side in pencil, 24 February 1915, Ritman Scrapbook, R. H. Love Galleries Archives, Chicago.

37. Ibid.

38. Lloyd Wendt and Herman Kogan, *Lords of the Levee* (Garden City, NY: Garden City Publishing Co., Inc., 1943), pp. 322-25.

39. C. H. Burkholder to Mrs. Edwin M. Bruce, Chicago, 23 February 1915, Director [Pro Tem] NHC, Letter Book, October 17, 1914-April 18, 1915, p. 760.

40. "Ritman's Sunlit Gardens," unidentified newspaper clipping, Ritman Scrapbook, R. H. Love Galleries Archives, Chicago.

41. Lena M. McCauley, "Art and Artists," *Chicago Evening Post*, 25 February 1915, p. 6.

42. Ibid.

43. As usual, the show was a joint venture managed by the Art Institute and the Municipal Art League of Chicago.

44. Unidentified newspaper clipping (spring 1915).

45. This exhibition was presented by the Terre Haute Art Association, headquartered at the Emeline Fairbanks Memorial Library in Terre Haute. At that time, Francis M. Stalker was president of the association.

46. Newton H. Carpenter to Louis Ritman, Chicago, 31 March 1915, Director [Pro Tem] NHC, Letter Book, October 17, 1914-April 18, 1915, p. 922 (reverse).

47. C. H. Burkholder (signed for N. H. Carpenter) to Professor D. O. Coate, Chicago, 3 May 1915, Director [Pro Tem] NHC, Letter Book, April 15-June 15, 1916, p. 64.

48. The exhibition at the John Herron Art Institute was entitled "Paintings by Odilon Redon and Louis Ritman" and ran from 6 April through 2 May 1915.

49. "Chase, Indiana Artist, Talks of Modern Art," *The Indianapolis News*, 24 April 1915.

50. Ibid.

51. In the official catalog of the Department of Fine Arts published for the San Francisco Exposition, the brief biography stated that Ritman had studied with Richard Miller; there was no mention of Chase or the Ecole des Beaux-Arts or Frieseke. The catalog listed two paintings known as *Early Morning in a Garden* and *Breakfast*, numbered 419 and 4127 respectively.

52. Kenneth W. Luckhurst, *The Story of Exhibitions* (New York: The Studio Publications, 1951), p. 159.

53. Ibid.

54. Eugene Neuhaus, *The Galleries of the Exposition* (San Francisco, CA: Paul Elder and Co., 1915), p. 83.

55. Richard H. Love, *Theodore Earl Butler: Emergence from Monet's Shadow* (Chicago: Haase-Mumm Publishing Co., Inc., 1985), p. 379.

56. J. Nilsen Laurvik, *Catalogue Deluxe of the Department of Fine Arts, Panama -Pacific International Exposition*, ed. John E. D. Trask and J. Nilsen Laurvik (San Francisco: The Paul Elder and Company Publishers, 1915), vol. 1, p. 20.

57. Louis Weinberg, "Current Impressionism," *The New Republic*, 6 March 1915, p. 124.

58. *Déjeuner* was a title frequently used by Ritman at this time. Although this painting, depicting two figures seated at a table, is similar in subject and style to the ***Déjeuner*** (a single standing figure, ill. 16-3) shown in the Anglo-American exhibition, they are different images and must not be confused.

59. Wendt and Kogan, p. 327.

60. Quoted in Albert Parry, *Garrets and Pretenders: A History of Bohemianism in America* (New York: Dover Publications, Inc., 1960), p. 194.

CHAPTER EIGHTEEN: WAR AND ART

It appears that some time after his arrival in Chicago in 1914 Ritman had taken a teaching position with Werntz at the Chicago Academy of Fine Arts.[1] Little is known of his daily activities at the academy, but it is believed that he taught portrait painting. In this way, not only did he return to his alma mater, but he was also able to raise funds for his trip back to Giverny. The length of time he taught at the academy has not been determined on account of the scant extant records from this period in his career.

Perhaps, then, Ritman's income from teaching and the proceeds from the sale of his paintings were sufficient to finance his return to France. Before leaving Chicago, Ritman made plans with Parker, Reynolds, and other friends to submit paintings he left behind for various forthcoming exhibitions. The exact number of canvases that he entrusted to the care of others is unknown, but there were several.[2]

Some time in the late spring of 1915, apparently undaunted by the sinking of the *Lusitania* and the raging war in France, Ritman left Chicago. Again he took a train to New York and boarded a liner for Europe. Neither the name of the ship nor his port of entry is known, but he arrived safely in France and made his way to Paris. Either at this time or later in the fall, he made arrangements to serve as a volunteer in French military hospi-

tals. It seems Ritman's work in these medical centers — like that of Frieseke, who, in the early months of the war, had also volunteered to serve as an orderly — did not last long. Eventually the soldiers with less serious injuries were treated at medical field stations outside Paris nearer the frontlines, where they could be readily sent back into battle following recovery.[3] In Frieseke's area, this shift of hospital locations had already reduced the need for attendants, and he admitted to Ritman and others that he sought consolation for the sadness of war by returning to intensive painting in Giverny.[4] Perhaps Ritman suffered the same trauma, but if so, he left no record of his feelings. In any instance, he lost no time in getting back to his beloved Giverny, where he found Frieseke already at his easel.

Although most of Ritman's American expatriate friends had returned to the United States or had gone to Paris, a few persevered in Giverny with Monet and Frieseke. One of these was George Biddle, whom Ritman came to know quite well during the summer of 1915 and the following one. Having been acquainted with Frieseke for some time, Biddle was glad to take advice from him as he attempted to learn something about impressionism firsthand in Giverny. Like Ritman, whose foundation was academic, Biddle had a good deal to unlearn as Frieseke taught him in Giverny. "For several years my method of study, after carefully establishing my figures and composition in charcoal, was to draft them in hastily with a bold free wash in a few direct tones of color," Biddle explained. "I would then laboriously, bit by bit, with patient and uninspired integrity, patch my painting together, as if I were completing some enormous picture puzzle. Frieseke, on seeing a fresh, direct and living sketch, remarked that it was the best thing I had done all summer. I argued: 'yes, of course, but I am still a student . . . I must learn how to draw.' "[5] Frieseke understood Biddle's plight in learning the techniques of impressionism just as he had understood Ritman's need for help. Making little attempt to soften his criticism, Frieseke told Biddle: "Granted, George, that you must learn to draw . . . . But surely . . . it would seem to me...that, as you work further on a drawing or a painting, you should improve it, not make it worse!"[6]

For artists like Ritman and Biddle, who could learn from Frieseke's blunt criticism, impressionism became more than a dogmatic technique or skill: it became a general style that could be flexibly adapted to the creative tendencies of each receptive painter. Ritman had been committed to impressionism as a style and as a way of life for several years; Biddle had tried impressionism as an experiment, although he stated that he "fell into it as a duck takes to water, after the mud of Munich, Julien's, and the Pennsylvania Academy."[7] That summer of 1915 (and the following one), spent in the company of Frieseke and Ritman, must have been especially pleasant for Biddle, who surprisingly described it as "comparatively peaceful" in spite of the raging war to the east of them. These men worked in near isolation. Each day they made art and talked about it, also discussing the exhibitions, their patrons, and other artists, especially the master impressionist who worked nearby: "One watched old Claude Monet over his garden wall, as he tramped about among his fruit trees, or sat contentedly on a canvas stool in front of the little wooden bridge that spanned his water lilies."[8] Indeed, they were all impressionists during the summer of 1915, and although Ritman had only recently returned to Giverny, his memories of Chicago were already growing dim. Letters from home kept him aware of such news as the capsizing of the steamer *Eastland* in the Chicago River or Harry Thaw's release from a prison for the insane or gossip about the possibility of America's entry into the war while the seesawing frontlines seemed to move closer to Giverny with each passing day.

Ritman and his friends continued to paint; they posed their models in Frieseke's garden, under trees, or by the Epte, just as they had done when Giverny was crowded with expatriates. One picture that may emanate from this summer is a work known as *Quiet Afternoon* (Phoenix Art Museum, pl. 18-1). In several ways this painting reveals the influences of Frieseke, Miller, and Parker; but the obviousness of this amalgam has been eclipsed by Ritman's own resolution of subject and style. We see two women seated at a table in a garden, as we might expect from Frieseke; we see Ritman's primary model on the left, posed in a manner similar to Miller's; and we see a manner of execution that reveals the influence of Parker; but we also see a distinctive style, which is Ritman's. The most striking feature in Ritman's post–Chicago work is the quiltlike patterning which, executed in broadly brushed shingle strokes, covers the whole surface of the canvas. Expanding the general formula of impressionism to suit himself, Ritman turns every surface and space into decorative pattern, be it an already spotted dress heightened with spots of sunlight, the back of a chair, the still life on the table, or the leafy background. The effect is more like that of a quilt than a mosaic. Owing to his high-key palette, Ritman seems to languish in the luxury of multicolored, multitextured compositions, much in the way he enjoyed helping his father lay out fabric patterns. We can see how much his style has changed by comparing *Quiet Afternoon* with a work such as *Nude in a Chair*, dating from three years earlier when the influence of impressionism was just beginning to appear in his art. Although Ritman's sojourn in America had kept him absent from Giverny for only a few months, upon his return a change manifested itself in his work. Judging from *Quiet Afternoon*, we see that the change was basically stylistic, not radical, but distinct and decidedly more impressionistic and more personal.

One can imagine the discussions that took place among the artists still working at Giverny, especially in the circle of Frieseke, Ritman, and Biddle, as they criticized their own work and that of missing constituents. Not out of arrogant disregard for the war but out of determination to work in their beloved environment, these artists created works that revealed little of the horrors of armies locked in battle night and day to the east of them. As has been seen in the rather ironically titled *Quiet Afternoon*, during the summer of 1915 Ritman continued his predilection for posing his models out of doors, probably in Frieseke's backyard. Another example of this setting is *In Shadow* (ill. 18-1), an oil that was obviously created as a version of *Quiet Afternoon*. Which canvas served as the prototype is unknown, but the styles are quite similar, and both depict a summer scene, indicating that they were done not long apart in time. The most obvious difference is that Ritman's primary model, the figure at the left, is missing in *In Shadow*. The focal point would appear to be the boldly executed still life (a secondary element in *Quiet Afternoon*) on the large table top, which

Ill. 18-1. Louis Ritman. *In Shadow*. 1915. Location unknown. Courtesy of Christie's.

takes up the whole lower half of the image. On the other hand, the still life seems to be no more than a decorative foil for the real focal point, the model across the table. Ritman must have found the model's pose fascinating: with the exception of her dress, the model is identical to the one in *Quiet Afternoon*. We should also notice that from the viewer's perspective, one is not standing but is seated across the table from the subject. This compositional device has been used by Ritman in the past, but in this instance, we are once again reminded of numerous precedent compositions by Degas, who frequently posed subjects staring blankly into space, lost in thought, and aloof from the viewer. In fact, the composition of *Quiet Afternoon* has numerous precedents by Degas, and the format of *In Shadow* is similar to that of an early work by Degas (*Woman with a Bandage*, 1872/73, the Detroit Institute of Arts).[9] Ritman was inspired not only by Degas's compositions but by his skill in draftsmanship and his unique ability to draw figures with a brush, a technique learned from years of academic training. We see, then, that Ritman's inspiration derived from several lingering sources of the nineteenth century.

In August 1915, Germany proposed that a separate peace plan be implemented on the Eastern front. At about the same time, Secretary of State Lansing informed President Wilson of German espionage plans, a report that set off an intense spy inquiry and prompted new fears that the United States was being drawn into a world conflict in spite of its efforts to remain neutral. These worries were not unjustified, since the war seemed to engulf new countries each day; later that month, for example,

Italy declared war on Turkey, while the Russians retreated from Brest Litovsk, allowing the division of Poland into administrative districts.

Although Ritman knew of the holocaust around him from refugees, wounded soldiers, letters, newspapers, and reports from friends, he refused to be driven from Giverny; along with Frieseke, Biddle, and a few others, he remained faithful to his easel and committed to the production of more canvases. Indeed, this was a fine time to depict subjects in the late summer sun or indoors posed near a window. One outstanding example of Ritman's indoor scenes from this time is a large square canvas (39½ x 39½ inches) entitled *Sewing* (pl. 18-2). The general theme, that is, a young woman absorbed in a domestic activity, is well known to us, as is the model and the pose. Here, however, Ritman has virtually surrounded his subject with an amazing variety of patterned surfaces, nearly all of which are decorative dry goods — clothing, drapery, paper, and other materials. His attractive subject is positioned close up in the shallow pictorial space, and although her form seems nearly consumed by the complex array of multicolored stripes, circles, and blotches around her, one is impressed with Ritman's skill in creating a sophisticated and harmonic balance between her form and the limited environment. As in previous examples, the lower half of the composition seems to be made up of small circular forms and sweeping curves, while the upper half consists primarily of stripes and elongated rectangles. The cool palette is quite high in key, and the brushwork is exemplary. Ritman always gives greater emphasis to careful draftsmanship and to the delineation of form and space than to the impasto surface of his canvas. All in all, he has created a superb example of impressionism in depicting his model in a dignified manner in spite of her relatively menial task.

September of 1915 provided no rest for the war-weary. As a result of the gigantic concentration of troops and firepower on both sides, soldiers were being brutally annihilated by the thousands not far to the east of Giverny, and it was not unusual to see horse-drawn carts filled with hungry refugees escaping the frontlines where their homes had been demolished or taken over for military use. The sights and sounds of war were distressing, and young Ritman found it difficult to concentrate on his work. Concentration was not easy for Frieseke either, but he was older and more determined to continue with his career. In this regard, he was a pillar of strength to Ritman and probably to Biddle. At the end of the month, Frieseke wrote to Macbeth, his art dealer in New York, as though business and work were proceeding as usual: "I'm glad to hear of another sale in San Francisco . . . . You may find too many nudes among my last shipment but one cannot paint for the public entirely . . . . I should think Detroit of my home state [Michigan] should . . .try a picture for the musem . . . . I haven't been able to send you many important canvases as they have been bought from the salons—but shall have more in the future.

In October 1915, as Ritman continued to paint in Giverny, friends in Chicago submitted his work to a group show at the Fine Arts Building. Apparently he had become a member of the [Chicago] Artists' Guild as Parker had recommended, since the show was billed as "Special Exhibition of Paintings by the Members of the Artists' Guild."[11] The list of participating artists read, like a Who's Who of Chicago artists; there was Adam Emory Albright (Ivan's father), Bolton Brown, the impressionist Charles W. Dahlgreen, the Indiana dunes painter Frank V. Dudley, the well-known teacher Oliver Dennett Grover, the Indiana impressionists T. C. Steele and L. O. Griffith, the Chicago and Old Lyme impressionist Wilson Irvine, Alfred Juergens, Carl R. Krafft, Lawton Parker, Pauline Palmer, H. Leon Roecker, J. Allen St. John, the painter of Western scenes Birger Sandzen, the figurative impressionist Ada W. Shulz, the landscapist John F. Stacey, the Western genre painter Walter Ufer, Frank A. Werner, and others. Catering especially to the art community, back in 1906, the owners of the Fine Arts Building had established the Fine Arts Building Prize, an annual award of $500 that was given in amounts of $100 for five separate exhibitions.[12] Each guild member was allowed to submit only one entry; Ritman's was an oil, presently known only by its title, *In Pensive Mood*.[13] In spite of the stiff competition, the guild jury, consisting of members only, awarded the first prize to Ritman and honorable mentions to H. Leon Roecker and Pauline Palmer. For Ritman, this well-known prize was one more admirable award to add to his burgeoning list of Chicago credentials.

At about the same time, in October, *The Art Student* published an article on Lawton Parker written by Lena M. McCauley.[14] The writer mentioned Parker's recent award at the Panama-Pacific Exposition and made reference to other credentials, including his presidency of Chase's New York School of Art. She also wrote about his work at Giverny and his alternate home bases in Chicago and Paris, but most intriguing were the words she quoted from himself: "Outside of my painting, I am most interested in bettering the conditions for artists in this country through the correction of jury systems . . . . In Chicago I am most interested in the Artists' Guild where we have an organization composed of and controlled by artists."[15]

Back in Giverny, Ritman and his few expatriate friends continued their production of intimism in spite of the roar of cannons moving ever closer from the east. Later in the fall of 1915, as the German, Austrian, and Bulgarian armies drove deep into Serbia and the French strove valiantly to weaken the German positions around Verdun, Ritman left Giverny for Paris. He brought pictures to finish during the winter season. In Paris he again arranged to serve as a volunteer in a local hospital.[16] The extent of his duties in this role and his activities there are known only from the reminiscences of family members.

Apparently no one in Chicago submitted Ritman's work to the Art Institute Alumni Association exhibition in January 1916 (membership was for former students, not graduates only). Shortly thereafter, however, several paintings were sent to various national shows in America, one of which was the 111th Annual Exhibition of Paintings and Sculpture, held at the Pennsylvania Academy of the Fine Arts in Philadelphia from February through March. Ritman did not win an award for his work, but another Chicago artist, Karl Anderson, who had been in Giverny, received the $300 Lippincott Prize. Ritman and Frieseke were not the only expatriates trying to eke out a living by sending work to America, but most of their friends were back working in New York. Parker had been in Chicago for quite some time, but his activities were not and never had been circumscribed by the parameters of the city. For example, in the spring of 1916, he was elected associate member of the National Academy of Design, but he also wished to return to France.

Numerous artist friends tried to make themselves busy in New York while the war continued to consume their beloved France. Even the Giverny pioneer Theodore Butler remained with his family in New York while he worked on murals at the Vanderbilt mansion at 640 Fifth Avenue. The kind of work that had inspired Ritman and Frieseke in Giverny was a far cry from the work featured in March 1916 at the Anderson Galleries in New York City. This show, entitled "The Forum Exhibition of Modern American Painters," was guided by a board of progressive thinkers—personalities like Alfred Stieglitz, Dr. Christian Brenton, W. H. de B. Nelson, and the art critic Willard Huntington Wright. Intended to be trend-setting, the exhibition included works by such radical modernists as Andrew Dasburg, Arthur G. Dove, Marsden Hartley, Oscar Bluemner, Man Ray, John Marin, Morgan Russell, Stanton Macdonald Wright, and others. Indeed, the Forum Exhibition looked very modern in comparison to the shows with which the Giverny group had been submitting their canvases. Appropriately, the catalog opened with a foreword by W. H. de B. Nelson. "The battle of art today is being keenly contested as any battle in Europe, and reputation, if not men, go down in the process," he explained.[17] Reflecting on his words, one is prompted to remember Ritman's dictum that "War in art means progress," but the battles in art that were waged by the Giverny group were minor skirmishes in comparison with those that were engaged in by Dove, Hartley, Russell, and other avant-garde painters.

Like Ritman, the avant-garde painters were fascinated with color; but unlike him, they took their cues not from impressionism but from a much newer theoretical mode, one that the critic Guillaume Apollinaire had found in the work of Robert Delaunay and called *orphism*. The American expatriates Patrick Henry Bruce and Arthur Burdett Frost, Jr. had ceased following Matisse and began experimenting with orphism, while Morgan Russell and Stanton Macdonald-Wright had launched their own movement, called synchromism, three years earlier in Paris. Synchromism was based upon the orphic principles discussed by Apollinaire, but it was a brand-new theory in art, and even at the Forum Exhibition, some viewers found it too radical. Indeed, these innovators were the "soldiers" engaged in what W. H. de B. Nelson called "the battle of art," not artists like Ritman whose only real enemies were time and the war that threatened his beloved Giverny.

Ill. 18-2. John Sloan. *Six O'Clock*. Oil on canvas, 26 x 32 inches. The Phillips Collection.

If the erstwhile expatriates were unhappy about not working in Europe, few of them saw any real opportunities on the continent when the war threatened to tear it apart and to wrench America from its neutral position. Even a Francophile as devoted to Giverny as Frieseke had written to his dealer Macbeth in New York over a year

earlier, complaining that he had "done very little" because his work had "been so very badly interrupted."[18] The war had grown worse, and Frieseke and Ritman had learned to work in spite of it, yet the threat that they would be overrun by the Germans at any time seemed a

Ill. 18-3. John Sloan. *The Masses*. Cover, June 1914. R. H. Love Galleries Archives, Chicago.

very real prospect. Local newspapers reported that the Verdun area east of Paris was still held by the French, but that the German Crown Prince Frederick William was about to march his one-million-man German Fifth Army against the salient. Ritman's artist friends probably felt a good deal safer in Chicago than he did in Giverny when, at the end of February, the Germans unleashed their offensive and sustained its slow momentum through March and into late spring. Before it was over, this would be the bloodiest military engagement in history and the longest battle of the war; France would lose over 500,000 men, and Germany over 400,000.

War news did not always quickly reach Giverny and it took even longer for military reports to appear in Ameri-

Ill. 18-4. IWW Meeting, Union Square. Photograph. United Press International.

can newspapers, but citizens on both sides of the Atlantic were horrified by the gruesome events. Moreover, many Americans had relatives in battle. There was constant controversy over America's policy of neutrality, but at this point only the most conservative and liberal individuals spoke out against Wilson and Congress. Ritman usually kept his views to himself in discussions with Frieseke and Biddle, but he did express his strong pro-French sentiments. In the United States, a number of artists were devoted socialists. Several of them were associated with Robert Henri's circle, while others had become downright antiwar activists. John Sloan (ill. 18-2), H. J. Glintenkamp, and younger idealists like John Barber were not overly subtle in their images of social protest or about their political alliances, and in some ways their postures indirectly reflected President Wilson's

isolationist policy. On the other hand, artists like Robert Minor, a dedicated socialist turned anarchist and then communist, found unlimited subject matter in contemporary world events. Minor produced brutally satiric images for the socialist magazine *The Masses* (ill. 18-3), whose staff Floyd Dell joined in New York when he left Chicago. In both Chicago and New York, the flames of the socialist art group were fanned constantly by many nonartists who sought reform at any price, one of whom was Emma Goldman (ill. 18-4). In her own war against what she believed to be capitalistic bigotry, Goldman "left a significant number of casualties on its bloody battlefields. Her self-declared battle was a social one, and though she enjoyed the allied forces of *The Masses* and other intellectuals . . . her offensive drives were nearly single-handed combats against the conservative majority."[19] On 20 April 1916, during one of her lectures, Goldman was arrested. Soon she was put on trial and sentenced to a workhouse prison for daring to discuss birth control.

As a Jew from a Chicago ghetto, Ritman sympathized with the plight of the poor as Goldman did, but he could not have joined her circle. Artists like Art Young, who had spent time in Chicago, Robert Minor, H. J. Glintenkamp, Maurice Becker, and others, on the other hand, were willing to use their creative talents for socialist, communist, and anarchist propoganda, especially if it could be directed against the war in Europe. In spite of their general socialist leanings, however, these artists showed great diversity of motivations. Thus, after a schism had resulted in the resignation of Sloan and his group from the radical, even militant, *Masses* constituents, Stuart Davis recalled: "Apparently the battle between *pure art* and *art of ideas* is not merely a contemporary manifestation."[20]

Notes

1. An undated brochure, published by the Chicago Academy of Fine Arts, contains the reproduction of a black and white photograph of the artist and a discussion of his teaching position.

2. The Ritman family has no record of the number of canvases left in Chicago at this time, but there were the so-called residuals of the solo show, which were seen in later Midwest exhibitions. It is believed that both Parker and Reynolds were instrumental in getting Ritman's pictures to shows.

3. Frederick Frieseke to Macbeth Galleries, Paris, Macbeth Gallery Papers, Archives of American Art, Smithsonian Institution, Microfilm Roll No. NMc46, Frame 0195.

4. Ibid.

5. George Biddle, *An American Artist's Story* (Boston, MA: Little, Brown and Co., 1939), p.124.

6. Ibid.

7. Ibid, p. 149.

8. Ibid.

9. In various works Degas depicted a seated model separated from the viewer (also seated) by a table with a still life. See, for example, *Mme Jeantaud Before a Mirror* (Musée d'Orsay, Paris).

10. Frederick Frieseke to Macbeth Galleries, 29 September 1915, Macbeth Gallery Papers, Archives of American Art, Smithsonian Institution, Microfilm Roll. No. NMc46, Frame 0204.

11. This competitive exhibition opened on 11 October and continued until 31 October 1915. The Fine Arts Building was located at 412 South Michigan Avenue, where the galleries were open daily from 8:30 AM to 5:30 PM.

12. Traditionally, the annual $500 Fine Arts Building Prize was given for the exhibitions of the Society of Western Artists ("western" indicating west of the East Coast, not western United States and its romantic subject matter). According to the guild, the "Prizes are to be awarded for the most meritorious and important exhibit made by the artists and craft workers, according to the decision of a jury; the jury for paintings to be selected by a majority vote of the painter members." Honorable mention for this 1915 exhibition went to H. Leon Roecker and the quasi-impressionist Pauline Palmer. See Artist Guild exhibition brochure prepared by the Artist Guild Galleries, Chicago, 1915.

13. This may be the same work as the one previously discussed in chapter 15, *A Pensive Moment*, from the summer of 1913. The canvas illustrated here was sold in Sotheby's New York Sale in December 1988.

14. Lena M. McCauley, "Lawton S. Parker," *The Art Student*, October 1915, pp. 4-8. Published by the students of the Art Institute, the *Art Student* sold for fifteen cents per copy to a small local audience. The article included a portrait photograph of Parker and reproductions of two paintings.

15. Ibid, p. 8.

16. The identity of the hospital is unknown, but his service is accounted for by his biographer, Maurice Ritman. Maurice Ritman, interview with Richard Love, August 1987, R.H. Love Galleries Archives, Chicago.

17. W. H. de B. Nelson, in foreword to *The Forum Exhibition of Modern American Painters,* exhibition catalog (New York: Anderson Galleries, 1916).

18. Frederick Frieseke to Macbeth Gallery, Paris, 31 December 1914; Macbeth Gallery Papers, Archives of American Art, Smithsonian Institution, Microfilm Roll No. NMc46, Frame 0196.

19. Richard H. Love, *John Barber: The Artist, the Man* (Chicago: Haase-Mumm Publishing Co., Inc., 1981), p. 33.

20. Ibid., p. 30. Stuart Davis quoted from James Johnson Sweeney, *Stuart Davis* (New York: Museum of Modern Art, 1945); See also by the same author, *Three American Modernist Painters: Max Weber, Maurice Sterne, Stuart Davis* (reprint ed. New York: Arno Press, 1969), p. 12.

CHAPTER NINETEEN: TOTAL COMMITMENT TO HIGH IMPRESSIONISM

In late 1914, Ritman had left Giverny for America, only to realize in Chicago that in spite of all he had achieved, much still remained to be done. We have seen that by the summer of 1915 he was back in the village, producing excellent work with Frieseke and Biddle at his side. After spending the long winter season in Paris, he longed to return to Giverny in the spring of 1916. It was a calculated risk for all of the expatriates in the village.

Giverny remained physically undamaged by the war, but her citizens were emotionally drained. At first glance, a visitor might have assumed that there was little change in the village, for as photographs taken in Frieseke's garden reveal, life appeared to be running as smoothly as usual. The idealistic resolutions of the residents to carry on in spite of the dangers were not fulfilled without a price. The Givernyites, both the natives and the handful of remaining expatriates, were frightened of the increasing artillery barrage. While a few brave artists spared no effort to produce pictures that bore no traces of war, they had to adjust to the constant threat of violent death and destruction.

Monet's painting performance during the war hinged on how much help he could count on from those around him. He received crucial help from members of his family and the much needed support from Georges Clemenceau

who was at the top of the French Government. With the Butlers in New York, only Blanche was left to assist the old master as he attempted to carry on a painting routine. Claire Joyes notes that had it not been for "Blanche's patient support and Clemenceau's endless encouragement it is doubtful if the aging Monet would have survived these difficult years." Joyes explains that the war had isolated "Blanche and Monet at Giverny and brought many fresh anxieties for both of them." She continues: "Friends and family were scattered, and Monet waited anxiously for news of them . . . . Monet and Blanche waited for the post, listened to communiqués and at night heard the cannon thundering from Beauvais; meanwhile stretcher-bearers went past in an endless stream along the Chemin du Roy, bringing the wounded from the front. Monet followed the army's movements on a map and was resolved, at all cost, not to leave Giverny, although at one stage he considered putting his collection in safety."[1]

At the outset of this ordeal, Monet had thought little about painting, a circumstance of the war that Clemenceau was determined to correct: the great French statesman persuaded Monet to execute a series of large water-lily pictures—mural-sized, in fact—because he wanted them to be installed in a special building. So it was that a new studio had to be built, a project that was nearing completion probably about the time that Ritman reportedly arrived in Giverny in 1916 and resumed his contacts with Frieseke.

Frieseke was so engrossed in his artistic work that he had resolved to leave only with the last troops pulling out of the area. Over the years, Ritman had come to know the Frieseke family quite well. Even prior to his Chicago sojourn, Ritman spent many pleasant hours with his painter friend and his family. After his return to Giverny, their friendship continued as usual, and as in previous years, the Friesekes invited him to dine at their home. Frieseke's garden was still beautiful, just as Ritman remembered it from a few months earlier.

It is uncertain whether the younger artist stayed in Giverny regularly or traveled back and forth to Paris; but some time during the summer, Ritman was able to complete at least a few garden scenes. One work that probably emanates from this time at Giverny is a large square canvas (36 x 36 inches) entitled *Girl in a Garden* (pl. 19-1). Here, ironically, Ritman has succeeded in creating a quiet genre scene that contains no hint of the war that threatened the peace and tranquillity of Giverny. Thus we see that just as Frieseke attempted to execute Giverny images representing "life as usual," Ritman posed his adult model as though she heard no cannon thunder in the distance. As in earlier works, *Girl in a Garden* depicts a single female in a garden, but all similarity ends there. In this painting, a small, nearly imperceptible figure is seated half-hidden in a mass of colorful flowers in the middleground. Ostensibly she remains the focal point of the composition, but her form has been relegated to a near equal position with the environment. Apparently Ritman has radically changed his pictorial formula and the attendant style. Frieseke's influence was already evident in similar works from the previous summer, but it had become paramount during the summer of 1916, as we can see by comparing this work with Frieseke's *Wind and Sun*. It seems that Ritman had finally decided to take the advice that Monet once gave to Lilla Cabot Perry: "Forget what objects you have before you, a tree, a house, a field or whatever." He told her, "merely think, here is a little square of blue, here an oblong of pink."[2] In earlier works, Ritman's backgrounds had consisted of mosaic-like strokes of broken color, which prophesied this change, but *Girl in a Garden* reveals that Ritman was now more interested in the pure "impressionistic" quality of the picture surface than in the genre message — a radical departure for him. Depicting a colorful flower garden in bright summer sunlight, Ritman applied a relatively uniform layer of pigment from a palette of both high-key and saturated hues. To achieve this brilliantly decorative

ensemble, the artist juxtaposed a variety of strokes ranging from squarish shingle types to elongated ones. Especially skillful is his treatment of the foreground foliage, and once again, his method of application reminds us of Frieseke's or, in this instance, Monet's. In fact, in writing about Monet, the enthusiastic champion of impressionism Camille Mauclair might equally well have been writing about Ritman when he stated that the artist brought about "complete interfusion of drawing and coloration by accumulated touches of pure colour, disposing them in due perspective and modelling them, so to speak with the paint of his brush; touches, spots, irregular dabs, confidently dashed on, never applied in the stiff and frigid manner of the pointillists."[3]

The setting in *Girl in a Garden* is undoubtedly a Giverny garden resembling Monet's, but it is more likely that Ritman posed his model in Frieseke's garden nearby. It is also interesting to note that the whole composition is designed in actual and implied horizontal planes running parallel to the picture plane: they begin with the flat wall and its rectangular window shapes and end with the foreground path. Despite all the difficulties, Ritman's return to Giverny, where Monet, Frieseke, Biddle, and a few other painters worked in relative seclusion, resulted in one of his finest demonstrations of impressionism.

Like his Giverny constituents, Ritman was preoccupied with the war, but judging from a picture called *On the Epte* (pl. 19-2), just the opposite seems true. In this and other works from the period, Ritman's mood seems calm, like Biddle's, and unaffected by the wartime horrors raging not far away. Certainly one of his most beautiful compositions, this rather bucolic image exudes a mutual balance of natural and aesthetic harmony. Once again, Ritman abandons his old pictorial format to exploit a new style, which is more closely allied to that of Monet. Although Monet had been inspired by the Epte for many years, Ritman used the river as a reference point less frequently than did some of his constituents who regularly posed their models on its banks. As in *Girl in a Garden*, Ritman relegates his model to a lesser position in the middleground. With her pattern-covered form lost in the foliate texture of the background, the subject also becomes a less important focal point, but in this Ritman follows the ideal impressionist doctrine. Again, as in the case of *Girl in a Garden*, the artist has lined up the flat planes of his composition parallel with the picture plane. If the lovely subject and her boat seem to dissolve into the rich tapestry of the background foliage, the broadly executed foreground provides a textural balance to the decorative scheme. The mood of this masterful ensemble is quiet, in terms of both subject matter and limited color range, yet the work remains high-keyed. Indeed, *On the Epte*, created in the shadow of war, becomes one of Ritman's finest examples of pure impressionism.

Judging from his pictures, one might speculate that in some strange way the war prompted Ritman to paint with a freedom that he had never experienced before. Whether because of the turmoil around him or simply because of an evolution in his style, Ritman purged all references to academicism from his methodology. Working outside the academic limits, Ritman expressed himself fully, uniquely as an impressionist. One canvas that shows his stylistic expansion is a vertical composition known simply as *Woman Gardening* (pl. 19-3). A striking departure even from the previously discussed works, the painting indicates that Ritman's style had changed drastically over quite a short period. As never before, the artist covers his canvas with rich, luscious pigment. This brilliantly colored work demonstrates a striking broken-color technique, strongly influenced by Monet and actually leaning somewhat toward the neo-impressionism frequently seen in the work of Signac's still influential circle.

In *Woman Gardening*, Ritman continues to isolate the figure, but now the woman is older and pushed irreverently into the middleground. No longer important as an individual, she is distant enough to remain featureless, but her purpose is obvious as she walks slowly in her luxuriant flower garden. We see that the overall theme is similar to that of a work from the previous summer, *Gathering Flowers*, but a comparison of the two pictures reveals strikingly different styles and images. In *Woman Gardening* there is no hint of intimism: an obsession to record the beauty of a lovely young lady has been replaced by a fascination with surface and color—brilliant, high-keyed, and full color, brushed in thick dabs, strokes, and crescent swirls to provide a mosaiclike summer fantasia for the leisure activities of his genre figure. Ritman provides his model some dignity of individual form, but it is clear that in works like these from the summer of 1916, he has no interest in giving his figures individuality—in these works he has finally become an impressionist in the manner of Monet (pl. 19-4).

That Ritman was totally committed to this new style of high impressionism is demonstrated in another vertical canvas entitled *Picking Flowers* (pl. 19-5). Here we probably see the same model in the same flower garden. This time the subject is brought much closer to the viewer, but she still remains faceless; the focus of the image is not on her femininity. Once again, what is important to Ritman here is the surface of his canvas, the richness of pigment, and his skill in producing art through the effects of pigment, color and light. Bringing an otherwise natural mixture of color and form into an arbitrary, nearly

abstract, realm of subjectivity, Ritman uses the subject as a mere reference point in his brilliant display of broken color. Close examination of the surface reveals the artist's amazing technical skill and his consummate understanding of impressionism. The figure is executed in a brushy, spontaneous manner while other areas of the canvas show a similar surface, indicating that he worked into his impasto surface from a uniform layer of thinner pigment. This technique had little to do with the precedents set by Renoir and a lot to do with those set by Monet.[4] In certain areas, we find hints of dragging pigment and a scumbling procedure, but mostly Ritman applied his dabs and strokes with fully loaded brushes, even with a palette knife here and there. As before, we must assume that in this work Ritman tried consciously to adopt Monet's style. Certainly he worked en plein air as usual, perhaps setting his canvas aside for slight touchup later. There is no doubt that Ritman's skill enabled him to create works of figurative impressionism that were quite superior to those executed by many of his constituents; on the other hand, we must not lose sight of the fact that his significant contribution came more than forty years after the debut of impressionism in Paris. Biddle was in Giverny during the summer of 1916, and he spent a good deal of time with both Ritman and Frieseke. Once when Biddle jokingly announced that "this nude of mine with black stockings looks nearly as good as a Degas," Frieseke angrily replied: "No, it does not. It looks—almost—like a Biddle."[5]

Ritman and other brave expatriates made every effort to remain productive as artists, but World War I made it nearly impossible to paint. As fall brought 1916 to a close, Ritman and a few others returned to Paris. Back in the city, they found it difficult to work on their Giverny canvases when they could do so much to help the war effort. To this end, Ritman resumed his volunteer work in a local hospital. By the end of January 1917, Germany had made it clear to President Wilson that "unrestricted submarine war" would begin on the high seas. Soon the United States terminated relations with the German government. Determined to remain neutral, however, even after American ships had been sunk by German submarines, the administration and Congress refrained from military action. By the first week of April 1917, there was no alternative but to declare war! President Wilson's patience had paid off; by this time only the most radical pacifists—some of whom were artists at the *Masses* in New York—were against an official call to arms. "It is probable that many did not understand exactly the ideals that actuated Wilson, but nine persons out of ten believed it absolutely necessary to fight."[6]

With the United States joining the war, the expatriate

Pl. 18-2. Louis Ritman. *Sewing*. Oil on canvas, 39½ x 39½ inches. Private Collection. Courtesy R. H. Love Galleries, Chicago.

Pl. 19-1. Louis Ritman. *Girl in a Garden*. Ca. 1916. Oil on canvas, 36 x 36 inches. Private Collection. Courtesy R. H. Love Galleries, Chicago.

Pl. 19-2. Louis Ritman. *On the Epte*. Oil on canvas, 32 x 32 inches. Pearce Collection. Courtesy R. H. Love Galleries, Chicago.

Pl. 19-3. Louis Ritman. *Woman Gardening*. Oil on canvas, 36¼ x 28¾ inches. Fifield Collection. Courtesy R. H. Love Galleries, Chicago.

Pl. 19-4. Louis Ritman. *Reflected Light*. 1916. Oil on canvas, 36 x 29 inches. Mr. and Mrs. L. J. Berger Collection. Courtesy R. H. Love Galleries, Chicago.

Pl. 19-5. Louis Ritman. *Picking Flowers*. 1916. Oil on canvas, 26¼ x 28¾ inches. Private Collection. Courtesy R. H. Love Galleries, Chicago.

Pl. 19-6. Louis Ritman. *In a Garden*. 1917. Oil on canvas, 32 x 32 inches. Geist Collection. Courtesy R. H. Love Galleries, Chicago.

Pl. 19-7. Louis Ritman. *Woman Before Mirror*. 1918. Oil on canvas, 36 x 36 inches. New Britain Museum of American Art.

world in Paris became increasingly involved in providing entertainment and other kinds of support, first to American volunteers and then to the regular troops of the American Expeditionary Forces in France. Numerous expatriates had friends or relatives serving in the military forces or in supporting services such as the American Red Cross.

The Friesekes had friends and relatives both in military service and among American Red Cross workers. Birthday parties and similar events became occasions for all generations of American expatriate families to entertain American soldiers in France. Ritman left no written accounts of these events, but Frieseke's daughter Frances has provided a vivid description of one such party given at her aunt's place in Paris, where a student of Isadora Duncan gave a dance performance for American officers and soldiers. Not to be outdone in patriotic fervor by her elders, the three-year-old Frances imitated Isadora Duncan's student the best way she could and was rewarded with thunderous applause. One of the American generals present on the occasion remarked that there was a need for such entertainment in wartime and sent Frances a doll.[7]

Overwhelmed by nostalgic memories of an idyllic life back home, many a member of the fresh contingents of American troops in France greatly appreciated a chance to meet expatriate Americans. Ritman made many such acquaintances during his volunteer service. He was especially friendly with Chicago soldiers. A chance encounter between an American soldier and Mrs. Frieseke on the Champs Elysées in Paris resulted in the following conversation as reported later by her daughter, Frances:

> SOLDIER: "You don't mean to say that you're living over here and you don't have to?" He looked half stunned. My mother [Mrs. Frieseke] smiled.
> MRS. FRIESEKE: "What part of America do you come from?" she asked.
> SOLDIER: "I live in Ovid, Illinois. You're going back aren't you?"
> MRS. FRIESEKE: "Well, perhaps later on, we may."
> SOLDIER: "It's the nicest little town in the whole United States. Golly! I wouldn't take half of France, I wouldn't take the whole of France for that one little house in Ovid." He turned away, abruptly touching his cap.[8]

In Paris, Ritman and other artists who stayed there until spring had no opportunities to show or sell their work. Nevertheless, they remained optimistic, making as many pictures as possible while they waited for the war to end. Still working as a hospital volunteer, Ritman finished a few canvases and lined them up against his studio wall.[9]

In New York, only eleven days after Wilson declared war on Germany, the newly organized Society of Independent Artists held its huge premier exhibition in the Grand Central Palace. The hierarchy of the society was made up of a strange mixture of conservatives and liberals ranging from the President William Glackens (a former member of the Ash Can circle turned impressionist) to Vice President Charles Prendergast (brother of the neo-impressionist Maurice Prendergast), Treasurer Walter Pach (Armory Show organizer), and other members. Directors included important names like George Bellows, Rockwell Kent, Man Ray, and some from Stieglitz's group—John Marin, Joseph Stella, and others. The society and its events were modeled after the *Société des Artistes Indépendants* in Paris and its annual exhibition; but carrying the influence even farther, the American Society elected several important French artists as directors, a move that it hoped would bring experience, credibility, and prestige to the enterprise. Indeed, at the outbreak of the war, many of these artists, like Ritman, had left France, but unlike Ritman, they had remained in America. There was Marcel Duchamp, whose *Nude Descending the Staircase* still inspired serious discussion about modern art, and Francis Picabia, an intellectual artist known also to be subversive, skeptical, and occasionally involved in scandal. For all of his skepticism, however, Picabia believed that the American public's traditional interest in something new would help the cause of the modernists. Jacques Villon was another French director who had once contributed drawings to *Le Chat Noir, Gil Blas*, and other reviews and avant-garde magazines that had inspired the organizers of *The Masses*. Now, however, Villon was a leading member of avant-garde French groups and experimented with Robert Delaunay in *Section d'Or*, a gathering concerned with theoretical application for the expansion of Cubist principles.[10] Although these forward-looking French artists had not yet become confirmed French expatriates in the United States, as Ritman was an American expatriate in France, they understood modern art and its direction, and their chances of becoming famous were even better in New York than Ritman's were in Paris. Of course, some commentators feared that just as the Americans had gone to Paris to work in the mecca of modern art, certain French artists were beginning to look to New York as the new center of world culture, especially now that Paris had buckled under the impact of the war. No, said others, Paris would not fall from its lofty cultural plateau; in the minds of most observers, even Americans, Paris would never lose hold on its position of cultural leadership.

Ritman's activities in 1917 are obscure; apparently he spent most of his time in Paris. How he made a living is unknown. One assumes, however, that he had saved enough from the sales of his paintings in Chicago to remain in France at this time. Although the frontlines never reached Paris, he balanced his time between volunteer service and painting. Ritman did his best painting en plein air, but it was not easy to get to the Paris suburbs where trees and shrubs provided a Giverny-like setting, so he found the best alternative in the city's parks. We may speculate that as a result of wartime conditions and transportation difficulties, Ritman frequented the parks and gardens that were located closer to Montparnasse, where he lived. A short distance north of Montparnasse, were the beautiful and spacious Luxembourg Gardens, with their imposing Palace of Luxembourg, the showcase of paintings purchased by the French government. It is quite possible that Ritman painted there.

One of Ritman's most interesting works probably emanates from his painting routine in the Parisian parks at this time: a square canvas entitled *In a Garden* (pl. 19-6). Here as never before, he concentrates not on one female, but on two figures: one, his regular model, is standing nearly in the center of the picture space; the other, a man (perhaps a self-portrait), is seated on a bench at the far left. This is unusual—a different scene, a different composition. Taking his cue from Degas, Ritman provides a snapshot glimpse of a young couple who appear to have paused for a moment on a Sunday afternoon stroll in a Parisian park. This is a decidedly candid view, almost as if it illustrated a precise moment in the relationship of two lovers. The man appears to be bored or lost in thought as he remains seated on the bench; the young woman, having just risen from her place next to him, is attracted by something beyond our view. Our interest is piqued—this genre is so unique that we speculate about its iconography. Did Ritman intend a subtle meaning here? Does the male figure prophesy the mood of disillusionment that will soon overtake numerous American painters? Does the standing female symbolize Paris, with her attention riveted on something beyond her immediate environs, namely, the war?

If this is overspeculation, we see the facts of the image: Ritman has employed a high-key palette, but one in which the hues are severely limited. Emphasizing the blues and purples of impressionism, he creates a mosaiclike leafy backdrop executed with elongated strokes of two colors, blue and yellow. The result is a typical view-limiting curtain, which vibrates and shimmers in the sunlight and seems to swirl up and around the standing woman, the focal point of the picture, who appears to have turned her back on her escort. Ritman emphasizes his protagonist in another way—by spotlighting her in bright sunshine, while relegating the male figure to the shadowy left. He flecks each figure with Renoiresque sunspots, a device he has used earlier, but clearly focuses on the lovely pink flesh of the young woman. The brushwork in this painting is outstanding in that it ranges from the skillful handling of the figure's drapery to the broadly rendered neo-impressionistic strokes of the leafy backdrop to the expressionistic treatment of the ground plane in the lower right spandrel of the picture. *In a Garden* is a very contemporaneous view of Ritman's environment, one still clinging to the vicissitudes of the good life in France, a scene ostensibly unaffected by war.

While eastern France was being crushed by the Germans in 1917, no one was safe, not even in sleepy Giverny, where Monet and a few of his American counterparts were trying to paint. Frieseke had the added misfortune of his wife's illness, a condition probably made worse by wartime shortages. Leaving their daughter, Frances, with Mrs. Frieseke's sister's family, the Friesekes went to Dax, a resort on the Mediterranean coast of France, for a period of convalescence during the summer of 1917. Theodore Butler and the Monet-Hoschedé family vacationed in this town in the early days of the Giverny art colony. When Mrs. Frieseke's health improved in a few months, Frances rejoined her parents, and before long they all returned to Giverny.[11]

It is quite likely that Ritman also spent the summer of 1917 in Giverny, as he had done in 1915 and 1916. He hoped to complete at least a few pictures. Whatever he did was always accomplished against a background of cannon thunder.

The second Aisne offensive had resulted in a French defeat and a recorded loss of some 130,000 French soldiers. Afterwards, an extensive mutiny had broken out among the French forces, but the unrest was soon quelled and the war continued. There would be a third Aisne assault, but for the time being, Allied strategists were deeply involved in stalling the German diversionary attack at Arras.

No paintings by Ritman have been positively identified as having been executed in the summer and fall of 1917, although a few seem to fit that period in terms of style. It was perhaps at this time in Giverny that Ritman painted a war propaganda scene, intended to symbolize the friendship between the United States and France. He showed a French soldier and an American soldier shaking hands in their unified war effort.[12]

Ritman was not the only artist to make a statement on canvas about the war. Indeed, both at home and abroad, numerous pictures were made that dealt, to some degree, with America's involvement in Europe's long conflict.[13] In distinct contrast with rather calm scenes like Hassam's *Early Morning on Fifth Avenue, May 1917*, or C. B. Falls's *Books Wanted*, there were allegories like Edwin Blashfield's *Carry On*, or battlefield scenes like Harvey E. Townsend's *A Wounded Torch*, Wallace Morgan's *Americans Mopping Up in Cierges*, and J. André Smith's *On Hill 204—Southwest of Château-Thierry*. Less brutal works were produced by George Harding, Maxfield Parrish, George Bellows, and Henry Reuterdahl; but although those who were most moved by the war tried valiantly to make some of their art propagandist, seldom was it truly as successful as their regular efforts.

Back in Chicago on Tuesday, 8 January 1918, the *Chicago Daily Tribune* reported that George K. Spoor, the filmmaker and owner of Essanay Studios had offered plans "of a trench machine" for frontline soldiers to the United States War Department. This was the kind of war news that had dominated Chicago newspapers for many months, but occasionally there were art events that inspired headlines. Such was the case in January when the Art Institute mounted its first Alumni Exhibition. In a preview article, Chicago art critic Louis Bargelt reported that the show consisted of paintings and sculpture by artists who had "been students in the school during some time of its existence," which had begun thirty-nine years earlier.[14] "Many distinguished names may be found in the list of exhibitors," the critic wrote. "There is George Gray Barnard, the sculptor of the much discussed Lincoln statue . . . Arthur B. Davies . . . Albert Sterner, Orson Lowell . . . and the Leyendeckers among the illustrators."[15] In a subsequent article, Bargelt was more specific about the art, reporting that visitors would see "*Abandoned* by Wilson Irvine, an Illinoisan by birth . . . . H. S. Hubbell, who is represented in the Luxembourg, Paris, . . . Victor Higgins." Briefly describing certain paintings, she singled out a "quiet, sunny landscape" by Carl R. Krafft and "one of the most exquisite nudes I have ever seen" by Louis Ritman.[16] Thus, in spite of his continued expatriate status, even during wartime Ritman kept his reputation alive in America by having a friend submit one of the works still left from his solo debut at the Art Institute or by sending an occasional canvas back across the Atlantic.

In her discussion of the alumni show, Bargelt offered a kind of overview of the current art world—"a brief survey," as she put it: "Art conditions in the world at the start of this year 1918 shows no decided change over the last three years except that prospects are perhaps more vague and indefinite than before. Still, in the eyes of optimists, there is much ground for hope in the renewed activities of France and England. In 1914 the art treasures of Paris, and London, and Venice, and Antwerp were hurriedly embedded in sandbags, hidden in cellars, buried deep in the earth. There they still remain. Public exhibitions of art have practically ceased in Paris. There have been few salons since 1914 . . . . Recently, however, in both Paris and London, private and public art auctions have brought high prices . . . . In America art conditions are still about normal. Indeed they might even be considered above normal, for the highest price ever received for a portrait will be paid to John Singer Sargent by the executors of Sir Hugh Lane for the portrait of President Wilson."[17]

When the German spring offensive of 1918 reached its full force under General Ludendorff, the threat to Giverny became greater than ever. In March the Germans captured Peronne, Noyon, and other key cities directly east of Giverny. Less than a month later, they took Armentières. If in the past it had been difficult to maintain a disciplined painting schedule, now it was nearly impossible to work as the roar of heavy guns gained in intensity. As we have seen, Frieseke and Ritman showed a tenacity to paint in Giverny that had persisted throughout the war. Though only three years old at the time, Frances Frieseke remembered the anxiety and uncertainty overtaking area residents.

One morning her father was attempting to pose his young French model, Louise, for a painting. The girl was distracted by the bursts of artillery fire.

> "Louise, if you jump so every time the cannon booms," gently remonstrated my father, "I will not be able to paint. Head a lit-tle bit this way; no, not so far; that's it."
> My father drew back from his canvas and squinted, looked at the frightened little model, whose pretty head tilted charmingly against the sunny background, and rubbed his brush on the pallette. Then carefully, very carefully, he pointed his brush to the middle of his canvas. "Very difficult!" he murmured. "Now, don't move, don't—hum— there!" Boom! went the cannon.
> "Ah! mon Dieu! oh! pardon Monsieur!" Louise settled again, her lips pouted slightly in spite of herself and her lashes were shiny with tears.
> "Your head, not so tense," corrected my father. "Let it droop more; not so much—that's it! You are a good little model Louise. Now just this little—Oh, dear!"
> "Ah! mon Dieu! Oh! pardon Monsieur!" quavered Louise, arranging her drapery.
> The gate clanged. Two ragged little children ran

in and addressed me."We want some shoes please, we are refugees, the cart is right outside the door. Can we see your Mama?"I was used to such appeals; for days, the road had been covered by a long procession of carts of every description. The horses, sweating and winded, tottered slowly on, carrying thin, pale women, nude babies, and hungry children. We disappeared in the house.

"Ah! mon Dieu! oh! par—" sobbed Louise, her blonde head resting on her knees. This was painting under difficulties. "You may rest a while," sighed my father. "Go and find Madame and see what she can do."[18]

Apparently Ritman shared such experiences with Frieseke—at least part of the time. In spite of such wartime distractions and uncertainties, he knew that above all, his career must continue. At this time, Ritman received considerable praise for the first major showing of his work in New York City. In this important debut, he shared the spotlight with another expatriate, impressionist William H. Singer, in a two-artist show presented by Folsom Galleries at 396 Fifth Avenue. The exhibition opened 16 February and continued through 6 March 1918. Exactly how Ritman came to make arrangements with Folsom Galleries to show his work is unclear, but he was fortunate to be represented by such a prestigious art establishment (ill. 19-1).

Singer had spent most of his expatriate career in Norway, not Paris, but Ritman may have known him through their mutual friend Walter Griffin (ill. 19-2). It is also possible that Folsom Galleries intended nothing more than to contrast the work of the two painters, since this exhibition of impressionism consisted of tonalist Norwegian landscapes and brightly colored figurative subjects from France (ill. 19-3). The show was also good publicity for Ritman because he was associated with Singer, a highly respected associate of the National Academy and a well-exhibited painter whose works were included in the permanent collections of numerous museums.[19] In addition to reviews of their work in the New York press, various Chicago newspapers gave accounts of the exhibition. A writer for the *Chicago Evening Post* reported that Singer's "scenes are deep in snow and the tranquility of a windless winter day rests upon them." He pointed out that Ritman had studied at the Ecole des Beaux-Arts and described his *Harmony in Lavender and Yellow* as showing "a young woman seated at a window through which is obtained a glimpse of a garden. A table with a tea set and fruit dish is in the foreground."[20] Ritman's *Tea in*

The Folsom Galleries

396 FIFTH AVENUE, NEW YORK

(Opposite Tiffany's)

REQUEST THE HONOR OF YOUR PRESENCE AT THE

SPECIAL EXHIBITION

OF THE RECENT WORKS OF

WILLIAM H. SINGER, A. N. A.

AND

LOUIS RITMAN

FROM

SATURDAY, FEBRUARY 16th, TO WEDNESDAY, MARCH 6th, INCLUSIVE 1918

Ill. 19-1. Cover of the catalog published for the exhibition at Folsom Galleries in 1918. R. H. Love Galleries Archives, Chicago.

the Garden, which had been exhibited in his solo show at the Art Institute, was also seen at the Folsom event, a fact that leads one to conclude that the Ritman selection was a mix of old and new works.[21] This deduction is confirmed by another work included in the New York show, an unusual oil known as *Mother and Child*, probably executed four years earlier and shipped to Chicago with the works for his 1915 solo show.

Back in Giverny and Paris, Ritman attempted to make new pictures for exhibitions, but the constant impact of war made a daily routine nearly impossible. People fervently longed for the end of the war. Finally, in June 1918, good news arrived from the front: the American Second Division had joined the French to smash a well-planned German advance at Château-Thierry. In July, the German invaders gained little ground against the combined French and American armies in the second battle of the Marne. During this period Ritman often stayed in Paris, but the city was a dull reflection of its former self. Art, once an integral part of Parisian culture, no longer seemed important. Like his French comrades, Ritman longed for peace. In the meantime, he did not relent in his efforts to make images of the good life, by now only a distant memory. Unfortunately, in this hectic period he did not indicate when or where his canvases were executed. Only a few works from this time are dated, and these provide stylistic clues that allow us to make conjectures about the execution of others.

An exemplary composition dated 1918 is a square work entitled *Woman before Mirror* (pl. 19-7). Seated and facing the viewer with her arms folded, the subject is partially reflected in a large wall mirror, a favorite motif for the artist and one also employed by Degas and by Ritman's former neighbor Theodore Butler. Positioned in this manner, the mirror expands the visual dimension of the room, functioning in the way that windows had in some of Ritman's earlier works. Again the artist lines up all of the objects in the room flat against the wall, parallel to the picture plane. Perhaps the most notable stylistic feature is a certain broadening of the brushwork. Ritman's system of broken color is still pronounced, but his juxtaposed strokes are larger and bolder, approaching regularity. We find here a system that is far different from the expressive manipulation of pigment seen in Ritman's earlier Giverny works. This work proves that his period of high impressionism was exceedingly brief.

As the war enveloped his world, Monet stayed at his estate in Giverny, where he painted the irises in his colorful garden. He worked on other flower subjects too, the water lilies, for example, and the wisteria that climbed over the Japanese footbridge. In spite of the dangers of war, the presence of Monet in Giverny served as an inspiration to Ritman and other expatriates. The Butler family maintained close ties with Monet and even became involved in wartime relief for French artists: apparently Marthe Butler forwarded money from their friends the Hales in Boston to Paul Signac in France, as is evident from the following excerpt from Marthe's letter: "Signac sends me his sincere and heartfelt thanks for the money and tells me that he will send a good part of it to poor artists who have been taken prisoner since the beginning of the war and who have been suffering terribly!"[22]

In Paris, Ritman, his model, and perhaps some of his

Ill. 19-2. Walter Griffin. *Morning Sunlight, Stroudwater River, Portland, Maine.* 1921. Oil on canvas, 33 x 36 inches. Private Collection. Courtesy R. H. Love Galleries, Chicago.

friends boarded a train for Giverny when they were lucky enough to find one running. Getting back and forth was so difficult that on several occasions during the war years, Ritman found himself stranded either in the city or in the country. That transportation was frequently a difficult matter was discovered by another Chicago painter, Alson Skinner Clark, about this time. Clark, who had painted in Giverny many times over the years, had been commissioned as an ensign in the Navy and sent to Paris, where he specialized in aerial photography. His train to Paris was stalled by a German raid during a blackout at night, and Clark was forced to walk. Later he reported: "All along the route, the work of the anti-aircraft guns were in operation, and the Bosches were peppering down the bombs thick and fast . . . it scarcely occurred to me to think of being hit, for I was so mad because I had to walk in the thick darkness. My intense anger and hatred of the Germans was uppermost in my mind, I hated them for everything, especially just that moment."[23]

A painting that Ritman probably executed in Giverny in the summer of 1918 is another square canvas entitled simply *Nude, Study No. 1* (pl. 19-8). Here, as in *Woman before Mirror*, we note the distinct broadening of brushwork and the same horizontal layerlike treatment of the water in the background. Once again Ritman exploits the sunspot effect, but these bright impasto patches of color tend to resemble the large strokes which make up the surrounding foliage. In a pose seen before, the model's arms are raised as she dresses her hair; her rather healthy form is silhouetted against three distinct horizontal zones — the foreground, the boat, and the water. Her organic vertical form is repeated in the sweeping tree trunks at the right. The colors are bright and achieved boldly, emphasizing the effect of sunlight, but Ritman's style has undergone an obvious change, as is evident in the somewhat deeper pigment applied in broader, flatter patchlike patterns.

In spite of the war, Giverny had retained its charm. Frieseke's old-fashioned garden was still an outstanding setting for intimism, and even the walls around Ritman's cottage seemed to enclose a kind of bucolic environment protected from the war. Indeed, the nearby hills and fields were no longer dotted with parasol-covered easels and carefree painters as in prewar times. Ritman made use of indoor space when necessary. An example of his indoor paintings is a canvas known as *Lady by a Window* (pl. 19-9). This rather transitional work is signed and dated 1918 at the lower right. Here we see the back of Ritman's model as she dresses standing by a table. In the middleground an open window provides a glimpse of foliage. The same plant stand and potted plant that are seen in other works form a striking compositional device that draws our attention to the focal point of the picture. Although he makes use of the direct light source as usual, Ritman's palette is deeper-keyed. Once again we notice broadly executed planes, with certain areas achieved with a palette knife. In general, the scene is composed of the same elements that Ritman had used for several years, but his palette and method of execution have changed from the typical broken-color method of impressionism to a Cézannesque manner. In the production of his pictures, Ritman was not theoretically driven as Cézanne was, but the older master's style apparently moved him, because from about this time, we see the growing influence of his style as it slowly replaces Ritman's impressionism (pl. 19-10). Ritman had already acted upon the advice that Cézanne had given Louis Le Bail; namely, "go and study Veronese and his technique in the Louvre." Now, however, Ritman was more interested in Cézanne's aesthetic resolutions than in those of the Italian master (pl. 19-11). Like Cézanne, Ritman had no use for theories that could not be translated into imagery, for as Cézanne once wrote to Emile Bernard, theories "are always easy; it is only the proof of what one thinks that presents serious obstacles."[24]

By October 1918, newspapers reported that the end of the war was imminent. The Germans still staged impressive drives, but their momentum had slackened. Under General John Pershing, the American forces held a seventeen-mile front from Forges on the Meuse River to the center of the Argonne Forest. It was about this time that Sergeant Alvin C. York from Fentess County, Tennessee — armed with only an automatic revolver and a Springfield rifle — captured a fortified hill, killing 20 Germans, forcing 132 others to surrender, and taking 35 machine guns. Reflecting on York's courage, Marshal Foch said that his action was "the greatest thing accomplished by any private soldier of all the armies of Europe."

Ill. 19-3. William Singer. *Quiet Meadow.* Pastel on board, 18 x 21½ inches. Private Collection. Courtesy R. H. Love Galleries, Chicago.

All Americans, but especially the expatriates in France like Ritman, were proud of York and the Pershing forces. Everywhere newspapers carried glowing reports of heroism and optimistic predictions of a decisive Allied victory. In the United States, George Creel, former editor of the *Kansas City Independent*, and now chairman of the Committee on Public Information, fueled the hot flames of anti-German vengeance by publishing millions of hate pamphlets.[25] In Paris, the war-weary population dreamed of liberation at the hands of the American forces, while artists, including Ritman, dreamed of the good old days, the resumption of the spring and fall salons, and even the critics' reviews.

By late October 1918, the Argonne Forest was cleared and the American forces had advanced ten miles. At the same time, the German fleet mutinied at Kiel, and soon revolution in military ranks broke out in Munich. At the beginning of November, the Americans and the French moved forward to Sedan; the Belgians forced the Germans out of Ostende; and finally on 11 November 1918, at 11:00 AM, the armistice was signed, and World War I was over!

The news of peace reached Ritman and the few remaining American expatriates in Giverny through the voice of the village crier. Ritman was working in his studio and Frieseke was painting in his walled garden with the same intensity that he had displayed at the outbreak of the war. Frieseke and his wife were in the garden when they heard the fanfare of old Père Sauce's drum. The ancient messenger of Giverny went marching by with all the appearance of military pomp in spite of his debilitating age, announcing the armistice. Ritman and nearly every citizen in Giverny began celebrating. The whole Frieseke household, servants and the omnipresent Madame Honette included, broke into a spontaneous dancing and hugging spree on the lawn.[26] It was time for a massive outpouring of patriotism.

Great rejoicing began throughout Europe and America. The European edition of the *New York Herald* of Tuesday, 12 November, reported that "a thousand church bells clanged out the news in joyous peals at eleven o'clock yesterday morning, while 1,200 guns told in thundering tones of the victorious end of the war . . . . Soon the streets were avenues of color, flags were waving from every apartment in the city, and the physiognomy of Paris was transformed as though by a magic wand. Who shall describe the delirious demonstrations of popular joy." In New York and Chicago, throngs celebrated victory with great ticker-tape parades, and artists in both cities captured the unique beauty, color, and excitement of it all.

Before sunrise on the morning of 13 December 1918, the presidential liner *George Washington* and its convoy came into view at the port of Brest in France. Later an impressive luncheon party for important dignitaries took place aboard ship. The guests included President Wilson's daughter, Margaret, who had been entertaining troops in Europe. By one o'clock shore batteries thundered deafening greetings to Woodrow Wilson, former schoolmaster and twenty-eighth president of the United States, the first American president to set foot on European soil during his term in office. From that point onward, Europeans demonstrated nothing short of hysteria wherever President Wilson appeared. Among military bands, marine guards, banners, the press, and throngs cheering at the top of their lungs for "the Champion of the Rights of Man" and "the Apostle of International Justice," there were proud American expatriates who felt that they had contributed their fair share to the campaign that ended

the reign of the Hohenzollerns, the architects of modern Germany. The demonstration of appreciation for President Wilson in Brest seemed small in comparison with that in Paris. Thousands of immaculately uniformed French troops lined the guests' entry to the city, while thousands more crowded behind to get a glimpse of the American savior. "No one ever heard such cheers," reported the British journalist William Bolitho, who stated that he had seen General "Foch pass, Clemenceau pass, Lloyd George, generals, returning troops, banners, but Wilson heard from his carriage something different, inhuman — or superhuman."[27]

Ritman, Frieseke, Miller, Parker, and other expatriates were proud and patriotic as never before on 14 December 1918, when President and Mrs. Woodrow Wilson arrived at the Gare du Bois de Boulogne in Paris, and Parisians everywhere saw the American leader as a hero. The Wilsons were met by President Raymond Poincaré of France as they made their way past the cheering throngs and booming cannon. Some American painters recorded the events on canvas. At a luncheon with President Poincaré, Wilson delivered the following toast: "From the very beginning of this war the thoughts of the people of America turned toward something higher than the mere spoils of war." He told his distinguished audience that the "thought" of America "was directed toward the establishment of the eternal principles of right and justice."

Indeed, these principles had motivated Wilson in his efforts to end the war, but soon the harsh postwar realities would become a more pressing issue. Wilson's idealism would result in the concept of the League of Nations, a great organization that would be able to solve the problems of modern Europe. But everyone wondered exactly what President Wilson had in mind when he spoke so eloquently about "the establishment of the eternal principles of right and justice." While attending the Peace Conference at Versailles, the Wilsons were guests of the French government in the Murat Mansion. Soon Europe learned of Wilson's vision as he outlined the Fourteen Points of his plan for a new Europe. "Self-determination was reiterated in clause after clause and it soon became apparent that the leaders of allied nations were not all in accord with his plan."

In Paris Ritman resumed the routine of finishing the canvases he had brought back from Giverny. Now, he thought, Paris would soon regain its strength. The winter art season lay ahead and the future looked bright for him and his Giverny friends.

Notes

1. Claire Joyes, *Monet at Giverny* (New York: The Two Continents Publishing Group, Mathews Miller Dunbar, 1976), pp. 39-40.

2. Lilla Cabot Perry, "Reminiscences of Claude Monet from 1889 to 1909," *The American Magazine of Art*, XVIII, no. 3 (March 1927), p. 120.

3. Camille Mauclair, *Claude Monet*, trans. J. Lewis May (London: John Lane the Bodley Head Limited, 1927), p. 35.

4. For a general study of the topic, see Bernard Dunstan, *Painting Methods of the Impressionists* (New York: Watson-Guptil Publications, 1976).

5. George Biddle, *An American Artist's Story* (Boston, MA: Little Brown and Co., 1939), p. 149.

6. Charles Seymour, *Woodrow Wilson and the World War* (New Haven, CT: Yale University Press, 1921), p. 116.

7. Frederick C. Frieseke (1874-1939), Reminiscences, Writings, Price Lists; Frances Frieseke, "It's Only the Cannon," Microfilm Roll No. N737, Frames 0038-0040, Archives of American Art, Smithsonian Institution, Washington, DC.

8. Ibid., Frames 0028-29.

9. Maurice Ritman, interview with Richard Love, September 1987, R. H. Love Galleries Archives, Chicago,

10. Sherry A. Buckberrough, *Robert Delaunay: The Discovery of Simultaneity* (Ann Arbor, MI: UMI Research Press, 1982); see also Gabrielle Buffet, "La Section d'Or," *Art d'aujourd'hui*, May-June 1957, pp. 74-76.

11. Frederick C. Frieseke (1874-1939), Reminiscences, Writings, Price Lists; Frances Frieseke, "It's Only the Cannon," Microfilm Roll N737, Frames 0041-43.

12. Little is known of this work. The picture's existence has been described by the artist's biographer, Maurice Ritman, who reports that the picture forms part of the collection of the village hall of Giverny.

13. One of the best sources for such pictures is a rare publication by Albert Eugene Gallatin, *Art and the Great War* (New York: E. P. Dutton & Co., 1919). Note that the author, Gallatin, was the chairman of the committee on exhibitions, Division of Pictorial Publicity, U. S. Government Committee on Public Information.

14. Louise James Bargelt, "Art: Noted Artists on List at Exhibition of Institute Alumni," *Chicago Sunday Tribune*, 6 January 1918, Part VIII, p. 3.

15. Ibid.

16. Louise James Bargelt, "Art Institute Alumni's Work on Exhibition," *Chicago Daily Tribune*, 8 January 1918, p. 5.

17. Louise James Bargelt, "Art: Noted Artists on List at Exhibition of Institute Alumni," p. 3.

18. Frederick C. Frieseke (1874-1939), Reminiscences, Writings, Price Lists. "It's Only the Cannon" by Frances Frieseke, Microfilm Roll N737, Frames 0044-45.

19. Born in Pittsburgh on 5 July 1868, William (Billie) Singer, Jr., was expected to enter the family business, the Singer-Nimich Works in Pittsburgh, part of the multimillion- dollar Carnegie industrial conglomerate. After his school years, Singer sought art as a profession and spent time in Old Lyme, Connecticut, becoming a quasi-student under Hassam, Walter Griffin, and others. After a stint at the Julian Academy, Singer went to Laren, Holland, where he met the Norwegian-American Martin Borgord. Their friendship resulted in a trip to Norway, the country that became Singer's second home. Until he died in Olden, Norway, in 1943, Singer spent his summers there, as Ritman spent his summers in Giverny. See *The American Painter W. H. Singer, Jr., and His Position in the World of Art*, reviews selected by J. Siedenburg (Amsterdam, Netherlands: Frans Buffa and Sons, 1928).

20. "From Here and There," *Chicago Evening Post*, 5 March 1918, p. 11.

21. The canvas **Tea in the Garden** was a hit in Chicago for quite some time after Ritman's triumphant return from France in 1915. Although the picture was not sold, it was reproduced in a number of Chicago newspapers. For example, see "Literature and Art," *Chicago Sunday Herald*, 10 January 1915, p. 7. Probably written by the critic Maude I. G. Oliver, the caption to **Tea in the Garden** read as follows: "One of the colorful canvases, recording phases of Giverny coloring, which Louis Ritman has at present on exhibition in Lawton Parker's studio on Pearson Street, is the charming record reproduced above."

22. Marthe Butler to Lillian and Philip Hale, New York, 15 April 1918, Philip Leslie Hale Papers, Microfilm Roll D98, Archives of American Art, Smithsonian Institution, Washington, DC.

23. Alson Skinner Clark, quoted from Jean Stern, *Alson S. Clark* (Los Angeles, CA: Petersen Publishing Co., 1983), p. 34.

24. John Rewald, *Cézanne* (New York: Harry N. Abrams, Inc., 1986), p. 228.

25. George Cabel, born in Lafayette County, Missouri in 1876, held this post from 1917 to 1919. He was active in the WPA in later years. In 1916 he published *Wilson and the Issues*.

26. Frederick C. Frieseke (1874-1939), Reminiscences, Writings, Price Lists. "It's Only the Cannon," by Frances Frieseke, Microfilm Roll N737, Frames 0051-52.

27. William Bolitho quoted from Edmund Stillman, "Retreat from Versailles," in *The American Heritage History of the 1920s and 1930s* , ed. Ralph K. Andrist (New York: Bonanza Books, 1987), p. 12.

CHAPTER TWENTY:
BUILDING A DURABLE REPUTATION

The war had no sooner ended than many artists in America made arrangements to return to Paris. Some expatriates had never left France, and a number of these—John Dos Passos, for example, volunteered their services to their adopted land. A few artists, such as Ritman, had divided their time between painting and service in hospitals. Some had served in other civilian jobs. In the words of Milton Brown, "these artists were defending a way of life, a culture which they loved intensely, the symbol of an ideal artistic existence which they found nowhere else in the world, certainly not in the land of their birth."[1] In the great City of Lights, Ritman and other artists were free again to create with or without the guidelines of tradition.

Meantime, in the United States, artists who had once been very vocal pacifists were completely eclipsed by postwar patriotism and optimism. With the end of the war, protest publications like *The Masses* had been put out of circulation, so that no real direction existed for the artists who produced protest art. Others were convinced more than ever before that the only place to succeed was France or England. For those who saw no future in America, the trend marked the beginning of the nation's era of postwar disillusionment. The end of the great war, which should have brought new life and vigor to a previously optimistic society, offered very little hope. Indeed, during postwar times, interest in cultural matters yielded to concern with more practical issues. Without sufficient outlets or opportunities to show their products, once again many American artists looked to Europe as a better place to work than Chicago and New York. The American government was incapable of responding adequately to the crisis in the arts. For example, the National Arts Committee was given the responsibility of commissioning eight artists to paint portraits of important wartime political and military leaders. The move seemed fitting and proper even to those who had hoped to remain neutral in Europe's conflict, but it was little more than a bandage stuck on a gaping cultural wound.

Ritman stayed in France for the better part of 1918. He found that as he had expected, Paris breathed new life and was reasserting its artistic prominence as never before: the once great mecca of Western art was in the process of becoming even more magnificent than it had been before the war. As never before, exhibitions were planned and mounted as American artists from everywhere streamed back to Paris; indeed, they came back in droves to Montparnasse in an attempt to reestablish their careers. Ritman witnessed the exodus from America with anticipation, for although his tenacity as an expatriate had given him somewhat of a head start, he was anxious to proceed with his career at full speed.

By this time Ritman was experienced in the ways of the art world. In the three years that had passed since his splendid performance in Chicago and the greater Midwest, he had gained distinction as a new star. He had also developed contacts with patrons — no small requirement for a successful expatriate artist. One of his admirers was J. S. Carpenter, a prominent industrialist and art patron in Des Moines, Iowa. Carpenter was president of the Iowa Bridge Company as well as of the recently founded Des Moines Fine Arts Association. Keenly interested in the fortunes of American expatriates in France, Carpenter had corresponded regularly with Ritman, Frieseke, Miller, and Henry O. Tanner during World War I, but he seemed to be devoting extra attention to Ritman as time went on. During the war, apparently, Carpenter wrote more often to Ritman and Frieseke than to others.[2] With new patrons like Carpenter at home, Ritman felt more confident in expanding his performance.

Perhaps it was no more than a need to change his career as he was changing his art style that prompted Ritman to seek new avenues of promotion in New York when others were returning to Paris. On the other hand, he may have felt compelled to be represented by a New York dealer, or he may simply have been homesick after the long grueling war years. In any instance, some time in the winter of 1918-19, Louis Ritman left Paris for New York with the purpose of finding a gallery to handle his work, as Frieseke had suggested. Ritman's earlier success at Folsom's had been gratifying, and perhaps it was that show that now prompted the Macbeth Gallery to take some interest in his work. However it came about, by early 1919 Ritman had entered into an agreement with Macbeth's for a solo show in March. We assume that he went on to Chicago after finishing up his business in New York, but his whereabouts during the spring of 1919 are unknown.

Back in Paris during this period, the lights burned long into the night at President Wilson's residence at the Hôtel de Murat, where he struggled with the issues of the Peace Conference (his Fourteen Points were being altered and amended) and the organization of the League of Nations. At home, European ethnic and special interest groups in every city found little agreement with the president. The newly elected Republican majorities in the House and Senate also showed displeasure with his policies of New Freedom and were anxious to ambush any attempts at a third term by their Democratic leader. After a period back in the United States in February and March 1919 — at which time Ritman was preparing for his one-artist show at Macbeth's — President Wilson returned to Paris, determined to keep intact his program for peace. The President was ill, however, and obvious physical signs indicated that he might be failing mentally as well. By early May 1919, the peace treaty was ready; the document bore little resemblance to Wilson's draft with its Fourteen Points. The German representatives came to Versailles, where they signed the treaty ending World War I in the Hall of Mirrors on 28 June 1919 — the British painter William Orpen recorded the important event on canvas (ill. 20-1).

Ill. 20-1. William Orpen. *Signing of the Peace Treaty.* Oil on canvas. Imperial War Museum, London.

At the Hôtel Baudy in Giverny, where Ritman had painted his patriotic picture of the French and the American soldiers shaking hands, Madame Baudy eagerly welcomed the returning guests, many of whom were Ritman's friends. Even the tennis courts could be used after some refurbishing. Through it all, Monet, encouraged by Clemenceau, not only had worked on his mural-sized water-lily pictures but also had stacked away many other canvases in his large new studio. When the war ended, Monet had asked Clemenceau to offer two of his new works to France in commemoration of the armistice. When Ritman was back in America in early 1919, Monet was embarking upon a series of paintings of the Japanese footbridge. Once again the French master was very worried about his eyesight, but he was yet to produce some outstanding works.

Ritman joined many Americans who were resuming their exhibition actvities in Paris during the spring of 1919; he had submitted some pictures to shows before he left, and others were submitted by friends. He had entered a painting in the Champ de Mars Salon for the spring show. It was a genre scene featuring his model on a burgundy sofa. Although he was absent during the exhibition, Ritman achieved another bright star in his dossier when he was elected a member of the Société Nationale des Beaux-Arts (National Society of the Fine Arts), the sponsoring body for the Champ de Mars Salon. Originally founded by Puvis de Chavannes, Meissonier, and Eugène Carrière, the society had the reputation of being more liberal than the Old Paris Salon, sponsored by the Société des Artistes Français (Society of the French Artists), but the Champ de Mars jury also rejected many entries each year. The salon also had a reputation of showing progressive American art, sometimes too much of it, in the opinion of certain French art critics.[3] Ritman's work was quite conservative by contemporary standards, but even the Champ de Mars group had become traditional. Thus Ritman became an official member of a prestigious French art society. By being elected to the society and by exhibiting at the Champ de Mars Salon, Ritman gained the kind of recognition that he had been struggling for in France for so many years.

Back in America, Ritman could not have hoped for a better dealer than Macbeth. Not only was Macbeth highly respected in the American and French art communities, but he also sold many pictures; and for these reasons, his gallery represented the biggest names. For example, Ritman joined a list of artists that included, in addition to Frieseke and Miller, the following painters: Emil Carlsen, John F. Carlson, Arthur B. Davies, Paul Dougherty, Childe Hassam, Robert Henri, Gari Melchers, Gardner Symons, Dwight Tryon, J. Alden Weir, Guy Wiggins, and a host of others over the years. At this time, Macbeth's Gallery was located at 450 Fifth Avenue (at Fortieth Street). The arrangement between Ritman and Macbeth was probably set up on a trial basis. In the meantime, Ritman was keeping Carpenter and others informed about his moves.[4] The Des Moines industrialist was constantly in touch with artists whose works he liked and whose causes he defended — Ritman was one of those fortunate individuals. Carpenter often visited Chicago and invited artists to flashy parties in Des Moines, events eagerly reported by the local press. Ritman's exhibition at Macbeth Galleries was an event not to be missed.

Opening on Wednesday, 5 March 1919, this show was Ritman's first solo performance in New York City, and along with several others, it initiated the 1919 spring exhibition season. A small brochure published by Macbeth, entitled simply *Paintings by Louis Ritman*, gave a brief and, alas, erroneous biography, including mention of the silver medal he had won at the Panama-Pacific Exposition.[5] The show consisted of twenty pictures, one of which, *A French Girl*, was reproduced in the brochure in black and white. This painting is similar to a previously discussed work entitled *Sunspots*; it features the same model, shown seated at an outdoor table on which a colorful still life has been carefully arranged.

The artist could not have planned a more successful New York solo debut. With his work highly praised by the public and critics alike, Ritman was thrust immediately toward the front rank of contemporary painters. From the critics' comments, Ritman's work seemed to typify everything that the Giverny impressionists had been achieving for several decades. In a review published in the April issue of *International Studio*, the critic C. H. Waterman wrote that "Ritman is far defter of touch, more exquisite in pattern, more richly varied, and sensitive of surface than Frieseke."[6]

This was the first time Ritman's work had been featured in a major article published for an international audience, so Waterman was careful to qualify his comparison of Ritman's art with Frieseke's: It was "not necessary to destroy Frieseke that Ritman may stand, but since the charge will no doubt recur, it becomes important in the interest of a true appreciation of this remarkable young painter that it be met." He stated that "to see the difference, one need only compare the still life painted by these two men. In a Frieseke, forms disintegrate and become powdered colour spots." Implying a formula more French than American, Waterman pointed out that Frieseke's "dresses, china, fruit, flowers, all lose their individuality of texture and modelling." Waterman's comparison also underlines the basic difference between Frieseke and Ritman: the former diffused form into a shimmering colorful mass in a distinctively French manner, obviously the result of Monet's influence, while Ritman preferred to give his forms greater solidity in a manner more typical of Parker and a few other progressive American impressionists. Waterman observed that "Frieseke knows his Monet, but seems totally unaware of Cézanne. Ritman is always plastic . . . . He has learnt that the painting of light and atmosphere need not imply the annihilation of form; that light as often as not, reveals the beauty of modelling in objects and that the movement of the planes in a teapot or a dress helps reveal the loveliness of the light which plays at different angles upon every facet."[7]

The show at Macbeth's consisted of certain new works as well as some older ones. This range of style made Waterman distinctly aware of the artist's stylistic evolution, something very evident even at this early date in the total scope of Ritman's career, but at a late date in the history of his impressionism. The greatest change in Ritman's work was in his choice and application of color—everything else remained primarily the same. "For a colourist with a colourist's temptations," Waterman observed, "his drawing is remarkably good." He concluded: "For Ritman is so much the colourist that he will on no account nag his surfaces. His very patchiest areas have a painter's sure touch in every stroke, in the direction and shape of the stroke as well as in its colour." Having examined the surfaces of Ritman's paintings thoroughly, the writer pointed out: "His brushwork . . . varies throughout his canvases, so that the surface of his pictures is most pleasing to the eye. Here the brushing is easy and flowing, there it is staccato and crisp. In one place it is rich in impasto, in another broad and flat. And every stroke evokes line, colour, form, light and air simultaneously."[8]

One of the works in the Macbeth exhibition is still known as *Sun Kissed*. Impressed by the picture, Waterman thought it might be called *Light Kissed* as should all the paintings in which the "kiss of the light is soft and caressing. It is playful and capricious. It is intense and passionate." This critic was straightforward in reporting that Ritman's themes were "few and simple and oft repeated." However, when "arranged in sequence," as they were in the exhibition, the paintings were "a song cycle in the leisurely moods of a midsummer's day." Ritman was "blazing no new paths either in the subject matter or in treatment," Waterman wrote. Nonetheless, he said "he brings to his work a sure taste, sensitive touch, and a fine synthesis of rich colour, beautiful surface and exquisite composition." At the end of his long article, Waterman paid Ritman his highest compliment in stating that his pictures were like "so much of the work of our younger men most markedly under French influence, but if Ritman fulfills the promise of these canvases, he will be the Vermeer of the Impressionist school."[9]

How long Ritman stayed in the United States on this visit is unknown. His activities in Chicago, if any, have not been established, since there are no documents to provide information. It is clear, however, that he had returned to Paris by the early summer of 1919, and that he was soon back in Giverny. Here, Ritman made every effort to fulfill the promise, to become the "Vermeer of the impressionist school." Considering his postwar successes, Ritman had only a bright future ahead of him, both in France and in America. He continued to execute paintings of typical genre subjects, which nearly always featured a single female figure.

One of Ritman's canvases from the early summer of 1919 is known as *The Blue Bench* (also as *Summer Afternoon*) (pl. 20-1). Here and in the works that follow, we see a gradual evolution in Ritman's art: his former delicate strokes of broken color are replaced by bold, sometimes Cézannesque patches of strong hue. Upon close examination, we discover that in some places, Ritman laid on his paint with a palette knife. In effect, by employing both brush and palette knife to render broken color, he has altered his technique significantly. Even this relatively safe departure from traditional technique is a large step for someone as conservative as Louis Ritman. In this image, he has allowed a good deal of the raw canvas to show through. We can also see some of the underlying charcoal drawing which has been smeared here and there. At this point, his technique seems to be experimental and not necessarily successful. Brushwork is thin in some areas, scumbled in others, and overall there is a kind of arbitrary execution. In essence, he has displayed a certain hesitancy in arriving at this adulterated impressionism.

Fully clothed and seated on a bench (a motif he frequently employs at this time), the typical female subject has been brought so far up into the foreground in *The Blue Bench* that her legs have been truncated by the lower edge of the picture—in this we are reminded of Degas.[10] Having initiated it some time during World War I, Ritman occasionally poses his subjects frontally on a bench. In this instance, the artist provides an interesting compositional format, in that he poses his model at the apex of a "V" created by two background trees, but this is the extent of his creativity in this work. It is true that the figure is seated in the shade of trees: however, Ritman's color values appear lifeless, owing to his palette of deeply saturated hues with no addition of white. All in all, then, this nonimpressionistic, low-keyed painting is an interesting experiment.[11]

In retrospect, we see that Ritman was not alone in his experiments. His rather broad Cézannesque manner was also seen in the work of other impressionists who clung to the style long after its movement was over and helped to make something different out of the worn-out formula as Cézanne had hoped. Even so, Giverny still served as a kind of incubator for impressionism—a warm, snug place where everyone felt comfortable in the tradition of the aesthetic, deviating a bit here and there. Actually, most members of the Giverny group aspired to a basically common goal—that is, to succeed as American expatriate painters in the art communities on both sides of the Atlantic, with one painter usually quite willing to help another. A November 1919 letter from Frieseke to Macbeth in New York underscores this fact; apparently, since his solo show in New York City, Ritman had been accepted for permanent representation by the gallery: "Ritman tells me he has been fortunate enough to have you take up his work—I hope you can do something for him—he has been a sort of pupil of mine for a number of years as no doubt he told you. I have never consented to take pupils but helped Ritman all I could as he seemed to have talent."[12]

For Ritman, creating impressionism in Giverny meant not only painting but also a way of life that did more than keep him working with his friends in the country; it allowed him to experiment, to exhibit his art with acclaim in Paris, New York, and Chicago, and to make a living. For him it was not as difficult as it was, perhaps, for others because he was exceedingly talented, humble, and willing to follow the advice of his older mentors. Macbeth planned to continue promoting Ritman's name with solo shows. Apparently the gallery sold enough of his work to provide him a modest living—at least all he needed to continue his work, traditional or otherwise, in Giverny. Occasionally Ritman sold a picture to a Chicagoan. These transactions were usually arranged through friends or members of his family.

Ritman enjoyed the relatively conservative life in the Norman village, although he also socialized with friends in the hustle and bustle of Paris. Both before and after the war, Giverny fostered a kind of rural bohemia. In its transplantation from Paris, New York, or Chicago, however, this bohemia became a very calm, if not nearly indistinguishable kind of society. As a result, its lifestyle was a mere shadow of the original bohemian endeavors. Ritman's place was always quite singular, even solitary at times, in spite of his close associates. Like his married friends Frieseke and Miller, Ritman maintained a comfortable and attractive studio cottage. He lived with his model. Only artists like Monet and Butler could remember when a slice of bohemia from Montparnasse could fit comfortably into the Hôtel Baudy, and soon even that had changed, so that Giverny became more of an elitist art colony, replete with dilettantes, than a microcosm of the Latin Quarter. Ritman had known something of Chicago's bohemia, "which mirrored the grassroots optimism of the young West," even before he went to Paris, but once he began living in Montparnasse, the difference between his raison d'être and that of many bohemian friends became obvious immediately. Ritman's concept of success had been formed long before he lived in Paris: from the time he was a teenager in Miss Benedict's class, he expected to succeed in academic art—so he did, and he was continually rewarded for his skill in rendering beautiful imagery, never for his concepts, never for his innovations. The bohemian milieu in Chicago produced literary realists like Thorsten Veblen, Arthur Davison Fiche, Theodore Dreiser, and others, but no profound thinkers appeared in art until they had imbibed the nectar of Greenwich Village or the Latin Quarter. For Ritman, who sought success more through extraordinary skill than through innovation, the stable body of academicism and then impressionism were the nuclei around which all other trendy movements orbited; moreover, the art community reinforced this time-honored modus operandi. Indeed, his formative years in art had been spent in Chicago where, since the time prior to the World's Columbian Exposition, leading members of the art community maintained close contact with Monet in Giverny.[13] With important members of the Art Institute hierarchy like Martin Ryerson and the Palmers visiting Monet, it is no wonder that Ritman gravitated toward impressionism and Giverny: it had become a tradition for many aspiring painters who cut their artistic teeth in Chicago.

Therefore, Ritman gravitated to that which he did and understood best, namely, impressionism, and the best place to make that kind of art was in Giverny, where Monet, the inventor, and all his American adherents gathered in cultlike serenity. Even after World War I, a good deal of aesthetic inquiry went on there, but it was very catholic and out of date. The bohemianism found in Giverny was a lot like Ritman's life there—unconventional but comfortable and safe, as it had been even earlier for struggling artists like Miller and Frieseke, and now Ritman.

When he returned to Paris, Ritman could not miss the amazing resurgence of American expatriatism and its bohemian trappings. The Latin Quarter swelled with a brand new generation of painters, writers, and intellectuals, all of whom were anxious to trade the Chicago and New York copies of bohemia for the Paris original. Many expatriates had already launched new careers in Paris, but many more were just arriving. For example, it was at this time in late 1919 that Sylvia Beach opened the bookshop Shakespeare and Company on Rue Dupuytren, an establishment that later became a meeting place for many expatriates, including Gertrude Stein, Cole Porter, Ezra Pound, Ernest Hemingway, Archibald MacLeish, Thornton Wilder, Sherwood Anderson, and many others (ill. 20-2). As he traveled in Paris art circles, Ritman came to know many of the newly arrived American avant-gardes. It was about this time that Cole Porter married Linda Lee Thomas. Wealthy and fluent in French, the Porters made their apartment on rue Monsieur the talk of Paris, with walls covered in zebra hide and red chairs lined with white kid. Later, Porter's *Within the Quota* was a success at the Théâtre des Champs Elysées, and that musical would be

Ill. 20-2. Sylvia Beach (third from left) and friends with Ernest Hemingway (fourth from left) in front of her bookshop in Paris. Photograph. Princeton University Library, Princeton, New Jersey.

followed by another smash hit, *Greenwich Village Follies*. Soon, too, there would be another great cultural success, a book entitled *America and the Young Intellectual* by Harold Stearns, a writer of about Ritman's age. In a future issue of the *Atlantic Monthly*, Stearns would defend the "moral idealism" of the younger generation of American expatriates, but in time he became just one more talent who drifted from café to café, accomplishing little until he ended up writing a column on horse racing for the *Chicago Tribune*. Ritman knew many of those who had come to find their places in the mecca of Western culture, but he also observed that some made it and others went home obscure and forgotten.

For all of the literary greats who resumed their careers in Paris, there were just as many artists, some of whom, like Ritman's friend Clara Kretzinger and others he would meet made no impact at all on the art community. The expatriate experience, however, seemed to demand that an artist of any sort carve out as much play time as work time — at least tradition had it that way. There were the usual places for them to meet — cafés like La Coupole, Le Select, and La Rotonde. Still, the Café du Dôme remained the favorite gathering spot.[14] Postwar expatriates, no less than their earlier counterparts, found the Dome irresistible, although a few, especially Sinclair Lewis, were not particularly flattering in their descriptions. "Nowhere in America itself," Lewis wrote, "is this duty-ridden earnestness of the artist and his disciples so well shown as at the Brevoort and cathedral of American sophistication, the Café Dome in Paris." He continued: "It is on a corner charmingly resembling Sixth Avenue at Eighth Street, and all the waiters understand Americanese, so that it is possible for the patrons to be highly expatriate without benefit of Berlitz. It is, in fact,

the perfectly standardized place to which standardized rebels flee from the crushing standardization of America."[15] All in all, for many Americans, Paris was once again the center of the cultural world, and Ritman had mastered the modus operandi; he knew the city well, its art system, its art hierarchy, its struggling painters, its galleries, museums, cafés, and, of course, the studio-apartments of many expatriate friends who, like him, intended to become famous.

In America life for the artist was a different story — in fact, the immediate postwar period proved to be exceedingly difficult. The focus was on the economy and on the president. President Wilson was only in his early sixties, but he had been "harrowed by the physical and mental ordeal of the Presidency, the responsibility of the war, and the endless wrangling in Paris."[16] Totally exhausted, Wilson had suffered a stroke in Pueblo, Colorado, in late September of 1919 and was being rushed back to Washington when a second stroke resulted in paralysis. Lying helpless, the president was attended by his wife and personal physician for several months as a few loyal Democrats did what they could to shore up power against the prevailing forces of Henry Cabot Lodge. Finally it became apparent that "domestic discord in 1919 mirrored the collapse of Wilson's moral world. A calendar of violence marked the decline of original progressive hopes."[17] Against a backdrop of constant strikes and clashes between business and labor unions, race riots erupted in cities across the nation. The most serious of the riots occurred in Chicago, where 38 people were killed and over 500 were injured. This kind of violence seemed ironic, at least to those who recalled President Wilson's definition of the progressive task a few years earlier: "Our duty is to cleanse, to reconsider, to correct the evil without impairing the good, to purify and humanize every process of our common life without weakening it or sentimentalizing it." To artists and most other citizens, that kind of task had been demolished by the war and its aftermath; there seemed to be no practical way to "correct the evil without impairing the good."

In Chicago and the Midwest, which Ritman still called home, the local art community openly reflected the same kind of confusion and disillusionment that had prompted artists from across the entire nation to go to Paris to start new careers. This prevalent mood was typified in Lena M. McCauley's review of the Thirty-second Annual Exhibition of Paintings and Sculpture at the Art Institute: "Artists in the United States have arrived at the parting of ways. They stand at the 'Great Divide' between achievements and promise with no prophecy of what is to come." Cynically but honestly, she reported: "The viewer looks in vain for superb accomplishment at this period in the evolution of the hundred years of American art. Where is the canvas or sculpture possessing that original effloresence [sic] of genius that thrills admiration or reverence, and awakens expectation of artistic nobility to change the trend of the commonplace in a war-weary world? Painters and sculptors alike are suffering stupefying reactions following the excitement of the world war that marked the close of a golden age in earth's history, when peace and prosperity attended the nations. The destructive elements paralyzed the imagination and blighted creative genius. Human activities are occupied with realities and the whirl of artificial stimuli to divert attention away from the truth. Honest craftsmanship and idealism mourn in the shadows."[18]

Ritman's canvases were the kind that seemed to have been created by an artist who clung to prewar ideals of excellence, with the result that they attracted collectors. Neither Arthur J. Eddy nor John Quinn were interested in intimism, but other, more moderate collectors were anxious to own his canvases. To Carpenter in Iowa and to local buyers, Ritman was a highly regarded Chicago painter who lived and worked in faraway Giverny near Monet and was handled by a famous New York gallery, facts that lent his work a certain romantic credibility in spite of its lack of modernity. Actually Ritman was becoming somewhat of a local artistic legend, as Parker had before him; some observers even thought of him as Parker's protégé, but all collectors thought of him as an impressionist.

In February 1920, Macbeth Gallery arranged another one-artist show of Ritman's work for the Grand Rapids Art Association. The Michigan exhibition was a smaller selection of the paintings previously seen in New York. The *Monthly Calendar Bulletin* informed its membership: "It is a distinct honor to the Grand Rapids Art Association that it has been included in the circuit of this very rare exhibition. It took some persuasion to convince the Macbeth Galleries that an exhibition of this quality would be appreciated in Grand Rapids. It is up to us to show them."[19] It was apparent to many members of the Chicago art community that Ritman was fast becoming one of the city's premier artists, but Macbeth's traveling show to places like Grand Rapids did wonders for Ritman's career elsewhere in the Midwest.

Another case that points to his burgeoning reputation was the mounting of his work in a two-artist show at the Art Institute of Chicago a couple of months later. Whether the exhibition was arranged by Macbeth in New York is unknown, but Ritman shared the Chicago limelight with another impressionist, W. Elmer Schofield, an older expatriate and former student at the Pennsylvania Academy of the Fine Arts.[20] Their canvases were hung in the east gallery at the institute near an exhibition of wash drawings by Henry G. Keller, a painter from Cleveland who specialized in animal subjects and taught at the Cleveland School of Art. Ritman's fourteen works had been done "in the manner of Frieseke," art critic Lena M. McCauley reported. "Whether this fashion was born at Giverny, in a garden on the Seine, or in some other neighborhood in France it matters not. It follows a formula of sunlight and color adjustments which Mr. Ritman has carried out conscientiously. To escape from the trammels of a style and to adventure with one's own rush-light into the world [of] picture-making spells independence."[21]

The American expatriates were not the only ones to demonstrate their independence; diverse factions of American society were struggling for the same goal, and like the artists, some were successful and others failed miserably. To unionists, for example, it seemed that every step they made forward was countered by riots, while the Ku Klux Klan swelled to unprecedented strength from self-generated bigotry and racism. Colonel William J. Simmons led Klansmen in cross-burning rituals, the victims of which included Jews, blacks, Catholics, and any "intellectually mongrelized liberals." While many government officials "looked the other way" when the Klan resorted to terrorism, President Wilson's Attorney General A. Mitchell Palmer did just the opposite when it came to communists on home soil. Warning Americans of "the blaze of revolution," Palmer regarded every alien as an anarchist and saw a Red agitator behind every union organizer. Initiating a "Red hunt," he destroyed left-wing presses and banned liberal professors from teaching. Other signs of independence came into play as a result of women's suffrage, the most obvious manifestation of which was the soon-to-be-ratified Nineteenth Amendment, which guaranteed women the right to vote in national elections. Suffragists predicted that their voters would uplift the moral level of modern politics. In any instance, the "new American woman" of postwar America wanted above all to demonstrate her independence not only in her unabashed exploitation of cosmetics and shortened skirts but also in her poise and enlightenment—these were not the kind of women Giverny painters had been depicting. If the new woman surprised society, the novel *This Side of Paradise*, by the young writer F. Scott Fitzgerald, was bound to shock Victorian mothers when they read descriptions of "petting." These were not the young women Ritman depicted, at least not outwardly.

During the election year of 1920, it became quite obvious even to the most loyal Democrats that their president's time was over, and that there was no man in their party to take his place. On the other hand, numerous capable

Pl. 19-8. Louis Ritman. *Nude, Study No. 1*. Oil on canvas, 36⅜ x 28⅝ inches. (reverse of *By the Brook*) Private Collection. Courtesy R. H. Love Galleries, Chicago.

Pl. 19-9. Louis Ritman. *Lady by a Window*. 1918. Oil on canvas, 47 x 39½ inches. Private Collection. Courtesy R. H. Love Galleries, Chicago.

Pl. 19-10. Louis Ritman. *Morning Walk*. 1918. Oil on canvas, 36 x 29 inches. Burke Collection. Courtesy R. H. Love Galleries, Chicago.

Pl. 19-11. Louis Ritman. *A Day in July*. 1918. Oil on canvas, 36 x 36 inches. Private Collection. Courtesy R. H. Love Galleries, Chicago.

Pl. 20-1. Louis Ritman. *The Blue Bench*. Oil on canvas, 32 x 32 inches. Patricia Hall Collection. Courtesy R. H. Love Galleries, Chicago.

Pl. 20-2. Edwin Blashfield. *Allegory of the Arts*. Oil on canvas, 89⅞ x 44⅛ inches. Richard H. Love Collection. Courtesy R. H. Love Galleries, Chicago.

Pl. 20-3. Louis Ritman. *Morning Leisure*. Oil on canvas, 32 x 32 inches. Private Collection. Courtesy R. H. Love Galleries, Chicago.

Pl. 20-4. Louis Ritman. *Paris View*. Oil on canvas, 32 x 25½ inches. Private Collection. Courtesy R. H. Love Galleries, Chicago.

Republicans were visible, distinguished individuals such as General Leonard Wood, Governor Frank Lowden of Illinois, Charles Evans Hughes (narrowly beaten by Wilson in 1912), and even Herbert Hoover. At this time, a great deal of maneuvering was going on in preparation for the primary conventions. Even then most politicians were in favor of a *laissez-faire* government in America—a system that promoted big business, big money, and as some knew, one that had an even bigger potential for corruption.

Later, in September 1920, the fourteen canvases that Ritman had shown with those of Schofield in the two-artist show at the Art Institute of Chicago became part of a large exhibition mounted at the Memorial Art Gallery in Rochester, New York.[22] The Art Institute had selected Ritman's canvases as one show of a four-part exhibition that included "A Collection of Paintings purchased by the Friends of American Art" for the institute, a collection of paintings and drawings by Captain George Harding, U.S.R., and portrait busts in bronze of leaders of World War I by Jo Davidson. The paintings that had been purchased for the institute by the "Friends" included some important names—artists like George Bellows, Randall Davey, Daniel Garber, Charles Hawthorne, Frederick J. Waugh, William Wendt, and others. Ritman knew the sculptor Jo Davidson in Paris, where they had met at the Café du Dôme. Like Ritman, Davidson was still an expatriate in Paris and only recently had taken a new studio on the avenue du Maine—they saw each other occasionally.

During the fall of 1920, Ritman sent work to the Thirty-third Annual Exhibition of American Paintings at the Art Institute of Chicago. It was a large and impressive show, which still consisted primarily of works revealing the influence of impressionism. Portraiture ranged from Abbott Thayer's *Young Woman in Olive Plush* to Louis Betts's likeness of James B. Forgan, and to "the dashing adventures of George Luks's Otis Skinner," as one critic put it. Then, too, there were outstanding paintings by Wayman Adams, Oliver Dennett Grover, Henry R. Rittenberg, Victor Higgins, Leopold Seyfert, Emil Carlsen, Helen M. Turner, Ernest Blumenschein, H. V. Poore, and others. A local critic observed that "subject painting with figures seems to be running a race with landscape in popularity." He also pointed out that "Childe Hassam's characteristic, 'The New York Winter Window,' with a figure, and Louis Rittman's [sic] fine 'Sunlit Window' are in a class by themselves."[23] Ritman's work was well spoken of by other critics, but it was Frederick Frieseke who received the Potter Palmer Gold Medal and $1,000 from the Art Institute. The prize was for the canvas entitled *Torn Lingerie*, the same work that had won the W. M. R. French Memorial Gold Medal. Such an award must have made it quite clear to Ritman that in spite of his own recent successes, Frieseke and other well-known impressionists were still the frontrunners in the minds of most of the jurists for national shows, even those in Chicago.

Of all the distinguished gentlemen who were available to run for the presidency on the Republican ticket in 1920, none was chosen as a result of a hopelessly deadlocked convention. Summoned to a smoke-filled room at two o'clock in the morning, an unlikely politician from Ohio, Warren Gamaliel Harding, was asked if there were any skeletons in his closet which would keep him from accepting the nomination. Unaware that his young mistress, Nan Britton, was living in Chicago with Harding's illegitimate daughter, the committee chose him as their alternative candidate. He and his running mate Calvin Coolidge, the governor of Massachusetts, were nominated on the tenth ballot. Later in November America elected Warren Harding as the twenty-ninth president. The women's vote was a deciding factor in the election—many said they had found him "handsome."

During the 1920s, Ritman continued to work in quiet Giverny and dynamic Paris. Many of the canvases he painted were sent across the Atlantic for exhibitions in America. First through Macbeth Galleries and then through Milch Galleries, he maintained close ties to the New York art scene. As a result, he became a well-known and highly respected member of the New York art milieu and the Chicago scene, to which he had become a major contributor. Ritman exhibited his work in numerous national shows including the one at the National Academy of Design. Once again, he sent work to the Paris Salon. In the spring of 1921, for example, three of his canvases lined the walls of the Salon. Paintings by the expatriate Myron Barlow (ill. 20-3) and others hung nearby while the entries of Frieseke, Elizabeth Nourse, Walter Gay, and other well-known expatriates were shown in adjacent galleries. This forum was still an excellent place for Ritman. Each spring, news of the salons was eagerly received and printed in the art pages of American newspapers.

Like Frieseke, Ritman entrusted his New York dealer Macbeth with the placement of most of his work. Unlike some of his more aggressive friends, Ritman did not always see to it that his pictures were shown in other major exhibitions in large urban centers. In certain instances, of course, these were invitational shows and not open to him. For example, in July 1921, the Museum of Fine Arts, Boston, mounted an exhibition of war portraits by American artists, which had been commissioned by a special committee. Ritman was not selected as a con-

Ill. 20-3. Myron Barlow. *Portrait of a Young Woman.* Oil on canvas, 30 x 30 inches. Private Collection. Courtesy R. H. Love Galleries, Chicago.

tributor, but a number of other impressionists with whom he had exhibited (Cecilia Beaux, Joseph DeCamp, Tarbell, Irving Wiles) were, and their portraits received praise in various publications.[24]

The inauguration of Warren G. Harding on 19 March 1921 was well covered by the American press. The event was ritualized by his riding with the outgoing President Woodrow Wilson in an open Pierce-Arrow cabriolet to Capitol Hill, where the role of leadership was passed on. In obviously failing health, Wilson bore only a faint resemblance to the once great leader who had charged his country with grave ideological responsibilities. The contrast between the two men was enormous in every way, since Harding, relatively limited in intellectual capacity, asked of Americans nothing except a return to "normalcy." His attitude appealed to the average American, who was worn out from three years of world war and its lackluster aftermath. Ritman, while not active in politics, was fiercely proud of being an American—especially an expatriate—and he and his friends discussed the affairs in Washington regularly. In recent years, the war, Wilson's term, and the great changes that had occurred in the cultural life of both Europe and the United States had been of serious concern to most artists, Ritman no less. Usually, however, he was a good deal less vociferous about the events in Washington, DC, than were friends like Parker or Frieseke and the many compatriots he sat with at the Café du Dôme and other haunts. Harding's "nor-

malcy" was not a quality Ritman had lost sight of, but it may have become protracted by years of life away from home. For Ritman, normalcy was the excitement that he had witnessed in art circles before the war, and he too was glad that life was returning to normal.

In 1922, Ritman, though still an expatriate in France, exhibited frequently in America. That spring he won the Julius Hallgarten Prize at the National Academy of Design in New York. This was an important award for him because it represented a confirmation of his artistic skills by his highest ranking American peers.[25] Ritman had never been a student at the Academy, but to have one's work shown at its annual exhibitions was the most official recognition an American artist could receive. The great allegorical painter Edwin Blashfield (pl. 20-2) was still president of the institution, and only a few weeks earlier he had held a series of conferences with the chancellor of New York University, with the view of coordinating National Academy courses with university courses to provide a Bachelor of Arts degree in the practice of art.[26] President Blashfield and other members of the academy hierarchy realized only too well that the institution had to effect some sort of policy changes that would strengthen its image. Of course, Ritman could boast of no degrees, and although the Hallgarten Prize was the first National Academy award to be conferred upon him, it marked the first of many official recognitions, which would eventually include full membership in the grand old institution; indeed, this was the most significant degree that Ritman would receive. In 1922, the Academy was nearing its centennial year, and Ritman, then only 33 years old, was obviously one artist who demonstrated the kind of potential that the academy still admired.

Although nearly a decade had elapsed since the revolutionary Armory Show, Chicago, like New York, cherished its tradition of academicism in art. If it had not been obvious to most observers, the establishment of the John H. Vanderpoel Art Association in the master's memory in the fall of 1922 underscored the fact. The twenty founders of the association paid official homage to Vanderpoel's academic mastery and even established an art collection in his name, which was housed in Beverly on Chicago's South Side.[27] Ritman was not one of the organizers of the Vanderpoel Association, but several of his artist friends were; these included a few expatriates who continued to work in France, painters like Karl Buehr, Lawton Parker, and some artists from New York and elsewhere, such as Gardner Symons, J. C. Leyendecker, William Wendt, Henry Salem Hubbell, Pauline Palmer, Jules, and others.

In the fall of 1922, Ritman exhibited at the Thirty-fifth

Annual Exhibition of American Paintings at the Art Institute. He received no award for his intimism, but it was obvious that the Chicago art community still enjoyed impressionism, for Frank W. Benson was awarded the Frank G. Logan medal and $1,500, while John Singer Sargent won the Potter Palmer Gold Medal and $1,000 for his portrait of Mrs. Swinton. To the average visitor, the Art Institute was exhibiting as many impressionist works as it had prior to the Armory Show. Most modernist works were exhibited primarily in New York.

Although awards went to more famous impressionists, Ritman was given another one-artist show at the Art Institute of Chicago in February and March of 1923. By this time he was no longer considered a young struggling artist; he was ranked as a very successful expatriate whose paintings were being shown to a local audience. Critics praised his work, and he sold some pieces. At this time a high price for a canvas was $500, but collectors bought his work regularly. He also participated in a group show entitled "Paintings by Contemporary American Artists" at the Art Gallery of Toronto. Later in the fall of 1923 he exhibited at the Memorial Art Gallery in Rochester, New York. The show consisted of three parts — a group of paintings by the Canadian Seven, loaned by the National Gallery of Canada in Ottawa; a number of canvases by the Russian-American Leon Gaspard; and fifteen works by Ritman. Actually the whole exhibition was a kind of broad view of impressionism in that most of the Canadian Seven revealed influences of the aesthetic as did both Gaspard and Ritman. The work of the two American painters was loaned to Rochester by Milch Galleries in New York. Interestingly, both Ritman and Gaspard were of Russian origin and each of them had exhibited extensively in Chicago. They had also shared similar experiences in their early lives.[28]

Perhaps the life of someone like Ritman, the successful expatriate artist living in France, was not altogether utopia, but relative to the times, it was as close to it as an artist could hope for. In Giverny, Ritman and his friends lived, worked, and played in bucolic bliss, while in Paris they joined in the festive and intellectual bohemianism of their adopted city. This idyllic lifestyle was so appealing that it drew painters from many different places in America, but especially Chicago. There were males and females, novices and veterans, poor and wealthy, single and married, but all were seeking to learn more about the art spirit that enveloped Giverny. The Chicago painter Herbert T. Lewis, for example, had studied at the Julian and Delecluse academies in Paris and spent the summer of 1922 in Giverny. Lewis and his wife enjoyed the life in Giverny while he received advice from Ritman about his art.[29] Artists like Lewis frequently sought Ritman's help in familiarizing themselves with the expatriate experience, just as Ritman had received Parker's help a dozen years earlier.

American expatriates in France were fully aware that their homeland was still in the difficult throes of finding itself culturally, but most of them also knew that it was making amazing progress. The majority of these artistic expatriates were proud of their heritage. Furthermore, business was booming, and America's private sector promised to support art as never before. The society also was moving at a much more rapid pace than it had prior to the war. The short-lived depression of 1921 had come and gone, and by 1922 the Big Bull Market was emerging as Warren G. Harding died surrounded by rumors of impending disgrace. In spite of the optimism, however, vastly greater numbers of American artists went to Paris than returned. Nevertheless, the "*Scènes de la vie de Bohême*" were quite different from those described by Henri Murger, because that once avant-garde lifestyle had become stereotypically traditional, even ordinary by contemporary standards.

Vice President Calvin Coolidge, or "Silent Cal" as he was known, took over the reins of government and promised to continue his friendship with business. Careful not to overwork himself, Coolidge designed his own rules of protocol and saw to it that the nation's business machinery stayed well oiled. For the first time in many years, America's future looked bright (ill. 20-4). The gross national product was growing, the stock market attracted citizens from all walks of life, and to many of them, art appeared to be a "good investment." In fact, although the Metropolitan Museum had received lavish praise for its new American wing, a gift of Robert Weeks De Forest, New Yorkers and Chicagoans were competing to pay unprecedented high prices for French paintings, especially those by Monet, Degas, and other pioneer impressionists. The businessman (cultured or otherwise) saw himself as the new American "soldier," now fighting for profit, not freedom. Some observers said that Rotary meetings had become more important than church. If the Edwardian years had made an impact on American life, the 1920s were to eclipse those influences and dictate new lifestyles. "It was a time of ballyhoo and whoopee, overlying a stratum of moral disorientation and cynicism, especially among the young and especially in urban areas."[30] These were new and fast-moving times, when Americans sought to cultivate a new and fast-moving way of life that was often shocking and vulgar as young men and women scorned the old-fashioned Victorian standards of polite behavior. From it all came new art, poetry, literature, movies, and music — all American, distinctly American! Generated in Chicago and especially in Green-

Ill. 20-4. Construction of new buildings on Michigan Avenue in Chicago, during the late 1920s. Photograph. R. H. Love Galleries Archives, Chicago.

wich Village in New York, the new styles made their way to Paris via the ever-growing expatriate circuit. In time, these artful manifestations would have an effect on the European art community, but for now their impact was somewhat tenuous on Ritman and his expatriate comrades. They all agreed that for various reasons life was still better in France. In later years, when asked by a reporter why she preferred Paris to Chicago, Ritman's artist friend Clara Kretzinger explained: "There never was time in Chicago to sit and talk over the tea cups. Greetings between friends were always superficial because they were hasty."[31]

During the early 1920s, Ritman concentrated on his painting in Giverny. His American exhibitions were usually handled by Milch Galleries in New York, while Papa Foinet in Paris took care of the shipment of his canvases to America. Ritman still visited Paris frequently and met with his friends at the Café du Dôme and other artist haunts in Montparnasse. By this time, postwar neobohemianism was in full swing, and Montparnasse was crowded; indeed, more Americans than ever before sought new experiences in the Latin Quarter. Among them were scores of other Midwestern painters who had come to try their luck in Paris. Rubbing shoulders with venerable old masters or with students, artists had an opportunity to meet the most creative minds in the Western Hemisphere. It was not only painters and sculptors that youngsters might meet but also famous writers like John Dos Passos, James Joyce, Ezra Pound, and Wyndham Lewis. Of course, there were scores of lesser names, such as Edna St. Vincent Millay, who, under the pen name of Nancy Boyd, had just published an article titled "Diary of an American Art Student in Paris."[32] This new wave of disillusioned American expatriates found it thrilling to rekindle and share in the bohemianism they had heard so much about. Their general attitude is reflected in a letter written by Ernest Hemingway to Sherwood Anderson, whom he had recently met in Chicago:

> Dear Sherwood and Tennessee [Sherwood Anderson's wife]: Well here we are. And we sit outside the Dome Café, opposite the Rotunda that's being redecorated, warmed up against one of those charcoal brazziers and it's so damned cold outside and . . . the rhum enters into us like the Holy Spirit. And when its a cold night in the streets of Paris and we're walking home down the Rue Bonaparte we think of the way the wolves used to slink into the city and Francois Villon and the gallows at Montfaucon. What a town.[33]

Later Janet Flanner would take up permanent residence at the Hotel Saint-Germain-des-Prés, from which she would write her first "Letter from Paris" for editor Harold Ross of the *New Yorker*.[34] In time she wrote about a dancer who had made her debut in Chicago, one Isadora Duncan: "Two decades before, her art, animated by her extraordinary public personality, came as close to founding an aesthetic renaissance as American morality would allow."

Veteran expatriates like Ritman mingled with hundreds of others, old-timers or newcomers, who hailed the resurgence of the City of Lights, its Eiffel Tower, cafés, Louvre, taxis, Opéra House, gendarmes, Champs Elysées, and Latin Quarter, still the testing grounds for all artists, writers, painters, sculptors, dancers, and musicians, in fact, for all creative Americans. Indeed, Virgil Thomson's Paris sojourn was as typical of the times as that of any painter or writer and perhaps more reflective of Parisian bohemianism than was Ritman's. Thomson had arrived in France a couple of years earlier as a member of the

Harvard Glee Club. After a stint with Nadia Boulanger, he took a modest fifth-floor room in a brothel, which allowed him to compose while his "neighbors were out, dining late, or dancing, love-time for kept girls being afternoon. The grand piano in his room was mounted on blocks, so he could write counterpoint standing up, using for a desk the piano's level top." Like many of his American friends, Thomson returned to the United States, but after a brief period at Harvard, he went back to the same room in Paris, saying that if he had to starve, he preferred to do so where the food was good. Later, Gertrude Stein and Alice B. Toklas heard him and his career was set.

So many creative Americans lived in Paris who were struggling to find inspiration, guidance, and forums for their artistic creations that many future theses will still not tell the whole tale of these golden years. Ritman was truly one of the experienced who was devoted to his career and no longer overwhelmed by the distractions of the fascinating environment. His talent had taken him over most obstacles, but he eventually had become a seasoned veteran who knew how to take advantage of every opportunity. This led him to paint many images that looked more French than American and to exhibit them as regularly as possible. At the Salon des Tuileries in 1923, Ritman was listed in the official catalog as an American and showed four very typical canvases: *Balcony, Toilette, Summer,* and *Poppies.*[35]

During the time that Ritman resided in France, the art world changed. Just as Monet grew old, so did impressionism. Ritman and many of his associates tried to alter the structure of the aesthetic to match Cézanne's efforts, that is, "to make something solid and durable out of impressionism," something "like the art of the museums." They faced an impossible task: the art world was moving at an unprecedented rate of speed, and it was too late! Although Ritman and his older constituents in Giverny continued to create beautiful genre work featuring lovely models, their paintings were not done in the delicately rendered intimist style that had propelled them meteorically to the top ranks of impressionism during its waning years. Perhaps a local Chicago critic perceived the change in Ritman's work best: the artist, he reported, "appears definitely to have abandoned himself to formula—of treatment and color." The writer lamented: "It is a pity; for in addition to believing that his paintings show he has the making of a good artist, the present exhibition demonstrates, I believe, that in a measure he is able to shake himself free of his formula." He concluded: "When he is most completely in the grip of his formula of treatment, Ritman is very little concerned with the question of form and greatly engrossed in the laying

in of more or less flat shapes with his preconceived color harmonies and restrictions mainly in view as an end."[36]

Ritman and many of his impressionist friends, changed their style to conform with a growing trend to modernize the fifty-year-old aesthetic via Cézanne's lead: they reduced the key of their palettes by removing white and eliminated most or all of their broken-color technique in order to render form in bold, quiltlike patterns of flat color. They could deviate from Monet's formula only so far as to assimilate Cézanne; they could not imitate Picasso, and they never dreamed of working like Wassily Kandinsky. Yet, their alteration of impressionism via Cézanne's mode resulted in a new trend, not a radical one but an acceptable one indeed—and one that marked the death of American impressionism.

For Ritman, then, the early 1920s mark the beginning of a strange, albeit fashionable, conservative style and the rapid demise of his own impressionism. In retrospect, we see that in spite of his youth, Ritman was at the peak of his powers for about six years, from 1913 until 1919 (between the ages of 24 and 30), when he was painting his own unique brand of intimism in Giverny. He never changed his predilection for intimism, and his draftsmanship actually improved over the years; but when he abandoned his brilliant expressions in high-key broken color to follow the prevailing trend in Paris, he lost the impressionistic spirit and harmonic sensitivity of his early Giverny period. This loss was obvious to most observers, as we glean from the words of an anonymous critic who reviewed his solo show at Milch Gallery in 1924 for the *New York Times*: "Louis Ritman paints landscape and figure as still life painted for the picturesque surface reason, lacking any inner significance, the play of light spots through the trees on flesh or flesh round and modeled against water and lily pads." The writer added that Ritman's pictures "curiously evade description because with all their modeled fleshness they are impersonal and with all the obvious search for the picturesque, they are as decorations not too successful in design." He concluded: "The color is original and personal, a pleasing and diffused light, as though the sun were comfortably warm and not too hot. Wanting in esthetic qualities of sufficient importance they still have something of a tactile appeal."[37] On account of the fact that, like Ritman, many of his impressionist friends who tried to abandon the well-known formula were generally unsuccessful, art historians have basically ignored the evolution of the style that occurred in the early 1920s, the years of its amazing transformation, but there is much to be gained from research in this area of expatriate work. Ritman was one of the foremost proponents of this evolution.

Ill. 20-5. Rue Campagne Première with a view toward the boulevard de Montparnasse. Ritman lived on the rue Champagne Première in the 1920s. Postcard; exact date and origin unknown. R. H. Love Galleries Archives, Chicago.

During the decade of the 1920s, Ritman continued to live in France (ill. 20-5); he corresponded with J. S. Carpenter and enjoyed the patronage of other collectors; and he was represented in New York by Milch Galleries.[38] Ritman made return trips to the United States, however, and maintained his contacts on both sides of the Atlantic. In this routine, he followed in the footsteps of Lawton Parker, Frederick Frieseke, Theodore Robinson, Mary Cassatt, and the most exemplary of all, John Singer Sargent, who died in 1925, only a year before the death of the great Monet, master of Giverny.

In the late 1920s, Ritman enjoyed the company of many important artists, writers, and intellectuals in France. He basked in the light of their camaraderie and shared secrets with them. He was close to Marc Chagall, Amedeo Modigliani, Chaim Soutine, and other members of the so-called Paris School. Unlike these artists, however, Ritman was never a true bohemian. In all this time, he had never married — that would happen later in his career — but he spent a great deal of time with his longtime friend Irene Hudson, who later married Louis Stern,

the great Philadelphia collector and patron of the arts.[39]

Even after Monet's death, a large contingent of American expatriates still worked in a quasi-impressionist style and a few others clung tenaciously to the broken-color technique. Yet, with the passing of Monet, the flame that had set Giverny on fire was gone; the embers glowed for quite some time, but Giverny and its group of American intimists gradually became less visible in the international art community.

Ritman was still comparatively young. He was ambitious and, indeed, for all intents and purposes, at the peak of his career. He knew, however, that he would not be able to remain indefinitely in the sleepy village — in fact, he spent considerable time in Paris, where he also painted. Perhaps his loyalty to Giverny owed more to the quality of life that he found there than to anything else, and perhaps this was the driving motivation for the entirety of his expatriate experience, for it was not art alone that kept him in Giverny for nearly twenty years. In the words of his brother and biographer Maurice, "Giverny became his 'idyllic trek.' As he experienced the tranquility of Giverny and its surroundings in the spring, summer, and fall, and his winters in Paris with the varied fantasies of such artists, writers, and composers as Chagall, Modigliani, Derain, Joyce, Fitzgerald, Stein, Copland, Revel, and others of similar caliber, life in this village became for him, as Ernest Hemingway aptly put it, 'A Moveable Feast.'[40]

So it was that 1929 marked the end of Ritman's French period after nearly twenty years of continued productivity in Paris and Giverny, although he would return to France many times. In March of that year, he sailed back to New York to be present at a solo exhibition at Milch Galleries. That his paintings were well received was indicated in a *Herald Tribune* review, in which change in "Figure compositions like *Sewing* and the portrait *Jullien* are emphatically pictorial . . . . Ritman's interiors are never so delicate as the similar ones of Frieseke, for instance. He is too vigorous for that. There is a touch of modernity in his broad defining of forms, but he is a man who also keeps his eye upon the object."[41] The fact that Ritman made some outstanding works in the late 1920s (and he continued to do so in the 1930s) is exemplified by the oil entitled *Jullien* (Butler Institute of American Art, Youngstown, OH), which was exhibited in the Milch show. The portrait would later win the Second Logan Prize and the William M. R. French Memorial Gold Medal at the Art Institute of Chicago in 1930.[42] After visiting the Ritman show at Milch Galleries, the great art writer Lloyd Goodrich summed up in essence the first half of the artist's career: "Judging by some of his earlier pictures included in the exhibition, he has evolved from a pleasant, modified impressionism suggestive of Frieseke to the use of stronger color and more lively brushwork. His work if not particularly distinguished color and the verve of his handling are attractive"[43] (pl. 20-3; pl. 20-4).

Goodrich's words also serve as a prophetic review of the second half of Ritman's career. At the time, the full mode of American realism was pursued tenaciously by a declining number of Chicago artists, who exploited the late Salon style to its very end. American artists, such as

Ill. 20-6. Kenneth Shopen. *Chicago: Backyard.* 1935. Etching on paper, 9¾ x 11½ inches. R. H. Love Galleries, Chicago.

Kenneth Shopen (ill. 20-6), were the heirs apparent of artists like Wellington J. Reynolds, and they depicted Chicago in a literal fashion. Ritman was successfully changing with the times to an amazing extent, but his achievement had little to do with impressionism, the style of Giverny's golden years.

Apparently Ritman had intended to return to Paris after the Milch show. Instead, fifteen years after the death of W. M. R. French, he was persuaded by Director William B. Harshe of the Art Institute of Chicago, to accept the position of instructor of portrait and figure painting for the 1930-1931 season. Ritman would remain in Chicago for the next thirty years, making scores of powerfully executed genre pictures of women and even some highly successful landscapes. During these years Louis Ritman was considered an American master of broadly executed realism. That art came in the second half of his career, in the mature years which followed his impressionist period in Giverny.

Notes

1. Milton W. Brown, *American Painting from the Armory Show to the Depression* (Princeton, NJ: Princeton University Press, 1972).

2. J. S. Carpenter to Henry O. Tanner, Des Moines, Iowa, February 24, 1919, Henry O. Tanner Papers, Microfilm Roll D306, Frame 0204, Archives of American Art, Smithsonian Institution, Washington, DC.

3. See Charles Morice, "Les Salons de la Nationale et des Français," *Mercure de France,* June 1904, pp. 686-705.

4. J. S. Carpenter to Henry O. Tanner, Des.Moines, Iowa, February 24, 1919, Henry O. Tanner Papers, Microfilm Roll D306, Frame 0204, Archives of American Art, Smithsonian Institution, Washington, DC.

5. *Paintings by Louis Ritman*, exhibition brochure (New York: Macbeth Gallery, 1919). The inaccuracies in the brochure are slight and biographical in nature.

6. C. H. Waterman, "Louis Ritman," *International Studio*, LXVII, no. 267 (April 1919), pp. LXII-LXIV.

7. Ibid., p. LXIV.

8. Ibid.

9. Ibid.

10. Numerous compositions exist in which the legs of the subject extend below the lower edge of the picture. Two important examples are *Estelle Musson de Gas* (1872-73, Chester Dale Collection, National Gallery of Art, Washington, DC) and *Combing the Hair* (1892-95, National Gallery, London).

11. On the reverse of this picture, entitled *Summer Afternoon* (also called *The Blue Bench*), is the inscription "Summer Afternoon, Louis Ritman, Milch 108 W 57."

12. Frieseke to Macbeth, 8 November 1919, Macbeth Gallery Papers, Microfilm Roll no. NMc46, Frame 0291, Archives of American Art, Smithsonian Institution, Washington, DC.

13. André Masson, Grace Seiberling, and J. Patrice Marandel, *Paintings by Monet*, exhibition catalog (Chicago: The Art Institute of Chicago, 1975). See J. Patrice Marandel, "Monet in Chicago," pp. 41-44.

14. Later in the 1920s, the Café Falstaff became a very popular place with Americans in Montparnasse. A British ex-boxer known as "Jimmy the Barman" and Joe Hildesheim, an American from Brooklyn called "Joe the Bum," ran the Falstaff in a rather casual manner. It was a favorite place for artists and writers, especially F. Scott Fitzgerald and Ernest Hemingway. Eventually Café Falstaff became a convenient alternative to the Café du Dôme.

15. Sinclair Lewis, *American Mercury,* October 1925.

16. Edmund Stillman, "Retreat from Versailles," in *The American Heritage History of the 1920s & 1930s,* ed. Ralph K. Andrist (New York: Bonanza Books, 1987), p. 17.

17. John L. Thomas, "Nationalizing the Republic," Part Five in Bernard Bailyn, David Brian Davis, David Herbert Donald, John L. Thomas, Robert H. Wiebe, and Gordon S. Wood, *The Great Republic: A History of the American People* (Boston, MA: Little, Brown and Co., 1977), p. 1046.

18. Lena M. McCauley, "Art in America Is at 'Great Divide,' " *Chicago Evening Post*, 11 November 1919, p. 11.

19. *Monthly Calendar Bulletin*, "On Wednesday, February 4th at 4:00 p.m. — Opening Tea for the Exhibition of Paintings by Louis Ritman from the Macbeth Galleries of N.Y.," The Grand Rapids Art Association, February 1920.

20. Walter Elmer Schofield was born in Philadelphia on 9 September 1867. He studied at the Pennsylvania Academy of the Fine Arts and later in Paris under Edmond Aman-Jean and Henri Lucien Doucet. Schofield won the Sesnan Gold Medal of Honor in 1903. During World War I, he served in the British Army and married into an English family. He maintained a studio in Cornwall during the latter part of his life.

21. Lena May McCauley, "News of the Art World: At the Art Institute," *Chicago Evening Post*, 18 May 1920, p. 17.

22. *Catalog of a Collection of Paintings Purchased by the Friends of American Art for the Art Institute of Chicago: Oil Paintings by Louis Ritman, Paintings and Drawings by Capt. George Harding, U.S.R. and Portrait Busts in Bronze of Leaders of the World War by Jo Davidson*, exhibition catalog (Rochester, NY: The Memorial Art Gallery, 1920), p. 4.

23. *Chicago Evening Post*, 9 November 1920, p. 11.

24. The exhibition was circulated under the direction of the American Federation of Arts. There were twenty portraits of soldiers and statesmen who figured prominently in World War I. The exhibition in Boston was hung in the Renaissance Court during July and remained on view until August 1921. See "War Portraits by American Artists," *Museum of Fine Arts, Boston, Bulletin* , XIX, no. 114 (August 1921), p. 46 (Reprint: New York: Arno Press, 1971).

25. The Julius Hallgarten Prize was established by Mr. Hallgarten in 1883 with an endowment of $12,000 to be used for prizes for the best paintings shown at the academy by artists under 35 years of age.

26. The affiliation, providing for a B.A. earned jointly between New York University and the National Academy of Design, was approved 3 April 1922. See Eliot Clark, *History of the National Academy of Design 1825-1953* (New York: Columbia University Press, 1954), p. 203.

27. This impressive Vanderpoel collection is still maintained and exhibited at the Beverly Arts Center in Chicago. The members of the organization are active in promoting the Vanderpoel heritage.

28. Gaspard first began sketching when he crisscrossed Siberia with his fur-trading father of Huguenot descent. As a protégé of Bouguereau, Gaspard exhibited at the prestigious Georges Petit Galleries in Paris. After sustaining injuries in aerial combat while serving in the French forces during World War I, he rejoined his American wife in the United States. In 1918 they settled in the Taos art colony in New

Mexico, where he became friends with the Taos Society of Artists. Victor Higgins and Walter Ufer, both acquaintances of Ritman, were leading members of the Taos group and frequent exhibitors with Gaspard in the "Chicago and Vicinity" shows.

29. Herbert T. Lewis to Robert Harshe, Art Institute of Chicago Archives, Chicago.

30. Stillman, "The Great Euphoria," in *The American Heritage History of the 1920s and 1930s,* p. 80.

31. Margot, "Clara Kretzinger Deserts Her Montparnasse Studio to Do Murals in Ireland," *Chicago Daily News,* 9 September 1932.

32. Nancy Boyd, "Diary of an American Student in Paris," *Vanity Fair,* 19, no. 3 (November 1922), pp. 44, 106, 108.

33. Brian N. Morton, *Americans in Paris: An Anecdotal Street Guide* (Ann Arbor, MI: The Olivia and Hill Press, 1984), p. 152.

34. Janet Flanner's column for the *New Yorker* was signed Genet, a nom de plume chosen by Harold Ross.

35. Ernest L. Heitkamp, "Cleverness makes Canvases of Oliver Dennett Grover 'Cold,' " *Chicago Herald and Examiner,* 30 December 1923, part 5, p. 4.

36. Ibid.

37. "Art: Exhibitions of the Week," *New York Times,* 13 April 1924, p. 10.

38. J. S. Carpenter to Henry O. Tanner, Des Moines, Iowa, March 8, 1927, Henry O. Tanner Papers, Microfilm Roll D306, Frames 0461-0462, Archives of American Art, Smithsonian Institution, Washington, DC.

39. For more information on this famous collector, see Henry G. Gardiner, Kneeland and McNulty, and Jean Gordon L'ec, *The Louis E. Stern Collection,* collection catalog (Philadelphia, PA: Philadelphia Museum of Art, 1964).

40. Maurice Ritman, "Introduction," in Maurice Ritman, "My Brother Louis Ritman," unpublished manuscript, Chicago, August 1987, p. 1, R. H. Love Galleries Archives, Chicago.

41. *New York Herald Tribune,* 17 March 1929.

42. The Second Logan Prize was awarded by the Chicago Art Institute and consisted of $1500. Royal Cortissoz mentioned Ritman's award for *Jullien* and stated that "these annual exhibitions at Chicago are rich in prizes." Royal Cortissoz, "A Visit to Chicago and San Francisco," *New York Herald Tribune,* 23 November 1930. The M. R. French Memorial Gold Medal was an annual award given since 1917 to a student or a former student of the Chicago Art Institute and awarded by a special committee selected by the Alumni Association.

43. Lloyd Goodrich, "Reviewer's Notebook," *New York Times,* 17 March 1929.

CHRONOLOGY

1863	Solomon Ritman and Rebecca Saltzman are born; parents of Louis Ritman.
1868	Lawton Parker is born in Fairfield, Michigan.
1873	Frederick Carl Frieseke is born in Owosso, Michigan.
	Parker family moves to Kearney, Nebraska.
	Richard Miller is born in St. Louis, Missouri.
1881	Frieseke family moves to Jacksonville, Florida.
1886	Lawton Parker wins amateur drawing competition and enters the School of the Art Institute of Chicago.
	Theodore Robinson and Willard Metcalf visit Giverny.
1889	Lilla Cabot Perry paints with Monet in Giverny.
	Louis Ritman is born in Kamenets-Podolsky, Russia.
1890	Parker enrolls at the Art Student's League in New York.
1892	Theodore Robinson leaves Giverny.
1893	Frieseke enrolls at the School of the Art Institute of Chicago.
	Miller attends night classes at the St. Louis School of Fine Art.

1894	*Crumbling Idols* includes a chapter on "Impressionism" by Hamlin Garland, the first important defense of impressionism in the United States.
1897	Parker is awarded the prestigious Studio Prize.
	Miller becomes an artist-reporter for the St. Louis Post Dispatch.
	Miller enrolls at the Julian Academy in Paris.
1900	Frieseke settles in Giverny.
	The Ritman family emigrates to America and settles in Chicago ca. 1900.
1901	Louis Ritman attends classes at Hull House.
1903	Begins working with the Thomas Cusack Company; paints banner portait of Mayor Harrison; promoted to picture illustrator and master craftsman.
1905	Enrolls in an evening life class at the School of the Art Institute of Chicago.
1907	Awarded the Chicago Academy of Fine Arts Scholarship; begins studies under Wellington J. Reynolds; makes first contact with Lawton Parker.
1908	*Girl in Brown* exhibited at Twelfth Annual Exhibition at the Art Institute of Chicago, "Works by Chicago Artists."

1908   Awarded the William L. Elkins Tuition Scholarship to the Pennsylvania Academy of Fine Arts; leaves for Philadelphia during the summer; returns to Chicago in November; re-enters the Chicago Academy of Fine Arts.

1909   Enrolls in Vanderpoel's morning life class at the School of the Art Institute of Chicago.

Portrait of W.J. Reynolds and *Portrait of Norbert Heerman* exhibited at the Thirteenth Annual Exhibition at the Art Institute of Chicago, "Works by Chicago Artists."

Travels to France; enrolls at the Ecole des Beaux-Arts in Paris.

1910   Begins friendship with Richard Miller at Café du Dôme; makes the acquaintance of Leo Stein.

Portrait of M. Norbert Heerman exhibited at the Spring Salon in Paris.

Portrait exhibited at the Fourteenth Annual Exhibition at the Art Institute of Chicago, "Works by Chicago Artists."

1911   *La Toilette* and *Portrait* exhibited at the Spring Salon in Paris.

Visits Giverny for the first time; meets with Miller and Frieseke.

Portrait selected by Sara Hallowell for exhibition at the Art Institute of Chicago.

1912   *Before the Ball* and *Portrait of the Artist and His Model* exhibited at the Spring Salon in Paris.

Visits Giverny in the spring; returns to Paris in the fall.

1913   *Nue* and *Le Matin* exhibited at the Spring Salon in Paris.

Visits Giverny in the spring; returns to Paris in the fall.

1914   Joins Independents in Giverny following the Spring Salon in Paris.

Returns to Chicago in the fall.

Exhibits work at Lawton Parker's studio in Chicago.

1915   First solo exhibition at the Art Institute of Chicago.

Dormitory Breakfast sells for $500, the highest amount paid during a group show at the Art Association of La Crosse, Wisconsin.

Early Morning in a Garden and *Déjeuner* exhibited at the Panama-Pacific Exposition in San Francisco; wins Silver Medal.

Returns to Paris; spends the summer in Giverny.

Awarded First Prize from the Chicago Artists'

Guild for work entitled *In Pensive Mood*.

Begins friendship with Des Moines industrialist, art collector and patron J.S. Carpenter.

1916   Leaves Paris for a summer in Giverny; returns to Paris in fall.

1917   Exhibits at Folsom Galleries.

1918   Returns to Giverny for the summer.

1919   Returns to the United States

Elected a member of the Société Nationale des Beaux-Arts in Paris.

Given first New York one-artist show by Macbeth Galleries; reviewed in *International Studio*.

Exhibits at the Champ de Mars Salon in Paris.

1920   *Sunlit Window* exhibited at the Thirty-Third Annual Exhibition of American Paintings at the Art Institute of Chicago.

One-artist show for the Grand Rapids Art Association.

Exhibits with William H. Singer in a two-artist show at the Art Institute of Chicago.

Exhibits at the Memorial Art Gallery in Rochester, New York.

Accepted for permanent representation by Macbeth Galleries.

1921   Exhibits three paintings at the Spring Salon in Paris.

Awarded Julius Hallgarten Prize from the National Academy of Design in New York.

One-artist exhibition at the Art Institute of Chicago.

Exhibits in "Paintings by Contemporary American Artists" at the Art Gallery of Toronto.

Exhibits at the Memorial Art Gallery in Rochester, New York.

Returns to Giverny for the summer.

1923   *Balcony, Toilette, Summer,* and *Poppies* exhibited at the Salon des Tuileries in Paris.

1924   Establishes friendships with such important writers and artists as Chaim Soutine and Marc Chagall.

One-artist show at Milch Galleries.

1926   Returns to New York.

1929   One-artist show at Milch Galleries

Awarded Second Logan Prize for *Jullien*.

1930   Awarded the William M.R. French Memorial Gold Medal from the Art Institute of Chicago for *Jullien*.

Appointed Instructor of Portrait and Figure Painting at the Art Institute of Chicago.

LIST OF BLACK AND WHITE ILLUSTRATIONS AND COLORPLATES

the late 1890s. R.H. Love Galleries Archives, Chicago.

Ill. 2-11. Theodore Robinson. *The Wedding March.* 1892. Oil on canvas, 22 x 26 inches. Terra Museum of American Art. Daniel J. Terra Collection.

Colorplates

Pl. 2-1. Claude Monet. *Spring in Giverny.* Oil on canvas, 25¹¹/₁₆ x 32 inches. Sterling and Francine Clark Institute, Williamstown, Massachusetts.

Pl. 2-2. Theodore Earl Butler. *New Road, Giverny.* 1902. Oil on canvas, 25½ x 32 inches. Private Collection. Courtesy R.H. Love Galleries, Chicago.

CHAPTER THREE

Ill. 3-1. William Butler Ogden, first mayor of Chicago. R.H. Love Galleries Archives, Chicago.

Ill. 3-2. Thomas H. Stevenson. *Untitled.* 1859. Oil on canvas, 29 x 39¾ inches. Private Collection. Courtesy R.H. Love Galleries, Inc., Chicago.

Ill. 3-3. Martin A. Ryerson and Claude Monet in the garden at Giverny. Photograph. Courtesy the Art Institute of Chicago.

Ill. 3-4. Map of downtown Chicago, showing the location of the Interstate Industrial Exposition, 1890. R.H. Love Galleries Archives, Chicago.

Ill. 3-5. Doorway of the Tree Studio Building. Photograph. R.H. Love Galleries Archives, Chicago.

Ill. 3-6. Detail: doorway of the Tree Studio Building. Photograph. R.H. Love Galleries Archives, Chicago.

Ill. 3-7. Lorado Taft in his studio. Photograph. Chicago Historical Society.

Ill. 3-8. A scene of Bohemian life in an etching from a design by Montader appearing in Henri Murger's book *The Bohemians of the Latin Quarter.*

CHAPTER FOUR

Ill. 4-1. Map of the World's Columbian Exposition of 1893, Chicago. R.H. Love Galleries Archives, Chicago.

Ill. 4-2. Albert Fleury. *Wabash Avenue.* Oil on canvas, 9¾ x 13 inches. Private Collection.

Ill. 4-3. The Palace of Mechanic Arts and Electricity. World's Columbian Exposition of 1893, Chicago. R.H. Love Galleries Archives, Chicago.

Ill. 4-4. Interior view of the Women's Building. World's Columbian Exposition of 1893, Chicago. R.H. Love Galleries Archives, Chicago.

Ill. 4-5. Fine Arts Building. World's Columbian Exposition of 1893, Chicago. R.H. Love Galleries Archives, Chicago.

Ill. 4-6. Interior View: 1892 construction of the Manufactures and Liberal Arts Building, in preparation for the World's Columbian Exposition of 1893, Chicago. R.H. Love Galleries Archives, Chicago.

Ill. 4-7. The Ferris Wheel. World's Columbian Exposition of 1893, Chicago. R.H. Love Galleries Archives, Chicago.

Ill. 4-8. Interior Detail: Fine Arts Building, sculpture wing with central view of *The Angel of Death and the Sculptor,* by Daniel C. French. World's Columbian Exposition of 1893, Chicago. R. H. Love Galleries Archives, Chicago.

Ill. 4-9. Bertha Honoré Palmer, a leader in the Chicago art world. R.H. Love Galleries Archives, Chicago.

Ill. 4-10. Halsey C. Ives, director of the Department of Fine Arts. World's Columbian Exposition of 1893, Chicago. R.H. Love Galleries Archives, Chicago.

Ill. 4-11. Interior Detail, Art Gallery: United States, section no. 3. World's Columbian Exposition of 1893, Chicago. R.H. Love Galleries Archives, Chicago.

Ill. 4-12. Theodore Robinson. *Summer Hillside, Giverny.* Oil on canvas, 18 x 24 inches. Private Collection. Courtesy R. H. Love Galleries, Inc., Chicago.

Ill. 4-13. J. Ottis Adams. *Sycamores, All in Yellow Clad.* Oil on canvas, 20 x 30 inches. Courtesy ACA Galleries, New York.

Ill. 4-14. Will H. Low. Photograph. R.H. Love Galleries Archives, Chicago.

Colorplates

Pl. 4-1. Charles Francis Browne. *Indiana Autumn.* 1897. Oil on canvas, 16 x 24 inches. Collection of Dan and Nancy Schneider. Courtesy R.H. Love Galleries, Chicago.

CHAPTER FIVE

Ill. 5-1. Kenyon Cox. Photograph. R. H. Love Galleries Archives, Chicago.

Ill. 5-2. Childe Hassam. Photograph. R. H. Love Galleries Archives, Chicago.

Ill. 5-3. Ernest Lawson. Photograph. R. H. Love Galleries Archives, Chicago

Ill. 5-4. Theodore Earl Butler. *Jimmy in a Garden.* 1894. Oil on canvas, 26 x 32 inches. Private Collection. Courtesy R. H. Love Galleries, Chicago.

Ill. 5-5. Lawton Parker. Photograph. R. H. Love Galleries Archives, Chicago.

Ill. 5-6. Frederick Carl Frieseke. Photograph. R. H. Love Galleries Archives, Chicago.

Ill. 5-7. Richard Miller. *Along the River, Sunset.* Oil on academy board, 12 x 16 inches. Private Collection. Courtesy R. H. Love Galleries, Chicago.

Ill. 5-8. Paul Gauguin in the early 1890s. Photograph. R.H. Love Galleries Archives, Chicago.

Ill. 5-9. Willard L. Metcalf. *The Pool.* 1904. Oil on canvas, 36 x 36 inches. Private Collection. Courtesy R. H. Love Galleries, Chicago.

Ill. 5-10. Mary Cassatt. *Mother and Child.* Oil on canvas, 36⅛ x 29 inches. The Metropolitan Museum of Art. George A. Hearn Fund, 1909.

Ill. 5-11. Lawton Parker. *Woman in a Garden.* Oil on canvas, 24 x 24 inches. Private Collection. Courtesy R. H. Love Galleries, Chicago.

Ill. 5-12. Theodore Earl Butler. *Jimmy Butler and His Dog.* 1895. Oil on canvas, 42 x 34½ inches. Mr. and Mrs. James P. Liautaud Collection.

Ill. 5-13. Lucien Doucet. R. H. Love Galleries Archives, Chicago.

Ill. 5-14. Richard Miller. Photograph. R. H. Love Galleries Archives, Chicago.

Colorplates

Pl. 5-1. Claude Monet. *Haystack at Sunset , near Giverny.* 1891. Oil on canvas, 28¾ x 36¼ inches. Museum of Fine Arts, Boston. Julia Cheney Edwards Collection. Bequest of Robert J. Edwards in memory of his mother.

Pl. 5-2. Lilla Cabot Perry. *Haystacks.* Ca. 1896. Oil on canvas, 25¾ x 32 inches. Private Collection. Courtesy R. H. Love Galleries, Chicago.

Pl. 5-3. Richard Miller. *Interior.* Ca. 1910. Oil on panel, 24 x 26 inches. Private Collection. Courtesy R. H. Love Galleries, Chicago.

CHAPTER SIX

Ill. 6-1. Hester Street, New York, around 1900. Photograph. R. H. Love Galleries Archives, Chicago.

Ill. 6-2. The Solomon Ritman family after their arrival in Chicago. Louis Ritman is standing at the far right (top row). His mother Rebecca is in the center, with her arm resting on Solomon's shoulder. Photograph. Courtesy Maurice Ritman.

Ill. 6-3. Carter H. Harrison, Jr., mayor of Chicago. R. H. Love Galleries Archives, Chicago.

1920s. Photograph. R. H. Love Galleries Archives, Chicago.

Ill. 20-5. Rue Campagne Première with a view toward the boulevard de Montparnasse. Ritman lived on the rue Champagne Première in the 1920s. Postcard; exact date and origin unknown. R. H. Love Galleries Archives, Chicago.

Ill. 20-6. Kenneth Shopen. *Chicago: Back-yard*. 1935. Etching on paper, 9¾ x 11½

inches. R. H. Love Galleries, Chicago.

Colorplates

Pl. 20-1. Louis Ritman. *The Blue Bench*. Oil on canvas, 32 x 32 inches. Patricia Hall Collection. Courtesy R. H. Love Galleries, Chicago.

Pl. 20-2. Edwin Blashfield. *Allegory of the Arts*. Oil on canvas, 89⅞ x 44⅛ inches. Richard H. Love Collection. Courtesy R. H.

Love Galleries, Chicago.

Pl. 20-3. Louis Ritman. *Morning Leisure*. Oil on canvas, 32 x 32 inches. Private Collection. Courtesy R. H. Love Galleries, Chicago.

Pl. 20-4. Louis Ritman. *Paris View*. Oil on canvas, 32 x 25½ inches. Private Collection. Courtesy R. H. Love Galleries, Chicago.

BIBLIOGRAPHY

BOOKS

Allan, Tony. *The Glamour Years, Paris, (1919-40)*. New York: Gallery Books, 1977.

The American Heritage History of the 1920s and 1930s. Ed. Ralph R. Andrist. New York, Bonanza Books, 1987.

Andreas, A.T. *History of Chicago from the Earliest Period to the Present Time*. Vol. III. Chicago, 1884-86.

The Annals of America, 1905-1915. Vol. 13. Chicago: Encyclopedia Britannica, 1976.

The Armory Show, International Exhibition of Modern Art, 1913. Vol. III, *Contemporary and Retrospective Documents*. New York: Arno Press, 1972.

Bacon, Henry. *A Parisian Year*. Boston, MA: Robert Bros., 1882.

Bailyn, Bernard, et al. *The Great Republic: A History of the American People*. Boston, MA: Little Brown & Co., 1977.

Baur, John I.H. "The Traditional: Impressionism and Romantic Realism." *In Revolution and Tradition in Modern American Art*. New York: Praeger Publishers, 1967.

Benjamin, S.G.W. *Contemporary Art in Europe*. New York: Harper, 1877.

Bennett, Francis Cheney, ed. *History of Music and Art in Illinois*. Société Universelle Lyrique, 1904.

Berry, C.B. *Chicago*. 1982.

Biart, Lucien. *Mes promenades à travers l'Exposition, souvenir de 1889*. Paris, France: A. Flennuyer, 1890.

Biddle, George. *An American Artist's Story*. Boston, MA: Little, Brown and Company, 1939.

Boggs, Jean Sutherland, et al. *Degas*. New York: The Metropolitan Museum of Art, 1988.

Boime, Albert. *The Academy & French Painting in the Nineteenth Century*. London: Phaidon Press, Ltd., 1971.

Boyle, Richard J. *American Impressionism*. Boston, MA: New York Graphic Society, 1974.

_____ . *In This Academy, The Pennsylvania Academy of the Fine Arts, 1805-1976*. Philadelphia, PA: The Pennsylvania Academy of the Fine Arts, 1976.

Brown, Milton W. *American Painting from the Armory Show to the Depression*. Princeton, NJ: Princeton University Press, 1972.

_____ . *The Story of the Armory Show*, 2nd ed. New York: Abbeville Press Publishers, 1988.

Buckberrough, Sherry A. *Robert Delaunay: The Discovery of Simultaneity*. Ann Arbor, MI: UMI Research Press, 1982.

Burke, Doreen Bolger. *J. Alden Weir, An American Impressionist*. New York: Cornwall Books, 1983.

Burnham, Daniel, and Edward Bennet. *Plan of Chicago*. Chicago, 1909.

Caffin, Charles H. *American Masters of Sculpture*. Garden City, NY: Doubleday, Page & Co., 1903.

Cahill, Holger. *Max Weber*. New York: Downtown Galleries, 1930.

Chasse, Charles. *Les Fauves et leur temps*. Lausanne-Paris: Bibliothèque des Arts, 1963.

Clapp, Jane. *Art Censorship*. Metuchen, NJ: The Scarecrow Press, 1972.

Clark, Eliot. *History of the National Academy of Design, 1825-1953.* New York: Columbia University Press, 1954.

_____ . *John Twachtman.* New York: Frederick Fairchild Sherman, 1924.

_____ . *Theodore Robinson, His Life and Art.* Chicago: R. H. Love Galleries, 1980.

Cooper, James Fenimore. *The Leatherstocking Saga.*

Cox, Annette. *Art-as-Politics: The Abstract Expressionist Avant-Garde and Society.* Ann Arbor, MI: UMI Research Press. 1982.

A Critical Triumvirate. *Five Hoosier Painters.* Chicago: Central Art Association, 1894.

_____ . *Impressions on Impressionism.* Chicago: Central Art Association, 1894.

Davis, Allen R. and Mary Lynn McCree, eds. *Eighty Years at Hull House.* Chicago: Quadrangle Books, 1969.

Dawson-Watson, Dawson. "The Real Story of Giverny." Appendix in Eliot Clark, *Theodore Robinson, His Life and Art.* Chicago: R. H. Love Galleries, 1980, pp. 65-68.

De Veer, Elizabeth; and Richard J. Boyle. *Sunlight and Shadow: The Life and Art of Willard L. Metcalf.* New York: Abbeville Press, 1987.

Donnelley, Reuben H. *The Lakeside Annual Directory of the City of Chicago.* Chicago, 1912.

Dorter, M.G. *Toulouse-Lautrec et son oeuvre.* New York: Collectors Editions, 1971.

Duis, Perry. "Chicago and the Movies" in *Chicago Creating New Traditions.* Chicago: Chicago Historical Society, 1976.

Dunstan, Bernard R. A. *Painting Methods of the Impressionists.* New York: Watson-Guptil Publications, 1976.

Eddy, Arthur Jerome. *Cubists and Post-Impressionists.* Chicago: A.C. McClurg, 1914.

Exposition Annuelle des Beaux-Arts, Salon de 1911. Paris: Société des Artistes Français, 1911.

Fairbrother, Trevor. *The Bostonians: Painters of an Elegant Age, 1870-1930.* Boston, MA: Northeastern University Press, 1986.

Fitzgerald, Richard. *Art and Politics.* Westport, CT: Greenwood Press, 1973.

Gallatin, Albert Eugene. *Art and the Great War.* New York: E.P. Dutton & Co., 1919.

Garland, Hamlin. *Crumbling Idols.* Reprinted; Cambridge, MA: The Belknap Press of Harvard University Press, 1960.

_____ . *Roadside Meetings.* New York: The Macmillan Co.,1930.

Gerdts, William H. *American Impressionism.* New York: Abbeville Press, 1984.

_____ . *The Great American Nude.* New York: Praeger Publishers, 1974.

Gilder, Rosamond, ed. *The Letters of Richard Watson Gilder.* Boston, 1916.

Giry, Marcel. *Fauvism: Origins and Development.* New York: Alpine Fine Arts, 1982.

Goodrich, Lloyd. *Pioneers of Modern Art in America: The Decade of the Armory Show, 1910-1920.* New York: Frederick A. Praeger, 1963.

Goodyear, Frank H., Jr., et al. *In this Academy: The Pennsylvania Academy of the Fine Arts, 1805-1876.* Philadelphia, PA: The Pennsylvania Academy of the Fine Arts, 1976.

Gordon, Robert, and Andrew Forge. *Monet.* New York: Harry N. Abrams, Inc., Publishers, 1983.

Haas, Willy. *Die Belle Epoque.* Munich, Germany: Verlag Kurt Desch, 1967.

Haftmann, Werner. *Painting in the Twentieth Century,* Vol. 1. *An Analysis of the Artists and Their Work.* New York: Frederick A. Praeger, Publishers, 1965.

Hanson, Anne Coffin. *Manet and the Modern Tradition.* New Haven, CT: Yale University Press, 1977.

Harper's Chicago and the World's Fair. ed. Julien Rolph. New York: Harper and Brothers Publishers, 1893.

Harrison, Carter H. *Stormy Years.* New York: The Bobbs-Merrill Co., 1935.

_____ . *Growing Up With Chicago.* Chicago: Ralph Fletcher Seymour, 1944.

Hartlaub, G. F. *Zauber des Spiegels.* Munich, 1951.

Hartmann, Sadakichi. *A History of American Art.* Vol. 2. Boston, MA: L.C. Page and Co., 1902.

Henri, Robert. *The Art Spirit.* Compiled by Margery Robertson. Philadelphia, PA: J.B. Lippincott Co., 1930.

Herbert, Eugenia W. *The Artist and Social Reform, France and Belgium, 1885-1898.* New Haven, CT: Yale University Press, 1961.

Herbert, Robert L. *Neo-Impressionism.* New York: The Solomon R. Guggenheim Museum, 1968.

Hines, Thomas S. *Burnham of Chicago, Architect and Planner.* Chicago: The University of Chicago Press, 1974.

Hitchcock, Ripley, ed. *The Art of the World Illustrated in the Paintings, Statuary, and Architecture of the World's Columbian Exposition.* New York: D. Appleton and Co., 1896.

Homer, William Innes. *Robert Henri and His Circle.* Ithaca, NY: Cornell University Press, 1969.

Hoopes, Donelson F. *The American Impressionists.* New York: Watson-Guptil Publications, 1972.

Howat, John K. *The Hudson River and Its Painters.* New York: Penguin Books, 1978.

Huyghe, René, ed. with Bazin Germain. *Histoire de l'art contemporain: La peinture.* Paris, France: Librairie Félix.

Huysmans, J.K. *Revue de l'Exposition universelle de 1889,* May 1988.

Impressionism, The California View. Oakland, CA: The Oakland Museum Art Department, 1981.

Ingram, J.S. *The Centennial Exposition.* Springfield, MA: Hubbard Bros., 1876.

Irving, Washington. *A Tour on the Prairies.* 1835, reprint. New York: Pantheon, 1967.

Isham, Samuel. *The History of American Painting.* New edition with supplemental chapters by Royal Cortissoz. New York: The Macmillan Co., 1936.

Joyes, Claire. "Giverny's Meeting House, the Hotel Baudy." In David Sellin. *Americans in Brittany and Normandy, 1860-1910.* Phoenix, AZ: Phoenix Art Museum, 1982.

_____ . *Monet at Giverny.* London: Mathews Miller Dunbar, Ltd., 1975.

Jullian, Phillipe. *Montmartre.* New York: E.P. Dutton, 1977.

Kampf, Avram. *Jewish Experience in the Art of the Twentieth Century.* South Hadley, MA: Bergin and Garvey Publishers, Inc., 1984.

Kampis, Antal. *The History of Art in Hungary.* Translated by Lily Halapy. Budapest, Hungary: Corvina Press, 1966.

Klüver, Billy, and Julie Martin: *KiKi's Paris: Artists and Lovers, 1900-1930.* New York: Harry N. Abrams, Inc. Publishers, 1989.

Kreymborg, Alfred. *Troubadour: An American Autobiography.* New York: American Century, 1957.

Lamb, Ella Condie. "1881 to 1884." In *Fiftieth Anniversary of the Art Students League of New York.* New York, 1925.

Landgren, Marchal. *Years of Art: The Story of the Art Students League of New York.* New York: Robert M. McBride and Company, 1940.

Lerman, Leo. *The Museum.* New York: The Viking Press, 1969.

Letters Home: 1859-1906, The Letters of William Blair Bruce. Ed. Joan Murray. Moonbeam, Ontario, Canada: A Penumbra Press Book, 1982.

Levy Florence N., comp. & ed. *American Art Annual 1898.* New York: The Macmillan Co., 1899.

_____ . *American Art Annual, 1905-06.* New York: American Art Annual, Inc., 1905.

_____ . *American Art Annual, 1910-11.* New York: American Art Annual, Inc., 1911.

_____ . *American Art Annual, 1916.* Washington, DC: The American Federation of Arts, 1916.

Lindberg, Richard. *Chicago Ragtime: Another Look at Chicago, 1880-1920.* South Bend, IN: Icarus Press, 1985.

Love, Richard H. *John Barber: the Artist, the Man.* Chicago: Haase-Mumm Publishing Co., Inc., 1981.

_____ . *Cassatt: The Independent.* Chicago: R. H. Love Galleries, 1980

_____ . *Theodore Earl Butler: Emergence from Monet's Shadow.* Chicago: Haase-Mumm Publishing Co., 1985.

Low, Will H. *A Chronicle of Friendships.* New York: Charles Scribners Sons, 1908.

Luckhurst, Kenneth W. *The Story of Exhibitions.* New York: The Studio Publications, 1951.

Mare, Marie de. *G.P.A. Healy, American Artist.* New York: David McKay Co., Inc., 1954.

Mark, Norman. *Mayors, Madams & Madmen.* Chicago: Chicago Review Press, 1979.

Marquis, Albert Nelson, comp. and ed. *Who's Who in Chicago: The Book of Chicagoans, A Biographical Dictionary of Leading Living Men and Women of the City of Chicago and Environs, 1926.* Chicago: A.N. Marquis and Co., 1926.

Mathews, Marcia M. *Henry Ossawa Tanner, American Artist.* Chicago: The University of Chicago Press, 1969.

Mauclair, Camille. *Claude Monet.* Trans. by J. Lewis May. London, England: John Lane the Bodley Head Limited, 1927.

Mayer, Harold M., and Richard C. Wade. *Chicago: Growth of a Metropolis.* Chicago: The University of Chicago Press, 1969.

McMullen, Roy. *Victorian Outsider: A Biography of J. A. M. Whistler.* New York: E. P. Dutton & Co., Inc., 1973.

Meeker, Arthur. *Prairie Avenue.* New York: Alfred A. Knopf, 1949.

Meyers, Jerome. *Artists in Manhattan.* New York: American Artist Group, Inc., 1904.

Moffatt, Frederick C. *Arthur Wesley Dow (1857-1922).* Washington, DC: Smithsonian Institution Press, 1977.

Monroe, Harriet. *John Wellborn Root: A Study of His Life and Work.* New York, 1896. Facsimile edition. Park Forest, IL: Prairie School Press, 1966.

Morgan, H. Wayne, ed. *An American Art Student in Paris: The Letters of Kenyon Cox, 1877-1882.* Kent, OH: Kent State University Press, 1986.

_____ . *New Muses, Art in American Culture, 1865-1920.* Norman, OK: University of Oklahoma Press, 1978.

Morton, Brian N. *Americans in Paris: An Anecdotal Street Guide.* Ann Arbor, MI: The Olivia and Hill Press, 1984.

Moure, Nancy Dustin Wall. *Publications in Southern California Art, No. 3: Dictionary of Art and Artists in Southern California Before 1930.* Los Angeles, CA: Dustin Publications, 1984.

Mumford, Lewis. *The Brown Decades, A Study of the Arts in America, 1865-1895.* New York: Dover Publishers, 1931.

Murger, Henri. *The Bohemians of the Latin Quarter (Scènes de la vie de Bohême).* London, England: Vizetelly and Co., 1883.

Neuhaus, Eugene. *The Galleries of the Exposition.* San Francisco, CA: Paul Elder and Co., 1915.

Newton, Judith Vale. *The Hoosier Group, Five American Painters.* Indianapolis, IN: Eckert Publications, 1985.

Novak, Barbara. *Nature and Culture, American Landscape and Painting, 1825-1875.* New York: Oxford University Press, 1980.

Osborne, Carol, M. et al. *The Impressionists and the Salon (1874-1886).* Los Angeles, CA: Los Angeles County Museum of Art, 1974.

Panofsky, Erwin. *Problems in Titian.* New York: New York University Press, 1969.

Parry, Albert. *Garrets and Pretenders, A History of Bohemianism in America.* Rev. ed. New York: Dover Publications, Inc., 1960.

Pierce, Patricia. *The Ten.* Concord, NH: Rumford Press, 1976.

Pisano, Ronald G. *A Leading Spirit in American Art, William Merritt Chase, 1849-1916.* Seattle, WA: Henry Art Gallery, University of Washington, 1983.

President Wilson's Great Speeches and Other History Making Documents. Chicago: Stanton and Van Vliet Co. Publishers, 1917-18.

Pringle, Henry F. *The Life and Times of William Howard Taft: A Biography.* Vol. I. New York: Farrar & Rinehart, Inc., 1939.

Quick, Michael. *American Expatriate Painters of the Late 19th Century.* Dayton, OH: The Dayton Art Institute, 1976.

Rearick, Charles. *Pleasures of the Belle Epoque.* New Haven, CT: Yale University Press, 1985.

Reff, Theodore. *Degas: The Artist's Mind.* New York: Harper and Row, 1976.

Reid, B.L. *The Man From New York: John Quinn and His Friends*. New York: Oxford University Press, 1968.

Report of the Board of General Managers of the Exhibit of the State of New York at the World's Columbian Exposition. Albany, NY: James B. Lyons, State Printers, 1894.

Rewald, John, ed. *Camille Pissarro: Letters to His Son Lucien*. Translated by Lionel Abel. New York: Pantheon Books, Inc., 1943.

_____ . *Cézanne*. New York: Harry N. Abrams, Inc., 1986.

_____ . *The History of Impressionism*. New York: The Museum of Modern Art, 1961.

_____ . *Post-Impressionism from Van Gogh to Gauguin*. New York: The Museum of Modern Art, 1956.

Richardson, E. P. *Painting in America, From 1602 to Present*. New York: Thomas Y. Crowell Co., 1965.

Richardson, Edgar P., and Otto Wittmann, Jr. *Travelers in Arcadia, American Artists in Italy, 1830-1865*. Detroit, MI: The Detroit Institute of Arts and the Toledo Museum of Art,1951.

Riedy, James L. *Chicago Sculpture*. Urbana, IL: University of Illinois Press, 1981.

Rothenstein, William. *Men and Memories, A History of the Arts, 1872-1900*. Vol. 1. New York: Tudor Publishing Co., 1931.

Rudorff, Raymond. *Belle Epoque: Paris in the Nineties*. London, England: Hamilton Publishing Co., 1972.

Saarinen, Aline B. *The Proud Possessors*. New York: Random House, 1968.

Scully, Vincent. *New World Visions of Household Gods & Sacred Places*. Boston, MA: Little, Brown and Co., 1988.

Sellin, David. *Americans in Brittany and Normandy, 1860-1910*. Phoenix, AZ: Phoenix Art Museum, 1982.

Seymour, Charles. *Woodrow Wilson and the World War*. New Haven, CT: Yale University Press, 1921.

Shakespeare, William. *Love Poems and Sonnets of William Shakespeare*. Garden City, NY: Doubleday & Co., 1957.

Sheldon, G. W. *American Painters*. New York: D. Appleton and Co., 1879.

Siedenburg, J., comp. *The American Painter W.H. Singer, Jr. and His Position in the World of Art*. Amsterdam, Holland: Frances Buffa and Sons, 1928.

Smith, Corinna Lindon. *Interesting People*. Norman, OK: University of Oklahoma Press, 1962.

Stebbins, Theodore E., Jr. *The Life and Works of Martin Johnson Heade*. New Haven, CT: Yale University Press: 1975.

Steele, Selma N., and Wilbur D. Peat. *House of the Singing Winds*. Indianapolis, IN: Indiana Historical Society, 1966.

Stein, Gertrude. *The Making of Americans*. Paris: Contact Editions, 1925.

Stern, Jean. *Alson S. Clark*. Los Angeles, CA: Peterson Publishing Co., 1983.

Stillman, Edmund. "The Great Euphoria." in *The American Heritage History of the 1920's and 1930's*. New York: Bonanza Books, 1987.

Stuckey, Charles F., ed. *Monet, A Retrospective*. New York: Hugh Lauter Levin Associates, Inc., 1985.

Sweeney, James Johnson. *Stuart Davis*. New York: Museum of Modern Art, 1945.

_____ . *Three American Modernist Painters: Max Weber, Maurice Sterne, Stuart Davis*. Reprint ed. New York: Arno Press, 1969.

Sweet, Frederick A. *Miss Mary Cassatt, Impressionist from Pennsylvania*. Norman, OK: University of Oklahoma Press, 1966.

Taft, Robert. *Artists and Illustrators of the Old West, 1850-1900*. New York: Scribner, 1953.

Tallmadge, Thomas E. *Architecture in Old Chicago*. Chicago: University of Chicago Press, 1941.

Tappan, Henry P. *A Step From the New World to the Old, and Back Again*. New York, 1852.

Tharp, Louise Hall. *Saint-Gaudens and the Gilded Era*. Boston, MA: Little, Brown and Company, 1969.

Tocqueville, Alexis de. *Journey to America*. Translated by George Lawrence and edited by J. P. Meyer. Garden City, NY: Doubleday, 1971.

Tuckerman, Henry T. *Book of the Artists*. 1867, reprint; New York: James F. Carr, 1966.

Vanderpoel, John H. *The Human Figure*. Chicago: The Inland Printer Co., 1907.

Véron, Eugène. *Aesthetics*. Translated by W.H. Armstrong. London, 1879.

Vlaminck, Maurice de. *Dangerous Corner*. London: Elek Books, 1961.

Waller, Frank. *First Report of the Art Students League of New York*. New York, 1886.·

Warshawsky, Abel G. *The Memories of an American Impressionist*. Kent, OH: The Kent State University Press, 1980.

Weimann, Jeanne Madeline. *The Fair Women*. Chicago: Academy Chicago, 1981.

Weitzenhoffer, Frances. *The Havemeyers: Impressionism Comes to America*. New York: Harry N. Abrams, Inc., 1986.

Wendt, Lloyd and Herman Kogan. *Lords of the Levee*. Garden City, NY: Garden City Publishing Co., Inc., 1943.

White, Bouch. *The Book of Daniel Drew*. 1910.

White, Harrison C., and Cynthia A. White. *Canvases and Careers*. New York: John Wiley and Sons, Inc., 1965.

Wildenstein, Daniel. *Claude Monet, Biographie et catalogue raisonné*. Vols. I-IV. Lausanne-Paris: La Bibliothèque des Arts, 1974-1979.

_____ . *Monet's Giverny*. New York: The Metropolitan Museum of Art, 1978.

Yochim, Louise Dunn. *Role and Impact: The Chicago Society of Artists*. Chicago: Chicago Society of Artists, 1979.

Young, Dorothy Weir. *The Life and Letters of J. Alden Weir*. Ed. Lawrence W. Chisholm. New Haven, CT: Yale University Press, 1960.

CATALOGS

The Art Institute of Chicago. *Catalogue of an Exhibition of Works by Chicago Artists*. Exhibition catalog. Chicago, 1907.

The Art Institute of Chicago. *Catalogue of Students 1905-1906*. Chicago, 1905.

The Art Institute of Chicago. *Catalogue of the 22nd Annual Exhibition of Oil Paintings and Sculpture by American Artists.* Exhibition catalog. Chicago, 1909.

Art Institute of Chicago. *Exhibition of Paintings by Louis Ritman.* Exhibition catalog. Chicago, 1915.

The Art Institute of Chicago School Catalogue, 1908-09. Chicago: The Art Institute of Chicago, 1908.

Artist Guild Exhibition. Exhibition catalog. Chicago: Artist Guild Galleries, 1915.

Art Students League of Chicago. *13th Annual Exhibition Catalog.* Exhibition catalog. Chicago, 1907.

Baur, John I. H. *Theodore Robinson (1852-1896).* Exhibition catalog. Brooklyn, NY: The Brooklyn Museum, 1946.

Bulletin officiel de l'Exposition universelle de 1889, 7 August 1889.

Catalog of a Collection of Paintings Purchased by the Friends of American Art for the Art Institute of Chicago: Oil paintings by Louis Ritman, Paintings and Drawings by Capt. George Harding, U.S.R. and Portrait Busts in Bronze of Leaders of the World War by Joe Davidson. Exhibition Catalog. Rochester, NY: Memorial Art Gallery, 1920.

Coke, F. Van Deren. *Impressionism in America.* Exhibition catalog. Albuquerque, NM: University of New Mexico, 1965.

Corn, Wanda M. *The Color of Mood, American Tonalism 1880-1910.* Exhibition catalog. Washington, DC: Smithsonian Institution Press, 1975.

Cowart, Jack, and Juan Hamilton. *Georgia O'Keeffe: Art and Letters.* Exhibition catalog. Washington, DC: National Gallery of Art, 1987.

De Fleur, Nicole. *Louis Ritman, 1892-1963, American Painter.* Exhibition catalog. Random Lake, WI: The Louis Ritman Estate in association with Times Publishing Co., 1967.

Distel, Anne. *Renoir.* Exhibition catalog. London: Arts Council of Great Britain, 1985.

Domit, M. Moussa. *American Impressionist Painting.* Exhibition catalog. Washington, DC: National Gallery of Art, 1973.

———. *Frederick Frieseke, 1874-1939.* Exhibition catalog. Savannah, GA: Telfair Academy of Arts and Sciences, 1974.

Exposition annuelle des Beaux-Arts, Salon de 1910. Exhibition catalog. Paris: Société des Artistes Français, 1910.

Feld, Stuart P. *Lilla Cabot Perry, A Retrospective Exhibition.* Exhibition catalog. New York: Hirschl & Adler Galleries, Inc., 1969.

Fink, Lois Marie. "American Renaissance: 1870-1917." *Academy: The Academic Tradition in American Art.* Exhibition catalog. Washington, DC: Smithsonian Institution Press, 1975.

The Forum Exhibition of Modern American Painters. Exhibition catalog. New York: Anderson Galleries, 1916.

The Frick Collection, An Illustrated Catalogue, Vol. I, *Paintings.* New York: The Frick Collection, 1968.

Gardiner, Henry G., Kneeland, and McNulty, and Jean Gordon. *The Louis E. Stern Collection.* Collection catalog. Philadelphia Museum of Art, 1964.

Garland, Hamlin. "Art Conditions in Chicago," introduction in *Catalogue, United Annual Exhibition of the Palette Club and the Cosmopolitan Art Club.* Exhibition catalog. Chicago: The Art Institute, 1895.

Gordon, Irene, Lucile M. Golson, Leon Katz, et al. *Four Americans in Paris: The Collections of Gertrude Stein and Her Family.* Exhibition catalog. New York: The Museum of Modern Art, 1970.

Ives, Halsey C. *The Art of the World, Illustrated in the Paintings, Statuary, and Architecture of the World's Columbian Exposition.* Ed. Ripley Hitchcock. New York. D. Appleton & Co., 1896.

John Quinn, 1870-1925, Collection of Paintings, Water Colors, Drawings and Sculpture. Collection catalog. Huntington, NY: Pidgeon Hill Press, 1926.

Kilmer, N., and B. L. Summerford. *A Retrospective Exhibition of the Works of F. C. Frieseke.* Exhibition catalog. San Francisco, CA: Maxwell Galleries, 1982.

Laurvik, J. Nilsen. *Catalogue Deluxe of the Department of Fine Arts, Panama-Pacific International Exposition.* Exhibition catalog. Edited by John E. D. Trask and J. Nilsen Laurvik. San Francisco, CA: The Paul Elder and Company Publishers, 1915. Vol. I.

Love, Richard H. *The Paintings of Louis Ritman (1889-1963).* Exhibition catalog. Chicago: Signature Galleries, 1975.

Marcel Duchamp. Exhibition Catalog. Chicago: Art Institute of Chicago.

Masson, André, Grace Seiberling, and J. Patrice Marandel. *Paintings by Monet.* Exhibition catalog. Chicago: The Art Institute of Chicago, 1975.

Mauclair, Camille. *Impressionist and Symbolist Painters.* Exhibition catalog. Paris: Le Barc de Boutteville Gallery, 1893.

Meixner, L. L. *An International Episode: Millet, Monet, and Their North American Counterparts.* Exhibition catalog. Memphis, TN: Dixon Art Gallery, 1982.

The One Hundred and Forty-Seventh Annual Exhibition of Painting and Sculpture. Exhibition catalog. Philadelphia, PA: The Pennsylvania Academy of the Fine Arts, 1952.

Osborne, Carol M., et al. *The Impressionists and the Salon, 1874-1886.* Exhibition catalog. Los Angeles, CA: Los Angeles County Museum of Art, 1974.

Painting in the United States, 1943. Exhibition catalog. Pittsburgh, PA: Carnegie Institute, 1943.

Painting in the United States, 1944. Exhibition catalog. Pittsburgh, PA: Carnegie Institute, 1944.

Painting in the United States, 1945. Exhibition catalog. Pittsburgh, PA: Carnegie Institute, 1945.

Paintings by Lawton Parker Exhibited at the Art Institute of Chicago, March 5 to March 27, 1912. Exhibition catalog. Chicago: The Art Institute of Chicago, 1912.

Paintings by Louis Ritman. Exhibition brochure. New York: Macbeth Gallery, 1919.

Philadelphia: Three Centuries of American Art. Exhibition catalog. Philadelphia, PA: Philadelphia Museum of Art, 1976.

Quick, Michael, and Eberhard Ruhmer. *Munich and American Realism in the 19th Century.* Exhibition catalog. Sacramento, CA: E.B. Crocker Art Gallery, 1978.

Rich, Daniel, Morris Cotton, George North, et al. *A Century and a Half of American Art.* Exhibition catalog. New York: National Academy of Design, 1975.

Rubin, William, ed. *Pablo Picasso, A Retrospective.* Exhibition catalog. New York: The Museum of Modern Art, 1980.

Twachtman in Gloucester, His Last Years. Exhibition catalog. New York: Ira Spanierman Gallery, 1987.

Weller, Allen S. *Frederick Frieseke, 1847-1939.* Exhibition catalog. New York: Hirschl & Adler Galleries, 1966.

Works of Chicago Artists, 1909. Exhibition Catalog. Chicago: The Art Institute of Chicago, 1909.

PERIODICALS

Amaya, Mario. "Art: Women in the Boudoir: A Glimpse into Private Settings." *Architectural Digest.* September 1979.

"American Art at the Anglo-American Exposition." *International Studio*, LIII, n. 212 (October 1914).

"American's Work Superb." *New York Times*, 1 May 1912.

Anderson, Donald James. "Those Haunting Trees." *Inland Architect*, 25, no.5 (June 1981), pp. 4-11.

Anonymous. "Boston Art and Artists." *The Art Amateur.* 17, no. 5 (October 1887), p. 93.

Anonymous. *Nation*, 50 (3 May 1890).

Anonymous. *New York Tribune*, 4 April 1963.

"Another Look at Foreign Pictures in New York." *Nation*, 2 (11 January 1866), pp. 55-56.

Architectural Record, 1910.

"Art." Unidentified newspaper clipping. Palette and Chisel Club Log Book, 1906-1915, Vol. 2, p. 100.

Art Amateur, no. 32 (March 1895), p. 107.

"Art Awards and Art." Unidentified newspaper clipping, c. 27 October 1914.

"Art: Exhibitions of the Week." *New York Times*, 13 April 1924, p. 10.

"Art in Chicago." *The Art Journal*, May 1876, p. 160.

Art Institute of Chicago Report, 5 June 1895. Chicago, 1895.

"Artists Give Cubist Play." *Chicago Daily Tribune*, 27 March 1913.

Baker, Martha S. "The Art Students League." *Brush and Pencil*, I, no. 3 (December 1897), pp. 61-77.

Bargelt, Louis James. "Art. Noted Artists on List at Exhibition of Institute Alumni." *Chicago Sunday Tribune*, 6 January 1918, Part VIII, p.3.

_____ . "Art Institute Alumi's Work on Exhibition." *Chicago Daily Tribune,* 8 January 1918, p. 5.

Beale, Bertha F. "Art Students Life in Paris." *Sketch Book*, IV, no.2 (October 1904), pp. 56-58, and IV, no. 8 (June 1905), pp. 251-52.

"Boston Art and Artists." *The Art Amateur*, 17, no. 5 (October 1887), p. 93.

Bowles, J.M. "Impressionalism." *Modern Art*, Winter 1893.

Boyd, Nancy W. "Diary of an American Art Student in Paris." *Vanity Fair*, November 1922.

Breck, Edward. "Something More of Giverny." *Boston Evening Transcript,* 9 March 1895.

Buell, James Ford. "Chicago's Fifteenth Annual Art Exhibition." *Brush and Pencil*, XI, no. 1 (October 1902), p. 298-299,302.

Buffet, Gabrielle. "La Section d'Or." *Art d'aujourd'hui*, May-June 1957, pp. 74-76.

Bulletin of the Metropolitan Museum of Art, IX, no. 12 (December, 1914). pp. 252-56.

Caffin, Charles. "The Art and Influence of Paris To-Day." *Artist,* 29 October 1900.

Casseres, Benjamin de, "The Unconscious in Art." *Camera Work*, 36 (October 1911), p. 17.

"Chase, Indiana Artist, Talks of Modern Art." *The Indianapolis News*, 24 April 1915.

"The Chicago Academy of Fine Arts." *The Sketch Book*, III, no. 8 (April 1904), p. 265.

"Chicago Artist Starts Revolt." *Chicago Daily Tribune*, 24 March 1913, p. 15.

Chicago Daily News, 14 February 1974.

Chicago Evening Post, 9 November 1920, p. 11.

Chicago Herald, 14 January 1915.

Chicago Herald, 25 February 1915, p. 7.

Chicago Sunday Herald, 10 January 1915, p. 7.

Chicago Tribune, 18 January 1891.

Chicago Tribune, 24 March 1889.

Chicago Tribune, 20 August 1893.

Chicago Tribune, 4 March 1894.

"Chicago's Art Advance to Be Told at Dinner." *Palette and Chisel Club Log Book*, 1906-1915, no. 2, p. 105. Unidentified newspaper clipping. Special Collection, Newberry Library, Chicago.

"Claude Monet to Thiébault-Sisson." *Le Temps*, 27 November 1900.

"Clara Kretzinger Deserts Her Montparnasse Studio to Do Murals in Ireland." *Chicago Daily News*, 9 September 1932.

Condit, Ida M. "Art Conditions in Chicago and Other Western Cities." *Brush and Pencil,* XI, no. 1 (October 1902), p. 298.

Cook, Clarence. "The Cry from the Studios." *Galaxy*, 3 (15 February 1867), pp. 439-440; 4 (1899), pp. 7-11.

_____ . "The Impressionist Pictures." *Studio,* 21 (17 April 1886).

Cortissoz, Royal. *New York Tribune*, February 17, 23, 1913.

_____ . "The Post-Impressionist Illusion." *Century.* LXXXV (April 1913), p. 813.

_____ . "A Visit to Chicago and San Francisco." *New York Herald Tribune*, 23 November 1930.

Cosmopolitan Art Journal, III (December 1859), p. 236.

Cox, Kenyon. "The Modern Spirit in Art." *Harper's Weekly*, LVII (15 March 1913), p. 10.

The Crayon, III (May 1856), p. 150.

The Crayon, V (February 1858), p. 59.

Daulte, F. "Le marchand des impressionnistes." *L'Oeil,* June 1960.

DeKay, Charles. "French and American Impressionists." *New York Times*, 31 January 1904, p. 23.

Denis, Maurice. "Gauguin, ses amis, l'école de Pont-Aven et l'académie Julian." *Gazette des Beaux-Arts*, Paris, n.d.

Didymous. "Little Sunny Spots." *Forest and Stream*, 21 (December 1895), p. 534.

Dorival, Bernard. "Fauves: The Wild Beasts Tamed." *Art News Annual*, 1952-53.

Dorra, Henri. "The Wild Beasts: Fauvism and Its Affinities at the Museum of Modern Art." *Art Journal*, XXXVI/I (Fall 1976).

"Eight Independent Painters to Give an Exhibition of Their Own Next Winter." *New York Sun*, 15 May 1907.

Eldredge, Charles. "Connecticut Impressionists: The Spirit of Place." *Art in America*, 62, no. 5. (September-October 1974), pp. 84-90.

"Fair Play for Insurgent Art." *The Chicago Evening Post*, 24 March 1913, p.6.

Fénéon, Félix. *La Revue Indépendante*, July 1888.

"The Fine Arts." *Chicago Herald*, 1 February 1915, p. 10.

"The Fine Arts." *Chicago Herald*, 22 February 1915.

"The Fine Arts." *Chicago Herald*, 25 February 1915, p.10.

"Fine Arts: The Society of American Artists." *Nation*, 50 (8 May 1890), p. 382.

"Former Poor Art Student Wins Victory in Chicago." Unidentified newspaper clipping. Ritman Scrapbook. R.H. Love Galleries Archives, Chicago.

"French Funeral Set for Tomorrow." *Chicago Daily Tribune*, 4 June 1914, Sec. I, p. 2.

"The French Impressionists." *New York Daily Tribune*, 10 April 1886.

French, M.D.R. [sic]. "The Art School of the Art Institute of Chicago." *The Sketch Book*, II, no. 6. (July 1903), pp. 7-8.

French, W.M.R. "Frightfulness in Art." *American Magazine of Art*, VII (April 1917), pp. 244-245.

"From Here and There." *Chicago Evening Post*, 5 March 1918, p. 11.

Garland, Hamlin. "Productive Conditions of American Literature." *Forum*, XVII (August 1884), p. 690.

Gilder, Richard Watson. "Some Other Pictures." *Scribner's Monthly*, no. 10 (May-October 1875), p. 253.

Goldstein, Jesse. "Two Literary Radicals: Garland and Markham in Chicago, 1893." *American Literature*, XVII, 2 (May 1945), p. 160.

Goodrich, Lloyd. "Reviewer's Notebook." *New York Times*, 17 March 1929.

"Gossip of the Ateliers, Being Sundry Notes of Interest Picked Up in Studios and Art Schools." *The Sketch Book*, III, no. 2 (October 1903), p. 61.

"A Great Art Leader." *New York Times*, 6 June 1914, p. 8.

"The Greatest Exhibition of Insurgent Art Ever Held." *Current Opinion*, no. 54 (March 1913), pp. 230-232.

Hackett, Francis. "Hull House—A Souvenir." *Survey*, 1 June 1925.

Heitkamp, Ernest L. "Cleverness Makes Canvases of Oliver Dennett Grover Cold." *Chicago Herald and Examiner*, 30 December 1923, part 5, p.4.

Henri, Robert (Robert H. Cozad). "A Letter From Young America." *Hundredth Meridian*, 28 November 1876.

Henrotin, Ellen M. "An Outsider's View of the Woman's Exhibit." *The Cosmopolitan*, XV (1893).

Hovey, Richard. "La-Bas." *Le Courrier Innocent*, no. 6 (1897).

"Hull House Classes." *Hull-House Bulletin*, VI, no. 1 (Mid-Winter, 1903-4), pp. 2-3.

Huth, Hans. "Impressionism Comes to America." *Gazette des Beaux-Arts*, 29 (April 1946), pp. 225-252.

Inter Ocean, 25 March 1913, p.2.

"Interview with Kenyon Cox." *New York Times*, 16 March 1913, pt. 6.

Ives, A. E. "Mr. Childe Hassam on Painting Street Scenes." *Art Amateur*, 27 October 1892, pp. 116-17.

Jean, René. "Les Salons de 1911, Le Salon de la Société des Artistes Français." *Gazette des Beaux-Arts*, 2 (1911), p. 420.

_____ . "Les Salons de 1911: Société Nationale des Beaux-Arts." *Gazette des Beaux-Arts*, 2 (1911), p. 364.

Landon, Herman. "Hark! Hark! The Critics Bark! The Cubists Are Coming!" *The Sunday Record Herald* (Chicago), 23 March 1912, pt 2.

Leavitt, Thomas W. "Let the Dogs Bark: George Loring Brown and the Critics." *American Art Review*, I, no. 2 (January-February 1974).

Leroy, Louis. "The Impressionist Exhibition." *Le Charivari*, 25 April 1874; English translation from Charles F. Stuckey, ed. *Monet, a Retrospective*. New York: Hugh Levin Associates, Inc., 1985.

Lewis, Sinclair. *American Mercury*. October 1925.

"Literature and Art." *Chicago Opinion*, LIV (April 1913), p. 316.

"Literature and Art." *Chicago Sunday Herald*, 10 January 1915, p.7.

MacChesney, Clara. "A Poet-Painter of Palestine." *International Studio*, I (July 1913), p. XII.

Marks, Montague. *Art Amateur*, 1885.

Mather, Frank J., Jr. "The Present State of Art." *Nation*, 93 (4 December 1911), pp. 584-87.

Morice, Charles. "Les Salons de la Nationale et des Français." *Mercure de France*, June 1904, pp. 686-705.

_____ . *Mercure de France*, 15 April 1905.

McCauley, Lena M. "Art and Artists." *Chicago Evening Post*, 25 February 1915, p. 6.

_____ . "Art in America is at 'Great Divide'" *The Chicago Evening Post*, 11 (November 1919), p. 11.

_____ . "Lawton S. Parker." *The Art Student*, October 1915, pp. 4-8.

_____ . "Nerves of the Art World: At the Art Institute." *Chicago Evening Post*, 18 May 1920, p. 17.

_____ . "News of the Art World: At the Art Institute." *Chicago Evening Post*, 18 May 1920, p.17.

_____ . "Wellington J. Reynolds—Painter." *The Sketch Book*, V, no. 7 (May 1906), pp. 334-336.

_____ . *Chicago Tribune*, 22 October 1904.

Monroe, Harriet. "Art Exhibition Opens in Chicago." *Chicago Tribune*, 25 March 1913.

_____ . "Cubist Art, a Protest Against Narrow Conservatism." *Chicago Sunday Tribune*, 8 April 1913, p. 11.

_____ . "Chicago Letter." *Critic*, no. 22 (29 December 1894), p. 450.

Monroe, Lucy B., "Art in Chicago." *The New England Magazine*, New Series VI (1892), pp. 427-428.

Monthly Calendar Bulletin. The Grand Rapids Art Association, February, 1920.

Morice, Charles. *Mercure de France*, 15 April 1905.

Moulton, Robert H. "Lorado Taft, Dean of Chicago Sculpture." *Art and Archeology*, XII (1921), pp. 243-252.

Mowrer, Paul Scott. "How U. S. Artists See Their Confrères." *The [Chicago] Daily News*, 3 February 1914.

"Mrs. Louis Stern Dies." *The Art Digest*, October 1, 1938.

New York Herald, 27 June 1906.

New York Herald, 21 December 1910.

New York Herald Tribune, 17 March 1929.

"New York School of Art." *The Sketchbook*, January 1904, p. 143.

New York Telegraph, 21 December 1910.

New York Times, 29 April 1875.

New York Times, 30 October 1877.

New York Times, 2 and 4 December 1883.

New York Times, 9 January 1898.

New York Times, 25 December 1910.

New York Times, 23 February 1913, Part VI, p. 15.

" York Times, 16 March 1913.

New York Tribune, 4 April 1863.

New York Tribune, 16 January 1867.

New York Tribune, 23 January 1867.

Oliver, Maude I.G. "Gossip of the Artists." *Chicago Sunday Herald*, 27 December 1914.

_____ . "Of Art and Artists." *Sunday Record Herald* (Chicago), 6 April 1913.

_____ . "Work of School of the Art Institute, Chicago." *International Studio*. (September 1909), pp. LXXVIII- LXXIX.

Parker, Lawton S. "Another View of Art Study in Paris." *Brush and Pencil*, XI, no. 1 (October 1902), pp. 11-15.

Perry, Lilla Cabot. "Reminiscences of Claude Monet from 1889-1909." *The American Magazine of Art*, XVIII, no. 3 (March 1927), p. 119.

Philpott, A. J. *Boston Sunday Globe*, 29 October 1933.

Powell, J. "American Landscape Painting." *Connoisseur*, 206, no. 827 (January 1981).

Quilibit, Philip. "Art at the World's Fair." *Galaxy*, no. 21 (February 1876), p. 272.

R. A. "American Art at the Anglo-American Exposition." *International Studio*, LIII, p. 3.

Rensselaer, M.G. Van. "The New York Art Season." *Atlantic Monthly*, 48 (August 1881), pp. 193-202.

Rich, D. G. "Chicago Makes Prize Awards; Annual American Exhibition." *Art News*, 9 (November 8, 1930).

Ritman Scrapbook, unidentified newspaper clipping, R.H. Love Galleries Archives, Chicago.

"Ritman's Sunlit Gardens." Unidentified newspaper clipping, Ritman Scrapbook, R.H. Love Galleries Archives, Chicago.

Roger-Marx, Claude. "Le vernissage du Salon de la Société des Artistes Français." *La Chronique des Arts et de la Curiosité*, no. 17 (29 April 1911), p. 132.

_____ . "Le Vernissage du Salon de la Société des Artistes Français." *La Chronique des Arts et de la Curiosité*, no. 18 (4 May 1912), p. 140.

_____ . "Le Vernissage de Salon de la Société des Artistes Français." *La Chronique des Arts et de la Curiosité*, May 1913, p. 140.

Sarcey, Francisque. "Murger and Bohemia." *The Cosmopolitan Magazine*, XX, no. 4 (February 1896), pp. 332-33.

Stanton, Theodore. "Europe at the World's Fair—The French Section." *North American Review*, 156 (1893).

Stark, Otto. "The Evolution of Impressionism." *Modern Art*, 3 (Spring 1895).

Steele, T. C. "Impressionism." *Modern Art*, 1 (Winter 1893).

"Students at French Funeral." *Chicago Daily Tribune*, 5 June 1914.

"Studio Talk." *International Studio*, LV, no. 228 (April 1912), pp. 222-23.

Sturgis, Russell. "What Is Art Criticism." *Art Journal*, no. 5 (January 1879), p. 29.

_____ . "The Recent Comparative Exhibition of Narrative and Foreign Art." *Scribner's Magazine*, XXXVII, no. 2 (February 1905), p. 253.

Sweet, Frederick A. "Great Chicago Collections." *Apollo*, 84 (1966), pp. 190-228.

"Table Talk". *Appleton's Journal*, no. 6 (December 16, 1871), p. 695.

"A Tale of a Night for the Actives." *The Cow Bell*, 4, no. 3, p.2.

Taylor, E. A. "The American Colony of Artists in Paris." *International Studio*, 52 (May 1911).

Teall, Gardner C. "Our Western Painters: What Chicago Is Doing Toward the Development of a Vital National Spirit in American Art." *The Craftsman*, XV (1908), pp. 139-153.

Thiébault-Sisson. *Le Temps*, 29 April 1911.

Thompson, Irma. "The Art Academy of Chicago." *The Sketch Book*, III, no. 7 (March 1904), p. 214.

Toulgouat, Pierre. "Skylights in Normandy." Trans. Robert M. Coates. *Holiday*, August 1948.

Travers, Innez. "Art." Unidentified newspaper clipping, dated in pencil 24 February 1915, Ritman Scrapbook. R.H. Love Galleries Archives, Chicago.

Unidentified newspaper clipping, 7 May 1892. Quoted in John I. H. Baur, *Theodore Robinson, 1852-1896*, exhibition catalog (Brooklyn, NY: The Brooklyn Museum, 1946).

Upton, George P. "Art in Chicago." *Western Monthly*, IV (December 1870).

Van Brundt, Henry. "Architecture at the World's Columbian Exposition." *Century Magazine*, 44 (1892), pp. 81-89.

Vandoyer, Jean-Louis. *La Chronique des Arts et de la Curiosité*, 15 May 1909, p. 159.

Van Rensselaer, M. G. "Artistic Triumph of the Fair Builders." *Forum*, 14 (1892), pp. 81-89.

_____ . "The New York Art Season." *Atlantic Monthly*, 48 (August 1881), pp. 193-202.

"War Portraits by American Artists." *Museum of Fine Arts Boston Bulletin, XIX*, no. 114 (August 1921). Reprint: New York: Arno Press, 1971.

Waterman, C. H. "Louis Ritman." *International Studio, LXVII*, no. 267, (April 1919), pp. LXII-LXIV.

Webster, H. Effa. *Chicago Examiner*, 1 April 1913.

_____. "Paris Lauds Chicago Boy—Ghetto Artist Wins Honor." Unidentified newspaper clipping from *The Chicago Examiner*.

Webster, J. Carson. "The Technique of Impressionism—A Reappraisal." *College Art Journal*, November 1944.

Weinberg, H. Barbara. "Nineteenth Century American Painters at the Ecole des Beaux-Arts." *American Art Journal*, 13 (Autumn 1981).

Weinberg, Louis. "Current Impressionism." *The New Republic*, 6 March 1915, p. 124.

Weller, Allen S. "Frederick Carl Frieseke: The Opinions of an American Impressionist." *The Art Journal, XXVII*, no. 2 (Winter 1968-69).

_____. "Sources of Style: The Impressionists." *Art in America*, 51 (June 1963).

White, Charles Henry. "Student Humor in Paris." Sketch Book, III, no. 2 (October 1903).

"William Merritt Chase Forced Out of New York School: Triumph for the New Movement Led by Robert Henri." *New York American*, 20 November 1907, p. 3.

"William Merritt Chase, His Life and Work." *Arts for America*, 7 (December 1897).

"William M. R. French Sinking." *Chicago Daily Tribune*, 2 June 1914.

Wuerpel, E. H. "American Artists' Association of Paris." *The Cosmopolitan Magazine*, XX, no. 4 (February 1896), pp. 402-409.

Zug, George B. "Among the Art Galleries." *The Inter Ocean*, 6 April 1913, p. 5.

_____ . "The Art of Lawton Parker." *International Studio*, LVII (December 1915).

Dissertations and Theses

Brown, Elizabeth. "American Paintings and Sculpture in the Fine Arts Building of the World's Columbian Exposition." Ph.D. dissertation, University of Kansas, 1976.

Goldstein, Leslie. "Art in Chicago and the World's Columbian Exposition of 1893." Master's thesis. The University of Iowa, 1970.

Hale, John Douglass. "The Life and Creative Development of John Henry Twachtman." Ph.D. dissertation. Ohio State University, 1957.

Sparks, Esther. "A Biographical Dictionary of Painters and Sculptors in Illinois, 1808-1945." Ph.D. dissertation. Northwestern University, 1971.

Whitridge, Eugenia Remelin. "Art in Chicago: The Structure of the Art World in a Metropolitan Community." Ph.D. dissertation. University of Chicago, 1946.

Documents

Academy Enrollment Records, Archives of the Pennsylvania Academy of Arts.

Director WMRF, Letter Books, Vols. December 27, 1899—April 18, 1915, General Correspondence, Archives of the Art Institute of Chicago, Chicago.

Director [Pro Tem] NHC, Letter Book, October 17, 1914—June 15, 1916, Archives of The Art Institute of Chicago, Chicago.

Frederick Frieseke File. R.H. Love Galleries Archives, Chicago.

Love, Richard H., to Bruce Bachman, memo, August 1987, R.H. Love Galleries Archives, Chicago.

Louis Ritman to Charles T. Ramsey, Curator of Schools, 20 November 1908, Chicago. Archives of the Pennsylvania Academy of the Fine Arts, Philadelphia, PA.

Louis Ritman Scrapbook, R.H. Love Galleries Archives, Chicago.

Nicholas Kilmer. Frederick Frieseke Questionnaire. R.H. Love Galleries Archives, Chicago.

Palette and Chisel Club Log Book, 1906-1915, Special Collection, Newberry Library, Chicago.

Student Record Card (1908-9) for Louis Ritman, Art Institute of Chicago Archives, Chicago.

Interviews

James Daugherty, interview with Ronald G. Pisano, quoted in Pisano, *A Leading Spirit in American Art, William Merritt Chase, 1849-1916.* Seattle, WA: Henry Art Gallery, University of Washington, 1983.

Maurice Ritman, interviews with Richard Love, June-September 1987, R.H. Love Galleries Archives, Chicago.

Taped Interviews, Eliot C. Clark to Richard H. Love, 1978-1979. R.H. Love Galleries Archives, Chicago.

Taped Interviews, Jean-Marie Toulgouat with Richard H. Love, 24 November 1984.

Papers

Chicago Academy of the Fine Arts, October-November 1908. Registrar.

Cox Papers, Avery Architecture Library, Columbia University, New York City.

Frederick Frieseke. Reminiscences, Writings, Price Lists. Microfilm Roll No. N737. Archives of American Art, Smithsonian Institution, Washington, DC.

Mrs. George. "Lawton Parker, Artist." Lawton Parker File. R.H. Love Galleries Archives, Chicago.

Henry O. Tanner Papers. Archives of American Art, Smithsonian Institution, Washington, DC.

James Carroll Beckwith Diary. Microfilm Roll No. 800. Archives of American Art, Smithsonian Institution. Washington, DC.

Jane Addams Papers. Series 1, Supplement, Swarthmore College Peace Collection, Swarthmore, PA.

Macbeth Gallery Papers, 1911-1933, Archives of American Art, Smithsonian Institution, Washington, DC.

Philip Leslie Hale Papers. Microfilm Roll D98. Archives of American Art, Smithsonian Institution, Washington, DC.

Ritman, Maurice. "My Brother Louis Ritman." Typescript. August 1987. R.H. Love Galleries Archives, Chicago.

Weber, Max. "The Reminiscences of Max Weber. Manuscript in the Weber Collection, Oral History Research Office, Columbia University, New York.

INDEX